Issues in Race and Ethnicity

THIRD EDITION

CQ PRESS

A Division of Congressional Quarterly Inc., Washington, D.C.

SELECTIONS FROM THE **CQ RESEARCHER**

D1417943

CQ Press
1255 22nd Street, NW, Suite 400
Washington, DC 20037

Phone: 202-729-1900; toll-free, 1-866-4CQ-PRESS (1-866-427-7737)

Web: www.cqpress.com

Cover designer: Kimberly Glyder
Cover photo: Getty Images/Nick Clements

♾ The paper used in this publication exceeds the requirements of the American National Standard for Information Sciences—Permanence of Paper for Printed Library Materials, ANSI Z39.48-1992.

Printed and bound in the United States of America

10 09 08 07 06   1 2 3 4 5

A CQ Press College Division Publication

Director	Brenda Carter
Acquisitions editor	Charisse Kiino
Marketing manager	Christopher O'Brien
Production editor	Anne Stewart
Compositor	Olu Davis
Managing editor	Stephen Pazdan
Electronic production manager	Paul Pressau
Print and design manager	Margot Ziperman
Sales manager	James Headley

ISBN-10: 1-933116-83-8
ISBN-13: 978-1-933116-83-9

Contents

Annotated Contents

The 12 *CQ Researcher* reports reprinted in this book have been reproduced essentially as they appeared when first published. In the few cases in which important new developments have since occurred, updates are provided in the overviews highlighting the principal issues examined.

RACE

Affirmative Action

A major battle over the use of race in college admissions ended with split decisions from the U.S. Supreme Court. The high court rulings came in suits by unsuccessful white applicants to the University of Michigan's undergraduate college and law school. They challenged policies that gave an advantage to minority applicants. The university said the policies were needed to ensure racial and ethnic diversity on campus. The Supreme Court upheld law school policies that gave individualized consideration to each applicant, but it ruled that the undergraduate admissions system operated too much like a racial quota. Officials at Michigan and other elite universities said the rulings would result in only minor changes in admissions policies. But former Justice Sandra Day O'Connor called for minority preferences to end in twenty-five years.

Race in America

Many people believe the end of legal discrimination gave African-Americans the same chance of success as other Americans. And by any measure, blacks' social, economic and political standing has vastly improved since the civil rights upheavals of the 1950s and 1960s. Yet, by all the same measures — wealth, income, life expectancy, school success, crime rates — blacks lag far behind whites. Many African-Americans — and many whites — say discrimination, whether due to institutional habits or deliberate prejudice, prevents them from attaining jobs and homes equal to those enjoyed by whites. The 2003 Supreme Court decision upholding affirmative action heartened many blacks. But racially tinged incidents — notably the response to Hurricane Katrina in 2005 — periodically shatter the complacency of all Americans about race.

Redistricting Disputes

Disputes over partisan redistricting, or gerrymandering, date back to the nation's earliest days, and the once-a-decade process was as contentious as ever following the 2000 census. New computer technology now gives map drawers unprecedented precision to make districts nearly impregnable by stuffing them with party loyalists. Republican-drawn maps in some key states helped the GOP gain House seats in the 2002 midterm congressional elections, which saw significantly less turnover than in similar elections during the last 30 years. Then, in an unusual move, Republicans reopened the redistricting process in Colorado and Texas, prompting the Democrats to try to get mid-decade remappings declared unconstitutional. However, a deeply divided Supreme Court in April 2004 upheld a redistricting plan that sought to give the Republican Party an edge in Pennsylvania's congressional races. The court also refused to bar court challenges to such partisan redistricting in future cases. Some citizens' groups say that using independent bodies to redraw the maps would ensure partisan fairness, competitiveness and stability.

School Desegregation

In April 2004, the nation celebrated the fiftieth anniversary of the Supreme Court's landmark decision declaring racial segregation in public schools unconstitutional. But the promise of equal educational opportunity for all offered by the once-controversial *Brown v. Board of Education* ruling is widely viewed as unfulfilled. Today, an increasing percentage of African-American and Latino students attend schools with mostly other minorities — a situation that critics blame on recent Supreme Court decisions easing judicial supervision of desegregation plans. Black and Latino students also lag far behind whites in academic achievement. School-desegregation advocates call for stronger steps to break down racial and ethnic isolation and to upgrade schools that serve minority students. Critics of mandatory desegregation, however, say stronger accountability, stricter academic standards and parental choice will do more to improve education for all students.

Black Colleges

Before the 1950s, most black Americans had little choice but to attend colleges and universities founded for blacks. The outlawing of segregation over fifty years ago gave black students more education options, and many took them. But the nation's 103 historically black colleges and universities (HBCUs) still enroll about 14 percent of African-American students. Supporters say black colleges offer important educational and social benefits over predominantly white institutions. Some critics, however, say many HBCUs are academically inferior institutions and do not prepare students for living in a diverse society. Whatever their advantages or disadvantages, many black colleges are in trouble today because of shaky finances and sagging enrollments.

Reparations Movement

After the Civil War, efforts to compensate former slaves were blocked. In recent years, calls have gotten louder for payments to the ancestors of slaves to help the nation come to terms with a gross historical injustice. But opponents worry that reparations would only widen the divide between the races. In January 2004, an Illinois federal court dismissed a lawsuit brought by slave descendents against corporations said to have profited from slavery, but the court still left the door open for further litigation. Meanwhile, survivors of the Nazi Holocaust have had considerable success in obtaining restitution from governments and corporations linked to Hitler's "Final Solution." Seeking reparations is not about money, they say, but about winning justice for the victims. But some Jewish Americans argue that the reparations movement has turned a historical tragedy into a quest for money. Other mistreated groups have picked up the call for reparations, including World War II "comfort women." In November 2002, the Australian government offered reparations to Queensland Aborigines.

Environmental Justice

Toxic-waste dumps, sewage-treatment plants and other pollution sources rarely are found near middle-class or affluent communities. Inner-city neighborhoods, rural Hispanic villages and Indian reservations are far more likely to suffer. For the last twenty-five years, a movement to combine environmental and human rights concerns has sought to help poor communities across the country to close the door on unwelcome dumps and factories. Charging that they are victims of environmental racism, activists are winning court battles on the grounds that siting polluting facilities among disadvantaged people violates Title VI of the 1964 Civil Rights Act. But business representatives and residents of some affected minority communities say that the movement is stifling their opportunities for economic development and growth. And the cause of environmental justice has lost some momentum, in part because of a lack of enforcement at the federal level, but also because environmental activists have turned their attention to other issues such as global warming.

Rebuilding New Orleans

Five months after Hurricane Katrina flooded most of New Orleans, some 80 percent of the "Crescent City" remained unrepaired. Damage was estimated at $35 billion. Most schools and businesses were still closed, and two-thirds of the 460,000 residents had moved out. How many will return remains troublingly uncertain. Questions about who will help the city's poorer residents — many of them African-American — hang over the city, along with concern about how much of New Orleans' storied popular culture will survive. Meanwhile, as a new hurricane season approaches, efforts to repair and strengthen the protective system of levees, canals and pumps lag behind schedule.

ETHNICITY AND IMMIGRATION

Illegal Immigration

More than 10 million illegal immigrants live in the United States, and 1,400 more arrive every day. Once concentrated in a few big states like Texas and California, they are rapidly moving into non-traditional areas such as the Midwest and South. Willing to work for low wages, the migrants are creating a backlash among some residents of the new states, which have seen a nearly tenfold increase in illegal immigration since 1990. While illegal immigrants only make up about 5 percent of the U.S. workforce, critics of the nation's immigration policies say illegal immigrants take Americans' jobs, threaten national security and even change the nation's culture by refusing to assimilate. But immigrants' advocates say illegal migrants fill the jobs Americans refuse to take and generally boost the economy. Proposals for increased immigration controls and a guest-worker program have divided Congress even as massive demonstrations in cities across the country have polarized the issue among the public.

Latinos' Future

Latinos have moved ahead of African Americans to become the nation's largest minority. But while Hispanics already exert enormous influence on American life their political clout has yet to catch up. An intense congressional debate brought tens of thousands of Latinos to the streets in 2006 in support of immigrant rights, but an equally powerful backlash has kept them from achieving the legislative goal of amnesty for many illegal aliens. Politicians are wary of offending the sensibilities of such a fast-growing segment of the population — and Latinos in recent years have spread far beyond the traditional ends of the immigrant journeys in states such as California, New York and Florida. Hispanics say their widely praised work ethic, high rate of English-language fluency and proud self-identification as Americans show they already embrace the nation's values. Still, they have engendered a good deal of fear because of post-September 11 concerns about border security, as well as anxiety that illegal immigrants are driving down wages because of their willingness to work for sub-minimum wages. Latinos are clearly an increasingly important force in U.S. political life and the national economy, but equality of income, educational attainment and complete cultural acceptance remain, for the time being, elusive.

Gang Crisis

Once an urban problem, street gangs have now infiltrated U.S. communities large and small. Gang experts say at least 21,500 gangs — with more than 731,000 members — are active nationwide. Long-established domestic gangs like the Bloods and the Crips remain powerful, but the problem has worsened dramatically in recent years. Heavy immigration, particularly from Latin America and Asia, has introduced highly violent gangs like Mara Salvatrucha and the Almighty Latin Kings Nation. Bound by tight ethnic and racial ties, they often stymie police investigations by assaulting or killing potential witnesses. Having already diversified from illegal drugs into auto theft, extortion, property crimes and home invasion, some East Coast gangs have begun trafficking in fraudulent identification papers that could be used by terrorists. While experts agree gangs are more pervasive than ever, few agree on a remedy. Proposed legislation would increase penalties for gang membership and gang crimes, but critics say it won't solve the problem.

American Indians

Winds of change are blowing through Indian Country, improving prospects for many of the nation's 4.4 million Native Americans. The number of tribes managing their own affairs has increased dramatically, and an urban Native-American middle class is quietly taking root. The booming revenues of many Native American-owned casinos seem the ultimate proof that Native Americans are overcoming a history of mistreatment, poverty and exclusion. Yet most of the gambling houses don't rake in stratospheric revenues. And despite statistical upticks in socioeconomic indicators, Native Americans are still poorer, more illness-prone and less likely to be employed than their fellow citizens. Meanwhile, tribal governments remain largely dependent on direct federal funding of basic services — funding that Native-American leaders and congressional supporters decry as inadequate. But government officials say they are still providing essential services despite budget cuts.

Preface

As minority populations continue to grow, and concerns about U.S. border security and immigration intensify, issues in race and ethnicity resonate ever more profoundly with Americans. These topics confound even well-informed citizens and often lead to cultural and political conflicts, because they raise the most formidable public policy questions: Are blacks still economically disadvantaged due to racism? Should illegal immigrants in the United States be allowed to acquire legal status? Is the federal government neglecting Native Americans? To promote change and hopefully reach viable resolution, scholars, students and policymakers must strive to understand the context and content of each of these issues, as well as how these debates play out in the public sphere.

With the view that only an objective examination that synthesizes all competing viewpoints can lead to sound analysis, this third edition of *Issues in Race and Ethnicity* provides comprehensive and unbiased coverage of today's most pressing policy problems. It enables instructors to fairly and comprehensively uncover opposing sides of each issue, and illustrate just how significantly these issues impact citizens and the government they elect. This book is a compilation of twelve recent reports from *CQ Researcher*, a weekly policy backgrounder that brings into focus key issues on the public agenda. *Researcher* fully explains complex concepts in plain English. Each article chronicles and analyzes past legislative and judicial action as well as current and possible future maneuvering. Each report addresses how issues affect all levels of government, whether at the local, state or federal level, and also the lives and futures of all citizens. *Issues in Race and Ethnicity* is designed to promote in-depth discussion, facilitate further research and help readers think critically and formulate their own positions on these crucial issues.

This collection is organized into two sections: "Race" and "Ethnicity and Immigration." Each section spans a range of important public policy concerns. These pieces were chosen to expose students to a wide range of issues, from political gerrymandering to illegal immigration. Over half of the reports are new to this edition, including four updated reports, "Race in America," "Environmental Justice," "Illegal Immigration" and "Latinos' Future." We are gratified to know that *Issues in Race and Ethnicity* has found a following in a wide range of departments in political science and sociology.

CQ RESEARCHER

CQ Researcher was founded in 1923 as *Editorial Research Reports* and was sold primarily to newspapers as a research tool. The magazine was renamed and redesigned in 1991 as *CQ Researcher*. Today, students are its primary audience. While still used by hundreds of journalists and newspapers, many of which reprint portions of the reports, *Researcher*'s main subscribers are now high school, college and public libraries. In 2002, *Researcher* won the American Bar Association's coveted Silver Gavel award for magazine excellence for a series of nine reports on civil liberties and other legal issues.

Researcher staff writers — all highly experienced journalists — sometimes compare the experience of writing a *Researcher* report to drafting a college term paper. Indeed, there are many similarities. Each report is as long as many term papers — about 11,000 words — and is written by one person without any significant outside help. One of the key differences is that writers interview leading experts, scholars and government officials for each issue.

Like students, staff writers begin the creative process by choosing a topic. Working with *Researcher*'s editors, the writer identifies a controversial subject that has important public policy implications. After a topic is selected, the writer embarks on one to two weeks of intense research. Newspaper and magazine articles are clipped or downloaded, books are ordered and information is gathered from a wide variety of sources, including interest groups, universities and the government. Once the writers are well informed, they develop a detailed outline, and begin the interview process. Each report

requires a minimum of ten to fifteen interviews with academics, officials, lobbyists and people working in the field. Only after all interviews are completed does the writing begin.

CHAPTER FORMAT

Each issue of *Researcher*, and therefore each selection in this book, is structured in the same way. Each begins with an overview, which briefly summarizes the areas that will be explored in greater detail in the rest of the chapter. The next section, "Issue Questions," is the core of each chapter. It chronicles important and current debates on the topic under discussion and is structured around a number of key questions, such as "Is discrimination still a problem in the United States?" and "Does illegal immigration hurt American workers?"

These questions are usually the subject of much debate among practitioners and scholars in the field. Hence, the answers presented are never conclusive but detail the range of opinion on the topic.

After "Issue Questions" is the "Background" section, which provides a history of the issue being examined. This retrospective covers important legislative measures, executive actions and court decisions that illustrate how current policy has evolved. Next, the "Current Situation" section examines contemporary policy issues, legislation under consideration and legal action being taken. Each selection concludes with an "Outlook" section, which addresses possible regulation, court rulings and initiatives from Capitol Hill and the White House over the next five to ten years.

Each report contains features that augment the main text: two to three sidebars that examine issues related to the topic at hand, a pro-versus-con debate between two experts, a chronology of key dates and events and an annotated bibliography detailing major sources used by the writer.

ACKNOWLEDGMENTS

We wish to thank many people for helping to make this collection a reality. Tom Colin, managing editor of *CQ Researcher*, gave us his enthusiastic support and cooperation as we developed this third edition. He and his talented staff of editors and writers have amassed a first-class library of *Researcher* reports, and we are fortunate to have access to that rich cache. We also thankfully acknowledge the advice and feedback from current readers and are gratified by their satisfaction with the book.

Some readers may be learning about *Researcher* for the first time. We expect that many readers will want regular access to this excellent weekly research tool. For subscription information or a no-obligation free trial of *Researcher*, please contact CQ Press at www.cqpress.com or toll-free at 1-866-4CQ-PRESS (1-866-427-7737).

We hope that you will be pleased with the third edition of *Issues in Race and Ethnicity*. We welcome your feedback and suggestions for future editions. Please direct comments to Charisse Kiino, Chief Acquisitions Editor, College Division, CQ Press, 1255 22nd Street, N.W., Suite 400, Washington, D.C. 20037, or ckiino@cqpress.com.

— *The Editors of CQ Press*

Contributors

Thomas J. Colin, managing editor of *CQ Researcher*, has been a magazine and newspaper journalist for more than 30 years. Before joining Congressional Quarterly in 1991, he was a reporter and editor at the *Miami Herald* and *National Geographic* and editor in chief of *Historic Preservation*. He holds a bachelor's degree in English from the College of William and Mary and in journalism from the University of Missouri.

Mary H. Cooper recently retired after 22 years as a *CQ Researcher* staff writer specializing in environmental, energy and defense issues. She formerly was a reporter and Washington correspondent for the Rome daily newspaper *l'Unità* and is the author of *The Business of Drugs* (CQ Press, 1990). Cooper graduated from Hollins College with a bachelor's degree in English.

Alan Greenblatt is a staff writer for Congressional Quarterly's *Governing* magazine, and previously covered elections and military and agricultural policy for *CQ Weekly*. A recipient of the National Press Club's Sandy Hume Memorial Award for political reporting, he holds a bachelor's degree from San Francisco State University and a master's degree in English literature from the University of Virginia.

Kenneth Jost, associate editor of *CQ Researcher*, graduated from Harvard College and Georgetown University Law Center, where he is an adjunct professor. He is the author of *The Supreme Court Yearbook* and editor of *The Supreme Court A to Z* (both published by CQ Press). He was a member of the *CQ Researcher* team that won the 2002 American Bar Association Silver Gavel Award.

Peter Katel is a veteran journalist who previously served as Latin America bureau chief for *Time* magazine, in Mexico City, and as a Miami-based correspondent for *Newsweek* and the *Miami Herald*'s *El Nuevo Herald*. He also worked as a reporter in New Mexico for eleven years and wrote for several non-governmental organizations, including International Social Service and The World Bank. He has won several awards, including the Interamerican Press Association's Bartolome Mitre Award. He is a graduate of the University of New Mexico in university studies.

Patrick Marshall is a freelance writer based in Bainbridge Island, Washington, who writes about public policy and technology issues. His recent *CQ Researcher* reports include "Policing the Borders" and "Marijuana Laws."

David Masci is a senior fellow at the Pew Forum on Religion and Society in Washington, D.C. He previously was a staff writer for *CQ Researcher*, specializing in social policy, religion and foreign affairs, and a reporter at Congressional Quarterly's *Daily Monitor* and *CQ Weekly*. He holds a bachelor's degree in medieval history from Syracuse University and a law degree from the George Washington University.

William Triplett is a veteran writer and former *CQ Researcher* staff writer who is now the Washington correspondent for *Variety*. He previously covered science and the arts for such publications as *Smithsonian*, *Air & Space*, *Washingtonian*, *Nature* and the *Washington Post*. He holds a bachelor's degree in journalism from Ohio University and a master's degree in English literature from Georgetown University.

1

Affirmative Action

Kenneth Jost

First-year engineering students at the University of
Michigan–Ann Arbor gather during welcome week.
A federal judge ruled in December 2000 that the
school's race-based admissions system in 1995 was
illegal but that a revised system adopted later was
constitutional. The case went before the Supreme Court
in 2003.

J ennifer Gratz wanted to go to the University of Michigan's flagship Ann Arbor campus as soon as she began thinking about
college. "It's the best school in Michigan to go to," she explains.
The white suburban teenager's dream turned to disappointment
in April 1995, however, when the university told her that even
though she was "well qualified," she had been rejected for one of
the nearly 4,000 slots in the incoming freshman class.

Gratz was convinced something was wrong. "I knew that the
University of Michigan was giving preference to minorities," she
recalls. "If you give extra points for being of a particular race, then
you're not giving applicants an equal opportunity."

Gratz went on to earn a degree from Michigan's less prestigious
Dearborn campus and a job in San Diego. But she also became the
lead plaintiff in a showdown legal battle in the long-simmering conflict over racial preferences in college admissions.

On the opposite side of Gratz's federal court lawsuit was Lee
Bollinger, a staunch advocate of race-conscious admissions policies
who served as president of the University of Michigan for five-and-
a-half years before leaving in June 2002 to assume the presidency of
Columbia University.

"Racial and ethnic diversity is one part of the core liberal educational goal," Bollinger says. "People have different educational experiences when they grow up as an African-American, Hispanic or white."

Gratz won a partial victory in December 2000, when a federal
judge agreed that the university's admissions system in 1995 was
illegal. The ruling came too late to help her, however, and Judge
Patrick Duggan went on to rule that the revised system the university adopted in 1998 passed constitutional muster.

From *CQ Researcher*,
September 21, 2001.

Despite Progress, Minorities Still Trail Whites

A larger percentage of young adult African-Americans and Hispanics have completed college today than 20 years ago. But college completion rates for African-Americans and Hispanics continue to be significantly lower than the rate for whites. Today, the national college completion rate — 30 percent — is more than triple the rate in 1950.

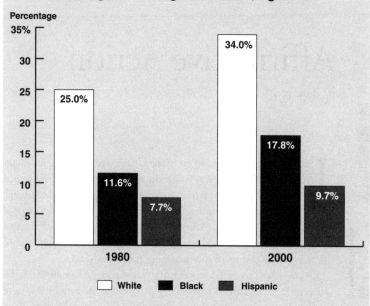

Percentages of College Graduates, Ages 25–29

Source: U.S. Department of Education, "Digest of Education Statistics," 2001 edition.

U.S. Supreme Court. Then, in a dramatic day at the high court, the justices issued companion rulings on June 23, 2003, that upheld the law school's policies, but struck down the college's system.

The law school system satisfied constitutional standards, Justice Sandra Day O'Connor wrote in the 5-4 decision, because it was narrowly tailored to achieve the goal of attaining a diverse student body. Writing for a different 6-3 majority, however, Chief Justice William H. Rehnquist said the college's admissions system was unconstitutional because it awarded minority candidates a fixed numerical bonus without individualized consideration of the applicants' backgrounds and records.[1]

The rulings were aimed at resolving legal uncertainty stemming from the long time span — 23 years — since the Supreme Court's only previous full-scale ruling on race-based admissions policies: the famous *Bakke* decision. In that fractured ruling, *University of California Regents v. Bakke*, the high court in 1978 ruled that fixed racial quotas were illegal but allowed the use of race as one factor in college admissions.[2]

Some three months later, however, another federal judge ruled in a separate case that the admissions system used at the university's law school was illegal. Judge Bernard Friedman said the law school's admissions policies were "practically indistinguishable from a quota system."

The decision came in a suit filed by Barbara Grutter, who unsuccessfully sought admission to the law school in December 1996 while in her 40s after having raised a family and worked as a health care consultant. Grutter, who is white, blamed her rejection on minority preferences used by the law school.

The two cases — *Gratz v. Bollinger* and *Grutter v. Bollinger* — went on to be argued together before the federal appeals court in Cincinnati and then again before the

After *Bakke*, race-based admissions policies became widespread in U.S. higher education — "well accepted and entrenched," according to Sheldon Steinbach, general counsel of the pro-affirmative action American Council on Education.

Roger Clegg, general counsel of the Center for Equal Opportunity, which opposes racial preferences, agrees with Steinbach but from a different perspective. "Evidence is overwhelming that racial and ethnic discrimination occurs frequently in public college and university admissions," Clegg says.[3]

Higher-education organizations and traditional civil rights groups say racial admissions policies are essential to ensure racial and ethnic diversity at the nation's elite universities — including the most selective state schools, such as Michigan's Ann Arbor campus. "The overwhelming majority of students who apply to highly selective institutions are still white," says Theodore Shaw, director of the NAACP Legal Defense and Educational Fund, which represented minority students who intervened in the two Michigan cases. "If we are not conscious of selecting minority students, they're not going to be there."

Opponents, however, say racial preferences are wrong in terms of law and social policy. "It's immoral. It's illegal. It stigmatizes the beneficiary. It encourages hypocrisy. It lowers standards. It encourages the use of stereotypes," Clegg says. "There are all kinds of social costs, and we don't think the benefits outweigh those costs."

The race-based admissions policies now in use around the country have evolved gradually after the passage of federal civil rights legislation in the mid-1960s. By 1970, the phrase "affirmative action" had become common usage to describe efforts to increase the number of African-Americans (and, later, Hispanics) in U.S. workplaces and on college campuses.[4] Since then, the proportions of African-Americans and Hispanics on college campuses have increased, though they are still underrepresented in terms of their respective proportions in the U.S. population. (*See chart, p. 4.*)

Michigan's efforts ranged from uncontroversial minority-outreach programs to an admissions system that explicitly took an applicant's race or ethnicity into account in deciding whether to accept or reject the applicant. The system formerly used by the undergraduate College of Literature, Science and the Arts had separate grids for white and minority applicants. It was replaced by a system that used a numerical rating with a 20-point bonus (out of a total possible score of 150) for "underrepresented minorities" — African-Americans, Hispanics and Native Americans (but not Asian-Americans). The law school's system — devised in 1992 — was aimed at producing a minority enrollment of about 10 percent to 12 percent of the entering class.

Critics of racial preferences say they are not opposed to affirmative action. "Certainly there are some positive aspects to affirmative action," says Michael Rosman, attorney for the Center for Individual Rights in Washington, which represented the plaintiffs in the Michigan cases. Rosman says he approves of increased recruitment of minorities and reassessment by colleges of criteria for evaluating applicants. But, he adds, "To the extent that suggests that they have carte blanche to discriminate between people on the basis of race, it's not a good thing."

Higher-education officials respond that they should have discretion to explicitly consider race — along with a host of other factors — to ensure a fully representative student body and provide the best learning environment for an increasingly multicultural nation and world. "Having a diverse student body contributes to the educational process and is necessary in the 21st-century global economy," Steinbach says.

As colleges and universities examine the impact of the Supreme Court's rulings in the University of Michigan cases, here are some of the major questions being debated:

Should colleges use race-based admissions policies to remedy discrimination against minorities?

The University of Michigan relies heavily on high school students' scores on standardized tests in evaluating applications — tests that have been widely criticized as biased against African-Americans and other minorities. It gives preferences to children of Michigan alumni — who are disproportionately white — as well as to applicants from "underrepresented" parts of the state, such as Michigan's predominantly white Upper Peninsula.

Even apart from the university's past record of racial segregation, those factors could be cited as evidence that Michigan's admissions policies were racially discriminatory because they had a "disparate impact" on minorities. And the Supreme Court, in *Bakke*, said that racial classifications were constitutional if they were used as a remedy for proven discrimination.

But Michigan did not defend its racial admissions policies on that basis. "Every public university has its share of decisions that we're now embarrassed by," Bollinger conceded. But the university defended its use of race — along with an array of other factors — only as a method of producing racial diversity, not as a way to remedy current or past discrimination.

Some civil rights advocates, however, insist that colleges and universities are still guilty of racially biased policies that warrant — even require — explicit racial preferences as corrective measures.

"Universities should use race-conscious admissions as a way of countering both past and ongoing ways in which the admission process continues to engage in practices that perpetuate racism or are unconsciously racist,"

Minority Enrollments Increased

African-Americans and Hispanics make up a larger percentage of the U.S. college population today than they did in 1976, but they are still underrepresented in comparison to their proportion of the total U.S. population. Hispanics comprise 12.5 percent of the population, African-Americans 12.3 percent.

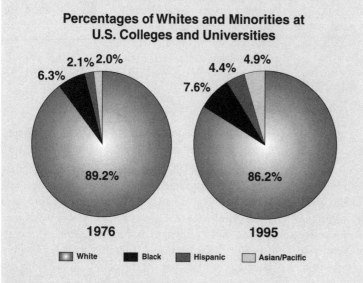

Percentages of Whites and Minorities at U.S. Colleges and Universities

Note: Percentages do not add to 100 due to rounding.

Source: U.S. Dept. of Education, "Digest of Education Statistics," 2001 edition.

says Charles Lawrence, a professor at Georgetown University Law Center in Washington.

Opponents of racial preferences, however, say colleges should be very wary about justifying such policies on the basis of past or current discrimination against minorities. "The Supreme Court has been pretty clear that you can't use the justification of past societal discrimination as a ground for a race-based admissions policy at an institution that did not itself discriminate," says Stephen Balch, president of the National Association of Scholars, a Princeton, N.J.-based group of academics opposed to racial preferences.

Balch defends alumni preferences, the most frequently mentioned example of an admissions policy that disadvantages minority applicants. "It's not at all unreasonable for colleges and universities to cultivate their alumni base," Balch says. In any event, he adds, "As student bodies change, the effect of that policy will change."

For his part, Rosman of the Center for Individual Rights says racial preferences are not justified even if colleges are wrong to grant alumni preferences or to rely so heavily on standardized test scores. "If you have criteria that discriminate and are not educationally justified, then the appropriate response is to get rid of those criteria, not to use 'two wrongs make a right,'" Rosman says.

Minority students intervened in both the undergraduate and law school suits to present evidence of discrimination by the university and to use that evidence to justify the racial admissions policies. In the undergraduate case, evidence showed that the university refused to desegregate fraternities and sororities until the 1960s, allowed white students to refuse to room with black students and did not hire its first black professor until 1967. The evidence also showed that black students reported continuing discrimination and racial hostility through the 1980s and into the '90s.

In his Dec. 13, 2000, ruling, Judge Duggan acknowledged the evidence but rejected it as a justification for the admissions policies. The racial segregation occurred too long ago to be a reason for current policies, Duggan said. He also rejected the minority students' argument that the racial impact of alumni preferences, standardized test scores and other admissions criteria justified preferences for minority applicants.

Judge Friedman rejected similar arguments in the final portion of his March 27, 2001, ruling in the law school case. "This is a social and political matter, which calls for social and political solutions," Friedman wrote. "The solution is not for the law school, or any other state institution, to prefer some applicants over others because of race."

Should colleges use race-based admissions policies to promote diversity in their student populations?

Michigan's high schools graduated some 100,000 students in 1999. Out of that number, only 327 African-

American students had a B-plus average and an SAT score above 1,000 — the kind of record needed to make them strong contenders for admission to the University of Michigan's Ann Arbor campus based on those factors alone.

University officials cited that stark statistic to underline the difficulty in admitting a racially diverse student body — and to justify their policy of giving minority applicants special consideration in the admissions process. Without the bonus for minority applicants, the number of African-American and Hispanic students "would drop dramatically" from the current level of about 13 percent of undergraduates to "somewhere around 5 percent," according to Elizabeth Barry, the university's associate vice president and deputy general counsel.

Opponents of racial preferences dismiss the warnings. "It's certainly not inevitable that the number of students from racial and ethnic minorities will decline" under a color-blind system, Rosman says. In any event, he says that diversity is "not a sufficiently powerful goal to discriminate and treat people differently on the basis of race."

The dispute between supporters and opponents of racial admissions policies turns in part on two somewhat rarefied issues. Supporters claim to have social-science evidence to show that racial and ethnic diversity produces quantifiable educational benefits for all students — evidence that opponents deride as dubious at best. *(See story, p. 14.)* The opposing camps also differ on the question of whether the *Bakke* decision allows colleges to use diversity as the kind of "compelling government interest" needed to satisfy the so-called strict-scrutiny standard of constitutional review. *(See story, p. 7.)*

Apart from those specialized disputes, opponents of racial preferences argue simply that they constitute a form of stereotyping and discrimination. "We don't believe that there is a black outlook or an Asian outlook or a white experience or a Hispanic experience," Clegg

Gratz v. Bollinger: Race and College Admissions

Jennifer Gratz, a white woman, sued the University of Michigan contending she was improperly denied admission because of race. The lawsuit is shaping up as a key battle in the long-simmering conflict over racial preferences in college admissions.

"I see benefits from different opinions, different thoughts on any number of subjects. But I don't think that's necessarily race coming through. I don't think like every other white person. . . . Your race doesn't mean that you're going to think this way or that way."

Jennifer Gratz, B.S., University of Michigan, Dearborn

"You get a better education and a better society in an environment where you are mixing with lots of different people – people from different parts of the country, people from different parts of the socioeconomic system, people from abroad, and people from different races and ethnicities."

Lee Bollinger, former president, University of Michigan

says. "Students are individuals, and they should be treated as individuals, not as fungible members of racial and ethnic groups."

Some critics — including a few African-Americans — also say racial preferences "stigmatize" the intended beneficiaries by creating the impression that they could not be successful without being given some advantage over whites. "There is no way that a young black at an Ivy League university is going to get credit for [doing well]," says Shelby Steele, a prominent black critic of racial preferences and a research fellow at the Hoover Institution at Stanford University. "There's no way that he's going to feel his achievements are his own."

Supporters of racial admission policies, however, say that race plays an independent and important role in American society that colleges are entitled to take into account. "It is reasonable for educational institutions to believe that race is not a proxy for something else," Bollinger says. "It is a defining experience in American life — and therefore an important one for this goal" of educational diversity.

White supporters of affirmative action generally deny or minimize any supposed stigmatization from race-conscious policies. Some blacks acknowledge some stigmatizing effects, but blame white racism rather than affirmative action. "The stigmatizing beliefs about people of color," Professor Lawrence writes, "have their origin not in affirmative action programs but in the cultural belief system of white supremacy."[5]

The two judges in the Michigan cases reached different conclusions on the diversity issue. In his ruling in the undergraduate case, Duggan agreed with the university's argument that a "racially and ethnically diverse student body produces significant education benefits, such that diversity, in the context of higher education, constitutes a compelling governmental interest under strict scrutiny."

Ruling in the law school case, Judge Friedman acknowledged that racial diversity may provide "educational and societal benefits," though he also called for drawing "a distinction . . . between viewpoint diversity and racial diversity." Based on his interpretation of *Bakke*, however, Friedman said these "important and laudable" benefits did not amount to a compelling interest sufficient to justify the law school's use of race in admissions decisions.

Should colleges adopt other policies to try to increase minority enrollment?

Texas and Florida have a different approach to ensuring a racial mix in their state university systems. Texas' "10 percent plan" — adopted in 1997 under then-Gov. George W. Bush — promises a spot in the state university to anyone who graduates in the top 10 percent of any high school in the state. Florida's plan — adopted in 1999 under Gov. Jeb Bush, the president's brother — makes the same commitment to anyone in the top 20 percent.

The plans are drawing much attention and some favorable comment as an ostensibly race-neutral alternative to racial preferences. But major participants on both sides of the debate over racial admissions policies view the idea with skepticism.

"It's silly to suggest that all high schools are equal in terms of the quality of their student body," Clegg says. "And therefore it makes no sense to have an across-the-board rule that the top 10 percent of every high school is going to be admitted."

Both Clegg and Rosman also say that a 10 percent-type plan is dubious if it is adopted to circumvent a ban on explicit racial preferences. "Any neutral policy that is just a pretext for discrimination would have to survive strict scrutiny," Rosman says.

Supporters of race-based admissions are also unenthusiastic. "The only reason they work is because we have segregated high schools, segregated communities," Shaw says. "From a philosophical standpoint, I'd rather deal with race in a more honest and upfront way and make a more principled approach to these issues."

In the Michigan lawsuits, the university cited testimony from a prominent supporter of racial admissions policies in opposition to 10 percent-type plans. "Treating all applicants alike if they finished above a given high school class rank provides a spurious form of equality that is likely to damage the academic profile of the overall class of students admitted to selective institutions," said former Princeton University president William G. Bowen, later president of the Andrew W. Mellon Foundation in New York City.

Rosman looks more favorably on another alternative: giving preferences to applicants who come from disadvantaged socioeconomic backgrounds. "It's not a bad idea to take into account a person's ability to overcome obstacles," he says. "That's useful in assessing a person's qualifications."

In his testimony, however, Bowen also criticized that approach. Youngsters from poor black and Hispanic families are "much less likely" to excel in school than those from poor white families, Bowen said. On that basis, he predicted that a "class-based" rather than race-based admissions policy "would substantially reduce the minority enrollments at selective institutions."

For its part, the University of Michigan stressed that its system gave up to 20 points to an applicant based on socioeconomic disadvantage — the same number given to minority applicants. "We consider a number of factors in order to enroll a diverse student body," Barry said while the system was in use, "because race is not the only element that's important to diversity in education."

In their rulings, Duggan and Friedman both favorably noted a number of alternatives to race-based admissions policies. Friedman suggested the law school could have increased recruiting efforts or decreased the emphasis on

What Does *Bakke* Mean? Two Judges Disagree

The Supreme Court's 1978 decision to prohibit fixed racial quotas in colleges and universities but to allow the use of race as one factor in admissions was hailed by some people at the time as a Solomon-like compromise.

But the meaning of the high court's famous *Bakke* decision was sharply disputed. And the disagreement lay at the heart of conflicting rulings by two federal judges in Michigan on the legality of racial preferences used at the University of Michigan's flagship Ann Arbor campus.

In upholding the flexible race-based admissions system used by the undergraduate College of Literature, Science and the Arts in December 2000, Judge Patrick Duggan said *Bakke* means that colleges can evaluate white and minority applicants differently in order to enroll a racially and ethnically diverse student body.

But Judge Bernard Friedman rejected that widely held interpretation in his March 2001 decision striking down the law school's use of race in admissions. Friedman — like Duggan an appointee of President Ronald Reagan — said that racial and ethnic diversity did not qualify as a "compelling governmental interest" needed under the so-called strict scrutiny constitutional standard to justify a race-based government policy.

The differing interpretations stem from the Supreme Court's unusual 4-1-4 vote in the case, *University of California Regents v. Bakke*. Four of the justices found the quota system used by the UC-Davis Medical School — reserving 16 out of 100 seats for minorities — to be a violation of the federal civil rights law prohibiting racial discrimination in federally funded institutions. Four others — led by the liberal Justice William J. Brennan Jr. — voted to reject Alan Bakke's challenge to the system.

In the pivotal opinion, Justice Lewis F. Powell Jr. found the UC-Davis admissions system to be a violation of the constitutional requirement of equal protection but said race could be used as a "plus" factor in admissions decisions. The "attainment of a diverse student body," Powell wrote, "clearly is a constitutionally permissible goal for an institution of higher education."

Under Supreme Court case law, it takes a majority of the justices — five — to produce a "holding" that can serve as a precedent for future cases. In a fractured ruling, the Court's holding is said to be the "narrowest" rationale endorsed by five justices. But Brennan's group did not explicitly address the question of diversity. Instead, they said that race-based admissions decisions were justified to remedy past discrimination — a proposition that Powell also endorsed.

Critics of racial preferences in recent years have argued that the Brennan group's silence on diversity means that they did not join Powell's reasoning. On that basis, these critics say, Powell's opinion cannot be viewed as a controlling precedent. They won an important victory when the federal appeals court in New Orleans adopted that reasoning in the so-called *Hopwood* case in 1996 striking down the University of Texas Law School's racial preferences.

In his ruling in the Michigan law school case, Friedman also agreed with this revisionist view of *Bakke*. "The diversity rationale articulated by Justice Powell is neither narrower nor broader than the remedial rationale articulated by the Brennan group," Friedman wrote. "They are completely different rationales, neither one of which is subsumed within the other."

But in the undergraduate case, Duggan followed the previous interpretation of *Bakke*. Brennan's "silence regarding the diversity interest in *Bakke* was not an implicit rejection of such an interest, but rather, an implicit approval of such an interest," Duggan wrote.

The two judges also differed on how to interpret later Supreme Court decisions. Duggan cited Brennan's 1990 majority opinion in a case upholding racial preferences in broadcasting — *Metro Broadcasting, Inc. v. Federal Communications Commission* — as supporting the use of diversity to justify racial policies. But Friedman said other recent rulings showed that the Supreme Court had become much more skeptical of racial policies than it had been in 1978. Among the decisions he cited was the 1995 ruling *Adarand Constructors Inc. v. Pena* that overruled the *Metro Broadcasting* holding.

Reporters follow Alan Bakke on his first day at the University of California-Davis Medical School on Sept. 25, 1978. The Supreme Court ordered him admitted after ruling that the school violated his rights by maintaining a fixed quota for minority applicants.

AP Photo/Walt Zeboski

undergraduate grades and scores on the Law School Aptitude Test. He also said the school could have used a lottery for all qualified applicants or admitted some fixed number or percentage of top graduates from various colleges and universities. Friedman said the law school's "apparent failure to investigate alternative means for increasing minority enrollment" was one factor in rejecting the school's admissions policies.

For his part, Duggan noted the possibility of using race-neutral policies to increase minority enrollment when he rejected the minority students' critique of such policies as alumni preferences. "If the current selection criteria have a discriminatory impact on minority applicants," Duggan wrote, "it seems to this court that the narrowly tailored remedy would be to remove or redistribute such criteria to accommodate for socially and economically disadvantaged applicants of all races and ethnicities, not to add another suspect criteria [sic] to the list."

BACKGROUND

Unequal Opportunity

African-Americans and other racial and ethnic minority groups have been underrepresented on college campuses throughout U.S. history. The civil rights revolution has effectively dismantled most legal barriers to higher education for minorities. But the social and economic inequalities that persist between white Americans and racial and ethnic minority groups continue to make the goal of equal opportunity less than reality for many African-Americans and Hispanics.

The legal battles that ended mandatory racial segregation in the United States began with higher education nearly two decades before the Supreme Court's historic ruling in *Brown v. Board of Education*.[6] In the first of the rulings that ended the doctrine of "separate but equal," the court in 1938 ruled that Missouri violated a black law school applicant's equal protection rights by offering to pay his tuition to an out-of-state school rather than admit him to the state's all-white law school.

The court followed with a pair of rulings in 1950 that similarly found states guilty of violating black students' rights to equal higher education. Texas was ordered to admit a black student to the state's all-white law school rather than force him to attend an inferior all-black

school. And Oklahoma was found to have discriminated against a black student by admitting him to a previously all-white state university but denying him the opportunity to use all its facilities.

At the time of these decisions, whites had substantially greater educational opportunities than African-Americans. As of 1950, a majority of white Americans ages 25-29 — 56 percent — had completed high school, compared with only 24 percent of African-Americans. Eight percent of whites in that age group had completed college compared with fewer than 3 percent of blacks. Most of the African-American college graduates had attended all-black institutions: either private colleges established for blacks or racially segregated state universities.

The Supreme Court's 1954 decision in *Brown* to begin dismantling racial segregation in elementary and secondary education started to reduce the inequality in educational opportunities for whites and blacks, but changes were slow. It was not until 1970 that a majority of African-Americans ages 25-29 had attained high school degrees.

Changes at the nation's elite colleges and universities were even slower. In their book *The Shape of the River*, two former Ivy League presidents — Bowen and Derek Bok — say that as of 1960 "no selective college or university was making determined efforts to seek out and admit substantial numbers of African-American students." As of 1965, they report, African-Americans comprised only 4.8 percent of students on the nation's college campuses and fewer than 1 percent of students at select New England colleges.[7]

As part of the Civil Rights Act of 1964, Congress included provisions in Title IV to authorize the Justice Department to initiate racial-desegregation lawsuits against public schools and colleges and to require the U.S. Office of Education (now the Department of Education) to give technical assistance to school systems undergoing desegregation. A year later, President Lyndon B. Johnson delivered his famous commencement speech at historically black Howard University that laid the foundation for a more proactive approach to equalizing opportunities for African-Americans. "You do not take a person," Johnson said, "who, for years, has been hobbled by chains and liberate him, bring him up to the starting line of a race and then say, 'You are free to compete with all the others,' and still justly believe that you have been completely fair."[8]

Affirmative Action

Colleges began in the mid-1960s to make deliberate efforts to increase the number of minority students. Many universities instituted "affirmative action" programs that included targeted recruitment of minority applicants as well as explicit use of race as a factor in admissions policies. White students challenged the use of racial preferences, but the Supreme Court — in the *Bakke* decision in 1978 — gave colleges and universities a flashing green light to consider race as one factor in admissions policies aimed at ensuring a racially diverse student body.

The federal government encouraged universities to look to enrollment figures as the criterion for judging the success of their affirmative action policies. By requiring universities to report minority enrollment figures, the Nixon administration appeared to suggest that race-conscious admissions were "not only permissible but mandatory," according to Bowen and Bok. But universities were also motivated, they say, to remedy past racial discrimination, to educate minority leaders and to create diversity on campuses.

As early as 1966, Bowen and Bok report, Harvard Law School moved to increase the number of minority students by "admitting black applicants with test scores far below those of white classmates." As other law schools adopted the strategy, enrollment of African-Americans increased — from 1 percent of all law students in 1965 to 4.5 percent in 1975. Similar efforts produced a significant increase in black students in Ivy League colleges. The proportion of African-American students at Ivy League schools increased from 2.3 percent in 1967 to 6.7 percent in 1976, Bowen and Bok report.[9]

Critics, predominantly but not exclusively political conservatives, charged that the racial preferences amounted to "reverse discrimination" against white students and applicants. Some white students challenged the policies in court. The Supreme Court sought to resolve the issue in 1978 in a case brought by a California man, Alan Bakke, who had been denied admission to the University of California Medical School at Davis under a system that explicitly reserved 16 of 100 seats for minority applicants. The 4-1-4 decision fell short of a definitive resolution, though.

Justice Lewis F. Powell Jr. cast the decisive vote in the case. He joined four justices to reject Davis' fixed-quota approach and four others to allow use of race as one fac-

AP Photo

President Lyndon B. Johnson signs the Civil Rights Act on July 2, 1964. Race-based admissions policies now in use around the country evolved gradually from the landmark law.

tor in admissions decisions. In summarizing his opinion from the bench, Powell explained that it meant Bakke would be admitted to the medical school but that Davis was free to adopt a more "flexible program designed to achieve diversity" just like those "proved to be successful at many of our great universities."[10]

Civil rights advocates initially reacted with "consternation," according to Steinbach of the American Council on Education. Quickly, though, college officials and higher-education groups took up the invitation to devise programs that used race — in Powell's terms — as a "plus factor" without setting aside any seats specifically for minority applicants. The ruling, Steinbach says, "enabled institutions in a creative manner to legally provide for a diverse student body."

The Supreme Court avoided re-examining *Bakke* after 1978, but narrowed the scope of affirmative action in other areas. The court in 1986 ruled that government employers could not lay off senior white workers to make room for new minority hires, though it upheld affirmative action in hiring and promotions in two other decisions that year and another ruling in a sex-discrimination case a year later. As for government contracting, the

CHRONOLOGY

Before 1960 *Limited opportunities for minorities in private and public colleges and universities.*

1938 Supreme Court says Missouri violated Constitution by operating all-white law school but no school for blacks.

1950 Supreme Court says Texas violated Constitution by operating "inferior" law school for blacks.

1954 Supreme Court rules racial segregation in public elementary and secondary schools unconstitutional; ruling is extended to dismantle racially segregated colleges.

1960s–1980s *Civil rights era: higher education desegregated; affirmative action widely adopted, approved by Supreme Court if racial quotas not used.*

1964 Civil Rights Act bars discrimination by federally funded colleges.

1978 Supreme Court rules in *Bakke* that colleges and universities can consider race as one factor in admissions policies.

1980s Supreme Court leaves *Bakke* unchanged.

1990s *Opposition to race-based admissions policies grows.*

1995 President Clinton defends affirmative action; University of California ends use of race and sex in admissions.

1996 University of Texas Law School's use of racial preferences in admissions ruled unconstitutional in *Hopwood* case; California voters approve Proposition 209 banning state-sponsored affirmative action in employment, contracting and admissions.

1997 Texas Gov. George W. Bush signs law guaranteeing admission to University of Texas to top 10 percent of graduates in state high schools.

1998 Washington state voters approve initiative barring racial preferences in state colleges and universities.

1999 Gov. Jeb Bush of Florida issues executive order banning racial preferences but granting admission to state colleges to top 20 percent of graduates in all state high schools.

2000s *Legal challenges to affirmative action continue.*

Dec. 4, 2000 University of Washington Law School's former admissions system — discontinued after Proposition 200 — is upheld by federal court.

Dec. 13, 2000 University of Michigan undergraduate admissions policies upheld by federal judge, though former system ruled illegal.

March 26, 2001 Supreme Court agrees to hear new appeal in *Adarand* case.

March 27, 2001 University of Michigan Law School admissions policies ruled unconstitutional by federal judge.

June 2001 Supreme Court declines to review conflicting rulings in *University of Washington, University of Texas* cases.

Aug. 27, 2001 Federal appeals court in Atlanta rules University of Georgia admissions system giving bonuses to all non-white applicants is unconstitutional.

May 2002 University of Michigan Law School admissions system upheld by federal appeals court in Cincinnati by 5-4 vote; court issues no ruling in challenge to admissions policies at Michigan's undergraduate college.

Dec. 2002 Supreme Court agrees to take up challenges to admissions policies for undergraduates and law students at University of Michigan.

June 23, 2003 Supreme Court upholds, 5-4, use of race in admissions at University of Michigan Law School, but rules racial preferences in undergraduate admissions unconstitutional by 6-3 vote; in pivotal opinion, Justice Sandra Day O'Connor calls for racial preferences to end in 25 years.

court ruled in 1989 that state and local governments could not use racial preferences except to remedy past discrimination and extended that limitation to federal programs in 1995.[11]

All of the court's decisions were closely divided, but the conservative majority made clear their discomfort with race-specific policies. Indeed, as legal-affairs writer Lincoln Caplan notes, none of the five current conservatives — Chief Justice William H. Rehnquist and Associate Justices Sandra Day O'Connor, Antonin Scalia, Anthony M. Kennedy and Clarence Thomas — had ever voted to approve a race-based affirmative action program prior to the Michigan cases.[12]

Negative Reaction

A political and legal backlash against affirmative action emerged with full force in the 1990s — highlighted by moves in California to scrap race-conscious policies in the state's university system and a federal appeals court decision barring racial preferences in admissions in Texas and two neighboring states. But President Bill Clinton rebuffed calls to scrap federal affirmative action programs. And colleges continued to follow race-conscious admissions policies in the absence of a new Supreme Court pronouncement on the issue.

In the first of the moves against race-conscious admissions, the 5th U.S. Circuit Court of Appeals in New Orleans in March 1996 struck down the University of Texas Law School's system that used separate procedures for white and minority applicants with the goal of admitting a class with 5 percent African-American and 10 percent Mexican-American students.[13] The ruling in the *Hopwood* case unanimously rejected the university's attempt to justify the racial preferences on grounds of past discrimination. Two judges also rejected the university's diversity defense and directly contradicted the prevailing interpretation of Bakke that diversity amounted to a "compelling governmental interest" justifying race-based policies.[14]

The ruling specifically applied only to the three states in the 5th Circuit — Louisiana, Mississippi and Texas — but observers saw the decision as significant. "This is incredibly big," said John C. Jeffries Jr., a University of Virginia law professor and Justice Powell's biographer. "This could affect every public institution in America because all of them take racial diversity into account in admissions."[15]

Four months later, the University of California Board of Regents — the policy-making body for the prestigious, 162,000-student state university system — narrowly voted to abolish racial and sexual preferences in admissions by fall 1997. The 14-10 vote approved a resolution submitted by a black businessman, Ward Connerly, and supported by the state's Republican governor, Pete Wilson. Connerly was also the driving force behind a voter initiative — Proposition 209 — to abolish racial preferences in state government employment and contracting as well as college and university admissions. Voters approved the measure, 54 percent to 46 percent, in November 1996.

In the face of opposition from UC President Richard Atkinson, the move to scrap racial preferences was delayed to admissions for the 1998-1999 academic year. In May 1998, the university released figures showing a modest overall decline in acceptances by non-Asian minorities to 15.2 percent for the coming year from 17.6 percent for the 1997-1998 school year. But the figures also showed a steep drop in the number of black and Hispanic students in the entering classes at the two most prestigious campuses — Berkeley and UCLA. At Berkeley, African-American and Hispanic acceptances fell to 10.5 percent from 21.9 percent for the previous year; at UCLA, the drop was to 14.1 percent from 21.8 percent.

The Supreme Court did nothing to counteract the legal shift away from racial preferences in education. It declined in 1995 to review a decision by the federal appeals court in Richmond, Va., that struck down a University of Maryland scholarship program reserved for African-American students. A year later, the justices refused to hear Texas' appeal of the *Hopwood* decision; and a year after that they also turned aside a challenge by labor and civil rights groups to Proposition 209. Instead, the high court concentrated on a series of rulings beginning in June 1993 that limited the use of race in congressional and legislative redistricting.[16] And in June 1995 the court issued a decision, *Adarand Constructors, Inc. v. Pena*, that limited the federal government's discretion to give minority-owned firms preferences in government contracting.[17]

With affirmative action under sharp attack, Bowen and Bok came out in 1998 with their book-length study of graduates of selective colleges that they said refuted many of the criticisms of race-based admissions. Using a

Minority Preferences: Will They Disappear in 25 Years?

We take the Law School at its word that it would "like nothing better than to find a race-neutral admissions formula" and will terminate its race-conscious admissions program as soon as practicable. . . . It has been 25 years since Justice Powell first approved the use of race to further an interest in student body diversity in the context of public higher education. Since that time, the number of minority applicants with high grades and test scores has indeed increased. . . . We expect that 25 years from now, the use of racial preferences will no longer be necessary to further the interest approved today.

Justice Sandra Day O'Connor, majority opinion,
Grutter v. Bollinger

I agree with the Court's holding that racial discrimination in higher education admissions will be illegal in 25 years. . . . For the immediate future, however, the majority has placed its *imprimatur* on a practice that can only weaken the principle of equality embodied in the Declaration of Independence and the Equal Protection Clause. . . . It has been nearly 140 years since . . . the Nation adopted the Fourteenth Amendment. Now we must wait another 25 years to see this principle of equality vindicated.

Justice Clarence Thomas, separate opinion,
Grutter v. Bollinger

However strong the public's desire for improved education systems may be, . . . it remains the current reality that many minority students encounter markedly inadequate and unequal educational opportunities. Despite these inequalities, some minority students are able to meet the high threshold requirements set for admission to the country's finest undergraduate and graduate educational institutions. As lower school education in minority communities improves, an increase in the number of such students may be anticipated. From today's vantage point, one may hope, but not firmly forecast, that over the next generation's span, progress toward nondiscrimination and genuinely equal opportunity will make it safe to sunset affirmative action.

Justice Ruth Bader Ginsburg, separate opinion,
Grutter v. Bollinger

database of some 80,000 students who entered 28 elite colleges and universities in 1951, 1976 and 1989, the two former Ivy League presidents confirmed the increase in minority enrollment at the schools and the impact of racial preferences: More than half the black students admitted in 1976 and 1989 would not have been admitted under race-neutral policies, they said. But they said dropout rates among black students were low, satisfaction with their college experiences high and post-graduation accomplishments comparable with — or better than — white graduates.[18]

The Bowen-Bok book buttressed college and university officials in resisting calls to scrap racial preferences. While voters in Washington state moved to eliminate race-based admissions with an anti-affirmative action initiative in 1998, no other state university system followed the UC lead in voluntarily abolishing the use of race in weighing applications.

In Texas, then-Gov. George W. Bush sought to bolster minority enrollment in the UT system after *Hopwood* by proposing the 10 percent plan — guaranteeing admission to any graduating senior in the top 10 percent of his class. (Florida Gov. Jeb Bush followed suit with his 20 percent plan two years later.) Many schools — both public and private — re-examined their admissions policies after *Hopwood*. But, according to Steinbach, most of them "found that what they had was satisfactory."

Legal Battles

Critics of race-based admissions kept up their pressure on the issue by waging expensive, protracted legal battles in four states: Georgia, Michigan, Texas and Washington. The cases produced conflicting decisions. The conflict was starkest in the two University of Michigan cases, where two judges, both appointed in the 1980s by President Ronald Reagan, reached different results in evaluating the use of race at the undergraduate college and at the law school.

The controversy in Michigan began in a sense with the discontent of a longtime Ann Arbor faculty member, Carl Cohen.[19]A professor of philosophy and a "proud" member of the American Civil Liberties Union (ACLU), Cohen had been troubled by racial preferences since the 1970s. In 1995 he read a journal article that described admissions rates for black college applicants as higher nationally than those for white applicants. The article prompted Cohen to begin poking around to learn about Michigan's system.[20]

As Cohen tells the story, administrators stonewalled him until he used the state's freedom of information law to obtain the pertinent documents. He found that the admissions offices used a grid system that charted applicants based on high school grade point average on a horizontal axis and standardized test scores on a vertical axis — and that there were separate grids or different "action codes" (reject or admit) for white applicants and for minority applicants. "The racially discriminatory policies of the university are blatant," Cohen says today. "They are written in black and white by the university. It's just incredible."

Cohen wrote up his findings in a report that he presented later in the year at a meeting of the state chapter of the American Association of University Professors. The report also found its way to a Republican state legislator, Rep. Deborah Whyman, who conducted a hearing on the issue and later held a news conference to solicit unsuccessful applicants to challenge the university's admissions system. They forwarded about 100 of the replies to the Center for Individual Rights, a conservative public-interest law firm already active in challenging racial preferences.

Gratz and a second unsuccessful white applicant — Patrick Hamacher — were chosen to be the named plaintiffs in a class-action suit filed in federal court in Detroit in October 1997. The center filed a second suit on behalf of Grutter against the law school's admissions system in December 1997. Grutter thought she deserved admission based on her 3.8 undergraduate grade point average 18 years earlier and a respectable score on the law school admission test (161, or 86th percentile nationally). After the rejection, she did not enroll elsewhere.

The cases proved to be long and expensive. By fall 2000, the university said it had spent $4.3 million

defending the two suits, not counting personnel costs; the center had spent $400,000, including salaries, and also received the equivalent of $1 million in pro bono legal services from a Minneapolis firm helping to litigate the suits. Among the key pieces of evidence was a long report by an Ann Arbor faculty member — psychology professor Patricia Gurin — concluding that diversity in enrollment has "far-reaching and significant benefits for all students, non-minorities and minorities alike." The center countered with a lengthy study issued under the auspices of the National Association of Scholars that analyzed the same data and found "no connection . . . between campus racial diversity and the supposed educational benefits."

In the meantime, the university revised its undergraduate admissions system, beginning with the entering class of 1999. The race-based grids and codes were replaced by a numerical system that assigned points to each applicant based on any of a number of characteristics. An applicant from an "underrepresented minority group" — African-Americans, Hispanics and Native Americans — was given 20 points. (One hundred points was typically required for admission, according to Cohen.) The same number was given to an applicant from a disadvantaged socioeconomic status, to a white student from a predominantly minority high school or to a scholarship athlete, according to university counsel Barry. The most important single factor, she added, was an applicant's high school grades.

Judge Duggan's Dec. 13, 2000, ruling in the undergraduate case sustained the plaintiffs' complaint against the system used when Gratz and Hamacher had been rejected. Duggan said that the "racially different grids and codes based solely upon an applicant's race" amounted to an "impermissible use of race." But Duggan said the revised system was on the right side of what he called "the thin line that divides the permissible and the impermissible."

Three months later, however, Judge Friedman on March 27, 2001, struck down the law school's admissions system. Evidence showed that the school had used a "special admissions" program since 1992 aimed at a minority enrollment of 10 percent to 12 percent.

Friedman relied on a statistical analysis that showed an African-American applicant's relative odds of acceptance were up to 400 times as great as a white applicant's. Friedman rejected the use of diversity to justify the racial

Evidence of Diversity Benefits Disputed

The University of Michigan defended its race-based admissions policies not only with law but also with evidence of the educational benefits of having a racially mixed student body. But opponents of racial preferences dismissed the evidence as distorted and biased.

The largest of the studies introduced as evidence in the two federal court lawsuits over the university's undergraduate and law school admissions policies runs 850 pages. Written by Patricia Gurin, chair of the Psychology Department, it contains detailed statistics derived from a national student database and surveys of Michigan students. Gurin contends that students "learn more and think in deeper, more complex ways in a diverse educational environment.[1]

In addition, Gurin says students "are more motivated and better able to participate in an increasingly heterogeneous and complex democracy." And students who had "diversity experiences" during college — such as taking courses in Afro-American studies — also had "the most cross-racial interactions" five years after leaving college.

The National Association of Scholars, which opposes racial preferences, released two lengthy critiques of Gurin's study after the trials of the two suits. The studies were included in a friend-of-the-court brief filed in the appeals of the rulings.[2]

In the major critique, Thomas E. Wood and Malcolm J. Sherman contend that the national student database actually shows "no relationship" between the proportion of minorities on campus and educational benefits. They also say that "diversity activities" had only a "trivial impact" on educational outcomes.

The university also included "expert reports" from William G. Bowen and Derek Bok, the two former Ivy League university presidents who co-authored the pro-affirmative action book *The Shape of the River*. Bowen and Bok repeat their conclusions from the 1998 book that black students admitted to the "highly selective" colleges and universities studied did "exceedingly well" after college in terms of graduate degrees, income and civic life.[3] About half of the blacks admitted to the schools would not have been admitted under race-neutral policies, Bowen and Bok say.

In their reports for the Michigan suits, Bowen and Bok briefly acknowledge that black students at the schools had lower grades and lower graduation rates than whites. In an early critique of the book, two well-known critics of racial preferences — Abigail and Stephan Thernstrom — call Bowen and Bok to task for glossing over the evidence of poor performance by black students. They note that the dropout rate for black students — about 20 percent — was three times higher than for whites and that black students' grades overall were at the 23rd percentile — that is, in the bottom quarter.[4]

The studies are the tip of a large iceberg of academic literature that has sought to examine the effects of diversity in colleges and universities. In one of the most recent of the studies to be published, a team of authors from Pennsylvania State University concluded that the evidence is "almost uniformly consistent" that students in a racially or ethnically diverse community or engaged in "diversity-related" activities "reap a wide array of positive educational benefits."[5] In their own study of students at seven engineering schools, the scholars found what they called "a small, if statistically significant, link between the level of racial/ethnic diversity in a classroom and students' reports of increases in their problem-solving and group skills."

University of Michigan student Agnes Aleobua speaks out against a court ruling in March 2001 that the law school's race-based admission policy is illegal.

AP Photo/Paul Sancya

[1] Gurin's report can be found on the university's Web site: www.umich.edu.

[2] Thomas E. Wood and Malcolm J. Sherman, "Is Campus Racial Diversity Correlated With Educational Benefits?," National Association of Scholars, April 4, 2001 (www.nas.org). Wood is executive director of the California Association of Scholars; Sherman is an associate professor of mathematics and statistics at the State University of New York in Albany.

[3] William G. Bowen and Derek Bok, *The Shape of the River: Long-Term Consequences of Considering Race in College and University Admissions*, 1998. Bowen is a former president of Princeton University, Bok a former president of Harvard University.

[4] Stephan Thernstrom and Abigail Thernstrom, "Reflections on *The Shape of the River*," *UCLA Law Review*, Vol. 45, No. 5 (June 1999), pp. 1583-1631. Stephan Thernstrom is a history professor at Harvard; his wife is a senior fellow at the Manhattan Institute and a member of the Massachusetts Board of Education.

[5] Patrick T. Terenzini *et al.*, "Racial and Ethnic Diversity in the Classroom: Does It Promote Student Learning?," *Journal of Higher Education* (September/October 2001), pp. 509-531. Terenzini is a professor and senior scientist with the Center for the Study of Higher Education at Pennsylvania State University.

preferences, but in any event said the law school's system was not "narrowly tailored" because there was no time limit and there had been no consideration of alternative means of increasing minority enrollment.

The two Michigan cases took on added significance in June 2001 when the Supreme Court declined for a second time to hear Texas' appeal in the *Hopwood* case or to hear the plaintiffs' appeal of a ruling by the 9th U.S. Circuit Court of Appeals upholding a discontinued system of racial preferences at the University of Washington Law School. Then on Aug. 27, 2001, the 11th U.S. Circuit Court of Appeals issued a ruling striking down the University of Georgia's admissions system.[21]

The 6th U.S. Circuit Court of Appeals decided to hear the two Michigan cases together in October 2001 before the full court instead of three-judge panels. Seven months later, the appeals court on May 14, 2002, issued a sharply divided, 5-4 decision upholding the law school admissions system. The majority said the school considered race along with other factors in an effort to admit enough minority students so that all students could enjoy "the educational benefits of an academically diverse student body." The dissenting judges maintained that the procedures were indistinguishable from a numerical quota.

The appeals court did not rule on the undergraduate case at the same time and issued no explanation for the omission. The Center for Individual Rights asked the Supreme Court to review the law school ruling and later — with the college case still undecided — asked the justices to bypass the appeals court and take jurisdiction of Gratz's case too. The university opposed reviewing the law school case, but agreed that if review was granted the two cases should be heard together.

The Court granted certiorari in both cases on Dec. 2, 2002. By the time the cases came to be argued, they had attracted a record number of friend-of-the-court briefs: eighty-one in all, more than two-thirds of them support-

Ethnicity at the University of Michigan

Undergraduate Enrollment, Fall 2000 (by percentage)

- 65.8% White
- 7.4% Unknown
- 8.4% African-American
- 13.1% Asian
- 4.7% Hispanic
- 0.6% Native American

Note: Percentages do not add to 100 due to rounding

Source: University of Michigan

ing the university. Court watchers noted in particular briefs filed by a group of retired military officers stressing the importance of affirmative action in producing a racially diverse officer corps and a separate brief by the Michigan-based General Motors Corp. defending affirmative action as a means of a diverse workforce at supervisory and managerial levels. On the opposite side, the Bush administration urged the Court to hold procedures at both schools unconstitutional but did not call for prohibiting any consideration of race in admissions.

CURRENT SITUATION

Split Decisions?

The Supreme Court's rulings in the Michigan cases — issued together on June 23, 2003 — appeared at quick glance to be a compromise of sorts: upholding the law school policies while ruling the college's admissions system unconstitutional. On closer examination, though, affirmative action supporters stressed that the law school decision squarely held — and the undergraduate case acknowledged — that universities could use individualized race-conscious admissions procedures to promote the compelling government interest in diversity.

Writing for the majority in *Grutter*, Justice O'Connor said the law school's admissions policies satisfied the constitutional requirement that any government use of race be "narrowly tailored" to achieve a compelling interest — in this case, attaining a diverse student body. The law school, she wrote, "engages in a highly individualized, holistic review of each applicant's file, giving serious consideration to all the ways an applicant might contribute to a diverse educational environment."

In contrast to the undergraduate admissions procedures, O'Connor said, the law school "awards no mechanical, predetermined diversity 'bonuses' based on race or ethnicity." Under the law school program, an applicant's race or ethnicity was not "the defining feature" of his or her application, she wrote. And even though the law school explicitly sought a "critical mass" of minority admittees, O'Connor said that the admissions program "does not operate as a quota."

O'Connor ended her opinion, though, by suggesting that race-conscious admissions policies should not be permanent. Colleges and universities, she said, should include "sunset provisions" and "periodic reviews" to determine whether racial preferences are still needed to achieve student body diversity. Citing the twenty-five year period since *Bakke*, O'Connor concluded, "We expect that 25 years from now, the use of racial preferences will no longer be necessary to further the interest approved today." O'Connor's opinion was joined by the court's four liberal-leaning justices: John Paul Stevens, David H. Souter, Ruth Bader Ginsburg and Stephen G. Breyer. The four dissenting justices — William H. Rehnquist, Antonin Scalia, Anthony M. Kennedy and Clarence Thomas — each wrote opinions explaining why they disagreed with the decision to uphold the law school's admissions program.

Writing for all four, Rehnquist said the procedures appeared to be "a carefully managed program designed to ensure proportionate representation of applicants from selected minority groups." Rehnquist also faulted the majority for what he called "unprecedented" deference to the law school's defense of its program. In a lone opinion, Kennedy also criticized the majority for what he called a "perfunctory" review of the program. But Kennedy explicitly agreed that racial diversity was a constitutionally legitimate goal in higher education.

In the longest of the dissents, Thomas strongly criticized affirmative action on both legal and practical grounds. Referring to diversity as "classroom aesthetics," Thomas said the majority made "no serious effort" to explain its educational benefits. In practice, he said, racial preferences provoked resentment among unsuccessful applicants while most blacks admitted under the policies were "tarred as undeserving." Thomas also warned the decision would produce further "controversy and litigation." Scalia joined Thomas's opinion and wrote a shorter dissent of his own.

Both Thomas and Scalia did note their agreement with the Court's suggestion that race-conscious admissions policies should be terminated in twenty-five years. From the other side, Ginsburg wrote a concurring opinion somewhat discounting the deadline: " . . . [O]ne may

hope, but not firmly forecast, that over the next generation's span, progress toward nondiscrimination and genuinely equal opportunity will make it safe to sunset affirmative action." Breyer joined her opinion.

Writing for the majority in *Gratz*, Rehnquist said the program violated the Equal Protection Clause because its use of race was "not narrowly tailored to achieve the interest in educational diversity that [university officials] claim justifies their program." The automatic distribution of 20 points, he said, had the effect of making race the decisive factor "for virtually every minimally qualified underrepresented minority applicant."

Rehnquist rejected the college's argument that the volume of applications made it "impractical" to adopt the kind of individualized review of applications approved by the Court in the law school case. "The fact that the implementation of a program capable of providing individualized consideration might present administrative challenges does not render constitutional an otherwise problematic system," he wrote.

Rehnquist was joined by the other three dissenters from the law school case and O'Connor. In a concurring opinion, O'Connor said the undergraduate admissions system was "a nonindivdiualized, mechanical one" that did not provide for "a meaningful individualized review of applicants." Breyer concurred in the judgment; he said he concurred in O'Connor's opinion "except insofar as it joins that of the Court."

The dissenters objected on procedural and substantive grounds. Procedurally, Stevens and Souter said that Gratz and Hamacher had no standing to seek to enjoin the further use of the admissions policies because they had both graduated from different schools and were no longer seeking admission. On the merits, Souter and Ginsburg both said they would uphold the admissions program. In her opinion, Ginsburg said racial policies aimed at "inclusion" should be treated more favorably than policies aimed at "exclusion." Breyer said he joined that part of Ginsburg's opinion.

OUTLOOK

Reform or Status Quo?

The Supreme Court's decisions in the Michigan cases heartened supporters of affirmative action and disappointed opponents. For their part, university officials

Should colleges eliminate the use of race in admissions?

YES Thomas E. Wood
Executive Director, California Association of Scholars, co-author of California Prop. 209

Written for *CQ Researcher*, September 2001

Colleges should eliminate the use of race in admissions. One cannot prefer on the basis of race without discriminating against others on the basis of race. Treating people differently on the basis of their race violates the Constitution's guarantee of equal protection under the laws.

There is only one national database for higher education that is in a position to adequately address this question whether, or to what extent, campus racial diversity is a necessary component of educational excellence. So far, the American Council on Education/Higher Education Research Institute database has failed to find any connection between campus racial diversity and any of the 82 cognitive and non-cognitive outcome variables incorporated in the study.

Proponents claim that the abandonment of racial classifications will result in the resegregation of higher education. Since preferences have been used to increase the number of minorities in the past, their abandonment will lead in the near term to lower numbers for minorities (though only in the most elite institutions of higher education).

But the claim that abandoning the use of race in college admissions will lead to resegregation implies that all or virtually all minorities who are presently enrolled in the most elite institutions are there only because they have been given preferences, which is both untrue and demeaning. The claim also ignores the fact that the country was making significant progress toward diversity *before* the advent of racial preferences in university admissions in the mid-to-late 1970s.

This analysis is confirmed by the experience of Texas, California and Washington, which already have bans on racial classifications in university admissions. The experience in these states has been that while there is an initial decline when racial classifications are abandoned (though only in the most elite institutions), the underlying trend toward greater diversity resumes after the initial correction.

For some, of course, any regression from the numbers that are obtainable through the use of preferences is unacceptable. At its heart, this is the view that racial diversity is a value that trumps all others. But that is a view that has clearly been rejected by the courts, and for good reason. Diversity is an important public policy goal, but there is a right way and a wrong way to pursue it. Racial classifications are the wrong way.

NO Angelo Ancheta
Director, Legal and Advocacy Programs, Civil Rights Project, Harvard Law School

Written for *CQ Researcher*, September 2001

Affirmative action policies advance the tenet that colleges, like the workplace and our public institutions, should reflect the full character of American society. Race-conscious admissions policies not only promote the integration ideal first realized in *Brown v. Board of Education* but also help create educational environments that improve basic learning and better equip students for an increasingly diverse society.

The U.S. Supreme Court upheld race-conscious admissions over 20 years ago in *Regents of the University of California v. Bakke.* Yet, affirmative action opponents, armed with the rhetoric of quotas and tokenism for the unqualified, persist in trying to undermine *Bakke.* Educators know that quotas are illegal under *Bakke* and that granting admission to the unqualified serves no one's interest. Colleges have been highly circumspect, employing carefully crafted policies that consider all applicants competitively and that use race as only one of many factors in admissions decisions.

Nevertheless, recent litigation challenging affirmative action in Texas, Washington, Georgia and Michigan portends that the Supreme Court will soon revisit *Bakke.* But the case that promoting educational diversity is, in the language of the law, "a compelling governmental interest" and that race-conscious admissions policies can best serve that interest has only strengthened in recent years.

The latest findings show that student-body diversity significantly improves the quality of higher education. Studies at the University of Michigan have found that diverse learning environments can enhance students' critical-thinking skills, augment their understanding and tolerance of different opinions and groups, increase their motivation and participation in civic activities and better prepare them for living in a diverse society. Several studies support these findings and further show that interaction across races has positive effects on retention rates, satisfaction with college, self-confidence and leadership ability.

Without race-conscious admissions, the student-body diversity necessary to advance these educational outcomes would be lost. The declining enrollment of minority students at public universities that have abandoned affirmative action strongly suggests that the "color-blind" path is not the path to equal opportunity; nor is it the path to the highest-quality education.

Affirmative action policies reflect the reality that race has always shaped our educational institutions. Justice Blackmun's admonition in *Bakke* thus remains as vital as ever: "In order to get beyond racism, we must first take account of race. There is no other way."

across the country generally said the rulings would allow them to continue using racial preferences in admissions with only minor modifications if any.

Affirmative action supporters were beaming after announcement of the decisions. "This is a wonderful day," University of Michigan president Mary Sue Coleman told reporters on the Supreme Court plaza. The decisions, she said, provided "a green light to pursue diversity" and "a road map to get us there."

Liberal interest groups also praised the decisions. "The Court has reiterated America's commitment to affirmative action, and the nation is better off for it," said Vincent Warren, a staff attorney with the American Civil Liberties Union who worked on the cases. "They're not willing to turn the clock back," said Theodore Shaw of the NAACP Legal Defense and Educational Fund. "That's the message for the nation."

Conservative groups, which had generally expected a clear-cut victory in the cases, tried to conceal their disappointment by depicting the rulings as a partial win. Terrence Pell, president of the Center for Individual Rights, said the rulings would make it "more difficult" for universities to use race-based admissions procedures. Clint Bolick, vice president of the libertarian Institute for Justice, said the decisions "will leave the nation racially polarized."

Both Pell and Bolick also contended that the rulings did nothing to address racial gaps in elementary and secondary education. "Racial preferences in post-secondary education make us think that we are solving that problem when in fact it is growing," Bolick said. "For that reason, this decision is a tragedy for all Americans."

President Bush cautiously praised the decisions for recognizing "the value of diversity" while requiring universities to "engage in a serious, good faith consideration of workable race-neutral alternatives."

Coleman told reporters that the university would quickly revise its undergraduate admissions policies in line with the Court's ruling in time for the class entering the college in 2004. Officials representing other colleges and universities said the decisions cleared up legal confusion over the issues and predicted the decisions would lead to few changes.

The ruling "has the effect of defining current practices as constitutional," said Barmak Nassirian, associate executive director of the American Association of Collegiate Registrars and Admissions Officers. "There are very few institutions that would be negatively affected by the undergraduate decision."

But Pell warned universities not to use the rulings as a "fig leaf" to preserve the status quo. "Some schools are determined to continue to take race into account, and it's business as usual for them," Pell said. He said the center would monitor responses to the decisions and challenge any schools that used a "mechanistic" formula to favor minority candidates.

NOTES

1. For extensive information on both cases, including the texts of the two rulings and other legal documents, see the University of Michigan's Web site (www.umich.edu) or the Web site of the public-interest law firm representing the plaintiffs, the Center for Individual Rights (www.cir-usa.org).

2. The legal citation is 438 U.S. 265; Supreme Court decisions can be found on a number of Web sites, including the court's official site: www.supreme-courtus.gov. For background, see Kenneth Jost, "Rethinking Affirmative Action," *CQ Researcher*, April 28, 1995, pp. 369-392.

3. See Robert Lerner and Althea K. Nagai, "Pervasive Preferences: Racial and Ethnic Discrimination in Undergraduate Admissions Across the Nation," Center for Equal Opportunity, Feb. 22, 2001 (www.ceo-usa.org).

4. For background, see David Masci, "Hispanic Americans' New Clout," *CQ Researcher*, Sept. 18, 1998, pp. 809-832; David Masci, "The Black Middle Class," *CQ Researcher*, Jan. 23, 1998, pp. 49-72; and Kenneth Jost, "Diversity in the Workplace," *CQ Researcher*, Oct. 10, 1997, pp. 889-912.

5. Charles R. Lawrence III and Mari J. Matsuda, *We Won't Go Back: Making the Case for Affirmative Action* (1997), p. 127. Matsuda, Lawrence's wife, is also a professor at Georgetown law school.

6. For background, see Joan Biskupic and Elder Witt, *Guide to the U.S. Supreme Court* (3d ed.), 1997, pp. 362-363. The cases discussed are *Missouri ex rel. Gaines v. Canada*, 305 U.S. 337 (1938); *Sweatt v. Painter*, 339 U.S. 629 (1950); and *McLaurin v. Oklahoma State Regents for Higher Education*, 339 U.S. 637 (1950).

7. William G. Bowen and Derek Bok, *The Shape of the River: Long-Term Consequences of Considering Race in College and University Admissions* (1998), pp. 4-5. Bowen, a former president of Princeton University, is now president of the Andrew W. Mellon Foundation in New York City; Bok is a former president of Harvard University and now a university Professor at the John. F. Kennedy School of Government at Harvard.

8. Reprinted in Gabriel J. Chin (ed.), *Affirmative Action and the Constitution: Affirmative Action Before Constitutional Law, 1964-1977*, Vol. 1 (1998), pp. 21-26.

9. Bowen and Bok, *op. cit.*, pp. 6-7.

10. Description of the announcement of the decision taken from Bernard Schwartz, *Behind* Bakke: *Affirmative Action and the Supreme Court* (1988), pp. 142-150.

11. The cases are *Wygant v. Jackson Bd. of Education*, 476 U.S. 267 (1986); *Johnson v. Transportation Agency of Santa Clara County*, 480 U.S. 646 (1987); *City of Richmond v. J.A. Croson Co.*, 488 U.S. 469 (1989); and *Adarand Constructors, Inc. v. Pena*, 575 U.S. 200 (1995).

12. Lincoln Caplan, *Up Against the Law: Affirmative Action and the Supreme Court* (1997), p. 16.

13. The case is *Hopwood v. Texas*. Some background on this and other cases in this section is drawn from Girardeau A. Spann, *The Law of Affirmative Action: Twenty-Five Years of Supreme Court Decisions on Race and Remedies* (2000).

14. The legal citation is *Hopwood v. Texas*, 78 F.2d 932 (5th Cir. 1996). In a subsequent decision, the appeals court on Dec. 21, 2000, reaffirmed its legal holding, but upheld the lower court judge's finding that none of the four plaintiffs would have been admitted to the law school under a race-blind system. See *Hopwood v. Texas*, 236 F.2d 256 (5th Cir. 2000).

15. Quoted in Facts on File, March 28, 1996.

16. For background, see Jennifer Gavin, "Redistricting," *CQ Researcher*, Feb. 16, 2001, pp. 113-128; Nadine Cahodas, "Electing Minorities," *CQ Researcher*, Aug. 12, 1994, pp. 697-720.

17. The legal citation is 515 U.S. 200.

18. For a critique, see Stephan and Abigail Thernstrom, "Reflections on the Shape of the River," *UCLA Law Review*, Vol. 46, No. 5 (June 1999), pp. 1583-1631.

19. For a good overview, see Nicholas Lemann, "The Empathy Defense," *The New Yorker*, Dec. 18, 2000, pp. 46-51. See also Carl Cohen, "Race Preference and the Universities — A Final Reckoning," *Commentary*, September 2001, pp. 31-39.

20. "Vital Signs: The Statistics that Describe the Present and Suggest the Future of African Americans in Higher Education," *The Journal of Blacks in Higher Education*, No. 9 (autumn 1995), pp. 43-49.

21. The Washington case is *Smith v. University of Washington Law School*, 9th Circuit, Dec. 4, 2000; the Georgia case is *Johnson v. Board of Regents of the University of Georgia*, 11th Circuit, Aug. 27.

BIBLIOGRAPHY

Books

Bowen, **William G., and Derek Bok,** ***The Shape of the River: Long-Term Consequences of Considering Race in College and University Admissions,*** **Princeton University Press, 1998.**
The book analyzes data on 80,000 students admitted to 28 selective private or public colleges and universities in 1951, 1976 and 1989 to examine the impact of race-based admissions on enrollment and to compare the educational and post-graduation experiences of white and minority students. Includes statistical tables as well as a nine-page list of references. Bowen, a former president of Princeton University, heads the Andrew W. Mellon Foundation; Bok is a former president of Harvard University and now a professor at Harvard's John F. Kennedy School of Government.

Caplan, Lincoln, ***Up Against the Law: Affirmative Action and the Supreme Court,*** **Twentieth Century Fund Press, 1997.**
The 60-page monograph provides an overview of the Supreme Court's affirmative action rulings with analysis written from a pro race-conscious policies perspective. Caplan, a longtime legal-affairs writer, is a senior writer in residence at Yale Law School.

Chin, Gabriel J. (ed.), ***Affirmative Action and the Constitution: Affirmative Action Before Constitutional Law, 1964-1977*** **(Vol. 1);** ***The Supreme Court "Solves" the Affirmative Action Issue, 1978-1988*** **(Vol. 2);**

Judicial Reaction to Affirmative Action, 1988-1997 (Vol. 3), Garland Publishing, 1998.
The three-volume compendium includes a variety of materials on affirmative action from President Lyndon B. Johnson's famous speech at Howard University in 1965 to President Bill Clinton's defense of affirmative action in 1995 as well as the full text of the federal appeals court decision in the 1995 *Hopwood* decision barring racial preferences at the University of Texas Law School. Chin, who wrote an introduction for each volume, is a professor at the University of Cincinnati College of Law.

Edley, Christopher Jr., *Not All Black and White: Affirmative Action, Race, and American Values,* Hill & Wang, 1996.
Edley, a Harvard Law School professor, recounts his role in overseeing the Clinton administration's review of affirmative action in 1995 as part of a broad look at the issue that ends with measured support for affirmative action "until the justification for it no longer exists."

Schwartz, Bernard, *Behind* Bakke: *Affirmative Action and the Supreme Court,* New York University Press, 1988.
Schwartz, a leading Supreme Court scholar until his death in 1997, was granted unusual access to the private papers of the justices for this detailed, behind-the-scenes account of the *Bakke* case from its origins through the justices' deliberations and final decision.

Spann, Girardeau A., *The Law of Affirmative Action: Twenty-Five Years of Supreme Court Decisions on Races and Remedies,* New York University Press, 2000.
The book includes summaries — concise and precise — of major Supreme Court decisions from *Bakke* in 1978 to *Adarand* in 1995. Spann is a professor at Georgetown University Law Center.

Steele, Shelby, *A Dream Deferred: The Second Betrayal of Black Freedom in America,* HarperCollins, 1998.

Steele, a prominent black critic of affirmative action and a research fellow at the Hoover Institution at Stanford University, argues in four essays that affirmative action represents an "extravagant" liberalism that "often betrayed America's best principles" in order to atone for white guilt over racial injustice.

Articles

Lawrence, Charles R. III, "Two Views of the River: A Critique of the Liberal Defense of Affirmative Action," *Columbia Law Review,* Vol. 101, No. 4 (May 2001), pp. 928-975.
Lawrence argues that liberals' "diversity" defense of affirmative action overlooks "more radical substantive" arguments based on "the need to remedy past discrimination, address present discriminatory practices, and re-examine traditional notions of merit and the role of universities in the reproduction of elites." Lawrence is a professor at Georgetown University Law Center.

PBS NewsHour, "Admitting for Diversity," Aug. 21, 2001 (www.pbs.org/newshour).
The report by correspondent Elizabeth Brackett features interviews with, among others, Barbara Grutter, the plaintiff in the lawsuit challenging the University of Michigan Law School's race-based admissions policies, and the law school's dean, Jeffrey Lehman.

Thernstrom, Stephan, and Abigail Thernstrom, "Reflections on *The Shape of the River,*" *UCLA Law Review,* Vol. 46, No. 5 (June 1999), pp. 1583-1631.
The Thernstroms contend that racial preferences constitute a "pernicious palliative" that deflects attention from real educational problems and conflicts with the country's unrealized egalitarian dream. Stephan Thernstrom is a professor of history at Harvard University; his wife Abigail is a senior fellow at the Manhattan Institute and a member of the Massachusetts State Board of Education. An earlier version appeared in *Commentary* (February 1999).

For More Information

American Council on Education, 1 Dupont Circle, N.W., Suite 800, Washington, D.C. 20036; (202) 939-9300; www.acenet.edu. The council was the lead organization in a friend-of-the-court brief filed by 30 higher-education groups in support of the University of Michigan's race-conscious admissions policies.

Center for Equal Opportunity, 14 Pidgeon Hill Dr., Suite 500, Sterling, VA 20165; (703) 421-5443; www.ceousa.org. The center filed a friend-of-the-court brief in support of the plaintiffs challenging University of Michigan admissions policies.

Center for Individual Rights, 1233 20th St., N.W., Suite 300, Washington, D.C. 20036; (202) 833-8400; www. cir-usa.org. The public-interest law firm, founded in 1989, represents plaintiffs in the University of Michigan and other cases challenging race-conscious admissions policies.

NAACP Legal Defense Fund, 99 Hudson St., Suite 1600, New York, N.Y. 10013; (212) 965-2200; www.naacpldf. org. The Legal Defense Fund, which traces its history to the NAACP's earliest civil rights litigation in the early 1900s, represents the minority student intervenors in the two suits contesting admissions policies at the University of Michigan.

National Association of Scholars, 221 Witherspoon St., Second Floor, Princeton, N.J. 08542-3215; (609) 683-7878; www.nas.org. The organization studies and advocates on academic issues including race-based admissions policies.

2

Race in America

Alan Greenblatt

Benny Robinson hugs his daughter Jada after he and other African-Americans in Tulia, Texas, were released from prison in June. Some three-dozen residents — mainly blacks — were convicted of drug charges based on the now-discredited testimony of a racist policeman. Although African-Americans have made economic, political and social progress over the last four decades, such incidents periodically erupt, shattering Americans' complacency about race.

From *CQ Researcher,*
July 11, 2003 (updated May 2006).

When Hurricane Katrina tore into the Gulf Coast in late August 2005, it quickly became both a symbol and an awakening — reminding Americans that their age-old project of achieving racial equality was far from completed. Race, as much as floodwaters and damaged homes, became the center of discussion regarding the storm and its impact.

Americans realized that there were people trapped in New Orleans not just by the storm but also by generations of poverty — and that these people were predominantly black. "So poor . . . and so black," as CNN commentator Wolf Blitzer put it. [1] Other commentators debated whether it was demeaning to refer to those left homeless by the storm as "refugees," while some objected to the endless cable news coverage of black looters.

Beyond all of this was a sense among many African-Americans that members of their race were left to suffer in abominable conditions simply because they were members of that race. "You want to know why all those black people are stuck there dying," asked Yvette Brown, a black refugee from New Orleans. "If they were white, they'd be gone. They'd be sending in an army of helicopters, jets and boats." [2] Rapper Kanye West drew national attention when he declared during a fundraiser for the victims, "George Bush doesn't care about black people."

President Bush denied that race had anything to do with the government's response to the storm — which was universally acknowledged as slow and inadequate (although federal, state and local officials spent a good deal of time trying to shift blame to one another). "When those Coast Guard choppers, many of whom were the first on the scene, were pulling people off roofs, they didn't check the color of a person's skin," he said. [3]

White Students Are the Most Isolated

The average white student in the United States attends a school made up of 80 percent whites. Similarly, most black students attend schools in which the majority of their fellow students are the same race as themselves. Asians are the most integrated in American schools.

Racial Composition of Schools Attended by the Average . . .

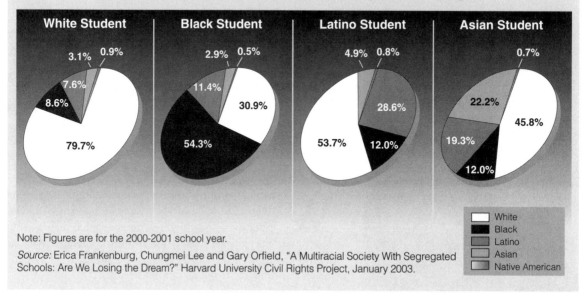

Note: Figures are for the 2000-2001 school year.

Source: Erica Frankenburg, Chungmei Lee and Gary Orfield, "A Multiracial Society With Segregated Schools: Are We Losing the Dream?" Harvard University Civil Rights Project, January 2003.

Nevertheless, the fact that so many black people were on those roofs — living in low-lying areas that suffered much of the worst damage — led many people to suspect that race was an underlying cause of much of the human suffering. At the time of the storm, the population of New Orleans was two-thirds black — and nearly a third of its residents were living in poverty. "So-called natural disasters reproduce or reveal sociological arrangements," says David Wellman, a professor of community studies at the University of California, Santa Cruz. "Katrina showed that wealthy people and white people are located strategically — geographically as well as economically — so they don't get hurt in the same way."

Many white Americans believe that race no longer matters in America, now that public schools have been integrated, blacks can vote and race-based job and housing discrimination are illegal. Yet racial incidents continue to erupt, periodically shattering Americans' complacency about race and signaling to many observers that racist sentiments still linger in some psyches.

Often the eruptions spill into the streets — usually in response to allegedly racist police actions — such as the riots that broke out in Cincinnati in April 2001 or in Benton Harbor, Mich., in 2003.

Lately, some of the incidents — particularly in the South — appear to represent a longing by some for the pre-1960s era of segregation. In Georgia, white high-school students held a prom at which African-American students pointedly were excluded — a year after the school's first integrated prom. That followed the downfall of Sen. Trent Lott of Mississippi, who was forced to resign as majority leader in 2002 after saying America would have been better off if then-Gov. Strom Thurmond of South Carolina had won the presidency in 1948, when he ran as an ardent segregationist.

And some of the racially tinged incidents have been particularly conscience-searing: the murder of James Byrd Jr., chained behind a truck in Jasper, Texas, and dragged to death in 1998; the broomstick sodomizing of Haitian immigrant Abner Louima in 1997 and the shooting of unarmed African immigrant Amadou Diallo by New York policemen in 1999; the beating in Los Angeles of Rodney King in 1991 and subsequent riots the following year. More than three-dozen, mostly black residents of the West Texas town of Tulia were convicted of drug crimes in 1999 solely on the since-discredited testimony of an undercover police officer widely labeled as racist. [4]

Such cases bring into dramatic focus the often diametrically opposing ways in which whites and blacks view race relations in America, especially when the criminal-justice system is involved. Many whites saw the 1995 acquittal of O.J. Simpson in the murder of his ex-wife Nicole Simpson and her friend Ron Goldman as a miscarriage of justice, while blacks generally viewed it as a triumph over racist police tactics.

Allegations of rape involving a black woman and white members of the Duke lacrosse team in 2006 offered yet another example. "This is becoming an inkblot test," wrote Dahlia Lithwik in *The Washington Post*. "We look to the facts to confirm our preexisting suspicions about what happens between men and women, rich people and poor people, black people and white people." [5]

Similarly, 63 percent of blacks said problems with the Katrina relief effort were an indication of continuing racial equality — a notion rejected by more than seven in 10 whites, according to a *Washington Post*-ABC News poll. [6]

And even the Supreme Court's landmark approval in 2003 of the University of Michigan's use of affirmative action in law-school admissions was viewed differently by some blacks and whites.

But many Americans — whites as well as blacks — say the nation's racial problems go beyond racial preferences and the criminal-justice system. They say discrimination still exists despite civil-rights laws, undercutting blacks educationally and economically. Although African-Americans have made economic, political and social progress over the last four decades, by several objective measures they are trailing whites:

- Median income among black men is only 73 percent as high as that of white men, and only 84 percent for black women compared with white women. [7]
- Blacks are 60 percent less likely than whites to receive access to sophisticated medical treatments such as coronary angioplasty and bypass surgery. [8]
- Minorities are far more likely to pay higher, "predatory" mortgage rates than whites. [9]
- A majority of black students score below the basic level in five out of seven subject areas on the National Assessment of Educational Progress (NAEP) tests, compared to only about 20 percent of white students. [10]
- One in five black men spends part of his life in prison — seven times the rate for whites. [11]

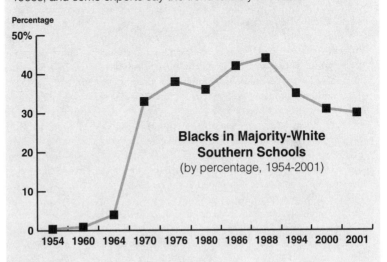

School-Integration Trend Reversing

The Supreme Court's landmark 1954 *Brown v. Board of Education* ruling declared racial segregation in public schools unconstitutional. But after more than three decades, the desegregation trend in U.S. schools reversed after 1988 — particularily in the South. Then a series of Supreme Court decisions between 1991 and 1995 eased the pressure on school dristricts to continue desegregation efforts. Today U.S. classrooms are almost as segregated as they were in the late 1960s, and some experts say the trend is likely to continue.

Percentage

Blacks in Majority-White Southern Schools
(by percentage, 1954-2001)

1954 1960 1964 1970 1976 1980 1986 1988 1994 2000 2001

Source: Southern Education Reporting Service

Are Blacks Losing Political Clout?

Even at age 100, Sen. Strom Thurmond, R-S.C., was a lightning rod for debates about racism. In Washington, powerful Mississippi Sen. Trent Lott lost his job as majority leader last year for waxing nostalgic for segregation at a 100th birthday party for Thurmond, who died in June 2003. Lott told the celebration he wished the centenarian had won the presidency back in 1948, when he ran as a segregationist.

And in South Carolina this spring, GOP state legislators angered some of their Democratic colleagues by including several pictures of a young Thurmond in the state legislative manual. "Nobody could dispute the fact that Strom Thurmond was probably the No. 1 racist Dixiecrat of the day," says state Sen. Robert Ford.

Ford, an African-American and veteran of the civil-rights movement, believes Thurmond sincerely tempered his views on race later in his career. Still, Ford took to the Senate floor to express his dismay over the pictures of a younger, unreconstructed Thurmond in the manual.

Several Republican legislators said Ford was making a big deal out of nothing, or, worse, that he was unnecessarily criticizing a man revered as an icon throughout South Carolina. "They don't want to hear anything negative about Strom Thurmond," Ford says. "They are living in another world."

In fact, whites in the state literally do live in a different world. Because of redistricting maneuvers, South Carolina blacks live in predominantly black political districts. Conversely, most districts are so dominated by whites that politicians representing those districts have no practical incentives to consider the needs or historical sensitivities of African-Americans. This political segregation encourages both black and white politicians to pick fights over racially charged matters — such as disputes about pictures of Thurmond or whether to allow the Confederate flag to fly over state buildings — because they get high-profile coverage back home.

"On both sides of the aisle, they log onto largely symbolic issues," says Dick Harpootlian, former chairman of the South Carolina Democratic Party.

"If you want to get re-elected and you're black, you don't want to talk to white voters," Harpootlian says. "If you're white and running for re-election, you don't want to talk to blacks. We've institutionalized this idea that race predominates over any other interest."

The Voting Rights Act of 1982 encouraged some blacks to join with Republicans to create majority-black districts after the 1980 and 1990 censuses — mostly in the South. The deal allowed African-Americans to create districts that would likely elect blacks. For Republicans, concentrating black voters into a relatively few districts weakened Democratic candidates' chances in neighboring districts.

Partly as a result, there are about 600 black state legislators in the United States today — twice as many as there were in 1970. But now that Democrats are losing power in the South, black legislators in the South are in the dubious position of becoming more important in a national party that has become less powerful.

"African-Americans now have a seat at the table but no plate, no forks and nothing to eat," Harpootlian says. "African-Americans have no influence in our legislature now — zero, nada, none."

- Blacks are 13 percent of the U.S. population, but make up more than 40 percent of the prisoners on Death Row. [12]

Meanwhile, some social critics warn that Latinos and Arabs increasingly experience discrimination in the United States. Latinos, who emerged as the nation's largest minority group in 2003, struggle with levels of poverty and education similar to those of blacks. And Arabs and civil-liberties advocates say the nation's war on terrorism subjects Middle Easterners to widespread harassment.

Some social scientists say that civil-rights laws are working and that blacks' lack of achievement is often due to lack of hard work and criminal behavior, not racism.

Moreover, they point to progress in a number of areas, including the decision by New Jersey and other states to stop racial profiling by state troopers.

Gary Orfield, co-director of the Harvard Civil Rights Project, says the racial divide still appears to be widest in public education. Despite decades of court-ordered school integration, more than one in six black children attends a school comprised of 99-100 percent minority students; by comparison, less than 1 percent of white public-school students attend such schools.

Many observers have expected the Republican Party to adopt a more conciliatory stance toward blacks, who overwhelmingly favor Democrats in elections for all levels of

Although today there are more black elected officials at all levels of government than in earlier years, the trend appears to have peaked, at least for now. Over the last 40 years, only one African-American — L. Douglas Wilder of Virginia — has been elected governor, and only three have been elected to the U.S. Senate — Edward W. Brooke, R-Mass., and Illinois Democrats Carol Moseley Braun and Barack Obama. A Yale University study published in 2006 found that white Republicans are more likely to vote Democratic for senator if the GOP nominee is black — on average, by 25 percentage points. White Democrats are also 38 percentage points more likely to abandon their party and vote for Republicans in House races if the Democratic nominee is black.[1] However, the leading Republican candidates for governor in 2006 in Pennsylvania and Ohio (Lynn Swann and Kenneth Blackwell, respectively) were African-American.

Blacks have enjoyed the most real political power at the city level — but even that power is receding. New York, Chicago,

Former Sen. Carol Moseley Braun, D-Ill., one of only three blacks ever elected to the U.S. Senate in modern times, is seeking the Democratic presidential nomination.

Denver, Cleveland, St. Louis, Baltimore, Seattle, Minneapolis, Dallas, Houston and numerous other cities had black mayors during the 1980s and '90s but have white mayors today.

Ronald Walters, director of the African American Leadership Institute at the University of Maryland, says that as increasing numbers of blacks moved out of the center cities, whites have gained the upper hand because they vote in greater numbers. "It's sort of a cycle of expectations that didn't pan out," Walters says. "There was a lot of euphoria around the first generation of black mayors and what they could accomplish."

But just as blacks were taking the reins of power, Walters points out, urban populations began declining, and aid to cities began drying up. "The irony was that they couldn't accomplish a whole hell of a lot. The whole conservative movement at the state and national level robbed them of the ability to do much."

---

[1] Richard Morin, "Whites Take Flight on Election Day," *The Washington Post*, April 14, 2006, p. A2.

---

office. Indeed, a day after 12 of the Tulia defendants were released from prison, the Bush administration barred federal officers from using race or ethnicity as a factor in conducting investigations (except in cases involving terrorism or national security).[13]

But some African-American leaders question the Bush administration's commitment to fighting racism. "Bush represents anathema to our struggle for social justice," says civil-rights activist Jesse Jackson. "He would not permit [Secretary of State Colin] Powell to go to the U.N. conference on racism in South Africa; he has sought to stock the courts with anti-civil rights judges; he is anti-affirmative action. . . . We are simply on different teams."[14]

Less than a month after Lott stepped down, President Bush spoke out against the University of Michigan's use of racial preferences.

Bush's supporters, however, say he has appointed as many women and minorities to top government jobs as Bill Clinton, whose administration was the most racially diverse in history. "The president is very committed to diversity of thought, of professional background, of geography, ethnicity and gender," said Clay Johnson, who coordinated appointments for Bush. By March 2001, he noted, 27 percent of Bush's selections were women, and 20 to 25 percent were minorities.[15]

The relatively liberal *New Republic* did give Bush

Most Inmates Are Black, Hispanic

Minorities represented nearly two-thirds of the 1.9 million American men over age 18 in local jails and state or federal prisons in 2004.

Men in U.S. Jails and Prisons
(as of April 2005)

		Percentage of Inmate Total	Percentage of Race in U.S. Population
White	695,800	35.7%	67.4%
Black	842,500	43.3	12.8
Hispanic	366,800	18.8	14.1
Total	**1,947,800**		

Note: American Indians, Alaska Natives, Asians, Native Hawaiians and other Pacific Islanders are included in the total.

Source: U.S. Department of Justice, Bureau of Justice Statistics, "Prison and Jail Inmates at Midyear 2004," April 2005 and U.S. Census Breau, "Statistical Abstract of the United States." www.census.gov/prod/www/statistical-abstract.html. Accessed May 8, 2006.

credit in 2006 for being "the first Republican president since the civil rights movement more interested in winning votes from blacks and Latinos than in winning votes by running against them." [16] Bush improved on his vote total among African-Americans during his 2004 reelection campaign, but his showing was still barely into the double digits. And he has never recovered his standing among blacks following what many viewed as his indifferent initial response to Katrina.

Like many conservatives, Bush believes that the interests of blacks, as well as whites, are best served by race-neutral policies. "As we work to address the wrong of racial prejudice, we must not use means that create another wrong, and thus perpetuate our divisions," he said.

Indeed, Heather Mac Donald, a senior fellow at the Manhattan Institute, says "the white establishment is doing everything it can to hire as many black employees as it can. If you are a black high-school student who graduates with modest SATs today, you're going to have colleges beating down your door to try and persuade you to come."

But Wellman, a white professor of community studies at the University of California, sees an opposite reality. "Race not only matters, but whites have an advantage because blacks have a disadvantage," says Wellman, co-author of the 2005 book *Whitewashing Race.* "That's the dirty little secret that nobody wants to talk about anymore.

"Everyone wants to believe that racism has been essentially solved through legislation," he insists. "Unfortunately, when you look at the evidence in terms of education, crime and welfare, it's just shocking how important race continues to be."

Some scholars argue that, absent overt discrimination, blacks must share much of the blame if their circumstances are not equal to whites. "The grip of the Cult of Victimology encourages the black American from birth to fixate upon remnants of racism and resolutely downplay all signs of its demise," writes John McWhorter, another senior fellow at the Manhattan Institute. [17]

Faith Mitchell, director of the National Research Council's Division on Behavioral and Social Sciences, acknowledges that her fellow African-Americans have made much progress — but only to a point. "Yes, you have a growing black middle class," she says, "but it's still disproportionately small relative to the rest of the black population. The lower class is growing faster." [18]

As blacks and whites examine race relations in the United States, here are some of the questions they are asking:

Is discrimination still a problem in the United States?

In 1988, when a residential treatment center opened in Indianapolis for convicted child molesters, neighbors accepted it with little comment. But three years later, when it was converted into a facility for homeless veterans — half of them black — neighborhood whites vandalized a car and burned a cross.

"An all-white cadre of child molesters was evidently acceptable," wrote Randall Kennedy, a black Harvard law-school professor, "but the presence of blacks made a racially integrated group of homeless veterans intolerable!" [19]

The Indianapolis case was unusually overt, says Leonard Steinhorn, an American University professor and co-author of the book *By the Color of Our Skin: The Illusion of Integration and the Reality of Race.* Most opposition to racial integration is much more subtle, he says. "Today, a black person moves in and most white people accept it, or even like it," Steinhorn says. "But one or two families get nervous and move out. More blacks may move in, because they see that the first blacks have been accepted. Then a couple more whites say we better move.

"It's a slow and gradual phenomenon, not the spontaneous, overnight reaction we saw in the past," Steinhorn explains. Even if the African-Americans share the same socioeconomic footing as the whites, most whites will not stay in a neighborhood once it becomes more than 10 to 15 percent black, he says.

But some observers argue that segregation today is more a matter of choice than of bigotry. "White flight is just as widespread as ever," says Jared Taylor, editor of *American Renaissance* magazine, who has been described as a white nationalist. "Even if few people acknowledge it, people prefer the company of people like themselves, and race is an important ingredient. Given the chance, they spend their time in homogeneous groups. It is part of human nature."

Taylor's sentiments are echoed by Carol Swain, a black professor of law and political science at Vanderbilt University. "Clearly, discrimination exists,

Predatory Lending on the Rise

The number of subprime home-mortgage loans — or loans with high interest rates, exorbitant fees and harmful terms — has skyrocketed in recent years. The increase in these so-called predatory loans has been most dramatic in minority communities, particularily among Latinos. At the same time, the number of prime, or lower-rate, loans decreased for blacks but increased for whites and Latinos. Subprime loans are intended for people who are unable to obtain a conventional prime loan at the standard bank rate. The loans have higher interest rates to compensate for the potentially greater risk that these borrowers represent, but Fannie Mae (Federal National Mortgage Association) estimates that as many as half of all subprime borrowers could have qualified for a lower-cost mortgage. Elderly homeowners, communities of color, and low-income neighborhoods are the most severely affected by such practices. Subprime loans represented 9 percent of all conventional home-purchase loans in the U.S. in 2001.

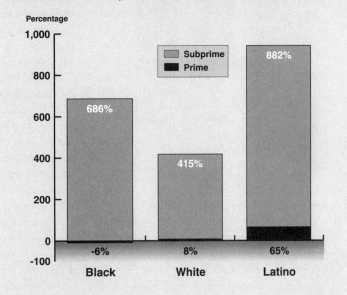

Increases in Subprime and Prime Lending, 1995-2001

Source: ACORN (Association of Community Organizations for Reform Now), "Separate and Unequal: Predatory Lending in America," November 2002

and in very subtle ways," she says, but it is "human nature for people to favor their own group." Indeed, many "black separatists" argue that African-Americans can achieve more by running their own businesses in their own communities, rather than seeking opportunities among whites.

Whites Earn the Most

The average white worker made $126 a week more than the average black worker in 2002, and $201 a week more than the average Hispanic.

Median Weekly Income
(by race, in 2002)

White	$624	
Black	$498	
Hispanic	$423	

Source: Bureau of Labor Statistics

"I would prefer to see more integration," says Bob Zelnick, chairman of the Boston University journalism department and a member of the conservative Citizens' Initiative on Race and Ethnicity. "But I don't think it's a mark of failure if people prefer to live among their own kind. There's some lingering discrimination [in the United States], but I think the determined middle-class or upper-middle-class minority family that seeks to live in a white neighborhood can do so."

Zelnick is "not overly concerned" about segregated patterns of residential living, but only "so long as you have real opportunity for African-Americans to get access to educational opportunity and institutions of higher learning, and as long as you have access to employment opportunities after college or high school."

But others are quick to point out that educational opportunities are not, in fact, allocated evenly to all races.

They cite a recent decision in which the New York Court of Appeals found that the city's longstanding system of providing less money to inner-city schools than to wealthier suburban schools violates the state Constitution because it deprives students of an equal education. The court gave the state 13 months to change the funding formulas that provide less money for urban students — a common practice in American school districts. [20]

Meanwhile, Harvard history Professor Stephan Thernstrom says studies show residential segregation has been declining since the 1960s. "[Segregation] is now at the lowest level since 1920," he says. Real estate agents and home sellers are more interested in closing the deal than engaging in discrimination. If residential segregation exists, he says, it's largely a matter of choice.

But some racial separation may not be by mutual choice. A recent Urban Institute analysis of home-loan applications in Chicago and Los Angeles found that information was withheld from blacks and Hispanics in "statistically significant patterns of unequal treatment" that "systematically favor whites." [21] In another study, African-American women had access to about half as many rental properties as white males because of disparities in the information the women received. [22]

Meanwhile, Southern public schools are "re-segregating." According to researchers at the Harvard Civil Rights Project, the proportion of black students in majority-white Southern schools has reached its lowest level since 1968. [23]

Moreover, American University's Steinhorn says, many forms of de facto discrimination still are practiced today, such as requiring black job applicants — but not whites — to take writing tests; department store security guards following blacks more closely than whites; and drug stores failing to carry African-American hair-care products to discourage their patronage.

"It doesn't have to be legalized, high-profile segregation to be meaningful," Steinhorn says. "This is the stuff of life. If it's death by a thousand cuts, that's as powerful as being told you have to sit at the back of the bus."

Are blacks still economically disadvantaged due to racism?

Nearly everyone agrees that blacks, generally, are far better off financially than they were 40 years ago. But blacks still hold a fraction of whites' accumulated assets. For instance, the proportion of blacks that own their own homes has doubled since 1940, but it is still about a third below the rate for whites. [24]

Are these financial disparities between the races due to racism or to socioeconomic factors and differences in education levels? Steinhorn and others say the persistent separation of the races has negative financial consequences for blacks. Segregation, for instance, can prevent blacks from having access to the social networks that can lead to good jobs. Some economists also argue that urban blacks suffer from "spatial mismatch" — unequal access to suburban jobs located near white residential areas. High crime rates also hamper black wealth creation.

"Crime depresses the property values in cities and neighborhoods that blacks tend to live in," says George R. La Noue, a political scientist at the University of Maryland, Baltimore County.

Much of the racial disparity in wealth is the result of the historical legacy of segregation, according to Steinhorn and others. Black families simply have not had time to accrue wealth to match the generations of inherited property and other assets enjoyed by whites. Blacks also have a harder time investing in major assets, such as real estate.

"There is no question that minorities are less likely than whites to obtain mortgage financing and that, if successful, they receive less generous loan amounts and terms," concluded a 1999 Urban Institute study. [25]

Education is perhaps the biggest factor affecting black incomes. Blacks consistently trail behind whites on standardized tests, and people who achieve higher test scores usually can command higher salaries.

But the University of California's McWhorter says the disparity in education levels can't be attributed solely to racism. "A cultural trait is the driving factor in depressing black scholarly performance," he writes. "A wariness of books and learning for learning's sake as [being] 'white' has become ingrained in black American culture." [26]

Harvard's Thernstrom, co-author of a 2003 book on racial disparities in education, *No Excuses: Closing the Racial Gap in Learning*, says the education gap largely explains the income gap. Too many studies unfairly compare income levels for blacks and whites who have completed the same level of education, he argues. But blacks score more poorly on standardized tests than whites at the same grade level, indicating that they are not receiving the same level of instruction.

"When you measure educational achievement — not by the time you've spent under a school roof, but by

Demonstrators reflect both sides of the affirmative-action debate following the Supreme Court's June 23 ruling supporting the University of Michigan's use of race as a factor in admissions.

what you know — the disparity in racial income mostly disappears," he says. "People of different races with equal levels of cognitive skills have earned about the same amount of money in our society for the past 25 years. Even if employers aren't discriminating at all on the basis of race, they are paying higher-skilled workers more."

Thernstrom believes that blacks' poor test scores are not so much due to racism but to flaws in K-12 public education in general. He says concentrating efforts on improving schools would aid education in general while also aiding blacks and other minorities.

"In a society committed to equal opportunity, we still have a racially identifiable group of educational have-nots — young African-Americans and Latinos," write Thernstrom and his wife and co-author, Abigail Thernstrom, a senior fellow at the Manhattan Institute

Few Changes Seen in Racial Admissions Plans

College and university officials expect few changes in admissions practices following the Supreme Court's qualified approval of affirmative action. But opponents of affirmative action vow to continue their fight in court and elsewhere.

Most undergraduate and graduate schools with race-conscious admissions policies use an individualized application process akin to the University of Michigan Law School's system approved by the high court on June 23, education officials and experts say. They add that only a few schools award all minority applicants a fixed, quantitative bonus similar to the point system used at Michigan's undergraduate college, which the court found unconstitutional.

The court's ruling "has the effect of defining current practices as constitutional," says Barmak Nassirian, associate executive director of the American Association of Collegiate Registrars and Admissions Officers. "There are very few institutions that would be negatively affected by the undergraduate decision."

The head of the conservative public-interest law firm that represented unsuccessful white applicants to Michigan, however, says the court's action will make it more difficult for universities to use racial preferences by precluding the mechanistic formulae that he believes are common. Terence Pell, president of the Washington-based Center for Individual Rights, warns universities not to use the rulings as a "fig leaf" to preserve the status quo.

"Some schools are determined to continue to take race into account, and it's business as usual for them," Pell said after the court's decisions. The center plans to monitor responses to the decisions, Pell said, and challenge any schools claiming to review applicants individually but still using a "mechanistic" formula to favor minority candidates. [1]

Immediately after the rulings, Michigan President Mary Sue Coleman greeted reporters at the Supreme Court with a broad smile. "This is a wonderful day," she said, adding that the undergraduate college would be able to change its system to comply with the court's decision by the fall. [2]

The court's 6-3 ruling in the undergraduate case — *Gratz v. Bollinger* — faulted the College of Literature, Science and the Arts for awarding minority applicants a fixed bonus of 20 points out of a maximum score of 150, with 100 points needed to qualify for admission. By contrast, the 5-4 majority in the law-school case — *Grutter v. Bollinger* — found that the admissions process used by the law school was constitutional because officers considered race or ethnicity as only one factor in trying to achieve a "critical mass" of minority candidates needed for a diverse student body.

Nassirian says the rulings will speed a movement already under way among colleges and universities toward what admissions officers call "full-folder review" of applicants. "Most applicants want to be treated fairly," he says, "and they don't want to be eliminated on the basis of only two or three data elements like grade point average and standardized test scores."

and vice chair of the U.S. Civil Rights Commission. "They place some blame on members of these groups for failing to place an emphasis on education and for a cultural work ethic that sometimes equates achievement with "acting white or selling out."

But the Thernstroms place heavier blame on schools for failing to adapt to group cultural differences and for not demanding high standards from their students. "Plenty of white and Asian kids are also being short-changed," they write, "but it is the black and Hispanic [statistics] that suggest appalling indifference." [27]

Many people on the other side, however, citing the recent New York appeals court decision, point out that

American school-funding policies — which unlike any other industrialized country are based on property values — are clearly lopsided against poorer school districts, which often are made up primarily of blacks, Latinos and other minorities.

However, William E. Spriggs, former executive director of the National Urban League's Institute for Opportunity and Equality, says even highly educated blacks suffer higher unemployment rates than whites. "Year after year, the unemployment rate for [black] college graduates has continued to climb," Spriggs says, "whereas for whites, it's been fairly stable."

But the disparities don't end there, adds Spriggs, now

But Bradford Wilson, executive director of the National Association of Scholars, in Princeton, N.J., notes that the undergraduate college defended its fixed-bonus system on the grounds that individualized review was impossible given its large volume of applications. "I just don't see how it's possible to do what the Supreme Court called meaningful, individualized review without having a virtual army of [undergraduate] admissions officers reviewing applicants," says Wilson, whose group opposed both Michigan admissions procedures.

The court's rulings came after a period of retrenchment on affirmative action in some states, including three with big public-university systems: Texas, California and Florida. Texas had to suspend racial preferences in admissions after a March 1996 federal appeals-court decision in a suit against the University of Texas Law School. [3] California voters approved an initiative in November 1996, Proposition 209, which barred consideration of race or national origin in admissions. And in February 2000, Gov. Jeb Bush, R-Fla., adopted a so-called "One Florida" program that similarly ended the use of race in admissions at state universities.

In Texas, the president of the university's Austin campus said the school has resumed a form of racial admissions policy. [4] University of California President Richard Atkinson, however, said the school would continue to comply with the state's initiative barring race-based admissions. In Florida, Bush also reaffirmed the policy against considering race in university admissions.

All three states also adopted so-called percentage plans for state universities to admit any high-school graduate with a class rank above a fixed cutoff point — the top 10 percent, for example, in Texas. In a brief opposing the Michigan admissions policies, the Bush administration endorsed the ostensibly race-neutral alternative to racial preferences. Percentage plans are designed to create diversity by ensuring representation from all schools, including those that are predominantly black or Hispanic.

But in her majority opinion in the Michigan law-school case, Justice Sandra Day O'Connor said such approaches "may preclude" individualized assessment of applicants and prevent universities from achieving diversity in other respects besides race.

— **Kenneth Jost**

---

[1] Quoted in Diana J. Schemo, "Group Vows to Monitor Academia's Responses," *The New York Times,* June 24, 2003, p. A22. For other statements and materials, see the center's Web site: www.cir.org.

[2] For the text of a letter on the ruling that Coleman sent to the university community and other materials, see the university's Web site: www.umich.edu/~urel/admissions/.

[3] The case is *Hopwood v. University of Texas Law School,* 78 F.3d 392.(5th Cir. 1996). The ruling, which the U.S. Supreme Court declined to review, also covered the states of Louisiana and Mississippi.

[4] Reaction from the three states is compiled in Jeffrey Selingo, "Decisions May Prompt Return of Race-Conscious Admissions at Some Colleges," *The Chronicle of Higher Education,* July 4, 2003, p. S5.

---

with the Economic Policy Institute. Blacks with the same skills as whites earn 10 to 20 percent less, he says. "Every hour at work, to make 80 cents on somebody else's dollar is a huge disadvantage," he says. "You can't start the race 20 percent behind."

William Rodgers, an economics professor at the College of William and Mary in Williamsburg, Va., and former chief economist at the Department of Labor in the Clinton administration, agrees that economic disparities cannot be explained entirely by differences in education. "Even if they come in with skills and education like their white counterparts, minorities are still experiencing labor-market discrimination," he says, with blacks receiving fewer callbacks and job offers.

The University of Maryland's La Noue admits that racism and discrimination persist, but he says other factors — such as limited educational opportunities — also can affect members of all races. Thus he opposes trying to alleviate income disparities through racial quotas or special race-based programs, because he says they are unfair to whites with limited opportunities.

For the same reason, La Noue opposes government programs that set aside a certain percentage of contracts for minority-owned companies. "Too often in this area, we created race-based solutions that are not really congruent with the problems we're trying to solve, and based

C H R O N O L O G Y

1940s-1950s *World War II and its aftermath presage big changes for African-Americans as the migration north intensifies and the civil-rights movement takes off.*

1941 World War II causes an immediate shortage of industrial labor at home, increasing the migration of Southern African-Americans to Northern urban areas.

1947 Jackie Robinson joins the Brooklyn Dodgers, becoming the first black to play Major League Baseball.

July 26, 1948 President Harry S Truman ends racial segregation in the armed forces.

1954 The Supreme Court's landmark *Brown v. Board of Education* ruling overturns the previous "separate but equal" policy in public education.

1955 Rosa Parks refuses to give up her seat on a city bus to a white man, sparking the Montgomery, Ala., bus boycott. The Rev. Dr. Martin Luther King Jr. emerges as a civil-rights leader.

1960s *The civil-rights movement prompts Congress to enact legislation aimed at ending discrimination.*

1961 President John F. Kennedy uses the term "affirmative action" for the first time, ordering federal contractors to give preferential treatment to minorities in hiring.

1963 Dr. King gives his stirring "I Have a Dream" speech at the Lincoln Memorial in Washington.

1964 The Civil Rights Act prohibits job discrimination based on race, sex or national origin.

1965 President Lyndon B. Johnson signs the Voting Rights Act. In September he orders federal contractors to actively recruit minorities.

1968 Dr. King is assassinated, touching off race riots in many U.S. cities.

1970s-1980s *New policies like affirmative action are*

adopted, prompting a backlash among whites.

1970 President Richard M. Nixon requires contractors to set goals for minority employment.

1978 In *University of California Regents v. Bakke*, the Supreme Court rules that universities can use race as a factor in admissions, but may not impose quotas.

1980 Affirmative-action foe Ronald Reagan is elected to the presidency. The Justice Department begins attacking racial quotas.

1990s-2000s *As affirmative action is challenged in the courts, racist-tinged incidents continue to shock the nation.*

1991 Black motorist Rodney King is kicked and beaten by white Los Angeles police officers; their acquittal in 1992 touches off major rioting. Eventually they are convicted of civil-rights violations.

1993 Supreme Court rules in *Shaw v. Reno* that race cannot be used as the "predominant" factor in drawing political districts.

1996 Voters in California approve Proposition 209 outlawing the use of race or gender preferences at all state government institutions.

1998 Three white men in Jasper, Texas, drag black James Byrd Jr. to death behind their pickup truck. Two are sentenced to death; a third is sentenced to life in prison.

2002 Sen. Trent Lott says the country would have been better off if then-segregationist Gov. Strom Thurmond had been elected president in 1948; after outcry, Lott steps down as Senate majority leader.

Jan. 15, 2003 President Bush announces that his administration sides with affirmative-action opponents against University of Michigan admissions policies.

June 2003 Supreme Court upholds the University of Michigan's qualified use of race as a factor in admissions. ... Blacks riot in Benton Harbor, Mich., to protest allegedly racist police tactics.

on gross generalizations that all people of one race are privileged and all people of another race are disadvantaged," he says.

Is the criminal-justice system racially biased?

Black comedian Richard Pryor used to joke about going to court seeking justice in America. "And that's exactly what I saw," he said. "Just us."

Indeed, blacks comprise 13 percent of the country's population but more than 40 percent of the U.S. prison population, according to the Washington-based Sentencing Project. A black male born in 2001 stands a 32 percent chance of spending time in prison, compared with 6 percent for white males. [28] In 1995, one in three black men between the ages of 20 and 29 was either in prison, on probation or on parole. [29]

Many African-Americans argue that more blacks are in jail because police and prosecutors target blacks. Many blacks say they have been pulled over for the "crime" of "driving while black." "Nothing has poisoned race relations more," writes Harvard's Kennedy, "than racially discriminatory policing, pursuant to which blacks are watched, questioned and detained more than others." [30]

Lawsuits challenging the constitutionality of racial profiling have led to settlements in California, Maryland and other states, many of which have revised their policies for stopping motorists. [31] In March 2003, New Jersey became the first state to ban profiling. [32] And in June of that same year, President Bush banned racial profiling at the federal level — except in cases involving terrorism and national security.

But the Manhattan Institute's Mac Donald, author of *Are Cops Racist?* says police don't target blacks because of race. "It's not racism that sends police departments into black neighborhoods," she says. "It's crime."

Merely comparing numbers of stops and arrests with raw census data is an exercise in false logic, she argues. "The way the anti-police activists are spinning numbers is very clever," Mac Donald says. Comparing arrest records for blacks and whites is just as spurious as complaining that too few senior citizens are arrested, despite the fact that they don't commit as many violent crimes as younger people, she says.

Complaints about profiling, Mac Donald warns, can make police officers wary of going after black offenders, for fear of exceeding their allowable quota of African-American arrests. In Cincinnati, where police changed

their tactics after blacks rioted in 2001, arrests dropped by 30 percent in 2002, but homicides reached a 15-year high, she notes. [33]

In a widely cited study, Michael Tonry, a law professor at the University of Minnesota, maintains that more blacks are locked up because they commit more "imprisonable crimes." [34]

Perhaps more poignantly, Jesse Jackson once said, "There is nothing more painful for me at this stage in my life than to walk down the street and hear footsteps and start to think about robbery and see it's somebody white and feel relieved." [35]

Still, some critics say when blacks do commit crimes, they can't get a fair shake from the criminal-justice system. Although even critics of the system admit that data is scarce comparing how blacks and whites are sentenced for committing the same crimes, the University of California's Wellman cites studies in Georgia and New York that show racial differences in the prison terms imposed for similar offenses.

Members of the Congressional Black Caucus — including Rep. John Conyers, D-Mich., the ranking Democrat on the Judiciary Committee — often complain that sentencing guidelines are much harsher for crack cocaine, predominantly used and sold by blacks, than for powder cocaine, used primarily by whites. But critics of that argument note the Black Caucus pushed hard for tough laws against crack precisely because it is a scourge in predominantly black communities. [36]

But the biggest disparities result because of where police concentrate their enforcement efforts, says Marc Mauer, assistant director of the Sentencing Project. "Drug use and abuse cuts across race and class lines, but drug-law enforcement is primarily located in the inner cities," Mauer says. Moreover, he points out, white suburban teenagers caught with drugs might be sent to treatment programs instead of being prosecuted, but similar treatment isn't offered to blacks: "In a low-income community, those resources aren't provided to the same extent, so [drug possession] is much more likely to be defined as a criminal-justice problem."

Critics of the criminal-justice system also argue that street crimes are prosecuted more harshly than white-collar crimes, which primarily are committed by whites. But that's because tax fraud and securities abuse are less of a societal concern than armed robbery, says Harvard sociologist Christopher Jencks. "Given a choice, almost

The N-Word and Other Racist Symbols

If you want to rile up black folk," says jazz singer Rene Marie of Atlanta, Ga., "wave the Confederate flag, sing 'Dixie' or say 'nigger.' "

Marie notes that the words to "Dixie" are not objectionable in and of themselves. But they hold negative connotations for her fellow African-Americans because it was the South's Civil War anthem and was sometimes sung by white Southerners in reaction to the civil-rights movement. Marie wants to reclaim "Dixie" to protest her feelings of being excluded from mainstream Southern culture even though she was born in the region. (Her parents participated in an effort to desegregate restaurants in Warrenton, Va.) "That song talks about longing for the South. Well, a majority of black people are from the South — they should be able to express those feelings, too."

Marie's emotionally vulnerable version, though, speaks to different memories of the Old South. On stage, she segues from "Dixie" into "Strange Fruit," the graphic song about lynching made famous by jazz singer Billie Holiday. But with its pounding rhythm and wrenching cries, Marie's rendition is more aggressive than Holiday's.

Marie remembers being nervous about how audiences would respond to the medley, particularly black listeners. Now, when she starts "Dixie," her fans applaud. Still, the combined effect of the two songs is harrowing, an angry reminder of the uglier legacies of the South.

Some black performers and other African-Americans have sought to reconfigure the meaning of "nigger," which Los Angeles prosecutor Christopher Darden famously called the "filthiest, dirtiest, nastiest word in the English language" during the O.J. Simpson murder trial. It has been "a familiar and influential insult" at least since the 1830s, writes Harvard University Professor Randall Kennedy in his recent book about the hateful word. [1]

Today, many blacks use the term to mean "friend" or simply to signify a black person. [2] "When we call each other 'nigger,' it means no harm," says the rap star and actor Ice Cube. "But if a white person uses it, it's something different, it's a racist word." [3]

Black comedian Chris Rock jokes about the differences between black people and "niggers," yet follows that up with a story in which he punches a white fan for repeating the same material. For blacks, whites using the word are offering an insulting reminder that they are perceived as inferior, a caste at a level to which whites can never sink. (Sen. Robert C. Byrd, D-W. Va., who as a young man belonged to the Ku Klux Klan, had to apologize for twice referring to "white niggers" during a Fox TV appearance in 2001.)

In recent years, local governments from Baltimore to San Jose have passed resolutions denouncing the use of the word. [4] Indeed, it remains such a potent insult that some white people claim not to be racist just because they refrain from saying it. A mobster who referred to blacks as "spades," "shines" and "coons" insisted to author Studs Terkel that he was nonetheless not a racist. "Did you ever hear me say 'nigger'? Never!" [5]

Whites and blacks also remain in conflict over the Confederate flag. For African-Americans, the "stars and bars" are a reminder not only of the South's fight to preserve slavery but also its resistance to desegregation. Some states returned to waving Confederate flags, or added aspects of it to their official state flags, during the 1950s and '60s to symbolize their defiance of civil-rights pressures.

---

everyone would rather be robbed by a computer than at gunpoint," he writes. [37]

Racial disparities also exist in the use of the death penalty, according to a recent Maryland study. It found that blacks who murdered whites were far more likely to face the death penalty than either white killers or blacks who killed other blacks. [38] A court-appointed committee in Pennsylvania announced in March 2003 that the state should halt executions pending a study of racial bias. [39] Several other states have commissioned studies to determine whether the death penalty is applied more often or unfairly to blacks.

"Generally, discrimination based on the race of the defendant has tremendously declined," says David Baldus, a University of Iowa law professor who has studied racial bias in the death penalty. "But discrimination based on the race of victim has continued."

BACKGROUND

Road to Emancipation

By 1619, the first African slaves had been brought to Virginia, and by the 1640s slavery was well-established,

Since 1999, the National Association for the Advancement of Colored People (NAACP) has organized economic boycotts of states that fly the Confederate flag. South Carolina has since taken the flag down from its Capitol, while Mississippi voters opted to keep it flying. In Georgia, Republican Gov. Sonny Perdue was elected in 2002 largely on his pledge to let voters decide whether to restore the Confederate cross to the state flag. [6] Voters approved a compromise flag design in 2004.

Many Southern whites argue that the Confederate flag, which some Southerners call the "battle flag," is not meant to be racist, but represents their heritage and is an expression of pride.

"Actually, in the South the battle flag is so ubiquitous it doesn't have a single meaning," says William Rolen, Southern-heritage defense coordinator for the Council of Conservative Citizens in Tennessee. Not only is the emblem found on countless bumper stickers, but Confederate flag T-shirts marketed to children are million-

Georgia voters will decide in March whether to restore the traditional Confederate battle symbol (shown above in the 1956 flag) to the state flag.

sellers. But dozens of Southern school districts have banned them. [7]

"It's just totally inconceivable that any other group that stood for something so vile and was defeated would be given this place of honor," says William Spriggs, former executive director of the National Urban League's Institute for Opportunity and Equality, referring to Southern capitals that fly the flag. "One could not imagine that the mayor of Paris would fly a Nazi flag because the Germans ruled France for part of World War II."

[1] Randall Kennedy, *Nigger: The Strange Career of a Troublesome Word* (2002), p. 4.

[2] Clarence Page, "A Word That Wounds — If We Let It," *Chicago Tribune*, Oct. 12, 1997, p. 25.

[3] Quoted in Kennedy, *op. cit.*, p. 41.

[4] Sarah Lubman, "Black Activists in S.J. Mount Campaign to Eliminate Slur," *San Jose Mercury News*, Jan. 28, 2003, p. A1.

[5] Studs Terkel, *Race: How Blacks and Whites Think and Feel About the American Obsession* (1992), p. 5.

[6] See "Phew," *The Economist*, May 3, 2003, p. 33.

[7] "Dixie Chic," *People*, March 10, 2003, p. 100.

mostly in the Southern colonies. Between 1680 and 1750, the colonies' blacks — who were virtually all slaves — grew from just under 5 percent of the population to more than 20 percent. [40] As slavery grew, so did the repressiveness of racial laws governing non-slaves. In the early 18th century, free blacks endured higher taxes and more severe criminal punishments than white colonials, with several Southern states denying them suffrage.

However, whites turned to blacks for support in their war against the British during the American Revolution. In part, this was a natural outgrowth of the egalitarian ideals that had become the rallying call for the Americans

— even though the Continental Congress had struck anti-slavery language from Thomas Jefferson's draft of the Declaration of Independence.

"How is it that we hear the loudest yelps for liberty among the drivers of Negroes?" mocked British author Samuel Johnson. [41]

But British commanders had promised freedom to any slave who fought on their side, so the Americans matched the offer. By 1775, George Washington, who had originally opposed recruiting black soldiers, wrote: "Success will depend on which side can arm the Negroes the faster." [42]

The Rev. Dr. Martin Luther King Jr. delivered his stirring "I Have a Dream" address during the March on Washington in August 1963. The assassination of the civil-rights leader five years later touched off race riots in many cities.

By war's end, most colonies and the Continental Congress were enlisting blacks, with the understanding that freedom would be their reward for fighting. Thousands served as soldiers and laborers, while thousands more took advantage of the confusion of war to flee from white masters in the South.

But the promises of freedom turned out, in many cases, to be empty ones. After the war, most of the New England states banned slavery, but the Southern states, of course, continued the practice.

Many of the economic gains made by blacks during the war were short-lived, and their political and legal status soon slipped as well. The Fugitive Slave Law of 1793 pledged the aid of federal courts in returning escaped slaves to their masters. With fear of slave revolts growing, abolitionism never took root in the South, and by the early 19th century several Northern states had disenfranchised free blacks.

A number of frontier states barred not just slaves but all blacks, purely out of racial hatred, as contemporary debates made clear. Then a new Fugitive Slave Act in 1850 expanded the role of the federal government in the search for escaped slaves.

Life for freed blacks was tenuous, indeed, a situation made abundantly clear by the Supreme Court's 1857 *Dred Scott* decision. The infamous ruling determined that runaway slaves like Scott remained the property of their masters, even after they had escaped to free states.

The court also said persons of African descent could never become citizens with the right to sue, and overturned bans on slavery in the frontier territories.

In early 1861, Congress approved a constitutional amendment protecting the institution of slavery, but it was never ratified by the requisite three-quarters of the states. The measure apparently was designed to allay Southerners' fears that the 1860 election of President Lincoln — who had advocated banning slavery in the territories — threatened slavery in the South. Unconvinced, 11 Southern states seceded from the Union, beginning in 1861. The country was soon at war.

Rise of "Jim Crow"

On Jan. 1, 1863, Lincoln issued his Emancipation Proclamation, freeing all slaves in the territories and Border States. Although Lincoln had not wanted to make slavery the central issue of the conflict between the North and the South, the Confederacy still focused on it. Even before issuing the proclamation, Lincoln — like Washington — recognized that putting blacks to use as soldiers had become "a military necessity."

After the North's victory, Congress passed the 13th, 14th and 15th amendments to the Constitution, which vacated the *Dred Scott* decision and gave blacks citizenship and the vote. Southern states wishing to rejoin the Union had to ratify the amendments.

After an anti-abolitionist assassinated Lincoln in 1865, his successors were reluctant to advocate further civil rights for blacks, and the Supreme Court did little to encourage enforcement of the civil-rights laws that existed.

In fact, emboldened by court interpretations that elevated states' rights above those of blacks, Southern states passed a series of so-called Jim Crow laws stripping blacks of stature and legal protections. Named after a minstrel character, the legislation was carefully written in race-neutral language to pass constitutional muster. Most infamously, the Supreme Court in 1896 upheld segregation laws, ruling in *Plessy v. Ferguson* that "separate but equal" accommodations did not intrinsically benefit one race over another.

Oklahoma soon required "separate but equal" telephone booths. New Orleans kept black and white prostitutes segregated. Florida and North Carolina made it illegal for whites to read textbooks that had been used by blacks. [43] Meanwhile, throughout the first half of the 20th century, Southern schools for blacks received only a fraction of what was spent to educate whites. As Mississippi Gov. James K. Vardaman put it in 1909, "Money spent today for the maintenance of public school for Negroes is robbery of the white man, and a waste upon the Negro." [44]

In many places, blacks were systematically deprived of the right to vote, and between the post-Civil War Reconstruction period and the turn of the century their turnout dropped 90 percent or more in some Southern states. The Supreme Court, increasingly influenced by Justice (and ex-klansman) Edward White, was deaf to the loudest complaints about voting-rights abuses.

Some Southern leaders even bragged about the region's concerted efforts to marginalize — and even eliminate — blacks. "We have done our level best," said Ben Tillman of the South Carolina Constitutional Convention. "We have scratched our heads to find out how we could eliminate the last one of them. We stuffed ballot boxes. We shot them. We are not ashamed." [45]

By the turn of the century, lynchings were more common in some years than legal executions. In a 2002 history of lynching, author Philip Dray notes that more than 3,400 blacks were lynched between 1882 and 1944. "Is it possible for white America to really understand blacks' distrust of the legal system, their fears of racial profiling and the police, without understanding how cheap a black life was for so long a time in our nation's history?" Dray asks. [46]

Blacks began to move north searching for better jobs and more political opportunity. Racial tensions during the economic upheaval that followed World War I led to riots in 1919 in about two dozen Northern cities. But whites were unable to drive the blacks out, despite dozens of fire-bombings of black homes.

Instead, beginning in the 1920s, whites left the cities in droves, a phenomenon called "white flight." Jobs often followed the whites to the suburbs. By 1940, 80 percent of the country's urban blacks lived in segregated neighborhoods, compared to less than a third in 1860. [47] Meanwhile, none of the five Deep South states — home to 40 percent of the nation's black population — had even a single black policeman. [48]

Civil-Rights Era

As in the Revolutionary and Civil wars, the pressures of World War II helped move desegregation forward. In 1941, as thousands of African-Americans were planning to march on Washington to protest hiring discrimination in the defense industries, President Franklin D. Roosevelt signed an executive order barring such discrimination and creating a Fair Employment Practices Committee (FEPC) to investigate such complaints. (Although the planned march was canceled, the idea was to re-emerge in 1963, providing the occasion for civil-rights leader Martin Luther King Jr.'s celebrated "I Have a Dream" speech.)

Meanwhile, Southern blacks continued migrating by the millions to Northern cities in search of factory jobs; more than 3 million African-Americans moved north between 1940 and 1960. [49]

In 1948, President Harry S Truman — bowing to pressure from blacks, whom he needed for political support, but also motivated by his personal revulsion at how some black veterans were physically attacked when they returned home from the war — signed an executive order desegregating the armed services. His action, coupled with a strong civil-rights plank in the Democratic Party's presidential platform that year, prompted many Southerners to walk out of the Democratic convention to protest the party's new commitment to civil-rights. South Carolina Gov. Strom Thurmond then ran for president as the nominee of the States' Rights Party, better known as the Dixiecrats, as an opponent of integration. Thurmond carried four Southern states.

On May 17, 1954, in the landmark *Brown v. Board of Education* decision, the U.S. Supreme Court unanimously declared that separate educational facilities are "inherently unequal" and thus violate the Constitution's 14th Amendment, which guarantees all citizens "equal protection under the law." The court ordered schools to be desegregated "with all deliberate speed." But the South was recalcitrant. Several years after the decision, less than 2 percent of Southern black students attended integrated schools. [50]

But if Southern whites were defiant, so, increasingly, were Southern blacks. In 1955 in Montgomery, Ala., Rosa Parks refused to give up her bus seat to a white man. Her arrest sparked a bus boycott led by King, which eventually prompted a Supreme Court decision banning segregation on buses.

Other blacks pressed their demands for equal rights through lunch-counter sit-ins, marches and "freedom rides." They were met with violence, as were orders to desegregate schools. In 1957 President Dwight D.

Fostering Integration on Campus and Beyond

Irini Bekhit was born in Egypt, but she feels right at home at the New Jersey Institute of Technology (NJIT) in Newark. When her fellow students socialize, some separate along racial or ethnic lines, but Bekhit says most students are working so hard they don't have time for the racial rivalries that mark many other campuses. Even many of the fraternities are racially mixed. "Everyone here is so different, it becomes a non-issue," Bekhit says. "You get used to it just from walking around."

U.S. News & World Report magazine ranked NJIT the eighth-most-diverse doctorate-granting campus in the nation. [1] The school is 20 percent Asian, 9 percent black, 9 percent Hispanic and 18 percent foreign-born. Dean of Students Jack Gentul says the school has fewer racial problems than New York University — which has the country's largest proportion of international students — where he ran diversity programs for 15 years.

"The degree of integration here is much greater, and I don't know why," he admits. "I would certainly get another Ph.D. if I could explain it well. I wish I could bottle it."

Most successfully integrated institutions work hard to create and maintain an inclusive atmosphere. The armed services, desegregated by President Harry S Truman in 1948, are often touted as an exceptionally strong example of integration — and one of the rare places in American life where whites routinely take orders from blacks.

"There are aspects of military culture that were conducive to change despite massive resistance," says Sherie Merson, co-author of a study of military integration. Those aspects include the military's culture of meritocracy; its sense of shared purpose, to which individuals subordinate their individual identities; and its command-and-control structure, which can impose programs over the objections of those individuals.

Moreover, the Department of Defense diligently runs racial-awareness programs to keep biases from coloring decisions. "What really makes the difference is the training we give. It helps officers realize they have to treat each person fairly and with respect, and they don't allow any embedded biases to cause them to treat one person better than another," says Capt. Robert Watts, a former commander of the Defense Equal Opportunity Management Institute.

Weldon Latham, who runs the corporate-diversity practice at Holland & Knight, one of the nation's biggest and most diverse law firms, says that although blacks are still underrepresented in corporate America, many big companies have taken major strides toward integrating their work forces. "The enlightened CEOs get it — and get it for the right reason, the same reason they get everything else — the bottom line," Latham says.

America's shifting demographics and the ever-increasing pursuit of markets overseas have made it advantageous for

Eisenhower federalized the Arkansas National Guard to force the entry of nine black students into Little Rock's Central High School. Five years later, President John F. Kennedy made the same decision in response to white violence when James Meredith became the first black to enroll in the University of Mississippi.

On June 11, 1963, after a confrontation over Gov. George Wallace's refusal to allow black students to register at the University of Alabama, Kennedy announced in a televised address that he would push Congress to pass a civil-rights bill that had been languishing for years. As was often the case during the 1960s, Kennedy couched the importance of the bill in terms of improving America's image abroad — an important strategic consideration during the Cold War.

Five months later Kennedy was assassinated, and President Lyndon B. Johnson vowed that passing the civil-rights bill would be a fitting memorial. Johnson eventually outlasted the filibuster — the obstructionist tactic typically employed by Southern senators — against such bills. [51] The Senate voted to close debate and passed the most important piece of civil-rights legislation in the nation's history — the Civil Rights Act of 1964 — outlawing discrimination in employment and public accommodations. [52]

However, King and others continued a series of nonviolent protests in the South, including a 1965 march from Selma to Montgomery, Ala., to protest state and local discrimination against blacks seeking the right to vote. They were met by state troopers wielding cattle prods, nightsticks and rubber hoses wrapped in barbed wire.

companies to have staffs that match, to some extent, the profile of their customers, he points out.

Yet even organizations that strive to recruit blacks find that racial disparities can slip back into their midst. Blacks have never been as well represented in the military officer corps as among enlisted personnel, and even their share of the enlisted ranks has been slipping in recent years as the job market has improved.

The U.S. armed services, desegregated by President Harry S Truman in 1948, are generally considered a strong example of successful integration.

Affluent Shaker Heights, Ohio, is often touted for having bucked the trend toward residential segregation that is pronounced in the Cleveland area. The city has long devoted about a half-million dollars annually to providing low-interest loans to people willing to buy houses in neighborhoods where their race is underrepresented. "Shaker Heights has been as aggressive as any place in trying to address the issue," says Ronald Ferguson, who teaches at Harvard University's Kennedy School of Government and is senior research associate at Harvard's Weiner Center for Social Policy. "It's try-

ing to maintain racial and, to a lesser degree, socioeconomic diversity."

Yet city officials say their vaunted loan program has found fewer takers of late, largely because interest rates are so low generally. As a result, locals worry about the re-segregation of many blocks. They are especially concerned that white parents have begun pulling their children from the public schools.

NJIT's Gentul finds it heartening to know that in little pockets effort at racial integration and understanding can work. But Harry Holzer, a labor economist at Georgetown University, finds himself discouraged by the fact that such situations are difficult to replicate, or sustain. "You can end your career with a broken heart," he says, "because there are great model programs here or there, and you try to re-create them or bring them up to scale, and they fail."

---

[1] "Step 2: Choose the Right School," *U.S. News & World Report*, Sept. 13, 2002, p. 45.

In response, Johnson proposed a law to "strike down restrictions to voting in all elections — federal, state and local — which have been used to deny Negroes the right to vote." The Voting Rights Act, cleared by Congress in 1965, outlawed literacy tests and similar qualification devices used to keep blacks off the rolls. Johnson signed the bill in full knowledge that it might weaken his party in the South.

That same year, Johnson ordered federal contractors to take "affirmative action to ensure that [black] applicants are employed." He had declared earlier, "You do not take a person who, for years, has been hobbled by chains and liberate him, bring him up to the starting line in a race and then say, 'you are free to compete with all the others.' " [53]

After King was assassinated in 1968, blacks rioted in 125 cities, mostly in the North. Within days, Congress passed an open-housing law — the Fair Housing Act — which had previously languished, but included no enforcement provisions. [54]

A Dream Deferred?

The Johnson administration proved to be the high-water mark for civil-rights legislation, although new versions of the Civil and Voting Rights acts have since been passed.

By the 1970s, de jure (legal) segregation was finished, voting rights for blacks were secure for the first time in U.S. history and economic improvements for many blacks had become irreversible. By 1970, 22 percent of black men and 36 percent of black women were holding white-collar jobs — four to six times the percentages, respectively, in 1940.

But some of the laws had little or no enforcement power. The rigor with which anti-discrimination laws were enforced would vary from one administration to the next. Meanwhile, the focus of anti-discrimination efforts broadened to include women, Hispanics, Native Americans and the young. (The voting age was lowered from 21 to 18 in 1970 as part of a Voting Rights Act extension.)

One of the major controversies between the races during the 1970s concerned the attempt to force integration by busing children out of their home neighborhoods in order to balance schools' racial demographics. Some of the stiffest resistance occurred in the North, notably in Boston, where a photograph of a white crowd holding a black man and attempting to impale him with an American flag won a Pulitzer Prize. The focus of numerous court challenges, busing has since been discontinued.

Since the 1970s, Johnson's prediction about Southern whites bolting the Democratic Party has largely come true. President Richard M. Nixon, a Republican, initially opposed the 1970 Voting Rights extension, responding to pressure from Southerners objecting to aspects of the law that applied only to their region. In the face of a growing political backlash against race-based preferential treatment in education or employment, the once solidly Democratic South has turned to a modern Republican Party that favors color-blind policies of equal opportunity for all. Beginning in 1968, working-class whites began to abandon the Democrats in presidential politics, and the party would go on to lose four out of the next five presidential contests.

Republicans aggressively encouraged the exodus of disaffected white voters from the Democratic Party. In 1980, GOP presidential nominee Ronald Reagan was accusing "strapping young bucks" and Cadillac-driving "welfare queens" of abusing the welfare system. "If you happen to belong to an ethnic group not recognized by the federal government as entitled to special treatment, you are the victim of reverse discrimination," he said. [55]

Reagan slashed funding for federal equal-protection agencies, but his administration was unable to limit affirmative-action programs. Meanwhile, in 1996, a federal court ruled that the University of Texas law school could not use affirmative action to create a diverse student body. That same year, California voters barred the state from using race as a factor in employment, contracts or university admissions. Black freshman enrollment dropped throughout the University of California system, but has since recovered except at the Berkeley and Los Angeles campuses. [56]

Even many African-Americans worry that affirmative-action programs have primarily helped the most affluent blacks instead of the most needy. And the policy has not lowered poverty rates among African-Americans: Since 1970, the overall poverty rate for blacks has not budged, dragged down by ever-burgeoning numbers of households headed by single women. [57]

Persistent Poverty

Both liberal and conservative writers blame persistent poverty on high rates of unwed pregnancy, particularly among teenagers. But while liberals generally blamed the pregnancies on poverty, conservatives blamed what they felt were wrong-headed welfare policies that rewarded out-of-wedlock births, perpetuating cycles of poverty from generation to generation. In 1996, Congress changed the welfare law to limit the lifespan of benefits and require recipients, including mothers, to work. Republicans claim that the new law has done more to lift black families out of poverty than any of the Johnson-era Great Society programs. [58]

Despite persistent poverty, a black middle class has arisen, primarily the result of public and nonprofit-sector employment, with middle-class blacks disproportionately entering jobs in government, the postal service, teaching and social work. In 2000, African-Americans made up 35 percent of the nation's postal clerks and 25 percent of the social workers, but only 5 percent of the lawyers and engineers and 4 percent of the dentists. [59] Yet, even critics of affirmative action agree that it helped accelerate, albeit slowly, the entry of African-Americans into the professional class.

In 1990, concerned that a series of Supreme Court rulings had weakened employment-discrimination law, Congress passed a tough, new Civil Rights Act to counteract the decisions. After lengthy negotiations and a major fight over the appointment of African-American Clarence Thomas to the Supreme Court, an initially reluctant President George H.W. Bush signed the new law in 1991. [60] The law expanded the anti-discrimination law to cover women and the disabled, as well as racial groups, and boosted the power of the Equal Employment Opportunity Commission (EEOC).

The Supreme Court was heavily involved in racial politics during the 1990s as well. The Justice Department had interpreted the 1982 Voting Rights Act to mean that, whenever possible, legislative districts with a high likelihood of electing blacks or other minorities should be drawn. After the redistricting cycle of the early 1990s, this led to large increases in the numbers of African-Americans elected to Congress and state legislatures.

However, the Supreme Court took exception to the Justice Department's earlier interpretation. In cases involving majority-minority congressional districts, the court ruled in the 1990s that such districts violated the 14th Amendment rights of white voters and said race could not be used as a "predominant" factor in drawing legislative districts. [61] In another voting-rights controversy, the U.S. Civil Rights Commission investigated hundreds of complaints stemming from the 2000 presidential election alleging racial discrimination in Florida and elsewhere.

Those complaints were echoed following the 2004 presidential election, when there were widespread allegations that poor and black voters were harassed or otherwise discouraged from voting in Ohio, a key swing state. "I've had hearings with all sorts of witnesses, many of whom were convinced of fraud and conspiracy," said John Conyers, ranking Democrat on the House Judiciary Committee. No definitive proof was offered, however. [62]

Meanwhile, the age-old debate continues about the harmful effects the legacy of slavery might be having on today's African-Americans. Since 1989, Rep. Conyers repeatedly has introduced legislation calling for reparations — payments to the descendants of slaves — sparking controversy in the states and on college campuses. [63]

With racial discrimination outlawed by the federal government, the political goals of blacks seeking to improve their standing in society became less clear. An age-old split widened between African-Americans who favored confrontation or reparations and those who favored individual improvement. As a result, many

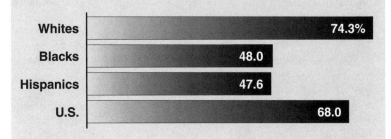

Minority Homeownership Lags

Despite increases in minority homeownership during the 1990s, large gaps remain between whites, blacks and Hispanics. Nearly three-quarters of whites owned homes in 2002, compared with less than half the blacks and Hispanics.

U.S. Homeownership Rates
(percentage of each race that owns a home)

Whites	74.3%
Blacks	48.0
Hispanics	47.6
U.S.	68.0

Sources: The White House (www.whitehouse.gov); U.S. Census Bureau

observers argue that black conservatives have "sold out"; others say civil-rights activists continue to be pessimistic about race relations to serve their own cause.

In essence, the "double-consciousness" for black Americans that the celebrated civil-rights leader and author W.E.B. Du Bois wrote about a century ago — "to be both a Negro and an American, without being cursed and spit upon by his fellows, without having the doors of opportunity closed roughly in his face" — continues today. [64]

CURRENT SITUATION

Affirmative-Action Ruling

The Supreme Court's June 2003 decisions involving two University of Michigan admissions policies turned on the question of whether racial preferences are discriminatory toward other groups, such as whites.

By a 5-4 vote in *Grutter v. Bollinger*, the court granted continuing legal favor to the law school's practice of affirmative action. The case centered on a challenge to the law school's policy of using race as a "plus factor" in accepting students. The court found that using race as one factor among many in determining individual admissions was acceptable.

Anti-Arab Sentiment on the Rise

For Yashar Zendehdel, an Iranian student at the University of Colorado, confusion over the number of academic credits he listed on his immigration paperwork led to a harrowing 26 hours in a federal jail. He was eventually cleared of any wrongdoing, but remains furious that he was treated like a criminal. [1]

"I couldn't believe it," Zendehdel said. "It was awful. I have never been to jail before. Government officials are wasting American people's tax money, my time, their time." [2]

"Discrimination against Arab-Americans and those perceived to be Arab-American has been a much bigger problem" since the Sept. 11, 2001, terrorist attacks by 19 Arab Muslims, says Laila Al-Qatami, of the American-Arab Anti-Discrimination Committee. "We've seen a lot more discrimination and hate-crime cases and a greater variety of cases."

In 2001, the FBI recorded 481 attacks against Middle Easterners, Muslims and Sikhs, compared with 28 attacks reported the previous year. [3] Job-discrimination complaints from Muslims roughly doubled after Sept. 11, from 542 in 2001 to 1,157 in 2002, according to the U.S. Equal Employment Opportunity Commission. [4]

And despite President Bush's declaration that Islam is a "religion of peace," some prominent politicians and religious leaders have made inflammatory remarks about Islam and Muslims. The Rev. Franklin Graham, son of the Rev. Billy Graham, called Islam "a very evil and wicked religion." Jerry Vines, former president of the Southern Baptist Convention, denounced the Islamic prophet Muhammad as a "demon-possessed pedophile." [5]

And then-Rep. John Cooksey, R-La., recommended that airline personnel selectively question Arab passengers. "If I see someone who comes in that's got a diaper on his head and a fan belt wrapped around the diaper on his head, that guy needs to be pulled over," Cooksey told a Louisiana radio interviewer. [6]

Moreover, some of the government's post-9/11 anti-terrorism programs have exacerbated Arabs' feelings of persecution and discrimination. The FBI began monitoring American mosques and encouraging thousands of Arab-Americans to undergo voluntary interviews. Many were arrested when they showed up. Recently, the FBI interviewed 5,000 Iraqis in the U.S. in an attempt to pre-empt terrorism related to the war in Iraq. [7]

The controversial domestic spying campaign, revealed in 2005 and conducted by the National Security Agency, allowed the agency to intercept international telephone and Internet communications without a court order, leaving many Arab Americans feeling targeted. Federal officials continue to check mosques for radiation levels.

The recent National Security Entry-Exit Registration System (NSEERS) — created by Attorney General John Ashcroft under a congressional mandate — required tens of thousands of mostly Arab and Muslim men living in the United States to be fingerprinted by the government during so-called special-registration sweeps. [8]

The program also has begun registering foreigners at U.S. borders who meet government criteria as potential threats or persons of interest. So far, the programs have documented visitors from 155 countries, says Jorge Martinez, a Justice Department spokesman.

In some instances, large Arab turnouts at registration locations have overloaded officials and forced them to detain hundreds of people until they could be fully documented, complains James Zogby, president of the Washington-based Arab American Institute.

"If you take all these pieces and you put them together, it produces a lot of fear in the Arab-American community," adds Al-Qatami.

But in *Gratz v. Bollinger*, by a 6-3 vote, the justices found unconstitutional the undergraduate school's practice of granting 20 points, on a 150-point scale, to blacks and Latinos just because of their race. Quantifying race as a universal value, the court said, was unacceptable.

"In order to cultivate a set of leaders with legitimacy in the eyes of the citizenry," wrote Justice Sandra Day O'Connor in the majority opinion in *Grutter*, "it is necessary that the path to leadership be visibly open to talented and qualified individuals of every race and ethnicity." The law school engages in a "highly individualized, holistic review of each applicant's file," she wrote, in which race counts as a factor but is not used in a "mechanical way." For that reason, O'Connor explained, the policy was in keeping with a 1978 court ruling on affirmative action that permits using race as a "plus factor."

The court's ruling that decisions can be made based on race as long as they are not done in a purely quantita-

Others say the registration programs are tantamount to racial profiling, a practice recently banned by the Bush administration. "The NSEERS program and special registration was a disaster," Zogby says, "and it clearly targeted Muslims and Arabs."

But the Justice Department insists registration programs only targeted people from countries that sponsor terrorism or harbor Al-Qaeda members. "The registration programs have absolutely nothing to do with race or religion," Martinez says. "People from certain countries were registered because they presented a higher national-security threat, and it's just coincidence that those countries happen to be a majority Arab and Muslim."

But Al-Qatami responds, "The reality is that if you are an Arab male, you are automatically registered, while people of other ethnic backgrounds will have to register according to the discretion of a Customs and Border Protection officer. Therefore this pattern is not, as the DOJ spokesperson says, just a coincidence."

Others doubt the efficacy of registration programs. "So far, registration programs haven't netted much," Al-Qatami says. "If we just focus on certain ethnic or racial characteristics, we're going to miss other people who also commit crimes and terrorism," such as Richard Reid — the British Al-Qaeda sympathizer convicted of trying to destroy an airliner with a shoe bomb.

Government officials counter that national security trumps concerns over racial profiling. "When it relates to a national-security investigation, efforts to identify terrorists may include factors like race and ethnicity," Martinez says.

On a more positive note, law enforcement has won praise for prosecuting backlash crimes against Arab-Americans. Martinez notes the Justice Department has investigated more than 500 alleged backlash crimes, and 13 have been prosecuted successfully.

"Clearly, after Sept. 11 there was a directive that the government would take backlash crimes against Arab-Americans and Muslims seriously in an effort to stem hate crimes," Zogby says.

To strengthen ties with the Arab community, the FBI recently established an Arab-American Advisory Committee in Washington similar to committees in several other cities. [9] "Both law enforcement and the Arab-American community believe that a community-policing situation was the ideal way to break down the barriers of mistrust," says Zogby, a member of the D.C. advisory committee. "We've been able do some good stuff together."

Others are more cautious. "Some positive things have come out of the experience," Al-Qatami says, "but we still have a long way to go."

— Benton Ives-Halperin

[1] Eric Hoover, "Closing the Gates: A Student Under Suspicion," *The Chronicle of Higher Education*, April 11, 2003, p. 12.

[2] Maria Bondes, "Foreign Students to Leave U. Colorado?" *Colorado Daily*, Jan. 7, 2003.

[3] Darryl Fears, "Hate Crimes Against Arabs Surge, FBI Finds," *The Washington Post*, Nov. 26, 2002, p. A2.

[4] Equal Employment Opportunity Commission fact sheet, June 11, 2003.

[5] Laurie Goodstein, "Seeing Islam as 'Evil' Faith, Evangelicals Seek Converts," *The New York Times*, May 27, 2003, p. A1.

[6] "National Briefing South: Louisiana: Apology From Congressman," *The New York Times*, Sept. 21, 2001, p. A16.

[7] "Under Suspicion," *The Economist*, March 29, 2003.

[8] Patrick J. McDonell, "Nearly 24,000 Foreign Men Register in U.S," *Los Angeles Times*, Jan. 19, 2003, p. A22.

[9] Alan Lengel and Caryle Murphy, "FBI, Arab Community Join Forces With Panel," *The Washington Post*, March 29, 2003, p. B1.

tive manner struck some observers as hazy. But the biggest complaints were lodged by those who thought the court had given credence to the notion that members of some races should be granted advantages that are not enjoyed by all.

"Racial classifications in the United States have a long and ugly history," wrote U.S. Civil Rights Commissioner Thernstrom. "Racial subordination was all about double standards, with different entitlements depending on your racial identity. Nevertheless, the highest court in the land has now embraced them. It is a bleak day in American constitutional law." [65]

Affirmative-action supporters, however, echoed O'Connor's assertion that creating a diverse leadership class through more racially balanced admissions to top universities was a societal good worth preserving. For them, the court's decision was a cheering answer to a long series of attacks on affirmative action, including

Should colleges be allowed to use race as a factor in admissions?

YES David W. DeBruin
Attorney, Jenner & Block

Excerpted from a Brief filed in the U.S. Supreme Court, *Grutter v. Bollinger*, Feb. 18, 2003.

Diversity in higher education is a compelling government interest not only because of its positive effects on the educational environment itself, but also because of the crucial role diversity in higher education plays in preparing students to be the leaders this country needs in business, law and all other pursuits that affect the public interest. ...

[B]y enriching students' education with a variety of perspectives, experiences and ideas, a university with a diverse student body equips all of its students with the skills and understanding necessary to succeed in any profession. Those skills include the ability to understand, learn from, and work and build consensus with individuals from different backgrounds and cultures. ...

There are several reasons for the importance of maintaining diversity in higher education. First, a diverse group of individuals educated in a cross-cultural environment has the ability to facilitate unique and creative approaches to problem-solving arising from the integration of different perspectives.

Second, such individuals are better able to develop products and services that appeal to a variety of consumers and to market offerings in ways that appeal to those consumers. Third, a racially diverse group of managers with cross-cultural experience is better able to work with business partners, employees and clientele in the United States and around the world. Fourth, individuals who have been educated in a diverse setting are likely to contribute to a positive work environment, by decreasing incidents of discrimination and stereotyping.

Overall, an educational environment that ensures participation by diverse people, viewpoints and ideas will help produce the most talented workforce. The thrust of the government's position is that it is permissible to take affirmative steps to ensure educational diversity — a goal that itself includes consideration of race. The United States defends particular admissions programs it prefers in Texas, Florida and California explicitly on the ground that those programs allegedly continue to produce, at least in raw numbers, the same racial and ethnic diversity in enrollment.

Institutions of higher learning must be allowed to prepare students to thrive in an increasingly diverse environment. The best way to do this is to ensure that students learn in an environment of diversity, including racial and cultural diversity. Accordingly, institutions of higher learning should be able to use "competitive consideration of race and ethnic origin" in pursuit of a diverse student body.

NO George W. Bush
President of the United States

Excerpted from remarks made on Jan. 15, 2003

Our Constitution makes it clear that people of all races must be treated equally under the law. Yet we know that our society has not fully achieved that ideal. Racial prejudice is a reality in America. It hurts many of our citizens. As a nation, as a government, as individuals, we must be vigilant in responding to prejudice wherever we find it. Yet, as we work to address the wrong of racial prejudice, we must not use means that create another wrong, and thus perpetuate our divisions.

America is a diverse country, racially, economically and ethnically. And our institutions of higher education should reflect our diversity. A college education should teach respect and understanding and goodwill. And these values are strengthened when students live and learn with people from many backgrounds. Yet quota systems that use race to include or exclude people from higher education and the opportunities it offers are divisive, unfair and impossible to square with the Constitution. ...

The University of Michigan has established an admissions process based on race. At the undergraduate level, African-American students and some Hispanic students and Native American students receive 20 points out of a maximum of 150, not because of any academic achievement or life experience, but solely because they are African-American, Hispanic or Native American. To put this in perspective, a perfect SAT score is worth only 12 points in the Michigan system. Students who accumulate 100 points are generally admitted, so those 20 points awarded solely based on race are often the decisive factor.

At the law school, some minority students are admitted to meet percentage targets while other applicants with higher grades and better scores are passed over. This means that students are being selected or rejected based primarily on the color of their skin. The motivation for such an admissions policy may be very good, but its result is discrimination, and that discrimination is wrong.

Some states are using innovative ways to diversify their student bodies. Recent history has proven that diversity can be achieved without using quotas. Systems in California and Florida and Texas have proven that by guaranteeing admissions to the top students from high schools throughout the state, including low-income neighborhoods, colleges can attain broad racial diversity. In these states, race-neutral admissions policies have resulted in levels of minority attendance for incoming students that are close to, and in some instances slightly surpass, those under the old race-based approach.

Is the Confederate flag a racist symbol?

YES   Sanford Cloud, Jr.
President and CEO, National Conference for Community and Justice

Excerpted from the NCCJ Web Site, dated 2002

Historically, the Confederate flag was a symbol during the Civil War of the Confederate States of America, which defended the rights of individual states that maintained their economy through slave labor. Although the Civil War ended 138 years ago, the battle over the legacy of slavery, segregation and civil rights continues.

Through the years, the Confederate flag has taken on additional negative connotations because it was used as a symbol of resistance during the civil-rights movement and is currently a prominent symbol of active white-supremacist groups. This is not to say that all individuals who bear the Confederate flag are racist. However, the symbolic meaning of the flag is that of white domination and Southern pride.

Some people assert that the Confederate flag is a symbol of their heritage; however, for many people of color and religious minorities across the United States and other communities around the world, it represents hatred, bigotry, racism, and anti-Semitism. This symbol is a very powerful nonverbal communication tool that, according to the Anti-Defamation League (ADL), generates deep meaning, intent and significance in a compact, immediately recognizable form. Members of racist organizations often use the symbol along with more specific images associated with their groups. Independent racists can avoid association with a specific group, and perhaps prosecution of that group by law enforcement, by opting for more universal racist symbols.

The National Conference for Community and Justice (NCCJ) maintains that the Confederate flag is a visible, confrontational racist symbol that represents racial oppression, segregation and slavery. As noted by Kweisi Mfume, president and CEO of the National Association for the Advancement of Colored People, "The [Confederate] flag is representative of an era that epitomized everything that was wrong and inhumane in this country and should be stripped of any sovereignty context and placed into a historical context." NCCJ concurs with this sentiment and calls for the removal of the Confederate flag from all public properties with allowances for its usage in appropriate historical and educational contexts.

All people of goodwill need to recognize that the Confederate flag ... is an attack on the freedoms of our nation. Similarly, racism has no boundaries, and this issue cannot be confined to the Southern states. NCCJ therefore calls on all residents of the United States to actively oppose the usage of the Confederate flag and denounce it as a visible public statement that is offensive in nature.

NO   William Rolen
Director and Southern Heritage Defense Coordinator, Council of Conservative Citizens

Written for *CQ Researcher*, May 2003

For thirty years, the 1956 Georgia flag flew peacefully over every public building in the state. Not many people seemed disturbed by the large Confederate portion of the flag, which was put there in 1956 to honor the Southern soldiers who had fought and died defending Georgia against the atrocities of Gen. Sherman.

Then in 1991, the NAACP national convention passed a resolution condemning the Confederate flag as racist. From that year on, the Confederate flag and other Confederate icons have been subjected to relentless vitriolic wrath. One by one, Confederate flags have been removed, banned or desecrated simply because threats from the NAACP terrify the political status quo in virtually every Southern state.

The problem with the Confederate flag does not involve illicit connections with the klan or any other "guilt by association" flummery. The NAACP took aim at the Confederate flag because the emblem is revered by most Southerners. Confederate flag decals stick on every type of vehicle from trucks to tricycles. Confederate-flag clothing, from Dixie Outfitter T-shirts to G.R.I.T.S. (Girls Raised In The South) swimsuits are ordinary sights. The images of celebrities like Elvis and Hank Williams are superimposed on Confederate flags sold at truck stops and souvenir shops. Only a very jaundiced eye sees racism lurking behind every Southern-cross belt buckle and bandana worn on race day at Talledega.

Certainly, the Confederate flag honors the Southern soldier and the memory of generals Lee, Jackson, and Beauregard. More significantly, the Confederate flag represents the continuum of Southern experience. Does the flag have a racial dimension? Yes, but the racial connotations are no more negative than the FUBU (For Us, By Us) clothing that is designed, marketed and intended only for blacks.

The Confederate flag is not an aggressive symbol. No one is trying to hoist the Confederate colors over the Capitol of Vermont, nor are Confederate flag ski jackets a fashion statement on the slopes of Aspen. The Confederate flag is largely a regional phenomenon, and one of multiple interpretations. The NAACP, however, allows for only one, narrow viewpoint.

The time has come to honor and respect the Confederate flag for all the sacrifices Southerners have made over the last 20 years to display the symbol with honor, dignity and pride. And a word of caution to the NAACP: The harder you try to pull it down, the higher it will fly.

Police Tactics Spark Riots

The racially tinged incidents that periodically break out across the country are often provoked by outrage in the black community over police tactics that are seen by many African-Americans as heavy-handed and racist. At least five homes were torched and up to 15 people injured during a riot in Benton Harbor, Mich., in mid-June following the death of a black motorcyclist during a police chase (top). Police arrest a demonstrator during a protest march outside Cincinnati in June 2001. (bottom). The march followed riots sparked by the fatal shooting of an unarmed black man by a white policeman.

state-ballot initiatives banning the practice in California and elsewhere.

"A diverse and racially integrated campus benefits all students and ultimately, all of America," says Marc Morial, president of the National Urban League. "The court clearly upheld the argument that the government has a compelling interest in promoting diversity in education and the workplace."

Thus, the notion of helping members of minority groups, such as blacks and Latinos, through some formal process rather than relying on "color-blind" admissions and hiring policies, is, legally, here to stay. However, O'Connor also expressed the hope that race-based admissions policies would no longer be necessary in 25 years.

Advocates of such policies point to public universities in California, Florida and Texas that have devised new formulas for continued minority enrollment after dumping affirmative action. Admission is either guaranteed to the top students from each high school, including those where students are predominantly minorities, or they seek out low-income students, who are disproportionately black or Latino. The university systems have maintained or even increased their minority enrollments, except at their flagship campuses. [66]

The cases in many ways demonstrate the shifting political dynamics when race is at issue. When the court considered affirmative-action policies in *University of California Regents v. Bakke* in 1978, hardly any corporations engaged in the issue. In the Michigan case, however, a group of five-dozen *Fortune* 500 companies filed an *amicus* brief with the court, arguing that diverse campuses better prepare future workers for a global economy, especially in a country whose demographic trends suggest that whites no longer will account for a majority of the population by 2050.

Three days after the Michigan ruling, the Supreme Court used a Georgia case, *Georgia v. Ashcroft*, to signal a new direction in the ways blacks and other minorities can be represented politically. For the past 20 years, Justice Department officials have interpreted the Voting Rights Act to mean that whenever a legislative district could be created with a majority of minority voters, such districts should be created. Majority-minority districts have led to more black and Latino representation in both Congress and state legislatures over the past dozen years.

But some blacks and Democrats argued that majority-minority districts actually weaken political representation for blacks: By "packing" most black voters within racially separate districts, politicians from neighboring "bleached" (all-white) districts have no natural incentive to represent black interests. The state of Georgia created a map of state Senate districts that broke up some majority-black districts, in favor of creating more districts in which blacks could compete politically.

It's now widely believed that black politicians can win office in districts where blacks make up less than a majority of the electorate. Giving blacks a real opportunity, rather than an assured win, is good enough to protect their interests in the current racial climate, according to Swain of Vanderbilt Law School and other black scholars.

The Justice Department opposed Georgia's map, but the high court upheld the plan, 6-3. Writing for the majority, Justice O'Connor wrote that "various studies have suggested that the most effective way to maximize minority voting strength may be to create" districts "where minority voters may not be able to elect a candidate of choice but [can] play a substantial, if not decisive role, in the electoral process."

Bush Administration

Many people predicted that after Lott lost his Senate leadership post for pro-segregationist remarks, the Republicans might show an increased interest in '60s-style civil-rights legislation. That has not been the case. With the momentum for race-specific programs slowing, the Congressional Black Caucus and African-American advocates have begun focusing on seeking equal treatment under laws and programs that apply to all Americans, advocating increased funding for domestic priorities like education and health. Meanwhile, Republicans continue to argue that race-neutral, market-based proposals will work better than further government intrusions into private-sector practices.

President Bush opposes race-specific government-aid programs. In response to the Supreme Court's affirmative-action decisions and O'Connor's comments about the need for affirmative action fading after 25 years, Bush said he was glad that the court shared his vision of a color-blind America.

In June 2003, Bush announced a new policy designed to severely curtail racial profiling by federal law-enforcement officers. Agents running auto-theft or drug investigations, for instance, cannot stop black or Latino motorists based on the "generalized assumption" that members of those racial or ethnic groups are more likely to commit such crimes.

If a specific description identifies a suspect as black, however, the agents can target blacks as part of their search. The new policy also exempts national-security cases in "narrow" circumstances. Immigration officers, for example, can continue to require registration by visitors from Middle Eastern countries thought to foster terrorism.

Skeptics, though, wonder whether cash-strapped states and the federal government will pick up a larger tab for funding anti-poverty programs and other measures that apply not only to blacks but also to a much-expanded pool of disadvantaged citizens of all races.

At a 2003 forum, Stephen Goldsmith, who was then a special adviser to the president, said, "There is now a broad consensus that a work-based benefit system is where we want to be." But he acknowledged that even if there is consensus about work being the best way to help low-income Americans, there isn't agreement about how much money to provide for such a system. [67]

Black and Latino activists are concerned that states are not properly monitoring civil rights in the current welfare-reform law's assistance programs. They want Congress to beef up enforcement, claiming that African-American and Hispanic women have not been given support services equal to members of other races.

Similarly, as Congress considers amendments to the Workforce Investment Act of 1998, which consolidated dozens of job-training programs into block grants to the states, members of the Congressional Black Caucus are concerned that the law's data-collection requirements make it harder to determine whether African-Americans are being discriminated against.

Some black advocates claim that blacks, Asians and Hispanics are being steered toward less-useful training — into areas such as résumé writing — rather than more potentially lucrative occupational job training.

Activists have also criticized the Bush administration for its handling of civil and voting rights cases. Political appointees to the Justice Department overruled staff attorneys who found that Republican-engineered voter identification and redistricting plans in Georgia and Texas hurt minority voters. The department subsequently "barred staff attorneys from offering recommendations in major Voting Rights Act cases." [68] A number of veteran voting and civil rights attorneys have quit the department over such policy disagreements. [69]

Action in the States

California, Maryland and New Jersey in recent years have revised their racial-profiling policies in an effort to discourage bias among their troopers. Mac Donald, at the Manhattan Institute, argues that the increasing number of states and cities requiring police to record interactions with civilians on the basis of race will have a "chilling effect . . . on legitimate police work," as police officers avoid "all but the most mandatory and cursory interactions with potential minority suspects." [70] Nevertheless, about 20 other states have set up commissions to study racial profiling or have considered legislation to curb the practice.

Meanwhile, as part of the ongoing debate about whether the descendants of slaves should receive reparations, several states also are considering establishing commissions to determine the effects of slavery on contemporary African-Americans.

In some states, the most pressing racial issues are largely symbolic. In his successful 2002 campaign for governor of Georgia, Republican Sonny Perdue promised voters a referendum on restoring a Confederate emblem to the state flag that had been removed in 2001. Voters approved a compromise flag design in 2004.

OUTLOOK

Lingering Problems?

The nation's historic blend of European colonialists, displaced Native Americans, African slaves and immigrants from around the world has made for an often-volatile racial mix. Given current predictions that by 2050 no racial group will comprise a majority of the population, racial relations are expected to evolve in complex ways.

Optimists believe that the demographic changes, along with the changes in social norms that make open discrimination against blacks taboo, will eventually lead to a society that is less divided and concerned about race. "It may be no accident," says Harvard's Thernstrom, "that the first state to bar racial preferences by constitutional amendment, California, is also the state with the most complex racial mix."

But even some optimists say racism will remain potent for a long time. "Hopefully, we've set in motion enough positive activities where we do ultimately get to a color-blind society," says Weldon Latham, corporate-diversity director at the giant Holland & Knight law firm. "But it's many decades from now."

Similarly, while University of California, Berkeley public policy professor Jack Glaser sees racism declining, "Sadly, I can't imagine that it will ever go away," he says. "People are pretty hard-wired to see things in categories. You can put people into very arbitrary groups, and they know it's arbitrary, but they will still show favor to members of their group."

During his tenure as president of the American Bar Association (ABA) from 1999 to 2000, Oklahoma City attorney William G. Paul made diversity his top priority because, he said, his profession is 88.6 percent white. [71] He has been heartened by the scholarship fund the ABA established and by data showing that blacks and other minorities are better represented in law schools than they are, as yet, in the legal profession itself.

"I didn't find anyone voicing any opposition," recalls Paul, who is white. Yet he admits that habits and the status quo are so ingrained that achieving equality even in his high-profile profession is "going to require a multi-decade effort."

Indeed, the most pessimistic observers of race relations predict that there could yet be a new backlash against blacks and minorities, mirroring the historic setbacks blacks faced following the Revolutionary and Civil wars. "I don't really think the white population is going to lose its powers or prestige because its numbers are going down," says *Two Nations* author Andrew Hacker.

Even without ill will or conscious discrimination, recent history suggests that institutions long dominated by whites will continue to be dominated by whites, with few exceptions. "If you assume attitudes and expectations are institutionalized," says Mitchell, of the National Research Council, "time won't make a difference."

NOTES

1. Rosa Brooks, "Our Homegrown Third World," *Los Angeles Times*, Sept. 7, 2005, p. B13.

2. William Neikirk and Mike Hughlett, "Critics Say Bias Delayed Relief to Disaster Area," *Chicago Tribune*, Sept. 3, 2005, p. 1.

3. Michael A. Fletcher and Richard Morin, "Bush's Approval Rating Drops to New Low in Wake of Storm," *The Washington Post*, Sept. 13, 2005, p. A8.

4. Sara Mosle, "The Case of the Lone Star Witness," *The New York Times*, Oct. 30, 2005, p. 7:15.

5. Dahlia Lithwik, "At Duke, Just Pick Your Facts," *The Washington Post*, April 23, 2006, p. B2.

6. Fletcher and Morin, *op. cit.*

7. Andrew Hacker, *Two Nations: Black & White, Separate, Hostile, Unequal* (3rd ed. 2003, originally published 1992), p. 111.

8. Sheryl Gay Stolberg, "Cultural Issues Pose Obstacles in Cancer Fight," *The New York Times*, March 14, 1998, p. A1.

9. Margery Austin Turner and Felicity Skidmore, ed., "Mortgage Lending Discrimination: A Review of Existing Evidence," The Urban Institute, June 1999, p. 1.

10. Stephan Thernstrom and Abigail Thernstrom, *America in Black and White: One Nation, Indivisible* (1997), p. 222. See "The Nation's Report Card," National Assessment of Educational Progress, National Center for Education Statistics. http://nces.ed.gov/nationsreportcard/.

11. Bruce Western, Becky Pettit and Josh Guetzkow, "Black Economic Progress in the Era of Mass Imprisonment," in Marc Mauer and Meda Chesney-Lind, eds., *Invisible Punishment: The Collateral Consequences of Mass Imprisonment* (2002), p. 170.

12. Thernstrom and Thernstrom, *op. cit.*, p. 274.

13. Eric Lichtblau, "Bush Issues Racial Profiling Ban But Exempts Security Inquiries," *The New York Times*, June 18, 2003, p. A1.

14. Quoted in Bettijane Levine, "Harry Belafonte won't retreat from slavery remarks," *Chicago Tribune*, Oct. 23, 2002, p. 1.

15. See Ellen Nakashima and Al Kamen, "Bush Official Hails Diversity," *The Washington Post*, March 31, 2001, p. A10.

16. Peter Beinart, "Mexican Standoff," *The New Republic*, April 10, 2006, p. 6.

17. John McWhorter, *Losing the Race: Self-Sabotage in Black America* (2000).

18. For background, see David Masci, "The Black Middle Class," *CQ Researcher*, Jan. 23, 1998, pp. 49-72.

19. Randall Kennedy, *Nigger: The Strange Career of a Troublesome Word* (2002), p. 27.

20. See Greg Winter, "State Underfinancing Damages City Schools, New York Court Finds," *The New York Times*, June 27, 2003, p. A1. For background on school funding issues, see Kathy Koch, "Reforming School Funding," *CQ Researcher*, Dec. 10, 1999, pp. 1041-1064.

21. Office of Policy Research and Development, "All Other Things Being Equal: A Paired Testing Study of Mortgage Lending Institutions," U.S. Department of Housing and Urban Development, April 2002, p. 10, www.huduser.org/Publications/PDF/aotbe.pdf.

22. Douglas S. Massey and Garvey Lundy, "Use of Black English and Racial Discrimination in Urban Housing Markets: New Methods and Findings," *Urban Affairs Review 36* (2001): 470-96.

23. Erica Frankenberg, Chungmei Lee and Gary Orfield, "A Multiracial Society With Segregated Schools: Are We Losing the Dream?" Harvard University Civil Rights Project, January 2003, p. 28, www.civilrightsproject.harvard.edu/research/reseg03/AreWeLosingtheDream.pdf.

24. Thernstrom and Thernstrom, *op. cit.*, p. 199. See also "Historical Census of Housing Tables," U.S. Census Bureau, www.census.gov/hhes/www/housing/census/historic/ownershipbyrace.html.

25. Turner and Skidmore, *op. cit.*

26. McWhorter, *op. cit.*

27. Thernstrom and Thernstrom, *op. cit.*

28. Thomas P. Bonczar, "Prevalence of Imprisonment in the U.S. Population, 1974-2001," Bureau of Justice Statistics, Aug. 2003.

29. Mark Mauer, "The Crisis of the Young African-American Male and the Criminal Justice System," testimony submitted to the U.S. Commission on Civil Rights, April 15-16, 1999.

30. Randall Kennedy, *Race, Crime, and the Law* (1997), p. x.

31. For background, see Kenneth Jost, "Policing the Police," *CQ Researcher*, March 17, 2000, pp. 209-240.

32. David Kocieniewski, "New Jersey Adopts Ban on Racial Profiling," *The New York Times*, March 14, 2003, p. B5.

33. The Associated Press, "Cincinnati Police Want Community Pact Ended," *The Washington Post*, April 30, 2003, p. A8.

34. Michael Tonry, *Malign Neglect: Race, Crime, and Punishment in America* (1995), p. 79.

35. Quoted in Kennedy 1997, p. 15. See Clarence Page, "Message to Jackson: The Word Is Crime, Not Black Criminals," *Chicago Tribune*, Jan. 5, 1994, p. 15.

36. See Kennedy 1997, pp. 370 ff.

37. Quoted in Kennedy 1997, p. 14.

38. Adam Liptak, "Death Penalty Found More Likely If Victim Is White," *The New York Times*, Jan. 8, 2003, p. A12.

39. Henry Weinstein, "Panel Urges Halt to Executions in Pa.," *Los Angeles Times*, March 5, 2003, p. 15.

40. Philip A. Klinkner with Rogers M. Smith, *The Unsteady March: The Rise and Decline of Racial Equality in America* (1999), p. 12.

41. Quoted in Philip S. Foner, *From Africa to the Emergence of the Cotton Kingdom* (1975), p. 303.

42. Quoted in Klinkner and Smith, *op. cit.*, p. 18.

43. Lerone Bennett, Jr., *Before the Mayflower: A History of Black America* (5th ed., 1984; originally published 1962), p. 257.

44. Quoted in Thernstrom and Thernstrom, *op. cit.*

45. Quoted in Bennett, *op. cit.*

46. Philip Dray, *At the Hands of Persons Unknown: The Lynching of Black America* (2002), p. iii.

47. Klinkner and Smith, *op. cit.*

48. Thernstrom and Thernstrom, *op. cit.*

49. *Ibid.*, p. 79.

50. Gerald N. Rosenberg, *The Hollow Hope: Can Courts Bring About Social Change?* (1991), p. 50.

51. Thurmond had led a record-breaking filibuster of 24 hours and 18 minutes against the Civil Rights Bill of 1957.

52. *Congress and the Nation, Vol. 1*, p. 1635.

53. *Congress and the Nation, Vol. 2*, p. 356.

54. Niel J. Smelser, William Julius Wilson and Faith Mitchell, eds., *America Becoming: Racial Trends and Their Consequences, Vol. 1* (2001), p. 321.

55. Quoted in Klinkner and Smith, *op. cit.*

56. Carol Pogash, "Berkeley Makes Its Pitch to Top Minority Students," *Los Angeles Times*, April 20, 2003, Part 2, p. A6.

57. Thernstrom and Thernstrom, *op. cit.*

58. For background, see Sarah Glazer, "Welfare Reform," *CQ Researcher*, Aug. 3, 2001, pp. 601-632.

59. Hacker, *op. cit.*, p. 130.

60. *Congress and the Nation, Vol. VIII*, p. 757.

61. For background see Jennifer Gavin, "Redistricting," *CQ Researcher*, Feb. 16, 2001, pp. 113-128.

62. William Raspberry, "What Happened in Ohio," *The Washington Post*, January 10, 2005, p. A17.

63. For background, see David Masci, "Reparations Movement," *CQ Researcher*, June 22, 2001, pp. 529-552.

64. W.E.B. Du Bois, *The Souls of Black Folk* (1933).

65. Abigail Thernstrom, "Court Rulings Add Insult to Injury," *Los Angeles Times*, June 29, 2003, p. M1.

66. Mitchell Landsberg, Peter Y. Hong and Rebecca Trounson, " 'Race-Neutral' University Admissions in Spotlight," *Los Angeles Times*, Jan. 17, 2003, p. 1.

67. Quoted in David Callahan and Tamara Draut, "Broken Bargain: Why Bush May Be Destroying A Hard-Won Consensus on Helping the Poor," *The Boston Globe*, May 11, 2003, p. H1.

68. Dan Eggen, "Staff Opinions Banned in Voting Rights Cases," *The Washington Post*, Dec. 10, 2005, p. A3.

69. Dan Eggen, "Civil Rights Focus Shift Roils Staff at Justice," *The Washington Post*, Nov. 13, 2005, p. A1.

70. Heather Mac Donald, "A 'Profiling' Pall on the Terror War," *The Washington Post*, May 5, 2003, p. A21.

71. Leonard M. Baynes, "Don't Let the Present Dictate the Future," *Business Law Today*, Nov-Dec. 2005.

BIBLIOGRAPHY

Books

Correspondents of *The New York Times*, How Race Is Lived in America, Times Books, 2001.
A collection of the *Times'* Pulitzer Prize-winning series of reporting about how issues of race still affect American society.

Hacker, Andrew, *Two Nations: Black & White, Separate, Hostile, Unequal*, 3rd ed. 2003 (originally published 1992).
A political scientist finds race to be an "obdurate" problem, portraying an America in which blacks and whites

are still separate and unequal, with illustrations drawn largely from census figures.

Kennedy, Randall, *Nigger: The Strange Career of a Troublesome Word*, Pantheon, 2002.
A Harvard Law School professor examines the history and usage of "the paradigmatic slur" and what it expresses about racial enmities.

Kennedy, Randall, *Race, Crime, and the Law*, Pantheon, 1997.
The Harvard law professor analyzes issues at the intersection of race and the criminal-justice system, including anti-drug laws, the death penalty and jury selection.

Klinkner, Philip A., with Rogers M. Smith, *The Unsteady March: The Rise and Decline of Racial Equality in America*, University of Chicago Press, 1999.
The authors survey African-American rights from Colonial times to the late 1990s and conclude that each period of advancement for blacks has been followed by a lengthy backlash. Klinkner teaches government at Hamilton College; Smith teaches race and politics at Yale University.

McWhorter, John , *Losing the Race: Self-Sabotage in Black America*, Free Press, 2000.
A linguistics professor at the University of California, Berkeley argues that African-Americans cling to a "Cult of Victimology" that keeps them fixated on racism at the expense of making improvements in their own lives.

Patterson, Orlando, *The Ordeal of Integration: Progress and Resentment in America's "Racial" Crisis*, Civitas/Counterpoint, 1997.
A Harvard sociologist examines the state of progress among Afro-Americans and the impact various ideologies have on public policy.

Smelser, Neil J., William Julius Wilson and Faith Mitchell , eds., *America Becoming: Racial Trends and Their Consequences, Vols. I and II*, National Academy Press, 2001.
Essays from a National Research Council conference on race cover trends in housing, labor, income, justice and other issues.

Steinhorn, Leonard, and Barbara Diggs-Brown, *By the Color of Our Skin: The Illusion of Integration and the Reality of Race*, Dutton, 1999.
Two American University professors — one white, one black — conclude that America has not successfully integrated.

Thernstrom, Stephan, and Abigail Thernstrom, *America in Black and White: One Nation Indivisible*, Simon & Schuster, 1997.
The authors trace the history of U.S. race relations and political, social and economic trends since the civil-rights movement. They argue that race-neutral policies are a better cure for society's ills than race-conscious ones. Stephan Thernstrom teaches history at Harvard; Abigail Thernstrom is a senior fellow at the Manhattan Institute.

Reports and Studies

Frankenberg, Erika, Chungmei Lee and Gary Orfield, "A Multiracial Society With Segregated Schools: Are We Losing the Dream?" *Civil Rights Project*, January 2003; www.civilrightsproject.harvard.edu/research/reseg03/AreWeLosingtheDream.pdf.
Harvard researchers find that schools are re-segregating, with most whites attending predominantly white schools and many blacks and Hispanics attending "apartheid schools" with almost entirely minority student bodies.

Office of Policy Research and Development, All Other Things Being Equal: A Paired Testing Study of Mortgage Lending Institutions, U.S. Department of Housing and Urban Development, www.huduser.org/Publications/PDF/aotbe.pdf, April 2002.
The report concludes that blacks and Hispanics often receive less favorable treatment than whites when applying for mortgages.

Rawlston, Valerie A., and William E. Spriggs, "Pay Equity 2000: Are We There Yet?" National Urban League Institute for Opportunity and Equality, April 2001; www.nul.org/departments/inst_opp_equality/word/reports_statistics/pay_equity_report.doc.
A study of federal contractors finds that women and minorities make about 73 cents for every dollar earned by non-Hispanic white men, in large part due to differences in the types of work they do. White men are still paid more, however, for doing the same jobs.

For More Information

American Civil Rights Institute, P.O. Box 188350, Sacramento, CA 95818; (916) 444-2278; www.acri.org. A group dedicated to educating the public about programs that promote race and gender preferences.

Center for Equal Opportunity, 14 Pidgeon Hill Dr., Suite 500, Sterling, VA 20165; (703) 421-5443; www.ceousa.org. A think tank promoting color-blind policies.

Center for Individual Rights, 1233 20th St., N.W., Suite 300, Washington, DC 20036; (202) 833-8400; www.cir-usa.org. A public-interest law firm that has challenged affirmative-action policies.

Center for New Black Leadership, 202 G St., N.E., Washington, DC 20002; (202) 546-9505. An advocacy organization supporting policies that "enhance the ability of individuals and communities to develop market-oriented, community-based" solutions to economic and social problems.

The Civil Rights Project, 124 Mt. Auburn St., 500 North, Cambridge, MA 02138; (617) 496-6367; www.civilrights project.harvard.edu. A Harvard-affiliated think tank.

Joint Center for Political and Economic Studies, 1090 Vermont Ave., N.W., Suite 1100 Washington, DC 20005; (202) 789-3500; www.jointcenter.org. Founded to train black elected officials, it studies issues of importance to black Americans.

Leadership Conference on Civil Rights, 1629 K St., N.W., 10th Floor, Washington, DC 20006; (202) 466-3311; www.civilrights.org. A coalition of 180 national organizations promoting civil-rights legislation and policy.

The Manhattan Institute, 52 Vanderbilt Ave., New York, NY 10017; (212) 599-7000; www.manhattan-institute.org. A think tank that fosters "greater economic choice and individual responsibility."

National Association for the Advancement of Colored People, 4805 Mt. Hope Dr., Baltimore, MD 21215; (877) NAACP-98; www.naacp.org. Century-old organization committed to improving the civil rights of African-Americans and other minorities.

National Conference for Community and Justice, 328 Flatbush Ave., Box 402, Brooklyn, NY 11217; (718) 783-0044; www.nccj.org. Formerly the National Conference of Christians and Jews, it fights bias and racism in America.

National Urban League, 120 Wall St., 8th Floor, New York, NY, 10005; (212) 558-5300; www.nul.org. Consortium of community-based organizations that promotes access to education, economic activity and civil rights among African-Americans.

Southern Poverty Law Center, 400 Washington Ave., Montgomery, AL 36104; (334) 956-8200; www.splcenter.org/. A group that fights discrimination through educational programs, litigation and its maintenance of the Civil Rights Memorial.

U.S. Commission on Civil Rights, 624 Ninth St., N.W., Washington, DC 20425; (202) 376-7700; www.usccr.gov. Government agency that investigates complaints about discrimination.

3

Redistricting Disputes

Kenneth Jost

What part of "NO!!" do they understand?

Democratic lawmakers from Texas, led by Sen. Leticia Van de Putte, display voter mail last summer opposing redistricting plans that could give Republicans 22 of the state's 32 House seats this November. Democratic lawmakers staged an exodus from the state last summer in an unsuccessful effort to block voting on the new boundaries. Redistricting normally occurs every 10 years, but Texas and Colorado Republicans regained control of their legislatures and decided to redistrict mid-decade.

AP Photo/Jake Schoellkopf

From *CQ Researcher,*
March 12, 2004.

artin Frost knows redistricting. The longtime Democratic congressman from Dallas-Fort Worth helped state lawmakers draw a congressional districting map in the early 1990s that gave Democrats control of Texas' delegation in the U.S. House of Representatives for a decade. Critics called the artfully drawn map a blatant "gerrymander."

During the 2001-2002 redistricting cycle, Frost had a chance to really help Democrats — as leader of the party's efforts to reshape congressional districts across the country.

But last year, Texas Republicans decided it was time to teach Frost a lesson about redistricting he would never forget. Aided by two other redistricting pros from Texas — House Majority Leader Rep. Tom DeLay and President Bush's top political adviser, Karl Rove — they redrew congressional districts so artfully that GOP congressional candidates could win 22 of the state's 32 House seats this November.[1]

As for Frost, his once-safe 24th District was decimated, its loyal Democratic voters in Fort Worth's Hispanic and African-American neighborhoods dispersed. Frost decided his best bet to win a 14th term this year would be to move to another district. He set his sights on the new, east-of-Dallas 32nd District and Rep. Pete Sessions — a four-term, conservative incumbent. The campaign is likely to be one of the most expensive, closely watched House contests this fall.

Frost avoids accusing the Republicans of singling him out. "I think they were trying to eliminate as many Democrats as possible," he says. "I happened to be one of the many Democrats that they were targeting."

For his part, Sessions says he is "surprised" that Frost decided to

GOP-Drawn Map Threatens Texas Democrats

Texas' new congressional redistricting plan, adopted by a Republican-controlled legislature, put 10 incumbent House Democrats in new, politically less favorable districts. One Democrat decided not to seek re-election, and another switched parties; the others are all running for new terms.

Democratic U.S. House member	Term	New political situation
Martin Frost	13th	Old Dallas-Fort Worth district carved up; seeking re-election in new 32nd District against four-term Republican.
Charles W. Stenholm	13th	Senior Agriculture Committee member lost two-thirds of his old Central/West Texas district; running against freshman Republican in 69 percent GOP district.
Ralph M. Hall	12th	Longtime conservative switched to GOP after more Republicans added to East Texas district.
Chet Edwards	7th	Lost major parts of his Central Texas district; new district is 64 percent GOP.
Gene Green	6th	Anglo representing Hispanic-majority Houston district; new district more Hispanic; ran unopposed for renomination in March 9 primary.
Lloyd Doggett	5th	Liberal representative from Austin; new district, heavily Hispanic, stretches to Mexican border; easily won renomination over Hispanic opponent in March 9 primary.
Max Sandlin	4th	East Texas district is 63 percent Republican, with 40 percent of previous constituency.
Jim Turner	4th	Old district virtually eliminated; Turner decided not to run.
Nick Lampson	4th	Lost major parts of his Houston suburban district.
Chris Bell	1st	White freshman elected from mixed Houston district redrawn into majority-black district; Bell lost bid for renomination against black opponent in March 9 primary.

Source: *Politics in America 2004* (CQ Press)

Legislators Redraw Most Congressional Districts

In 40 states, the legislature or governor redraws new district lines, but the legislators have the final say. In three states, redistricting panels draw the maps and submit them to the legislatures for approval.* In seven states, special commissions control both drawing and approving the maps. Seven low-population states have only one congressional district, so they do not regularly go through the process. ** A significantly larger number of states use independent commissions to redraw state legislative district lines.

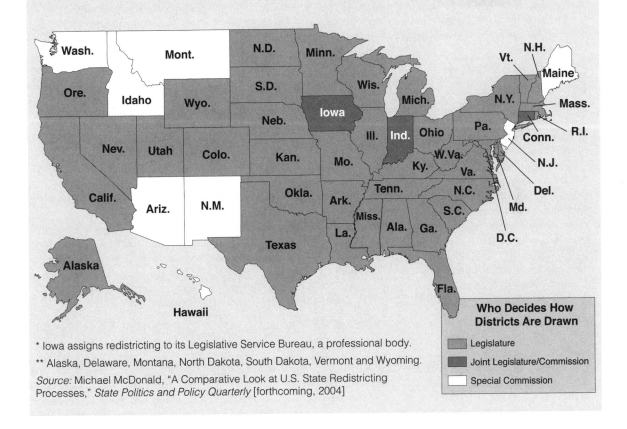

Who Decides How Districts Are Drawn

Legislature
Joint Legislature/Commission
Special Commission

* Iowa assigns redistricting to its Legislative Service Bureau, a professional body.

** Alaska, Delaware, Montana, North Dakota, South Dakota, Vermont and Wyoming.

Source: Michael McDonald, "A Comparative Look at U.S. State Redistricting Processes," *State Politics and Policy Quarterly* [forthcoming, 2004]

run against him, but adds, "I welcome him, red carpet rolled out. It won't be easy."[2]

Frost is among more than a half-dozen House Democrats who were thrown into new districts against each other or against Republican incumbents or stripped of large segments of their old constituencies. Meanwhile, Republicans in several safe districts shed some of their voters to aid the party's chances in others.

What happened in Texas could determine whether the Democrats regain control of the House next year. The new Texas map (*see p. 70*) could shift the state's House delegation from its current 16-16 partisan balance to a GOP margin as wide as 22-10. A six- or seven-vote pickup for the Republicans would all but dash Democrats' already slim hope of regaining control of the House in November.

Republicans make no secret of their partisan motivations, but insist they were merely trying to bring the state's congressional delegation into line with Republican dominance throughout the state.

"We increased the number of Republican-opportunity districts to reflect the voting trend in the state of Texas," says Andy Taylor, a Houston attorney who represents the state in defending the redistricting plan in

Reformers Target 'Winner-Take-All' System

About 40 percent of the population in Amarillo, Texas, is African-American or Latino, but during the 1990s no black or Hispanic sat on the school board. To help minority groups elect a candidate of their choice, the League of United Latin American Citizens (LULAC) and the NAACP jointly filed a federal court suit asking to replace the system of at-large elections with single-member districts.

In a settlement with the Amarillo Independent School District, however, the two groups agreed instead to a different system known as cumulative voting, which allows voters in a multi-office election to cast multiple votes in any combination. For example, in an election for four school board seats, a voter could spread four votes among four candidates or cast all four for the same candidate.

The new system produced the hoped-for results. An African-American and a Hispanic won two of the four seats being filled in the first cumulative-voting election for the seven-member board, held in May 2000. Many voters had cast multiple votes for their respective minority candidates to enable them to win.

"The fact that we got two minorities on the board is awesome," said Nancy Bosquez, a local LULAC leader. "History was made in Amarillo."[1]

Amarillo's experience is often cited by the small number of academic experts and political reformers who want to replace the predominant use of single-member districts and winner-take-all elections for multimember bodies with some form of so-called limit voting designed to enhance representation for political, racial or ethnic minorities.

"Winner-take-all is horse-and-buggy technology," says Steven Hill, Western regional director of the Center for Voting and Democracy. "One side wins all the representation; the other side wins nothing."

Cumulative voting is one of three election systems suggested by reformers as alternatives to winner-take-all, according to Richard Engstrom, a professor of political science at the University of New Orleans.[2] Often imprecisely labeled "proportional representation," the proposed systems differ from those used in Israel and Europe, which allot parliamentary seats to party candidates in mathematical proportion to the party's overall vote. Rather, the U.S. reformers' methods would still focus on individual candidates, but change the methods of casting and counting votes.

Cumulative voting would give cohesive minority groups a chance to aggregate their votes for a select number of candidates. A second, less common method — known as limited voting — would allow voters to vote for fewer candidates than the total number of positions at stake, thus preventing a majority from taking every seat in a multi-

federal court. "We undid a Democratic gerrymander instead of creating a Republican gerrymander. We brought balance back to the districts because of the partisan shift in the way Texas voters vote."

But Democrats insist the GOP plan is indeed a partisan gerrymander and should be struck down. "The sole motivation of the Texas plan was to maximize partisan advantage, to discriminate against nearly half of the voters on the basis of their political affiliation," says Sam Hirsch, a Washington attorney representing Democrats challenging the plan. "This map is designed to lock down 22 out of 32 seats for the Republicans for the rest of the decade."

The bitter redistricting fight came after most observers thought the rough-and-tumble game of redrawing congressional district maps — which normally occurs every 10 years after a new census is released —

was over until 2011.[3] But after gaining control of their state legislatures in 2002, Republicans in Texas and Colorado decided to revisit the task anew. GOP leaders in both states insisted they acted because their legislatures had deadlocked on redistricting in 2001, forcing courts to draw the districting plans used in the 2002 elections.

The unusual maneuver prompted Democrats — and many political observers — to say that redistricting is, or should be, allowed only once every 10 years. But Republicans and some academic experts say the Constitution's command to reapportion House seats among the states every 10 years based on census revisions does not limit redistricting to once per decade. Moreover, they say, mid-cycle remappings are more frequent than critics acknowledge.

One thing is certain: Redistricting can mean political life or death.

member election by eliminating the "sweep effect." A voter might get three votes, for example, if four seats are being filled.

A third, more complicated system, known as preference voting, would allow voters to write in a specified number of candidates in order of preference. After an initial tally of the first-preference votes, one or more candidates are eliminated, and the ballots for those candidates are redistributed according to the voters' second preferences. The counting continues until the number of candidates remaining equals the number of seats being filled.

Besides beefing up minority representation, Hill and Engstrom say, the alternatives avoid some of the redistricting problems experienced today. "Alternative election systems take the emphasis off the lines," Engstrom explains.

Some critics say the proposals are too complex, but Engstrom says, "There's nothing all that complicated. That's largely a red herring."

In Amarillo at least, voters appear satisfied. "It's a new system, and it takes some explaining, but we haven't had any resistance to it," Amarillo Assistant School Superintendent Les Hoyt remarked recently.[3]

Cumulative or limited voting has been instituted in 100 communities, according to Engstrom — typically in response to minority groups' suits brought under the federal Voting Rights Act. But Hill says the benefits go beyond minority representation: The alternatives would improve campaign discourse and increase political participation.

Winner-take-all encourages "negative campaigning," Hill says, because candidates are as interested in driving voters away from a rival as attracting voters to themselves. The alternative systems require candidates to "define themselves more precisely," he says.

Alternative systems would also increase turnout, he says, because they would increase competition. "All voters are swing voters, instead of a small select number of voters," he says.

But so far the proposals are only blips on the nation's political radar screen. A bill sponsored by Rep. Melvin Watt, D-N.C., in 1999 would have allowed states to choose House members from multimember districts with alternative voting arrangements. Watt, the African-American candidate elected from the majority-black district that was the focus of the Supreme Court's first ruling on racial redistricting in 1993, got a hearing on the bill, but it advanced no further.[4]

---

[1] Sonny Bohanan, "Voting System Lauded," *The* (Amarillo) *Globe-News*, May 8, 2000. The seven-member board now includes two Hispanics and one African-American.

[2] See Richard L. Engstrom, "The Political Thicket, Electoral Reform, and Minority Voting Rights," pp. 36-44, in Mark E. Rush and Richard L. Engstrom, *Fair and Effective Representation? Debating Electoral Reform and Minority Rights* (2001).

[3] Quoted in Zeke MacCormack, "Like a Candidate? Vote for Him Twice," *San Antonio Express-News*, May 1, 2003, p. 1B.

[4] See Engstrom, *op. cit.*, pp. 51-52.

"It's no secret why everybody fights so hard," says Mark Braden, a Washington attorney for the Republican National Committee. "How you draw the lines has a huge impact on who sits in legislative chambers."

"You can devise districts in such a way that you can not only predict the outcome of the next election but also how they're going to perform in a series of elections over a decade," says Gerald Hebert, a Washington-area lawyer for Democrats. "You can actually rig elections in such a way that you can produce an electoral outcome almost regardless of what happens on Election Day."

Fights over redistricting date back to the nation's earliest days, but they have become more complex since the Supreme Court launched the reapportionment revolution in the 1960s, requiring the states to draw congressional and legislative districts with roughly equal populations. The high court introduced a new measure of complexity in the 1990s by limiting the use of race to create districts with majority-black or Hispanic populations. (*See box, p. 60.*)

Now the court is considering a constitutional challenge that could fundamentally alter redistricting. Pennsylvania Democrats argue the Republican-written congressional redistricting plan is unconstitutional because it gerrymanders on political — rather than population or racial — grounds. Republicans gained a 12-7 majority in Pennsylvania's congressional delegation under the new map. The court heard arguments in the case on Dec. 10, 2003. The case is *Vieth v. Jubelirer*, 02-1580.

Meanwhile, courts in Colorado and Texas were asked to announce a "once-per-decade" rule to strike down the new GOP redistricting plans. Democrats won in Colorado but failed with a similar argument in Texas. Democrats are appealing to the Supreme Court, but the

Court Redistricting Decisions Affecting Race

The Supreme Court issued a series of decisions beginning in 1993 limiting states' ability to consider race in drawing majority-minority congressional and legislative districts.

Case	Date of Vote	Vote

***Shaw v. Reno*, 509 U.S. 630 (1993); 5-4** — White voters were allowed to challenge a highly irregular-shaped congressional district under the Constitution's Equal Protection Clause as an effort to separate voters by race; the challenge to North Carolina's majority-black 12th District was sent back to the lower court for trial.

***Miller v. Johnson*, 515 U.S. 900 (1995); 5-4** — Use of race as predominant factor in drawing voting-district lines can be upheld only if it serves a compelling government interest and is narrowly tailored to serve that interest; the ruling struck down a Georgia plan with three majority-black districts.

***Bush v. Vera*, 517 U.S. 952 (1996); 5-4** — Three majority-minority congressional districts in Texas were ordered redrawn because they were primarily motivated by race and not justified by legitimate state interests; in a fractured decision, majority of justices nevertheless said states can deliberately create majority-minority districts in some circumstances.

***Shaw v. Hunt*, 517 U.S. 899 (1996); 5-4** — North Carolina's 12th District was ruled unconstitutional because it was racially motivated and not justified by state interests; state responded by redrawing a more compact district with 47 percent black population; in new challenge, a three-judge court ruled the redrawn district was unconstitutional without full trial.

***Hunt v. Cromartie*, 526 U.S. 541 (1999); 9-0** — Federal court must hold a trial in racial gerrymandering case if the state's motivation for creating a challenged districting plan is in dispute; ruling sent challenge to North Carolina's redrawn 12th District back to lower court for full trial.

***Easley v. Cromartie*, 532 U.S. 234 (2001); 5-4** — Redistricting plan challenged on racial grounds must be upheld unless plaintiffs show state had ways to achieve legitimate political objectives with significantly greater racial balance; decision upheld North Carolina's redrawn 12th District.

***Georgia v. Ashcroft*, 539 U.S.___ (2003); 5-4** — States can reduce the number of blacks in majority-minority districts if they offset the reduced voting strength with gains in minority groups' political influence elsewhere; ruling sent challenge to redistricting plan for Georgia Senate back for trial on other issues; three-judge court in February 2004 ruled plan invalid because of excessive population deviations between districts.

Source: Supreme Court Collection, CQ Press

justices refused to issue a stay — meaning the new map will be used for the Nov. 2 elections.

Political map-drawing is all the more intense today because of computers. "Partisan gerrymandering is becoming easier because of the sophistication of the technology," says Nathaniel Persily, a law professor and redistricting expert at the University of Pennsylvania. Using detailed census maps with racial and ethnic break-downs and past election results, redistricters can customize a district neighborhood by neighborhood — even block by block.

Moreover, Persily says, "partisan preferences are more stable" today. Predictable voting patterns allow redistricters to use two common techniques for partisan advantage. "Packing" a rival party's voters into overly safe districts gives one's own party a better shot in others, while "cracking" a rival party's voters — dispersing them into several districts — can make the targeted district politically competitive for the party drawing the lines.

Some citizens' groups — such as Common Cause and the League of Women Voters — say that if independent bodies redrew the maps, partisan wrangling would be reduced and political competition enhanced. The Center for Voting and Democracy, in Takoma Park, Md., advocates replacing the single-member, winner-take-all system of congressional and legislative districts with some form of proportional or cumulative voting in multimember districts. Although voters would probably show little interest, politicians would probably adamantly resist either change. (*See sidebar, pp. 58-59.*)

Meanwhile, some academics say redistricting is not really a big problem. "The political system does recover," says Mark Rush, a professor of political science at Washington and Lee University in Lexington, Va. Over time, voting behavior changes, incumbents retire and new candidates emerge, he says. "Elections go back and forth. The system works."

As redistricting cases work their way through the courts, and redistricting issues continue to divide political parties, here are some of the major questions being debated:

Should states redraw congressional district lines in the middle of a decade?

When Colorado's legislature deadlocked on a congressional redistricting plan in 2002, a federal court re-drew the maps that were used for the seven House races that November. The result was a GOP-controlled legislature, and in May 2003 it adopted a new plan that favored Republicans in two politically competitive districts.

Democrats sued, complaining that both federal and state constitutions — as well as established political custom — limit redistricting to once a decade following the federal census. In December 2003, the Colorado Supreme Court agreed and threw out the new plan.

But Colorado appears to be one of only about a dozen states with such prohibitions. The Texas constitution limits legislative — but not congressional — redistricting to the session following a census. Constitutional or statutory redistricting provisions in other states are either silent or ambiguous on mid-decade enactments.

The U.S. Constitution requires that House seats be reapportioned among the states after the census. But neither the Constitution nor federal law explicitly says when congressional maps can be — or must be — redrawn.

Republicans in both Colorado and Texas insist they were merely fulfilling their constitutional responsibilities in order to replace court-crafted plans following the earlier legislative deadlock. "The legislature hadn't done its job this decade," says Texas attorney Taylor. "It fell to a federal court, and that court created a plan that we believe was a simple interim solution, not one designed for the remainder of the decade."

Hirsch, the Democrats' lawyer, counters that a redistricting plan approved at the start of a decade should be retained, whether adopted by the legislature or by a court. "If you redistrict more often, you're taking away [voters'] chance to vote for incumbents who've served them well — or against incumbents who've served them poorly," he says.

Many academic experts say successive redistrictings serve no purpose other than the partisan interests of the majority party. "No one in his right mind believes there's a good reason to do mid-decade redistricting except for political gain," says Bernard Grofman, a professor of political science at the University of California, Irvine.

"Redistricting occupies a lot of resources, it engenders litigation — all at taxpayer expense," Rush says. "The taxpayers' coffers are being drained to allow incumbents

The term gerrymander was coined after Massachusetts Gov. Elbridge Gerry approved an irregularly shaped legislative district in 1812 that a critic said resembled "a salamander;" another critic promptly dubbed it "a gerrymander." This cartoon-map first appeared in the *Boston Gazette* on March 26, 1812.

of one party to put incumbents of the other party out of business."

"Reapportionment and redistricting are done every 10 years," says Paul Herrnson, director of the Center for American Politics and Citizenship at the University of Maryland, College Park. "That is the written law and a norm, practiced for a very long time."

Herrnson acknowledges that legislatures occasionally redraw maps mid-decade after a court strikes down lawmakers' first attempt. "What's taken place in Colorado and Texas goes beyond that," he says. "Basically, it's a power grab."

GOP lawmakers in Texas, however, insist they were merely bringing district lines into conformity with the state's predominantly Republican voting pattern. "We tried to make it consistent with general voting patterns," says state Rep. Phil King, R-Weatherford. "We took it from 15 seats to maybe 19, 20, or 21 or 22. That's a long way from a coup."

Grofman scoffs. "The Republican plan will exaggerate the extent to which Texas is a Republican state rather than mirror the politics of the state," he says.

Hebert, the Democrats' lawyer, says the Constitution envisions congressional lines being redrawn only in conjunction with reapportionment of House seats after the decennial census. "The Census Clause makes it pretty clear that the Framers intended for the House to be electorally stable," he says.

"There's no rule against it," counters GOP lawyer Braden. "Maybe there should be, but there isn't."

Academic opinion — even among critics of mid-decade redistricting — appears to side with the Republicans. "It makes sense to have it once a decade, but it's clear that there's no legal rule against it in most states," says Michael McDonald, a professor of government and politics at George Mason University, in Fairfax, Va.

And there's nothing in the Constitution about redistricting at all, Persily notes. "The Constitution does not mandate how the states draw district lines at all."

Democrats plan to press their argument by appealing the Texas decision to the U.S. Supreme Court. Declaring that redistricting should occur only once a decade is "one thing the court could do if it is looking for some clear way to put some brakes on the redistricting process — which has gone completely haywire," Hebert says. Braden notes that Congress also could limit congressional redistricting to once a decade.

But Taylor insists public disapproval is enough to deter legislators from successive redistrictings. "Public sentiment is a sufficient check and balance on the legislative redistricting front," the GOP lawyer says. "If voters don't think state legislatures should be changing districts, they'll let them know, either before or after."

Should courts limit partisan gerrymandering?

After Republicans gained control of both houses of the Pennsylvania legislature in 2000, they began drawing new congressional districts, cutting two districts to reflect declining statewide population. The GOP-crafted plan maximized the party's advantages. It paired Democratic incumbents in three redrawn districts — forcing them to fight against each other. It also put another Democratic incumbent in a district drawn to favor a senior Republican House member, and created two new open seats favorably situated for up-and-coming GOP state senators.

The strategy paid off. The state's congressional delegation shifted from a narrow 11-10 Republican majority in 2000 to a lopsided 12-7 edge for the GOP in 2002.

The Pennsylvania shift, combined with Republican gains from another GOP-drawn redistricting plan in Michigan, helped the Republicans pick up six additional House seats — an unusual midterm gain for a party controlling the White House.

Democrats complained in federal court that by "packing" Democratic voters into Democratic districts, the Republicans locked in a GOP advantage in most districts, regardless of any partisan shift in the statewide population.

"Republican votes count twice as much as a Democrat's vote," says Hirsch, one of the attorneys for Pennsylvania Democrats in the case now before the U.S. Supreme Court. In House races, he contends, "We Democrats could capture a majority of the votes, [but] Republicans would get two-thirds of the seats."

Republicans counter that the new map simply reflects a statewide trend toward the GOP. The state has two Republican senators although it has voted Democratic in the past three presidential elections.[4]

"The state itself was becoming more Republican," says John Krill, a Harrisburg attorney for the Republicans. The predominantly Democratic cities of Philadelphia and Pittsburgh have lost population, and people have moved into Republican areas, such as central Pennsylvania, he says. "The legislature [had to accommodate] very significant demographic shifts."

Democrats have asked the high court to breathe life into a 1986 decision, *Davis v. Bandemer*, which allowed federal challenges to political gerrymandering.[5] A redistricting scheme could be unconstitutional if it caused "continued frustration of the will of a majority of the voters or effective denial to a minority of voters of a fair chance to influence the political process," Justice Byron R. White wrote in the main opinion.

"The standard is very hard to meet," says Washington and Lee's Rush. In fact, the Supreme Court upheld, 7-2, the Indiana congressional redistricting plan at issue in the case. Since then, no federal court has used the *Davis v. Bandemer* case to strike down a legislative or congressional redistricting plan.[6]

Critics of gerrymandering hope the Supreme Court will use the Pennsylvania case to establish a new standard that challengers could more readily meet. The Pennsylvania Democrats say a plan drawn by one party should be held unconstitutional if "the rival party's candidates could be consigned to fewer than half the seats even if its candidates consistently won a majority of votes statewide."

Grofman endorses the Democrats' test. "It's a gerrymander when an even split always means one party wins," he says.

Somewhat oddly, Republicans at the national level are not averse to the court limiting partisan gerrymandering. Attorney Braden says he is "sympathetic" to the goal of getting "useful" standards from Bandemer and suggests a plan be struck down if the lines are "totally lacking in legitimate state interests."

Some experts, however, caution against judicial intervention in gerrymandering disputes. "There is a real risk that it will seriously affect the integrity of the judiciary," Persily says. Courts "are going to be in this incredible position of having to decide . . . which representatives live and die," he continues. "It would make confirmation fights more difficult, and it would reduce somewhat the impression of an impartial judiciary."

Rush says courts should avoid partisan gerrymandering disputes because — in contrast to racial lines in redistricting cases — voting patterns and voting behavior are inherently changeable. "History indicates that the damage done by a partisan gerrymander simply is not as clear as critics suggest," Rush says. For example, within a few years after Indiana Democrats failed to overturn the GOP-crafted redistricting plan challenged in Bandemer, the Democrats had regained a majority of the state's congressional delegation, he notes.

Critics of partisan gerrymandering are doubtful about the outcome of the Pennsylvania case. "It's clear from the questions of the justices that they were searching for a standard, and they can't find one," Grofman says.

Krill urged the justices to flatly overrule Bandemer. "Any extreme attempts at partisan redistricting are self-correcting," he says, "sometimes in a very short time."

If the court chooses not to limit partisan gerrymandering, Congress could establish new redistricting standards. Congress passed a law in 1901 requiring "contiguous and compact" House districts but it lapsed after 1929.

Should states use nonpartisan or bipartisan bodies to oversee redistricting?

Arizona voters in 2000 approved creation of an independent, five-member, bipartisan commission to draw congressional and state legislative district lines that would encourage competitive political contests.

In January, however, Maricopa County Superior Court Judge Kenneth Fields agreed with Hispanic plaintiffs that the commission had hampered political competition by packing Hispanic voters into Democratic districts, thus giving Republicans too much of an edge elsewhere.[7]

The episode illustrates the difficulty of objective redistricting. Good-government groups — such as Common Cause and the League of Women Voters, which promoted the Arizona initiative — earnestly call for nonpartisan or bipartisan bodies to take the politics out of the process.

Many academic experts agree. Nonpartisan bodies "remove the prima facie basis for challenging a redistricting plan as being predatory," Washington and Lee's Rush says.

"Incumbents are looking to benefit themselves, and their parties are looking for partisan advantage," says the University of Maryland's Herrnson, who calls himself "a big fan" of using commissions.

But others insist that neutrality is simply unattainable in such an inherently partisan undertaking. "You can't just give off to technicians the responsibility for a plan," says the University of California's Grofman. "Any plan involves tradeoffs. These are political questions, not purely technical matters."

Currently, 21 states use bipartisan or nonpartisan bodies for either congressional or legislative redistricting. Iowa assigns the task to its professional Legislative Service Bureau. The others use special bipartisan commissions. Typically, commission members include the attorney general, secretary of state or other government officials, or members appointed by the governor or legislative leaders.

The Arizona measure aimed to minimize partisan influence by using a judicial-appointments body to select a pool of potential commission members. Republican and Democratic legislative leaders appoint two members each from the pool. The fifth member is then chosen by the other four.

In some states, commissions propose districting maps for the legislature to consider; in others, the commission itself is the decision-making body. In Florida and Kansas, lawmakers submit a plan to the state supreme court, which can approve it or draw its own.

Iowa is often cited as proof that politics can be removed from the redistricting process. Four out of Iowa's five congressional districts are potentially competitive — a much higher percentage than in other states.

CHRONOLOGY

Before 1960 *Reapportionment and redistricting engender political conflicts; Congress and Supreme Court leave issues mostly to states.*

1787 Constitution requires House of Representatives to reapportion seats following decennial censuses.

1842, 1872, 1901 Congress requires single-member, contiguous districts for House seats; subsequent versions require districts to be nearly equal in population (1872) and "compact" (1901). House declines to void elections for violations; law lapses after 1929.

1946 Supreme Court declines to nullify Illinois' malapportioned congressional districts; main opinion says court should stay out of "political thicket" of redistricting.

1950s Cities, suburbs gain population, but most states fail to redraw districts to reflect shift.

1960s *Supreme Court launches reapportionment revolution; states forced to redraw legislative, congressional districts, shifting power to cities and suburbs.*

1962 Supreme Court rules that redistricting challenges are "justiciable" in federal courts (*Baker v. Carr*).

1963, 1964 Supreme Court establishes equal-population requirement — "one person, one vote" — for congressional districts and state legislatures.

1970s-1980s *Redistricting becomes routine, along with court challenges; partisan maneuvering, incumbent protection are dominant considerations.*

1983 Supreme Court limits population deviations for congressional districts unless required for legitimate state interests.

1986 High court opens door slightly to federal court challenges to partisan gerrymandering (*Davis v. Bandemer*); separately, court sets standards for "minority vote dilution" cases under federal Voting Rights Act.

1990s *Supreme Court limits use of race in redistricting.*

1993 In *Shaw v. Reno*, Supreme Court rules that white voters can challenge the use of race to create "majority-minority" districts.

1995, 1996 Supreme Court tightens strictures on racial redistricting in cases from Georgia, Texas.

2000-Present *With Republican gains, partisan conflicts over redistricting intensify.*

2001-2002 Democrats redraw congressional districts in Georgia to their advantage; Republicans do the same in Michigan, Pennsylvania; lesser partisan shifts approved in other states; Democrats challenge Pennsylvania plan as unconstitutional partisan gerrymander.

Nov. 2002 Redistricting helps Republicans pick up seats in U.S. House; GOP also gains in gubernatorial and state legislative contests.

May 2003 GOP-controlled Colorado state legislature adopts new congressional map to replace court-drawn plan; Democrats file state, federal challenges.

Oct. 2003 Texas legislature, controlled by Republicans, ends months of partisan rancor by approving new congressional map aimed to give Republicans 20-22 out of 32 House seats; Democrats challenge plan in federal court.

Dec. 2003 Colorado Supreme Court bars second-in-decade redistricting on state constitutional grounds (Dec. 1) . . . U.S. Supreme Court hears arguments in Pennsylvania case on constitutional limits to partisan gerrymandering (*Vieth v. Jubelirer*, Dec. 10); decision expected by June 2004.

2004 Three-judge federal court rejects challenge to Texas' second-in-decade congressional redistricting (*Sessions v. Perry*, Jan. 6); Supreme Court refuses to stay ruling, allowing the plan to be used in the Nov. 2 elections.

"If you believe in representation and accountability, and that political competition leads to that, that's hard not to notice," Herrnson says.

Other experts, however, note that the Iowa legislature has thrice rejected redistricting maps drawn by the professional staff. They also say the Iowa system's relative success stems mostly from the state's somewhat less partisan political culture. "Nothing about the institutional form insulates it from partisan pressures," says Persily, at the University of Pennsylvania. "If you transfer that to New York, it wouldn't be nonpartisan."

Iowa does not have the same kind of racial and ethnic diversity that creates problems in other states, says McDonald, who supports the commission approach. "Iowa is like white bread," he says. "It doesn't matter how you slice it; you get back Iowa."

Elsewhere, commissions either split along party lines and produce a plan that favors the dominant party or reach a "compromise" favorable to both parties. "They tend to behave just like legislatures," Persily says.

GOP attorney Braden is dubious about reform proposals. "Bipartisan commissions are possible," he says, "but they've not been notoriously successful. It's a tricky matter to make it work. Some good intentions have been disasters."

Democratic lawyer Hebert, however, says independent bodies "ultimately are the solution," if they are truly nonpartisan. "It's an idea that needs to be studied."

BACKGROUND

Political Conflicts

In structuring the new national legislature, the Framers of the Constitution crafted a compromise to balance the interests of large and small states. Congress was to consist of a Senate, with two members from each state, and a House of Representatives, with each state allotted a number of representatives tied to its population. Although the plan eased the way for ratification of the Constitution, it also set the stage for recurrent political conflicts over reapportionment and redistricting.[8]

Article I, Section 2, initially allocated 65 representatives among the 13 original states and required population-based reapportionment "within every subsequent term of ten years" — now done after each decennial census. However, the Constitution contained no instructions about how states were to draw congressional districts — or even whether districts were required at all.

Nevertheless, the Framers apparently envisioned the division of states into congressional districts with equal population. In *The Federalist Papers No. 57*, for example, James Madison said each representative "will be elected by five or six thousand citizens." In the absence of a specific requirement, however, the states adopted varying practices. Six states elected representatives by districts, while five used at-large elections. Delaware and Rhode Island each were allotted only a single House member.[9]

More than a century of trial-and-error produced the current system of apportioning representatives among the states. Debates swirled around the size of the House and the method of allocating seats among the states, given the inevitability of "fractional remainders" — the leftover fraction when a state's population is divided by the population of an ideal-size district.[10]

At first, leftover fractions were disregarded (1790-1830). A method used only in 1840 allotted an additional seat to any state with a surplus fraction greater than one-half the size of the ideal district. From 1850-1900, a new plan specified the size of the House with each new decade, allocated whole-number seats and assigned any leftover seats to states with the largest leftover fractions.

In 1910, Congress voted that the House would permanently consist of 435 members, and that seats would be apportioned using a system called "major fractions." A decade later, a Congress dominated by members from rural states stalemated when it appeared reapportionment would combine with the fixed-size provision to shift power to more urban states. For the only time in U.S. history, Congress went an entire decade without reapportioning House seats.[11]

Meanwhile, a debate between leading mathematicians produced a new apportionment method, which was eventually adopted in 1950 and remains in use today. The so-called Huntington method — named after its inventor, Edward Huntington of Harvard University — was deemed fairer than the earlier method. It assigns seats to the states based on a division of each state's population by $n(n-1)$, with n being the number of seats given so far to the state. The Supreme Court upheld this method in 1992 in a suit brought by Montana, which lost its second seat under the formula but would have been entitled to two seats under a different method.[12]

Racial, Ethnic Politics Complicate Redistricting

Reps. Howard L. Berman and Brad Sherman represent adjoining congressional districts in Los Angeles County's San Fernando Valley, an area with a rapidly growing Hispanic population. The two Anglo Democrats back Latino positions on such issues as immigration and regularly receive Hispanic support in elections.

When it came time to redraw California's congressional map after the 2000 census, however, neither Berman nor Sherman wanted to have too many Latinos in his district — for fear of a successful challenge from a Latino opponent. Fortunately for Berman, the state's Democratic lawmakers had entrusted the task of redrawing congressional districts to his brother Michael, a behind-the-scenes force in the powerful local Democratic machine.

The new map, approved by the state legislature in September 2001 with support from most Latino lawmakers, shifted enough Hispanics out of Berman's district to protect him from a potential Latino rival. But Sherman, who now had double the number of Latino registered voters in his district, opposed the plan, although it still left Latinos far short of the numbers required to threaten him.[1]

The Mexican American Legal Defense and Educational Fund (MALDEF) challenged the configuration in court, arguing that the legislature deliberately fragmented Latino voters, creating "vote dilution" prohibited by the federal Voting Rights Act. MALDEF charged that the legislature had violated the act by removing thousands of Latino voters from Berman's district and placing them in Sherman's.

A three-judge federal court rejected the suit on the ground that Anglo prejudice against Latino candidates has diminished in recent years. "Whites and other non-Latinos are currently far more willing to support Latino candidates for office than in the past," the court ruled.[2]

The episode illustrates some of the complexities of racial and ethnic politics in the redistricting process, especially as it affects the nation's two largest minorities: Hispanics and African-Americans. Race-conscious redistricting in the 1990s contributed to a marked increase in blacks and Hispanics elected to the House. But a series of Supreme Court decisions now limits state legislatures' discretion to create so-called majority-minority districts.[3]

Meanwhile, the partisan implications of racial redistricting have become more evident. For Republicans, creating majority-minority districts can help GOP prospects in other districts with reduced minority voting strength. For Democrats, while the strategy helps elect African-Americans and Hispanics, it can put Anglo incumbents at risk — either from minority challengers in districts with concentrated minority populations or from Republican opponents in districts with fewer minority voters.

In Texas, partisan maneuvering meant that neither of the major parties supported Latino groups' call for an additional Latino majority district in South and West Texas. A Republican-drawn map reduced the Latino voting-age population in one district — the 23rd — below 50 percent to safeguard incumbent Republican Henry Bonilla. The five-term Hispanic Republican depended on Anglo votes to narrowly beat a Hispanic Democrat in 2002.

Democrats opposed the GOP-drawn map as a partisan gerrymander, but did not support the call for a new Latino district. Instead, they focused on line drawing elsewhere that put Anglo Democrats' political fortunes in jeopardy.

"In this round of redistricting, there was less willingness to create Latino-majority districts and little support from either political party to do it," says Nina Perales, a MALDEF regional counsel in San Antonio. "In terms of the redistricting struggle, there are Republicans, there are Democrats and there are Latinos. And our interests don't

---

Congress followed a similarly meandering path on districting issues. In the early 1800s, the Senate three times approved a constitutional amendment requiring single-member congressional districts, but it failed to reach a vote in the House. Nevertheless, by 1840 most states were using single-member districts. In 1842, Congress required contiguous, single-member districts. The law lapsed after 1850 but was approved again in 1862. A

decade later, Congress enacted a seemingly stricter law that required contiguous, single-member districts "as nearly as practicable" equal in population. That requirement was re-enacted in 1881 and 1891 and again in 1901 with an added requirement that districts be "compact."

But none of the laws were enforced. The House in 1844 voted — on partisan lines — to seat representatives from four states that had used at-large elections

line up with either of the other two groups."

The push to create majority-minority districts began during the administration of the first President George Bush. The Justice Department interpreted the Voting Rights Act to require states to draw districts with majority-black populations wherever feasible. To comply, some Southern states — with Democratic-controlled legislatures — created bizarre-shaped districts to cover widely separated African-American neighborhoods.

Beginning in 1993, the Supreme Court set limits on the practice, ruling that race could not be the predominant factor in drawing district lines. In 2001, however, the high court gave states somewhat greater leeway by ruling that North Carolina had legitimate political reasons for creating a congressional district challenged on racial grounds.[4]

The court eased the state rules again in 2003 in a ruling on Georgia's Democratic-drawn plan for state Senate districts. Supported by 10 of 11 black senators — all Democrats — the plan reduced the African-American population in some senatorial districts to help spread the predominantly Democratic voters into others. But the Justice Department had said the plan improperly reduced minority voting strength.

Minorities Gained in Redistricting

Race-conscious redistricting in the 1990s contributed to a marked increase in the number of blacks and Hispanics elected to the U.S. House of Representatives. But recent Supreme Court decisions now limit legislatures' discretion to create so-called "majority-minority" districts.

African-American and Hispanic Members of U.S. House of Representatives

Year	Blacks	Hispanics
1991	26	11
2001	37	19
2003	37	22

Sources: CQ.com, *CQ Weekly, American Political Leaders: 1789-2000*, CQ Press.

In a 5-4 decision, the high court ruled that states could indeed move black voters out of "majority-minority" districts in order to increase the black population in "minority-influence" districts.

"The State may choose," Justice Sandra Day O'Connor wrote for the majority, "that it is better to risk having fewer minority representatives in order to achieve greater overall representation of a minority group by increasing the number of representatives sympathetic to the interests of minority voters."[5]

[1] For background, see David Rosenzweig and Michael Finnegan, "Latino Voter Lawsuit Rejected," *Los Angeles Times*, June 13, 2002, p. A1., and Kenneth Reich, "Latino Groups Sue Over Redistricting," *Los Angeles Times*, Oct. 2, 2001, Part 2, p. A1.

[2] The case is *Cano v. Davis*, 211 F.Supp.2d 1208 (C.D. Cal. 2002).

[3] For background, see Nadine Cohodas, "Electing Minorities," *CQ Researcher*, Aug. 12, 1994, pp. 697-720.

[4] The decision is *Hunt v. Cromartie*, 526 U.S. 541 (2001). The most important of the earlier decisions are *Shaw v. Reno*, 509 U.S. 630 (1993); *Miller v. Johnson*, 515 U.S. 900 (1995) and *Bush v. Vera*, 517 U.S. 952 (1996).

[5] The decision is *Georgia v. Ashcroft*, 539 U.S. ___ (2003). The ruling sent the case back to a three-judge federal court for further consideration. The court struck the plan down because of population deviations. See Rhonda Cook, "Redistricting Shot Down," *The Atlanta Journal-Constitution*, Feb. 13, 2004.

despite the law requiring single-member districts. In 1901, a House committee rejected a challenge to the election of a Kentucky congressman on the grounds that the state's redistricting law did not conform to federal statutes. Seven years later, a House committee approved a somewhat similar challenge involving a Virginia congressman, but the full House never acted on the recommendation.

The 1901 single-member districting requirement was not re-enacted when it expired in 1929, but a new version was adopted in 1967, which also barred at-large elections. By then, however, the Supreme Court had transformed the legal landscape by requiring that legislative and congressional districts be roughly equal in population — the "one person, one vote" standard.

James Madison recommended in *The Federalist Papers No. 57* that each representative to Congress "will be elected by five or six thousand citizens." *The Federalist Papers*, written with Alexander Hamilton and John Jay in 1787-88 and published in several New York newspapers, argued for ratification of the proposed Constitution.

Court Battles

Initially, the Supreme Court decided to stay out of what Justice Felix Frankfurter famously called the "political thicket" of legislative and congressional redistricting. In a series of momentous decisions in the 1960s, however, it ruled that federal courts had jurisdiction over equal-protection claims attacking malapportioned districting schemes and required states to devise districts essentially equal in population.

In its first brush with the issue, the Supreme Court in 1932 left standing a Mississippi redistricting law that was challenged as a violation of the 1911 federal statute. The majority ruled that the 1911 law had expired, but four other justices said they would have dismissed the suit "for

want of equity" — in effect, a discretionary decision not to exercise jurisdiction.[13]

In 1946, the court shelved a broader attack claiming that an Illinois legislative districting scheme favoring rural areas violated the voting rights of urban and suburban voters under the Equal Protection Clause. Three justices said the court had no jurisdiction. "Courts ought not enter this political thicket," Frankfurter wrote, although three other justices said they would have heard the case. Casting the deciding vote, Justice Wiley Rutledge concluded that courts could hear such claims, but that in this instance the court should refrain because of the potential "collision" with other branches of government.[14]

In the absence of judicial pressure, state lawmakers often did not bother to redistrict, leaving the nation's growing urban and suburban areas underrepresented. The disparity was greatest in state legislative districts: By 1960, all the nation's legislatures featured at least a 2-to-1 disparity between the most and the least heavily populated districts. Congressional districts were less imbalanced, but several states had lopsided plans. The most heavily populated congressional district in Texas, for instance, had four times as many inhabitants as its least populated, while Arizona, Maryland and Ohio had 3-to-1 disparities between districts.

Once again, city-dwellers took the equal-protection issue to the courts, this time in Tennessee, which had not reapportioned its legislature since 1901. The state courts declined to act, as did a lower federal court — citing the Supreme Court's 1946 decision. But the high court reversed itself in 1962, in its landmark *Baker v. Carr* decision. The urban residents' claim that the failure to reapportion violated their equal-protection rights presented "a justiciable constitutional cause of action upon which [they] were entitled to a trial and a decision," Justice William J. Brennan Jr. wrote in the 6-2 ruling.[15]

The decision set no standard and sent the case back to Tennessee. A year later, however, the high court was more explicit. In a legislative-reapportionment suit from Georgia, Justice William O. Douglas wrote for the majority that political equality "can mean only one thing — one person, one vote." The next year, the high court applied the same standard to congressional districting in another case from Georgia. "[A]s nearly as practicable, one man's vote in a congressional election is to be worth as much as another's," Justice Hugo Black wrote.[16] The dual rulings forced state lawmakers subsequently to redraw legislative and congressional district maps — significantly shifting power from rural to urban and suburban areas.

In applying the one-person, one-vote standard, the Supreme Court moved gradually toward strict mathematical equality for congressional districts, while allowing a bit more leeway for legislatures. The series of decisions on congressional maps culminated with a 1983 ruling in a New Jersey case, *Karcher v. Daggett*, which struck down a districting scheme where the disparity between the most and the least populous district was a tiny 0.69 percent — or 4,400 people. The court said that even small deviations were prohibited unless they were necessary to achieve some legitimate state interest.[17]

In separate opinions, Justice John Paul Stevens, who joined the majority, and Justice Lewis F. Powell Jr., who dissented, said they were more concerned about the partisan gerrymandering in New Jersey's plan. The court took up that issue more directly in Indiana's Bandemer case three years later, but the split decision fell short of a constitutional command against politically driven districting.

The 6-3 vote established that federal courts could entertain and rule on constitutional claims against political gerrymandering, but the fact that Indiana's politically driven congressional districting plan was upheld — plus the strict legal test set out in the main opinion — gave federal courts scant encouragement to review partisan gerrymandering cases.[18]

Building Blocs

Racial politics, partisan gamesmanship and computerized demographics combined in the 1990s to transform both congressional redistricting and judicial oversight of the process. Under pressure from a Republican Justice Department in the early 1990s, states used newly available, block-by-block census maps to draw intricate schemes concentrating minority voters in select districts to help elect African-American or Hispanic candidates.

White voters challenged the bizarrely shaped districts as "racial gerrymanders" that violated their equal-protection rights. The Supreme Court recognized the claims and told states that race could not be "the predominant factor" in drawing district lines.

Computer-aided redistricting was first proposed in the 1960s as an antidote to overly partisan line-drawing, according to Mark Monmonier, a geography professor at

Syracuse University's Maxwell School of Citizenship and Public Affairs and author of a book on the subject.[19] Beginning with the 1970 population count, the Census Bureau started producing computerized street maps that could be used in an interactive computerized process to draw increasingly precise district lines. With the 1990 census, the bureau produced what Monmonier calls "a more powerful and precise database." These electronic files, he explains, enabled redistricters to follow streets, streams, railways or other boundaries to produce districts with specified population counts — and predictable demographic makeups.

Meanwhile, slow, expensive "mainframe" computers were replaced by fast, cheap personal computers, spawning a growing niche industry that gave legislators, political parties, interest groups and others the data needed to fine-tune redistricting schemes to maximize their respective interests.

The new demographic information became available just as the Justice Department — under the first President George Bush — was advancing a new interpretation of the federal Voting Rights Act, which required states to maximize the number of majority-minority congressional and legislative districts. Legally, the department said it was acting to prevent "minority vote dilution," as defined by a pivotal 1986 decision by the Supreme Court.[20] But the legal position also served Republican interests by packing minority voters — overwhelmingly Democratic — into a few districts. Minority groups supported the government's position. Democrats had little choice but to go along, given their dependence on African-American votes.

States subject to the Voting Rights Act's "preclearance" requirement for redistricting plans met the Justice Department directive after the 1990 census by stitching minority neighborhoods together in sprawling, comically intricate districts. North Carolina's 12th wound snake-like through the center of the state to pick up African-American neighborhoods in three cities. Georgia's 11th stretched from Atlanta eastward to pick up black neighborhoods in Augusta and Savannah on the coast. Louisiana's 4th gained the nickname "the mark of Zorro" for its Z-shaped path along the state's northern and eastern borders. Texas produced a congressional map with districts resembling Rorschach inkblots — some designed to elect African-American or Hispanic candidates, others aimed at protecting incumbents.

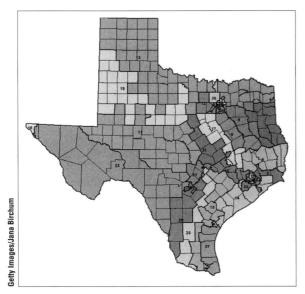

Getty Images/Jana Birchum

Texas' new congressional map threw several House Democrats into new districts against each other or against Republican incumbents or stripped them of large segments of their old districts. Voting in November in Texas could eliminate the Democrats' hopes of regaining control of the House next year.

The Supreme Court had countenanced some use of racial criteria in legislative districting in a 1974 decision. But the racial redistricting of the 1990s — often discarding the traditional principle of compactness — did not sit well with the court's conservative majority. A series of 5-4 decisions challenging the North Carolina, Georgia and Texas maps established constitutional bounds on the practice.

First, the court ruled in the North Carolina case — Shaw v. Reno — that white voters could challenge racially drawn districts that were "highly irregular in shape." Two years later, in the Georgia case, the court said a redistricting plan had to meet the high constitutional standard of "strict scrutiny" if race was "the predominant factor" in placing "a significant number of voters" in or outside a district. A year later, the court made clear that the constitutional test was stringent by rejecting Texas' argument that its racially drawn districts were justifiable efforts to preserve minority voting strength or to protect incumbents in other districts.[21]

The court also helped resolve a second reapportionment-related issue over the use of statistical "sampling" in the population counts used to allocate congressional seats. The Census Bureau and most demographers argued that enumerators could not possibly find everybody in a nationwide count and that sampling techniques were reliable methods to adjust for the inevitable "undercount."[22] Democrats agreed, but Republicans said sampling was unreliable, unnecessary and illegal. In 1999, the court sided with the GOP, ruling 5-4 that the Census Act did not allow sampling in congressional apportionment.[23]

By decade's end, the court's decisions in the racial redistricting cases had forced Georgia, North Carolina and Texas to redraw the challenged congressional districts and prompted other states to re-examine the use of race in map drawing. Meanwhile, political winds were blowing in a Republican direction. The GOP gained control of the House in 1994 and held on for the rest of the decade. In 2000, Republicans gained control of the White House and both chambers of Congress and improved their positions in statehouses and state legislatures. The GOP began the new century in a favorable posture and saw an opportunity for further gains in the coming redistricting cycle.

Escalating Warfare

Political pundits expected the post-2000 redistricting season to be the most contentious ever. Three years later, the predictions had proven well-founded. As both parties sought to maximize whatever political control they had over the process, the courts were again called in to referee, but the judiciary appeared reluctant to rein in partisan gerrymandering or limit redistricting to once a decade.

In Texas, a divided state legislature — with a Democratic-controlled House and GOP-controlled Senate — adjourned its regular session in May 2001 without seriously trying to redraw the congressional map to incorporate the two new seats Texas was apportioned following the 2000 census. GOP Gov. Rick Perry decided not to reconvene the legislature for a special session — leaving the matter up to the courts. In approving a new map on Nov. 14, a three-judge federal court relied heavily on the existing, Democratic-drawn map in order to protect incumbents.[24]

Colorado followed a similar course after the Republican-controlled House and Democratic-controlled Senate deadlocked. A state judge adopted a Democratic-

Should federal courts limit partisan gerrymandering?

YES
Sam Hirsch
Counsel for Appellants in Vieth v. Jubelirer, *Jenner & Block LLP*

Written for *CQ Researcher,* February 2004

Inviting federal courts to wade deeper into the "political thicket" always raises difficult issues of federalism and separation of powers. But sometimes the risks are worth taking. That was the case in the 1960s, when malapportionment had effectively doubled the voting strength of rural voters, at the expense of city-dwellers and suburbanites. It is the case again today, when partisan gerrymandering has effectively doubled the power of a class of voters defined solely by their political viewpoint. Like malapportionment 40 years ago, severe gerrymandering today threatens to make a mockery of our democratic system.

In the first general elections after the 2001-2002 redistricting, only four congressional challengers ousted incumbents — a record low. In California, none of the 50 general-election challengers garnered even 40 percent of the vote. Indeed, in 80 of the 435 districts nationwide, one of the two major parties did not even field a candidate. This lack of competition was peculiar to House elections, where redistricting has an impact: On the same day when barely one out of 12 House elections were decided by 10 percentage points or less, roughly half of all gubernatorial and Senate elections were that close. Most of the House is now locked in cement.

While historic levels of uncompetitiveness infected redistricting nationally, severe partisan bias was confined to a handful of states where one political party had unilateral control over the legislature and the governorship. For example, although Florida, Pennsylvania, Ohio and Michigan are all highly competitive "toss-up" states, redistricting handed the Republican Party 51 of their 77 House seats — an artificial 2-to-1 advantage.

Partisan gerrymandering is also transforming Congress. With little reason to fear voters, representatives increasingly cater to party insiders and donors, rather than to the political center where most Americans reside. Bipartisan compromise around moderate policies takes a backseat to party loyalty, resulting in historic levels of polarization. And further polarization only fuels the bitterness that promotes more gerrymandering.

The partisan-gerrymandering wars have spilled out of the legislatures and into the courtrooms. But with little prospect of prevailing on a forthright claim of partisan gerrymandering, aggrieved partisans instead often allege racial gerrymandering or minority-vote dilution under the Voting Rights Act. The incentive to couch partisan disputes in racial terms corrodes our politics. By putting teeth into the constitutional limits on partisan gerrymandering, federal courts can halt the racializing of redistricting, while restoring to the American people a House of Representatives worthy of its name.

NO
John P. Krill, Jr.
Counsel for Appellants in Vieth v. Jubelirer, *Jenner & Block LLP*

Written for *CQ Researcher,* February, 2004

Court-imposed limits on partisanship in redistricting would create, not solve, problems. Redistricting is inherently political. Any line drawn anywhere has partisan repercussions, and no criteria are "neutral." For example, trying to follow county and municipal lines would give preference to 19th-century political boundary decisions, while disfavoring emerging communities of interest in our sprawling, non-compact suburbs.

Turning judicial preferences into constitutional principles would create a drag on democratic change. Although legislators are free to envision the future, the judicial role is essentially to apply precedent and past legislative policy choices to restrict future conduct. If the courts had intervened in an earlier age, and had applied principles of so-called partisan fairness based on past electoral strength, they might well have kept the Whig Party from collapsing. But a party whose base is shrinking should not be propped up by judges giving weight to the past preferences of voters who have died, moved or switched.

If judges start second-guessing elected legislatures about fundamental choices for future representation, the judiciary will inevitably be criticized for partisanship. Although the courts often redraw maps in one-person, one-vote cases, they must use past legislative districting decisions as guidance, so as to avoid making political choices. But if the courts start making such policy choices themselves, the unavoidable partisan impact will put judicial legitimacy at risk. We can't afford to have respect for the courts turn into cynicism about political bosses in black robes.

In any event, redistricting, even with the aid of modern computers, cannot control the choices of voters. Good candidates vector toward the politics of their districts, regardless of their party affiliation. That is why Congress has conservative Democrats and liberal Republicans and vice versa. Some districts will elect a conservative regardless of party and vice versa. Recognizing this point leads to the realization that partisan affiliation is not the be-all, end-all of elections, except to the parties themselves. The parties care about partisan control of legislative bodies more than about the politics of the members of their caucuses. Voters care more about the responsiveness and personalities of their representatives.

The states have used districting for partisan effect since the ratification of the Constitution. For example, Pennsylvania enacted different plans for congressional elections in 1788, 1790, 1792 and 1794, as Federalists struggled with Anti-Federalists for control of the delegation. Partisan conflict is no fiercer now. Judicial restraint is just as important now.

backed plan in January 2002 that largely protected the state's six incumbent House members — four Republicans and two Democrats — while favoring a Democratic candidate in a newly created district around Denver.[25]

Democrats already had won a victory in Georgia, where a Democratic-controlled legislature had adopted a redistricting plan. By "packing" GOP districts and pairing incumbent Republicans in two of them, Democrats hoped to shift the state's congressional delegation from an 8-3 GOP majority to a 7-6 Democratic edge.[26]

Some Pennsylvania Republicans cited the Democrats' Georgia remap as grounds for retaliation in their own state later that year. Facing the loss of two of Pennsylvania's 21 House seats, the GOP-controlled legislature threw two pairs of Democratic incumbents together and put another Democrat into a district with an incumbent Republican. The map, approved in early January 2002, appeared likely to enlarge the GOP's narrow 11-10 edge to a more comfortable 12-7 margin.[27]

Michigan, another GOP-controlled state that lost seats after the 2000 census, followed Pennsylvania's example by pairing six Democratic incumbents in three redrawn districts. Likewise, Democratic-controlled legislatures in North Carolina and Tennessee approved maps likely to net their party one seat in each, while a Democratic plan in Maryland added a hefty chunk of Democrats to the district of longtime moderate Republican Rep. Constance A. Morella. In other states, incumbent protection appeared the dominant goal. As the redistricting cycle ended, Republicans and Democrats alike pronounced themselves largely satisfied.

In November, however, redistricting appeared to be a significant factor — along with President Bush's popularity and the population shift toward predominantly Republican Sun Belt states — in producing a net pickup of six House seats for the GOP.[28] It was only the third time since the Civil War that the president's party gained House seats in a midterm election.

Democrats lost six seats in Michigan and Pennsylvania, while Republicans gained new seats in Florida and Texas (two each) and Arizona and Nevada (one each). In Maryland, Morella fell to a Democratic opponent, but Democrats did not match their expectations in other states. Notably, Republicans held onto an 8-5 majority in the expanded Georgia delegation. In Colorado, a Republican eked out a surprise 122-vote victory for the new seat.

Republicans also made gains in state legislative contests and, significantly, won majority control of both chambers of the Colorado and Texas legislatures. Meanwhile, House Majority Leader DeLay hatched a plan for a second round of redistricting in Texas. Ironically, the idea bore fruit first in Colorado, where a Republican-crafted redistricting plan was introduced, approved and signed into law within five days in early May. Colorado's Democratic attorney general, Ken Salazar, promptly vowed to challenge the mid-cycle redistricting in court.

The path to the second-in-a-decade redistricting in Texas was more protracted. Republicans pushed the measure to the top of the House calendar as the regular legislative session was ending in May. But Democrats thwarted passage by decamping en masse to a motel in Oklahoma for the final four days — putting them beyond the reach of Texas authorities and leaving the chamber without a quorum. When Gov. Perry convened a special legislative session, the Senate's 12 Democrats staged a similar exodus to New Mexico. But the month-long boycott ended on Sept. 2 when one of the Democrats decided to come back home after concluding that Perry could outlast them by calling a succession of special sessions.[29]

The legislature finally adopted the plan on Oct. 13. Democrats immediately sued, claiming the mid-decade redistricting violated the U.S. and state constitutions. Along with the Mexican American Legal Defense and Educational Fund (MALDEF), Democrats also contended that the map improperly diluted minority voter strength in violation of the Voting Rights Act. Republicans countered that the measure actually created a new, third "minority-opportunity" district for African-Americans in Houston and maintained the number of Hispanic opportunity districts at six.

Meanwhile, Pennsylvania Democrats were challenging the redistricting plan the GOP had pushed through in the regular post-census cycle. The measure was an unconstitutional gerrymander, they claimed, even under the Supreme Court's stringent *Davis v. Bandemer* standard. A three-judge federal court rejected the claim in January 2003, but the high court agreed in June to take up the case and scheduled oral arguments for Dec. 10.

As the December arguments approached, the stage was set for some of the most significant legal battles over redistricting since the start of the reapportionment revolution four decades earlier.

CURRENT SITUATION

Designing Districts

Pennsylvania Democrats want the Supreme Court to give courts more power to strike down political gerrymandering, but they ran into strong resistance from several justices during arguments on Dec. 10, 2003. Even justices sympathetic to the Democrats' claim of unfairness appeared uncertain about what standard courts could use to police the practice. Meanwhile, lawyers for GOP legislators and the state urged the justices to bar partisan gerrymandering cases from federal courts altogether or give legislatures free rein in drawing district lines for partisan advantage.[30]

For the Democrats, Washington attorney Paul Smith opened the hour-long session by saying that lower courts had "effectively overruled" the high court's 1986 decision allowing challenges to partisan gerrymandering by setting an "impossible" burden of proof for plaintiffs. He urged that redistricting maps be ruled unconstitutional if plaintiffs showed it was "very clear" one party could win a majority of votes but have "no chance" of securing a majority of the seats.

Three justices openly disagreed with Smith — starting with the pivotal moderate conservative Sandra Day O'Connor, a dissenter in the original Bandemer decision. "Maybe the way to go is to just say hands off these things," O'Connor declared.

Justice Antonin Scalia reached the same conclusion after noting that the Constitution lets the states or Congress itself prescribe the "time, place, and manner" of House elections. "That suggests to me it is none of our business."

Chief Justice William H. Rehnquist, another of the dissenters in Bandemer, also sharply rejected Smith's proposed standard. "You're just pulling this thing out of a hat," he said.

For his part, Justice Anthony M. Kennedy conceded that the GOP-drawn congressional map might be "unfair . . . in common parlance," but still wondered what test courts could use. "It seems to me that we're at sea," he said.

"The government has no business discriminating against people based on their partisan affiliation or their political viewpoint," Smith answered later. "There has to be an outer boundary."

Harrisburg attorney Krill, representing the GOP legislative leaders, urged the justices to bar federal courts from policing politically driven redistricting. Any test "requires inherent political choices" that are "inappropriate for the judiciary to make," Krill said.

Justice John Paul Stevens — who had voted in 1986 not only to allow legal challenges to gerrymandering but also to strike down the Indiana map at issue in the case — asked Krill whether a redistricting plan should be subject to challenge if "maximum partisan advantage" were the only justification for a line-drawing.

Yes, Krill answered, "It's a permissible legislative choice." When Stevens again asked whether the legislature had "any duty" to try to draw districts "impartially," Krill said the Constitution does not require fairness, but that "political forces" might pull lawmakers "in a multitude of directions."

In any event, Krill added, "The system is self-correcting," noting that Indiana Democrats gained control of the state's congressional delegation within a few years of losing their redistricting challenge. In Pennsylvania, he added, Democrats had won the House race in a district seemingly drawn to favor the GOP incumbent. "Voters are not disenfranchised," he concluded.

Representing Pennsylvania, Senior Deputy Attorney General J. Bart DeLone said "the simplest and cleanest way" for the justices to "get out of the political thicket" was to overrule the Bandemer decision.

By the close of the argument, court-watchers counted four votes seemingly against the Democrats: Rehnquist, O'Connor, Scalia and the conservative Clarence Thomas, who followed his customary practice of asking no questions. Kennedy, a moderate conservative, seemed a likely fifth vote to reject the Democrats' claim.

Meanwhile, among the four liberal justices, only Stevens strongly favored an aggressive role for the courts on gerrymandering, and he did not embrace the standard proposed by Smith. Justices David H. Souter and Ruth Bader Ginsburg seemed possible votes for the Democrats' position, but Justice Stephen G. Breyer, an active questioner, had asked skeptical questions of both Smith and Krill.

"I expect the Supreme Court will reject the plaintiffs' cause of action," the University of Pennsylvania's Persily commented after attending the arguments. The justices, he said, "are afraid that they will get even more deeply into the political thicket."

A decision is due by July.

Taking Seconds

Democrats are one for two in challenging the mid-cycle congressional redistricting plans approved by GOP legislatures and governors in Colorado and Texas. But the Colorado Supreme Court's decision barring a second-in-a-decade redistricting set no broad precedent, because it depended on a provision in the state's constitution. So Democrats will have only a limited victory unless they can persuade the U.S. Supreme Court to overturn the Texas federal court ruling that the Constitution does not limit congressional redistricting to once every 10 years.

The Colorado court's decision, announced Dec. 1, came on a 5-2 vote, with the court's two Republican-appointed justices dissenting.[31] The ruling relied on a provision in Colorado's constitution requiring the general assembly to redistrict congressional seats whenever "a new apportionment shall be made by Congress." Writing for the majority, Chief Justice Mary Mullarkey said the provision mandated redistricting immediately after the census and barred a second remap — even if the new plan was drawn by a court following a legislative deadlock.

"The state constitution limits redistricting to once per census, and nothing in state or federal law negates this limitation," Mullarkey wrote in her 63-page opinion. "Having failed to redistrict when it should have, the General Assembly has lost its chance to redistrict until after the 2010 federal census."

Mullarkey also cited previous state practice and policy considerations as weighing against a second-in-a-decade redistricting. "The Framers knew that to achieve accountability there must be stability in representation," she wrote. "Limiting redistricting to once per decade maximizes stability."

Justice Rebecca Kourlis, one of the two dissenters, argued that the state constitution's provision specifying redistricting "when" Congress reapportions did not prohibit a subsequent re-map, nor did the state court's adoption of new congressional maps prevent the legislature from "reclaiming its authority to redistrict."

In the Texas case, all three federal judges said mid-decade redistricting is not prohibited by the Constitution, federal statute, Texas law or tradition — at least when a new map substitutes for a court-drawn plan. But two of the judges recommended Congress ban the practice, citing "compelling arguments" why states should "abstain from drawing district lines mid-decade."[32]

The judges divided sharply, however, on whether the redistricting violated the Voting Rights Act by improperly weakening Hispanics' political clout. Two Republican-appointed judges upheld the decision to disperse Hispanic voters from a South Texas district held by a Republican incumbent — a Hispanic — because the move was offset by creation of a new Hispanic-majority district. The Democratic-appointed judge on the panel disagreed.

In the main opinion, Judge Patrick Higginbotham — a federal appeals court judge appointed in 1982 by President Ronald Reagan — rejected the Democratic plaintiffs' arguments that the Census Clause limits redistricting to once per decade. The clause, Higginbotham wrote, "does not mention the states or their power to redistrict, and we fail to see how it can limit a power it never references." The Democratic-appointed judge on the panel, John Ward, also said mid-decade redistricting was prohibited, but added, "There may be legitimate state interests advanced by the effort."

In the main opinion, Higginbotham rejected claims by Democrats and minority-advocacy groups that the Voting Rights Act was violated by dispersing blacks and Hispanics — changes affecting 11 of the state's previous districts, including Frost's old 24th. Higginbotham wrote that because the two groups together constituted only 46 percent of the voting-age population in the old district — less than a majority — the argument against the reconfiguration was political, not racial or ethnic.

Higginbotham also upheld the redrawing of GOP Rep. Henry Bonilla's 23rd district to reduce its Hispanic voting-age citizen population to 46 percent from 57 percent — chiefly by splitting the border city of Laredo. The move was aimed at boosting Bonilla, who won only 8 percent of the Hispanic vote when he narrowly defeated a Hispanic Democrat in 2002. But Higginbotham said the offsetting creation of a new Hispanic-majority district — the 25th, stretching 300 miles from the Austin suburbs south to the border — satisfied the Voting Rights Act. Ward — a federal district judge appointed by President Bill Clinton — said the redrawn 23rd district violated Supreme Court rulings against "minority vote retrogression."

Democrats asked the Supreme Court to stay the effect of the ruling and leave the existing districting map in place for the 2004 election, but the justices declined without comment. Democrats now plan a full appeal to the Supreme Court, but Republicans are confident about the outcome.

"We are in very good shape," says GOP lawyer Taylor. If the court does hear the case, oral arguments would not be held until fall 2004.

OUTLOOK

Winners Take All?

The House of Representatives undergoes some turnover at the start of each decade when seats are reapportioned among states and districts redrawn within the states. But House elections in 2002 saw considerably less turnover and less political competitiveness than in comparable years in any of the previous three decades — and, in fact, less turnover and less competitiveness than in a typical election year.

Only 16 incumbent House members were defeated in 2002 — compared to an average of 35 following redistricting in 1972, 1982 and 1992. In addition, fewer members retired: 35 in 2002 compared to an average of 48 for the first post-redistricting elections in the previous three decades. And — in a telling statistic compiled by Democratic attorney Hirsch — 338 of the House's 435 members were elected in 2002 with at least 60 percent of the vote in their districts.[33]

Hirsch views the lack of political competitiveness as a consequence of partisan gerrymandering and the courts' refusal to rein in the practice. He wants courts — federal or state — to consider the political effects of redistricting plans and require what he calls "a reasonable degree" of partisan fairness, competitiveness and stability.

Surprisingly, perhaps, Republican attorney Braden agrees on the diagnosis, but not on the cure. "Turnover in 2002 was way too low," Braden says. He blames "partisan" gerrymanders, where both parties used control of the process to protect incumbents, as well as "bipartisan" gerrymanders, where Republicans and Democrats combined to spare incumbents from competitive races.

But Braden says he is "adamantly opposed to the courts getting more politicized." States may want to add competitiveness to the factors to be considered in redrawing districts, he says, but federal courts should keep hands off. "My concern doesn't make it a constitutional issue," he says.

Supporters of redistricting reforms — such as independent commissions or the more far-reaching step of devising some form of proportional representation — also cite lawmakers' self-preservation instinct as a drawback of current practices. Academic experts who worry about the problem see no easy solution.

"No politician likes competitive seats," says the University of California's Grofman. "It's hard to imagine a situation where you will have a lot of seats that will shift back and forth.'

"Incumbents are quite powerful," says Washington and Lee's Rush. "How to repair that, I can't say."

For now, most Supreme Court-watchers do not expect the justices to use the Pennsylvania case to increase the judicial review of partisan gerrymandering. "I'm not very optimistic that Bandemer is going to be resuscitated," Grofman adds. "It's more likely that the final nail will be laid."

Without any judicial controls, partisan gerrymandering is likely to continue and perhaps increase, the University of Maryland's Herrnson predicts. "Once the precedent allows for extremely selfish behavior on the part of politicians, it will be followed until things become so out of hand that reform is ultimately enacted," he says.

Predictions about the future of mid-decade redistricting are more tentative. Some experts say if the courts give the practice a green light, both parties will draw new maps for partisan advantage whenever and wherever they can. Others question whether legislators of either party have much stomach for reopening the partisan warfare unless forced to.

For his part, state Sen. Todd Staples, a Republican architect of Texas' mid-decade redistricting, says he has no desire to redraw congressional maps anytime soon. "I want to take up redistricting again in the year 3011," Staples quips.

But Democratic attorney Hirsch notes that GOP lawmakers have not promised to stick with the map approved in 2003, which was designed to elect 22 Republicans. "If they get only 20 or 21 seats, it will be interesting to see if they try again in 2005 or 2007," he says.

Hirsch's Democratic colleague Hebert agrees judicial intervention is necessary to check partisan-driven redistricting. "It won't get better as long as the fox guards the district and just makes more foxes," he says. "It's time for the Supreme Court to step in; it's not going to happen in any other fashion."

But GOP attorney Krill in Pennsylvania says a Supreme Court decision allowing greater review of redistricting cases would damage the political process and the judicial system itself.

"If they adopt a more relaxed standard, then there's litigation all over the country," says Krill — not only over Congress but also over state legislatures, city councils, school districts and so forth. "It will be wasteful litigation that will immerse judges in every level — federal, state and local. It will be bad for the public perception of the judicial system."

NOTES

1. For detailed information, including maps, see the Web site of the Texas Legislative Council: www.tlc.state.tx.us.

2. Quoted in Dave Leventhal, "Sessions, Frost Ready to Rumble," *The Dallas Morning News*, Jan. 18, 2004, p. 1B.

3. For background, see Jennifer Gavin, "Redistricting," *CQ Researcher*, Feb. 16, 2001, pp. 113-128.

4. "Candidate and Office Histories," CQ Voting and Elections Collection, CQ Electronic Library, accessed Feb. 26, 2004; http://library2.cqpress.com/elections/histories.php.

5. *Davis v. Bandemer*, 478 U.S. 109 (1986).

6. In the only decision to cite *Davis v. Bandemer* to mandate an electoral change, a federal court in North Carolina required the state to elect state supreme court justices by district rather than statewide; the court said at-large elections disenfranchised Republicans. See *Republican Party v. Martin*, 980 F.2d 943 (4th Cir. 1992).

7. Chip Scutari and Robbie Sherwood, "Legislative Districts Map Thrown Out; Judge Orders New Boundaries Drawn," *The Arizona Republic*, Jan. 17, 2004, p. 1B. The ruling upheld the commission's congressional district map. For background on the initiative, see Chip Scutari, "Citizens Panel to Redraw Districts," *The Arizona Republic*, Nov. 8, 2000, p. 11E.

8. Background drawn from "Reapportionment and Redistricting," in *Congressional Quarterly's Guide to Congress* (5th ed., 2000), pp. 891-911. See also David

Butler and Bruce Cain, *Congressional Redistricting: Comparative and Theoretical Perspectives* (1992), pp. 17-41.

9. "Reapportionment and Redistricting," *op. cit.*, p. 900. States with districts were Maryland, Massachusetts, New York, North Carolina, South Carolina and Virginia; at-large states included Connecticut, Georgia, New Hampshire, New Jersey, and Pennsylvania.

10. A chart summarizing the various formulas can be found in Butler and Cain, *op. cit.*, p. 19.

11. For a history, see Charles W. Eagles, *Democracy Delayed: Congressional Reapportionment and Urban-Rural Conflict in the 1920s* (1990).

12. The case is Department of *Commerce v. Montana*, 503 U.S. 442 (1992).

13. *Wood v. Broom*, 287 U.S. 1 (1932).

14. *Colegrove v. Green*, 328 U.S. 549 (1946).

15. The citation is 369 U.S. 186 (1962). For a history of the case, see Gene Graham, *One Man, One Vote: Baker v. Carr and the American Levelers* (1972).

16. The cases are *Gray v. Sanders*, 372 U.S. 368 (1963), and *Wesberry v. Sanders*, 376 U.S. 1 (1964).

17. The citation is 462 U.S. 725 (1983). The leading case on population deviations in legislative redistricting is *Mahan v. Howell*, 410 U.S. 315 (1973), which approved a Virginia plan with a 16 percent variation between the largest and smallest population districts.

18. The citation is 478 U.S. 109 (1986). Stevens and Powell dissented from the decision to uphold Indiana's districting plan.

19. Mark S. Monmonier, *Bushmanders and Bullwinkles: How Politicians Manipulate Electronic Maps and Census Data to Win Elections* (2001). Background drawn from "What a Friend We Have in GIS [Geographic Information Systems]," pp. 104-120.

20. The case is *Thornburg v. Gingles*, 478 U.S. 30 (1986). The decision held that minority plaintiffs could establish a claim of improper "vote dilution" under the Voting Rights Act by proving racially polarized voting, a legacy of official discrimination in voting or other areas, and campaign appeals to racial prejudice.

21. The citation for *Shaw v. Hunt* is 509 U.S. 630 (1993). The other cases are *Miller v. Johnson*, 515 U.S. 900 (1995) (Georgia) and *Bush v. Vera*, 517 U.S. 952 (1996) (Texas).

22. For background, see Kenneth Jost, "Census 2000," *CQ Researcher*, May 1, 1998, pp. 385-408.

23. The case is *Department of Commerce v. United States House of Representatives*, 503 U.S. 442 (1999).

24. See Mary Clare Jalonick, "Court-Ordered Remap Aids Texas Incumbents," *CQ Weekly*, Nov. 17, 2001, p. 2758.

25. Gregory L. Giroux, "Judge's Ruling Puts New House District Up for Grabs," *CQ Monitor News*, Jan. 25, 2002.

26. Gregory L. Giroux, "Georgia Remap Merges 2 GOP-Held Districts," *CQ Weekly*, Oct. 6, 2001, p. 2001.

27. Jonathan Allen, "GOP Scores Major Win in Pennsylvania Redistricting," *CQ Monitor News*, Jan. 4. 2002.

28. See Gregory L. Giroux, "Redistricting Helped GOP," *CQ Weekly*, Nov. 9, 2002, p. 2934. See also Gregory L. Giroux, "Redistricting Increases Polarization," in *Politics in America 2004: The 108th Congress* (2003), p. xxiii.

29. See Gregory L. Giroux, "Texas GOP Outlasts Renegades, Prepares for New Congressional Map; Democrats Put Their Hope in Court," *CQ Weekly*, Sept. 6, 2003, p. 2145; Gebe Martinez, "In Texas Redistricting Game, DeLay Holds the High Cards," *CQ Weekly*, July 12, 2003, p. 1728.

30. For coverage, see Stephen Henderson, "Spirited Debate at High Court on Pa. Redistricting," *Philadelphia Inquirer*, Dec. 11, 2003, p. A19; Michael McGough, "Justices Treading Warily in Pa. Case," *Pittsburgh Post-Gazette*, Dec. 11, 2003, p. A12.

31. The decision is *Salazar v. Davidson*, 03SA133. For the most extensive coverage in Colorado newspapers, see John J. Sanko, "Dems Are Big Winners on Congressional Map," *Rocky Mountain News*, Dec. 2, 2004, p. 6A.

32. The decision is *Sessions v. Perry*, 2:03-CV-354. For the most extensive coverage in Texas newspapers, see David Paztor and Chuck Lindell, "Map Survives Court Challenge," *The Austin American-Statesman*, Jan. 7, 2004, p. A1.

33. Sam Hirsch, "The United States House of Unrepresentatives: What Went Wrong in the Latest Round of Congressional Redistricting," *Election Law Journal*, Vol. 2, No. 2 (November 2003), Table 1, p. 3.

BIBLIOGRAPHY

Books

Butler, David, and Bruce Cain, *Congressional Redistricting: Comparative and Theoretical Perspectives*, Macmillan, 1992.
Surveys the history and contemporary practices of U.S. congressional redistricting; compares practices in other democracies. Butler is a professor at Nuffield College, Oxford, England; Cain is director of the Institute of Governmental Studies, University of California, Berkeley.

Clayton, Dewey M., *African Americans and the Politics of Congressional Redistricting*, Garland, 2001.
An assistant professor of political science at the University of Louisville argues that the case for deliberately drawing majority-black congressional districts "remains compelling."

Grofman, Bernard (ed.), *Political Gerrymandering and the Courts*, Agathon Press, 1990.
Essays by 15 political scientists examine the Supreme Court's decision to allow federal challenges to gerrymandering. Includes 12-page list of references. Grofman is a professor of political science at the University of California, Irvine.

— (ed.), *Race and Redistricting in the 1990s*, Agathon Press, 1998.
Essays by 16 political scientists examine Supreme Court decisions in the 1990s limiting the use of race in redistricting.

Hill, Steven, *Fixing Elections: The Failure of America's Winner Take All Politics*, Routledge, 2002.
The Western regional director of the Center for Voting and Democracy strongly criticizes redistricting and the single-member, winner-take-all system, advocating proportional representation to increase political competition.

Kousser, J. Morgan, *Colorblind Injustice: Minority Voting Rights and the Undoing of the Second Reconstruction*, University of North Carolina Press, 1999.

A professor of social sciences at California Institute of Technology and frequent witness for minority groups in voting-rights cases analyzes the history of minority voting rights during post-Civil War Reconstruction and following passage of the Voting Rights Act in 1965. Includes 36-page bibliography.

Monmonier, Mark S., *Bushmanders and Bullwinkles: How Politicians Manipulate Electronic Maps and Census Data to Win Elections*, University of Chicago Press, 2001.

A professor of geography at Syracuse University's Maxwell School of Citizenship and Public Affairs examines the implications of high-tech, super-precise redistricting.

Rush, Mark E., *Does Redistricting Make a Difference? Partisan Representation and Electoral Behavior*, Johns Hopkins University Press, 1993.

A professor of politics at Washington and Lee University argues that concern about partisan gerrymandering is based on an inaccurate understanding of voting behavior and contributes to political divisiveness.

Rush, Mark E., and Richard L. Engstrom, *Fair and Effective Representation? Debating Electoral Reform and Minority Rights*, Rowman & Littlefield, 2001.

Two political science professors offer conflicting views on using proportional representation instead of winner-take-all, single-member districts. Includes excerpts from nine major Supreme Court decisions. Rush is at Washington and Lee University, Engstrom at the University of New Orleans.

Thernstrom, Abigail M., *Whose Votes Count? Affirmative Action and Minority Voting Rights*, Harvard University Press, 1987.

A senior fellow at the conservative Manhattan Institute argues that maximizing minority office-holding may inhibit political integration.

Articles

Hirsch, Sam, "The United States House of Unrepresentatives: What Went Wrong in the Latest Round of Congressional Redistricting," *Election Law Journal*, Vol. 2, No. 2 (November 2003), pp. 179-216.

A Washington lawyer for Democrats in redistricting cases strongly criticizes courts' reluctance to carefully scrutinize "severely partisan incumbent-protecting gerrymanders."

McDonald, Michael, "A Comparative Look at U.S. State Redistricting Processes," *State Politics and Policy Quarterly* [forthcoming, 2004].

An assistant professor of government and politics at George Mason University analyzes redistricting processes and lawmakers' use of them to influence electoral outcomes.

Persily, Nathaniel, "In Defense of Foxes Guarding Henhouses: The Case for Judicial Acquiescence to Incumbent-Protecting Gerrymanders," *Harvard Law Review*, Vol. 116 (2002), pp. 649-683.

A University of Pennsylvania law professor defends courts' deference to partisan-motivated redistricting.

"Reapportionment and Redistricting," in *Congressional Quarterly's Guide to Congress* (5th ed.), CQ Press, 2000, pp. 891-911.

Overview of relevant issues from the Constitutional Convention to present day. Includes selected bibliography.

For More Information

Center for Voting and Democracy, 6930 Carroll Ave., Suite 610, Takoma Park, MD 20912; (301) 270-4616; www.fairvote.org.

Common Cause, 1133 19th St., N.W., 9th Fl., Washington DC 20036; (202) 833-1200; www.commoncause.org.

Democratic National Committee, 430 South Capitol St., S.E., Washington, DC 20003; (202) 863-8000; www. dnc.org.

National Conference of State Legislatures, 7700 East First Place, Denver, CO 80230; (303) 364-7700; www. ncsl.org.

Republican National Committee, 310 1st St., S.E., Washington, DC 20003; (202) 863-8500; www.rnc.org.

4

School Desegregation

Kenneth Jost

Fifty years after the Supreme Court handed down its historic *Brown v. Board of Education* decision declaring racial segregation in public schools unconstitutional, most black and Latino students attend predominantly minority schools. At Birdwell Elementary in Tyler, Texas, 60 percent of the students are Hispanic.

Getty Images/Mario Villafuerte

From *CQ Researcher*,
April 23, 2004.

Civil rights advocates consider Louisville-Jefferson County, Ky., a model of desegregation — but don't tell that to David McFarland.

McFarland says the county's claimed success in racial mixing comes at the expense of his children's education. In his view, Stephen and Daniel were denied admission to the school of their choice simply because they are white. "Diversity should not be used as an excuse for discrimination," he says.

The county's 19 traditional schools — with their reputation for good discipline, structured teaching and parental involvement — are so popular that they cannot accommodate all the students who want to attend. So students are assigned to schools by lottery.

To keep enrollments at each school within racial guidelines, a separate list of African-American applicants is maintained. The county's voluntary "managed-choice" program — which replaced a court-ordered desegregation plan in 2000 — is designed to prevent any school from having fewer than 15 percent or more than 50 percent African-American students.

The program works. In a countywide system where African-Americans comprise about one-third of the 96,000 students, only one school has a majority-black enrollment.

Jefferson County was one of the first school systems in the country to begin integrating after the U.S. Supreme Court handed down its historic *Brown v. Board of Education* decision declaring racial segregation in schools unconstitutional.[1]

Today, as the 50th anniversary of the May 17, 1954, ruling approaches, Jefferson County stands in stark contrast to the ethnic and racial patterns in most other school districts. Across the coun-

Minority School Districts Receive Less Funding

School districts with high enrollments of minority or low-income students typically receive fewer funds compared to districts with more white or wealthier students. In 11 states, the funding gap between white and minority school districts is more than $1,000 per pupil.

Per-Pupil Funding Gaps Between Districts with High and Low Minority Enrollments

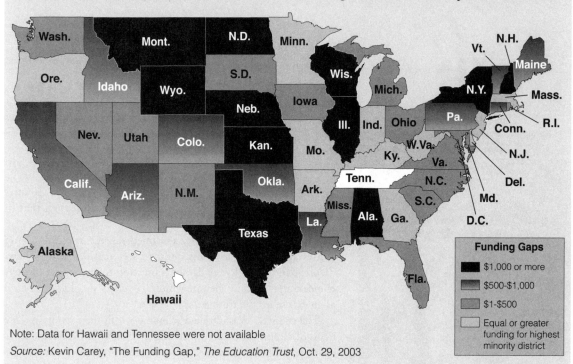

Funding Gaps
- $1,000 or more
- $500-$1,000
- $1-$500
- Equal or greater funding for highest minority district

Note: Data for Hawaii and Tennessee were not available

Source: Kevin Carey, "The Funding Gap," *The Education Trust*, Oct. 29, 2003

try today, most black students attend majority-black schools, and an even larger percentage of Latino students attend majority-Latino schools — evidence of what civil rights advocates call resegregation.

In Louisville, McFarland and three other families sued in federal court to bar the school system from using race in any student assignments.[2] "It can't be fair to discriminate against a white male because he's a white male," says Ted Gordon, the plaintiffs' attorney. "That can't be fair in anybody's book."

School administrators, however, say a ruling for McFarland would effectively bring back racial segregation in Louisville. "We would be back to majority-white suburban schools and majority-black inner-city schools," says Byron Leet, lead attorney for the school system.

"That would not be in the best interest of young people in the community, who have benefited greatly from attending desegregated schools."

The case is being closely watched at a time when school desegregation litigation nationwide is dormant, but parents in some areas are asking courts to block administrators from continuing to use race to promote integration.

"If the court decides that the sensitive way that Louisville has gone about trying to achieve integration is not acceptable, then I worry that there may be little or no way to reap the benefits of integration for our primary and secondary schools," says Chinh Quang Le, assistant counsel for the NAACP Legal Defense and Educational Fund, which filed a friend of the court brief on the side of the Louisville school system. The fund directed the court challenges against racial segregation that produced the *Brown* decision and remains the principal litigation center in school desegregation cases.

Today's pattern of school desegregation litigation underscores the changes in the nation's schools — and in the nation's attitudes toward race — since the *Brown* decision.[3] While the ruling is universally hailed, its promise is widely recognized as unfulfilled and its implications for educational policies today vigorously debated.

"*Brown v. Board of Education* is one of the signal legal events of our time," says Education Secretary Rod Paige, who himself attended racially segregated schools through college in his native Mississippi. But the ruling did not eliminate all the vestiges of segregation, Paige quickly adds. "If the goal was equality in education — to level the educational playing field for all children, especially children of color — we've yet to achieve that," he says.

"We have an unfulfilled promise of *Brown*," says Julie Underwood, general counsel for the National School Boards Association, which once resisted and now strongly supports desegregation. "If the civil rights people were actually seeking fully integrated public schools, we have not reached that point."

Civil rights advocates acknowledge that *Brown* fundamentally transformed American schools — and America itself. "Both whites and blacks have been in far more integrated settings than anyone would have imagined before *Brown*," says Gary Orfield, a professor at Harvard's Graduate School of Education and director of the Harvard Civil Rights Project.

But Orfield and other desegregation advocates also maintain that the hard-won progress of the post-*Brown* era has not merely stalled but is now being reversed.

School-Integration Trend Reversing

The Supreme Court's landmark 1954 *Brown v. Board of Education* ruling declared racial segregation in public schools unconstitutional. But after more than three decades, the desegration trend in U.S. schools reversed after 1988 — particularly in the South. Then a series of Supreme Court decisions between 1991 and 1995 eased the pressure on school districts to continue desegregation efforts. Today U.S. classrooms are almost as segregated as they were in the late 1960s, and some experts say the trend is likely to continue.

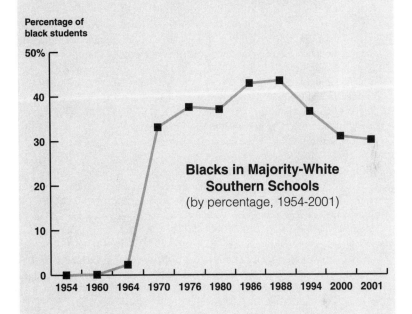

Percentage of black students

Blacks in Majority-White Southern Schools
(by percentage, 1954-2001)

Source: Gary Orfield and Chungmei Lee, "*Brown* at 50: King's Dream or Plessy's Nightmare?" The Harvard Civil Rights Project, January 2004

"We've been going backward almost every place in the country since the 1990s," Orfield says.

A coterie of educational conservatives from academia and various advocacy groups challenge both this view of present-day conditions and policies for the future. While praising the *Brown* decision, they argue that today's racial separation is not the result of law or policy and that race-conscious assignments violate *Brown's* central meaning.

Brown "stands for the principles of integration and color-blindness," says Curt Levey, director of legal and public affairs for the Washington-based Center for Individual Rights.

Latinos' Unheralded Struggles for Equal Education

When school board officials in Lemon Grove, Calif., became concerned in 1930 that Mexican-American students were slowing down the Anglo pupils, they hit upon a simple solution: build a new school solely for the Mexican-Americans.

To the board's surprise, however, Mexican-Americans in the small border community protested, deriding the new facility as a "barn." And — more than two decades before the Supreme Court declared racial segregation in public schools unconstitutional — they won a lower-court order forcing the school board to dismantle the plans for a dual system of education.[1]

The Lemon Grove incident is one of many efforts by Latinos to fight for educational equity well before the Supreme Court's landmark 1954 decision in *Brown v. Board of Education*. The history of those efforts, however, has gone largely untold. "These cases are not taught, even in law school," says Margaret Montoya, a professor at the University of New Mexico School of Law.

Today, Latinos continue to receive far less attention in school desegregation debates than African-Americans even though Latinos now comprise the nation's largest ethnic minority, and Latino students are somewhat more likely than blacks to be in ethnically identifiable schools.

"We don't see an equal commitment on the part of educational equity for Latinos," says James Ferg-Cadima, legisla-tive staff attorney for the Mexican American Legal Defense and Educational Fund (MALDEF) in Washington.

The Lemon Grove ruling was never appealed and had no further impact in California. Chicano families won a similar ruling from a lower court in Texas around the same time. It, too, did nothing to undo the advancing segregation of Mexican-American students in that state.[2]

In 1946, however, a federal appeals court in California ruled in favor of Mexican-American parents contesting school segregation in four districts in Orange County, south of Los Angeles. Ferg-Cadima says the case "could have been a precursor to *Brown v. Board of Education*," but the school districts decided not to appeal. The ruling did lead to a law in 1947, however, that barred school segregation in the state. The act was signed by then-Gov. Earl Warren, who later became chief justice and author of the *Brown* decision.[3]

Perversely, Mexican-American families prevailed in some of their early legal efforts on the grounds that they were white and could not be segregated as black students were. "We have not been treated as a white subgroup, and we don't think of ourselves as a white subgroup," Montoya says. "But when the litigation was being developed, that seemed to be a reasonable way of trying to get kids educational rights." One consequence, Montoya adds, has been "to drive a wedge between Latinos and African-Americans."

"It's unfortunate that in the past few decades we have abandoned those principles in favor of racial preferences," Levey says. "It's just another form of discrimination." The center has represented plaintiffs challenging affirmative action in higher education and, in one case from Minneapolis, racial guidelines in public schools.

"Most of our schools became substantially racially balanced," says David J. Armor, a professor at George Mason University School of Public Policy in Fairfax, Va., and the leading academic critic of mandatory integration. Armor acknowledges that there's been "some resegregation of schools" but attributes the trend to changes in ethnic and racial residential patterns and the higher percentages of blacks and Latinos in public schools.

The debate over desegregation is waged against the disheartening persistence of large gaps in learning and achievement between whites, blacks and Latinos. "The magnitude of the gap is simply appalling," says Abigail Thernstrom, a senior scholar at the Manhattan Institute and co-author with her husband Stephan Thernstrom of a book on the subject.[4]

"A typical black student is graduating from high school with junior high school skills," Thernstrom says, citing figures from the National Assessment of Educational Progress (NAEP) — informally known as "the nation's report card." Hispanics, she says, "are doing only a tad better."

Traditional civil rights advocates acknowledge the gap, but they say that closing the gap requires more thor-

The Supreme Court recognized Latinos as a separate group for desegregation purposes only in 1973 in a case from Denver.[4] By that time, however, the justices were about to pull back on school-desegregation remedies. "About the time we could have profited from *Brown* and used it ourselves, the protection starts crumbling," Ferg-Cadima says. Latinos have been the principal beneficiaries, however, of the Supreme Court's unanimous 1974 decision that school districts must make sure that non-English-speaking students are given language skills needed to profit from school attendance.[5]

Language is among the educational barriers distinctive to Latino students. Another, Ferg-Cadima says, is the migratory status of many Latino families, especially in agricultural areas in California, Texas and the Southwest.

Today, most Latino students attend majority-Latino schools in every region of the country, according to The Harvard Civil Rights Project.[6] As with African-American students, ethnic isolation for Latinos increased through the 1990s. The most intense segregation is found in the Northeast, where 45 percent of Hispanic students attend schools that are 90 to 100 percent Hispanic.

As for educational achievement, Latinos lag far behind white students and only slightly ahead of African-Americans. The average Latino student scored around the 25th percentile in both reading and mathematics in the 1999 National Assessment of Educational Performance — the so-called nation's report card.[7]

"The one lesson from *Brown* for all minority communities is that educational equity must be battled for on all fronts — it's something that has to be sought out," Ferg-Cadima says. "The schoolhouse gate isn't always open for our kids, so we have to fight for schools to be open and conducive to learning for all students."

---

[1] Robert R. Alvarez Jr., "The Lemon Grove Incident: The Nation's First Successful Desegregation Court Case," *The Journal of San Diego History*, Vol. 32, No. 2 (spring 1986). Alvarez is the son of the lead plaintiff in the case, *Alvarez v. Board of Trustees of the Lemon Grove School District*.

[2] See "Project Report: De Jure Segregation of Chicanos in Texas Schools," *Harvard Civil Rights-Civil Liberties Law Review*, Vol. 7, No. 2 (March 1972), pp. 307-391. The authors are Jorge C. Rangel and Carlos M. Alcala.

[3] See Vicki L. Ruiz, "'We Always Tell Our Children They Are Americans': *Méndez v. Westminster* and the California Road to *Brown v. Board of Education*," *The College Board Review*, No. 200 (fall 2003), pp. 20-27. See also Charles Wollenberg, *All Deliberate Speed: Segregation and Exclusion in California Schools, 1855-1975* (1976), pp. 108-135.

[4] The case is *Keyes v. Denver School District No. 1*, 413 U.S. 921 (1973).

[5] The case, brought by non-English-speaking Chinese students in San Francisco, is *Lau v. Nichols*, 414 U.S. 563 (1974).

[6] Gary Orfield and Chungmei Lee, "Brown at 50: King's Dream or Plessy's Nightmare?," Harvard Civil Rights Project, January 2004, p. 21.

[7] Cited in Abigail Thernstrom and Stephan Thernstrom, *No Excuses: Closing the Racial Gap in Learning* (2001), pp. 19-20.

---

oughgoing desegregation and better funding for schools with large numbers of minority or low-income students. But educational conservatives discount those solutions, calling instead for changing "school culture" by improving discipline, teaching and student behavior.

One path to those changes, conservatives say, is "school choice" — vouchers that help students pay for private school tuition and charter schools that operate with freedom from traditional regulations. Traditional civil rights groups generally oppose vouchers and voice some doubts about charter schools, saying they drain support from public schools and risk further resegregation of minority students.

The policy debates underscore the shared view that *Brown* — despite its iconic status — has not proved a complete success. "You have to say it was a partial failure," says James Patterson, a professor emeritus of history at Brown University and author of a new account of the ruling and its impact.

Theodore Shaw, director of the Legal Defense Fund, agrees: "*Brown* changed everything and yet did not change everything."

As the nation prepares to unite in celebrating *Brown*, here are some of the issues that divide Americans 50 years later:

Is racial imbalance in schools increasing due to court actions?

North Carolina's Charlotte-Mecklenburg County school system in 1971 became the first in the country to oper-

Minority Students Are Now More Isolated

The 1954 *Brown* ruling led to widespread school integration, but today, due to resegregation, an overwhelming percentage of African-American and Latino students attend schools with predominantly non-white student bodies. Segregation has increased nationwide since 1991, when the Supreme Court began to relax pressure on school districts to integrate.

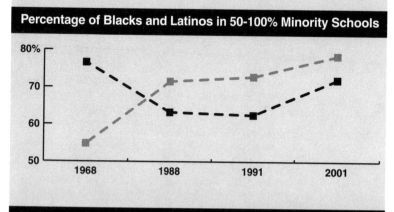

Percentage of Blacks and Latinos in 50-100% Minority Schools

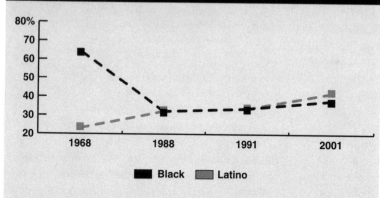

Percentage of Blacks and Latinos in 90-100% Minority Schools

■ Black ■ Latino

Source: "*Brown* at 50: King's Dream or Plessy's Nightmare?" The Civil Rights Project, Harvard University, January 2004.

attracting white students to majority-black schools by turning them into magnet schools. Then, at the end of the decade, white families successfully sued the school system, forcing it to dismantle the busing plan altogether.[6]

The result, combined with increasing percentages of African-American and Hispanic students in the system, has been a growing concentration of minorities in many schools. Today, more than one-third of the county's 148 schools have at least 80 percent non-white enrollment.

Civil rights advocates say Charlotte is one of many school systems where political and legal developments have contributed to a trend toward resegregation. "The federal court required Charlotte to resegregate," says Harvard's Orfield, "and they are resegregating — fast."

Critics of mandatory integration, however, say today's concentration of non-white students, particularly in urban school systems, largely reflects residential demographics. Nationwide, whites comprise only about 60 percent of students in public schools, compared to 80 percent in the late 1960s. In Charlotte today, 43 percent of the system's 114,000 students are black, and only 42 percent white.

"It's wrong to say that schools are segregated or becoming resegregated," says Abigail Thernstrom, a former member of the Massachusetts Board of Education. "Cities are becoming more heavily minority. There's nothing we can do about that. You can't helicopter kids in to get more white kids in the schools."

Orfield acknowledges that the increase in non-white enrollment poses "an obstacle" to racial mixing. But he and other desegregation advocates blame resegregation primarily on the courts, including the Supreme Court.

ate under a court-ordered desegregation plan using wide-scale busing to achieve racial balance in school populations. Under the plan, African-Americans comprised between 30 percent and 40 percent of the students at most of the schools through the 1970s and '80s.[5]

With public support for desegregation weakening, however, the school system shifted in the 1990s to voluntary measures to maintain racial balance — chiefly by

The percentage of black students attending majority-black schools was declining nationwide through the 1980s, Harvard Civil Rights Project reports show, but it increased during the 1990s — just as the Supreme Court was signaling to federal courts that they could ease desegregation orders. "The only basic thing that's changed since [the 1980s] is the Supreme Court of the United States," Orfield maintains.[7]

"This is a demographic process," responds Armor, "and has little to do with what the courts are doing in the desegregation area."

Education Secretary Paige also argues that court rulings are not responsible for the increasing racial isolation of blacks or Latinos. "It's not our impression that these patterns are the result of current legal practices," he says. "Ethnic communities cluster together because of a lot of different factors. Some of these factors include preferences; some are economic."

The Harvard civil rights report found that during the 1990s the trend toward integration was reversed, and the percentage of black students attending majority-black schools increased throughout the country. The percentage of Latino students attending majority-minority schools also increased in every region. Latinos are more likely than African-Americans to be in a racially or ethnically identifiable school, the report shows.

Educational conservatives, however, claim that Orfield presents a misleading picture by focusing exclusively on minority pupils' exposure to white students and not on white students' exposure to blacks and Latinos. "There are fewer white children who have no non-white classmates," says Stephan Thernstrom. "More and more white children have minority classmates."

More broadly, conservatives insist that talk of resegregation ignores the changes wrought by *Brown*. "There is no public school today that is segregated in the way that schools were routinely segregated before *Brown v. Board of Education*," says Roger Clegg, vice president and general counsel of the Center for Equal Opportunity, which opposes racial preferences. "Racial balance in a school that reflects the neighborhood is not segregation in the sense that we had segregation before *Brown*."

Shaw, of the Legal Defense Fund, counters that segregation never was eliminated completely and is increasing today. "The legal fiction is that we've severed the link between present-day segregation and our past segregated and discriminatory actions," Shaw says. "The truth is

Three high school students in Clinton, Tenn., peacefully register their feelings about their school becoming the first in Tennessee to integrate, on Aug. 27, 1956. Many other protests were violent.

that the effects of decades and decades of segregation and discrimination were to segregate housing and to segregate other aspects of life.

"The busing remedies didn't eliminate the effects of that discrimination; they neutralized them," Shaw continues. "Once you get rid of the desegregation plans, those effects become operative once again."

Shaw and Orfield both say school boards should be allowed to consider race and ethnicity in pupil-assignment plans in order to promote integration. But educational conservatives oppose policies to deliberately increase racial mixing.

"I like racially mixed schools better than racially homogeneous schools," Abigail Thernstrom says. "But I do not want computer printouts that say you have no choice as to where to send your kids."

Do minorities suffer educationally because of racial isolation?

Black and Latino youngsters lag significantly behind whites (and Asian-Americans) on every significant measure of academic achievement. The "racial gap" in learning deeply troubles advocates and experts on both sides of the desegregation debate.

Traditional civil rights advocates largely blame racial isolation for the lagging performance of blacks and Latinos.

CHRONOLOGY

Before 1950 *Racial segregation takes root in public schools — by law in the South, by custom elsewhere; NAACP begins challenging "separate but equal" doctrine in the 1930s.*

1950s-1960s *Supreme Court outlaws racial segregation; ruling provokes massive resistance in South.*

1950 Supreme Court bars racial segregation in public graduate education.

1954 Supreme Court rules racial segregation in public elementary and secondary schools unconstitutional on May 17, 1954 (*Brown I*).

1955 Court says schools must be desegregated "with all deliberate speed" (*Brown II*).

1957 President Dwight D. Eisenhower calls out Arkansas National Guard to maintain order when Little Rock's Central High School is integrated.

1964 Civil Rights Act authorizes federal government to bring school-desegregation suits and to withhold funds from schools that fail to desegregate.

1968 Impatient with limited desegregation, Supreme Court says school districts must dismantle dual school systems "now."

1970s-1980s *Desegregation advances, but busing triggers battles in many cities.*

1971 Supreme Court upholds use of busing as desegregation tool.

1973 Supreme Court orders Denver to desegregate, making it the first non-Southern city ordered to integrate.

1974 Supreme Court bars federal courts from ordering cross-district busing to achieve desegregation . . . Start of busing in Boston provokes fierce opposition.

1975 Coleman report blames white-flight from urban

public schools on court-ordered busing; desegregation advocates disagree.

Late 1980s Integration peaks, with most African-American students still attending predominantly black schools in each of five regions across country.

1990s *Many school systems freed from court supervision; race-conscious assignments challenged as "reverse discrimination."*

1998, 1999 Federal courts strike racial preferences used for Boston Latin School, "magnet" schools in two Washington, D.C., suburban districts.

1991 Supreme Court allows judges to lift court orders if segregation has been eliminated to all "practicable" extent.

1995 Supreme Court says judges in desegregation cases should try to end supervision of school systems.

2000-Present Brown's *promise hailed, impact debated.*

2001 President Bush wins passage of No Child Left Behind Act, providing penalties for school districts that fail to improve students' overall scores on standardized tests. . . . Federal court in September lifts desegregation decree for Charlotte-Mecklenburg schools in North Carolina.

2003 Supreme Court upholds affirmative action for colleges and universities. . . . Federal judge in December hears challenge to racial guidelines for Louisville-Jefferson County Schools; federal appeals court in same month considers suit to bar use of race as "tiebreaker" in pupil assignments in Seattle.

2004 *Brown* decision widely celebrated as 50th anniversary approaches; civil rights advocates decry "resegregation," while others say emphasis on racial balance is divisive and unproductive. . . . Federal appeals court to hear challenge in June to racial-balance transfer policy for Lynn, Mass., schools.

There is "a very systematic relation" between segregation and the learning gap, Orfield says. "No one has ever made separate schools equal in American history on any scale."

Some critics of mandatory integration, however, see no solid evidence that racially mixed classrooms significantly benefit learning. "There is absolutely no reason to assume that because schools are heavily Hispanic or black that these children can't learn, that they have to sit next to whites or Asians in order to learn," Abigail Thernstrom says.

The social-science evidence on the issue is voluminous but less than clear-cut. In his review of the literature, George Mason University's Armor concludes that racial composition "by itself" has "no significant effect on black achievement." When combined with other educational improvements, he says, desegregation has improved black achievement "to a limited but significant degree."[8]

Desegregation advocates strongly disagree with this minimalist view. Orfield says the effect of desegregation on achievement is "significant, but not transformative." But he adds that desegregation has a "huge" effect on "life chances," such as graduating from high school, going to college and "being able to live in an interracial world as an adult."[9]

In an examination of data from Charlotte-Mecklenburg schools, Roslyn Mickelson, a professor of sociology at the University of North Carolina in Charlotte, found that black and white students both had higher average scores on standardized tests if they had been in racially integrated schools. "There is a small but significant effect on test scores that cumulates over time," she says.[10]

Orfield and other desegregation advocates say the achievement gap for minority students results in part from underfunding of schools with high percentages of black or Latino students. "The resources aren't equivalent because those are often schools that have a badge of poverty," says Underwood of the school boards association. "So they have fewer resources." U.S. schools traditionally have received most of their funding from property taxes, so schools in wealthier neighborhoods usually had more resources than schools in districts with lower property values.[11]

Armor and the Thernstroms instead blame the racial gap primarily on social and cultural factors. "There are very strong correlations between single-parent households, low birth-weight and performance in school," says Abigail Thernstrom. Armor lists single-parent households as one of 10 "risk factors" for low academic achievement. Some of the others include poverty, limited education of parents, the size of the family and the age of the mother at pregnancy.[12]

The most incendiary aspect of the issue, perhaps, concerns the claim that some black students disdain academic achievement for fear of being accused by their peers of "acting white." The thesis is most often associated with the work of the late John Ogbu, an African-American professor of anthropology at the University of California, Berkeley, who died in 2003. Ogbu first aired the theory in a co-authored article about Washington, D.C., high school students in 1986 and repeated similar views in a book about students in the affluent Cleveland suburb of Shaker Heights.[13]

Education Secretary Paige subscribes to the theory based not only on Ogbu's research but also on his own experience as school superintendent in Houston. "I had a chance to see examples where some kids were not putting their best efforts into this in an effort to keep status among some of their peers," Paige says. "It exists."

Armor, however, discounts the theory, noting that the educational gap for African-Americans can be found at the earliest grades. Abigail Thernstrom also says the evidence is "not very good." She places greater blame on schools' failure to instill educational ambitions in minority youngsters. "Schools are delivering a wrong message — that this is a racist society, and there's a limit to how far you can go," she says.

But the Legal Defense Fund's Shaw says there is evidence of an "acting white" syndrome and says the issue needs more discussion among African-Americans. But he adds that some of the debate over the educational gap for black students has "the lurking sense of racial inferiority.

"If people come to this issue in good faith and they want to focus on the causes, the first thing they have to recognize is that there's still massive inequality," Shaw says. "By the time you get to high school, African-American students have had a completely different experience from white students. Let's not blame the victim. Let's fix the problem."

Would "school choice" policies help reduce the racial gap in educational achievement for African-Americans and Latinos?

President Bush touts school vouchers, not integration, as the best way to help disadvantaged students get a better education. "When we find children trapped in schools

Success Asian-American Style

Uncivilized, unclean and filthy beyond all conception . . . they know not the virtues of honesty, integrity or good faith," fulminated Horace Greeley, the 19th-century abolitionist and social reformer, describing Chinese immigrants.[1]

But the numbers today tell a different story. By any measure, Asian-Americans have been phenomenally successful academically. As a result, the concentration of Asian students in top American schools is wildly disproportionate to their ratio in the U.S. population.

For example, Asians make up approximately 70 percent of San Francisco's most prestigious public school, Lowell High, with Chinese-Americans alone constituting over 50 percent, although Chinese make up only 31.3 percent of the school district.

The excellent scholastic record of Asian students dates back at least to the 1930s, when California teachers wrote of "ideal" Japanese students who could serve as an example to other students. Their delinquency rate was one-third that of whites.

Today, although Asians make up only 3.8 percent of the U.S. population, Asian-Americans accounted for 27 percent of the freshman class at the Massachusetts Institute of Technology in the 2000-2001 school year, 25 percent at Stanford, 24 percent at the California Institute of Technology and 17 percent at Harvard; Asians were a phenomenal 40 percent of the freshmen at the University of California, Berkeley, in 1999. One in five American medical students is Asian.[2] Similarly, between 10 and 20 percent of the students at the nation's premier law schools are Asian.

The achievement gap between whites and Asians is greater than the gap between blacks and whites, by some measures. In 2001, 54 percent of Asian-Americans between ages 25 and 29 had at least a bachelor's degree, compared with 34 percent of whites and 18 percent of blacks.

Academics have long disputed the reasons for Asians' stellar performance. The controversial 1994 book, *The Bell Curve*, held that Asians did better because they were inherently more intelligent than others. But numerous academics attacked Richard J. Herrnstein and Charles Murray's methodology and racial conclusions. Some studies show that Asians, particularly Chinese, consistently score higher on IQ tests than other groups.[3] But there is increasing evidence that racial differences are minimal.[4]

Another explanation attributes the relative success of Asians in America to the socioeconomic and educational status of the Asian immigrants who were allowed to enter the United States. In 1965, immigration reforms allotted immigrant visas preferentially to people with needed skills. Many came from India or China with advanced degrees in medicine or technology.

The parents' educational and occupational attainments "far exceed the average for native-born Americans," according to Stephen L. Klineberg, a Rice University sociology professor studying Houston-area demographics.[5] With such parents, the children seem primed for success, but critics of socioeconomic explanations point out that even though many early Asian immigrants were mainly laborers and peasants, they still performed exceptionally well in school.

Most of those early Asian-Americans, mainly Chinese, lived in California, where school segregation developed quickly. By 1863, "Negroes, Mongolians and Indians" were prohibited from attending schools with white children.[6] Statewide restrictions were soon amended so non-white children could attend public schools with whites where no separate schools existed; in areas with fewer Chinese immigrants, they often attended schools with whites. San Francisco responded by building a separate school for Chinese children in 1885.

In 1906, Japanese and Koreans also were ordered to attend the so-called Oriental School in San Francisco, although the Japanese resisted, and by 1929 the vast majority of Japanese children attended integrated schools.[7] The courts and legislature ended legal segregation in California schools in 1947.

However, Chinese immigrants in California have staunchly opposed integration proposals that required their children to be bused out of local neighborhoods. "One time, in the 1960s and '70s, when integration of schools was the big issue, I almost got lynched in Chinatown by Chinese-Americans for supporting integration," said Ling-chi Wang, a professor of ethnic studies at Berkeley and veteran civil rights advocate.[8] More recently, Chinese-American parents successfully challenged a San Francisco school-integration plan, arguing that their children were losing out due to racial quotas at magnet schools.[9]

Today, regardless of their parents' income level or education, Asian students perform better academically than other groups, though their performance does improve as parental education and income increase. The persistent performance gap, even accounting for socioeconomic factors, leads to a third explanation for Asians' success:

the great emphasis put on education by Asian parents, higher academic expectations and the attitude that successful achievement is simply a question of hard work.

For instance, a study by Temple University's Laurence Steinberg of 20,000 Wisconsin and California students found that Asian-American students felt any grade below A- would anger their parents; for whites the anger threshold was B-, for blacks and Latinos a C-. And research shows that more than 50 percent of Asian-American high school seniors spend an hour or more per night on homework, compared to 30 percent of Latinos and less than 25 percent of whites.[10]

Education experts often blame the gap between how white children and new immigrants perform educationally on the language barriers faced by the immigrants. But evidence suggests that newly arrived Asians learn English faster than Latinos, thus breaking down those barriers faster. For instance, 1990 Census data showed that 90 to 95 percent of third-generation Asian-American children spoke only English at home, compared to only 64 percent of Mexican-Americans.[11]

But Asian immigrants are not a monolithic "model minority." Asians who arrive already speaking English, such as Filipinos or Indians, fare better educationally and economically. The poverty rate among Filipino immigrants — who come from a country with a 95 percent literacy rate — is only 6.3 percent, compared with 37.8 percent among the Hmong — a mostly uneducated ethnic group from Southeast Asia.

In Sacramento, where Hmong comprise about 8 percent of public school students, they are the lowest-performing

Asians were segregated from whites in California schools at the end of the 19th century. In 1885, San Francisco built a separate school for Chinese children.

Library of Congress

group, according to Suanna Gilman-Ponce, director of the school district's multilingual education department.[12] For example, only 3 percent of the Hmong had a bachelor's degree, according to the 1990 census, compared with 24 percent of the nation as a whole.

But there is progress: Among the 25-to-34 age group, the first Hmong generation to grow up in the United States, 13.5 percent had degrees. And of the Vietnamese, many of whom also arrived as refugees, 26.9 percent had a college degree; the national average is 27.5 percent.

— Kenneth Lukas

[1] Quoted in Andrew Gyory, *Closing the Gate* (1998), p. 17.

[2] Abigail Thernstrom and Stephan Thernstrom, *No Excuses: Closing the Racial Gap in Learning* (2003), p. 85.

[3] Jeff Wise, "Are Asians Smarter?" *Time International*, Sept. 11, 1995, p. 60.

[4] Natalie Angier, "Do Races Differ? Not Really, Genes Show," *The New York Times*, Aug. 22, 2000, p. F1 and Steve Olson, "The Genetic Archaeology of Race," *The Atlantic Monthly*, April 2, 2001, p. 69.

[5] Quoted in Mike Snyder, "Survey: Area Asians Have Head Start," *The Houston Chronicle*, Oct. 1, 2002, p. A1.

[6] For background on Asians in California, see Charles Wollenberg, *All Deliberate Speed: Segregation and Exclusion in California Schools, 1855-1975* (1976).

[7] Bill Hosokawa, *Nisei: The Quiet Americans* (2002), pp. 85-89.

[8] Quoted in Sam McManis, "Activist Fights for Asian Americans at U.S. Labs," *San Francisco Chronicle*, March 27, 2002, p. A1.

[9] David J. Hoff, "San Francisco Assignment Rules Anger Parents," *Education Week*, June 4, 2003, p. 9. See also "All Things Considered," National Public Radio, Aug. 10, 2002, and April 5, 2004.

[10] Thernstrom, *op. cit.*, p. 94.

[11] *Ibid.*, pp. 111-113.

[12] Quoted in Erika Chavez, "Hmong Cry for Help Has Been Heard," *Sacramento Bee*, May 28, 2002, p. B1.

What Americans Think About School Desegregation

While 60 percent of Americans think classroom racial diversity is "very important," 66 percent think school officials should not try to increase the diversity of local schools.

In elementary school, were your classmates of many different races, or mostly the same race?

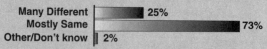

Many Different	25%
Mostly Same	73%
Other/Don't know	2%

Do the public elementary schools in your community today have kids mostly of the same race, or many different races?

Many Different	60%
Mostly Same	34%
Other/Don't Know	6%

Did the Supreme Court make the right decision to end racial segregation in schools?

Right	90%
Wrong	6%
Other/Don't know	4%

How did ending racial segregation affect the quality of America's schools?

Better	45%
Worse	12%
No Change	34%
Other/Don't know	9%

How important is it that students of different races are in class together?

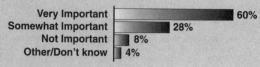

Very Important	60%
Somewhat Important	28%
Not Important	8%
Other/Don't know	4%

Should school officials try to increase the racial diversity of schools in your community?

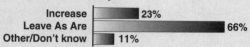

Increase	23%
Leave As Are	66%
Other/Don't know	11%

Source: Scripps Survey Research Center, Ohio University, www.newspolls.org. The national telephone survey of 1,013 people was taken Feb. 15-24, 2004.

that will not change, parents must be given another viable option," Bush told students and teachers at Archbishop Carroll High School in Washington on Feb. 13, 2004. The president used the appearance to plug a new law he had just signed to award vouchers to some 1,700 District of Columbia students per year to help pay tuition at private schools.[14]

Educational conservatives say "school choice" programs such as vouchers or charter schools will help improve schools by promoting innovation and overcoming resistance to change from public school administrators and teachers. Education Secretary Paige claims particular support for school choice among African-American families.

"My reading of the polls shows that African-American parents support choice, vouchers, strongly," Paige says. "The parents are supporters because the parents want the best education for the child."

The public school establishment strongly opposes vouchers, saying they would drain needed money from public schools. Underwood, the school boards association lawyer, says vouchers also "threaten any kind of diversity agenda that a school district may have." Private schools, she says, "can choose to discriminate. They can choose not to serve students with special needs or students who are poor or of a particular culture or ethnicity."

Local voucher programs are already operating in Milwaukee and Cleveland; Florida has a statewide program pushed by Gov. Jeb Bush, the president's brother. The programs are targeted to middle- and low-income families, but are small-scale because of limited funding. "Vouchers are going to be a sideshow for American education," Orfield says.

Charter schools — which operate under public auspices but free from some generally applicable regulations — are more widespread.[15] Some 2,700 charter schools were operating as of the 2002-2003 academic year. Many of them were established by black families and educators to serve the educational needs of African-American students. But Orfield and other desegregation advocates are skeptical that they will be better for black pupils than public schools.

"There is no evidence that charter schools are better than average," Orfield says, "and our studies show that they're more segregated than public schools."

Abigail Thernstrom counters that vouchers and charter schools "have the potential" to improve education for minority youngsters. "They have the potential for one very simple reason," she says. "They are out from under the constraints that make for such mediocre education in so many public schools."

Armor, however, sees no necessary benefit for minority youngsters from school choice programs. "I don't see personally why vouchers or charters would have any automatic impact on school quality," Armor says. "It might or might not. There's nothing intrinsic about charters that says those teachers are going to have a better subject mastery" than teachers at regular schools. As for vouchers, Armor says they "can also be used to go to a school that doesn't have better programs" than regular public schools.

Public-education groups cite underfunding as a major barrier to improving education for minority youngsters. Nationwide, schools with the highest minority or low-income enrollments receive $1,000 less per student than schools with the lowest minority or poverty enrollments, according to a report by the Education Trust, a Washington advocacy group. (*See map, p. 80.*)

"There is definitely a relationship between the amount of funding a district gets and academic performance," says Kevin Carey, a senior policy analyst with the group. "There are important issues besides money: organization, expectations for students, curricula, the way teachers are compensated. But money matters, too."

"We need to pay attention to sending resources where resources are needed," Underwood says, "so students with high educational needs get the resources they need to learn, so you really aren't leaving any child behind."

Pioneering civil rights attorney Thurgood Marshall, shown here in 1957, successfully argued the landmark *Brown v. Board of Education* case before the U.S. Supreme Court. President Lyndon B. Johnson appointed Marshall to the high court in 1967.

Library of Congress

But Paige and other educational conservatives discount the importance of funding. "I don't accept that the achievement gap is a function of funding issues," Paige says. "It is a factor, but it is not *the* factor. The more important factors are those factors embedded in the No Child Left Behind Act: accountability, flexibility and parental choice — and teaching methods that work."

Orfield, however, says the No Child Left Behind Act has produced "confusion and frustration" for local school districts with scant evidence of help for minority pupils.[16] And the Legal Defense Fund's Shaw insists that school choice proposals could help only some minority students while leaving most of them behind.

"Most African-American students, like most students, are going to remain in public schools," Shaw says. "The promise of *Brown* isn't going to be realized by focusing on those few students who can escape from public

Police escort school buses carrying African-American students into South Boston in 1974, implementing a court-ordered busing plan to integrate schools.

schools. If we don't talk about fixing public education, then I think we betray not only *Brown* but also the fundamental notion of what public education is all about."

BACKGROUND

Long, Hard Road

The Supreme Court's celebrated decision in *Brown v. Board of Education* marks neither the beginning nor the end of the campaign for equal education for black Americans. It was only a turning point in a struggle with roots in the 19th century that now extends into the 21st.[17]

Black youngsters received no education in the antebellum South and little schooling in the decades immediately after the abolition of slavery. Where blacks did go to school, they were segregated from whites in most (though not all) parts of the country, by law or custom. Some legal challenges to the practice in the 19th century succeeded, but the Supreme Court thwarted any broad attack on segregation with its 1896 decision in *Plessy v. Ferguson* upholding "separate but equal" in public transportation.

The NAACP — founded in 1909 — won its first victory against racial segregation in education in 1935, with a state court ruling to admit a black student to the University of Maryland's law school. Four years later,

one of the winning lawyers, Thurgood Marshall, was named to head a separate organization: the NAACP Legal Defense and Educational Fund, Inc. The Inc. Fund — as it was then known — won important victories from the Supreme Court with two unanimous decisions in 1950 striking down segregationist practices in graduate education at state universities in Oklahoma and Texas.[18]

Meanwhile, Marshall had been helping organize local campaigns against segregation in elementary and secondary education in four Southern and Border States. The four cases, which were consolidated in the *Brown* decision, differed in their facts and in their legal histories: Black schools in Clarendon County, S.C., were mostly ramshackle shanties; those in Topeka, Kansas, were more nearly comparable to schools for whites. The federal judge in the Prince Edward County, Va., case found "no hurt or harm to either race" in dual school systems; the state judge in the Delaware case declared that state-imposed segregation "adversely affected" education for blacks. The federal judge in Topeka also had agreed that separate schools were harmful for blacks but abided by Supreme Court precedent in rejecting any relief for the plaintiffs.

The four cases were argued before the Supreme Court twice — first in December 1952 and then again in December 1953. The justices were divided after the first argument. Five or six justices appeared inclined to declare segregation unconstitutional, according to later reconstructions of the deliberations.[19] But Chief Justice Fred M. Vinson hesitated to press for a final decision and accepted the suggestion of Justice Felix Frankfurter to ask for a reargument.

Vinson's death in September 1953 paved the way for the appointment of Chief Justice Earl Warren, who as governor of California had signed a law abolishing racial segregation in that state's public schools.[20] Warren used his considerable political skills to forge the unanimous decision on May 17, 1954, which buried the "separate but equal" doctrine, at least in public education. "Separate educational facilities," Warren wrote near the end of the 13-page opinion, "are inherently unequal."

A year later, the justices rejected both Marshall's plea to order immediate desegregation and a federal recommendation that a specific timetable for desegregation be established. Instead, the court in *Brown II* ruled that the four school districts be required to admit pupils on a racially non-discriminatory basis "with all deliberate speed."[21]

Public opinion polls indicated a narrow majority of Americans favored the ruling, but the court's gradualist approach allowed the formation of what became massive resistance. More than 100 members of Congress signed the "Southern Manifesto" in 1956 vowing to use "all lawful means" to reverse the ruling. Most school districts dragged their feet, while even token integration efforts brought forth scattered bombings and violence and more widespread intimidation and harassment. In the most dramatic instance, President Dwight D. Eisenhower had to call out National Guardsmen in September 1957 to maintain order at Central High School in Little Rock, Ark., after nine black students were enrolled. As of 1964, only 2 percent of black students in the South were attending majority-white schools.

Facing resistance both active and passive, the Supreme Court left local federal courts largely on their own for nearly a decade. In 1964, however, Congress included provisions in the landmark Civil Rights Act that authorized the federal government to file school desegregation suits and to withhold funds from school districts that failed to desegregate. Four years later, the court — with Marshall now serving as the first African-American justice — announced that its patience was at an end. The justices rejected a "freedom of choice" plan offered by a rural Virginia school board and declared that school districts had to develop plans to dismantle dual systems "root and branch" — and to do it "now."

Given patterns of residential segregation, many plans devised by federal judges inevitably involved busing — typically, transporting black students to schools in predominantly white areas. Many white parents objected, but the court — under a new chief justice, Warren Burger — unanimously ruled in the *Charlotte-Mecklenburg* case in 1971 that courts had discretion to order busing as part of a desegregation plan.

Bumps in the Road

In the 1970s and '80s, desegregation advanced generally in the South and in most of the rest of the country. But the use of busing as a principal tool for racial mixing provoked fierce protests in some cities and widespread opposition from officials and the public at large. Meanwhile, Latino enrollment in public schools began

to increase dramatically — and so, too, did the percentage of Latino students attending predominantly Latino schools.

The busing issue dominated the headlines and the policy debates in the 1970s, obscuring the less dramatic evidence of changes in public schools, especially in the South. From 1968 to 1988, the percentage of black students attending predominantly minority schools fell sharply in the South — from more than 80 percent to around 55 percent — and declined significantly in every other region except the Northeast.[22] As historian Patterson notes, most of the heavily black schools in the South were more nearly comparable to white schools by the end of the 1980s, salaries for black teachers were more nearly equal to those for whites and teaching staffs were integrated.

Public education in the South, he concludes, "had been revolutionized" — thanks to pressure from the then-Department of Health, Education and Welfare and rulings from federal courts.[23]

For many Americans, however, desegregation came to be understood only as court-ordered transportation of students out of their neighborhoods to distant schools of uncertain character and quality. The polarizing issue erupted most dramatically in ostensibly liberal Boston, where a federal judge ordered racial mixing between heavily white South Boston and predominantly black Roxbury. Patterson notes that on the first day of the plan in September 1974, only 10 of the 525 white students assigned to Roxbury High School showed up, while buses carrying 56 black pupils bound for South Boston High School were stoned.[24]

Busing had few vocal supporters. President Gerald Ford, a Republican, complained that busing "brought fear to black students and white students." President Jimmy Carter, a Democrat, was lukewarm toward the practice. Sociologist James Coleman — who authored an influential report in 1968 documenting the educational achievement gap for African-American students — added respectability to the anti-busing critique with a report in 1975 blaming "white flight" from central-city schools on court-ordered busing and calling instead for voluntary desegregation.[25]

Civil rights supporters countered that opponents were exaggerating the costs and disruption of court-ordered busing when their real objection was to racial mixing altogether. They also sharply disputed Coleman's "white

'We've Yet to Achieve' Equality of Education

Secretary of Education Rod Paige was interviewed on March 24, 2004, in his Washington office by Associate Editor Kenneth Jost. Here are verbatim excerpts from that interview.

On his experience attending racially segregated schools:

"The fact that [white students] had a gym was a big deal. They played basketball on the inside. They had a big gym with lights and stuff on the inside. We played basketball on the outside with a clay court. We played up until the time that you couldn't see the hoop any more. . . . I wanted to take band, but there was no music. I wanted to play football, but there was no football team [until senior year]. . . . The concept of separate but equal is not at all academic for me. It is very personal. And even today . . . I don't know what I missed."

On the impact of the *Brown v. Board of Education* decision:

"Was the goal to take 'separate but equal' away . . .? The answer would be [yes], in a very strong and striking way. If the goal was equality education, to level the educational playing field for all children, especially children of color, the answer is we've yet to achieve that."

On the resegregation of black and Latino students:

Secretary of Education Rod Paige

U.S. Dept. of Education

"Ethnic communities cluster together because of a lot of different factors. Some of these factors include preferences; some are economic. So our goal should be now to provide a quality education for a child no matter where they are in this system."

On efforts to promote racial balance in schools:

"If anybody is in a segregated school based on unfairness, then, yes, they should work against that. But . . . we don't want to get integration confused with educational excellence. We want to provide educational excellence to kids no matter what their location is [or] the ethnic makeup of their community."

On the use of race in pupil assignments:

"A person should not be disadvantaged because of the color of their skin. Nor should that person be advantaged because of the color of their skin. . . . That's the principle I would apply to any set of circumstances."

On "equal" opportunities for African-American and Latino students:

"I've got to come down on the side that there's a large amount of lower expectations for minority kids. . . . If there are lower expectations for a child, then the answer to your question has to be that there is not a fair opportunity."

On causes of the "racial gap" in learning:

"There are three drivers. One is the quality of instructional circumstances. . . . The second is the quantity of it . . . And the third one is student engagement. Learning is an active activity between the teacher and the student. So the student does have some responsibility here in terms of student engagement."

On underfunding of minority and low-income schools:

"I don't accept that the achievement gap is a function of funding issues. I think it is a factor, but it is not *the* factor. . . . The more important factors are those embedded in the No Child Left Behind Act: accountability, flexibility and parental choice — and teaching methods that work."

On school choice proposals — vouchers and charter schools:

"My reading of the polls show[s] that African-American parents support choice, vouchers, strongly. . . . The parents are supporters because [they] want the best education for the child. . . . Enforcing monopolistic tendencies on schools is a detriment to schools. The people who force these monopolistic tendencies on schools deny schools the opportunity to innovate, create and reach their potential."

Should the federal government do more to promote racial and ethnic diversity in public schools?

YES

Gary Orfield
Director, The Harvard Civil Rights Project
*Co-author, "*Brown *at 50: King's Dream or* Plessy's *Nightmare?"*

Written for *CQ Researcher*, April 2004

The federal government has taken no significant, positive initiatives toward desegregation or even toward serious research on multiracial schools since the Carter administration.

In fact, Presidents Richard M. Nixon, Gerald Ford, Ronald Reagan and both George Bushes were generally opposed to urban desegregation and named like-minded appointees to run the major federal civil rights and education agencies. Attorney General John Ashcroft, for example, fought desegregation orders in St. Louis and Kansas City, and Reagan Supreme Court appointee Chief Justice William H. Rehnquist has consistently opposed urban desegregation.

Between 1965 and 1970, federal leadership played a decisive role in ending educational apartheid in the South and transforming it into the nation's most desegregated region. Southern schools were the most integrated for more than three decades, during which time black achievement, graduation and college attendance increased, and educational gaps began to close. But those schools now are seriously resegregating.

President Nixon largely ended enforcement of the 1964 Civil Rights Act in schools and intentionally stirred up national division over busing as part of his "Southern strategy." Then, in two separate 5-4 decisions in 1973 and 1974, four Nixon justices helped block school-finance equalization and desegregation across city-suburban lines. The federal government never enforced the Supreme Court's 1973 decision recognizing Latinos' right to desegregation. And in the 1990s the Rehnquist court thrice ended desegregation orders, effectively producing resegregation. Nearly 90 percent of the heavily segregated minority schools produced by this process have high rates of poverty and educational inequality.

Federal policy could help reverse the resegregation trend. First, leaders must make the compelling case that desegregation, properly implemented, is valuable for all students, preparing them to live and work in a multiracial society. Second, judicial vacancies and civil rights enforcement agencies should be staffed with progressives. Third, the desegregation-aid program could be revived to help suburbs experiencing racial change without preparation or resources.

In addition, serious research needs to be done on resegregation. Educational choice programs should forbid transfers that increase segregation and reward those that diminish it. And magnet school programs should be expanded. Finally, fair-housing enforcement should be greatly increased and policies adopted to help stabilize desegregated neighborhoods.

NO

David J. Armor
Professor of Public Policy, School of Public Policy, George Mason University

Written for *CQ Researcher*, April 2004

To answer this question, we must ask three related questions. First, do legal constraints prevent the promotion of diversity in public schools? The answer is yes. The Supreme Court has provided a legal framework for using race in public policy, and the justices recently clarified that framework in two cases involving college admissions in Michigan. Racial diversity can be a compelling government purpose, but policies must be narrowly tailored to reflect the use of race or ethnicity as only one factor, not the predominant factor, in the policy.

Applying this framework to public schools, race could not be used as the primary basis for assigning students to schools (as in old-fashioned busing plans), unless a school district was remedying illegal segregation. The use of race might be justified for controlling enrollment in a voluntary magnet school on the grounds that students should be allowed to choose racially diverse programs, but even this limited use of race is being challenged in the courts. The Supreme Court has yet to rule on diversity for K-12 public schools.

Second, does diversity bring clear social and educational benefits to public school children? Diversity unquestionably has social value, since it allows children from different backgrounds to learn about other cultures and how to work together. However, it is hard to find social outcomes that have consistently benefited from desegregation. For example, race relations have sometimes worsened after desegregation programs, particularly if they involved mandatory busing. Moreover, the formal educational value of diversity has not been proven, since large-scale school-desegregation programs have not reduced the racial gap in academic achievement.

The third question we must ask is what kind of promotion, if any, might be appropriate for the federal government? Federal agencies have an important but limited role in policies for K-12 public schools. They conduct research, sponsor special programs, conduct assessment and recently adopted policies to raise academic standards and accountability under the No Child Left Behind Act. Given the legal constraints on diversity programs and the uncertain educational benefits of diversity in K-12 schools, I do not think promoting diversity should be a high priority at this time.

However, since there is still a debate over the educational benefits of racial diversity programs, it would be appropriate for the federal government to sponsor research to help resolve this important issue.

Stanton Elementary School, in Stanton, Ky., reflects the current status of school integration in most of the nation. Most public schools are as segregated today as they were in 1969. During the 2000-2001 school year, for instance, only 30 non-white students were enrolled in the 2,500-student Stanton school district.

flight" theory, insisting that the movement of whites to the suburbs — and the resulting concentration of African-Americans in inner cities — stemmed from social and economic trends dating from the 1950s unrelated to school desegregation.

The Supreme Court itself acknowledged the logistical problems of busing in some of its decisions, but the justices couched their emerging disagreements on desegregation in legalistic terms. In 1973, the court established a critical distinction between "de jure" segregation — ordered by law — and "de facto" segregation resulting only from residential segregation. The ruling allowed a lower court to enforce a desegregation plan, but only on the grounds that the school district had intentionally drawn zones to separate black and white pupils. (The ruling also recognized Hispanic students as an identifiable class for desegregation purposes.) In a partial dissent, Justice Lewis F. Powell Jr. criticized the distinction between "de facto" and "de jure" segregation, saying any racial separation of students was constitutionally suspect.

A year later, the court dealt integration advocates a more serious setback in a 5-4 ruling that barred transportation of students across school-district lines to achieve desegregation. The ruling struck down a desegregation plan for the heavily black Detroit school district and the predominantly white schools in surrounding Wayne County suburbs. For the majority, Chief Justice Burger said school district lines

"could not be casually ignored." In dissent, Marshall called the ruling "a large step backwards."

Three years later, the court dealt another blow to desegregation advocates by ruling — in a case from Pasadena, Calif. — that a school district was not responsible for resegregation of students once it had adopted a racially neutral attendance plan.

The rulings combined with political opposition and socioeconomic trends to stall further increases in racial mixing of students by the end of the 1980s. The percentage of black students attending predominantly minority schools increased after 1988 in the South and West and after 1991 in the Northeast, Midwest and Border States. The Supreme Court, under the leadership of conservative Chief Justice William H. Rehnquist, then eased the pressure on school districts to continue desegregation efforts with three more decisions between 1991 and 1995.

The rulings — in cases from Oklahoma City; suburban DeKalb County, Ga.; and Kansas City — effectively told federal judges to ease judicial supervision once legally enforced segregation had been eliminated to the extent practicable. For the majority, Rehnquist wrote in the Kansas City case that federal judges should remember that their purpose was not only to remedy past violations but also to return schools to the control of local and state authorities.

Reversing Directions?

By the mid-1990s, traditional civil rights advocates were strongly criticizing what they termed the resegregation of African-American and Latino students. Critics of mandatory integration replied that legal segregation and its effects had been largely eliminated and that apparent racial and ethnic separation reflected residential neighborhoods and the growing proportion of African-American and Latino students in public schools.

As federal courts backed away from desegregation suits, white students brought — and in a few cases won — so-called reverse-discrimination suits contesting use of race in school-assignment plans. Meanwhile, some civil rights supporters shifted direction by bringing school-funding cases in state courts.

School-desegregation litigation all but petered out during the 1990s. Nearly 700 cases remain technically alive nationwide, but a law professor's examination of the period 1992-2002 found only 53 suits in active litigation.[26] Professor Wendy Parker of the University of

Cincinnati College of Law also showed that school districts had succeeded in every instance but one when they asked for so-called unitary status — in order to get out from under further judicial supervision of desegregation decrees — even if enrollments continued to reflect racial imbalance.

In addition, Parker said judges were somewhat lax in requiring racial balance of teaching staffs and that any racial imbalance in teaching assignments invariably mirrored a school's racial composition: Schools with a disproportionate number of black teachers were predominantly black, those with disproportionate numbers of white teachers were predominantly white.

Meanwhile, a few federal courts were curbing school districts' discretion to consider race in assigning students to elite or so-called magnet schools. In 1998, the 1st U.S. Circuit Court of Appeals had ruled against the use of "flexible race/ethnicity guidelines" for filling about half of the places each year at the elite Boston Latin School. The court said the Boston School Committee had failed to show that the policy either promoted diversity or helped remedy vestiges of past discrimination.[27]

The next year, another federal appeals court ruled in favor of white students' claims that school boards in two suburban Washington, D.C., school districts — Montgomery County, Md., and Arlington, Va. — violated the Constitution's Equal Protection Clause by considering race in magnet-school placements. In both rulings, the 4th U.S. Circuit Court of Appeals said the use of race was not narrowly tailored to achieve the goal of diversity. The Supreme Court refused to hear the school districts' appeals.[28]

With federal courts seemingly uninterested in desegregation initiatives, civil rights groups put more resources into school-funding challenges before state legislatures or courts.[29] The various efforts, pushed in some 40 states, generally aimed at narrowing or eliminating financial disparities between well-to-do and less-well-off school districts. Funding-equity advocates succeeded in part in several states — sometimes through court order, sometimes by legislative changes spurred by actual or threatened litigation.

The initiatives helped cause a shift in education-funding sources away from the historic primary reliance on local property taxes. Today, just over half of local education funding comes from state rather than local revenues, according to Carey, of the Education Trust. Nonetheless, school districts with high minority or low-income enrollments still receive fewer funds compared to districts with more white or wealthier students.

The limited progress on funding issues gave civil rights advocates only slight consolation for the evidence of increasing racial imbalance in public schools. By 2001, at least two-thirds of black students and at least half of Latino students nationwide were enrolled in predominantly minority schools. Significantly, the Northeast is more segregated: More than half of black students (51 percent) and nearly half of Latino students (44 percent) attended intensely segregated schools with 90 to 100 percent minority enrollment. "We've been going backward almost every place in the country since the 1990s," Harvard's Orfield says.

Critics of mandatory integration, however, viewed the figures differently. They emphasized that white students' exposure to African-American and Latino students has continued to increase. In any event, they say, residential patterns, city-suburban boundary lines and the increasing percentages of African-American and Latino students in overall enrollment make it impractical to achieve greater racial mixing in many school districts.

"The proportion of minorities in large districts is growing," says George Mason's Armor. "When it crosses 50 percent, whatever your racial-assignment plan, you're going to have minority schools."

For his part, President Bush has pushed education reform aimed in part at helping low-income students but without adopting traditional civil rights goals or rhetoric. "American children must not be left in persistently dangerous or failing schools," Bush declared as he unveiled — on Jan. 23, 2001, his second full day in office — what eventually became the No Child Left Behind Act. Approved by Congress in May 2001, the law prescribes student testing to measure academic progress among public school students and provides financial penalties for school districts that fail to improve student performance.

Education Secretary Paige says the law seeks to continue the effort to improve educational opportunities for all students started by *Brown v. Board of Education*. The law passed with broad bipartisan support. By 2004, however, many Democrats were accusing the administration of failing to provide funding to support needed changes, while many school administrators were criticizing implementation of the law as excessively rigid and cumbersome.

CURRENT SITUATION

Race-Counting

Schools in Lynn, Mass., were facing a multifaceted crisis in the 1980s, with crumbling buildings, tattered textbooks, widespread racial strife and rapid white flight. To regain public confidence, the school board in 1989 adopted a plan combining neighborhood-school assignments with a transfer policy that included only one major restriction: No child could transfer from one school to another if the move would increase racial imbalance at either of the schools involved.

The Lynn school board credits the plan with stabilizing enrollment, easing race relations and helping lift academic performance throughout the 15,000-student system. But lawyers for parents whose children were denied transfers under the plan are asking a federal appeals court to rule that the policy amounts to illegal racial discrimination.

"They're denying school assignments based on the color of the kid who's asking for the assignment," says Michael Williams, a lawyer with the Boston-based Citizens for the Preservation of Constitutional Rights.

The case — expected to be argued in September 2004 before the 1st U.S. Circuit Court of Appeals in Boston — is one of several nationwide where school boards with voluntary integration plans are facing legal actions aimed at eliminating any use of race in student assignments. Attorneys for the school boards are vigorously defending race-conscious policies.

"You cannot ignore race and expect that the issue will not be present in your school system," says Richard Cole, senior counsel for civil rights in the Massachusetts attorney general's office, who is defending the Lynn plan. "The only way is to take steps to bring kids of different racial groups together."

Meanwhile, the federal appeals court for Washington state is considering a challenge to the Seattle School District's use of race as one of several factors — a so-called "tiebreaker" — in determining assignments to oversubscribed schools. The 9th Circuit appeals court heard arguments on Dec. 14, 2003, in a three-year-old suit by the predominantly white Parents Involved in Community Schools claiming that the policy violates equal-protection guarantees.[30]

Opposing experts and advocates in the desegregation debate are also closely watching the Louisville case, where

U.S. District Judge John Heyburn II is expected to rule by the end of the school year on Jefferson County's racial guidelines for pupil assignments. And in another case, a conservative public-interest law firm is in California state court claiming that a statewide initiative barring racial preferences prevents the Berkeley school system from asking for racial information from students and families or using the information for assignment purposes.[31]

Schools in Lynn, a gritty former mill town 10 miles north of Boston, were in "dire straits" in the 1980s before adoption of the integration plan, according to Cole. Attendance was down; violence and racial conflict were up. White students — who comprised more than 80 percent of the enrollment as of 1977 — were fleeing the schools at the rate of 5 percent a year. There was also evidence that white students were being allowed to transfer out of predominantly black schools in violation of the district's stated rules.

The school board adopted a multipronged strategy to try to stem white flight and improve schools for white and minority youngsters alike, Cole says. A neighborhood-school assignment plan was combined with the construction of new schools, including magnet schools, using funds under a state law to aid racial-balance programs. Cole says attendance rates and achievement levels are up, discipline problems down and enrollment stabilized. The district's students are 58 percent minority, 42 percent white.

The citizens' group, which had earlier filed a suit that forced Boston to drop its use of busing for desegregation, sued Lynn schools in August 1999. Williams acknowledges the school system's past problems and more recent progress. But he says all of the improvements resulted from "race-neutral stuff that could have happened if the plan had not included a racial element."

U.S. District Judge Nancy Gertner rejected the group's suit in a 156-page ruling in December 2003. "The Lynn plan does not entail coercive assignments or forced busing; nor does it prefer one race over another," said Gertner, who was appointed by President Bill Clinton. "The message it conveys to the students is that our society is heterogeneous, that racial harmony matters — a message that cannot be conveyed meaningfully in segregated schools."[32]

Legal Defense Fund Director Shaw calls the legal challenges to voluntary desegregation plans "Orwellian." "Our adversaries have this perverted sense of the law and the Constitution that holds mere race consciousness — even if it's in support of desegregation — as discriminatory," he says.

But Clegg of the Center for Equal Opportunity says schools should not assign students on the basis of race or ethnicity. "The social benefits to achieving a predetermined racial or ethnic mix are very small compared to the social costs of institutionalized racial and ethnic discrimination," he says.

Race-Mixing?

Some two-dozen Washington, D.C., high school students gathered on a school day in late February for a "dialogue" with the president of the American Bar Association and the city's mayor about *Brown v. Board of Education*. Dennis Archer, a former mayor of Detroit, is black — as is Washington's mayor, Anthony Williams. And so, too, are all but three of Woodson High School's 700 students.

The students — chosen from an advanced-placement U.S. history course — listen respectfully as Archer and Williams relate the story of the *Brown* case and the implementation of the ruling over the ensuing 50 years. The students' questions, however, make clear that they feel little impact from the ruling in their daily lives.

"Why is there such a small percentage of white students in D.C. schools?" Danyelle Johnson asks. Wesley Young echoes the comment: "I feel that to make it better we should be like Wilson [High School] and have different races in schools," he says, referring to a well-regarded integrated school in a predominantly white neighborhood.

"It's really hard for me to make [*Brown*] relevant to them," assistant principal Phyllis Anderson remarks afterward, "because they've been in an all-black environment all their lives, and their parents before them."

With 84 percent of its 65,000 public school students black, another 10 percent Hispanic and only 5 percent white, Washington provides an extreme, but not unrepresentative, example of the situation in central-city school districts throughout the country. Nationwide, central-city black students typically attend schools with 87 percent minority enrollment, according to the Harvard Civil Rights Project. For Latinos, the figure is 86 percent. This "severe segregation" results from residential segregation and the "fragmentation" of large metropolitan regions into separate school districts, the project's most recent survey explains.[33]

The Supreme Court's 1974 ruling barring court-ordered interdistrict desegregation plans virtually eliminated the possibility of racial mixing between inner cities and suburbs except in countywide systems like those in Louisville-Jefferson County and Charlotte-Mecklenburg County. The court's ruling in the Kansas City desegregation case in 1995 also limited federal judges' power to order costly improvements for central-city schools in an effort to attract white students from the suburbs.

Over the past decade or so, middle-class blacks and Latinos have themselves migrated to the suburbs, but because of residential segregation the movement has not fundamentally changed the pattern of racial isolation in the schools, according to the Harvard report. Even in the suburbs of large metropolitan areas, the typical black student attends a school that is 65 percent minority, the typical Latino a school that is 69 percent minority.[34]

Federal courts, meanwhile, have been freeing dozens of school districts from judicial supervision by declaring the segregated systems dismantled and granting the districts "unitary status." In an examination of 35 such districts, the Harvard study found that black students' exposure to whites had fallen in all but four — typically, by at least 10 percent. "Desegregation is declining rapidly in places the federal courts no longer hold accountable," the report concludes.[35]

The Legal Defense Fund's Shaw says the trends result from judicial solicitude for school districts that once practiced segregation. "If a snapshot reveals a desegregated district," he says, "the court can grant judicial absolution, and the district can return to a segregated status."

The Manhattan Institute's Abigail Thernstrom counters that the focus on racial mixing is beside the point. "Teach the kids instead of worrying about the racial composition of the school," she says. "Otherwise, we're chasing demographic rainbows. Cities aren't going to get whiter. And they're not going to get more middle-class."

OUTLOOK

Mixed Records

Fifty years after the Supreme Court declared the end of racial segregation, the four communities involved in the historic cases present mixed records on the degree of progress in bringing black and white children together in public schools.[36]

Topeka — home of Oliver Brown and his daughter Linda, then in elementary school — achieved "substantial levels of integration" while under a court-ordered desegregation plan, according to the Harvard Civil Rights Project. But integration has receded slightly since the system was declared unitary and judicial supervision was ended in 1999.

As of 2001, black students in Topeka were in schools with 51 percent white enrollment — down from 59 percent in 1991. Just outside the city limits, however, better-off suburban school districts have predominantly white enrollments. "The city was then, as it is now, physically and emotionally segregated," Ronald Griffin, a black professor at Washburn University Law School in Topeka, remarked at a symposium in 2002. "That has not changed."[37]

The Delaware case "led to the merger and full desegregation of all students" in Wilmington and adjoining suburban districts, the Harvard report says. The federal court lifted judicial supervision in 1996, but Wilmington and the entire state remain as some of the most integrated school systems in the country, according to the report.

The two Southern communities involved in the four cases present a sharp contrast. Prince Edward County, Va., resisted integration to the point of closing all public schools from 1959 until the Supreme Court ordered them reopened in 1964. Today, however, the school system has an integration level "far above the national average" and student achievement in line with other Virginia districts, despite a predominantly black enrollment, according to the Harvard report.

In Clarendon County, S.C., however, School District Number One in tiny Summertown has only 60 white students among a total enrollment of 1,100. Other white students attend a private academy set up at the start of desegregation in 1969. When an *Education Week* reporter recently asked Jonathan Henry — a great-great-grandson of one of the plaintiffs — about his interactions with white students, Henry seemed "bewildered. . . . He really doesn't know any."[38]

The legacy of the *Brown* cases is "mixed," according to historian Patterson. "It seems in the early 2000s to be somewhat more complicated, somewhat more mixed than anybody in the 1970s could have imagined."

"We are miles ahead because of *Brown*," Education Secretary Paige says. "But we have yet to achieve" the goal of equal educational opportunities for all students.

Whatever has or has not been accomplished in the past, the nation's changing demographics appear to be combining with law and educational policy to push ethnic and racial mixing to the side in favor of an increased emphasis on academic performance. Schools "are going to be more racially identifiable," the Legal Defense Fund's Shaw says. "I don't see any public policy right now that's going to turn that around."

Critics of mandatory integration applaud the change. "At the end of the day, what you want to ask is, 'Are the kids getting an education?'," Abigail Thernstrom says. "The right question is what are kids learning, not whom are they sitting next to."

The emphasis on academic performance makes the challenges for schools and education policy-makers all the more difficult, however, not less. "The black kid who arrives at school as a 5- or 6-year old is already way, way behind, and it just gets worse as they go on," historian Patterson says. "There's only so much the schools can do."

Latino youngsters enter school with many of the same socioeconomic deficits, often combined with limited English proficiency. In any event, the debates about educational policy have yet to catch up with the fact that Latinos are now the nation's largest minority group.[39] "We don't see an equal commitment on the part of educational equity for Latinos," says James Ferg-Cadima, an attorney for the Mexican American Legal Defense and Educational Fund.

"It's a major challenge for all of us to work together collegially to make sure that our children get the education they deserve," ABA President Archer says. "We're going to have to do a lot more to make sure all of our children in public schools — or wherever they are — graduate with a good education and can be competitive in a global economy."

NOTES

1. The decision is *Brown v. Board of Education of Topeka*, 347 U.S. 483 (1954). The ruling came in four consolidated cases from Topeka; Clarendon County, S.C.; Prince Edward County, Va.; and Wilmington-Kent County, Del. In a companion case, the court also ruled racial segregation in the District of Columbia unconstitutional: *Bolling v. Sharpe*, 347 U.S. 497 (1954).

2. The case is *McFarland v. Jefferson County Public Schools*, 3:02CV-620-H. For coverage, see Chris Kenning, "School Desegregation Plan on Trial," *The (Louisville) Courier-Journal*, Dec. 8, 2003, p. 1A, and subsequent daily stories by Kenning, Dec. 9-13. McFarland's quote is from his in-court testimony.

3. For background, see Kenneth Jost, "Rethinking School Integration," *CQ Researcher*, Oct. 18, 1996, pp. 913-936.

4. Abigail Thernstrom and Stephan Thernstrom, *No More Excuses: Closing the Racial Gap in Learning* (2003). For a statistical overview, see pp. 11-23.

5. Some background drawn from Roslyn Arlin Mickelson, "The Academic Consequences of Desegregation and Segregation: Evidence From the Charlotte-Mecklenburg Schools," *North Carolina Law Review*, Vol. 81, No. 4 (May 2003), pp. 1513-1562.

6. The decision is *Belk v. Charlotte-Mecklenburg Board of Education*, 269 F.3d 305 (4th Cir. 2001). For coverage, see Celeste Smith and Jennifer Wing Rothacker, "Court Rules That Schools Unitary," *The Charlotte Observer*, Sept. 22, 2001, p. 1A.

7. See Gary Orfield and Chungmei Lee, "*Brown* at 50: King's Dream or *Plessy's* Nightmare," The Civil Rights Project, Harvard University, January 2004.

8. David J. Armor, "Desegregation and Academic Achievement," in Christine H. Rossell *et al.*, *School Desegregation in the 21st Century* (2001), pp. 183-184.

9. See Orfield and Lee, *op. cit.*, pp. 22-26.

10. Mickelson, *op. cit.*, pp. 1543ff.

11. For background, see Kathy Koch, "Reforming School Funding," *CQ Researcher*, Dec. 10, 1999, pp. 1041-1064.

12. See David J. Armor, *Maximizing Intelligence* (2003).

13. See John Ogbu, *Black Students in an Affluent Suburb: A Study of Academic Disengagement* (2003).

14. Quoted in Justin Blum, "Bush Praises D.C. Voucher Plan," *The Washington Post*, Feb. 14, 2004, p. B2. For background, see Kenneth Jost, "School Vouchers Showdown," *CQ Researcher*, Feb. 15, 2002, pp. 121-144.

15. For background, see Charles S. Clark, "Charter Schools," *CQ Researcher*, Dec. 20, 2002, pp. 1033-1056.

16. See Gary Orfield *et al.*, "No Child Left Behind: A Federal-, State- and District-Level Look at the First Year," The Civil Rights Project, Harvard University, Feb. 6, 2004.

17. For a recent, compact history, see James T. Patterson, Brown v. Board of Education: *A Civil Rights Milestone and Its Troubled Legacy*, 2001. The definitive history — Richard Kluger, *Simple Justice: The History of* Brown v. Board of Education *and Black America's Struggle for Equality* — was republished in April 2004, with a new preface and final chapter by the author.

18. The decisions are *Sweatt v. Painter*, 339 U.S. 629, and *McLaurin v. Oklahoma State Regents for Higher Education*, 339 U.S. 637. Sweatt required Texas to admit a black student to its main law school even though a "black" law school was available; McLaurin ruled that the University of Oklahoma could not deny a black student use of all its facilities, including the library, lunchroom and classrooms.

19. For a recent reconstruction of the deliberations, see National Public Radio, "All Things Considered," Dec. 9, 2003.

20. See Charles Wollenberg, *All Deliberate Speed: Segregation and Exclusion in California Schools, 1855-1975* (1976), p. 108.

21. The case is *Brown v. Board of Education of Topeka*, 349 U.S. 294 (1955).

22. "*Brown* at 50," Harvard Civil Rights Project, *op. cit.*, Appendix: Figure 5.

23. Patterson, *op. cit.*, p. 186.

24. *Ibid.*, p. 173.

25. James S. Coleman, Sara D. Kelly and John A. Moore, *Trends in School Segregation, 1968-1973*, The Urban Institute, 1975. The earlier report is James S. Coleman, *et al.*, Equality of Educational Opportunity, U.S. Department of Health, Education and Welfare, 1966.

26. Wendy Parker, "The Decline of Judicial Decision-making: School Desegregation and District Court Judges," *North Carolina Law Review*, Vol. 81, No. 4 (May 2003), pp. 1623-1658.

27. The case is *Wessmann v. Gittens*, 160 F.3d 790 (1st Cir. 1998).

28. The decisions are *Tuttle v. Arlington County School Board*, 195 F.3d 698 (4th Cir. 1999) and *Eisenberg v. Montgomery County Public Schools*, 197 F.3d 123 (4th Cir. 1999).

29. See Koch, *op. cit.*

30. The case is Parents Involved in *Community Schools v. Seattle School District No. 1.* For coverage, see Sarah Linn, "Appeals Judges Told of Schools' Racial Tiebreaker," The Associated Press, Dec. 16, 2003.

31. The case is *Avila v. Berkeley Unified School District*, filed in Alameda County Superior Court. For coverage, see Angela Hill, "Suit Accuses District of Racial Bias," *The Oakland Tribune*, Aug. 9, 2003.

32. The decision is *Comfort v. Lynn Schools Committee*, 283 F Supp, 2d 328 (D.Mass. 2003). For coverage, see Thanassis Cambanis, "Judge OK's Use of Race in School Assigning," *The Boston Globe*, June 7, 2003, p. A1.

33. Orfield and Lee, *op. cit.*, p. 34.

34. *Ibid.*

35. *Ibid.*, pp. 35-39.

36. *Ibid.*, pp. 11-13, 39 (Table 21).

37. Quoted in Vincent Brydon, "Panel: Segregation Still Exists in U.S. Schools," *The Topeka Capital-Journal*, Oct. 26, 2002. The Topeka district has a Web site section devoted to the *Brown* case (www.topeka.k12.ks.us).

38. Alan Richard, "Stuck in Time," *Education Week*, Jan. 21, 2004.

39. For background, see David Masci, "Latinos' Future," *CQ Researcher*, Oct. 17, 2003, pp. 869-892.

BIBLIOGRAPHY

Books

Armor, David J., *Forced Justice: School Desegregation and the Law*, Oxford University Press, 1995.
A professor of public policy at George Mason University offers a strong critique of mandatory desegregation. Includes table of cases and seven-page bibliography.

Cushman, Clare, and Melvin I. Urofsky (eds.), *Black, White and Brown: The School Desegregation Case in Retrospect*, Supreme Court Historical Society/CQ Press, 2004.
This collection of essays by various contributors — including the lawyer who represented Kansas in defending racial segregation in *Brown* — provides an historical overview of the famous case, from a variety of perspectives.

Klarman, Michael J., *From Jim Crow to Civil Rights: The Supreme Court and the Struggle for Racial Equality*, Oxford University Press, 2004.
A law professor at the University of Virginia offers a broad reinterpretation of racial issues, from the establishment of segregation through the *Brown* decision and passage of the Civil Rights Act of 1964. Includes extensive notes and a 46-page bibliography.

Kluger, Richard, *Simple Justice: The History of Brown v. Board of Education and Black America's Struggle for Equality*, Vintage, 2004.
A former journalist and book publisher has written a definitive history of the four school-desegregation suits decided in *Brown v. Board of Education*. Originally published by Knopf in 1976, the book has been reissued with a new chapter by the author.

Ogletree, Charles J., Jr., *All Deliberate Speed: Reflections on the First Half Century of Brown v. Board of Education*, Norton, 2004.
A well-known African-American professor at Harvard Law School offers a critical examination of the unfulfilled promise of the *Brown* decision. Includes notes, case list.

Patterson, James T., Brown v. Board of Education: *A Civil Rights Milestone and Its Troubled Legacy*, Oxford University Press, 2001.
A professor emeritus of history at Brown University provides a new compact history of *Brown* and its impact.

Rossell, Christine H., David J. Armor and Herbert J. Walberg (eds.), *School Desegregation in the 21st Century*, Praeger, 2001.
Various academics examine the history and current issues involving desegregation. Rossell is a professor of political science at Boston University, Armor a professor of public policy at George Mason University and Walberg a professor emeritus of education and psychology at the University of Illinois, Chicago. Includes chapter notes, references.

Thernstrom, Abigail, and Stephan Thernstrom, *No Excuses: Closing the Racial Gap in Learning*, Simon & Schuster, 2003.
An academic-scholar couple provides a strongly argued case for adopting educational reforms, including school choice, instead of racial mixing to reduce the learning gap for African-American and Latino pupils. Abigail Thernstrom is a senior scholar at the Manhattan Institute; Stephan Thernstrom is a professor of history at Harvard. Includes detailed notes.

Articles

Cohen, Adam, "The Supreme Struggle," Education Life Supplement, *The New York Times*, Jan. 18, 2004, p. 22.
A *Times* editorial writer offers an overview of the 1954 *Brown* decision and its impact.

Henderson, Cheryl Brown, "*Brown v. Board of Education* at Fifty: A Personal Perspective," *The College Board Review*, No. 200 (fall 2003), pp. 7-11.
The daughter of Oliver Brown, first-named of the 13 plaintiffs in *Brown v. Board of Education of Topeka*, provides a personal reflection on the landmark case. Henderson is executive director of the Brown Foundation for Educational Equity, Excellence and Research in Topeka (www.brownvboard.org).

Hendrie, Caroline, "In U.S. Schools, Race Still Counts," *Education Week*, Jan. 21, 2004.
This broad survey of racial issues in public schools was the first of a five-part series marking the 50th anniversary of *Brown*. Other articles appeared on Feb. 18 (Charlotte-Mecklenburg County, N.C.), March 10 (Chicago; Latinos), April 14 (Arlington, Va., challenges of integration), with a final story scheduled for May 19 (parental choice).

Reports and Studies

Orfield, Gary, and Chungmei Lee, "*Brown* at 50: King's Dream or *Plessy's* Nightmare?" The Civil Rights Project, Harvard University, January 2004.
The project's most recent analysis of school-enrollment figures finds that racial separation is increasing among African-American and Latino students.

For More Information

Center for Equal Opportunity, 14 Pidgeon Hill Dr., Suite 500, Sterling, VA 20165; (703) 421-5443; www.ceousa.org. Opposes the expansion of racial preferences in education, employment and voting.

Center for Individual Rights, 1233 20th St., N.W., Suite 300, Washington, DC 20036; (202) 833-8400; www.cir-usa.org. A nonprofit, public-interest law firm that opposes racial preferences.

The Civil Rights Project, 124 Mt. Auburn St., 500 North, Cambridge, MA 02138; (617) 496-6367; www.civilrightsproject.harvard.edu. A leading civil rights advocacy and research organization.

Mexican American Legal Defense and Educational Fund, 1717 K St., N.W., Suite 311, Washington, DC 20036; (202) 293-2828; www.maldef.org. Founded in 1968 in San Antonio, MALDEF is the leading nonprofit Latino litigation, advocacy and educational outreach organization.

NAACP Legal Defense and Educational Fund, Inc., 99 Hudson St., Suite 1600, New York, NY 10013; (212) 965-2200; www.naacpldf.org. The fund's nearly two-dozen attorneys litigate on education, economic access, affirmative action and criminal justice issues on behalf of African-Americans and others.

National School Boards Association, 1680 Duke St., Alexandria, VA 22314; (703) 838-6722; www.nsba.org. The association strongly supports school desegregation.

5

Black Colleges

Kenneth Jost

Atlanta's Morris Brown College is among several of the nation's 103 historically black colleges and universities (HBCUs) facing academic or financial troubles. While well-known schools like Spelman and Morehouse are thriving, all the nation's HBCUs struggle to survive with far fewer resources than predominantly white schools. Critics say HBCUs are anachronisms in the age of integration, but fervent supporters say they provide higher education and support to a neglected group of Americans.

From *CQ Researcher*,
December 12, 2003.

The recorded message on the Morris Brown College switchboard assures callers that the 118-year-old institution is "still open — renewing and rebuilding." But visitors to the Atlanta campus find a school with massive debts, no president, fewer than 75 students and a perilously uncertain future.

Morris Brown has been on the ropes since late 2002 when the Commission on Colleges of the Southern Association of Colleges and Schools (SACS) revoked the school's accreditation because of financial mismanagement. Student enrollment — 2,700 — dropped by more than half within a month and plummeted further after a SACS appeals panel in April rejected Morris Brown's effort to overturn the revocation.

Since then, the school's athletic program has been eliminated, all classrooms and offices consolidated into a single building and the few remaining students told to settle accounts for the current semester before enrolling in the next. Meanwhile, a transition team is trying to devise a plan to repay the school's $27 million debt, including $5.4 million that the U.S. Department of Education says is owed for mishandled student-loan funds.

Among the school's financial mistakes: handing out scholarships without the funds to pay them, giving laptop computers to all students and applying for membership in the NCAA's elite Division I-A for intercollegiate athletics — an expensive proposition even for big state schools. "They didn't think thoroughly and clearly in terms of the financial impact," says Adam Gibbs, a former Bank of America executive now serving on a three-member transition team seeking to keep Morris Brown alive.

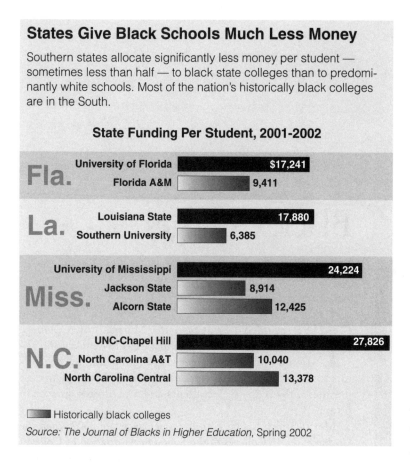

States Give Black Schools Much Less Money

Southern states allocate significantly less money per student — sometimes less than half — to black state colleges than to predominantly white schools. Most of the nation's historically black colleges are in the South.

State Funding Per Student, 2001-2002

Fla.
- University of Florida: $17,241
- Florida A&M: 9,411

La.
- Louisiana State: 17,880
- Southern University: 6,385

Miss.
- University of Mississippi: 24,224
- Jackson State: 8,914
- Alcorn State: 12,425

N.C.
- UNC-Chapel Hill: 27,826
- North Carolina A&T: 10,040
- North Carolina Central: 13,378

☐ Historically black colleges

Source: The Journal of Blacks in Higher Education, Spring 2002

Several other schools reportedly have financial problems serious enough to threaten sanctions from the accreditation body. [2]

More broadly, all of the nation's HBCUs — founded primarily during the late 19th and early 20th centuries — continue their ongoing struggle to survive with far less in financial and other resources than predominantly white colleges and universities, private or public. All told, the 103 HBCUs have endowments totaling about $1.6 billion — less than one-tenth of the $19 billion endowment held by Harvard University alone, the nation's wealthiest institution of higher learning. And in the Southern and Border states, which traditionally maintained dual systems of higher education, states continue to fund public black colleges at significantly lower rates than predominantly white schools — with white schools sometimes receiving more than twice as much per student as the black schools. (*See chart, p. 106.*)

The loss of accreditation was the final blow. The decision meant that Morris Brown students were no longer eligible for federal student loans, which account for a major part of the private school's revenues. "Once we lost accreditation, our survival was put in doubt," says Gibbs.

Morris Brown is among several of the nation's 103 historically black colleges and universities — widely referred to as HBCUs — undergoing high levels of financial, managerial or academic stress. Mary Holmes College — a private, two-year institution in West Point, Miss. — closed its doors in September after losing accreditation in December 2002, and more than 20 other black colleges have closed over the years. [1]

Meanwhile, Clark Atlanta University, which along with Morris Brown is part of a consortium of six Atlanta-based black schools, sent layoff notices to 157 non-tenured faculty members in August after incurring a $7.5 million budget deficit in the previous academic year.

Despite such challenges, fervent supporters of black colleges and universities tout historical legacies and current accomplishments to justify the schools' continued existence in the post-segregation era. By offering higher education to a "neglected, oppressed and segregated group of American citizens," HBCUs have been a "major force by which some of the disparity which exists among the races has been solved," says Frederick Humphries, president of the National Association for Equal Opportunity in Higher Education (NAFEO), which comprises virtually all of the historically black institutions.

William Gray — president of the United Negro College Fund (UNCF) — notes that HBCUs represent only 3 percent of the nation's 3,000-plus colleges and universities but account for nearly a third of the country's black college graduates each year. "If an educational institution is producing outstanding graduates and leaders who are helping make America strong, then it's worth having," says Gray, whose organization raises funds for 39 private member HBCUs.

The roster of HBCU alumni indeed includes some impressive names: from prominent government officials and well-known entertainers to high-profile journalists and top-ranked professional athletes. (*See chart, p. 109.*) Overall statistics, however, are less impressive. Some of the schools graduate fewer than one-third of the students in their entering classes. And graduation rates at even the most prestigious black institutions fall short of comparable figures for black students attending the most elite predominantly white schools. (*See chart, p. 107.*)

Some critics say the figures show that African American students who attend HBCUs lose more than they gain from the choice. "There is a certain amount of comfort at some of these institutions," says Gerald Foster, a professor of social work at historically black Virginia Union University in Richmond. "But what you give up is a certain amount of academic quality."

Graduation Rates Are Lower at Black Colleges

Black students at most top white colleges graduate at a higher rate than those who attend most black colleges. Administrators at black colleges point out that African Americans at elite white schools are often the second and third generations of their families to go to college, while students at black colleges are often the first.

Percentage of Black Students Who Graduate
(at selected colleges in 2002)

At Predominantly White Institutions		At Historically Black Institutions	
Amherst	93%	Spelman	76%
Harvard	92	Morehouse	63
Princeton	91	Fisk	59
Yale	87	Hampton	52
Wellesley	86	Howard	48
Dartmouth	86	Tuskegee	48
Georgetown	85	Florida A&M	44
MIT	81	North Carolina A&T	44
Grinnell	75	Tennessee State	42
Oberlin	66	Bennett	37
UNC-Chapel Hill	65	Grambling State	31
UC-Berkeley	65	Jackson State	31
UCLA	64	Cheyney	28
University of Michigan	61	Virginia Union	21
Carnegie Mellon	60	Texas Southern	10
Bates	59	University of D.C.	6

Source: The Journal of Blacks in Higher Education, Autumn 2002

Foster, author of a confrontational critique, *Is There a Conspiracy to Keep Black Colleges Open?*, believes racially identifiable schools have outlived their usefulness. "The whole purpose of civil rights was to get beyond the issue of segregation," says Foster, who is African American and earned degrees from Virginia Union and Howard University in Washington, D.C.

Some leading opponents of racial preferences — both black and white — also question the HBCUs' reasons for being. "These colleges were formed out of necessity," says Ward Connerly, president of the Sacramento-based American Civil Rights Institute, which opposes racial and gender preferences.

"From the standpoint of public policy, I have to think that they are an idea whose time has come and probably gone," at least with regard to public funding. Connerly,

who is African American, authored Proposition 209, the 1996 California initiative that barred racial preferences in admissions in the state's university system.

Roger Clegg, general counsel for the Center for Equal Opportunity, agrees. "Everyone would welcome the day when the rationale for historically black colleges would no longer apply," Clegg says, "when a special nurturing environment is no longer necessary, the problems of the inner city are not racially defined and where there are lots of institutions [focusing] on the contributions of a wide variety of different racial and ethnic groups." Clegg, who is white, has filed friend-of-the-court briefs opposing racial preferences on behalf of the center in several major cases.

President Bush and other administration officials, however, strongly support the HBCUs. Bush called for increased federal funding for HBCUs during his 2000 campaign. Education Secretary Roderick Paige, who is African American and a graduate of historically black Jackson State University in Mississippi, credits the HBCUs with helping narrow the continuing gap between college attendance and graduation rates for white and black students. "The situation would be much worse without our historically black colleges and universities," Paige told the Mississippi Association of Colleges recently. [3]

"Historically, they've done a better job of educating African American students to productive roles in American society," says Wilbert Bryant, executive director of the White House Initiative on Historically Black Colleges and Universities. "I don't think this nation would be the same without the large numbers of African American leaders that HBCUs have produced."

Bush has fallen short, however, in fulfilling his campaign pledge to raise federal aid to HBCUs by 77 percent over five years. [4] And bills to provide targeted aid for black colleges had mixed results in Congress. A proposal to provide computers stalled, and funding for historic preservation passed, but at less than the requested amount. (*See sidebar, p. 116.*) But prominent African Americans — many of them HBCU alumni — are rallying to raise funds for struggling black colleges. In August, nationally syndicated radio host Tom Joyner, a graduate of Alabama's Tuskegee University, donated $1 million in scholarship funds for students at embattled Morris Brown.

As the fundraising continues, and as black colleges and universities grapple with the challenges of an increasingly competitive academic environment, here are some of the major questions being debated:

Do historically black colleges and universities still serve a useful purpose?

When William Allen was about to become executive director of Virginia's higher-education policymaking panel in June 1998, the conservative African American suggested in a newspaper interview that it was time to reconsider the role of historically black colleges and institutions. "It's always important for people to go back and review their inheritance to see if it's what they want to embrace," Allen, an opponent of racial preferences in college admissions, told *The Washington Post.*

His comment immediately drew sharp criticism from, among others, former Virginia Gov. L. Douglas Wilder, himself an alumnus of Virginia Union University. In a

quick retreat, Allen told the *Post* the next day that he had a record of supporting historically black colleges and had no plans to review the status of the two black universities in the state system. [5]

The episode indicates both the strong support for historically black colleges among their alumni and the combative reaction from alumni and other supporters to any suggestion that the institutions are no longer needed. UNCF President Gray counters the idea by emphasizing that religiously founded schools survive today even though overt discrimination against Jews, Catholics and Mormons has largely disappeared.

"I'll close Morehouse and say it's no longer needed when you close Notre Dame," Gray says. "I'll close Spelman and say that it's no longer needed when you close Brigham Young."

Gray and other HBCU supporters insist the schools still serve a vital purpose by providing educational opportunities for all types of students — but, in particular, for African American students from economically or educationally disadvantaged backgrounds. "Some of the youngsters who are educated out of the urban inner cities or from rural, poor Southern roots would not have access to a college education but for the existence of an Alcorn or Tuskegee," says Walter Allen, a professor of sociology at UCLA.

As a result, supporters say, black colleges provide greater socioeconomic diversity than many or most predominantly white schools, mixing students whose parents are professionals with sons and daughters of tenant farmers. "This is very important learning in an increasingly globalized society," says Charles Willie, professor emeritus at Harvard's Graduate School of Education.

But Connerly, who served on the University of California Board of Regents, opposes any public funding for racially identified schools. "We as taxpayers ought to be providing the funding for our kids to get an education that is free from any consideration of race," Connerly says. "If they want to make [black colleges] a privately financed enterprise, God speed. [But] I don't personally ascribe to the rationale."

Supporters of HBCUs, however, deny that black colleges are themselves promoting racial separation. They note that HBCUs have never excluded whites, and in fact today have a higher percentage of white students (13 percent) and white faculty (28 percent) than comparable statistics for black students and faculty at predominantly

A Who's Who of HBCU Graduates

Some of the leading figures in the African American civil rights movement graduated from historically black colleges and universities, including Booker T. Washington (Tuskegee), W.E.B. DuBois (Fisk), Thurgood Marshall (Lincoln University of Pennsylvania, Howard Law School) and the Rev. Martin Luther King Jr. (Morehouse). Today, prominent HBCU alumni can be found in many walks of public life:

Politics and Government

Mfume

Paige

Kweisi Mfume, president, NAACP (Morgan State)

L. Douglas Wilder, former Va. governor (Virginia Union)

The Rev. Jesse L. Jackson Sr., president, Rainbow Coalition (North Carolina A&T)

Rod Paige, U.S. secretary of Education (Jackson State)

Vernon Jordan, attorney/lobbyist (Howard)

Henry Frye, former N.C. chief justice (North Carolina A&T)

Andrew Young, human-rights activist (Howard)

Marian Wright Edelman, president, Children's Defense Fund (Spelman)

Hazel O'Leary, former U.S. secretary of Energy (Fisk)

Steve Bullock, former acting president, American Red Cross (Virginia Union)

Arts and Entertainment

Lee

Winfrey

Spike Lee, film director (Morehouse)

Oprah Winfrey, media entrepreneur (Tennessee State)

Leontyne Price, opera singer (Central State)

Lionel Richie, singer/musician (Tuskegee)

Erykah Badu, singer (Grambling State)

Keenen Ivory Wayans, actor/director (Tuskegee)

Keshia Knight Pulliam, actress (Spelman)

Ossie Davis, actor/director (Howard)

Samuel L. Jackson, actor (Morehouse)

Sean "P Diddy" Combs, rap artist/producer (Howard)

All photos by Getty Images

Source: HBCUNetwork.Com

Science and Medicine

Satcher

David Satcher, U.S. surgeon general (Morehouse)

Jocelyn Elders, former U.S. surgeon general (Philander Smith)

Ronald McNair, astronaut (North Carolina A&T)

Alvin H. Crawford, director, pediatric orthopedics, Cincinnati Children's Hospital Medical Center (Tennessee State)

Louis Sullivan, former U.S. secretary of Health and Human Services; founder and former president, Morehouse School of Medicine (Morehouse)

Levi Watkins Jr., cardiac surgeon/associate dean, John Hopkins University (Tennessee State)

Journalism, Literature and Publishing

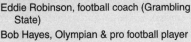

Morrison

Earl Graves, magazine publisher (Morgan State)

Ed Bradley, CBS News (Cheyney State)

Tony Brown, journalist (West Virginia State)

Toni Morrison, novelist (Howard)

Alice Walker, novelist (Morgan State)

Athletics

Rice

Eddie Robinson, football coach (Grambling State)

Bob Hayes, Olympian & pro football player (Florida A&M)

Edwin Moses, Olympic athlete and physicist (Morehouse)

Jerry Rice, pro football player (Mississippi Valley State)

Lou Brock, pro baseball player (Southern University A&M)

Walter Payton, pro football player (Jackson State)

---

white institutions. HBCUs "are diverse and integrated — more racially diverse than predominantly white institutions," Gray says.

For his part, Virginia Union's Foster forcefully makes a separate accusation of academic inferiority against what he depicts as the middle and bottom tiers of HBCUs. "There

Black Colleges Have Smaller Endowments

The United Negro College Fund's 39 member institutions had an average endowment of $22 million in 2001. By contrast, the average predominantly white American college had $340 million in 2002.

Market Value of Endowments
(in $ thousands)

Institution	Endowment Value (in 2000-2001)
Spelman	$228,993
Morehouse	100,325
Tuskegee	54,356
Dillard	42,920
Clark Atlanta	31,557
Xavier of LA	29,666
Stillman	24,045
Morris Brown	15,646
Fisk	13,533
Virginia Union	12,741
Bennett	11,322
Talladega	4,329

Source: United Negro College Fund

is an ethos of academic and administrative mediocrity," he writes, "that maintains and sustains an inefficient status quo of fifty years ago and drives away bright, young, energetic faculty who are ostracized rather than embraced."

Foster says the "top-tier" black schools "can compete on par with any other school of similar mission." But some of the lower-ranked schools, he says, may have outlived their usefulness. "The only thing that they're hanging their hat on is that they're black," Foster says. "That's ludicrous."

Supporters of HBCUs sharply dispute the critique. Black colleges "have been superlative with regard to the quality of teaching," says NAFEO President Humphries. "They had to be good teachers with what they had to work with. They might not have had as many resources

as the rest of higher education, but nothing has been slack about the teaching."

Asked if black colleges measure up to white schools, Professor Allen replies, "Absolutely." HBCUs are "underresourced" and might not compare favorably in terms of lab facilities or the like, he says. But, he adds, "Many of those colleges produce a better product in terms of black students because they have a core of dedicated teachers who believe in the capabilities and potential of those students and who motivate those students to succeed."

In any event, says Christopher Brown, an associate professor at Pennsylvania State University's Center for the Study of Higher Education currently on leave to work at UNCF's Frederick D. Patterson Research Institute, HBCUs have become an essential component of U.S. higher education.

"Those institutions play a tremendous role in the production of students, irrespective of race, and they play a tremendous role in the production in terms of race," Brown says. "If we remove these institutions, it would not be possible for the remaining institutions to absorb those students."

Do African American students benefit from attending a predominantly black college?

When white Americans think about historically black colleges, they naturally focus on the schools' distinctive racial identity. But for many African Americans attending HBCUs, race becomes a non-issue — perhaps for the first and maybe the only time in their lives.

"Because the vast majority of students are African American, it becomes less and less of an issue in daily interaction," says Christopher Elders, a Morehouse graduate studying at Oxford University in England this year as a Rhodes scholar. "You forget that everybody around you is African American."

HBCU supporters say that experience gives African American students both comfort and self-confidence. "The schools have always had to do a job of weeding out from the minds of black students that they were second-class citizens," Humphries says. "All they need is opportunity and a fair set of conditions, and they'll do as well as anybody else. But they need to be in an environment where people believe in them."

Critics, however, question both rationales. "In this nation, we're not supposed to get our comfort from being around people with the same melanin content as ourselves," Connerly says.

Foster says HBCUs "are harming more than they are benefiting students because [the schools] are not preparing them for what they will confront when they graduate."

Supporters of black colleges contrast the environment on HBCU campuses with the African American students' experiences at predominantly white schools. Black students "get to an integrated school and find they're segregated by race anyway," says Reginald Stuart, a graduate of Tennessee State University in Nashville and a longtime reporter, now a corporate recruiter with Knight Ridder Newspapers.

Work by two researchers published in the early 1990s does suggest that African American students fare better in many respects at HBCUs than at predominantly white schools, according to Laura Perna, an assistant professor of education policy at the University of Maryland in College Park. Perna, who is white and formerly worked at UNCF's Patterson Research Institute, says the researchers concluded that African American students who attend predominantly black schools experience "less social isolation, less alienation, less personal dissatisfaction and less personal racism than African Americans who attend predominantly white institutions." [6]

But Foster disputes the idea that black students generally have problems at predominantly white campuses. "If you find yourself in a campus environment that is so stressful or distressful," he says, "one would raise questions why you would stay there. Sometimes it's easier to stay, to assume victim status. That provides an excuse for you not to excel."

HBCU supporters also say the schools do a better job than predominantly white institutions of tailoring instruction and curricula to the needs of black students, many of whom come to college with weak educational backgrounds. Black colleges "continue to offer customized teaching for the African American student," says Komanduri Murty, a professor of sociology at Clark Atlanta and co-author of a 1993 study of HBCUs. "They get a lot of special attention that they would not get in other schools." [7]

Foster views this so-called "remediation" rationale less favorably. He says many of the lower-tier HBCUs admit far too many students who do not belong in college at all and are accepted only because they bring federal aid to the schools. "In this millennium," he writes, "there is

Spelman College in Atlanta is among only three HBCUs with an endowment valued in excess of $100 million, as of 2001. Black colleges have far smaller endowments than predominantly white private schools.

neither need nor reason for substandard, mediocre colleges — black or white." [8]

Some HBCU supporters concede that black students do make some tradeoffs by attending a black college. "You will get football, but you won't get the Rose Bowl," says Brown of the Patterson Institute. But, he adds, "In terms of the academics, more often than not, you're going to gain."

UCLA Professor Allen, who is black but attended predominantly white schools, acknowledges that black students may fare better in wealth and prestige by choosing an elite white school over one of the best black colleges. On those factors, Allen says, "Harvard trumps everywhere in the country." But, he adds, "If your emphasis is on social and other cultural indicators, Harvard loses out."

Rhodes scholar Elders, however, says he has no doubts about picking Morehouse over a predominantly white college. "The ultimate outcome of a successful education at a black school is that there's a real sense of security in your identity," he says. "There was no illusion that the rest of the world was like Morehouse. Everyone is aware that this is one aspect of their lives but not a microcosm for the rest of the world."

After studying the history of the Cold War at Oxford, Elders expects to return to the United States for law school and a public policy-oriented career. He says he has no concerns that his Morehouse degree leaves him at a disadvantage. "I couldn't imagine being in a better position than I am right now," he says.

Should the federal government increase support for historically black colleges?

Students leaving for college today pack many of the same things that their parents took with them a generation earlier; but at least half arrive on campus with something new: desktop or notebook computers. [9]

Computers are less widespread, however, at the nation's historically black colleges and universities. A Commerce Department survey in 2000 found that only a quarter of the students at the nation's HBCUs owned personal computers. The study was based on survey replies from three-fourths of America's HBCUs. [10]

To remedy what the study called "a digital-divide issue," HBCU supporters on Capitol Hill are pushing a bill to authorize $250 million per year for five years in targeted aid to historically black and other minority-serving colleges and universities. Before the bill stalled in a dispute over which agency should administer the program, it had drawn opposition from groups opposed to racial preferences.

The bill "uses racial classifications to address a problem that is not limited to institutions or individuals of a particular racial identity," Clegg and Connerly wrote in a July 29 letter to Sen. George Allen, R-Va., chief sponsor of the Senate bill. They proposed a rewritten version with neutral criteria that they said would nevertheless probably funnel most of the proposed funds to HBCUs. [11]

For HBCU supporters, however, the episode demonstrates the continuing need to remedy more than a century of underfunding of higher education for black Americans. "It's hard to overcome the historical advantage that white schools had," says NAFEO's Humphries. "There is a historical inadequacy that is going to take a long time to make up."

The financial gap results not only from historical inequities but also from present-day disadvantages, according to Gray of the UNCF and other HBCU supporters. HBCUs have to keep tuitions relatively low to be affordable to middle- and lower-income black families. Tuition at prestigious private black schools such as Morehouse College in Atlanta or Hampton University in Virginia is below $10,000 per year — significantly less than $26,854, the average tuition at private, predominately white schools today.

In addition, although firm figures are hard to come by, most studies show that lower percentages of African American graduates donate to their alma maters than alumni from predominantly white institutions. And, with a few notable exceptions — such as media entrepreneur Oprah Winfrey or magazine publisher Earl Graves Jr. — HBCU alumni lack the wealth to support their alma maters with the kind of six- or seven-figure contributions that predominantly white colleges sometimes receive from well-heeled alumni.

Initially, HBCUs sent a disproportionate number of graduates into lower-paying professions like teaching and academics — a legacy of their early mission of promoting basic education for African American students. Today more HBCU graduates are going into more lucrative professions such as business, law and medicine, but until recently their incomes were still limited because they primarily served black clienteles.

With limited alumni giving, HBCUs have been unable to amass endowments anywhere near those of predominantly white colleges and universities. Only three HBCUs had endowments valued in excess of $100 million as of 2001: Spelman, Morehouse and Howard. As Gray notes, a $1 billion endowment, even if conservatively invested, can spin off $50 million in income without any fundraising effort by the school's president or office of development.

"A black college president is trying to do a lot with practically nothing," Gray concludes. "They have to depend on fees, tuitions [federal aid] to make ends meet — unless they're public, and even then they don't get a fair share from the state legislatures."

In fact, a recent compilation shows that the predominantly white flagship state universities in nine states studied received as much as three times more per student than the historically black state schools. For example, the University of Florida in Gainesville received $17,241 per student per year compared to $9,411 for Florida A&M University in Tallahassee, one of the most prestigious of the public HBCUs. North Carolina A&T State University in Greensboro, another high-profile black school, received $10,040 per student — less than half the comparable figure of $27,826 for the University of North Carolina at Chapel Hill. (*See chart, p. 106.*) [12]

HBCU supporters are working to increase private and public support. Gray, who is resigning the UNCF post at the end of the year, has energized the center's fundraising over the past 10 years with glitzy events featuring black celebrities such as singer Lou Rawls. But he and other HBCU supporters say the federal government needs to do more. Specifically, they call for making Pell Grants available to all low-income students, increasing targeted funding for HBCUs under the so-called Title III program created in 1986, and helping HBCUs gain a greater share of federal research grants.

President Bush's budget requests have fallen short of his campaign promise to raise federal aid to HBCUs by 77 percent over five years. Since he took office in 2000, federal aid for historically black colleges — initially authorized under Title IIIB of the Higher Education Amendments of 1986 — has risen only 20 percent, from $230 million to the $277 million proposed for fiscal 2004. [13]

BACKGROUND

Separate and Unequal

Blacks had few opportunities for education at any level in the United States before the Civil War and only limited opportunities during the century of racial segregation that prevailed after the abolition of slavery in 1863. The segregated school systems, however, included fledgling black colleges — first private and later public institutions — that evolved by the mid-20th century into an important avenue of educational advancement for African Americans. [14]

Before the Civil War, African Americans, whether slave or free, were restricted from higher education by law in the South and — with limited exceptions — by social custom elsewhere. Blacks were admitted at only a few white colleges — notably, Berea in Kentucky and Oberlin in Ohio. Five of today's historically black colleges can trace their roots to the antebellum period, but only one — Wilberforce University in Ohio, founded in 1843 by the African Methodist Episcopal Church — actually awarded baccalaureate degrees before the Civil War. * All told, only 28 blacks received college degrees in the United States before 1861.

After the Civil War, missionary and church groups rushed to the South to lay the foundations for an educational system for the largely illiterate population of freed black slaves. By the end of the 19th century, more than 60 educational institutions for blacks had been founded, thanks to the efforts of Northern missionary societies, philanthropists and federal and state governments.

Although some schools, such as Fisk, had college departments from early on, most remained little more than elementary and secondary schools until the 1900s. For instance, Hampton, founded in 1868, did not award its first college degree until 1922. The differences between the early black and white colleges resulted from the black schools' limited financial resources, black students' limited educational preparation and deliberate decisions by Southern states to provide vocational instead of liberal arts curricula for black students.

Many of today's leading black private schools were established during this period and began as church-supported schools that emphasized training of ministers and teachers. Among those early church-funded schools were Atlanta University (1865), Fisk (1866), Talladega (1867) and Tougaloo (1868), all founded by the American Missionary Association; Hampton and Morehouse (1867) were supported by the American Baptist Home Mission.

The church groups had the support of the Freedmen's Bureau, the federal agency established to help the former slave population. The bureau itself started Howard University, chartered by Congress in 1867 and named after the bureau's commissioner, General O. O. Howard. But the bureau drew the wrath of Southern politicians and was abolished in 1872.

After the bureau's demise, some Southern and Border states began to establish separate public schools for blacks. Paradoxically, the movement was spurred in part by the Second Morrill Act of 1890, which prohibited federal aid to state systems that discriminated against blacks in tax-supported education. Within a decade, 17 of 19 Southern and Border states had responded to the law by establishing parallel higher-education systems for whites and blacks. Although the two systems were separate, they were demonstrably unequal. Virtually all of the public black colleges began as "normal" or "industrial" schools, and none initially offered baccalaureate degrees. They also received less state aid per student than their predominantly white counterparts — a tradition that continues to this day.

---

* The four other schools included the abolitionist-founded Institute for Colored Youth (1837, now Cheyney University) and the Ashmun Institute (1854, now Lincoln University), both now parts of the Pennsylvania state higher education system; the District of Columbia Teachers College (1851, merged in 1975 into the University of the District of Columbia); and St. Louis Normal College for Women (1856, now Harris-Stowe State College).

C H R O N O L O G Y

1901-1950 *Segregated black colleges and universities advance but still lag far behind white schools; first efforts to challenge racial segregation in courts.*

1928 Southern Association of Colleges and Schools (SACS) agrees to consider accrediting black institutions.

1944 United Negro College Fund (UNCF) formed, with 29 members.

1950 Supreme Court rules black students' rights violated by unequal treatment at state post-graduate schools in Oklahoma, Texas.

1951-1980 *Desegregation era; efforts begin to dismantle dual systems of public colleges and universities.*

1954 Supreme Court rules racial segregation in elementary and secondary schools unconstitutional; applies ruling to higher education two years later.

1964 Civil Rights Act of 1964 bars discrimination in federally funded programs by state and local governments (Title VI); Department of Health, Education and Welfare (HEW) cites provision in orders to 10 states in 1968 and 1969 to submit plans to dismantle dual systems of higher education.

1967 Harvard sociologists David Riesman and Christopher Jencks describe most black colleges as "academically inferior"; supporters of black colleges call critique inaccurate.

1970 Civil rights groups sue HEW to make states dismantle dual systems of higher education (*Adams v. Richardson*); three years later judge orders states to "eliminate vestiges of racial dualism."

1972 UNCF launches "A mind is a terrible thing to waste" public-awareness campaign.

1977 Federal court orders white University of Tennessee at Nashville to merge with historically black Tennessee State University.

1978 HEW develops desegregation criteria for state higher-education systems calling for desegregation of faculty, elimination of duplicative programs.

1980s *Higher-education desegregation suits falter. . . . Federal aid voted for historically black colleges and universities (HBCUs). . . . Enrollment at HBCUs declines.*

1986 Congress authorizes direct aid for HBCUs in Title III of Higher Education Amendments; funding initially set at $100 million, $5 million for black graduate institutions.

1987 Federal judge dismisses higher-education desegregation suit, saying plaintiffs lacked legal standing.

1990s *HBCU enrollment levels off.*

1992 Researchers find favorable social effects for African American students attending black colleges. . . . Supreme Court says states must take affirmative steps to dismantle dual systems of public higher education.

1996 Congress authorizes $29 million over five years for historic preservation at HBCUs.

2000-present *Many black colleges in trouble over finances.*

2000 GOP presidential candidate George W. Bush promises 77 percent increase in funding over five years for HBCUs; budget proposals as president fall short of promise.

2001 Southern Association of Colleges and Schools places three black colleges — Grambling State, Bennett and Talladega — on probation for financial irregularities.

2002 Morris Brown and Mary Holmes colleges lose accreditation due to inadequate financing.

2003 Mary Holmes College closes; Morris Brown opens fall semester with fewer than 75 students, works on plan to refinance debt and seek reaccreditation in 2004 . . . Bennett, Grambling, Talladega win lifting of probation.

The Supreme Court gave its legal blessing to mandatory racial segregation with its infamous 1896 decision, *Plessy v. Ferguson*, upholding a Louisiana law requiring separation of black and white passengers on railways. A decade later, the high court also sanctioned racial segregation in higher education. The lesser-known ruling in *Berea College v. Kentucky* (1908) upheld a state law that made it a crime to teach black and white students in the same school. [15]

By the turn of the century, private black colleges had awarded more than 1,100 baccalaureate degrees. In the early 1900s they began attracting significant financial support from white philanthropic organizations — notably, the Carnegie and Rockefeller foundations, the Peabody Education Fund, the Slater Fund and the Julius Rosenwald Fund. Despite the Morrill Act's anti-discrimination provision, however, black public colleges were significantly underfunded compared to white schools. A decade after enactment, white schools were reportedly receiving appropriations 26 times greater than black schools. [16]

Opening Doors

The legal battle against racial segregation began with court cases that successfully challenged discriminatory treatment of black students in higher education. The focus turned to elementary and secondary education, however, after the Supreme Court's historic 1954 decision outlawing segregation in public schools. Only in the 1970s did civil rights groups mount comparably broad challenges to the dual systems of higher education. Those cases left the separate black and white public colleges standing, but reduced some of the funding disparities that had disadvantaged the historically black schools.

The NAACP first focused on higher education in the 1930s as a glaring example of racial inequality and as a politically less explosive area than elementary and secondary education. The strategy yielded an initial victory in 1938 when the high court, by a 6-2 vote, ruled that the state of Missouri had violated black student Lloyd Gaines's equal-protection rights by offering to pay his tuition at an out-of-state law school rather than admit him to the state's all-white law school. The court went further in a pair of rulings in 1950, which ruled separate but evidently unequal treatment of black students unconstitutional. In one case, Texas sought to avoid admitting a black student to the University of Texas Law

School by creating a new all-black school; in the other, the University of Oklahoma admitted a black graduate student but assigned him to a special seat in the classroom and special tables in the library and cafeteria. [17]

The high court unanimously jettisoned the "separate but equal" doctrine for elementary and secondary education in its 1954 decision, *Brown v. Board of Education*. A year later, the court said in the so-called *Brown II* decision that public school systems did not need to desegregate immediately.

But in a higher-education case in 1956, the court said that no delay was allowed in admitting qualified black applicants to graduate professional schools on the same basis as white applicants. [18]

None of the higher-education decisions, however, addressed the status of the historically black public colleges and universities. That issue lay largely dormant until 1964 when Congress — in Title VI of the Civil Rights Act — prohibited racial discrimination by any state or local governmental program that received federal funding. [19] The Office of Civil Rights of the Department of Health, Education and Welfare (HEW) did not draw up regulations to enforce the law, but in 1968 and 1969 it ordered 10 states with dual higher-education systems to draft plans to dismantle the separate systems and create unitary systems in their place. Five states submitted plans deemed unacceptable; five others ignored the order. But the department failed to initiate enforcement proceedings against any of them.

Civil rights groups responded with a broad suit in 1970 aimed at requiring HEW to enforce Title VI. [20] The suit — filed in the name of Kenneth Adams, a black Mississippi student, against HEW Secretary Elliott Richardson — lasted for nearly 20 years but ultimately produced only limited effects. In an initial ruling, a federal judge in Washington in 1973 not only ordered HEW to enforce the law but also directed the 10 states "to eliminate the vestiges of racial dualism" in higher education. NAFEO replied with a friend-of-the-court brief that argued for correcting disparities but preserving the public black colleges as separate institutions.

In response to a second ruling, HEW in 1978 developed criteria that called on the states to desegregate faculty at both white and black schools and to reduce or eliminate programs at white schools that duplicated similar programs at nearby black schools. By the 1980s, however, enforcement slowed to a near halt. And in

Historic Buildings Get Little Help

In the years immediately after its founding in 1866, Fisk University was barely able to stay afloat. To raise funds, the Nashville school hit on the idea of sending the grandly named, 11-member Jubilee Singers on a European tour.

The tours — lasting from 1871 to 1878 — helped popularize the African American spiritual and ensure the survival of one of the oldest of the nation's historically black colleges and universities (HBCUs). Some of the money raised was used to build Jubilee Hall, the first permanent structure built expressly for black education in the South and still the centerpiece of the campus.

Despite its historic importance, Jubilee Hall deteriorated over the years — the victim of deferred maintenance by a university perennially low on cash. In spring 2003, however, the building re-emerged with its past glory after a multimillion-dollar renovation financed by a $4 million grant from the federal government and a matching anonymous gift. [1]

Fisk is one of the fortunate few among black universities that have been able to take on major renovations of historic buildings in advanced states of decay or disrepair. In a federal government survey in 1998, HBCUs identified 712 historically significant properties in need of restoration, at a total estimated cost of $755 million. [2] About half were listed in the National Register of Historic Places. [3]

Two years earlier, Congress had signaled an interest in the issue by authorizing $29 million over five years to finance restoration at HBCUs as part of an omnibus National Parks bill. The legislation required colleges to match the federal funds on a 50-50 basis.

Officials at black colleges welcomed the funding but also called it inadequate. "We were quite enthusiastic about the [original] program, but it was never funded at a high enough level," David Swinton, president of Benedict College in South Carolina, remarked in late 2002. [4] Many schools also said the 50-50 match was difficult to meet.

Congress reauthorized the program in 2003 at $10 million per year for seven years. But the Interior Department appropriations bill signed into law provides only $3 million. However, the bill does lower the amount colleges must raise on their own to 30 percent.

Bea Smith, vice president for government affairs at the National Association for Equal Opportunity in Higher Education (NAFEO), says the money will help but still falls short of the need. NAFEO had recommended an initial appropriation of $60 million.

"The needs were so great that we would like a large amount of money," Smith says. "Even at that, it was not going to address all the needs. We're concerned about the deferred maintenance. Many schools have buildings that are very much at risk."

"America's historically black colleges and universities have provided a strong foundation upon which generations of young African Americans have built their lives," says Richard Moe, president of the National Trust for Historic Preservation. "But now, those foundations are deteriorating. We need to take immediate action to preserve not just the historic structures that grace these campuses but also the important legacy of the schools themselves — the dreams they fulfill through the education they provide."

---

[1] For coverage, see Gail Kerr, "Jubilee Hall Renovation Breathes Life Into Fisk," *The* [Nashville] *Tennessean*, Nov. 18, 2002, p. 1B; The Associated Press, "Fisk Receives $4 Million Anonymous Donation to Renovate Historic Buildings," May 4, 2002.

[2] U.S. General Accounting Office, "Historic Preservation: Cost to Restore Historic Properties at Historically Black Colleges and Universities," February 1998 (GAO/RCED-98-51). For background, see Jacqueline Conciatore, "Fighting to Preserve Black History," *Black Issues in Higher Education*, July 20, 2000, p. 18.

[3] Conciatore, *ibid.*

[4] Quoted in Charles Dervarics, "HBCU Preservation Bill Dies in Congress," *Black Issues in Higher Education*, Dec. 19, 2002, p. 6.

1987 the court dismissed the case on the ground that the plaintiffs lacked legal standing to bring the suit.

Four higher-education desegregation suits in individual states also lasted for decades, with somewhat limited results. [21] In Tennessee, a federal court in 1977 ordered the merger of historically black Tennessee State University (TSU) in Nashville with the University of Tennessee at Nashville, a smaller school with a largely white and predominantly part-time student body. The ruling marks the only instance when a white school has been merged into an HBCU.

Suits in Alabama, Louisiana and Mississippi took countless twists and turns from the late 1960s through the '90s. Federal courts handling the suits generally tried to establish unitary standards for admissions, promote racial diversity in faculty hiring and reduce financial disparities. Broader changes were beaten back in at least two instances: the proposed elimination of the governing board for historically black Southern University in Louisiana and the proposed closing of HBCU Mississippi Valley State University.

Settlements in some of the suits stipulate that the black public colleges try to increase the percentage of whites in the student body, but the schools have fallen short of the goals — even while giving white applicants preferential admissions or scholarships. Tennessee State, for example, was to increase white enrollment to 50 percent, but whites comprised only 15 percent of the student body in 2001. Mississippi's three black public universities were to become eligible for additional funding if they reached 10 percent white enrollment, but as of 2001 none had. [22]

The Supreme Court addressed the higher-education desegregation issues only once, in a 1992 decision in the Mississippi desegregation case. In its 8-1 ruling in *United States v. Fordice*, the court held that the adoption of race-neutral policies was not sufficient to dismantle the state's dual system of higher education — five historically white schools and three HBCUs. The justices sent the case back to lower federal courts to consider, among other steps, eliminating duplicative programs or possibly closing one or more of the schools.

In a significant concurring opinion, Justice Clarence Thomas, the court's only African American member, stressed that the ruling did not require the closure of historically black schools. "It would be ironic, to say the least, if the institutions that sustained blacks during segregation were themselves destroyed in an effort to combat its vestiges," he wrote. [23]

Debating Quality

The court battles over desegregation played out against a background debate in educational circles over the HBCUs' role and academic quality. The debate was touched off by an article written in 1967 by two Harvard University sociologists sharply criticizing historically black colleges as academically inferior. HBCU supporters said the critique was unfounded — based on anecdotes more than research — and ignored the schools' contributions under adverse circumstances.

The debate has roots in a pedagogical dispute that raged in the late 19th and early 20th centuries between the first two great proponents of black education: Booker T.

Both Courtesy of Morehouse College

Morehouse College in Atlanta boasts three Rhodes scholars in recent years, including political science majors Christopher Elders (left), who plans a career in public policy after law school, and Oluwabusayo Folarin, who hopes to work for the United Nations.

Washington and W.E.B. DuBois. Washington (1856-1915), who founded Tuskegee Institute in 1880, advocated industrial-arts education for blacks. Vocational training, he argued, was the best way for blacks to improve their lives without unnecessarily confronting the white power establishment. DuBois (1868-1963), a professor at Atlanta University and one of the founders of the NAACP, favored instead a liberal arts education for what he called "the talented tenth" of the black population. He viewed this intellectual elite as the key to blacks' advancement and regarded Washington's philosophy as amounting to acceptance of second-class status. [24]

The disagreement is today widely viewed as more theoretical than concrete and probably mattered less at the time than practical issues of funding, staffing and leadership. As a Department of Education overview relates, much of the instruction being offered at black colleges in the early 20th century was at the elementary or secondary level. [25] The schools were predominantly controlled by white administrators and teaching staffs, many of whom tended to be overly authoritarian toward students and accommodationist toward their local white communities. And — despite support from northern philanthropists — they were woefully underfunded.

Some gains began by the 1920s. Howard got its first black president in 1926. The Southern Association of Colleges and Schools agreed in 1928 to consider accreditation for black institutions. Despite the Great Depression, enrollment at HBCUs increased by 66 percent during the 1930s — outpacing the 36 percent rise for all colleges — while expenditures more than doubled after adjustment for inflation. And in an important financial development Tuskegee President Frederick D. Patterson called in 1943 for other black college presidents to join in cooperative fundraising. Patterson's initiative resulted in the formation the next year of the United Negro College Fund, with 27 member colleges at the time.

By mid-century, black colleges and universities were still largely invisible to the white educational community, even though they enrolled about 90 percent of all African American higher-education students. The schools drew attention in the 1950s and '60s as some of their students took part in the growing civil rights movement. North Carolina A&T students, for example, mounted the seminal Greensboro sit-in campaign in 1960. But the visibility came at the price of political disfavor and in some instances retaliation. The Louisiana legislature demanded that Southern University expel all students and fire all teachers taking part in the demonstrations. [26]

Unfavorable attention of a different sort came in 1967 when a leading education journal published an article, "The American Negro College," written by two well-regarded Harvard University sociologists: Christopher Jencks and David Riesman. [27] Jencks and Riesman were critical of segregation and insightful and sympathetic toward the black colleges' financial and political difficulties. Still, their central conclusion was that the majority of black colleges were — and were likely to remain — "academically inferior institutions . . . in terms of student aptitudes, faculty creativity and intellectual and moral ferment." They added that they had "the impression" that black colleges "do even less than comparable white colleges to remedy their students' academic inadequacies."

African Americans were "outraged" by the article, according to Marybeth Gasman, an assistant professor at the University of Pennsylvania's Graduate School of Education in Philadelphia. They said the article used little research and relied on anecdotes and hearsay, she recalls. Riesman, in fact, told an education conference in 1976 that his views had changed. In a book-length response two years after that, Harvard's Professor Willie insisted Jencks and Riesman had made an unfair comparison to white schools. The real question, Willie

wrote, was, "How have black colleges and universities done so much, so well, with so little?" Phasing out black schools, Willie added, "would be an academic disaster." [28]

The controversy spurred efforts to raise the HBCUs' profile and strengthen their finances. The UNCF in 1972 launched a public-awareness campaign with its now-famous slogan, "A mind is a terrible thing to waste." Two years later, the fund staged its first telethon, which evolved in 1979 into Lou Rawls' "Parade of Stars" — now called "An Evening of Stars" and set to mark its 25th anniversary in January 2004. The ongoing desegregation suits sought in part to increase states' financial support for the public black colleges and universities. And in 1986 Congress approved the first general federal-aid program for HBCUs. Title IIIB of the Higher Education Amendments of 1986 authorized $100 million for HBCUs and $5 million for historically black graduate and professional schools.

Researchers in the early 1990s painted a more favorable picture of HBCUs than Jencks and Riesman had done a quarter-century earlier. In a broad study of colleges, researchers Ernest Pascarella and Patrick Terenzini found that black students performed better academically at HBCUs than at white undergraduate schools. Similarly, they found that attendance at HBCUs had a more positive effect on later educational attainment than attendance at a white school. [29] Two professors at historically black Clark Atlanta University — Julian Roebuck and Komanduri Murty — reported similar findings following a survey of HBCUs. The result, they wrote, was "a growing conviction that HBCUs can best prepare black students for service and leadership roles in the black community." [30]

CURRENT SITUATION

Aiming High

Florida A&M officials were flying high when *Time* magazine designated it as "College of the Year" for the 1997-98 academic year. Five years after capturing the title on the strength of its academics, the nation's largest single-campus black university took aim this summer at another prestigious distinction. It began the expensive process of applying for membership in the NCAA's elite Division I-A of intercollegiate sports.

Suddenly, however, school spirit on the Tallahassee campus has turned from upbeat to downcast amid financial turmoil and high-level administrative buck-passing. The university's financial books are off by $1.8 million. The school needs $1.5 million to pay overdue bills. Students are getting financial aid months late. And the state's financial chief temporarily cut off checks for the university's president and 18 top administrators until they turned over financial records that were six weeks late.

"All of this has been a tremendous blow to the university," Jim Corbin, chairman of the school's board of trustees, told the *St. Petersburg Times* in late November. "I don't think there's any excuse for it." [31]

Florida A&M's fall from academic celebrity to notoriety provides only one example — if the most dramatic — of an array of financial and managerial problems besetting several of the nation's historically black colleges and universities in fall 2003. [32] Three schools — Grambling State University in Louisiana, Talladega University in Alabama and Bennett College, a private women's school in Greensboro, N.C. — learned on Dec. 9 that the Southern Association of Colleges and Schools had rewarded their efforts to work out years of financial mismanagement by lifting academic probation imposed by the accrediting body in December 2001. Other schools, however, are facing bearish financial conditions, managerial disorder or both.

To stave off what its trustees called a potential "disaster," Clark Atlanta University decided in October to close five academic programs: the School of Library and Information Studies, the Systems Sciences doctorate program and the departments of Engineering, International Affairs and Development and Allied Health Professions. The effort was aimed at turning the college's $7.5 million deficit into a surplus by summer 2004. The school — formed by the 1989 merger of undergraduate Clark College and Atlanta University, then exclusively a graduate institution — is reported to have no financial reserves, be $55 million in debt and have only a $30 million endowment that President Walter Broadnax calls "a pittance." [33]

In Nashville, Fisk University is seeking a new president following the sudden resignation of Carolyn Reid-Wallace in October after having held the position for less than two years. Reid-Wallace, a Fisk alumna, was the third president to lead the school — one of the best known of the nation's HBCUs — since 1996. Reid-Wallace gave no reason for her departure, but a member of the school's board of trustees who resigned the next day hinted that micromanagement by the board might have been to blame. "At some point the board must take a hard look at itself to understand why Fisk continues to have a succession of presidents," trustee Del Glover wrote in his resignation letter. [34]

Meanwhile, public HBCUs throughout the South are facing the same budget squeezes plaguing most other state colleges and universities. [35] In Alabama, Gov. Bob Riley, a Republican who unsuccessfully sought voter approval of a tax increase, is also cutting aid to private schools in an effort to close a projected $675 million deficit. The cuts would eliminate grants to three HBCUs: Tuskegee, which received $4.7 million from the state in fiscal 2003; Talladega, with $485,000 at stake; and Miles College, facing a loss of $347,000. Riley would also cut a $5 million program that provides $600 to any Alabaman attending a private school in the state — aid deemed especially important to students at black colleges. [36]

The turmoil at Florida A&M includes unsavory finger-pointing between the school's current leaders — Corbin and university president Fred Gainous — and the previous president, Humphries. In his 16 years as president, Humphries gained a reputation for raising funds from big corporations, winning government grants, promoting academic excellence and personally recruiting and befriending students. He prided himself on regularly vying with Harvard for the best record in enrolling African American students designated as National Achievement Scholars.

Gainous succeeded to the post after Humphries resigned in 2001 to become president of NAFEO, the association that represents black colleges and universities. Gainous took steps to deal with financial problems by firing some administrators and instituting greater accountability. Today, Corbin says Humphries "left the place in a financial mess," while Humphries denies any responsibility. "I left no problems for FAMU," he told the *St. Petersburg Times.*

Whoever is to blame, Gainous has now put his ambition for Florida A&M to move up into the top rank of intercollegiate sports on hold to deal with more pressing problems. "There still is a lot to be done to move the university forward," Gainous said in late November. "We must get our financial house in order."

Philip Neely/Fisk University

The 2003 academic year for freshmen at Fisk University begins with the fall convocation. Graduation rates are significantly lower for students at HBCUs than for blacks at predominantly white schools.

Saving Morris Brown

Friends of Morris Brown College are trying to raise millions of dollars to dig the 118-year-old school out of a financial hole, which many blame on unsustainable ambition and inattentive oversight. Today the school is a shell of its previous self, and leading experts on black colleges doubt its ability to survive.

"It's going to be a very uphill fight," says Gray, president of the UNCF. "The fiscal mismanagement that apparently occurred there was so deep, so large that I don't know how they're going to overcome it very quickly."

Morris Brown's problems stem primarily from what transition team member Gibbs acknowledges were "errors in judgment" by past administrations. But they also are rooted, to some extent, in the school's governance structure and in its historical mission of serving economically and educationally disadvantaged African American youths.

The college was founded in 1885 by leaders of the African Methodist Episcopal (AME) Church and remains today one of the few black institutions to have been established and operated under African American patronage. The school began by serving a constituency that was "unskilled, untrained, and economically unstable," the college says in an historical overview posted on its Web site. When the civil rights revolution came along in the

1960s, Morris Brown was ahead of other schools — both black and white — in serving disadvantaged youth. [37]

The school's Web site boasts a handful of prominent alumni, including the Rev. Hosea Williams, the late civil rights leader; and James McPherson, the Pulitzer Prize-winning historian of the Civil War. But the college's supporters emphasize above all Morris Brown's continuing commitment to serving students who — as transition team member Watson puts it — "don't test so well" or "sometimes aren't as prepared as they could be or should be."

That philosophy translated into an admissions policy that looked beyond an applicant's grades, test scores or ability to pay. [38] Grateful alumni sang the college's praises, but the school lacked the reputation of the other HBCUs that comprise the six-member Atlanta University Center. Morris Brown was the only one of the undergraduate institutions in the consortium that did not make *Black Enterprise* magazine's most recent list of top 50 colleges for African Americans. [39]

The college was also financially challenged. The school faced a possible shutdown in 1993 over a $10 million shortfall, averted only by $7 million in emergency fund-raising and $2 million in budget cuts. The financial squeeze was exacerbated by a series of ambitious moves by Dolores Cross, who served as the college's president from 1998 to 2002. Under Cross, the college increased enrollment, decided to buy laptops for all students, and sought to move into the NCAA's top-ranked Division I-A.

Over the years, the Negro College Fund provided $24 million in aid to the college even though Gray says he warned against some of the policies. "All we can do is give money," Gray told one newspaper as the school faced loss of accreditation in 2002. "I cannot control how it is spent." [40] The fund also approved a special $1 million donation to Morris Brown in March 2003, as the college was appealing its loss of accreditation.

The Southern Association of Colleges and Schools cited an array of financial issues in placing the school on probation in December 2000. "Concerns were expressed about their financial status, the way they were handling student aid, planning, oversight," explains James Rogers, the association's executive director. "Those are all very serious areas."

Cross resigned in February after an additional disclosure that the college had withdrawn $8 million

Are racially identifiable colleges and universities good for the country?

YES
William H. Gray, III
President and CEO, United Negro College Fund

Written for *CQ Researcher*, November 2003

Historically black colleges and universities (HBCUs) play a critical role in American higher education. They produce a disproportionate number of African American baccalaureate recipients and the undergraduate degree-of-origin for a disproportionate share of Ph.D.s to blacks. These institutions perform miracles in elevating disadvantaged youth to productive citizenship. If they did not exist, we would have to invent them.

The landscape of American higher education is composed of a diverse array of institutions, each preserving and strengthening the cultural communities from which they emerged. The role of HBCUs in this commonwealth of cultures is similar to that of Notre Dame for Catholics, Brandeis for Jews, Smith for women and Haskell Indian Nations University for American Indians. These institutions enrich diversity in America by providing access and choice to college-goers.

HBCUs are diverse institutions. Over 13 percent of students at HBCUs are white while fewer than 6 percent of students at white colleges are black. More than 25 percent of faculty at HBCUs are white compared to less than 4 percent of black faculty at white colleges. More than 10 percent of deans and administrators at HBCUs are white compared to 2 percent at white institutions who are black. Many HBCUs recruit white students. In fact, several now have majority-white enrollments, including Bluefield State University (92 percent) and West Virginia State College (86 percent).

The nation's 105 HBCUs are public, private, two-year, four-year and graduate. While HBCUs comprise only 3 percent of the nation's 3,688 institutions of higher learning, they produce 24 percent of all bachelors' degrees. These institutions also account for nine of the top 10 colleges that graduate the most black students who go on to earn Ph.D.s, and four of the top five colleges that produce black medical-school acceptances. Students select HBCUs for their educational excellence, low costs and nurturing environments.

HBCUs have evolved into diverse institutions worthy of public support, just as Catholic, Jewish, Mormon and Methodist colleges have. Yet no one suggests that those religious institutions hurt diversity in public colleges and should be closed.

HBCUs are national treasures. For decades, they have enabled underprivileged students to transition from dependence to independence and have contributed immensely to building a more competitive and skilled America.

NO
Ward Connerly
Chairman, American Civil Rights Institute

Written for *CQ Researcher*, November 2003

The American people have a decision to make. Two different ideals, both popular but mutually exclusive of each other, are at war in our colleges and universities. The first is that racial diversity is an intrinsic good that should be promoted at every opportunity on every campus. This is the position of the federal government, after the Supreme Court ruled last summer that states have a "compelling interest" in fostering diversity. It is also the position of the overwhelming majority of college and university administrations, many of which submitted briefs to the court supporting this ideal. And polls show that a sizable number of Americans agree with them.

But directly opposed to the diversity ideal are historically black colleges and universities (HBCUs). An HBCU's entire reason for being is to not be diverse. Yet Americans support HBCUs as well, understandably so given their historic origins. We show our support by channeling federal funds to HBCUs every year. Here lies the dilemma.

Very few would call for a halt in federal funds to HBCUs, just as very few would like to see publicly funded universities cease to exist. But it is hypocritical to support the public funding of HBCUs and then turn around and criticize a "lack of diversity" at other public colleges and universities, since HBCUs, by their very nature, draw away many black students who would otherwise attend racially mixed schools and affect their "diversity."

Take the University of California, for instance. Although HBCUs tend to be located in the South — not California — many black California students seek out these institutions. These students definitely do not want diversity, and presumably don't think it will add much to their education. They're specifically seeking racial homogeneity.

It seems unfair, then, to immediately blame the UC system or the command in the California Constitution that prohibits racial discrimination or preferences to any UC applicant for any perceived "lack of diversity" in the UC student body. Surely the drain of talented black California students to HBCUs must lessen the numbers of talented black students in the UC system. And those HBCUs are funded, in part, by public dollars.

So before critics condemn the public UC system for a dearth of minorities and charge it with insensitivity, or even worse, racism, those critics should look at other actions our government undertakes that undermine the ideal they hold above all others.

from a federal student-aid account allegedly to pay overdue bills. After his arrival, the new president, Charles Taylor, estimated the school's debt at $23 million — and then upped it to $27 million. The U.S. Department of Education meanwhile was demanding repayment of $5.4 million in allegedly mishandled student-aid funds.

Taylor went on leave in September, yielding control to a transition team composed of financial executive Gibbs, attorney Aaron Watson and Adib Shakir, a former president of historically black Tougaloo College in Mississippi. The team's first priority is paying down the debt. "If we could raise and pay off $6 million to $7 million," Gibbs says, "we would be in a position to show SACS that we've repaid our short-term debt and are in a position to handle our long-term debt."

The AME Church has already chipped in $3 million and is asking member churches to pass the plate in February in hopes of raising at least $2.5 million more. Radio host Joyner's $1 million in student scholarship funds will also help. The Rev. Jesse Jackson Sr. recently came for a publicized pep rally, and in early December he agreed to serve on the college's Board of Trustees.

The few students who returned in fall 2003 are getting close personal attention. Stacey Barrett, a music major who chose to finish her education at Morris Brown, is the only student in her intermediate French class. "I'm getting a lot of one-on-one attention from my professors this semester," Barrett told a reporter. "It's a real family atmosphere." [41]

The college is trying to get creditors to agree to partial payments and negotiating with the Education Department over the amount of money owed because of mishandled student-aid funds. Gibbs says the school plans to apply for reaccreditation in April 2004, with hopes of gaining a vote in December 2004.

Rogers says it is "rare" for a college to regain accreditation. "It is a steep mountain, but there are other institutions that have been able to climb those steep mountains," he says.

OUTLOOK

Changing Times

When Oluwbusayo Folarin graduated from high school in Grand Prairie, Texas, in 2000, he expected to take a year off to travel before enrolling in college. But he changed his plans after Morehouse College flew him all-expenses paid to the historically black Atlanta college for a summer conference with other top-ranking African American students — and then offered him what amounted to a full scholarship.

Four years later, Folarin is about to graduate with a degree in political science and a ticket to Oxford University on a prestigious Rhodes scholarship. Having left Morehouse twice to study at predominantly white campuses — Bates College in Maine and the University of Cape Town in South Africa — Folarin also has no doubts about the quality of his education or the benefits of a predominantly black institution.

"Morehouse provides a bubble of empowerment," says Folarin, who grew up with his Nigerian father and American stepmother. "It gives people a chance to discover themselves. You have so many schools in the Northeast that are predominantly white and have so few African Americans."

Morehouse's mission, he continues, "is not to segregate. Its mission is to empower people who have been historically oppressed. There is still definitely a need for this kind of environment."

Folarin's story illustrates both the continuing appeal of historically black colleges for many African Americans and the intense recruiting efforts by many HBCUs to attract students in a competitive academic marketplace. Enrollment statistics yield a mixed picture of their success.

Total enrollment at HBCUs has increased about 10 percent during the 1990s, but the 218,000 black students enrolled in 2001 represent only 14 percent of all African Americans in college. That figure has been sagging for most of the decade. And the HBCUs have had only limited success attracting white students: The number of whites attending black colleges declined by about 15 percent over the past decade — from 29,000 in 1991 to 24,000 in 2001.

Recruiting is only one of the many challenges faced by historically black colleges today. Money is another — and the most pressing in many ways. Tight budgets and limited endowments cramp all of a school's programs and ambitions — even recruiting. Twenty HBCUs signed up to exhibit at the Heartland Black College Expo in Mt. Vernon, Ill., in October 2003, but only four showed up. The rest canceled because of budget constraints. [42]

Money is tight for all higher education institutions, HBCU supporters acknowledge — from public and private sources alike. But black colleges face special problems because of their history. Because most HBCUs have not had a lot of wealthy alumni or friendly corporate executives to give and help raise money, their endowments are sometimes perilously small. "Without some resources deliberately infused into black colleges," Harvard's Willie says, "we're going to lose a few."

Leaders of the two major HBCU organizations, however, are cautiously optimistic. NAFEO's Humphries looks to an economic turnaround to bring an end to the current conditions of pinched government funding and philanthropic giving. "We're going to come out of these things," Humphries says. "And when we do, black colleges will be stronger."

The UNCF's Gray agrees. "Hopefully, as opportunity gets equalized in American society, and we overcome the effects of our past history, then I think you're going to see these schools get stronger," he says. Gray acknowledges that some schools "probably will go by the wayside," but quickly adds, "Not because of their blackness but because of market forces."

Foster at Virginia Union also predicts that there may be fewer black colleges over time, but, unlike Gray, he welcomes the potential demise of schools among what he calls the bottom tiers of HBCUs. "If these schools are not selective in admissions criteria, are not graduating 75 percent of the students admitted, [and] are almost totally dependent on the federal trough for survival, then there is no need for them," he writes. [43]

For his part, Penn State's Brown sees a need for fundamental changes of a more positive nature — changes that will make the schools attractive to black and white students alike in a post-segregation world.

"We're going to have to reclaim our uniqueness of mission while identifying new niches of opportunity," Brown says. "We have to maintain and reassert this rich intellectual history that was burst out at a time of segregation and that did the yeoman's work of generating a national work force, and now — in the same space but at a different hour of the day — reaffirm that history, but be mindful and responsive to the fact that the segregation hour certainly by law has passed."

NOTES

1. For background, see Susan Phillips, "Troubled Times for Black Colleges," *CQ Researcher*, Jan. 7, 1994, p. 15. Historically black colleges and universities are defined in federal law as accredited institutions established before 1964 "whose principal mission was, and is, the education of black Americans." They include colleges in Southern and Border states stretching from Pennsylvania and Ohio to Texas, the District of Columbia and the Virgin Islands. The White House Initiative on Historically Black Colleges and Universities counts the number of HBCUs as 105, the National Association for Equal Opportunity in Higher Education puts the number at 103. The total NAFEO membership of 115 includes some "predominantly black institutions" established after 1964.

2. See Bill Maxwell, " 'We're in This Struggle Together,' " *St. Petersburg Times*, Sept. 21, 2003, p. 1D. The schools listed include one public university — Florida A&M in Tallahasee — and five private schools: Barber-Scotia College in Concord, N.C.; Philander Smith College in Little Rock; Saint Augustine's College in Raleigh, N.C.; Talladega College in Alabama; and Virginia Union University in Richmond. Knoxville College has operated without accreditation since 1997.

3. Quoted in "Black, White Performance Gap Widens, Study Finds," *Black Issues in Higher Education*, Nov. 6, 2003, pp. 6-7.

4. See "Bush Seeks More Money for Pell Grants and Black Colleges," *The Chronicle of Higher Education*, Sept. 8, 2000.

5. See Spencer S. Hsu, "Va. Support for Black Universities Challenged," *The Washington Post*, June 12, 1998, p. C1; "Va. Appointee Retreats From Comments on Black Schools," *The Washington Post*, June 13, 1998. p. C1. Allen served in the position until July 1999.

6. See Ernest P. Pascarella and Patrick Terenzini, *How College Affects Students: Findings and Insights From Twenty Years of Research* (1992).

7. Julian B. Roebuck and Komanduri S. Murty, *Historically Black Colleges and Universities: Their Place in American Higher Education* (1993).

8. Foster, *op. cit.*, p. 94.

9. See Kenneth C. Green, *Campus Computing Study* (1999). The study, completed in 1999, estimated that 49 percent of students in colleges nationwide personally owned their own computers.

10. U.S. Department of Commerce, National Telecommunications and Information Administration, "Historically Black Colleges and Universities: An Assessment of Networking and Connectivity," October 2000 (http://search.ntia.doc.gov/nafeo.pdf). The earlier study is Kenneth C. Green, *Campus Computing Study* (1999).

11. For coverage, see Andrea L. Foster, "Playing Catch-Up: A Bill in Congress Could Give Minority Institutions New Money for Computer Technology," *The Chronicle of Higher Education*, June 27, 2003, p. 27. The Senate approved the bill 97-0 on April 30, 2003.

12. Figures from the Center for Higher Education and Educational Finance at Illinois State University cited in "Jim Crow Entrenched: Unequal Funding of State-Operated Colleges in the South," *The Journal of Blacks in Higher Education*, spring 2002, p. 9.

13. See Bill Swindell, "President's 5-Percent Gesture Reignites Battle Over Black College Funding," *CQ Weekly*, Jan. 25, 2003, p. 211.

14. Background drawn from M. Christopher Brown II, *The Quest to Define Collegiate Desegregation: Black Colleges, Title VI Compliance, and Post-ADAMS Litigation* (1999); Julian B. Roebuck and Komanduri S. Murty, *Historically Black Colleges and Universities: Their Place in American Higher Education* (1993). See also Norman Anthony Meyer, "Historically Black Colleges and Universities: A Legacy of African American Educational Achievement," master's thesis, School for Summer and Continuing Education, Georgetown University, 1991 (thesis 6120, Georgetown University Libraries).

15. The citation is 211 U.S. 405 (1908).

16. John Sekora, "Murder Relentless and Impassive: The American Academic Community and the Negro College," *Soundings*, Vol. 51 (spring 1968), p. 259, cited in Meyer, *op. cit.*, p. 22.

17. See Joan Biskupic and Elder Witt, *Congressional Quarterly's Guide to the U.S. Supreme Court* (3d ed.), 1997, p. 631. The cases are *Missouri ex rel Gaines v. Canada*, 305 U.S. 337 (1938); *Sweatt v. Painter*, 339 U.S. 629 (1950) (Texas); and *McLaurin v. Oklahoma State Regents for Higher Education*, 339 U.S. 637 (1950).

18. The case is *Florida ex rel. Hawkins v. Board of Control of Florida*, 350 U.S. 413 (1956).

19. See Brown, *op. cit.*, pp. 22-23.

20. *Ibid.*, pp. 23-28; see also Roebuck & Murty, *op. cit.*, pp. 45-47. The two principal court rulings are *Adams v. Richardson*, 356 F.Supp. 92 (D.C. Circ. 1973), and *Adams v. Bennett*, 676 F.Supp. 668 (D.C. Cir. 1987).

21. See Brown, *op. cit.*, pp. 29-53.

22. See Janita Poe, "Traditional Black Colleges Struggle to Create Diversity While Preserving Proud Histories," *Atlanta Journal-Constitution*, Nov. 4, 2001, p. 1A; Jeffrey Gettleman, "New Era for Mississippi's Black Colleges," *Los Angeles Times*, May 1, 2001, p. 1A.

23. See *United States v. Fordice*, 505 U.S. 717 (1992). Justice Byron R. White wrote the court's opinion; Justice Antonin Scalia dissented.

24. See Roebuck & Murty, *op. cit.*, pp. 30-31.

25. National Center for Education Statistics, "Historically Black Colleges and Universities, 1976-90," July 1992 (NCES 92-640).

26. See Sekora, *op. cit.*

27. Christopher Jencks and David Riesman, "The American Negro College," *Harvard Educational Review*, Vol. 37, No. 1 (1967), pp. 3-60. The article was published as a chapter in their book *The Academic Revolution* (1968).

28. Charles V. Willie and Ronald R. Edmonds (eds.), *Black Colleges in America: Challenge, Development, Survival* (1978), p. xi.

29. Pascarella and Terenzini, *op. cit.*

30. Roebuck & Murty, *op. cit.*, p. 202.

31. Anita Kumar, "Financial Turmoil Racks FAMU," *St. Petersburg Times*, Nov. 30, 2003. Other background and quotes also drawn from article. For

"College of the Year" designation, see *Time/The Princeton Review*, "The Best College for You and How to Get In," 1998 edition, p. 76.

32. For compilation of news coverage of historically black colleges and universities, see The HBCU Network (www.hbcunetwork.com: click on "About Our Schools."

33. Dana Tofig and Patti Ghezzi, "Clark Atlanta votes to close 5 programs," *Atlanta Journal-Constitution*, Oct. 18, 2003, p. 1G.

34. See Michael Cass, "Fisk Trustee Quits, Cites 'Concerns' Over Board," *The* [Nashville] *Tennessean*, Oct. 10, 2003, p. 1A.

35. For background, see William Triplett, "State Budget Crisis," *CQ Researcher*, Oct. 3, 2003, pp. 821-844.

36. See Thomas Spencer, "State May Cut Private School Student Aid," *The Birmingham News*, Sept. 11, 2003, p. 1A.

37. "College Information — History," www.morris-brown.edu (visited December 2003).

38. Some background drawn from Audrey Williams June, "Endangered Institutions," *The Chronicle of Higher Education*, Jan. 17, 2003.

39. Sonya A. Donalds, "50 Best Colleges and Universities for African Americans," *Black Enterprise*, January 2003, p. 76. Morris Brown did rank 32nd in the magazine's 1999 list.

40. Gray's statement to the *New York Daily News* is quoted in June, *op. cit.*

41. Andrea Jones, "60 Students, Slim Faculty Keep Morris Brown Going," *Atlanta Journal-Constitution*, Sept. 12, 2003, p. 1C.

42. Gregory R. Norfleet, "Students at Black College Expo Experience Budget Cuts Firsthand," *The Register-News*, Oct. 20, 2003.

43. Foster, *op. cit.*, p. 24.

BIBLIOGRAPHY

Books

Brown, M. Christopher II, *The Quest to Define Collegiate Desegregation: Black Colleges, Title VI Compliance, and Post-ADAMS Litigation*, Bergin & Garvey, 1999.
Chronicles history of litigation to desegregate public higher education, concluding by arguing against efforts to eliminate "racially identifiable" institutions. Includes four-page list of cases, 17-page bibliography. Brown is a professor of education at Pennsylvania State University on leave in fall 2003 at the Frederick D. Patterson Research Institute, the research arm of the United Negro College Fund. For a more recent title, see M. Christopher Brown II and Kassie Freeman, *Black Colleges: New Perspectives on Policy and Practice* (Praeger, 2003).

Bullock, Henry Allen, *A History of Negro Education in the South: From 1619 to the Present*, Harvard University Press, 1967.
Comprehensive history of the education of African Americans in the South from Colonial era through the abolition of slavery and the early years of the civil rights revolution; originally published in 1934 and reissued in 1967. Bullock taught at several HBCUs before becoming the first black professor at the University of Texas in Austin in 1969; he died in 1973.

Foster, Gerald A., *Is There a Conspiracy to Keep Black Colleges Open?* Kendall/Hunt, 2001.
Strongly argues that many historically black colleges and universities (HBCUs) are academically mediocre and no longer needed. Foster, an African American, is a professor of social work at his alma mater, historically black Virginia Union University.

Garibaldi, Antoine M. (ed.), *Black Colleges and Universities: Challenges for the Future*, Praeger, 1984.
Sixteen contributors examine issues such as challenges faced by underfinanced private schools and by public schools on account of desegregation. Garibaldi held chief academic positions at two HBCUs — Xavier and Howard — before his current position as president of Gannon University.

Roebuck, Julian B., and Komanduri S. Murty, *Historically Black Colleges and Universities: Their Place in American Higher Education*, Praeger, 1993.
Survey reports positive features of HBCUs for black stu-

dents along with some criticisms of "authoritarian" administrators and unfavorable climate for white students and faculty; also includes good historical overview, individual profiles of schools and 10-page list of references. Roebuck is professor emeritus and Murty professor at Clark Atlanta University.

Articles

"African American College Graduation Rates: Intolerably Low, and Not Catching Up to Whites," *The Journal of Blacks in Higher Education*, autumn 2002, pp. 89-102.
Special report calls black students' graduation rates "dismally low" and shows figures for many HBCUs, both public and private, well below 50 percent.

Donalds, Sonya, "50 Best Colleges and Universities for African Americans," *Black Enterprise*, January 2003, p. 76.
Annual survey lists many HBCUs as among the best colleges or universities for African Americans.

"Jim Crow Entrenched: Unequal Funding of State-Operated Colleges in the South," *The Journal of Blacks in Higher Education*, spring 2002, pp. 8-10.
Shows that public HBCUs in nine Southern and Border states receive substantially less in state funds than white institutions.

Maxwell, Bill, " 'We're In This Struggle Together,' " *St. Petersburg Times*, Sept. 21, 2003, p. 1D.
Excellent overview of current conditions and problems of historically black colleges and universities.

Poe, Janita, "Traditional Black Colleges Struggle to Create Diversity While Preserving Proud Histories," *The Atlanta Journal and Constitution*, Nov. 4, 2001, p. 1A.
Relates efforts by black public colleges to attract white students.

Reports and Studies

U.S. Department of Commerce, National Telecommunications and Information Administration, "Historically Black Colleges and Universities: An Assessment of Networking and Connectivity," October 2000.
Most HBCUs responding to a government survey estimate that fewer than one-fourth of their students own personal computers.

U.S. General Accounting Office, "Historic Preservation: Cost to Restore Historic Properties at Historically Black Colleges and Universities," February 1998 (GAO/RCED-98-51).
Survey of HBCUs identifies 712 historically significant properties needing restoration estimated to cost $755 million.

Web Sites

Both major organizations representing HBCUs maintain Web sites with useful information and links. For the National Association for Equal Opportunity in Higher Education, see www.nafeo.org. For the United Negro College Fund, see www.uncf.org. In addition, the HBCU Network serves as a general resource for HBCUs. See www.HBCUNetwork.com.

For More Information

American Civil Rights Institute, P.O. Box 188350, Sacramento, CA 95818; (916) 444-2278; www.acri.org. A national organization opposed to racial and gender preferences.

Center for Equal Opportunity, 14 Pidgeon Hill Dr., Suite 500, Sterling, VA 20165; (703) 421-5443; www.ceousa. org. A think tank opposed to racially conscious public policies in education and immigration.

National Association for Equal Opportunity in Higher Education, 8701 Georgia Ave., Suite 200, Silver Spring, MD 20910; (301) 650-2440; www.nafeo.org. Represents historically black colleges and universities, both public and private.

United Negro College Fund, 8260 Willow Oaks Corporate Dr., Fairfax, VA 22031; 1-800-331-2244; www. uncf.org. Raises funds for 39 private black colleges and universities.

White House Initiative on Historically Black Colleges and Universities, 1990 K St., N.W., 6th floor, Washington, DC 20006; (202) 502-7900. www.ed.gov/ about/inits/list/whhbcu/edlite-index.html. Launched by President Ronald Reagan in 1981 to strengthen HBCUs.

6

Reparations Movement

David Masci

Children were among the survivors in April 1945 when Russian soldiers liberated the Nazi concentration camp at Auschwitz, Poland, where hundreds of thousands of Jews were murdered. Billions of dollars have been paid to Holocaust survivors.

From *CQ Researcher*, June 22, 2001.

Rep. John Conyers Jr. is not a man who gives up easily. Six times since 1989, the feisty 19-term Michigan Democrat has introduced a measure in the House of Representatives to create a commission to study paying reparations to African-American descendants of slaves. Each time, the bill has died.

But Conyers is optimistic. He claims that beating the same legislative drum so long has helped bring the reparations issue to the attention of the American people.

"Twelve years ago, most people didn't even know what reparations were, and now it's a front-burner issue," he says. "It's like those first [unsuccessful] bills making Martin Luther King's birthday a holiday: You have to build up a critical mass of support, or you don't get anyplace."

Indeed, several local governments have passed resolutions favoring reparations, and the issue has caught the attention of a growing cadre of prominent black advocates and scholars, who have begun holding conferences and symposia on the subject. "It's time to address this issue we've so long denied — the lingering effects of slavery," said Johnnie Cochran, former counsel for O.J. Simpson and a member of a "dream team" of attorneys preparing to sue the federal government and others for slavery reparations.[1]

In addition, several African nations are trying to put the issue on the agenda of the upcoming United Nations World Conference Against Racism, in Durban, South Africa. They hope the United States and former colonial powers like Britain and France will increase aid to African countries to compensate for centuries of slave trading.

Until 50 years ago, debates over reparations for victims of persecution were largely theoretical. But in the wake of World War II,

Seeking Justice for Australia's Aborigines

Australian Olympic gold medal winner Cathy Freeman knew all about the "stolen generation" of Aborigines. Her grandmother was one of the thousands of youngsters taken from their parents by white authorities.

Winning the 400-meter dash at last year's Summer Games gave Freeman a chance to speak out on the centuries of mistreatment of Australia's indigenous people.

Aborigines have lived in Australia for at least 40,000 years, most likely migrating from Southeast Asia. Their downfall as a people began in 1788, when British ships brought 1,000 settlers, including more than 500 convicts from overcrowded jails. Clashes began almost immediately, but the Aborigines' primitive weapons were no match for British guns and mounted soldiers.

Because the convicts provided free labor, the white settlers treated the Aborigines as little more than useless pests. Those who were not killed were driven away to fenced reservations in the most inhospitable parts of the "outback" territory. Crimes against Aborigines often went unpunished.

Aborigines, who make up 2 percent of Australia's largely white population of 19 million, were not allowed to vote until 1962; they were not counted in the census until 1967. Moreover, Aborigines' life expectancy is 20 years less than the national average and they occupy the lowest rung of the nation's economic ladder.

Olympic gold medalist Cathy Freeman has used her celebrity to call attention to her fellow Aborigines.

But in 1992, they won a significant victory when courts recognized that the Aborigines had "owned' Australia before whites arrived. Today, they own more than 15 percent of the continent, mostly in the remote northern territory.

Nevertheless, some Aboriginal leaders are seeking reparations for perhaps the worst injustice perpetrated against their group — the state-sponsored abduction of Aboriginal children from their parents.

From the early 1900s until the 1970s, as many as 100,000 Aboriginal children were taken from their parents to be raised among whites in orphanages or foster families. State and federal laws that permitted the practice were based on the belief that full-blooded Aborigines would eventually die out and that assimilating the children into white society was the best way to save them.

In 1997, the Australian Human Rights and Equal Opportunity Commission reported that many of the children had been physically and sexually abused and suffered long-term psychological damage from the loss of family and cultural ties.

But Australian Sen. John Herron called the 1997 report "one-sided" and said the stories about removing Aboriginal children from their families was greatly exaggerated."[1]

His comments stung Aden Ridgeway, the only Aborigine senator in Parliament, who angrily compared Herron's statements to "denying the Holocaust."[2]

"They were denying they had done anything wrong, denying that a whole generation was stolen," Freeman said. "The fact is, parts of people's lives were taken away."[3]

reparations increasingly have been seen as a viable means of addressing past injustices — not just to Jews slaughtered in the Holocaust but to Japanese-Americans, Native Americans and even Australian Aborigines. In fact, the debate over slavery reparations comes on the heels of a string of victories for groups seeking restitution.

Herron recognizes the removal of Aboriginal children as a blemish on Australia's history, but he claims many were taken with their parents' consent and for their own welfare. He believes amends are the responsibility of states and churches and has suggested that reparations claims be filed individually via the courts.

But reparations proponents say it is difficult to prove abuse in the absence of documents and witnesses. They cite the first stolen-generations case, brought last year, which was dismissed for lack of evidence.

AFP Photo/Torsten Blackwood

At a rally during the 2000 Olympics in Sydney, an Aborigine spokesman calls for the resignation of Prime Minister John Howard, who opposed reparations for mistreated indigenous Australians.

the Aboriginal and Torres Strait Islander Commission, which oversees indigenous affairs, wants the government not only to apologize but also to sign a treaty with the indigenous population that would provide limited autonomy for Aboriginal communities. His group cites similar treaties in the United States and Canada.

Howard says a treaty would be too divisive. "One part of Australia making a treaty with another part is to accept that we are in effect two nations," he said in a radio interview last year.[5]

Ridgeway supports the treaty. "I think the prime minister's kidding himself if he thinks that a treaty's going to be divisive. The goal is about a formal document that better defines black and white relations and the unfinished business of reconciliation."[6]

Many advocates for the Aborigines favor creation of a national compensation board to adjudicate all "stolen generation" claims.

But Prime Minister John Howard dismisses the idea. He refuses to issue an apology, stating today's Australians should not be held responsible for the mistakes of past generations. He also points to a $63 million government program designed to reunite families of the stolen generation.

However, former Prime Minister Malcolm Fraser says an apology is essential. "We can't undo the past, but we can, in an apology, recognize the fact that many actions in the past did a grave injustice to the Aboriginal population of Australia. We have a commitment to recognize that and other past injustices in walking together into a new future."[4]

Last year, the government spent $1.5 billion on health, education, housing and job-training programs for Aborigines.

But monetary payments and programs are not enough, say some reparations supporters. Geoff Clark, chairman of

A national election later this year is widely expected to usher in a new prime minister. Howard's rival has supported the idea of a government apology to the Aborigines.

— Scott Kuzner

[1] "Separated, But Not a Generation," *Illawarra Mercury*, Aug. 19, 2000, p. 9.

[2] Mitchell Zuckoff, "Golden Opportunity, Australian Aboriginal Activists Hope to Exploit the Olympics to Publicize Their Demands for an Apology, Cash Reparations and Limited Sovereignty," *The Boston Globe*, Sept. 18, 2000, p. 1E.

[3] Michael Gordon, "Beginning Of The Legend," *Sydney Morning Herald*, Sept. 25, 2000, p. 10.

[4] Malcolm Fraser, "Apology Must Be First Step," *Sydney Morning Herald*, April 8, 1999, p. 15.

[5] Tony Wright and Kerry Taylor, "PM Rules Out 'Divisive' Treaty," *The Age*, May 30, 2000, p. 2.

[6] *Ibid.*

In 1988, for instance, Congress passed a law authorizing the U.S. government to apologize for interning Japanese-Americans during the war and award $20,000 to each surviving victim. More recently, European countries and companies from Bayer AG to Volkswagen have paid billions of dollars to victims of Nazi

Germany's effort to exterminate Europe's Jews and other "undesirables."

Now it is time for slavery reparations, proponents say. Randall Robinson, author of the bestseller *The Debt: What America Owes to Blacks*, argues that acknowledging the nation's debt to African-Americans for slavery and a subsequent century of discrimination will help heal the country's existing racial divide. "We cannot have racial reconciliation until we make the victims of this injustice whole," says Robinson, president of TransAfrica, a Washington, D.C.-based black advocacy group.

Besides raising a moral question, reparations for slavery is also an economic issue, Robinson says. Many of the problems facing black America are directly linked to slavery and the 100 years of forced segregation that followed emancipation in 1865, he says. "It's foolish to argue that the past has nothing to do with the present," Robinson

> ## "Whites need to realize that we'll have no chance of cohering as a nation in the future unless we deal with this issue now."
> ### — Randall Robinson, President, TransAfrica

says. "There's a reason why so many African-Americans are poor: It's because a terrible wrong occurred in our history that produced a lasting inequality." Reparations will help right that wrong, advocates say, by helping black Americans reach social and economic parity.

But other black Americans warn that paying reparations for slavery will drive a new wedge between blacks and whites, leading to greater racial polarization. "Doing something like this would create a tremendous amount of resentment among whites," says Walter Williams, chairman of the Economics Department at George Mason University in Fairfax, Va.

Williams says whites and other Americans would understandably be opposed to paying restitution for a crime that ended more than 135 years ago and to a com-

munity now making great social and economic strides. "Blacks have come so far; this is nothing but counterproductive," he says.

Opponents also argue that, rather than correcting economic disparity, reparations would take money and attention away from more pressing social and economic issues facing black Americans, such as a substandard education system and high incarceration rates for young African-American men. "This would be such a huge waste of resources, at a time when so much needs to be done in education and other areas," Williams says.

To counter such arguments, slavery reparations advocates have begun modeling their efforts on successful techniques used by Holocaust victims. Recent battles for Holocaust-related reparations have netted survivors and their families more than $10 billion in compensation for slave labor, recovered bank accounts and unclaimed life insurance policies.

But some argue that compensating victims of injustice cheapens their suffering. Indeed, a group of mostly Jewish-American scholars and journalists has criticized some of the efforts to obtain relief for Holocaust survivors. They say the lawyers and Jewish groups involved have turned the legitimate quest for restitution into a shameless money grab that degrades the memory of the millions who perished.

"Fighting for money makes it much harder to see a tragedy in the right light," says Melissa Nobles, a professor of political science at the Massachusetts Institute of Technology (MIT) in Boston.

"They have hijacked the Holocaust and appointed themselves saviors of the victims — all in the name of money," says Norman Finkelstein, a history professor at Hunter College in New York City and author of *The Holocaust Industry: Reflections on the Exploitation of Jewish Suffering.*

Finkelstein points out that those representing the victims have used hardball tactics to "blackmail" Germany, Switzerland and other countries into paying huge sums to satisfy what are often dubious claims. Besides cheapening the historical legacy of the Holocaust, he argues, such actions could potentially trigger an anti-Semitic backlash in Europe.

Supporters say they are only working aggressively to obtain some small measure of justice for the victims. "We are trying to compensate slave laborers and return the assets of survivors," says Elan Steinberg, executive director of the World Jewish Congress, one of the groups leading the Holocaust reparations efforts. "In doing this, we must uncover the truth, which is often hard for these countries to confront."

He says Holocaust victims should not be denied their assets or rightful compensation just because confronting European countries with their past might lead to an anti-Jewish backlash. "Survivors have a right to pursue legitimate claims," he insists. "This is about justice."

"It is good that we try to make some effort to acknowledge someone's suffering, even if it is inadequate," says Tim Cole, a professor of 20th century European history at the University of Bristol in England. At the very least, reparations are important symbolic gestures to the victims from the victimizers, he adds.

As the debate over reparations continues, here are some of the questions experts are asking:

Should the United States pay reparations to African-American descendants of slaves?

For much of its 250-year history on these shores, slavery was America's most divisive and controversial issue. The Founding Fathers fought over the status of African slaves when drafting both the Declaration of Independence and the Constitution. And of course, in 1861 slavery helped trigger the nation's most costly conflict, a four-year Civil War that tore the country apart.

Today, few Americans of any race would disagree that slavery was the most shameful and tragic episode in American history. Many would also agree that African-Americans as a whole, including the descendants of slaves, are still suffering from its effects.

Proponents say compensation is justified on a variety of levels, beginning with the fact that African-Americans remain severely handicapped by the legacy of slavery, lagging behind the nation as a whole in virtually every measure. As a result, supporters say, they need and deserve extra help to overcome the economic and social disadvantages they face.

"Our entire economic sector has been and remains truncated because of slavery," says Ronald Walters, a political science professor at the University of Maryland. "We need something to help reverse this terrible harm done to blacks in this country."

"You have an enormous, static and fixed inequality in America due to a 350-year human-rights crime,"

Robinson says. "We have an obligation to compensate the people still suffering for the wrong that occurred."

Robinson, Walters and others argue that reparations are justified by the fact that the United States grew prosperous largely through the toil of unpaid African-Americans. "Exports of cotton, rice and tobacco swelled the coffers of the U.S. Treasury, yet the people who produced it were never paid," Robinson says.

However, an overwhelming majority of Americans do not believe the nation owes black Americans reparations. A March poll found that 81 percent of registered voters oppose reparations, while only 11 percent support them.[2]

Some Americans feel that the nation has already paid reparations for slavery by passing civil rights and affirmative action laws and by funding myriad social programs designed to help African-Americans and other

> "I can't think of a better fortification for racism than reparations to blacks."
>
> *— Walter Williams,*
> *Chairman, Economics Department,*
> *George Mason University*

disadvantaged peoples. "Since the War on Poverty in the 1960s, the nation has spent $6 trillion on fighting poverty," Williams says.

Others dismiss the whole idea of reparations for slavery out of hand, citing the potentially astronomical cost. Compensating for slavery's injustices could cost as much as $10 trillion, according to some estimates, dwarfing the estimated $10 billion paid to Holocaust victims so far.

Nevertheless, supporters say, reparations would ease African-Americans' feeling that the nation cares little about their plight. "The socio-economic inequality that exists today because of slavery means that the American promise of egalitarianism remains unfulfilled for blacks," Walters says. "It would make the idea of America and American democracy meaningful to blacks."

For Native Americans, a Different Struggle

Unlike African-Americans, Native Americans are not seeking a huge settlement to right the wrongs of the past. Instead, they're working on the present. "We don't want reparations," says John Echohawk, executive director of the Native American Rights Fund, an Indian advocacy group in Boulder, Colo. "What we do want is the government to honor its duty to us — and we want our land and our water back." They also want up to $40 billion they say the government owes them.

Tribes have been making land claims against the government for more than a century. Today, dozens of claims are being dealt with (*see p. 139*).

But the biggest fight for restitution has come over allegations of government mishandling of a huge trust fund for Native Americans. Indian advocates say the federal government will end up owing between $10 billion and $40 billion to Native Americans when the matter is cleared up.

Since 1887, the federal government's Bureau of Indian Affairs (BIA) has managed many of the natural resources on Indian lands, such as oil and mineral deposits and grazing and water rights. Proceeds from the sale or use of these resources are, in theory at least, put into a trust fund administered by the government on behalf of members of the tribes who own the assets — some 500,000 Native Americans throughout the country.

In the 1970s, Elouise Cobell, a member of the Blackfoot tribe, began to question the government's management of these accounts. Other Indians had long suspected mismanagement, but no one had challenged the BIA officials who controlled the fund.

Over the next two decades, Cobell, who has an accounting background, concluded that billions of dollars had been lost, and that many Indians were being cheated out of money that was rightfully theirs. Her efforts to get BIA officials to pay attention to the problem came to naught. "They tried to belittle me and intimated that I was a dumb Indian," she says.

In 1996, after years of what Cobell calls stonewalling by federal officials, she and four other Native Americans filed a class action suit in federal court against the Department of the Interior, which controls BIA. "The suit was a last resort, because no one would listen to us," Echohawk says. "No one did anything."

The plaintiffs charged that many records had been destroyed; that officials had improperly invested much of the money coming into the trust; and that no effort was made to keep individual Indians informed about the individual accounts the government kept for them.[1] These claims were later buttressed by a government official, who acknowledged that trust managers could not locate some 50,000 account holders because of poor recordkeeping.

Paying reparations would benefit the entire nation by creating a more conducive environment for racial reconciliation, supporters say. "We'll never have any harmony or stability between the races until there is commitment to make the victim whole," Robinson says. "Whites need to realize that we'll have no chance of cohering as a nation in the future unless we deal with this issue now."

Conyers agrees that paying reparations would encourage racial healing — for both blacks and whites. "This could create a bridge that unlocks understanding and compassion between people," he says.

But opponents say compensating slavery victims will have exactly the opposite effect — creating new grounds for racial polarization. "I can't think of a better fortification for racism than reparations to blacks," says George Mason University's Williams. "To force whites today,

who were not in any way responsible for slavery, to make payments to black people — many of whom may be better off [than the whites] — will create nothing but great resentment."

"It would create a huge backlash against black people, which is something they don't really need," says Glen Loury, director of the Institute of Race and Social Division at Boston University. "It would also be seen as just another example of black people's inability 'to get over it and move on.' "

Indeed, opponents say, reparations might even have the reverse effect: They could significantly weaken the nation's commitment to lifting poor black Americans out of poverty. "This would be a Pyrrhic victory for African-Americans," says Loury, who is black. "It would undermine the claim for further help down the road,

Even before the suit was filed, the federal government had made some attempts to address the problem. In 1994, Congress passed the Native American Trust Fund Accounting and Management Reform Act, authorizing the appointment of a special trustee to manage and reform the fund. But the first such trustee, former Riggs Bank President Paul Homan, resigned in protest in 1999, complaining that the Interior Department was not adequately committed to reform.

Meanwhile, Cobell's suit against the government succeeded. In December 2000, a federal court ruled against the Interior Department and took control of the trust fund. "The government kept arguing that they were doing the best they could, but that just wasn't true," Echohawk says. "Fortunately, the court didn't believe them."

Penny Manybeads stands beside her hogan at the Navajo Indian reservation in Tuba City. Ariz., in 1993. Native Americans want the government to pay for the mismanagement of their natural resources trust fund.

AP Photo/Jeff Robbins

The government lost a subsequent appeal. Most recently, the new Bush administration decided not to continue to appeal the ruling, ending resistance to a court-administered solution.

The parties now must decide how much the government owes the trust fund. "We hope we can avoid a protracted legal battle over damages and settle out of court," Echohawk says, adding that Bush's decision not to continue appealing the ruling is a good sign the administration is committed to solving the problem.

Still, Echohawk is wary. "I'm cautious because until now, the government has fought us every inch of the way," he says. "Federal stonewalling and neglect are part of the story of the American Indian."

---

[1] Colman McCarthy, "Broken Promises Break Trust," *The Baltimore Sun*, March 7, 1999.

because the rest of America will say: 'Shut up: You've been paid.' "

In addition, Loury says, pushing for restitution detracts from the real issues facing the black community. "This whole thing takes the public's attention away from important issues, like failing schools and the fact that so many African-Americans are in jail."

Have efforts to collect reparations for Holocaust victims gone too far?

In the last five years, efforts to compensate and recover stolen property for Holocaust victims and their heirs have increased dramatically. What started in the mid-1990s as an action to recover money in long-dormant Swiss bank accounts has snowballed into a host of lawsuits and settlements against European insurance companies, German and American manufacturers and art galleries around the world.[3]

By and large, these actions have been hailed as a great victory for victims of oppression. Yet a small but growing circle of critics questions the efforts. They charge the lawyers working on behalf of Holocaust victims — as well as the World Jewish Congress, the International Commission on Holocaust Era Insurance Claims (known as the Claims Conference) and other groups — with exploiting a historical tragedy for monetary gain.

"This whole thing has gone way too far," says Gabriel Shoenfeld, senior editor of *Commentary*, a conservative opinion magazine that examines issues from a Jewish perspective. "This is a case of a just cause that has been traduced by overzealous organizations and some rather unscrupulous lawyers."

Hunter College's Finkelstein goes further, branding those who work on behalf of survivors as "the Holocaust industry" and their actions "nothing short of a shakedown racket."

Shoenfeld and Finkelstein are troubled by the fact that Jewish groups and attorneys working on the cases have taken it upon themselves to represent Holocaust survivors. "Groups like the World Jewish Congress don't really represent anyone," Finkelstein says. "They weren't elected by anyone to do this, and most Jews don't even know who they are."

He argues that such groups are using the survivors' high moral status as a cudgel to beat countries and corporations into submission. "They've wrapped themselves in the mantle of the needy Holocaust victims against the greedy, fat Swiss bankers and Nazi industrialists," Finkelstein says. "They are out of control and reckless."

Shoenfeld says the claims often are either overblown, dubious or simply not valid. "It's clear that they're trying to humiliate these countries into giving in," he says.

Shoenfeld cites a recent case against Dutch insurers, who had already settled with the Netherlands' Jewish community for unpaid wartime insurance policies. "These guys then came in and tried to unfairly blacken Holland's reputation by painting their behavior during the war in an unfavorable light, without acknowledging all of the good things Dutch people did for Jews during that time," he says. "It was all an effort to blackmail them, to extract more money from them."

Even the much-publicized victory against the Swiss banks was marred by unscrupulous tactics, Finkelstein contends. After forcing the banks to set up a commission headed by former U.S. Federal Reserve Chairman Paul A. Volcker to investigate claims, they demanded a settlement before the commission finished its work, he says.

The Swiss caved in and paid $1.25 billion, Finkelstein says, because the groups were creating public hysteria and had American politicians threatening an economic boycott. "They honed this strategy against the Swiss and then turned to the French, Germans and others and used it successfully against them."

Such heavy-handed tactics create unnecessary ill will against European Jews, critics say. "By bludgeoning the Europeans into submission, the Holocaust industry is fomenting anti-Semitism," Finkelstein says.

Shoenfeld says the tactics have already spurred an anti-Semitic backlash in Germany and Switzerland.

"Don't Jews have enough problems in the world without bringing upon themselves the wrath of major European powers?" he asks.

But groups pursuing Holocaust reparations say their opponents are misguided. "How can anyone ask [if] we are going too far in attempting to get restitution for people who were driven from their homes, forced into hiding, persecuted and forced to work?" asks Hillary Kessler-Godin, director of communications for the Claims Conference in New York City.

Supporters also argue that their tactics are not "heavy-handed" or designed to blackmail European countries. "We're not out to humiliate anyone," says the World Jewish Congress' Steinberg. "But sometimes the truth is hard and difficult for everyone to accept."

For instance, it would not serve the truth or the victims to sugarcoat Holland's dismal record of protecting Jews during the Holocaust, Steinberg says. "Holland had the worst record of any Western European country," he argues. "Eighty percent of its Jews were wiped out."

He also points out that his group rushed to settle the Swiss case before the Volcker commission finished its work in order to begin repaying survivors before they died. "Many survivors are very old and dying at such a rapid rate — some 10,000 to 15,000 a year. We had to move on this," he says. The commission will continue its work, so that all 55,000 Holocaust-era accounts can be investigated and paid out, he adds.

Proponents also counter the criticism that their actions foment anti-Semitism. "Anti-Semitism is not caused by Jewish actions, but by people who don't like Jews," Kessler-Godin says. "To temper our actions on behalf of people who have suffered the worst form of anti-Semitism possible in the name of not causing anti-Semitism defies logic."

"Holocaust survivors should not have to abrogate their rights simply for political expediency," Steinberg adds, pointing out that most people, regardless of their religious background, understand and support his group's efforts. "At the end of the day, most non-Jews — except those who represent the banks or insurance companies — see this as an act of justice."

Does putting a price tag on suffering diminish that suffering?

On Dec. 7, 1998, the leader of one of the pre-eminent Jewish organizations in the United States shocked many

American Jews by publicly questioning efforts to obtain reparations for Holocaust survivors. In a *Wall Street Journal* editorial, Abraham Foxman, national director of the Anti-Defamation League, argued that when "claims become the main focus of activity regarding the Holocaust, rather than the unique horror of 6 million Jews, including 1.5 million children, being murdered simply because they were Jewish, then something has gone wrong."[4]

Foxman worried that the drive to obtain restitution would shift modern attitudes about the Holocaust from one of reverence for the victims and their suffering to an accounting of their material losses.

"I fear that all the talk about Holocaust-era assets is skewing the Holocaust, making the century's last word on the Holocaust that the Jews died, not because they were Jews, but because they had bank accounts, gold, art and property," he wrote. "To me that is a desecration of the victims, a perversion of why the Nazis had a Final Solution, and too high a price to pay for a justice we can never achieve."[5]

Foxman's editorial provoked an immediate response from many prominent Jews. Nobel Peace Prize winner Elie Wiesel argued that compensating Holocaust survivors does not sully their memory but is the right thing to do.

"It is wrong to think of this as about money," said Wiesel, a Holocaust survivor himself. "It is about justice, conscience and morality."[6]

But critics point out that reparations, almost by their nature, are tainted, because they mix the sacredness of a people's suffering and pain with the world's greatest source of corruption: money. "Although there might be a way to handle this whole thing with dignity, it inexorably becomes a sordid business," Finkelstein says. "I believe money always corrupts things."

"There is a real danger here that most people will say: Hey wait a minute. This is all really about money," says MIT's Nobles. "Money can profoundly obscure the nature of a tragedy."

Some critics also contend that monetary reparations can do victims more harm than good. "People who have been victimized need to become free internally in order to move beyond the tragedy that has occurred," says Ruth Wisse, a professor of Yiddish and comparative literature at Harvard University. "In this sense, reparations can be harmful because they make victims less dependent on themselves."

Instead of monetary payments, she says, nations should take steps to resolve the political problems that led to the suffering in the first place. "Reparations should be made on political terms, not economic terms," she says. For example, she said a country like Turkey, which many historians say exterminated more than a million Armenians at the beginning of the 20th century, might want to help protect Armenia from outside threats.

But advocates for reparations argue that the money is more a powerful symbol than a primary motive. "We're really talking about justice," says the University of Bristol's Cole. "It's a symbolic act, a gesture."

Although, Cole says, "no amount of money can ever compensate for the suffering of history's victims," restitution can aid them in some small way. "There are things we can do to ease people's suffering or bring them some sense that justice is being done."

"Of course you can't put a price tag on suffering," says the University of Maryland's Walters. "But what you can do is ask: What will bring the victims a measure of dignity? Isn't that the most important thing?"

Proponents also contend that, in the real world where victims of past oppression may still be suffering, monetary compensation can make a huge difference in their lives. For instance, says Kessler-Godin, many Eastern European Holocaust survivors live in poverty and need assistance. "It's OK for Abraham Foxman, living his comfortable American life, to say that it cheapens the memory of victims, but there are people who are living hand to mouth who don't have that luxury."

Finally, supporters say, forgoing reparations allows the victimizers to retain their financial wealth. "When you argue that a victim shouldn't pursue restitution, you are essentially rewarding the oppressors," Steinberg says.

BACKGROUND

Ancient Notion

The payment of reparations for genocide or other injustices is a relatively new phenomenon, which began with Germany's 1951 pledge to aid Israel and to compensate individual victims of the Holocaust. "Before World War II, nations saw what they did to other people during wartime as a natural byproduct of war," MIT's Nobles says. "The vanquished simply had to accept what had happened to them."

1945-1980 *After World War II, West Germany moves to pay restitution to Jewish survivors of the Holocaust.*

1948 Congress passes the Japanese-American Evacuations Claims Act to compensate Japanese-Americans who lost property as a result of being interned during World War II.

1951 West German Chancellor Konrad Adenauer proposes paying assistance to Israel and reparations to Jewish survivors of the Nazi Holocaust.

1953 Israel and West Germany agree on payment of reparations and aid. Over the next nearly 50 years, Germans will pay more than $60 billion in Holocaust-related restitution.

1956 Swiss government asks banks and insurers to reveal their Holocaust-related assets. The companies say such "dormant accounts" hold less than 1 million Swiss francs.

1962 A second request for an accounting of Holocaust-related assets leads to the discovery of about 10 million Swiss francs in dormant accounts.

1965 West Germany ends state-to-state payments to Israel. Holocaust survivors continue to receive payments from German government through the present.

1980s-Present *Oppressed groups begin seeking reparations.*

1980 Congress creates the Commission on Wartime Relocations and Internment of Civilians to study possible reparations for Japanese-Americans interned during World War II.

1987 National Coalition of Blacks for Reparations in America (N'COBRA) is founded.

1988 Congress passes the Civil Liberties Act, which apologizes for the wartime internment of Japanese-Americans and authorizes the payment of $20,000 to surviving internees. Eventually, 80,000 Japanese-Americans receive an apology and a check.

1989 Rep. John Conyers Jr., D-Mich., introduces legislation to create a commission to study the African-American reparation issue. He will reintroduce the bill five more times in the coming years.

1990 The first Japanese-American internees begin receiving reparations checks.

1995 European and American media exposés document the role of Swiss banks in financing the Nazi war effort and in failing to make restitution to Holocaust survivors.

Oct. 1996 Class action suit is filed in New York federal court against Swiss banks, seeking funds from "dormant accounts" of Holocaust victims.

1998 Though not an apology, President Clinton says in a speech at a Ugandan village school that it was wrong for European Americans to have received "the fruits of the slave trade."

Aug. 1998 Swiss government agrees to pay $1.25 billion to settle claims against Swiss banks.

Dec. 1998 In a *Wall Street Journal* op-ed piece, Anti-Defamation League national director and Holocaust survivor Abraham Foxman questions the tactics employed by those seeking reparations for Holocaust survivors.

Dec. 1999 The German government and corporations that used slave labor during the war establish a $4.3 billion fund to compensate surviving slave laborers.

2000 TransAfrica founder Randall Robinson publishes *The Debt: What America Owes to Blacks*, a bestselling book arguing for reparations for slavery.

2001 Conservative commentator David Horowitz creates a controversy on many American campuses when he tries to publish an ad in college newspapers entitled "Ten Reasons Why Reparations for Slavery is a Bad Idea — and Racist, Too."

2002 Prominent African-American attorneys promise to sue the federal government and private companies for slavery reparations.

But while the use of reparations may be a relatively new remedy, the ideas behind them have a long, if circuitous, intellectual pedigree stretching back for millennia. For instance, the ancient Greeks and Romans explored the notion that the weak and oppressed deserve sympathy and possibly assistance. The 4th century B.C. Athenian philosopher Plato addressed this issue in his most famous dialogue, *The Republic*. A generation later Aristotle, another Athenian philosopher, wrote that the best kind of government was one that helped those who had been deprived of happiness.[7]

Judeo-Christian doctrine also grappled with what individuals and society owe to the downtrodden and oppressed. For instance, in the New Testament, Jesus Christ singled out the persecuted as being particularly deserving of compassion and assistance.[8]

The first modern articulation of these principles came in the 18th century during the Enlightenment. Ironically, it was the intellectual father of free market economics — Scottish philosopher Adam Smith — who wrote most forcefully and eloquently about guilt and the resulting sympathy it causes.

In his 1759 treatise, *The Theory of Moral Sentiments*, he wrote: "How selfish soever man may be supposed, there are evidently some principles in his nature, which interest him in the fortunes of others, and render their happiness necessary to him, though he derives nothing from it, except the pleasure of seeing it. Of this kind is pity or compassion, the emotion we feel for the misery of others, when we either see it, or are made to conceive it in a very lively manner."[9]

Smith argued further that this sympathy is a cornerstone of justice. It is necessary for creating and maintaining general social order, he believed.

Native Americans

In the 18th and 19th centuries, compassion for the plight of others — whether out of Christian duty or to promote the greater good — fueled movements to abolish slavery and the slave trade in Europe and the United States. Later, these impulses led the United States, albeit very slowly, to consider compensating Native Americans for the government's taking of their land and the resulting destruction of much of their population and culture.

The expansion of the American frontier during the 19th century resulted in American Indians being forcibly moved to reservations, where many remain today. Millions of acres, primarily in the Great Plains, were taken from tribes with little or minimal compensation.

But the U.S. government did not consider compensating Native Americans for the loss of this property until 1946, when Congress established a Claims Commission to handle Indian land claims. The body soon became bogged down in the flood of claims, many of which were substantial. When the commission was eliminated in 1978, it had adjudicated only a fraction of the disputes between tribes and the government and had paid Native Americans only token compensation for the lost land.[10]

Meanwhile, the courts became much more sympathetic to Indian claims. In 1980, for instance, the Supreme Court awarded the Sioux $122 million for the theft of lands in South Dakota's Black Hills. It remains the largest award for a Native American land claim in U.S. history. (*See story, pp. 134-135.*)

Today, Native Americans are still pressing land claims, particularly in the Eastern United States. "Many of these claims revolve around treaties made between states and Indian nations early in the country's history," says John Echohawk, executive director of the Native American Rights Fund, an Indian advocacy group in Boulder, Colo. Since the U.S. Constitution leaves the power to negotiate Indian treaties with the federal government, many of these agreements with the states are now being challenged, he adds.

One of the biggest such disputes involves three bands of Oneida Indians, who are trying to recover 300,000 acres of land in central New York state. The case hinges on a treaty negotiated in 1838.

Restitution to "Comfort Women"

On the other side of the globe, victims of a more recent tragedy — Japan's sexual enslavement of thousands of Asian women during World War II — are also seeking restitution. An estimated 200,000 "comfort women" were forced to serve the Japanese military at its far-flung outposts. They claim they were kidnapped or tricked into working as sexual slaves for the Japanese soldiers, who beat and raped them.

In 1995, then Japanese Prime Minister Tomiici Murayama officially apologized for the practice, but the government has yet to pay any reparations to the surviving women.

THE WHITE HOUSE
WASHINGTON

A monetary sum and words alone cannot restore lost years or erase painful memories; neither can they fully convey our Nation's resolve to rectify injustice and to uphold the rights of individuals. We can never fully right the wrongs of the past. But we can take a clear stand for justice and recognize that serious injustices were done to Japanese Americans during World War II.

In enacting a law calling for restitution and offering a sincere apology, your fellow Americans have, in a very real sense, renewed their traditional commitment to the ideals of freedom, equality, and justice. You and your family have our best wishes for the future.

Sincerely,

GEORGE BUSH
PRESIDENT OF THE UNITED STATES

OCTOBER 1990

In October 1990, Japanese-Americans interned during World War II received this letter of apology from President George Bush, in addition to a check for $20,000.

Japanese-Americans

On Feb. 19, 1942, less than three months after the Japanese bombing of Pearl Harbor, President Franklin Delano Roosevelt signed Executive Order 9066, authorizing the removal of Japanese immigrants and their children from the western half of the Pacific coastal states and part of Arizona.

Within days, the government began removing 120,000 Japanese-Americans — two-thirds of them U.S. citizens — from their homes and businesses. Many were forced to sell their property at far below market value in the rush to leave. All were eventually taken to hastily built camps in Western states like California, Idaho and Utah, where most remained until the war was almost over. Some young Japanese-American men were allowed to leave the camps to serve in the armed forces — and many did so with valor — and a handful of mostly young internees were also permitted to relocate to Midwestern or Eastern states.

The camps were Spartan, but in no way resembled Nazi concentration camps or Stalinist Russia's gulags. Still, the internees were denied their freedom and, in many cases, their property.

During this time, internee Fred Korematsu and several other Japanese-Americans challenged the constitutionality of the internment. Korematsu's case ultimately found its way to the Supreme Court, which ruled that during national emergencies like war Congress and the president had the authority to imprison persons of certain racial groups.

After the war, Congress passed the Japanese-American Evacuations Claims Act of 1948 to compensate those who had lost property because of their internment. Over the next 17 years, the government paid $38 million to former internees.[11]

Other groups that have been victimized, like Armenians, also want restitution. And still others — like Latinos, Chinese-Americans and women in the United States — who suffered varying degrees of discrimination over the years, have not organized significant reparations movements, in part because their suffering is perceived as being different from the official policies that led to genocide or slavery.

But efforts to make the government apologize for its wartime actions and pay reparations to internees over and above the property claims remained on a back burner until the 1970s. During that decade, Japanese-American activists — led by the community's main civic organization, the Japanese-American Citizens League (JACL) — began building support for redress.

Initially, only about a third of Japanese-Americans favored reparations. Many felt the painful war years should be forgotten. Others worried that vocal demands, coupled with growing fears among the U.S. public over the rising economic power of Japan, would provoke another backlash against Japanese-Americans.[12]

But by the end of the decade, a majority of Japanese-Americans supported the effort, and the JACL began effectively lobbying Congress for redress. In 1980, Congress created the Commission on Wartime Relocations and Internment of Civilians to study the issue.

During public hearings over the next two years, the commission heard emotional testimony as former internees shared their personal sagas. Publicity generated by the hearings helped awaken the American public to the injustice done to the internees.

One former internee, Kima Konatsu, told about her family's experience while incarcerated near Gila River, Ariz. "During that four years we were separated [from my husband] and allowed to see him only once," Konatsu told the commission. Eventually he became ill and was hospitalized, she said. "He was left alone, naked, by a nurse after having given him a sponge bath. It was a cold winter and he caught pneumonia. After two days and two nights, he passed away. Later on, the head nurse told us that this nurse had lost her two children in the war and that she hated Japanese."[13]

In 1983, the commission concluded that there had been no real national security reason to justify relocating or incarcerating the Japanese-Americans, and that the action had caused the community undue hardship. A second report four months later recommended that the government apologize for the internment and appropriate $1.5 billion to pay each surviving internee $20,000 in reparations.[14]

That same year, a new National Council for Japanese-American Redress (NCJAR) emerged, which opposed what it saw as the JACL's accommodationist approach to reparations. NCJAR filed a class action suit against the

South Korean "comfort women" who were forced to provide sex for Japanese soldiers in World War II demand compensation during a protest at the Japanese Embassy in Seoul last April.

government on behalf of the internees, demanding $27 billion in damages. But the suit was dismissed in 1987 on procedural grounds.[15]

Nevertheless, the lawsuit created restitution momentum in Congress, where support had been building since issuance of the commission's 1983 reports. Because many former internees were elderly, proponents argued that something should be done quickly, before most of the intended beneficiaries died.[16]

In 1988, Congress passed the Civil Liberties Act, which authorized $1.25 billion over the next 10 years to pay each internee $20,000. The law also contained an apology to Japanese-Americans who had been incarcerated.[17] (*see p. 140*).

On Oct. 9, 1990, the government issued its first formal apologies and checks to Japanese-Americans in a moving ceremony in Washington, D.C. A tearful Sen. Daniel K. Inouye, D-Hawaii — a Japanese-American who lost an arm fighting for the United States during World War II — told the internees and assembled guests that day: "We honor ourselves and honor America. We demonstrated to the world that we are a strong people — strong enough to admit our wrongs."[18]

Since then, some 80,000 former internees have received compensation.[19]

The Holocaust

In many ways, the modern debate over reparations began on Sept. 27, 1951. On that day West German Chancellor

AFP Photo

Japanese-Americans wait for housing after being sent to the Manzanar, Calif., internment camp in March 1942 following the Japanese attack on Pearl Harbor. The U.S. later paid $20,000 to each person confined.

Konrad Adenauer appeared before the country's legislature, or Bundestag, and urged his fellow Germans to make some restitution for the "unspeakable crimes" Germany had committed against the Jewish people before and during World War II. His proposal — to provide assistance to the newly founded state of Israel as well as restitution to individual Holocaust survivors — was supported by both his own Christian Democratic party and the opposition Social Democrats.

Ironically, West Germany's offer of reparations was much more controversial in Israel, where a sizable minority, led by then opposition politician Menachem Begin, opposed taking "blood money" from Holocaust perpetrators. Begin and others argued that by receiving compensation from the Germans, Israel would literally be selling the moral high ground.[20]

But Israeli Prime Minister David Ben Gurion argued forcefully that Israel had a duty to see that Germany did not profit from its heinous crimes. "He understood that we are obligated to ensure that murderers are not inheritors," says the World Jewish Congress' Steinberg.

Ben Gurion prevailed, in part because Israel desperately needed funds to resettle European Jews who had survived the Holocaust. The German government began paying restitution to Holocaust survivors around the world in 1953 and has since paid out about $60 billion

for both individual claims and aid to Israel. The state-to-state payments ended in 1965, but the German government still sends monthly pension checks to about 100,000 Holocaust survivors.

After West Germany's agreement with Israel, little was done to obtain further restitution for Holocaust victims. Many who had survived the camps were more concerned with getting on with their new lives and wanted to forget about the past. In addition, the Soviet Union and its Eastern bloc allies — where most Holocaust victims had come from — made no effort to aid the quest for restitution. Even the United States was content to let the issue lie, partly in order to focus on integrating West Germany and other Western allies into a Cold War alliance.[21]

Still, the issue did not disappear entirely. In Switzerland — a banking and finance mecca and a neutral country during the war — the government was taking small, inadequate steps to discover the extent of Holocaust-related wealth. Many Jews killed by the Germans had opened accounts in Swiss banks and taken out insurance policies from Swiss companies before the war as a hedge against the uncertainty created by the Nazi persecution.

In 1956, the Swiss government surveyed its banks and insurance companies to determine the value of accounts held by those who had died or become refugees as a result of the Holocaust. The companies replied that there were less than a million Swiss francs in those accounts.

In 1962, the government once again requested an accounting of Holocaust-related assets. This time, the companies came up with about 10 million francs, some of which was paid to account holders or their heirs. In the 1960s, '70s and '80s, other efforts by individuals seeking to recover Swiss-held assets were largely unsuccessful because the banks and insurers required claimants to have extensive proof of account ownership, proof that often had been lost or destroyed during the war.

But in the 1990s the situation changed dramatically. First, the collapse of communist regimes throughout Eastern Europe opened up previously closed archives containing Holocaust-related records. In addition, many Holocaust survivors lost their reticence about pursuing claims, in part because films like "Schindler's List" brought greater attention to their plight and made it easier to go public.

Italian-Americans Were Also Mistreated

Japanese-Americans were not the only ethnic group to suffer from discrimination during World War II. Many Italian-Americans also were victimized in the name of national security.

The United States was at war with Italy from the end of 1941 until it surrendered to the Allies in 1943. During that time, some 600,000 Italian immigrants were classified as "enemy aliens," even though many had sons fighting for the United States against Italy, Germany and Japan.

Tens of thousands were subjected to search and arrest, and 250 were interned in camps. In California, an evening curfew was imposed on more than 50,000 Italian-Americans. Some 10,000 were forced to move away from areas near military installations. Authorities even impounded the boats of Italian-American fishermen.

While generally recognized as a gross violation of civil liberties, the federal government's mistreatment of Italians was much less far-reaching than the internment suffered by 120,000 Japanese. Indeed, more German-Americans were interned — about 11,000 in Texas, North Dakota and elsewhere. Perhaps that's why Italian-American groups have not demanded reparations. Instead, they have asked the government to "acknowledge" what happened.

In 2000, Congress agreed, passing legislation authorizing the Justice Department to conduct an investigation into the episode. The department's work is expected to be finished by the end of the year.

In the mid-1990s, journalists and scholars began uncovering evidence that Switzerland had been a financial haven for Nazi officials, who had deposited gold looted from Holocaust victims in Swiss banks. The investigation stimulated new interest in dormant bank accounts and insurance policies.

In 1996 a class action suit on behalf of victims and their heirs was filed in New York against Swiss banks and insurance companies. Swiss efforts to get the suit dismissed failed. Meanwhile, pressure from the U.S. Congress and local officials threatening economic sanctions against the companies forced the banks and insurers to acknowledge the existence of a large number of dormant accounts. By 1999, the Swiss had negotiated a settlement to set aside $1.25 billion to pay out dormant accounts and fund other Holocaust-related philanthropies.

The Swiss case prompted other Holocaust claims. For instance, in 1998 U.S. and European insurance regulators, Jewish groups and others formed a commission — headed by former Secretary of State Lawrence Eagleburger — to investigate claims against European insurance companies outside Switzerland.

The commission was an attempt to bypass lawsuits and to get the insurers — which include some of Europe's largest, like Italy's Generali and Germany's Allianz — to pay elderly claimants before they died. So far, the companies have paid out very little in compensation, because of bureaucratic wrangling at the commission and unwillingness on the part of survivors to accept what have in many cases been only small offers of restitution from the companies.[22]

Meanwhile, former prisoners who had been forced to work without pay for German manufacturers during the war began seeking restitution for their labor. The Nazis had drafted an estimated 12 million people — including 6 million mostly Jewish concentration camp inmates — to provide unpaid labor for some of the biggest names in German industry, including giant automaker Volkswagen. Many were worked to death.[23]

Initially Germany and then-Chancellor Helmut Kohl resisted efforts to pay reparations to slave laborers, citing the 1953 settlement with Israel. But in 1998 the country elected a new leader, Gerhard Schröeder, who authorized negotiations to settle the issue.

Last July, the German government and companies that had used slave labor established a $4.3 billion fund to compensate an estimated 1.5 million survivors. The deal, negotiated with German and American lawyers for the slave laborers and ratified in the Bundestag on May 30, indemnifies German industry from further lawsuits on behalf of slave laborers.

CQ/Scott Ferrell

Rep. John Conyers Jr., D-Mich., wants Congress to create a commission on reparations for descendents of slaves. "Twelve years ago, most people didn't even know what reparations were, and now it's become a front-burner issue," he says.

CURRENT SITUATION

Reparations for Slavery

Efforts to compensate African-Americans for slavery began formally on Jan. 16, 1865, months before the Civil War ended. On that day, Union General William Tecumseh Sherman issued Special Field Order 15, directing his soldiers — who were then marching through the South — to divide up confiscated Confederate farms into 40-acre plots and redistribute the land to slaves. Farm animals were also to be redistributed.

But Sherman's promise of "40 acres and a mule" was never realized. Four months after the order was signed, President Abraham Lincoln was assassinated. His successor, Southerner Andrew Johnson, largely opposed reconstruction and quickly rescinded Sherman's order. More than 40,000 slaves were removed from farms they had recently occupied.

In the years since Special Field Order 15, the idea of compensating African-Americans arose only occasionally in the public arena and attracted little attention. But lately the idea has gained considerable steam, propelled by several high-profile events, such as academic conferences on the subject and the threat of reparations lawsuits by prominent black attorneys.

In addition, Chicago, Detroit and Washington, D.C., have passed resolutions supporting federal reparations legislation. And slavery reparations has become a hot topic on college campuses, as more and more scholars study the idea. "This is the fourth paper I've delivered on reparations this year alone," University of San Diego Law Professor Roy Brooks said at a May conference on the issue. "That suggests there's much to say about the subject and that reparations is a hot issue internationally."[24]

The lawsuits being prepared by several prominent black attorneys and advocates are expected to be filed early next year. They are the brainchild of a legal team that includes TransAfrica's Robinson, O.J. Simpson attorney Cochran, Harvard University Law School Professor Charles Ogletree and Alexander Pires, who recently won a $1 billion settlement from the Department of Agriculture on behalf of black farmers who were denied government loans.

"The history of slavery in America has never been fully addressed in a public forum," Ogletree said. "Litigation will show what slavery meant, how it was profitable and how the issue of white privilege is still with us. Litigation is a place to start, because it focuses attention on the issue."[25]

The team wants the federal government to officially apologize for slavery and for the century of state-supported discrimination — such as the South's segregationist "Jim Crow" laws — that followed emancipation. Moreover, the lawyers are likely to ask for some kind of monetary remedy, although no agreement has been reached either on how much is owed or how reparations would be dispersed.

Estimates vary wildly over how much black Americans are owed for slavery. Larry Neal, an economics professor at the University of Illinois at Urbana-Champaign, has calculated that the United States owes African-Americans $1.4 trillion in back wages for work completed before emancipation. Georgetown University Business School Professor Richard America, however, estimates the debt is closer to $10 trillion.[26]

Should the U.S. government apologize to African-Americans for slavery?

YES Rep. Tony P. Hall
D-Ohio

Written for *CQ Researcher*, June 2001

America's history has changed the course of humanity. As an enemy of tyrants, an advocate of liberty and a defender of freedoms, America has proven herself again and again. Our achievements stir other peoples' pride, and our history bestows upon us the courage to conquer new challenges.

But our achievements and our history are blemished by the shameful decades when U.S. laws permitted the enslavement of African-Americans. This long chapter ensured that many of the hands that built our young nation were not those of full participants in an emerging American dream, but of men, women and children forced to obey the tyranny of "masters."

In recent years, we have apologized for racist medical experiments that inflicted pain and eventually death on many young, innocent men in Tuskegee, Ala. We have paid reparations for forcibly interning thousands of Japanese-Americans during World War II. And we helped to broker an apology and reparations for victims of the Holocaust.

Of course, the fact we have acknowledged these wrongs doesn't make up for the pain of the past. But if what we've done in these cases wasn't sufficient to fulfill that impossible goal, it was necessary to restore the goodwill needed to change our future. In giving these and other Americans the dignity of an honest admission that our nation was wrong, these apologies have given us all a measure of healing.

Nearly 14 decades after slavery was abolished, its legacy still reverberates through Americans' daily lives. Neither former slaves nor slave owners are alive today, and few Americans trace their own roots to slavery. But all Americans bear slavery's bitter burdens — the lingering racial tensions, the stubborn poverty and dysfunction that is disproportionately high among African-Americans, the persistence that justice has not yet been done.

"I am sorry" are the first words uttered by anyone sincere about righting a wrong. And yet in the case of our nation's greatest moral failing, we have yet to say these words. We have pursued countless policies toward the goal of racial healing. We have been enriched by the determination of African-Americans to overcome the problems rooted in their ancestors' enslavement. But neither their success, nor the blood spilled in our Civil War, excuses our country's continuing silence.

Some critics say an apology may open old wounds. Some say that paying reparations is essential to atonement. But no one can say those three words don't ring true.

NO Robert W. Tracinski
Fellow, Ayn Rand Institute, Marina del Rey, Calif.

Written for *CQ Researcher*, June 2001

An apology for slavery on behalf of the nation presumes that whites today, who mostly oppose racism and never owned slaves, still bear a collective responsibility — simply by belonging to the same race as the slaveholders of the Old South. Such an apology promotes the very idea at the root of slavery: racial collectivism.

Slave owners were certainly guilty of a grave injustice. But by what standard can other whites be held responsible for their ideas and actions? By what standards can today's Americans be obliged to apologize on the slaveholders' behalf? The only justification for such an approach is the idea that each member of the race can be blamed for the actions of every other member, that we are all just interchangeable cells of the racial collective.

Critics of the proposed apology oppose it, not because it embraces this racist premise but because it does not go far enough. They want to apply the notion of racial collectivism in a more "substantial" form, by increasing welfare and affirmative-action programs designed to compensate for the wrongs of slavery. Such compensation consists of punishing random whites, by taxing them and denying them jobs and promotions in order to reward random blacks.

The ultimate result of this approach is not racial harmony or a color-blind society but racial warfare. It is precisely this kind of mentality that has devastated the Balkans, with each ethnic tribe continually exacting revenge on the other in retaliation for centuries-old grievances.

The idea of a national apology for slavery merely reinforces this same kind of racial enmity in America. By treating all whites as the stand-ins or representatives for slaveholders, it encourages the view of blacks and whites as a collective of victims pitted against an opposing and hostile collective of oppressors, with no possibility for integration or peaceful coexistence.

The only alternative to this kind of racial Balkanization is to embrace the opposite principle: individualism. People should be judged based on their choices, ideas and actions as individuals, not as "representatives" of a racial group. They should be rewarded based on their own merits — and they must not be forced to pay, or to apologize, for crimes committed by others, merely because those others have the same skin color.

Americans both black and white should reject the notion of a collective guilt for slavery. They should uphold the ideal of a color-blind society, based on individualism, as the real answer to racism.

South Carolina Gov. Jim Hodges helps to break ground for an African-American monument last year in Columbia. In spite of efforts by several states to come to terms with the history and contributions of black Americans, many advocates for slavey reparations say that only restitution will close the racial divide.

Robinson doesn't want direct cash payments to African-Americans, especially people like himself, who are in the middle- or upper-income brackets. He favors establishment of a trust fund to assist underprivileged blacks. "The question we need to be asking is: How do we repair the damage?" Robinson asks. "We need a massive diffusion of capital to provide poor African-American youth with education — from kindergarten through college — and some sort of fund to promote economic development."

Most legal experts do not expect Cochran, Ogletree and the others to succeed, noting that the claim is almost 150 years old and thus the statute of limitations expired long ago.

"Even in a friendly court, there are going to be statute of limitations problems," Tulane University Law School Professor Robert Wesley says.[27] Moreover, experts point out, under the doctrine of sovereign immunity governments are protected from most legal actions.

Still, some legal scholars say the suit is not wholly a pipe dream, noting that civil rights attorneys in the 1950s and '60s also faced long odds in their battle to end race discrimination. "This will be a daunting task, but it is certainly not impossible," says Robert Belton, a Vanderbilt University law professor.

Even if the suit does not ultimately lead to redress or an apology, it may succeed on another level, says David Bositis, senior political analyst at the Joint Center for Political and Economic Studies, a think tank focusing on African-American issues. "Even if they just got some federal district judge to hear the case, it would become a much larger news item and so would stimulate discussion and debate," he says. "They would consider that a victory."

The black legal team is also planning to sue private companies that benefited from slavery, including banks, insurance companies, shipping firms and other businesses that may have profited from the slave trade.

Research by New York City lawyer and activist Deadria Farmer-Paellmann revealed that several insurance companies — including Aetna and New York Life — insured slave owners against the loss of their "property."

"If you can show a company made immoral gains by profiting from slavery, you can file an action for unjust enrichment," she said.[28] Her work coincides with a new California law requiring all insurance companies in the state to research past business records and disclose any connections to slavery.

In addition, a growing chorus of civil rights leaders, including the Rev. Jesse L. Jackson, has called on insurers to pay some form of restitution. "We call on the insurance companies to search their national files and disclose any and all policies issued to insure slave owners during the period of slavery," Jackson said.[29]

Some black leaders have suggested that culpable corporations establish scholarship funds for underprivileged black students.

But, while Aetna has publicly apologized for insuring owners against the loss of slaves, it has refused to provide compensation, arguing that slavery was legal when the policies were issued. New York Life is withholding comment until it finishes reviewing its historical records.

OUTLOOK

Starting a Dialogue

Those working to obtain reparations for slavery often compare the fight with the long, uphill struggle faced by civil rights activists in the 1950s and '60s. "The relative powerlessness of our community is not a new thing for

African-Americans," the University of Maryland's Walters says. "We've been here before and have won, and I think we're going to win this time, too."

"The uneasiness that some express about reparations is the same uneasiness that we had about integration and about a woman's right to choose," Harvard's Ogletree said. "We've gained some important mainstream viability, but these things take time."[30]

For now, reparations proponents say that they hope to get the government to consider the issue, just as it did for Japanese-American internees and Holocaust survivors. "Right now this is about process," Walters says. "With Japanese-Americans, nothing really happened until after the government took some time to study the issue."

But opponents and others are confident the effort will fail. "This is going to die out because it makes no sense," George Mason's Williams says. "Conyers' bill is languishing in Congress and will continue to languish in Congress, because white politicians cannot sell this to white America."

MIT's Nobles agrees. "The best they can hope for from Congress is some sort of formal apology," she says. A claim based on an injustice that occurred so long ago is simply too nebulous to warrant serious consideration by lawmakers or judges, she says. "This isn't like the case of Japanese-Americans, where you had direct survivors of the act in question. [The former internees'] suffering was identifiable and for a specific period of time — four years — making it much less complicated."

Efforts against private firms — like insurance companies — have a better chance of producing some monetary reward, she predicts. "Eventually, some company will feel the heat, cave in and set up some sort of trust fund or something," she says, adding that Cochran, Ogletree and the other attorneys are unlikely to quit without something to show for their efforts. "To prove that all of this [effort] was worthwhile, they're going to work for a real win."

Others agree the movement will probably achieve at least some of its goals. "The less sophisticated supporters may think that they're going to win reparations, but the more sophisticated ones know that, in the near term, the chance of this happening is very unlikely," says Bositis, of the Joint Center for Political and Economic Studies.

"For these more realistic people, the principal thing they are trying to do is to start a dialogue on the issue, to get people talking about it," he concludes.

NOTES

1. Quoted in Jane Clayson, "Some Civil Rights Leaders Say Descendants of Slaves Should Be Compensated," CBS News: "The Early Show," Jan. 11, 2001.

2. Larry Bivins, "Debate on Reparations for Slavery Gaining Higher Profile," Gannett News Service, April 21, 2001.

3. For background, see Kenneth Jost, "Holocaust Reparations," *CQ Researcher*, March 26, 1999, pp. 257-280.

4. Quoted in Abraham H. Foxman, "The Dangers of Holocaust Restitution," *The Wall Street Journal*, Dec. 7, 1998.

5. Quoted in *Ibid.*

6. Mortimer Adler, *Aristotle for Everybody* (1978), p. 126.

7. Quoted in Arthur Spiegelman, "Leaders of Fight for Holocaust Reparations Under Attack," *The Houston Chronicle*, Dec. 27, 1998

8. Matthew 5:10.

9. Adam Smith, *The Theory of Moral Sentiments* (1759), pp. 47-48.

10. Elazar Barkan, *The Guilt of Nations: Restitution and Negotiating Historical Injustices* (2000), p. 183.

11. Mitchell T. Maki, *et al.*, *Achieving the Impossible Dream: How Japanese-Americans Obtained Redress* (1999), p. 54.

12. Barkan, *op. cit.*, p. 34.

13. Maki, *op. cit.*, p. 107.

14. *Ibid.*

15. *Ibid.*, pp. 121-128.

16. Christine C. Lawrence, ed., *1988 CQ Almanac* (1988), p. 80.

17. *Ibid.*

18. Maki, *op. cit.*, p. 213.

19. *Ibid.*, p. 214.

20. Barkan, *op. cit.*

21. Jost, *op. cit.*

22. Henry Weinstein, "Spending by Holocaust Claims Panel Criticized," *Los Angeles Times*, May 17, 2001.

23. "Key Dates in Nazi Slave Labor Talks," *The Jerusalem Post*, May 21, 2001.

24. Quoted in Erin Texeira, "Black Reparations Idea Builds at UCLA Meeting," *Los Angeles Times*, May 12, 2001.

25. Quoted in Tamar Lewin, "Calls for Slavery Restitution Getting Louder," *The New York Times*, June 4, 2001.

26. Kevin Merida, "Did Freedom Alone Pay a Nation's Debt?" *The Washington Post*, Nov. 28, 1999.

27. Quoted in Tovia Smith, "Legal Scholars Considering Class Action Lawsuit to Seek Restitution for Descendants of African Slaves," Weekend Edition Saturday, National Public Radio, April 1, 2001.

28. Quoted in Lewin, *op. cit.*

29. Quoted in Tim Novak, "Jackson: Companies Owe Blacks," *The Chicago Sun Times*, July 29, 2000.

30. Quoted in Lewin, *op. cit.*

BIBLIOGRAPHY

Books

Barkan, Elazar, *The Guilt of Nations: Restitution and Negotiating Historical Injustices*, W.W. Norton (2000).
A professor of history at Claremont Graduate University has written an excellent and thorough history of restitution efforts in the 20th century, from attempts by Holocaust survivors to recover stolen property to the campaign to compensate "comfort women" forced to provide sex to Japanese soldiers. Barkan also examines the intellectual origins of the reparations movement.

Finkelstein, Norman G., *The Holocaust Industry: Reflections on the Exploitation of Jewish Suffering*, Verso, 2000.
Finkelstein, a professor of political theory at Hunter College, charges lawyers and Jewish groups with exploiting the Holocaust for financial and political gain, using unethical and immoral tactics. He contends that much of the money "extorted" from European companies and countries is not going to survivors, and that the entire process is degrading the historical legacy of the Holocaust.

Maki, Mitchell T., Harry H. L. Kitano and S. Megan Berthold, *Achieving the Impossible Dream: How Japanese Americans Obtained Redress*, University of Illinois Press (1999).
The authors trace the history of efforts to get the U.S. government to pay reparations to Japanese-Americans interned during World War II.

Robinson, Randall, *The Debt: What America Owes to Blacks*, Plume, 2000.
The president of TransAfrica argues for reparations for African-Americans, writing: "If . . . African Americans will not be compensated for the massive wrongs and social injuries inflicted upon them by their government, during and after slavery, then there is no chance that America can solve its racial problems — if solving these problems means, as I believe it must, closing the yawning economic gap between blacks and whites in this country."

Articles

Bivis, Larry, "Debate on Reparations for Slavery Gaining Higher Profile," Gannett News Service, April 21, 2001.
The article examines African-Americans' growing call for reparations.

Dyckman, Martin, "Our Country has Paid the Bill for Slavery," *St. Petersburg Times*, June 25, 2000.
Dyckman makes a strong case against reparations to black Americans, arguing that the Union soldiers who died in the Civil War to free the slaves paid the country's debt to African-Americans.

Jost, Kenneth, "Holocaust Reparations," *CQ Researcher*, March 26, 1999.
Jost gives an excellent overview of the debate over reparations for the survivors of the Nazi Holocaust. His description of the fight over dormant bank accounts and insurance policies in Switzerland is particularly illuminating.

McTague, Jim, "Broken Trusts: Native Americans Seek Billions They Say Uncle Sam Owes Them," *Barron's*, April 9, 2001.
McTague examines the Native American lawsuit against the federal government for decades of mishandling of the

trust fund derived from the lease and sale of natural resources on Indian lands. The tribe recently won a judgment against the federal government, and the suit may result in native tribes receiving up to $10 billion.

Merida, Kevin, "Did Freedom Alone Pay a Nation's Debt?" *The Washington Post*, **Nov. 28, 1999.**
Merida examines the movement to obtain reparations for the African-American descendants of slaves, providing a good historical overview of efforts to compensate newly freed slaves after the Civil War.

Schoenfeld, Gabriel, "Holocaust Reparations — A Growing Scandal," *Commentary Magazine*, **Sept. 2000.**
The magazine's senior editor takes Jewish groups to task for their hardball tactics against Germany and other European countries in their Holocaust reparations

efforts. He worries they will foment bad feeling in Europe against Jews and Israel.

Trounson, Rebecca, "Campus Agitator," *Los Angeles Times*, **April 10, 2001.**
The article chronicles the controversy surrounding recent attempts by conservative commentator David Horowitz to place ads in college newspapers that argue against reparations for African-Americans.

Zipperstein, Steven J., "Profit and Loss," *The Washington Post*, **Sept. 24, 2000.**
A professor of Jewish studies at Stanford University accuses author Norman G. Finkelstein of making wild and unsubstantiated charges in *The Holocaust Industry* (see above). "Imagine an old-style rant, with its finely honed ear for conspiracy, with all the nuance of one's raging, aging, politicized uncle," he writes.

For More Information

Anti-Defamation League, 823 United Nations Plaza, New York, N.Y. 10017; (212) 490-2525; www.adl.org. Fights anti-Semitism and represents Jewish interests worldwide.

Conference on Jewish Material Claims Against Germany, 15 East 26th St., Room 906, New York, N.Y. 10010; (646) 536-9100; www.claimscon.org. Pursues reparations claims on behalf of Jewish victims of the Nazi Holocaust.

Japanese American Citizens League (JACL), 1765 Sutter St., San Francisco, Calif. 94115; (415) 921-5225. www.jacl.org. The nation's oldest Asian-American civil rights group fights discrimination of Japanese-Americans.

Joint Center for Political and Economic Studies, 1090 Vermont Ave., N.W., Suite 1100, Washington, D.C. 20005; (202) 789-3500; www.jointcenter.org. Researches and analyzes issues of importance to African-Americans.

National Coalition of Blacks for Reparations in America, P.O. Box 90604, Washington, D.C. 20090-0604; (202) 291-8400; www.ncobra.com. Lobbies for reparations for African-Americans.

Native American Rights Fund, 1712 N St., N.W., Washington, D.C. 20036; (202) 785-4166; www.narf.org. Provides Native Americans with legal assistance for land claims.

TransAfrica, 1629 K St., N.W., Suite 1100, Washington D.C. 20036; (202) 223-1960; www.transafricaforum.org. Lobbies on behalf of Africans and people of African descent around the world.

U.S. Holocaust Memorial Museum, 100 Raoul Wallenberg Place, S.W., Washington, D.C. 20024; (202) 488-0420; www.ushmm.org. Preserves documentation and encourages research about the Holocaust.

World Jewish Congress, P.O. Box 90400, Washington, D.C. 20090; (212) 755-5770; www.worldjewishcongress.org. An international federation of Jewish communities and organizations that has been at the forefront of negotiations over Holocaust reparations.

7

Contaminated drainage ditches run through the largely African-American Hyde Park neighborhood in Augusta, Ga.

From *CQ Researcher*, June 19, 1998 (updated August 2006).

Environmental Justice

Mary H. Cooper and Alan Greenblatt

I n 1982, the state of North Carolina decided to do something about the "midnight dumpers" who were illegally spraying oil laced with polychlorinated biphenyls (PCBs), a highly toxic compound similar to dioxin, along roadways throughout the state. PCBs, a blend of up to 209 individual chemical compounds, are known to cause skin and immunological problems in humans and cancer in rats. State officials decided to concentrate PCBs in a 142-acre waste dump in Afton, which is in Warren County in the eastern part of the state. Needless to say, local residents were not thrilled.

More than 84 percent of the Warren County population was black and the county is significantly much poorer than North Carolina as a whole. It seemed as if in locating the site of the PCB dump — as in so many cases of chemical contamination — businessmen and politicians took the course of least political resistance, choosing an area whose residents appeared to lack the political or economic clout to engage in the kind of NIMBY ("Not in My Backyard") howling that makes site selection for controversial projects so difficult.

Environmental justice refers to cases where human rights and the environment impact each other, where communities become polluted by nearby refineries, chemical plants or other polluters. "The siting of the PCB landfill in Afton is a textbook case of environmental racism," according to Robert D. Bullard, executive director of the Environmental Justice Resource Center at Clark Atlanta University, and a leading scholar and proponent of the movement. [1]

But something surprising happened in Warren County. Residents may not have had many political tools, but they did march in protest of the new dump site, drawing national attention to their cause.

151

Residents of Chester, Pa., went to court to block construction of a waste facility in their community. The Supreme Court agreed on June 8 to decide whether the activists can bring suit in federal court alleging environmental racism.

The Warren County landfill not only illustrated the problem, but prompted a federal General Accounting Office study that confirmed that hazardous waste landfills throughout the South were disproportionately located in black communities. [2] Warren County residents started to hear many promises from state government officials that they would do something to mitigate or correct the environmental damage done to their area.

But it was not until 2003 that the land was actually cleaned up. State and federal agencies spent $18 million to detoxify the contaminated landfill, by digging up and burning 81,500 tons of oil-laced soil in an 800-degree kiln. [3]

This cleanup effort in Warren County, however delayed or incomplete, at least gave environmental justice advocates something to cheer about. They haven't enjoyed too many such occasions in recent years. Their greatest political victory came more than a dozen years ago, when President Clinton signed an executive order directing federal agencies concerned with health or the environment to take environmental justice concerns into effect. "All communities and persons across this nation should live in a safe and healthful environment," the president's order declared. [4]

Since then, however, the federal Office of Environmental Justice has been mostly moribund, with the Environmental Protection Agency's own inspector general complaining about lack of enforcement efforts.

In 2004, the inspector general concluded that EPA had not fully implemented Clinton's order "nor consistently integrated environmental justice into its day-to-day operation. [The agency] has neither defined nor developed criteria for determining [who is] disproportionately impacted." [5]

The inspector general's report defines "disproportionate impact" as the "adverse effects of environmental actions that burden minority and/or low-income populations at a higher rate than the general population." That's become a less useful term for the environmental justice movement in recent years because most of the environmental justice battles have been waged not in the political arena, but in the courts. During the 1980s and 1990s, the environmental justice movement set one precedent after another in presenting their lawsuits. But in 2001, the Supreme Court took a good deal of steam out of their legal strategy by determining in an Alabama case that plaintiffs filing actions under the Civil Rights Act must show "intentional" discrimination, rather than simply proving "disparate impact," which had meant, in environmental justice cases, that poor or minority residents are shown to suffer more than whites from pollution. [6] The Court's decision was good news for companies whose expansion or location plans had run afoul of the environmental justice movement in recent years. Since the first lawsuit of this type was filed in 1979 against a waste-dump operator in Houston, activists have turned increasingly to the courts on behalf of poor and minority communities seeking protection from pollution. [7]

Although environmental justice advocates had successfully lobbied companies to change their siting plans in a number of U.S. communities, they won their first legal victory in 1998. A Nuclear Regulatory Commission (NRC) hearing board rejected plans to build a uranium-enrichment plant in a poor, minority community in northwestern Louisiana.

That same year, Shintech Corporation, a Japanese-owned company, bowed to 18 months' worth of community pressure and legal maneuvers and canceled its plan to open a $700 million polyvinyl chloride (PVC) plant in Convent, Louisiana. Convent's population is more than 80 percent black, and the area was already burdened by other polluters. St. James Parish (Louisiana's term for counties) was already home to 11 fertilizer and chemical plants.

Indeed, the parish lies along a stretch of the Mississippi River between Baton Rouge and New Orleans that is so heavily industrialized it's known as "cancer alley." More than 130 chemical plants line the 120-mile river corridor, many of which have spewed thousands of tons of dioxin and other carcinogens into the air, water and soil for decades. Before Shintech decided against locating in St. James Parish, Richard Mason, an executive with the company, said, "We did not choose that site because there were African Americans there. We chose it because there was nobody there."

But Bullard and other activists argue that it is no accident that so many toxic polluters have zeroed in on the region. Throughout the country, they say, poor and minority communities are disproportionately exposed to noxious industry byproducts. Siting the Shintech plant in St. James Parish, they contend, would have amounted to yet another instance of environmental racism, another example of a poor community not benefiting from the nationwide improvements in environmental quality over the past three decades.

"This is our *Brown v. Board of Education*, our line in the dirt," says Bullard." This community is already over-burdened with toxic plants."

Despite the obstacles, it is victories like Shintech — which may have been years in coming — that keep environmental justice activists in the fight, despite the odds. Courts have cited the Clinton executive order in finding for plaintiffs in environmental justice cases. Meanwhile, the number of advocacy groups engaged in the issue continues to grow, as does academic interest. There are half a dozen environmental justice centers and legal clinics at universities, primarily in the South — but the University of Michigan offers the nation's only graduate degree in environmental justice.

"Citizens want control of their environment rather than money," says Robert Knox, former director of EPA's Office of Environmental Justice. "The time is past when companies could come in and pay for new school buses or other amenities in exchange for locating in poor, minority communities. Everyone understands about environmental pollution now, and they are not going to accept that any more."

As this chapter in the struggle for civil rights continues to unfold, these are some of the questions being asked:

Children play in a park across from a Shell Oil refinery in Norco, La.

Environmental Justice Resource Center

Do poor and minority populations suffer disproportionately from exposure to toxic materials?

"Poor and minority communities are where you find children with lead poisoning living near polluting industries, garbage dumps, incinerators, petrochemical plants, freeways and highways — all the stuff that other communities reject," says Bullard. "And the fact that the problem has existed for so many years seems to be still a matter of denial for a lot of people."

Statistics seem to confirm Bullard's view. A widely cited study of U.S. census data by the NAACP and the United Church of Christ Commission for Racial Justice found that people of color were 47 percent more likely than whites to live near a commercial hazardous-waste facility. The study also found that the percentage of minorities was three times higher in areas with high concentrations of such facilities than in areas without them. Moreover, the study suggested that minorities" exposure to environmental toxins was getting worse. [8]

The EPA found similar disparities in exposure to toxins depending on income and race. Ninety percent of the nation's 2 million farmworkers, the agency estimates, are people of color, including Chicanos, Puerto Ricans, Caribbean blacks and African Americans. Of these, more than 300,000 are thought to suffer from pesticide-related illnesses each year. Even air pollution affects minorities disproportionately, according to the EPA.

Sixty-five percent of African Americans and 80 percent of Hispanics live in counties that failed to meet at

An Indian Leader Speaks Out for the Land ...

Most instances of environmental racism that come to public attention involve black or Hispanic communities trying to keep polluting factories, sewage plants or toxic-waste dumps out of their communities. But an older and much less visible struggle is being fought by remote Indian tribes that are trying to clean up water supplies contaminated by mine tailings. Since the mid-19th century, miners and mining company executives have scoured the West for gold, silver and other minerals. They have left behind vast deposits of waste rock, or tailings, containing toxic materials. Cyanide and other chemicals used to separate some ores from rock also are left behind, usually in holding ponds. Over the years, rainwater carries these pollutants into streams and rivers, where they can be carried for miles, killing fish and contaminating drinking water.

Native Americans' pleas for environmental protection were ignored for decades, but now Indians are gaining a voice in the environmental justice movement. In what could turn out to be the most sweeping federal cleanup of pollution from mining activities ever undertaken, the Environmental Protection Agency (EPA) in February agreed to study the feasibility of designating the entire Coeur d'Alene River basin in Idaho as a Superfund site. The decision came largely as a result of the efforts of Henry SiJohn, environmental leader of the 1,600-member Coeur d'Alene tribe, whose reservation lies along the southern banks of Lake Coeur d'Alene. Staff writer Mary Cooper interviewed SiJohn by phone from his home in Plummer, Idaho.

How long has pollution in the Coeur d'Alene River basin been a problem?

In the 1920s and '30s, we noticed that the water potatoes, which grow along the lake, began to have a strange, metallic taste. We used to drink water from the lake, but we haven't since then.

How did government authorities react to your complaints about the water pollution?

The situation was different then because we were Indians, and everything was done by the superintendents of the Bureau of Indian Affairs. They had charge of us on our reservation. They said we didn't have any voice, that we couldn't buck the state or the federal government. They wouldn't do anything for us.

Do you think minority communities like yours are exposed to more pollution than white Americans?

I'm afraid that's true. It seems we have embedded an undercurrent of racism here in America. The Indian people have been for the longest time put into a situation whereby they were considered people who were unfamiliar with things. They couldn't participate in politics until 1924, when Congress allowed American Indians to have the vote. But even

least one of EPA's outdoor air-quality standards, compared with 57 percent of white. Blacks are twice as likely as whites, and Hispanics are three times more likely than non-Hispanic whites, to live in counties that did not meet EPA air quality standards for four specific pollutants. [9]

Some critics of the environmental justice movement say the stunning improvements in environmental quality brought by thirty years of anti-pollution legislation benefit everyone in the United States. They also claim that the remaining environmental threats do not necessarily impact poor or non-white Americans more than anyone else.

"Since toxic air emissions, pesticide runoffs and groundwater contamination cannot neatly select their victims by race or income, the inequities visited upon minorities afflict a great many others as well," writes Christopher H. Foreman Jr., a nonresident senior fellow at the Brookings Institution. "Indeed, the range of arguably significant environmental-equity comparisons is so broad that some doubtless cut the other way: Many Native Americans, for example, breathe cleaner air than urban Yuppies and live further from hazardous waste than New Jersey's white ethnics." [10]

Activists reject this reasoning as out of hand. "Sure, everyone is exposed to some level of toxins," says Knox, the former EPA official, "but exposure is disproportionate in poor and minority communities. He points to a

... An Interview with Idaho's Henry SiJohn

that didn't help for a long time because we had to establish our tribal government as an entity in itself and prove to people we knew what we were doing. Then we had to do assessment screenings to determine the pollution in the river basin.

Is the government responding adequately to your requests now?

I wish the EPA would protect the environment, especially of Indian people, through the enforcement arm of their agency. I feel they have been neglectful of punishing people that are the perpetrators of this pollution. If the Indians were the polluters, the public would have gotten up in arms and demanded that the Indians pay. However, this isn't the case. And the federal government has not protected the Indian people or the environment to the point where they enforce the law.

Has President Clinton's support of environmental justice affected your dealings with EPA?

By good fortune, I feel optimistic, in that someone is getting to the president of the United States with this issue. I have a lot of faith in Vice President Al Gore and his staff. I feel they truly have the interests of the environment at heart. But they can't move without the Congress of the United States. Congress is for corporate America, and corporate America is the segment of society that has dug this hole for us, and I don't know if we can escape.

Has the environmental justice movement helped your cause?

Environmental justice advocates are trying to help, but they don't have any idea how to go about it. I feel they and the Clinton administration could do more if they would only take a stand and tell the perpetrators they're the guilty ones.

Industry is polluting the rivers of America. People need to understand the Indian philosophy of the cycle of life. Fish have to spawn, and the spawning beds have to be protected, so they can complete the cycle of life. Because people don't understand this, they jeopardize the species to the point where they're endangered, and then we have this big to-do with the Endangered Species Act. So we have a political response rather than a natural response. Things would be different if people let animals complete the cycle of life.

Do you think EPA will accept your request to clean up the Coeur d'Alene River basin?

I'm very optimistic. If America doesn't wake up and take hold of things, it's going to put us all in jeopardy. People need to realize they can't survive without the environment. That's where the Indian philosophical view comes in. It perpetuates the purity of the environment. Without the natural resources of fish, animals, birds and the like we can't live. We will starve.

---

black neighborhood in Gainesville, Ga., that accounts for just 20 percent of the town's population but handles 80 percent of its waste. The predominantly black town of Chester, Pa., accounts for 7 percent of Delaware County's population but has 70 percent of the county's waste facilities. "That's clearly disproportionate," Knox says. "And it's not atypical for the country as a whole."

Some business representatives reject the notion that factory owners even look for communities of any kind to site their facilities. They say that when petrochemical companies flocked to southern Louisiana early in the century, for example, they were drawn primarily by the fact that such a long segment of the Mississippi

River was deep enough to enable oceangoing barges to transport large shipments of raw materials and finished products.

"No one lived near the Baton Rouge Exxon refinery, the oldest in Louisiana, when it was built in the early 1900s," says Dan S. Borne, president of the Louisiana Chemical Association in Baton Rouge. "It and other chemical plants were built in agricultural areas, and communities literally grew toward them because that's where the jobs were. What's inferred in this debate — that people of color are targeted for chemical plants simply because they're people of color — is repugnant and ridiculous."

Riverbank State Park was built on top of the North River Sewage Treatment Plant in West Harlem, N.Y.

Does President Clinton's 1994 executive order provide sufficient guarantees of environmental justice?

By the time President Clinton issued his 1994 environmental justice executive order, more than ten years had passed since the first complaints of environmental racism gained public attention. In November 1992, in response to growing pressure to address the concerns of communities exposed to toxins, President George H.W. Bush created the Office of Environmental Equity within EPA to study the problem.

But it was not until Clinton's 1994 policy statement that the goal of environmental justice gained formal recognition at the federal level. "[E]ach federal agency shall make achieving environmental justice part of its mission by identifying and addressing, as appropriate, disproportionately high and adverse human health or environmental effects of its programs, policies and activities on minority populations and low-income populations," Clinton declared.

The agencies were not only required to correct existing problems but also had to take steps to prevent environmental injustice from occurring in the first place. Clinton gave each federal agency a year to develop and submit its strategy for achieving environmental justice and another year to report on progress in implementing the strategy.

Even though the new policy directive did not change laws currently in force, environmental justice advocates thought it would strengthen both the 1964 Civil Rights Act and the 1969 National Environmental Policy Act, which calls for environmental information to be made available to citizens. "We have two important pieces of legislation on the books which, if used in tandem, can be very potent weapons against environmental racism," says Bullard, pointing to several instances in which plans to build polluting facilities in communities of color were rejected after Clinton issued his executive order.

"These decisions make a lot of states nervous because they haven't really enforced equal protection when it comes to permitting," he says. "They could even lose transportation dollars because environmental justice is not just incinerators and landfills. It's also construction of highways, which have definite impacts on low-income communities and communities of color."

The order has been lightly enforced, as EPA's inspector general reports. Nevertheless, it's had a measure of influence. According to Knox, Clinton's executive order changed the way states are dealing with the issue. Nearly half the states have created formal policies regarding environmental justice "and all but 13 . . . have enacted formal policy or programs that aim to fight discrimination in the placement of landfills, highways and industrial facilities," according to Stateline.org, a news service covering state governments. [11]

"They did this as a result of the executive order," Knox says. "They want to look at problem areas in the states so they can get ahead of the problem."

But some civil rights activists fear the policy may tip the scales in favor of those who want to keep industry out of poor areas at all costs, even when vital job opportunities are at stake. "In light of the executive order, environmental justice requires balancing economic benefit with environmental risks," writes Ernest L. Johnson, president of the Louisiana NAACP. "It is critical that we not succumb to outside pressure by those who have otherwise failed to promote their ideologies and now use the 'environmental race card' for their own agendas."

Does the focus on environmental justice distract attention from bigger health problems in poor and minority communities?

Some observers suggest that by single-mindedly opposing industrial development in poor communities, environmental justice activists may be hurting the very people they purport to represent. "It's very common to meet people in St. James, both black and white, who say their great-great-grandfather lived here," says Mason of Shintech. "They also say they want to continue living here with their families but that there are no job opportunities that will allow them to stay. Because the base of employment there now is the parish government and the existing chemical plants, the only way to find a job is if someone quits, retires or dies."

Not only are poverty and joblessness more serious problems for most minority communities than pollution, critics say, but so are a whole range of health and social ills. "Hypertension, obesity, low birth weights, inadequate prenatal care, substance abuse and violence are only some of the forces that arguably deserve pride of place in the struggle to improve the lives and health of communities of color," writes Foreman of Brookings. "That such forces are more intractable and harder to mobilize around than a Superfund site or a proposed landfill must not deter communities from asking . . . hard questions about overall health priorities." [12]

Activists say it is false logic to draw distinctions between their quest for environmental equity and these other goals of poor, minority communities. "Environmental justice is also about health," Bullard says. "The No. 1 reason why children in these communities are hospitalized is not because of drive-by shootings. It's because of asthma." The incidence of respiratory diseases has increased, especially among children and the elderly, in areas of high concentrations of ozone and particulate matter, notably urban neighborhoods close to major roadways. [13]

Bullard also points to lead poisoning as an environmental threat to health in minority communities. "The No. 1 threat to kids is lead poisoning, and this, too, is an environmental justice issue because African-American children are three to five times more likely to be poisoned by lead than are low-income white children," he says. "That's the direct result of residential segregation, so housing is another environmental justice issue."

Even crime and illiteracy can be traced to environmental racism, in Bullard's view. "There is a direct correlation between lead poisoning and learning disabilities, aggressive behavior and kids dropping out of school," he says. "So if you look at the root of many of the problems facing minority communities, both physical and environmental, you'll see they are all about health. It's no longer just a matter of a chemical plant."

Knox of the EPA agrees that environmental pollution has far-reaching effects on the quality of life in poor and minority neighborhoods. "Some people say the fight against crime should take precedence over other issues in these neighborhoods," he says. "But environmental problems only exacerbate such problems as crime and asthma in minority communities. Just because a community is poor doesn't mean the people there should not breathe clean air, drink clean water and be able to eat fruit from their gardens. You would not expect to find the same environmental quality in South Central Los Angeles that you find in Beverly Hills, but that doesn't mean that the people in South Central L.A. should not have clean air, clean water and clean soil."

BACKGROUND

Plight of the Poor

The poor have always suffered the health effects of inferior living conditions. Even before the Industrial Revolution unleashed the toxic byproducts of the manufacturing process in Europe and North America, serfs, slaves and farm laborers often lived amid farm animals in crowded, drafty hovels under unsanitary conditions that took a disproportionately heavy toll in the form of infant mortality and premature death among adults.

Industrialization added numerous new environmental threats to health and well-being that were borne overwhelmingly by the poor. As factories sprang up along the railroads and rivers in the center of towns and cities, wealthy families moved out of range of the smoke and foul odors they emitted. Lacking transportation or the money to move away from the industrial centers, poor factory workers had little choice but to live close to their places of work. Where factories sprang up in rural areas along rivers and other transportation corridors, new communities of workers and job-seekers grew up around them.

In the United States, race compounded poverty as a factor in determining exposure to industrial toxins. Beginning in the 1950s, when many black farmworkers moved to cities in the East and Midwest in search of better-paying jobs, they were drawn to downtown neighborhoods where housing was affordable and close to work. Hispanic immigrants also gravitated to low-cost, inner-city neighborhoods where manufacturing jobs could be found, or to farming communities in remote

Residents claim that Fort Lauderdale's Wingate Incinerator, now contaminated and a Superfund cleanup site, spewed ash and soot for over 25 years on the mostly African-American Bass Dillard neighborhood.

agricultural areas of the West — frequent sites of toxic-waste dumps and pesticide contamination.

Native Americans were exposed to inordinate levels of toxic waste by virtue of another historical phenomenon — the relegation of Indians to remote reservations, many of which were later found to harbor vast deposits of uranium, gold, silver and other minerals. Mine tailings exposed many tribes to toxic runoff that contaminated their water supplies.

Birth of a Movement

The environmental plight of poor and minority communities was not an immediate priority of the modern environmental movement, which took shape in the late 1960s. [14] The first Earth Day, held April 22, 1970, marked the start of a national campaign whose main legislative victories were the 1970 Clean Air Act, the 1972 Clean Water Act, the 1973 Endangered Species Act and the 1980 Superfund legislation (the Comprehensive Environmental Response, Compensation and Liability Act).

These basic environmental laws focused on reducing the sources of pollution but basically ignored the varying impact of pollution on different income or racial groups. The first official acknowledgement that poor, non-white Americans were disproportionately impacted by environmental degradation was a statement in the Council

on Environmental Quality's 1971 annual report that racial discrimination adversely affects the urban poor and the quality of their environment. [15]

That discrete communities could be disparately affected by environmental degradation became clear in 1978, when 900 families living in the Love Canal neighborhood of Niagara Falls, N.Y., discovered that their homes had been built near 20,000 tons of toxic waste. Initially rebuffed in their calls for reparations, residents demanded, and eventually won, relocation benefits. Their struggle also helped galvanize public support for federal legislation to clean up hazardous waste — the 1980 Superfund law.

Race and income were not the main issues at Love Canal. Working-class and mostly white, the neighborhood nonetheless served as a model for communities trying to ward off environmental threats. The first largely minority community to take up the challenge was the example first mentioned in Warren County, N.C., where residents in 1982 demonstrated against a state plan to dump 6,000 truckloads of soil laden with (PCBs). More than 500 protesters were arrested, calling national attention to the issue. Although the landfill was completed as planned, the protesters won an agreement from the state that no more landfills would be put in their county, the state's poorest. [16]

A series of reports on environmental threats to poor and minority communities followed the Warren County protest, helping galvanize the nascent movement for environmental justice. The General Accounting Office found in a 1983 study that three of four hazardous-waste facilities in the Southeast were in African-American communities. In 1987, the United Church of Christ issued a widely cited study showing that landfills, incinerators and other waste facilities were found disproportionately in or near poor or minority communities across the country. [17]

In 1990, Bullard published the first of his four books on the subject. Like most other early works on environmental justice, *Dumping In Dixie* focused on toxic wastes and their close association with black communities in the Southeast. Bullard also called attention to the fact that black Americans are far more likely to be exposed to lead than whites, and that Hispanics are more likely to live in areas with high soot pollution. In his efforts to help impacted communities, Bullard was joined by Benjamin Chavis Jr., former executive director of the NAACP, and also other civil rights groups as well as mainstream environmental organizations such as Greenpeace and the Sierra Club and Earthjustice, which sometimes works with poor communities.

The George H. W. Bush administration recognized the environmental justice movement's growing clout in 1990, when then-EPA Administrator William K. Reilly established the Environmental Equity Workgroup to study the issue. Two years later, the movement gained permanent federal status with the creation of the EPA's Office of Environmental Equity.

Clinton's Policies

President Clinton took office in January 1993 promising to restore federal environmental protections that he said had eroded during the previous twelve years of Republican administrations. His newly appointed EPA administrator, Carol M. Browner, declared that environmental justice would be a priority for the agency and renamed the Office of Environmental Equity, the Office of Environmental Justice.

"Many people of color, low-income and Native-American communities have raised concerns that they suffer a disproportionate burden of health consequences due to the siting of industrial plants and waste dumps, and from exposure to pesticides or other toxic chemicals at home and on the job, and that environmental programs do not adequately address these disproportionate exposures," she said shortly after taking office.

"EPA is committed to addressing these concerns and is assuming a leadership role in environmental justice to enhance environmental quality for all residents of the United States. Incorporating environmental justice into everyday agency activities and decisions will be a major undertaking. Fundamental reform will be needed in agency operations." [18]

On September 30, 1993, Browner established the National Environmental Justice Advisory Council (NEJAC), a 23-member group of representatives of environmental organizations, state and local agencies, communities, tribes, businesses and other interested parties to increase public awareness of the issue and help EPA develop strategies to ensure environmental equity. By rotating membership in NEJAC (pronounced "knee-jack," or "knee-jerk" by its critics) every three years, the agency is trying to involve as many interested parties as possible in the ongoing policy debate.

President Clinton elevated environmental justice to yet a higher plane with Executive Order 12898, which required each federal agency involved in public health or environmental matters to "make achieving environmental justice part of its mission," particularly as minority and low-income populations were affected. The order also directed Browner to create and chair an interagency working group on environmental justice to coordinate federal policies aimed at furthering environmental equity.

Recent Cases

The cause of environmental justice advanced on several fronts following President Clinton's 1994 executive order.

In northwest Louisiana in May 1997, a citizens' group blocked plans by a German-owned firm, Louisiana Energy Services, to build the first private uranium-enrichment plant in the United States. After nearly seven years of opposition, Citizens Against Nuclear Trash persuaded the Nuclear Regulatory Commission (NRC) to deny the company the required license based on evidence that race had played a part in site selection.

"The communities around that site are 97 percent black," says Bullard, who drafted a social and economic analysis of the area for the NRC. "The company didn't consider the fact that these people live off the land as subsistence hunters, fishermen and farmers whose water comes from wells. That plant would have been slam-dunk, in-your-face racism."

The company appealed the ruling, but a three-judge NRC panel rejected the appeal. Not only was there evidence that racial discrimination had played a role in the siting process, the judges ruled, but also that the NRC staff had failed to consider the plant's environmental and social impact on the surrounding community, as required by the executive order as well as by the 1969 National Environmental Policy Act.

"This was the first environmental justice case that we actually won in court outright," Bullard says. It was also the first time a federal agency had used President Clinton's executive order to deny a license or permit.

In Flint, Mich., environmental justice activists succeeded in 1997 in delaying the issuance of a permit for a power plant sited in a mostly black neighborhood. The case began after the Michigan Department of Environmental Quality issued a permit to Genesee County to build a cogeneration electric power plant

CHRONOLOGY

1960s *Jobs draw blacks to the industrial East and Midwest and Hispanics to agricultural areas of the West.*

1964 Congress enacts the Civil Rights Act. Title VI of the law prohibits discrimination based on race, color or national origin under programs supported by federal funds.

1969 The National Environmental Policy Act calls for information on pollutants to be made public.

1970s *The environmental movement produces major laws to curb pollution.*

April 22, 1970 The first Earth Day marks the start of a national campaign to improve environmental protection, starting with the Clean Air Act, passed the same year.

1971 The Council on Environmental Quality acknowledges that racial discrimination adversely affects the urban poor.

1972 Congress passes the Clean Water Act.

1978 Residents of the Love Canal neighborhood of Niagara Falls, N.Y., built atop a toxic-waste dump, demand, and eventually win, relocation benefits, establishing a model for later action by poor communities.

1979 The first lawsuit claiming environmental racism is filed against a waste-dump operator on behalf of a poor community in Houston.

1980s *Environmental justice movement takes off.*

1980 The Comprehensive Environmental Response, Compensation and Liability Act creates the Superfund to pay for the identification and cleanup of severely polluted sites.

Oct. 1982 More than 500 protesters are arrested after trying to block a landfill being created for soil laced with polychlorinated biphenyls (PCBs) in Warren County, N.C., the poorest county in the state.

1983 The General Accounting Office finds that three of four hazardous-waste facilities in the Southeast are in black communities.

1990s *Environmental justice gains federal support.*

Nov. 1992 President George H. W. Bush creates the Office of Environmental Equity within the Environmental Protection Agency (EPA).

1993 Newly appointed EPA Administrator Carol M. Browner renames the Office of Environmental Equity the Office of Environmental Justice and promises to promote environmental protection for all Americans.

Feb. 11, 1994 President Clinton directs all federal agencies with a public health or environmental mission to make environmental justice an integral part of their policies.

1998 Browner issues "interim guidance" to provide a framework for processing claims of environmental injustice, based on Title VI of the Civil Rights Act. . . . Shintech Corporation drops its plan to build a $700 million plastics plant in a predominantly African American Louisiana community.

2000s *The environmental justice cause is slowed by court rulings and Bush administration indifference.*

2000 *The Dallas Morning News* and the University of Texas at Dallas find that 870,000 federally subsidized apartments are within one mile of factories that emit toxins.

2001 The Supreme Court finds that plaintiffs seeking redress under Title VI must show evidence of intentional discrimination. . . . Monsanto settles a class action with 1,500 Anniston, Alabama, plaintiffs who complained about PCB contamination.

2002 Shell Oil agrees to buy properties from Norco, Louisiana, residents who live between its chemical plant and its refinery, allowing them to relocate.

2003 Monsanto, Solutia and Pharmacia agree to pay $700 million to settle state and federal lawsuits brought by 22,000 plaintiffs in Anniston, Alabama. . . . State and federal agencies complete an $18 million cleanup of PCB-contaminated soil in Warren County, North Carolina.

2004 EPA's inspector general finds that environmental justice policy is haphazardly addressed by the agency.

2005 Congress blocks EPA from spending money in ways that contradict Clinton's 1994 order . . . Dynegy Midwest Generation agrees to invest $545 million to reduce emissions from its power plants in Illinois to settle a lawsuit filed by the federal government and environmental groups.

fueled in part by wood scraps from building construction and demolition, which might have been contaminated with lead-based paint. The permit allowed lead emissions from the plant of 2.4 tons a year. The Flint chapter of the NAACP and other plaintiffs sued the department, charging that the surrounding community was already overburdened by lead contamination and that by issuing the permit the state had violated its mandate to protect the health of all citizens.

In response, the department reduced the allowable level of lead emissions, but the plaintiffs proceeded with the suit, charging the department with practicing racial discrimination in issuing the permit in the first place. According to Director Harding, the department agreed to comply with additional demands but refused to settle the case because the plaintiffs would not drop their charges of racial discrimination.

Both sides claimed a victory of sorts from the judgment, handed down on May 29, 1997, by circuit court judge Archie Hayman. Plaintiffs won an injunction against future permits, pending the state's performance of risk assessments to be paid for by applicants and the holding of broader public hearings when applications for toxic facilities are made. They also won recognition that compliance with air-quality standards under the Clean Air Act does not necessarily mean that a community is not adversely affected by air pollution.

For its part, the state claimed vindication on the racial discrimination charges. "The judge said there was no racial discrimination," Harding says. "In fact, he complimented my agency, saying our overall environmental regulatory system was sufficiently protective, though he directed the agency to do more initial determinations of environmental impact."

In Chester, Pa., residents complained that their predominantly African-American city had become the main waste dump for all of largely white Delaware County. In 1996, after the Pennsylvania Department of Environmental Protection issued a permit to Soil Remediation Services Inc. to build yet another waste facility in the city, Chester Residents Concerned for Quality Living sued the agency for racial discrimination in its permitting process.

Their suit, *Chester Residents Concerned for Quality Living v. Seif*, was the first filed against a state agency under Title VI of the 1964 Civil Rights Act, which prohibits agencies that receive federal funds from practicing racial discrimination, either deliberately or by effecting "policies or practices [that] cause a discriminatory effect."

On November 6, 1996, U.S. District Judge Stewart Dalzell dismissed the suit for technical reasons. On December 30, 1997, however, the court of appeals for the Third Circuit overturned the district court, allowing the suit brought by the citizens' group to proceed. The ruling also set an important legal precedent by enabling a low-income and minority community to pursue a charge of environmental racism regardless of whether the discrimination was deliberate. The Supreme Court agreed to hear the case, but didn't address the question of whether lawsuits alleging environmental racism can be brought in federal court. The Court simply declared the case moot in 1998, because the state had denied SRS its operating permit while the case was still under appeal.

Pressure on EPA

The court of appeals' ruling in the Chester case did not elaborate on the question of evidence needed to mount a successful environmental justice suit against a state agency. [19] With the proliferation of charges of environmental racism in the 1990s, the EPA has come under increasing pressure to clarify the procedures for dealing with such cases. "EPA had to respond to a backlog of complaints," said Robert Knox. "The agency had to do something to respond to this, so we issued guidelines to help identify who could bring claims and what constitutes a disparate impact on a community."

The backlogged complaints included the one in Louisiana brought against Shintech, which proposed in September 1997 to build a state-of-the-art plant to produce PVC, used to make a range of consumer products, such as plumbing pipes and shrink-wrap food wrapping. On May 23, 1997, the Louisiana Department of Environmental Quality issued three air permits for the facility. But on September 10, in response to a citizens' petition, EPA Administrator Browner took the agency's first formal action on the environmental justice issue.

She canceled one of the firm's permits and directed the state agency to take environmental justice into greater consideration when reissuing the permit. In addition, she ordered further investigation of charges that the choice of St. James Parish for the plant site amounted to environmental racism. "It is essential the minority and low-income communities not be disproportionately subjected to environmental hazards," Browner wrote in her decision. [20]

Fighting for Environmental Justice . . .

The ongoing controversy over plans by Shintech Inc. to open a new plastics plant in St. James Parish, La., is among the most visible environmental justice cases. The following are some of the other notable battles being waged around of the country:

Sierra Blanca, Texas — Residents of this West Texas community, located in the 10th poorest county in the nation, fought construction of a low-level nuclear-waste facility outside the town. The facility would be the final repository for radioactive wastes from hospitals and research facilities in Texas, Maine and Vermont. Opponents complained that Sierra Blanca already is home to a large sewage sludge dump and said its selection as a dumping ground for nuclear waste amounted to environmental racism against the area's predominantly Hispanic population. Residents called on Congress to reject the three-state compact authorizing the facility. (*See "At Issue," p. 164.*) They lost their battle April 1, when the Senate approved the House-passed plan after adding amendments requiring an environmental review of the proposed site and barring other states from dumping radioactive wastes there as well.

Brunswick, Ga. — Contamination from lead, mercury, polychlorinated biphenyls (PCBs) and other toxins around an inactive LCP Chemicals-Georgia Inc. plant led to a $40-million, EPA-directed cleanup of this industrial area several years ago. Afterwards, the agency led a detailed area study, called the Brunswick Initiative, which failed to turn up other pollution threats to neighboring communities. But an environmental justice group called Save the People rejected the study's findings. The group and many residents of a mostly black community adjacent to another chemical plant, owned by Hercules Inc., claim that their yards are contaminated by toxaphene, an insecticide that Hercules manufactured until it was banned two decades ago.

Oak Ridge, Tenn. — Residents of the predominantly black neighborhood of Scarboro attribute a range of diseases in their community to the nearby Department of Energy (DOE) Y-12 nuclear weapons plant. The federal Centers for Disease Control and Prevention is investigating a possible link between the plant and respiratory illnesses in Scarboro. The DOE has offered to pay for health assessments but has not yet taken responsibility for any illnesses reported, some of which are the subject of pending litigation.

Houston, Texas — Three decades ago, the Kennedy Heights neighborhood was built over abandoned oil pits once owned by Gulf Oil. Today residents of this African-American community claim that leakage of oil sludge into their water supply is responsible for at least 60 cases of serious diseases found there, such as cancer and lupus, as well as hundreds of other lesser health complaints. In a lawsuit brought against Chevron, which bought out Gulf Oil, plaintiffs claim a corporate document slating the contaminated site for "Negro residential and commercial development" proves that environmental racism is at the root of their medical problems. Chevron denies that the incidence of disease in Kennedy Heights is high enough to prove a link with oil contamination.[1]

Huntington Park, Calif. — After four years of community opposition, the operator of a concrete recycling plant was forced to close it. Similarly, black and Hispanic residents of South East Los Angeles are organizing to get rid of the growing number of recycling facilities in their part of the city. Glass-recycling ventures spew ground glass into the air, residents say, aggravating asthma and other respiratory diseases and killing trees. Metal crushers at car- and appliance-recycling plants cause walls of neighboring houses to crack and release tiny fragments of oil and metal that contaminate the soil.[2]

Pensacola, Fla. — The Escambia Treating Co. ran a wood-treating facility here for 40 years, depositing highly toxic dioxin into the soil and prompting a $4 million Superfund cleanup of the site. Residents of the primarily low-income, black neighborhood adjacent to the site objected to the cleanup, saying it exposed them to an even greater health threat by bringing toxins to the surface. A local activist group, Citizens Against Toxic Exposure, convinced the Environmental Protection Agency (EPA) to test the soil and, as the results proved compelling, pay for the relocation of all 358 households around the site, which is expected to cost $18 million.[3]

As noted earlier, Shintech resolved the issue in 1998 by deciding not to locate the plant in St. James Parish. It had been thought that the Shintech case would provide the test case for the EPA's interim guidance, or guidelines. Browner issued the guidance on February. 5, 1998, in the wake of the Chester ruling, seeking to clarify the

. . . From New Jersey to California

Newark, N.J. — A section of the city's East End, known as Ironbound, lies in one of the most polluted areas of the country. It is home to a garbage incinerator that serves all of Essex County and a sewage-treatment plant serving 33 municipalities and 1.5 million people. The area also contains the now-

Responding to public health concerns in a black neighborhood in Anniston, Ala., Monsanto has begun buying out residents and relocating them.

Environmental Justice Resource Center

closed Diamond Alkali plant, which once produced Agent Orange, the defoliant used in the Vietnam War. The area is thought to have among the highest concentrations of dioxin in the world. When Wheelabrator Technologies tried to build a $63 million sewage sludge treatment facility there, Ironbound's residents claimed that the placement of yet another waste plant in their community, home to many poor Portuguese immigrants, blacks and Hispanics, would constitute environmental racism. The Ironbound Committee Against Toxic Waste persuaded the state Department of Environmental Protection to deny the plant's final permits.[4]

Anniston, Ala. — In the low-lying industrial and residential neighborhood of Sweet Water, production of toxic PCBs had been going on since the 1930s. In 1996, the Alabama Department of Public Health declared Sweet Water and the adjacent community of Cobb Town a public health hazard. Monsanto stopped producing PCBs at the facility in 1971, eight years before EPA banned the chemical, a known carcinogen in laboratory animals. The company also began buying out residents and relocating them, even before agreeing with the state to do so and clean up the polluted areas. But the Sweet Valley-Cobb Town

Environmental Justice Task Force charges Monsanto with environmental racism against the black communities by knowingly releasing PCBs from the plant after the environmental threat became apparent in the late 1960s. About 1,000 residents have sued the company.

Coeur d'Alene, Idaho — Silver mining came to the pristine area around Lake Coeur d'Alene in the 1880s. By the 1920s, members of the Coeur d'Alene Indian tribe began noticing that the water and root vegetables had taken on a metallic taste. Ignored by the mining companies and governmental officials for decades, the 1,600-member tribe finally convinced the EPA in February to consider declaring the entire Coeur d'Alene River basin a Superfund site. If the agency adds the site to its list — which is strongly opposed by local businesses in this recreational area — it will become the largest federal cleanup ever undertaken, covering an area of 1,500 square miles including the Idaho Panhandle and part of western Washington, where mine tailings have also polluted the Spokane River.[5] (*See story, p. 154.*)

[1] See Sam Howe Verhovek, "Racial Tensions in Suit Slowing Drive for 'Environmental Justice,'" *The New York Times*, Sept. 7, 1997.

[2] See David Bacon, "Recycling — Not So Green to Its Neighbors," posted on EcoJustice's Web page, www.igc.org, July 28, 1997.

[3] See Joel S. Hirschhorn, "Two Superfund Environmental Justice Case Studies," posted on Ecojustice's Web page, *op. cit.*

[4] See Ronald Smothers, "Ironbound Draws Its Line at the Dump," *The New York Times*, March 29, 1997.

[5] See Michael Satchell, "Taking Back the Land That Once Was So Pure," *U.S. News & World Report*, May 4, 1998, pp. 61-63.

conditions under which a decision to issue a permit violates Title VI. The guidance describes a five-step process by which the EPA must identify the affected population, primarily on the basis of proximity to the site in question, determine the race or ethnicity of the affected population and decide whether the permitted activity will

Would constructing a low-level radioactive nuclear-waste dump near Sierra Blanca, Texas, constitute "environmental injustice"?

YES — Bill Addington
Rancher, farmer and merchant, Hudspeth County, Texas

From testimony before the House Commerce Subcommittee on Energy and Power, May 13, 1997.

I speak today on behalf of Save Sierra Blanca, our citizens group, and many people in West Texas who feel run over by the state and federal governments. These people are opposed to the forced placement of this risky radioactive-waste cemetery at Sierra Blanca near the Rio Grande River. ...

Most of the people in Hudspeth County and Sierra Blanca are poor — the median annual income is $8,000. Seventy percent of the people are of Hispanic origin, like myself. This is the reason Texas "leaders" have focused on our county for the dump site since 1983. This appeared to be the political path of least resistance. But there is strong resistance locally, regionally and internationally. There are about 3,000 people and 1,300 registered voters in the county, and every one of them who was asked signed the petition against the dump. ...

The siting of the Sierra Blanca dump by the state legislature was a violation of environmental justice and our civil rights. ...

If the radioactive-waste dump is approved in Sierra Blanca, it is likely that additional radioactive and hazardous facilities will follow. Westinghouse Scientific Ecology Group has entered into an option agreement to lease 1,280 acres of land adjoining the proposed Sierra Blanca site for radioactive waste processing and storage, possibly including incineration. There is also a proposal for an additional sludge dump in the community. This concentrating of hazardous facilities in communities is a characteristic of environmental injustice.

The proposed radioactive dump site is geologically fatally flawed. It is in an earthquake zone, and there is a buried fault underneath the proposed trenches. ...

The real reason for the compact is economic — to make it cheaper for nuclear power generators to bury their waste and shift their liability. It does not "protect Texas," as has been touted. ...

Texas began negotiations with ... Maine in 1988, and in 1992 passed the compact. Maine's and Vermont's legislatures have approved the compact. They failed to develop their own waste sites because of heavy opposition. Maine voters approved the compact by referendum, yet people in my home are not even heard or considered. We do not get to vote on the measure or placement of the dump like Mainers, who chose to dump on us, did.

NO — Sen. Olympia J. Snowe, R-Maine

From a Senate Floor Speech, April 1, 1998.

As the law requires, Texas, Vermont and Maine have negotiated an agreement that was approved by each state. ... So, we have before us a compact that has been carefully crafted and thoroughly examined by the state governments and people of all three states involved. Now all that is required is the approval of Congress, so that the state of Texas and the other Texas Compact members will be able to exercise appropriate control over the waste that will come into the Texas facility. ...

Opponents of the Texas Compact would have you believe that should we ratify this compact it will open the doors for other states to dump nuclear waste at a site, in the desert, located five miles from the town of Sierra Blanca, exposing a predominantly low-income, minority community to health and environmental threats.

The truth is that Texas has been planning to build a facility for its own waste since 1981, long before Maine first proposed a compact with Texas. That is because whether or not this compact passes, Texas still must somehow take care of the waste it produces. ...

The opponents of the compact would have you believe this issue is about politics. It is not about politics, it is about science: sound science. It is very dry in the Southwest Texas area, where the small amount of rainfall it receives mostly evaporates before it hits the ground. The aquifer that supplies water to the area and to nearby Mexico is over 600 feet below the desert floor and is encased in rock.

The proposed site has been designed to withstand any earthquake equaling the most severe that has ever occurred in Texas history. Strong seismic activity in the area is non-existent. All these factors mean that the siting of this facility is on strong scientific grounds.

Our opponents say we will be bad neighbors if we pass this compact because the proposed site is near the Mexican border. In fact, the U.S. and Mexico have an agreement, the La Paz Agreement, to cooperate in the environmental protection of the border region. The La Paz Agreement simply encourages cooperative efforts to protect the environment of the region.

Any proposed facility will be protective of the environment because it will be constructed in accordance with the strictest U.S. environmental safeguards.

impose an "undue burden" on the community. The agency will then identify any other permitted facilities in the vicinity that may compound the community's environmental threat.

Aid for "Brownfields"

The EPA's latest attempt to promote environmental justice may prove to be a double-edged sword. For while the interim guidance is intended to make it easier for minority and low-income communities to protect themselves from environmental threats to their health, it may also weaken economic development in these communities by discouraging companies from building new, non-polluting facilities in their midst that could provide needed employment. The EPA has led an effort to convert abandoned commercial and industrial sites into productive use.

Many of these so-called "brownfield" sites scare off investors, fearful of being held liable for potential lawsuits by users of the site. While the sites are polluted, they are not polluted enough to qualify for federally funded cleanup under the Superfund program. On January 25, 1995, EPA launched a program to encourage investors to build non-polluting businesses on brownfield sites, which tend to be in urban areas in or near poor or minority communities. Since the beginning of the brownfields program, EPA has awarded 883 assessment grants totaling $225.4 million, 202 revolving loan fund grants totaling $186.7 million, and 238 cleanup grants totaling $42.7 million.

"A lot of brownfields are in environmental justice communities," says Knox. "These communities see brownfields as providing an opportunity to get involved in the siting process and address problems in the city, an opportunity for jobs and a chance to reverse the fiscal deterioration that has drained resources from their neighborhoods. Most of all, brownfields allow communities to get their vision involved in development because they have a seat at the table."

In Knox's view, furthering environmental justice goes hand in hand with brownfield development. "The interim guidance actually helps," he says. "By ensuring that environmental justice has to be considered in the permitting process and bringing affected communities to the table, we are educating residents so they can take over their own communities and bring in clean industries."

The Southwest Network for Environmental and Economic Justice staged a protest in Phoenix, Ariz., in 1995.

CURRENT SITUATION

Recent Legislation

During the presidency of George W. Bush, environmental justice has lost much of the momentum the cause had built up during the Clinton years. For one thing, the issue has lost saliency in some eyes, with more donors attracted to combating Bush's desires to open up Alaska's Arctic National Wildlife Reserve to oil drilling. And global warming has taken pride of place on the larger green agenda.

The Supreme Court's 2001 ruling that, in order to sue under Title VI of the Civil Rights Act plaintiffs had to prove intentional discrimination — and not just disparate impact — has also had a chilling effect. But there have been some recent victories in longstanding cases. Anniston, Alabama, alone has seen two major settlements. In 2001, 1,500 plaintiffs from the Sweet Valley and Cobb Town neighborhoods settled with Monsanto Company for $42.8 million in a PCB contamination case. Two years later, Monsanto, Solutia and Pharmacia agreed to pay $700 million to settle state and federal lawsuits brought by 22,000 Anniston residents alleging harm from PCBs. Chemical and oil companies have also reached major settlements in Illinois, Louisiana and North Carolina.

In the political arena, environmental justice remains an official policy concern, if not a top-drawer issue. During deliberations over the EPA's budget for 2006, Rep. Alcee

S.C. Delaney/Environmental Protection Agency

Residents of Wagner's Point, a working-class enclave in South Baltimore, link the abnormally high cancer rates in their neighborhood to emissions from a nearby wastewater treatment plant, an oil refinery and other industrial sites.

Hastings, D-Fla., successfully added an amendment to the spending bill that blocks the agency from spending funds in any way that conflicts with Clinton's executive order. (Richard Durbin, D-Ill., sponsored similar language in the Senate). In addition, the House approved an amendment offered by Rep. Raul Grijalva, D-Az., to restore the 32 percent budget cut to the EPA's Office of Environmental Justice that the Bush administration had proposed in 2005. And most states have enacted policies designed to mitigate discrimination in the siting of landfills, highways and other polluting projects.

OUTLOOK

Troubling Disparities

Despite such shows of legislative support, however, it's not clear how vigorously the EPA intends to enforce the 1994 executive order. A series of studies in recent years have found that the agency has not focused on environ-

mental justice. According to Bullard, numerous communities have filed complaints with the EPA's Office of Civil Rights, "only to have their complaints languish for years in an administrative time warp." [21]

A 2004 report issued by the agency's own inspector general found that the executive order was inconsistently enforced. Similarly, the National Academy of Public Administration, in a 2001 study conducted at the Office of Environmental Justice's request, concluded that, "EPA does not now have a routine process for identifying high-risk communities and giving them priority attention to prevent pollution and reduce existing public health hazards." [22] And in 2003, the U.S. Commission on Civil Rights found that "Federal agencies still have neither fully incorporated environmental justice into their core missions . . . Moreover, a commitment to environmental justice is often lacking in agency leadership." [23]

If environmental justice is not a priority for officials in Washington, however, it remains a prime concern to residents of areas that appear to be heavily targeted by polluters. In 1999, the Institute of Medicine reported that communities with populations dominated by the poor and minorities are exposed to much higher levels of pollution than the nation as a whole — and they experience certain diseases much more frequently than residents of affluent white areas. [24]

Long before Hurricane Katrina slammed into the Gulf Coast in 2005, revealing to the nation disparate living conditions of African Americans and whites in Louisiana, local blacks had long complained about living in and around areas that were heavily polluted. Some 135 petrochemical plants that line the 85-mile stretch of the Mississippi River that runs from Baton Rouge to New Orleans, are often located closer to black neighborhoods than to white ones.

Southern Louisiana is hardly the only part of the country where African Americans are exposed to more environmental hazards. A 2005 Associated Press analysis of government research found that black Americans are 79 percent more likely than whites to live in neighborhoods where industrial pollution is suspected of posing great health dangers. Hispanics are more than twice as likely as non-Hispanics to live in the most polluted areas in twelve states, the AP found. [25]

In 2000, the *Dallas Morning News*, in a research study conducted with the University of Texas at Dallas, found that 870,000 federally subsidized apartments — nearly half out of 1.9 million total nationwide" are located within one mile of factories that reported emissions of toxic air pollutions." The paper found that 40 percent of public housing for the poor is located within a mile of at least one toxic waste site. Minorities were more likely to live in housing near toxic sites than whites. [26]

"Poor communities, frequently communities of color but not exclusively, suffer disproportionately," Carol Browner told the AP. "If you look at where our industrialized facilities tend to be located, they're not in the upper middle class neighborhoods."

A Bush administration official said that EPA isn't trying to reduce pollution affecting specific racial or income groups, but rather sees its mission as protecting anyone exposed to the highest risk. "We're going to get at those folks to make sure that they are going to be breathing clean air, and that's regardless of their race, creed or color," said Deputy EPA Administrator Marcus Peacock.

Residents of this African-American neighborhood built on top of the Agriculture Street Landfill in New Orleans are petitioning the EPA to relocate them from the area, now a Superfund site. Activists call this the "black Love Canal."

NOTES

1. Robert D. Bullard, "A Legacy of Injustice," in *The Quest for Environmental Justice: Human Rights and the Politics of Pollution* (2005), p. 40.

2. U.S. General Accounting Office, "Siting Hazardous Waste Landfills and Their Correlation with Racial and Economic Status of Surrounding Communities" (1983).

3. Bullard, p. 38.

4. Executive Order 12898, "Federal Actions to Address Environmental Justice in Minority Populations and Low-Income Populations," Feb. 11, 1994. For background, see "Cleaning Up Hazardous Wastes," *CQ Researcher*, Aug. 23, 1996, pp. 752-776.

5. Office of Inspector General, "EPA Needs to Consistently Implement the Intent of the Executive Order on Environmental Justice," Environmental Protection Agency Evaluation Report No. 2004-P-00007, March 1, 2004, p. i.

6. Linda Greenhouse, "Supreme Court Limits Scope of a Main Civil Rights Law," *The New York Times*, April 25, 2001, p. A14.

7. In *Bean v. Southwestern Waste Management*, residents of a predominantly black subdivision in Houston charged that Browning-Ferris Industries had practiced environmental discrimination by choosing their community to site a municipal solid-waste landfill. They lost the case.

8. Benjamin A. Goldman and Laura Fitton, "Toxic Wastes and Race Revisited, Center for Policy Alternatives," National Association for the Advancement of Colored People and United Church of Christ Commission for Racial Justice, 1994.

9. "Lung Disease Data in Culturally Diverse Communities," American Lung Association, February 2005; available at www.lungusa.org/site/pp.asp?c=dvLUK9O0E&b=308853.

10. Christopher H. Foreman Jr., "A Winning Hand? The Uncertain Future of Environmental Justice," *The Brookings Review*, Spring 1996, p. 24. Foreman's new book, "The Promise and Peril of Environmental Justice," is due to be published by the Brookings Institution in the fall.

11. Jessica Kitchin, "Environmental Justice: An Emerging State Issue," Stateline.org, Aug. 2, 2004; available at www.stateline.org/live/ViewPage.action?siteNodeId=137&languageId=1&contentId=15725.

12. *Ibid.*, p. 25.

13. See American Lung Association, "Health Effects of Outdoor Air Pollution," 1996.

14. For background, see "Environmental Movement at 25," *CQ Researcher*, March 31, 1995, pp. 283-307.

15. See Environmental Protection Agency, Office of Environmental Justice, Environmental Justice 1994 Annual Report: Focusing on Environmental Protection for All People, April 1995.

16. See Robert D. Bullard, *Unequal Protection* (1994), pp. 43-52.

17. General Accounting Office, "Siting of Hazardous Waste Landfills and Their Correlation with Racial and Economic Status of Surrounding Communities" (1983); United Church of Christ Commission for Racial Justice, "Toxic Wastes and Race in the United States" (1987).

18. Quoted in EPA, Environmental Justice 1994 Annual Report, p. 3.

19. See Andrew S. Levine, Jonathan E. Rinde and Kenneth J. Warren, "In Response to Chester Residents, EPA Releases Environmental Justice Rules," *The Legal Intelligencer*, Feb. 18, 1998.

20. See Paul Hoverten, "EPA Puts Plant on Hold in Racism Case," *USA Today*, Sept. 11, 1998.

21. Bullard 2005, p. xi.

22. "Environmental Justice in EPA Permitting: Reducing Pollution in High-Risk Communities is Integral to the Agency's Mission," National Academy of Public Administration, December 2001, p. 3.

23. "Not in My Backyard: Executive Order 12,898 and Title VI as Tools for Achieving Environmental Justice," U.S. Commission on Civil Rights," October 2003, p. iii.

24. Institute of Medicine, "Toward Environmental Justice: Research, Education, and Health Policy Needs," National Academy of Sciences, March 1, 1999. See chapter 1.

25. David Pace, "AP: More Blacks Live With Pollution," Associated Press, December 13, 2005.

26. Craig Flournoy and Randy Lee Loftis, "Toxic Traps: Public Housing and Pollution," *Dallas Morning News*, Oct. 1, 2000, p. 1A.

BIBLIOGRAPHY

Books

Bullard, Robert D., *Dumping in Dixie: Race, Class and Environmental Quality*, Harper Collins, 1996.
A leading activist in the environmental justice movement examines the enforcement of environmental-protection laws in the Southern United States, where poor, mostly black communities are commonly chosen as sites for waste dumps and incinerators.

Bullard, Robert D., ed., *The Quest for Environmental Justice: Human Rights and the Politics of Pollution*, Sierra Club Books, 2005.
This collection of essays updates a 1994 collection, demonstrating the progress and setbacks experienced by the environmental justice movement, and noting that interest has spread internationally.

Szasz, Andrew, *EcoPopulism: Toxic Waste and the Movement for Environmental Justice*, University of Minnesota Press, 1994.
The author describes the environmental justice movement's evolution from grass-roots activism to federal policy. By focusing on pollution prevention rather than cleaning up polluted sites, the movement is changing the focus of environmental policy.

Articles

Arrandale, Tom, "Regulation and Racism," *Governing*, March 1998, p. 63.
The Environmental Protection Agency's decision to overturn a state-issued permit to build a plastics plant near a poor, minority community in Louisiana last fall does not further the goal of environmental justice, the author writes, because it will discourage industry from bringing jobs to the very communities that are hardest hit by unemployment.

Kitchin, Jessica, "Environmental Justice: An Emerging State Issue," Stateline.org, August 2, 2004, www.state-

line.org/live/ViewPage.action?siteNodeId=136&language
Id=1&contentId=15725.
Nearly half the states have created policies on environmental justice, while all but thirteen have programs
designed to fight discrimination in infrastructure siting.

**Pace, David, "AP: More Blacks Live With Pollution,"
The Associated Press, Dec. 13, 2005.**
An Associated Press analysis of government research
finds that African American are 79 percent more likely
than whites to live in neighborhoods where industrial
pollution is suspected of posing grave health risks.

**Parris, Thomas M., "Spinning the Web of Environmen-
tal Justice," *Environment*, May 1997, pp. 44-45.**
This collection of Internet addresses provides a wealth of
sources, including Environmental Protection Agency (EPA)
reports and non-governmental studies, on efforts to combat
pollution that affects poor and minority communities.

**Reppy, Judith, "Environmental Change and Social
Justice," *Environment*, April 1997, pp. 12-20.**
The authors apply the tenets of environmental justice to
global environmental issues, including global warming.
Developed nations, which have contributed the most to
this problem, should help devise solutions that reduce
economic inequality between rich and developing
nations, the authors contend.

**Sachs, Aaron, "Upholding Human Rights and
Environmental Justice," *The Humanist*, March-April
1996, pp. 5-8.**
The author reviews the international movement for environmental justice that took off after the 1988 murder of
Chico Mendes, a Brazilian rubber tapper who fought for
the rights of rain forest inhabitants against the cattle
barons who were clearing the forests for grazing land.

**Schoeplfle, Mark, "Due Process and Dialogue:
Consulting with Native Americans under the National
Environmental Policy Act," *Common Ground*,
Summer/Fall 1997, pp. 40-45.**
The 1969 National Environmental Policy Act provides
standards for informing Indian tribes of environmental
hazards and taking steps to protect themselves from pol-
lutants.

**Shepard, Peggy M., "Comment: Environmental Racism
and Public Health," *American Journal of Public
Health*, May 1997, pp. 730-732.**
The authors call for further study of the disparate impact
of environmental hazards on poor, non-white communities and a broad public health initiative, similar in scope
to the anti-smoking campaign, to prevent and remove
toxins from these communities.

Reports and Studies

**Fitton, Laura, *Toxic Wastes and Race Revisited*,
Center for Policy Alternatives, 1994.**
This update of a 1987 report on the racial and socioeconomic characteristics of communities with hazardous-
waste sites finds that poor and minority communities are
even more disproportionately exposed to toxins than
before, despite the growth of the environmental justice
movement.

**National Academy of Public Administration,
"Environmental Justice in EPA Permitting: Reducing
Pollution in High-Risk Communities Is Integral to
the Agency's Mission," December 2001.**
An academy panel, as part of an ongoing environmental
justice project, found that the EPA still has not effectively incorporated the relevant issues into its permitting
process.

**National Environmental Justice Advisory Council,
*Environmental Justice, Urban Revitalization and
Brownfields: The Search for Authentic Signs of Hope*,
December 1996.**
An EPA advisory committee finds that the development
of brownfields — abandoned industrial sites that are not
polluted enough to warrant federal cleanup under the
Superfund program — is an important contribution to
the goal of environmental justice.

**Office of Inspector General, "EPA Needs to
Consistently Implement the Intent of the Executive
Order on Environmental Justice," U. S. Environmental
Protection Agency, March 1, 2004.**
The inspector general finds that the 1994 executive order
on environmental justice has not been fully imple-
mented, nor are environmental justice concerns well
integrated into the agency's day-to-day operations.

U.S. Commission on Civil Rights, "Not in My Backyard: Executive Order 12,898 and Title VI as Tools for Achieving Environmental Justice," October 2003.
The federal commission finds that "significant problems and shortcomings remain" in the way that four Cabinet-level departments assess and control the impact of pollution on communities of color and low-income populations.

U.S. Environmental Protection Agency, Office of Environmental Justice, "Serving a Diverse Society," November 1997.
This pamphlet summarizes the adverse impact of air pollution, pesticides, agricultural runoff and other environmental hazards on communities of color and suggests steps communities can take to minimize exposure.

For More Information

Center for Health, Environment and Justice, P.O. Box 6806, Falls Church, VA 22040; (703) 237-2249; www.chej.org. The center helps community-based groups fend off environmental hazards. It was founded by a former resident of Love Canal, N.Y., the community built near a toxic-waste dump.

Earthjustice, 426 17th Street, Oakland, CA 94612-2820; 1 (800) 584-6460; www.earthjustice.org. Formerly known as the Sierra Club Legal Defense Fund, this nonprofit law firm is active in cases involving environmental justice.

Environmental Council of the States, 444 N. Capitol St., N.W., Suite 445, Washington, D.C. 20001; (202) 624-3660; www.sso.org/ecos/. A membership group representing environmental officials of the states and the District of Columbia, ECOS opposes the EPA's new rules for handling environmental justice complaints.

Environmental Justice Resource Center, Clark Atlanta University, 223 James P. Brawley Dr. S.W., Atlanta, Ga. 30314; (404) 880-6911. Directed by Robert D. Bullard, a longtime environmental justice leader, the center helps communities protect themselves from pollution sources.

Greenpeace, 702 H St., N.W., Suite 300, Washington, D.C. 20001; (202) 462-1177; www.greenpeace.org. This research and activist group has recently become involved in several cases involving complaints of environmental racism.

National Black Environmental Justice Network, P.O. Box 15845, Washington, DC 20003; (202) 265-4919; http://www.nbejn.org/. A coalition, founded in 1999, that links environmental and health activists and attorneys in 33 states and the District of Columbia.

Office of Environmental Justice, U.S. Environmental Protection Agency, 401 M St., S.W., Washington, D.C. 20460; (202) 564-2515 or (800) 962-6215; es.epa.gov/environsense/oeca/oej.html. The OEJ coordinates EPA activities and provides technical assistance to communities threatened by environmental hazards.

8

Rebuilding New Orleans

Peter Katel

CQ Press/Peter Katel

The working-class Lower Ninth Ward was among the hardest-hit New Orleans neighborhoods. A rebuilding plan proposed by the Bring New Orleans Back Commission in early January would give residents a role in deciding whether heavily flooded neighborhoods would be resettled. An earlier plan by the Urban Land Institute sparked controversy among African-Americans when it proposed abandoning unsafe areas, including parts of the Lower Ninth.

From *CQ Researcher,*
February 3, 2006.

urricane Katrina's floodwaters surged through tens of thousands of houses in New Orleans, including Dennis and Linda Scott's tidy, two-story brick home on Farwood Drive. The first floor has since been gutted, the ruined furnishings and appliances discarded.

Five months after floodwaters breached the city's levees and drainage canals, every other house for miles around is in the same deplorable shape. [1]

Like the Scotts, most of the residents who evacuated the sprawling New Orleans East area cannot decide whether to return, uncertain if their solidly middle class, mostly African-American neighborhoods will ever come back to life.

The disaster that began when Katrina's Category 3 winds hit New Orleans on Aug. 29, 2005, grinds on. [2] Yet the Scotts and their neighbors feel lucky to be alive.

"I'm one of the fortunate ones," says Scott, 47, who fled to Houston with his wife before the storm hit.

Linda's teaching job was swept away when the floods closed down the schools, so she's staying in Texas while Dennis works on the house and goes to his job as a communications specialist at Louis Armstrong International Airport. Their next-door neighbors, an elderly couple who stayed home, were drowned. Some three-quarters of Louisiana's 1,070 Katrina deaths occurred in New Orleans, where about 70 percent of the victims were age 60 and older. [3]

But "the east" is not alone. Similar devastation also afflicts some older neighborhoods, where lush gardens and sprawling villas reflect the city's French and Spanish heritage. [4]

171

Flooding Affected Most of Greater New Orleans

Flood water up to 20 feet deep covered more than three-quarters of New Orleans when storm surges pushed by Hurricane Katrina breached levees in 34 places. The Lower Ninth Ward and the New Orleans East district were among the hardest-hit areas.

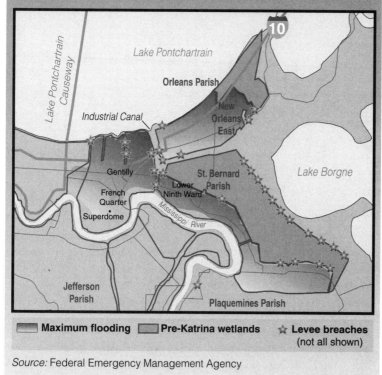

Maximum flooding   Pre-Katrina wetlands   ☆ Levee breaches
(not all shown)

Source: Federal Emergency Management Agency

Losses in destroyed and damaged property, added to losses resulting from the shrinkage of the city's economy, amount roughly to $35 billion, estimates Stan Fulcher, research director of the Louisiana Recovery Authority in Baton Rouge.

Most residents are still gone, largely because most jobs — except those that involve either tearing down houses or fixing them up — have disappeared. Plans are only starting to be made to rebuild the city, and no one knows how much reconstruction money will be available.

Does Scott have a future in New Orleans? "I'm on hold," he replies.

That response comes up a lot among the city's residents and evacuees, often accompanied by a sense that the rest of the country has moved on — or views the French-founded, majority-African-American city as somehow foreign or not worth rebuilding.

"This is America you're talking about," lawyer Walter I. Willard says in frustration.

So American, in fact, that jazz was born there — amid a culture formed by the peculiarities of the city's slavery and segregation traditions. [9] "The West Africans [slaves] were allowed to play their music in Congo Square on Sundays. That happened nowhere else in the United States," famed New Orleans-born trumpeter Wynton Marsalis says. [10]

Slavery's legacy of racial and class divide has been part of the Katrina story from the beginning. New Orleans is two-thirds African-American, and the thousands of impoverished residents who were without cars to flee the approaching hurricane were overwhelmingly black. [11] "As all of us saw on television," President Bush acknowledged, "there's . . . some deep, persistent poverty in this region. That poverty has roots in a history of racial discrimination, which cut off generations from the opportunity of America." [12]

The continuing devastation mocks President Bush's stirring promise two weeks after the storm to mount "one of the largest reconstruction efforts the world has ever seen." [5]

Indeed, when the Senate Homeland Security and Governmental Affairs Committee toured the city four months later, members were "stunned" to see that "so much hasn't been done," said Chairwoman Susan Collins, R-Maine. [6]

Floodwaters up to 20 feet deep covered about 80 percent of the city and didn't recede until late September. [7] Fully half the city's homes — 108,731 dwellings — suffered flooding at least four feet deep, according to the Bring New Orleans Back Commission (BNOBC) formed by Mayor Ray Nagin. In some neighborhoods, Hurricane Rita, which struck later in September, brought additional flooding. [8]

Bush also conceded that the federal response to Katrina amounted to less than what its victims were entitled to — a point reinforced in early 2006, when Sen. Collins' committee released a strikingly accurate prediction of Katrina's likely effects, prepared for the White House two days *before* Katrina hit. [13]

But in a sense, New Orleans was crumbling from within even before the floods washed over the city. "The city had a lot of economic and social problems before — economics, race, poverty, crime, drugs," says musician and Xavier University Prof. Michael White. "Our failure to deal with harsh realities has sometimes been the problem."

In 2004, for example, the city's homicide rate hit 59 per 100,000 — the nation's highest. [14]

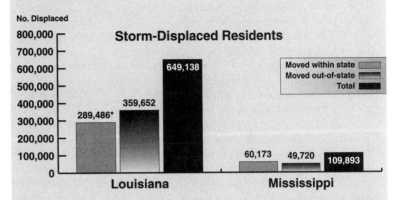

More Than 400,000 Residents Left Home States

Six times more Louisiana residents are still displaced from their homes than Mississippians. Of the more than 750,000 residents from both states displaced by Katrina, more than half are still living outside their home states.

Storm-Displaced Residents

Moved within state
Moved out-of-state
Total

Louisiana: 289,486*, 359,652, 649,138
Mississippi: 60,173, 49,720, 109,893

* Based on the number of FEMA aid applicants who have not returned to their pre-Katrina addresses.

Source: Louisiana Recovery Authority

In that post-Katrina climate — fed by bitter memories of institutional racism — the African-American community is concerned that developers are planning to reduce the black portion of the city's population. U.S. Housing and Urban Development Secretary Alphonso Jackson, who is African-American, intensified those fears when he said, "New Orleans is not going to be as black as it was for a long time, if ever again." [15]

The concern remained an issue into early 2006, when Mayor Nagin, also African-American, declared on Jan. 16 that the city "should be a chocolate New Orleans . . . a majority-African-American city. It's the way God wants it to be." [16] The following day, after furious reactions from both the white and black communities, Nagin apologized. [17]

Nagin's provocative language aside, fears of a demographic shift seem well-founded. In late January, sociologist John R. Logan of Brown University said he had conducted a study that showed about 80 percent of New Orleans' black residents were unlikely to come back, in part because their neighborhoods wouldn't be rebuilt. [18]

The BNOBC sparked the most recent chapter of the race and redevelopment debate. The commission's rebuilding plan, unveiled in early January, would give residents of the most heavily flooded neighborhoods four months to help figure out if their districts could be resettled. Homeowners in neighborhoods that can't be revived could sell their houses to a government-financed corporation for 100 percent of the pre-Katrina values, minus insurance payouts and mortgage obligations. The overall plan would cost more than $18 billion. [19] Federal, state and city approval is needed. [20]

Nowhere did the commission say that the poorest and most heavily damaged African-American neighborhoods should be abandoned. But the Washington-based Urban Land Institute (ULI), flatly recommended against extensive rebuilding in the most flood-prone areas, by implication including much of the working-class, largely African-American Lower Ninth Ward. [21]

Under the Jim Crow segregation system that lasted into the 1960s, residents point out, the Lower Ninth was the only place where African-Americans could buy property. "These people struggled to buy a little bit of land they could call home," says contractor Algy Irvin, 60, standing in the wrecked living room of his mother's house on Egania Street.

Irvin recalls earning $35 a week mopping hospital floors and paying $18 a week for his own $1,200 lot on

Can New Orleans' Musical Culture Be Saved?

Sunpie and the Louisiana Sunspots have the crowd at the House of Blues rocking as the group pounds out "Iko-Iko," a New Orleans standard with Creole lyrics and an irresistible beat.

The first night of Carnival is under way in the French Quarter, and the club is filling up for a long evening of music, with three more acts to follow. In the less touristy Marigny neighborhood, jazz pianist Ellis Marsalis is starting a slightly more sedate set at popular Snug Harbor.

Four months after Katrina hit, New Orleans is making music again. "So far, it's gone better than I would have thought, given the total lack of tourism," says Barry Smith, proprietor of the Louisiana Music Factory, where CDs and vinyl records of New Orleans artists account for some three-quarters of the stock of jazz, blues and gospel artists — both world-renowned and known only to locals. "I've definitely experienced a big increase in the number of local customers coming to the store, and a lot of the people who came here to work — from construction workers to Red Cross volunteers."

Few if any places in the United States come even close to New Orleans as an incubator of musical style and talent. As far back as 1819, a visitor wrote about the African music being played at Congo Square. And by the early 20th century, a musical tradition had formed in which Louis Armstrong — arguably the century's most influential musician — came of age. [1]

"All American music in the 20th century was profoundly shaped and influenced by New Orleans music," Tom Piazza writes in *Why New Orleans Matters.* [2]

The career of famed musician/producer Allen Toussaint illustrates the city's musical power. Toussaint wrote such 1960s hits as "Mother in Law" and produced and arranged the 1973 hit "Right Place, Wrong Time" for fellow New Orleans resident "Dr. John," as well as the disco standard "Lady Marmelade."

"He helped invent things we take as everyday in music — certain beats, certain arrangements," his partner in a record label said recently. [3]

Toussaint fled New Orleans after Katrina and has spoken optimistically of the city's future prospects. [4] But away from the club scene and music stores, the future looks less bright.

That's because the city's music springs from the very streets that Katrina emptied — the fabled "social aid and pleasure clubs," fraternal organizations that sponsor the Mardi Gras "Indian tribes," as well as the brass-band funeral processions that nourished jazz. All these influential institutions are maintained by people who mostly live paycheck to paycheck, says Michael White, a clarinetist and music scholar who holds an endowed chair in arts and humanities at New Orleans' Xavier University. [5]

nearby Tupelo Street — now also a ruin. "You can see why people don't want a fat-cat developer coming in, making millions," he says, giving voice to a common suspicion that declaring the neighborhood unsafe is merely a cheap means of clearing out its present inhabitants to make way for lucrative development. But Irvin adds, "If people are compensated, that's another story."

Post-Katrina television coverage also gave the impression that New Orleans' African-American population was uniformly poor. In fact, the city had a substantial black middle class. "I had no clue that people couldn't get out of here," says Anne LaBranche, an African-American from New Orleans East, who returned to the city in January after staying with friends in Birmingham, Ala. "I do not know a person who doesn't own a car."

The LaBranches are moving into a house owned by her father-in-law. Her physician husband Emile, whose family practice was destroyed by Katrina along with all the patients' records, has been looking for work. But other medical offices say they aren't hiring until they know how many people are coming back.

Across town, Cory Matthews, 30, a medical-technology salesman, also wonders whether he still has a place in the city. He is rebuilding the flood-damaged Uptown house he shares with his girlfriend, but as he puts up new Sheetrock and rewires, he worries that his physician customer base has shrunk. "I'm hoping we're making the right move," he says.

Certainly, nobody is expecting redevelopment to bring speedy population growth. An estimated 135,000 people remain in New Orleans — less than a third of the 462,000 pre-Katrina population. Nagin's commission

The New Orleans establishment recognizes the problem. "Financial losses for social aid and pleasure clubs, Mardi Gras Indian tribes and [brass band] second-line companies are conservatively estimated at over $3 million," the Bring New Orleans Back Commission reports. [6]

"These were poor people, but people who spent a lot of money on these events," says White, a New Orleans native who comes from a long line of musicians. "The thing of money is serious. If people don't have jobs, they're not going to be able to participate."

White himself suffered another kind of loss — his vast collection of vintage instruments and memorabilia that included a trumpet mouthpiece from jazz saint Sidney Bechet; 4,000 rare CDs and even rarer vinyl recordings; photographs of New Orleans musical legends and notes and tapes of interviews with musicians who have since died. All were stored at his house — and it's all gone.

Is resurrecting an entire popular culture any more possible than restoring White's collection? "It's not like there's

Legendary jazz pianist Ellis Marsalis is a popular performer in Old New Orleans, which was largely spared by the flooding.

a central entity that can be rebuilt," says Piazza. "What steps can be taken to repatriate as many members of the African-American community and other communities — people who don't have the same kinds of resources as others to come back and rebuild, or who lived in areas where logistical challenges to rebuilding are all but insurmountable? That is the most difficult question about cultural renewal."

---

[1] For background, see Geoffrey C. Ward and Ken Burns, *Jazz: A History of America's Music* (2000), pp. 7-16; 40-46.

[2] Tom Piazza, *Why New Orleans Matters* (2005), p. 37.

[3] Quoted in Deborah Sontag, "Heat, and Piano, Back in New Orleans," *The New York Times*, Sept. 20, 2005, p. E1; for additional background see, "Inductees: Allen Toussaint," Rock+Roll Hall of Fame and Museum, undated, http://rockhall.com/hof/inductee.asp?id=200.

[4] *Ibid.*

[5] Ward and Burns, *op. cit.*, pp. 7-16.

[6] "Report of the Cultural Committee, Mayor's Bring New Orleans Back Commission," Jan. 17, 2006, pp. 8-9, www.bringneworleansback.org.

---

projects 247,000 residents by September 2008, while a more optimistic consultant projects 252,000 by early 2007. [22] The totals, however, don't specify whether the residents will be laboring at construction sites or behind desks.

Jay LaPeyre, president of the Business Council of New Orleans and the River Region, says laborers are desperately needed "for every type of manual labor — from skilled electricians and plumbers to low-skilled apprentices and trainees to service jobs at Burger King."

That kind of talk makes white-collar New Orleanians nervous. Tulane University, one of the city's major high-end employers, laid off 230 of its 2,500 professors. [23] Nearly all 7,500 public school employees were laid off as well, though some were rehired by the handful of charter schools that have sprung up. [24]

"It's become a blue-collar market," says Daniel Perez, who lost his night-manager job at the swanky Royal Sonesta Hotel after business dropped off. Perez applied in vain for dozens of professional or managerial jobs. He had almost decided to leave New Orleans before finally landing a position as a sales manager for *USA Today.*

For now, at least, even the service-industry job market is thinning, though the profusion of help-wanted signs in the functioning parts of the city convey a different impression. A planned Feb. 17 reopening of Harrah's Casino, for example, will take place with only half the pre-Katrina payroll of 2,500, says Carla Major, vice president for human resources.

On his Jan. 11 visit, President Bush touted New Orleans as still "a great place to visit." But his motorcade

Katrina Costs Dwarf Previous Disasters

Hurricane Katrina cost the Federal Emergency Management Agency $25 billion in the Gulf Coast — nearly three times more than the 2001 terrorist attacks on the World Trade Center and eight times more than Hurricane Rita, which followed on the heels of Katrina. The money pays for such services as temporary housing, unemployment assistance, crisis counseling and legal aid.

Disaster	FEMA Cost Estimate* ($ in billions)
Hurricane Katrina (2005)	$24.6
World Trade Center (2001)	$8.8
Hurricane Rita (2005)	$3.4
Hurricane Ivan (2004)	$2.6
Hurricane Wilma (2005)	$2.5
Hurricane Georges (1998)	$2.3
Hurricane Andrew (1992)	$1.8
Hurricane Hugo (1989)	$1.3
Loma Prieta Earthquake (1989)	$0.87
Hurricane Alberto (2000)	$0.6

* Flood-insurance reimbursements not included

Source: FEMA, December 2005

ural landfill process, called silting — have exacerbated the problem. And sea levels are rising due to global warming. [26] As a result, writes Virginia R. Burkett of the U.S. Geological Survey's National Wetlands Research Center in Louisiana, by 2100 parts of New Orleans "could lie [about 23 feet] below water level during a Category 3 hurricane." [27]

Even so, the extensive levee system was designed to defend the entire metropolitan area from floods. So the Katrina disaster didn't grow out of the development of flood-prone lands that never should have been urbanized, say opponents of shrinking the footprint. Instead, they argue, the catastrophe grew out of human failure in engineering, construction or maintenance — or in all three.

"If we can build levees in Iraq, we can build levees on the Gulf Coast," says Sen. Mary Landrieu, D-La. "And if we can build hospitals in Baghdad and Fallujah, we can most certainly rebuild our hospitals in this metropolitan area." [28]

But congressional power brokers aren't in the mood to redevelop flood-prone areas. "We are committed to helping the people of Louisiana rebuild," said House Appropriations Committee member Rep. Ray LaHood, R-Ill. But, "we are not going to rebuild homes that are going to be destroyed in two years by another flood. We are not just going to throw money at it." [29]

Some who call the flood a man-made failure don't oppose redesigning the city in a more environmentally sensible way — even if it means abandoning their own neighborhoods. "It's not what I want, but I could live with it," says LaBranche, who with her husband owns a home, an office building and rental properties in New Orleans East. "I don't want to go through this again."

But who should decide? "The idea that everybody gets to have what they want" is not practical, says business leader LaPeyre. He wants the government to use its power of eminent domain — the right to condemn pri-

had skirted most of the devastation, going nowhere near, for instance, the Scotts' deserted neighborhood. [25]

"We can't move forward until we have positive information on what's happening," Scott says. "There are no banks, no schools, no electricity. We just want to be home."

As officials plan the city's future, here are some of the questions being debated:

Should some neighborhoods not be rebuilt?

The buzzword summing up the single toughest question about New Orleans' future is "footprint." That's urban-planner jargon for a city's shape and the amount of space it occupies. In New Orleans, the term has become code for the idea that flood-prone districts are best turned back into open-space "sponges" to absorb nature's future onslaughts.

But would that help? New Orleans and the entire Gulf Coast are sinking. New Orleans was built on sandy soil to begin with, but oil and gas extraction and upriver levee construction — which reduces the delta area's nat-

vate property and compensate the owner — to prevent redevelopment of areas unsuitable for residential and business use. [30]

Private companies, such as utility and insurance companies — will also influence decisions about where development will occur. "The market will do better than most people claim," he says. "If you're not going to have good services, most people will say, 'I don't want to live there.'"

Others argue that a neighborhood's residents should have a big voice. The Bring New Orleans Back Commission proposed letting residents of heavily damaged neighborhoods work with urban and financial planners to determine if their districts could be revived. The "neighborhood planning teams" would have until May to decide. The procedure grew out of opposition to the Urban Land Institute's recommendation against rebuilding in flood-prone areas.

"In an arbitrary and capricious manner to say that these areas — which were populated by black people because they were directed there — should now be turned into green space deepens the wound," says Councilwoman Cynthia Willard-Lewis, who represents several of the city's eastern neighborhoods. Many of the houses can be repaired and the communities brought back, she says, adding that she suspects the plan "was not based on what was safe but on whom they wanted to return."

William Hudnut, a former mayor of Indianapolis who holds the Urban Land Institute's public policy chair, says city leaders do not have the courage to tell residents what they don't want to hear. "The footprint has to be smaller and development more compact," he says. "An honest, tough-minded approach to rebuilding is part of what leadership is all about. It may be that some people would lose their political base or lose their jobs. But if a thing is worth doing, it's worth doing well and worth standing up for."

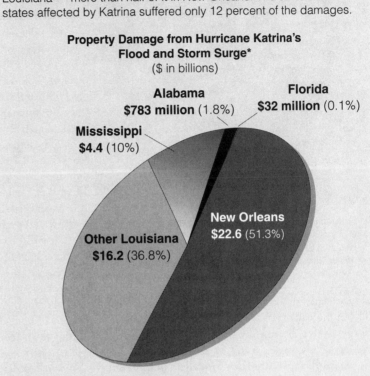

Katrina Saved Worst for New Orleans

Nearly 90 percent of Katrina's flood and storm damage occurred in Louisiana — more than half of it in New Orleans. The other three states affected by Katrina suffered only 12 percent of the damages.

Property Damage from Hurricane Katrina's Flood and Storm Surge*
($ in billions)

Alabama $783 million (1.8%)

Florida $32 million (0.1%)

Mississippi $4.4 (10%)

New Orleans $22.6 (51.3%)

Other Louisiana $16.2 (36.8%)

* Includes insured and uninsured damage

Source: AIR Worldwide Corp., September 2005

Ari Kelman, an environmental historian at the University of California at Davis, concedes that some neighborhoods should be abandoned. At the same time, he says, low-income African-American residents have well-founded fears that any planning and decision system will be stacked against them.

"People who don't have money also don't have power," says Kelman, author of a 2003 book on the interplay between human design and nature in New Orleans. "When politics get cooking in New Orleans, it's likely that the poor are going to get screwed."

Should the levee system be upgraded to guard against a Category 5 storm?

The levee system surrounding New Orleans was designed to withstand a Category 3 hurricane. Katrina

Skip LaGrange takes a break from cleaning out his flooded home in the Mid-City section of New Orleans, on Oct. 5, 2005. An estimated 135,000 people are now living in New Orleans — less than a third of the 462,000 pre-Katrina population.

had weakened to Category 3 by the time it made landfall, but the wall of water it sent ashore — the hurricane's "surge" — was born when the storm was still offshore and raging at Category 4 and 5 strength. [31]

So far, official attention has focused on possible errors in design, construction or maintenance of the levees. But many are also asking whether the system should be upgraded to protect against a Category 5 hurricane — the most powerful. Among Louisianans in general and New Orleanians in particular, support for a Category 5 system seems nearly universal.

"I would like to see the levees brought to Category 5 for my safety and that of my family and properties," says LaBranche, the displaced New Orleans homeowner.

But some government experts say a Category 5 levee system is a pipe dream. They point out Category 5 is open-ended, taking in all hurricanes whose winds exceed 155 mph and create storm surges greater than 18 feet. "What's the top end for a Cat 5 hurricane?" asked Dan Hitchings, director of Hurricane Katrina recovery for the Corps of Engineers. "There isn't one." [32]

That argument carries little weight in Louisiana. Some Louisiana lawmakers say that if the below-sea-level Netherlands can protect itself from floods, New Orleans shouldn't settle for less. "They built once-in-1,000-years

flood protection," Sen. Landrieu told a rally of some 75 displaced New Orleanians outside the White House last December. "We don't even have once-in-100-years [protection]."

No hurricanes strike in the North Sea, which surrounds the Netherlands. But the tiny country, some of which lies more than 20 feet below sea level, is vulnerable to powerful storms with winds that can reach 60 mph. Following a 1953 storm that killed more than 1,800 people, the country redesigned its protective system in ways that many New Orleanians say should serve as a model. [33]

The Netherlands system was designed to withstand a once-in-10,000-years storm. New Orleans' levees were designed for a once-in-200-300-years storm, says the Corps of Engineers. [34]

In addition, say Louisiana officials, a Category 5 system would probably cost about $32 billion. [35]

"It will probably be a pretty staggering price tag," acknowledges Craig E. Colten, a geography professor at Louisiana State University in Baton Rouge and author of a recent book on New Orleans' flood-protection history. But the long-term value of property protection would make an upgraded system a wise investment, he added, citing the prosperous Netherlands, an international shipping center.

But Rep. Richard Baker, R-La., cautions that debating a Category 5 upgrade now could distract from the immediate and urgent tasks facing New Orleans. "Construction toward a Category 5 standard would be a decade-long project," he says. "The statistical probabilities of a Category 5 hitting New Orleans are fairly small, especially since we just got hit. I think we have time."

No one denies the need for fixing the existing flood-protection system. The Bush administration has proposed $1.6 billion to restore the system to a Category 3 level of protection, and another $1.5 billion for further improvements. [36] Thus far, however, it has stayed out of the Category 5 argument. At a White House briefing on the new flood-protection plan, Donald E. Powell, the administration's coordinator of post-hurricane recovery projects, would only say that after the proposed improvements, "The levee system will be better, much better, and stronger than it ever has been in the history of New Orleans." [37]

The White House plan also includes a study, backed by Mayor Nagin, of whether a substantial upgrade to the system is needed. A preliminary report is due in May.

However, city officials argue that a system capable of protecting against a Category 5 storm is well within the range of engineering possibilities and would be good for both the city's and the country's economy. "We need to build toward Category 5 to provide . . . assurance to [potential] investors," says Gary P. LaGrange, director of the Port of New Orleans, and to protect the port, an essential part of the nation's trade system.

Should the nation pay for New Orleans to be rebuilt?

So far, Congress has committed $98.9 billion for post-hurricane recovery and rebuilding programs throughout the Gulf Coast, the Senate Budget Committee calculated. The funding came in two emergency appropriations in September totaling $62.3 billion, followed by several smaller spending authorizations. In December, expanding on a request by Bush, Congress redirected $23.4 billion in funds previously appropriated. [38]

It's uncertain, however, how much will go to New Orleans.

In any event, money appropriated so far includes $6.2 billion in Community Development Block Grants intended for Louisiana, and $22 billion for reimbursements to Gulf Coast homeowners from the federal flood-insurance program. But even with the emergency injections of cash, the flood-insurance program is "bankrupt," Senate Banking Committee Chairman Richard Shelby, R-Ala., said on Jan. 25. The acting director of the Federal Emergency Management Agency (FEMA) insurance division said the agency has paid out $13.5 billion in claims arising from the 2005 hurricane season — nearly as much as the agency has paid out in its 37-year existence. And 30 percent of the 239,000 claims have yet to be resolved. [39]

Federal hurricane-recovery coordinator Powell has been advocating directing much of the block grant money to the estimated 20,000 New Orleans homeowners who didn't have flood insurance because their neighborhoods weren't designated as flood plains. [40]

Given the huge costs involved and all the unknowns, lawmakers from other parts of the country are not exactly champing at the bit to pay for rebuilding New Orleans. The city's tenuous hydrological situation and the likelihood that it will be flooded again by other hurricanes lead some Americans to question whether the rest of the country should have to pay to rebuild the city in such a precarious location.

"There is a lot of — I suppose you can call it 'Katrina fatigue' — that people are dealing with out in the heartland," Rep. Henry Bonilla, R-Texas, told Louisiana Gov. Kathleen Babineaux Blanco, a Democrat, at a House Select Katrina Response Investigation Committee hearing last Dec. 14.

The situation has rekindled a long-simmering debate about whether Americans in the heartland should pay to constantly bail out people — usually those living on the coasts — who choose to live in areas prone to floods, hurricanes, landslides and earthquakes. "Is it fair to make people living in Pennsylvania or Ohio pay billions for massive engineering projects so that some of the people of New Orleans can go back to the way things were and avoid the hard choices that nature presents them?" asks economist Adrian Moore of the libertarian Reason Foundation of Los Angeles. [41]

Some lawmakers agree, although only a few have spoken out. "It looks like a lot of that place could be bulldozed," House Speaker Dennis Hastert, R-Ill. said shortly after the hurricane, raising hackles. He later explained he only meant that danger zones shouldn't be resettled. [42]

New Orleanians respond that other disaster-prone areas, including hurricane-exposed Florida coastal cities, get rebuilt with few questions asked about viability. "People build on mountainsides in California that fall in the ocean," notes Perez, the newspaper sales manager. "We're not the only vulnerable area in the country."

In addition, points out Republican Louisiana Sen. David Vitter, 25 percent of the nation's energy and most of the Midwest's grain exports are shipped through the port of New Orleans. "If people don't think there's a national stake in rebuilding New Orleans, that's fine. But they should get used to much higher gasoline prices," he said. "And people can forget about getting crops to foreign markets. You need a major city as the hub of all that activity."

But if federal funds are forthcoming to rebuild the city, they should have some serious accountability strings attached, given the city's long history of corruption and dysfunction, some argue. "A lot of . . . our constituents now are telling us that they [don't] want us to support funding for the Gulf region at this point without strong plans of accountability," Bonilla said.

Recognizing those sentiments — as well as the reality that the country is at war and its debt and deficits are rising — Louisiana politicians have proposed two major

CHRONOLOGY

1700s-1800s *From the time of its founding, New Orleans' vulnerability to nature is seen as the price of its incomparably strategic location.*

1718 New Orleans is founded on a natural levee along a bend in the Mississippi River.

1892 Adolph Plessy of New Orleans is arrested after testing segregation laws by riding in a "white" train car. U.S. Supreme Court later upholds his conviction in landmark *Plessy v. Ferguson* decision.

1900-1947 *A catastrophic flood reminds the city of its dangerous location.*

1927 Massive Mississippi floods see many African-Americans forced into levee-reinforcement work; two rural parishes are deliberately flooded to save New Orleans.

1929 The U.S. Army Corps of Engineers begins building a spillway on the Mississippi to channel floodwater away from New Orleans.

1930s *Expansion of city drainage systems allows urban expansion, but new neighborhoods are strictly segregated.*

Sept. 17-19, 1947 A Category 4 hurricane overwhelms levees, causing flooding over nine square miles of the city.

1950s-1970s *The city expands into drained wetlands, increasing its vulnerability to floods.*

1950 Land drained for suburban expansion reaches 49,000 acres.

Sept. 7, 1965 Hurricane Betsy slams the city with Category 3 winds, pushing a 10-foot storm surge through some levees.

Oct. 27, 1965 President Lyndon B. Johnson signs the Flood Control Act, which includes funding for a hurricane-protection system in New Orleans.

Aug. 17, 1969 Category 5 Hurricane Camille devastates Mississippi and Alabama, but reinforced protective systems keep most of New Orleans safe.

May 3, 1978 Heavy rainstorm flooding damages more than 70,000 homes.

1980s-1990s *Attempts by the city to guard against rainstorm floods prove inadequate, as fears of vulnerability to hurricanes begin to grow.*

April 1982 Rainstorm-caused floods damage 1,400 homes and other buildings.

1983 City expands pumping and drainage systems.

May 8-10, 1995 Flooding damages thousands of homes, causes six deaths.

2000-Present *Fears of hurricane vulnerability grow, as journalists and government officials warn about the weakness of the city's defenses.*

June 23-June 26, 2002 *Times-Picayune* warns of New Orleans' hurricane vulnerability.

Sept. 26, 2002 Hurricane Isidore hits Louisiana after weakening to a tropical storm, but still causes major flooding.

July 2004 FEMA officials conduct a drill featuring Category 3 "Hurricane Pam" hitting New Orleans and predict serious flooding, massive evacuation.

Aug. 29, 2005 Hurricane Katrina makes landfall east of New Orleans.

Sept. 15, 2005 President Bush visits New Orleans and pledges a massive disaster-recovery effort.

Jan. 11, 2006 Bring New Orleans Back Commission releases an "Action Plan" for re-creating the city.

Jan. 17, 2006 Senators of both parties visit New Orleans and criticize slow progress on recovery.

Jan. 26, 2006 President Bush explains why he refused to support the creation of a public corporation to buy flood-damaged homes.

June 1, 2006 Hurricane season begins; repairs and improvements to levee system due for completion.

plans that they say would lower the federal spending burden for rebuilding New Orleans and the rest of the state.

But the White House has already refused to back one of these plans. Its author, Rep. Baker, proposed establishing a public corporation to buy or finance repairs on storm-damaged property. Homeowners who sold their houses to the corporation would get 60 percent of the pre-Katrina value of their holdings. The corporation would then resell the homes, if possible, and turn the proceeds back to the Treasury. Nagin's BNOBC adopted the idea, which some of its members called crucial to reviving the city.

"We were concerned about creating additional federal bureaucracies, which might make it harder to get money to the people," Bush said, explaining his rejection of Baker's idea. [43]

On Feb. 1, according to Baker's office, three former Republican governors of Louisiana — Murphy J. "Mike" Foster, Charles E. "Buddy" Roemer III, and David Treen — urged Bush to change his mind concerning Baker's bill, which they called the only practical method of disposing of thousands of ruined residential and business properties.

The congressman has been vowing to press ahead with his proposal, sponsored in the Senate by Sen. Landrieu. Bush's negative response would "constrict the opportunities for rapid redevelopment, and that's tough," said Reed Kroloff, architecture dean at Tulane University and a BNOBC member. [44]

But developer Joseph Canizaro, who helped put together the commission's plan, said block grant money and other unspecified funds could be found for a property buyback. [45]

The other plan to lower direct federal spending is a longstanding proposal to boost the state's share of money that the federal government earns from petroleum leases on the Outer Continental Shelf in the Gulf of Mexico off Louisiana's coast. One-quarter of U.S. crude oil production comes from Louisiana's offshore waters. [46]

The cost of repairing the state's hurricane-protection system "can be paid for simply by giving Louisiana our fair share of oil and gas revenues from the Outer Continental Shelf," Gov. Blanco told Bonilla at the House Select Committee hearing.

Coastal states like Louisiana receive 27 percent of the revenues from oil and gas leases from waters within their three-mile jurisdictions (federal waters extend another 197 miles). By contrast, states with oil and gas production on public lands receive 50 percent of the federal revenues, leading coastal states to feel they are entitled to a larger share of offshore revenues. [47]

Sen. Landrieu last year pushed a bill to grant coastal states 50 percent of the take from oil and gas leases in the areas off their shores. The bill died at year's end, but she is planning to revive it this year (*see p. 188*).

Rather than creating a new revenue source, however, the proposal would merely divert money to the state before the funds reach federal coffers, which bothered Bonilla. "It is wise when states and local governments come before us to show what they are doing to help themselves in terms of raising whatever revenue dollars you can," Bonilla told Blanco. "People would want to know . . . what is Louisiana doing in terms of everything you possibly can do to help yourself and not just look at the federal government and say, 'We need you to help us pay for these things.' "

But, he added, Americans would not "turn their back on those who want to help themselves."

BACKGROUND

Island City

New Orleans has been battling with nature ever since explorer Jean-Baptiste Le Moyne de Bienville founded the city in 1718. Its original name, in fact, reflected the city's relationship to the four bodies of water surrounding it — the Mississippi River, Lake Pontchartrain, Lake Borgne and the Gulf of Mexico. He called it *L'Isle de la Nouvelle Orléans* — the Island of New Orleans. [48]

"His enthusiasm for the river's commercial benefits blinded him to many of the challenges of building a city in the delta," environmental historian Kelman writes. These included: epidemics; "terrible to nonexistent" drainage; dampness; and "the threat of catastrophic flooding."

Still, Bienville's insight into the river's economic importance was on the money. The Mississippi was unrivalled as a highway deep into the North American continent, and remains so today. Some 500 million tons of goods — including about 60 percent of U.S. grain exports — are shipped downriver to the southern Louisiana port complex, which includes New Orleans. [49]

Experts Blame Levees, Not Storm

The newspaper headlines blamed "Killer Storm Katrina" for devastating New Orleans. But engineers largely blame the levees designed and built by the U.S. Army Corps of Engineers.

A team of experts who examined the protective system found no fewer than 34 storm-induced levee breaches, indicating that the engineering failures were far wider than initial reports indicated. [1]

"The performance of many of the levees and floodwalls could have been significantly improved, and some of the failures likely prevented, with relatively inexpensive modification," the team concluded. The simple addition of concrete "splash slabs," for instance, might have prevented soil levee tops from eroding.

In fact, even a task force assembled by the Corps of Engineers itself concluded "integral parts of the . . . hurricane-protection system failed." [2]

With the June 1 start of the 2006 hurricane season approaching, the Corps is trying to patch the immediate problems. Engineers and lawmakers, meanwhile, are evaluating the system's performance. So far, a lethal combination of design, construction and maintenance errors appears to underlie the disaster.

Blame extends from state-appointed "levee boards" responsible for inspection and maintenance to the Corps of Engineers, Sen. George Voinovich, R-Ohio, told the Senate Homeland Security and Governmental Affairs Committee on Dec. 14. And Congress deserved blame too, he said: "We have been penny-wise and pound-foolish" on funding upkeep and completion of the New Orleans levee system.

The Lake Pontchartrain and Vicinity Hurricane Protection Project includes 125 miles of levees, floodwalls and other structures. The system was supposed to bar storm surges from Lake Pontchartrain and channel any flooding out of the city via a series of canals. [3]

Though Congress approved the project in 1965, it was unfinished when Katrina struck. In the city itself, construction was 90 percent complete, but the lack of completion has not been blamed for the system's failure. [4] Rather, the devastation was intensified by the environmental changes in southern Louisiana since the system was first designed, the *Times-Picayune* reported as early as 2002. [5]

As the oil and gas industry expanded, the Corps of Engineers built or approved the necessary navigation channels in southern Louisiana and the Gulf of Mexico. And the industry expansion swallowed one-third to one-half of the wetlands — which have been disappearing at a rate of at

---

The first of New Orleans' protective barriers — called levees from the French verb "to lift" — were natural. In fact, New Orleans exists in the first place because the Mississippi's waters helped create a high section of riverbank along the section of the river that forms a crescent embracing old New Orleans — known today as the French Quarter. The sloping, natural levee was only 12 feet above sea level.

Settlers soon began adding to nature's work. Throughout the 18th and early 19th centuries — during the first period of French rule, the Spanish colonial period that followed in 1768-1801 and the French restoration in 1801-1803 — levees were built far upstream, and raised continually after flooding.

The levee work continued after the United States bought the city and vast swaths of the new nation's interior in 1803 for $15 million, or about 3 cents an acre.

Nine years after the so-called Louisiana Purchase, Louisiana became a state.

From the beginning, many people realized that building ever-higher levees up and down the river prevented its energy from being dissipated naturally in periodic floods. By the time the Mississippi reached New Orleans, it would be dangerously high and flowing at maximum force.

"We are every year confining this immense river closer and closer to its own bed — forgetting that it is fed by over 1,500 streams — and regardless of a danger becoming every year more and more impending," State Engineer P. O. Herbert warned in 1846. He argued for flood outlets along the river, but landowners resisted, not wanting their plantations flooded. [50]

In 1849, the river broke through several upstream levees, one of them 17 miles above New Orleans. The

least 25 square miles a year. Experts now know wetlands play a critical role during hurricanes, slowing storms as they make landfall. [6]

So when Katrina made landfall across the region's depleted wetlands, the poorly designed and built levees and floodwalls couldn't withstand the full force of the storm surge.

A section of floodwall along the London Avenue Canal was so weakened that it likely would have been breached by the floodwaters — if the barrier on the opposite side of the canal hadn't failed first, an engineer told the Senate Environment and Public Works Committee on Nov. 17. "Multiple, concurrent failure mechanisms" were present, said Larry Roth, deputy executive director of the American Society of Civil Engineers. "The wall was badly out of alignment and tilting landward; as a result of the tilt, there were gaps between the wall and the supporting soil."

Additional pressure on the flood barriers came from the Mississippi River Gulf Outlet (MRGO), a 76-mile long canal built to give ships a shortcut from the Gulf to the Port of New Orleans. Instead, it gave Katrina a straight shot into the city — a "hurricane alley" — said Sen. David Vitter, R-La., who has called, along with others, for the canal's closure. The Corps says it will not conduct its annual dredging of the waterway, and hurricane experts say it may become less dangerous as it becomes shallower. [7]

Meanwhile, engineers have suggested that some residential areas be abandoned — to provide a flood-absorbing

floodplain — and building codes amended to require that houses be elevated.

But the levee system also must be dealt with, Roth said. "If we are to rebuild the city," he said, "we must also rebuild its protections." [8]

---

[1] The team was assembled by the National Science Foundation (NSF), the American Society of Civil Engineers (ASCE) and the University of California at Berkeley. See R. B. Seed, *et al.*, "Preliminary Report on the Performance of the New Orleans Levee Systems in Hurricane Katrina on Aug. 29, 2005," Nov. 2, 2005, Figure 1.4, p. 1-10, www.ce.berkeley.edu/~inkabi/KRTF/CCRM/levee-rpt.pdf.

[2] "Performance Evaluation Plan and Interim Status, Report 1 of a Series: Performance Evaluation of the New Orleans and Southeast Louisiana Hurricane Protection System," Interagency Performance Evaluation Task Force, Jan. 10, 2006, Appendix A, p. 2, https://ipet.wes.army.mil.

[3] *Ibid*, pp. 1.2-1.3; Seed, *et al.*, *op. cit.*, p. A-2.

[4] "Performance Evaluation Plan," *op. cit.*, Appendix A, p. 2.

[5] John McQuaid and Mark Schleifstein, "Evolving Danger; experts know we face a greater threat from hurricanes than previously suspected," *The Times-Picayune* (New Orleans), June 23, 2002, p. A1.

[6] John McQuaid and Mark Schleifstein, "Shifting Tides," *The Times-Picayune* (New Orleans), June 26, 2002, p. A1.

[7] John Schwartz, "New Orleans Wonders What to Do With Open Wounds, Its Canals," *The New York Times*, Dec. 231, 2005, p. A26; Seed, *et al.*, *op. cit.*, p. 3.1; Matthew Brown, "Corps suspends plans to dredge MRGO," *The Times-Picayune* (New Orleans), Breaking News Weblog, Nov. 21, 2005, www.nola.com/t-p/.

[8] For background, see Larry Roth statement to Senate Committee on Environment and Public Works, Nov. 17, 2005, http://epw.senate.gov/hearing_statements.cfm?id=249000.

---

resultant flooding in the lowest section of New Orleans forced 12,000 mostly poor residents to abandon their dwellings or try to coexist with the water.

Afterward, the city raised the levees higher still. But A. D. Wooldridge, the state engineer who succeeded Herbert, declared in 1850 that reliance on levees "will be destructive to those who come after us." By then, some rose 15 feet.

Dynamiting the Levee

The engineers' warnings came to pass in early 1927. A series of rainstorms, coupled with unusually heavy spring runoff, swelled the huge river and overwhelmed the levees. Floodwater inundated 28,545 square miles of the Mississippi Valley as far north as Illinois, killing 423 people. By mid-April, more than 50,000 people had fled their homes. [51]

In New Orleans, powerful pumps kept floodwaters at bay — until a bolt of lightning disabled the power plant that kept the pumps humming.

A group of city leaders, who had formed the Citizens Flood Relief Committee, began campaigning to stop the flooding of the city by blowing a hole in the levee some 12 miles downstream.

Residents of the two thinly populated wetland parishes downstream, St. Bernard and Plaquemines, largely made their living fishing and trapping muskrats for their fur. The New Orleans political class persuaded Louisiana Gov. Oramel Simpson that those rural activities were worth sacrificing to protect New Orleans. Simpson gave the "river parish" residents three days to clear out. Muskrat trapping took years to recover.

For the poor African-Americans living along the river's southern reaches, the 1927 flood left bitter memories of

Getty Images/Robyn Beck

Engineers inspect a Katrina-damaged section of the London Avenue Canal on Sept. 21, 2005, three days before Hurricane Rita hit and reopened some levees that had been partially repaired. The city's flood-control system may not be completely repaired by June 1, the start of the 2006 hurricane season.

racial oppression and death. Especially in Mississippi, thousands of black men were conscripted into labor gangs that shored up the levee, often working at gunpoint. Some drowned as they worked, and a community leader who refused a summons because he'd been working all night was shot on the spot.

The race-hatred exacerbated by the flood triggered a vast expansion of the "great migration" of African-Americans from South to North. [52] For the black community, 1927 established a connection between natural disaster, racism and black exodus — a chain of events that many would later see repeating itself with Katrina.

New Expansion

The 1927 disaster led to improved federal flood-control systems and also launched a continuing debate over whether all Americans should have to pay to protect people living in disaster-prone places. [53]

In New Orleans, the 1927 flood also undermined the total dependence on levees for protection. Two years later, the Corps of Engineers began building a spillway at Bonnet Carré that could release river water into Lake Pontchartrain if the Mississippi rose to 20 feet in New Orleans. The spillway was completed in 1936.

By then, New Orleans residents had other reasons to feel safer. Electric and gasoline-powered motors had relieved major drainage problems. In a city sitting below sea level in a swampy area, difficulties in disposing of human and other waste had long endangered health and lowered the quality of life. Mosquito-borne yellow fever alone killed about 41,000 people between 1817 and 1905.

Draining surrounding swampland also allowed the opening up of new lands for settlement. From the 1930s to the post-World War II years, acreage to the north, east and west of the original city were transformed from wetlands into tract-housing territory. The suburbanization expanded into Jefferson Parish, just outside of the city.

Within New Orleans itself, the amount of land that had been drained for settlement expanded from 12,349 acres in 1895 to more than 90,000 by 1983.

On a dry day, the newly drained territory appeared suitable for housing. But after Katrina, the local paper, the *Times-Picayune*, published an 1878 map showing that nearly every part of the city that flooded in 2005 had been uninhabited in the years before the land was drained. Early residents understood exactly where not to live, the paper concluded. [54]

Hurricanes and Floods

Since the city's founding, the protective levee system had aimed mainly at holding back Mississippi flooding. But beginning in the mid-20th century, a series of powerful hurricanes changed the perception of where danger lay.

In 1947, a 112-mile-an-hour hurricane (they didn't have names yet) brought two-foot floods in a nine-square-mile area. Hurricanes Flossy (1956) and Hilda (1964) caused some damage but were dwarfed by the 160-mile-an-hour winds of Hurricane Betsy in 1965. Floodwaters reached eight feet in parts of the city; 75 people died, and 7,000 homes suffered damage.

In response, Congress passed the Flood Control Act of 1965, which funded expansion of the levee and canal system in and around New Orleans to protect against what today would be classified as a Category 3 hurricane. [55]

In 1969, just as construction of the expanded system began, Hurricane Camille slammed the Gulf Coast. Mississippi was hit hardest, but a section of the New Orleans levee complex also failed, flooding part of the city.

In succeeding years, even rainstorms became problematic. Nine inches of rain during a 1978 storm caused flooding of up to 3.5 feet in low-lying sections, damaging 71,500 homes. A series of heavy rainstorms between 1979 and 1995 also caused widespread damage, and in 1998, Hurricane Georges, a Category 2 storm that barely touched New Orleans, brought a water surge to within a foot of topping the levees. [56]

Waiting for the Big One

The steady growth in the number and intensity of hurricanes during the 1990s fed unease in New Orleans and prompted the *Times-Picayune* to publish — at the beginning of the 2002 hurricane season — a series of articles unflinchingly examining the risks New Orleans faced. "Officials at the local, state and national level are convinced the risk is genuine and are devising plans for alleviating the aftermath of a disaster that could leave the city uninhabitable for six months or more," the authors presciently wrote. [57]

In January 2005, Ivor van Heerden, deputy director of the Louisiana State University (LSU) Hurricane Center, told a conference on "coastal challenges" that a Category 3 or above storm striking New Orleans or any other coastal Louisiana city would be a "disaster of cataclysmic proportion." [58]

By then, the city's new-and-improved flood-protection system consisted of about 125 miles of levees, floodwalls and flood-proofed bridges and other barriers. In Orleans Parish, the renovation work was 90 percent complete. [59]

On Aug. 28, as Hurricane Katrina was rolling through the Gulf and heading for New Orleans, the National Weather Service called it "a most powerful hurricane with unprecedented strength." After landfall, "Most of the area will be uninhabitable for weeks, perhaps longer." [60]

Mayor Nagin, a newcomer to politics, had ordered the city evacuated. But buses for the tens of thousands of elderly and poor residents who didn't own cars were never dispatched.

Even before Katrina touched down near New Orleans on the morning of Aug. 29, a storm surge breached the levees along the Inner Harbor Navigation Canal (the "Industrial Canal"). At about the same time, an 18-foot surge from Lake Borgne pushed through a wall along the Mississippi River Gulf Outlet east of St. Bernard Parish and the Lower Ninth Ward. The resulting flooding soon reached the Lower Ninth. [61]

Over the next few hours, additional surges over the Industrial Canal sent even more floodwater into the Lower Ninth. Then, with Katrina moving westward near Lake Pontchartrain, another section of levee along the Industrial Canal gave way, followed by a breach of the 17th Street Canal floodwall, flooding the western end of the parish. [62]

In the days following the storm, New Orleans became an international symbol of government dysfunction. Tens of thousands of residents unable to evacuate clung to rooftops or flocked to the New Orleans Superdome, which was unequipped to receive them. By Sept. 12, FEMA Director Michael Brown had resigned under pressure — only days after being congratulated by President Bush. Belatedly, federal officials organized bus convoys and flights out of the city. [63]

Then, on Sept. 24, Hurricane Rita, a Category 3 storm, hit the Gulf Coast. New Orleans didn't lie directly in the storm's path, but the hurricane reopened some partly repaired levee breaches. As a result, the Lower Ninth Ward and the Gentilly neighborhood flooded again. Elsewhere in Louisiana and East Texas, the damage was far worse, with tens of thousands left homeless. [64]

By early December, only 10 percent of the city's businesses were up and running, and 135,000 residents, at most, had stayed or returned. They had a name for the only fully functioning part of the city — a strip of high ground that includes the French Quarter and other sections of old New Orleans: Like explorer Bienville, they called it "the island." [65]

CURRENT SITUATION

Redevelopment Plans

On Jan. 11, the Bring New Orleans Back Commission released its "Action Plan" for rebuilding the city, but action doesn't seem to be on the near horizon.

The plan recommended the formation of 13 neighborhood-planning committees, with work on recommendations to start on Feb. 20, finish by May 20 and be submitted to the city for approval by June 20. Reconstruction would begin by Aug. 20. [66]

Within days of the plan's release, however, a FEMA official said updated floodplain maps of the city wouldn't be available until the summer, depriving crucial information to homeowners considering rebuilding.

"If I were putting my lifetime savings in the single, biggest investment I'll ever make, I'd want to make sure I had minimized every possible risk," said Tulane's Kroloff, chairman of the commission's urban-design sub-committee. [67]

The delay in obtaining the updated flood-zone information would slow the reconstruction timetable, Kroloff said, but wouldn't prevent the neighborhood committees from canvassing past and present residents. "There are some people who are going to return no matter what, and some who aren't," he said. [68]

Other obstacles could further slow the plan's execution. Congress may not approve Rep. Baker's proposal to create a public corporation to buy and sell distressed properties, although BNOB Commissioner Canizaro hopes funds can be rounded up from FEMA and elsewhere. [69] The Louisiana legislature would have to create the nonprofit entity, provisionally entitled the Crescent City Recovery Corp., and New Orleans voters would have to OK changes to the city charter to authorize it. [70]

That vote could come as soon as April. But it remains to be seen how receptive voters will be to measures recommended by Nagin and the commission, especially in light of the criticism that greeted the plan when it was unveiled. Some property owners attacked the proposal as a land grab.

"If you come to take our property, you'd better come ready," homeowner Rodney Craft of the Lower Ninth Ward told the commissioners. [71]

"I hear the politicians talk, and nothing is being said — nothing," says Gail Miller, a retired New Orleans police officer who has returned to her home in New Orleans East, living upstairs but cooking in a motor home she and her husband park in the driveway. "The political situation worries me — the levees don't worry me a bit."

Another widespread worry is education. Since the state took over 102 of the city's 117 schools by designating them as a "recovery district," only about 8,000 of 60,000 pre-Katrina students are attending the handful of public and parochial schools that are operating. [72]

"One of the barriers to families returning is that the state took over the schools and is not opening them," says Councilwoman Willard-Lewis.

Many residents say, however, that reopening the schools as they were wouldn't be much help. The Urban Land Institute reported that before Katrina the public school system had an "educational quotient" ranking of 1 out of 100 — the nation's lowest. [73]

"Everybody knew that public education was broken before the storm," says Heather Thompson, a New Orleans native and Harvard Business School student. A graduate of the public schools' only secondary-level crown jewel, Benjamin Franklin High School, Thompson helped organize a consulting project by four dozen of her fellow business students to recommend recovery ideas for schools and other elements of civic life. [74]

Meanwhile, the shortage of school space seems likely to continue. "I want to get the very best leaders and the very best teachers for every child in Orleans Parish," said State Education Superintendent Cecil Picard, adding that he expects 15,000 public-school students when classes reopen in August. [75]

Port Bounces Back

Giant cranes are swinging containers off and on ships, warehouses are filled with bundles of rubber and coils of steel, and trucks headed inland are filling up with coffee beans. The Port of New Orleans is back up and running, though only months ago a quick comeback seemed improbable.

"On Aug. 30, somebody told me it would be six months before we got the first ship back," port Director LaGrange says. "I said our goal was to be at 70 percent of pre-Katrina activity by March 1 — the six-month anniversary [of Katrina]. We're pushing 65 percent now."

Immediately after Katrina struck, while Americans watched thousands of human tragedies unfolding in real time on television, shippers and merchants focused on the southern Louisiana port complex — the country's fourth-largest. [76] "The longer the ports remained closed, the greater the risk that we'd all be paying higher prices for coffee, cocoa, lumber, steel, zinc, aluminum and any number of other things," said Mark M. Zandi, chief executive of the Economy.com research firm. [77]

In a seeming paradox, Katrina largely spared the river-front port area. Like the old French Quarter, most of the port sits atop the natural levee on which Bienville

Should New Orleans be completely rebuilt on its old footprint?

YES
Sen. Mary Landrieu, D-La.
Member, Senate Appropriations Committee

Written for *CQ Researcher*, January 2006

More than five months ago, Hurricane Katrina and the subsequent breaks in numerous flood-control levees decimated one of our nation's greatest cities, my hometown, New Orleans.

Some have since questioned whether or not we should rebuild New Orleans, saying that we should abandon a city that has contributed so much to our great nation.

New Orleans is the capitol of our nation's energy coast. It was put there for a reason. We did not go there to sunbathe. We went there to set up the Mississippi River, to tame that river, to create channels for this country to grow and prosper. New Orleans was established so the cities and communities along the Mississippi River would have a port to trade with the world.

The indispensible Higgins boats that saved us during World War II were built in New Orleans. Forty-three thousand people built those boats and headed them out to Normandy. We're going to rebuild our shipping industry. We're going to rebuild our maritime industry, we will maintain our great port and we will continue to provide the energy that keeps our lights on across the nation.

Just because parts of New Orleans are below sea level is no reason to allow this great city to die. The Netherlands is a nation that is 21 feet below sea level at its economic heart, yet they still operate Europe's largest port — just as we operate America's largest port system.

The Dutch have proved that you can live below sea level and still keep your feet dry. They believe in an integrated system of water management. After a flood destroyed their nation in 1953, the Dutch said "Never again," and today they have created the world's most advanced storm-protection and flood-control system. If a nation half the size of Louisiana can do it, then surely the United States of America can.

We can and should rebuild every neighborhood — but maybe not exactly the way we did it the first time. This time we can build better, smarter, stronger neighborhoods.

One fact is certain: Every, single American citizen who calls New Orleans home has a right to come back and rebuild their neighborhoods, and the federal government should generously support that right.

New Orleans helped build America, and now America must help rebuild New Orleans, because America needs that great city — right where it is.

NO
William Hudnut
Joseph C. Canizaro Chair in Public Policy, Urban Land Institute

Written for *CQ Researcher*, January 2006

There are those who understandably feel that New Orleans should be rebuilt in its entirety, and that blocks and neighborhoods throughout the pre-Katrina city should be rebuilt house by house as resources permit.

The emotional tug of going back to one's "roots" is strong. One cannot blame the City Council and others for demanding that all areas of the city, especially East New Orleans and the Lower Ninth, as well as Lakeview and Gentilly, be rebuilt simultaneously. But we need to ask: Is such a plan realistic? Does it make sense?

The city will not have the resources to take care of a widely dispersed population, and not all the evacuees will be returning. Critics of a smaller city dismiss such plans and ideas as "arrogant," "elitist" and "racist," because the low-lying areas are where mostly black and low-income residents lived before Katrina. But the questions persist.

I can think of two compelling reasons to envision a smaller New Orleans in the future. It will have a smaller population, and it will be safer.

As is often said, "Demography is destiny." If New Orleans once had 465,000 people, that was once and no more. The city was losing population before Katrina and has shrunk to a little over 100,000 today, with prospects of that number climbing to perhaps 250,000 by the time Katrina's third anniversary rolls around.

Is it prudent to think that this smaller number of people should occupy all the territory that almost twice that number did before August 2005, especially when the city will not have the financial resources, police, fire and EMS services and the like to care for such a scattered population? Two keys to a successful, vibrant city are diversity and density, which a sprawled-out land base does not provide.

Katrina has given New Orleans a chance to reinvent itself as a more compact, connected city on a smaller footprint. The city's recovering economy built on restored building blocks — culture, food, music, art, entertainment, tourism, bioscience and medical research, the port, energy production — will attract people back into mixed-use, mixed-income, racially balanced, pedestrian-friendly neighborhoods carefully planned by citizens, with parks, open space, new wetlands and light-rail transit added to the mix. All of that can be accomplished on less space than the city occupied heretofore.

Who was it that said, "Small is beautiful?"

founded the city. However, a major container terminal and a new cold-storage warehouse in eastern New Orleans were both destroyed.

Louisiana politicians frequently cite the port's importance to the economy as an argument for rebuilding New Orleans to its pre-Katrina scale. When she heard that the port might be able to function at full strength with a city somewhat smaller than pre-Katrina New Orleans, Sen. Landrieu, responded: "Where are the workers going to come from? You can't have a port without New Orleans."

LaGrange takes a more nuanced view. "You've got to have the work force here," he says, and they will need "the support services that a city provides — transit, schools, places to worship, grocery stores, gasoline stations. But if the city, for some reason, is smaller, I don't think that would be a tremendous effect on the output of the port."

Politics and Legislation

New Orleans' future lies in many hands, but federal lawmakers may be the most important, because they control the biggest money source.

"We are at your mercy," Gov. Blanco told Senate Homeland Security Committee members as they toured the disaster zone on Jan. 17. "We are begging you to stay with us." [78]

Landrieu plans to revive her proposal to channel 50 percent of offshore petroleum-lease revenues to the state. The money would be earmarked for post-Katrina reconstruction, says her spokesman, Adam Sharp.

Besides the Landrieu and Baker proposals, Louisiana politicians will continue to push for $2.1 billion in supplemental Medicaid funds to help pay for health care for Katrina victims — many suddenly homeless and unemployed — who had to enter the federally subsidized medical insurance program for low-income people. Congress adjourned at year's end without passing the Medicaid bill, but Landrieu says she'll also continue to push for that.

The fact that none of these proposals passed while Katrina's devastation was fresh would seem to show that the state's politicians "have some work to do" to get Congress' attention, said one of Baker's aides. Blanco, meanwhile, is preparing to call a special 12-day legislative session, beginning on Feb. 6. She wants state lawmakers to make the "levee boards" that supervise maintenance more accountable. The boards were widely criticized — even ridiculed — for laxity, following Katrina. [79]

Getting the schools going again remains a priority, and Blanco must hammer together by May a plan to reorganize the city's school system, now largely under state control. The state Board of Elementary and Secondary Education would have to rule on the plan. The BNOBC in January proposed a leaner administrative office — one superintendent and four or five assistants — and expanded authority for principals, who would be able to hire and fire their own staffs. Differences between "have" and "have-not" schools would be eliminated under the plan, and early-education programs would be initiated. [80]

Meanwhile, the often-criticized Blanco tangled with the City Council over what she called its resistance to installing FEMA-supplied trailers for needy families. The council was responding, in part, to complaints from some residents who objected to trailer villages in their neighborhoods.

"Disagreements over housing must end — and must end now," she told the council on Jan. 5. Council members denied that they had obstructed trailer installation. After a subsequent meeting between the governor and council members, sites for a total of 40,000 trailers were identified. [81]

Even the demolition of unsafe houses stirred controversy. When it appeared the city was about to bulldoze some Lower Ninth Ward houses deemed unsafe, residents and some council members sought a court order to stop it. U.S. District Judge Martin L. C. Feldman then OK'd a deal between the Nagin administration and Lower Ninth Ward residents requiring at least seven-days' notice before demolition. [82]

The court-approved settlement apparently resolved the demolition issues, but political conflicts between Nagin and the council remain. The beleaguered mayor is among the candidates up for re-election on April 22.

OUTLOOK

Pessimism and Paralysis

Optimism is in short supply in New Orleans, notwithstanding the brave talk of Louisiana politicians. The failure of the flood-protection system, the tragedy and chaos of the early days of the disaster and the devastated conditions that remain in much of the city five months after Katrina have not provided grounds for much hope.

President Bush, in his State of the Union address on Jan. 31, devoted 162 of the speech's 5,432 words to New Orleans, proposing no specific, new remedies. "As we meet . . . immediate needs, we must also address deeper challenges that existed before the storm arrived," Bush said, citing a need for better schools and economic opportunity. Among Louisiana politicians, even the president's fellow Republicans felt left out. "I was very disappointed at how small a part those national challenges — and I think are national challenges — were given in the speech," Sen. Vitter told the *Times-Picayune*.

"There's no sense of urgency from the city government, the state government or the federal government," says Dennis Scott, looking out on his devastated New Orleans East neighborhood.

Indeed, as of late January, the U.S. Army Corps of Engineers had completed only 16 percent of the levee repairs scheduled for completion by June 1, when the 2006 hurricane season begins. [83]

An outsider draws essentially the same conclusion as Scott. "The lack of unity in the political establishment is the paralyzing factor," says the Urban Land Institute's Hudnut. "There's almost a political stand-off between the governor's office, the mayor's office, the City Council and the Bring New Orleans Back Commission; but this is also partially a Washington issue. I don't see a lot of leadership coming from the White House team."

Republican Hudnut is one of many politicians and ordinary citizens to question the high cost of the war in Iraq with the needs of New Orleans. The war's direct cash cost alone through November 2005 was calculated at $251 billion, according to a study released in January by two former Clinton administration officials. [84] Thompson, the Harvard Business School student working on redevelopment plans, observes that the government ought to be able to "make money appear" for New Orleans in the same way as deficit financing is arranged for the war.

If talking openly about race relations holds promise for making them better, the New Orleans disaster might have served some purpose. Some black New Orleanians wonder aloud, though, if the color of the majority of the city's residents hasn't also slowed down the pace of recovery. Anne LaBranche, the doctor's wife from New Orleans East, can't think of any other reason.

"This was a man-made problem," she says, referring to the failure of the flood-protection system. And yet, previous hurricane damage in Florida and other Gulf Coast states has been paid for without debate on whether people should be living in such potentially risky areas, she says. "President Bush says he resents it when people say 'racism,' so tell me what it is," she says quietly. "Why the different treatment?"

If New Orleans has one advantage concerning race, it may be that the city's geography tends to throw people of different colors together more than in other locales. Another point in the city's favor is New Orleanians' loyalty to their city. It remains to be seen whether that's enough to overcome the economic, political and environmental obstacles.

Piano technician David Doremus has lived in New Orleans most of the past 30 years. He and his wife live in the unflooded Algiers neighborhood on the Mississippi's west bank, and they are committed to remaining in town with their daughters.

While he's unsure about how much piano tuning and rebuilding work he'll have in the near future, he can't imagine anywhere else that offers the pace of life, the social graces and the fishing that he enjoys in New Orleans — as well as the musical variety. "I work for a recording studio, and one of the first sessions I worked on after the storm was with Allen Toussaint and Elvis Costello," he says.

So Doremus is ready to commute 40 miles to work at a friend's piano business in Covington, La., for a year, if he has to, or even work at Home Depot. "My family back in Virginia thinks I'm nuts," he adds. "And my wife's family in Pittsburgh thinks she's nuts."

If the Doremuses are crazy, New Orleans needs all the nuts it can muster.

NOTES

1. Gary Rivlin, "Anger Meets New Orleans Renewal Plan," *The New York Times*, Jan. 12, 2006, p. A18.

2. When Hurricane Katrina made landfall at Buras, La., 35 miles east of New Orleans at about 6 a.m., it was originally rated at Category 4, the classification for storms with wind speeds of 131-155 mph. The National Hurricane Center later revised that classification down to Category 3, with winds of 111-130 mph. Some 24 hours before reaching Louisiana, Katrina varied between categories 4 and 5. For further detail, see Peter Whoriskey and Joby Warrick,

"Report Revises Katrina's Force," *The Washington Post*, Dec. 22, 2005, p. A3; Richard D. Knabb, *et al.*, "Tropical Cyclone Report: Hurricane Katrina, 22-30 August, 2005," National Hurricane Center, Dec. 20, 2005, p. 3, www.nhc.noaa.gov/pdf/TCR-AL1 22005_Katrina. pdf; and National Aeronautics and Space Administration, "Hurricane Season 2005: Katrina," www.nasa.gov/vision/earth/lookingatearth/h2005_katrina.html.

3. Nicholas Riccardi, "Most of Louisiana's Identified Storm Victims Over 60," *Los Angeles Times*, Nov. 5, 2005, p. A11; Nicholas Riccardi, Doug Smith and David Zucchino, "Katrina Killed Along Class Lines," *Los Angeles Times*, Dec. 18, 2005, p. A1.

4. While Katrina had weakened to Category 3 upon reaching Louisiana, the surges it created began when the storm was at categories 4 and 5 strength. For further detail, see "Tropical Cyclone Report," *op. cit.*, p. 9.

5. "President Discusses Hurricane Relief in Address to the Nation," White House, Sept. 15, 2005, www.whitehouse.gov/news/releases/2005/09/print/20050915-8.html.

6. Bill Walsh, "Senators say recovery moving at snail's pace," *The Times-Picayune* (New Orleans), Jan. 18, 2006, p. A1.

7. Ralph Vartabedian, "New Orleans Should be Dry by End of Week," *Los Angeles Times*, Sept. 19, 2005, p. A8; "Performance Evaluation Plan and Interim Status, Report 1 of a Series: Performance Evaluation of the New Orleans and Southeast Louisiana Hurricane Protection System," Interagency Performance Evaluation Task Force, Jan. 10, 2006, p. 1, https://ipet.wes.army.mil.

8. "Action Plan for New Orleans: The New American City," Bring New Orleans Back Commission, Urban Planning Committee, Jan. 11, 2006, Introduction, www.bringneworleansback.org.

9. "It was not unusual for slaves to gather on street corners at night, for example, where they challenged whites to attempt to pass. . . ," historian Joseph G. Tregle is quoted in Eugene D. Genovese, *Roll, Jordan, Roll: The World the Slaves Made* (1972), pp. 412-413.

10. Quoted in Reed Johnson, "New Orleans: Before and After," *Los Angeles Times*, Sept. 5, 2005, p. E1. For more background on Congo Square, see Craig E. Colten, *An Unnatural Metropolis: Wresting New Orleans From Nature* (2005), p. 72; and Gerald Early, "Slavery," on Web site for "Jazz," PBS documentary, www.pbs.org/jazz/time/time_slavery.htm.

11. "A Strategy for Rebuilding New Orleans, Louisiana," Urban Land Institute, Nov. 12-18, 2005, p. 17, www.uli.org/Content/NavigationMenu/ProgramsServices/AdvisoryServices/KatrinaPanel/ULI_Draft_New _Orleans%20Report.pdf.

12. "President Discusses Hurricane Relief," *op. cit.*

13. Joby Warrick, "White House Got Early Warning on Katrina," *The Washington Post*, Jan. 24, 2005, p. A2.

14. Steve Ritea and Tara Young, "Cycle of Death: Violence Thrives on Lack of Jobs, Wealth of Drugs," *The Times-Picayune* (New Orleans), p. A1; Adam Nossiter, "New Orleans Crime Swept Away, With Most of the People," *The New York Times*, Nov. 10, 2005, p. A1. Dan Baum, "Deluged, When Katrina hit, where were the police?" *The New Yorker*, Jan. 9, 2006, p. 59.

15. Quoted in, Joel Havemann, "New Orleans' Racial Future Hotly Argued," *Los Angeles Times*, Oct. 1, 2005, p. A14.

16. Brett Martel, The Associated Press, "Storms Payback From God, Nagin Says," *The Washington Post*, Jan. 17, 2006, p. A4.

17. Manuel Rog-Franzia, "New Orleans Mayor Apologizes for Remarks About God's Wrath," *The Washington Post*, Jan. 18, 2006, p. A2.

18. James Dao, "Study Says 80% of New Orleans Blacks May Not Return," *The New York Times*, Jan. 27, 2006, p. A16.

19. *Ibid.*; see also "Action Plan," (pages unnumbered); Frank Donze and Gordon Russell, "Rebuilding proposal gets mixed reception," *The Times-Picayune* (New Orleans), Jan. 12, 2006, p. A1.

20. Donze and Russell, *ibid.*; Rivlin, *op. cit.*

21. "A Strategy for Rebuilding," *op. cit.*; Frank Donze, "Don't write us off, residents warn," *The Times-Picayune* (New Orleans), Nov. 29, 2005, p. A1.

22. "Action Plan," Introduction, *op. cit.*; Gordon Russell, "Comeback in Progress," *The Times-Picayune* (New Orleans), Jan. 1, 2006, p. A1.

23. "Battered by Katrina, Tulane University forced into layoffs, cutbacks," The Associated Press, Dec. 9, 2005.

24. Susan Saulny, "Students Return to Big Changes in New Orleans," *The New York Times*, Jan. 4, 2006, p. 13; Steven Ritea, "School board considers limited role," *The Times-Picayune* (New Orleans), Dec. 7, 2005, p. A1.

25. Elizabeth Bumiller, "In New Orleans, Bush Speaks With Optimism But Sees Little of Ruin," *The New York Times*, Jan. 13, 2006, p. A12.

26. For background, see Marcia Clemmitt, "Climate Change," *CQ Researcher*, Jan. 27, 2006, pp. 73-96.

27. Virginia R. Burkett, "Potential Impacts of Climate Change and Variability on Transportation in the Gulf Coast/Mississippi Delta Region," Center for Climate Change and Environmental Forecasting, Oct. 1-2, 2002, p. 7, http://climate.volpe.dot.gov/workshop1002/burkett.pdf. Burkett is chief of the Forest Ecology Branch of the U.S. Geological Survey's National Wetlands Research Center, in Lafayette, La.

28. In 2006, the Bush administration does not plan to seek new funds for reconstruction in Iraq. See, Ellen Knickmeyer, "U.S. Has End in Sight on Iraq Rebuilding," *The Washington Post*, Jan. 2, 2006, p. A1.

29. Michael Oneal, "GOP Cools to Katrina Aid," *Chicago Tribune*, Nov. 12, 2005, p. A7.

30. For background, see Kenneth Jost, "Property Rights," *CQ Researcher*, March 4, 2005, pp. 197-220.

31. R. B. Seed, *et al.*, "Preliminary Report on the Performance of the New Orleans Levee Systems on August. 29, 2005," University of California at Berkeley, American Society of Civil Engineers, Nov. 2, 2005, pp. 1.2-1.4.

32. Schwartz, *op. cit.*

33. For details, see John McQuaid, "The Dutch Swore It Would Never Happen Again," "Dutch Defense, Dutch Masters," "Bigger, Better, Bolder," *The Times-Picayune* (New Orleans), Nov. 13-14, 2005, p. A1.

34. "Performance Evaluation Plan," *op. cit.*, appendix A-2. John Schwartz, "Category 5: Levees are Piece of $32 Billion Pie," *The New York Times*, Nov. 29, 2005, p. A1.

35. *Ibid.*

36. Richard W. Stevenson and James Dao, "White House to Double Spending on New Orleans Flood Protection," *The New York Times*, Dec. 16, 2005, p. A1.

37. *Ibid.*

38. President Bush said on Jan. 26 the congressional appropriations amounted to $85 billion. For background and detail, see Joseph J. Schatz, "End-of-Session Gift for the Gulf Coast," *CQ Weekly*, Dec. 26, 2005, p. 3401; "Cost of Katrina Nearing $100 Billion, Senate Budget Says," *CQ Budget Tracker News*, Jan. 18, 2006; "Senate Budget Committee Releases Current Tally of Hurricane-Related Spending," Budget Committee, Jan. 18, 2006, http://budget.senate.gov/republican. "Press Conference of the President," [transcript] Jan. 26, 2006, www.whitehouse.gov/news/releases/2006/01/20060126.htm.

39. Quoted in Jacob Freedman, "Additional Flood Funds Needed to Cover Extensive Gulf Coast Damage," *CQ Today*, Jan. 25, 2006; Statement of David I. Maurstad, Acting Director/Federal Insurance Administrator, Mitigation Division, Federal Emergency Management Agency, Committee on Senate Banking Housing and Urban Affairs, Jan. 25, 2006, http://banking.senate.gov/_files/ACF43B7.pdf.

40. Frank Donze, Gordon Russell and Lauri Maggi, "Buyouts torpedoed, not sunk," *The Times-Picayune* (New Orleans), Jan. 26, 2006, p. A1.

41. Adrian Moore, "Rebuild New Orleans Smarter, Not Harder," Reason Foundation, Jan. 11, 2006, /www.reason.org/commentaries/moore_20060111.shtml.

42. David Greising, *et al.*, "How Do They Rebuild a City?" *Chicago Tribune*, Sept. 4, 2005, p. A1.

43. "Press Conference of the President," *op. cit.*

44. Donze, Russell and Maggi, *op. cit.*

45. *Ibid.*

46. Robert L. Bamberger and Lawrence Kumins, "Oil and Gas: Supply Issues After Katrina," Congressional Research Service, updated Sept. 6, 2005, p. 1, www.fas.org/sgp/crs/misc/RS22233.pdf. For background on offshore leases, see Jennifer Weeks, "Domestic Energy Development," *CQ Researcher*, Sept. 30, 2005, pp. 809-832.

47. Marc Humphries, "Outer Continental Shelf: Debate Over Oil and Gas Leasing and Revenue Sharing," Congressional Research Service, Uupdated Oct. 27, 2005, pp. 1-4. http://fpc.state.gov/documents/organization/56096.pdf.

48. Unless otherwise indicated, all material in this section comes from Colten, op. cit.; and Ari Kelman, *A River and Its City: The Nature of Landscape in New Orleans* (2003).

49. Caroline E. Mayer and Amy Joyce, "Troubles Travel Upstream," *The Washington Post*, Sept. 5, 2005, p. A23.

50. Colten, *op. cit.*, pp. 25-26.

51. For background, see C. Perkins, "Mississippi River Flood Relief and Control," *Editorial Research Reports, 1927*, Vol. 2; and M. Packman, "Disaster Insurance," *Editorial Research Reports 1956*, Vol. I.

52. John M. Barry, *Rising Tide: The Great Mississippi Flood of 1927 and How it Changed America* (1998), pp. 311-317; p. 332

53. For background, see "Economic Effects of the Mississippi Flood," *Editorial Research Reports, 1928*, Vol. I.

54. Gordon Russell, "An 1878 Map Reveals that Maybe Our Ancestors Were Right to Build on Higher Ground," *The Times-Picayune* (New Orleans), Nov. 3, 2005, p. A1.

55. "Performance Evaluation Plan," *op. cit.*, Appendix A, p. 1; Willie Drye, " 'Category Five': How a Hurricane Yardstick Came To Be," *National Geographic News*, Dec. 20, 2005, http://news.nationalgeographic.com/news/2005/12/1220_051220_saffirsimpson.html.

56. John McQuaid and Mark Schleifstein, "The Big One," *The Times-Picayune* (New Orleans), June 24, 2002, p. A1.

57. *Ibid.*

58. Ivor van Heerden, "Using Technology to Illustrate the Realities of Hurricane Vulnerability," Jan. 25, 2005, www.laseagrant.org/forum/01-25-2005.htm.

59. "Performance Evaluation Plan," *op. cit.*, Appendix A, pp. 2-3.

60. "Urgent Warning Proved Prescient," *The New York Times*, Sept. 7, 2005, p. A21.

61. "How New Orleans Flooded," in "The Storm That Drowned a City," NOVA, WGBH-TV, October 2005, www.pbs.org/wgbh/nova/orleans/how-nf.html.

62. *Ibid.*

63. See Pamela Prah, "Disaster Preparedness," *CQ Researcher*, Nov. 18, 2005, pp. 981-1004.

64. "Rita's Aftermath," *Los Angeles Times*, Sept. 28, 2005, p. A1; Shaila Dewan and Jere Longman, "Hurricane Slams Into Gulf Coast; Flooding Spreads," *The New York Times*, Sept. 25, 2005, p. A1.

65. Anne Rochell Konigsmark, "Amid ruins, 'island' of normalcy in the Big Easy," *USA Today*, Dec. 19, 2005, p. A1; Gordon Russell, "Comeback in Progress," *The Times-Picayune* (New Orleans), Jan. 1, 2006, p. A1.

66. "Action Plan," *op. cit.*, Sec. 4, (pages unnumbered).

67. Gordon Russell and James Varney, "New flood maps will likely steer rebuilding," *The Times-Picayune* (New Orleans), Jan. 15, 2006, p. A1.

68. *Ibid.*

69. *Ibid.*

70. *Ibid.*

71. Russell and Donze, *op. cit.*, Jan. 12, 2006.

72. Ritea and Saulny, *op. cit.*

73. "A Strategy for Rebuilding New Orleans," *op. cit.*, p. 19.

74. For background, see, George Anders, "How a Principal in New Orleans Saved Her School," *The Wall Street Journal*, Jan. 13, 2006, p. A1.

75. Steve Ritea, "La. won't run N.O. schools by itself," *The Times-Picayune* (New Orleans), Jan. 3, 2006, p. B1.

76. Vanessa Cieslak, "Ports in Louisiana: New Orleans, South Louisiana, and Baton Rouge," Congressional Research Service, Oct. 14, 2005, p. 1, http://fpc.state.gov/documents/organization/57872.pdf.

77. Keith L. Alexander and Neil Irwin, "Port Comes Back Early, Surprisingly," *The Washington Post*, Sept. 14, 2005, p. D1.

78. Bill Walsh, "Senators say recovery moving at a snail's pace," *The Times-Picayune* (New Orleans), Jan. 18, 2006, p. A1.

79. Ed Anderson, "Special session set to begin Feb. 6," *The Times-Picayune* (New Orleans), Jan. 12, 2006, p. A2.

80. Steve Ritea, "Nagin's schools panel issues reforms," *The Times-Picayune* (New Orleans), Jan. 18, 2006, p. A1; "Rebuilding and Transforming: A Plan for World-Class Public Education in New Orleans," Bring New Orleans Back Commission, Jan. 17, 2006, pp. 10, 48.

81. Ed Anderson, "N.O. needs 7,000 more trailer sites,

Blanco says," *The Times-Picayune* (New Orleans), Jan. 9, p. A1.

82. Adam Nossiter, "New Orleans Agrees to Give Notice on Home Demolitions," *The New York Times*, Jan. 18, 2006, p. A10.

83. Spencer S. Hsu, "Bush's Post-Katrina Pledges," *The Washington Post*, Jan. 28, 2006, p. A12.

84. Linda Bilmes and Joseph Stiglitz, "The Economic Costs of the Iraq War: An Appraisal Three Years After the Beginning of the Conflict," http://ksghome.harvard.edu/~lbilmes/paper/iraqnew.pdf. Former Deputy Assistant Commerce Secretary Bilmes is now at the Kennedy School of Government at Harvard; Stiglitz, a Nobel laureate economist, teaches at Columbia University.

BIBLIOGRAPHY

Books

Colten, Craig E., *An Unnatural Metropolis: Wresting New Orleans from Nature*, Louisiana State University Press, 2005.
A Louisiana State University, Baton Rouge, geographer chronicles the city's ongoing efforts to tame its watery environment.

Dyson, Michael Eric, *Come Hell or High Water: Hurricane Katrina and the Color of Disaster*, Basic Civitas Books, 2006.
A professor of humanities at the University of Pennsylvania — and a prolific author and commentator on issues of race and culture — dissects what he views as structural racism, government incompetence and class warfare against the poor in the Katrina disaster.

Kelman, Ari, *A River and its City: The Nature of Landscape in New Orleans*, University of California Press, 2003.
Using New Orleans' long and complicated relationship with the Mississippi River as a framework, an environmental historian at the University of California, Davis, examines why New Orleans developed as it did.

Piazza, Tom, *Why New Orleans Matters*, Harper Collins, 2005.
A jazz historian, novelist and New Orleans resident who evacuated the city during Katrina argues that American culture will be poorer if the working people who keep the city's traditions alive are permanently uprooted from the city.

Ward, Geoffrey C., and Ken Burns, *Jazz: A History of America's Music*, Alfred A. Knopf, 2000.
An author of popular history (Ward) and a renowned documentary filmmaker provide — with contributions by jazz scholars — a one-volume history of America's major cultural creation, with much attention to New Orleans' role.

Articles

Baum, Dan, "Deluged: When Katrina hit, where were the police?" *The New Yorker*, Jan. 9, 2006, p. 50.
A writer recounts how police and city government coped — or failed to — in the post-hurricane disaster.

Cooper, Christopher, "Old-Line Families Escape Worst of Flood and Plot the Future," *The Wall Street Journal*, Sept. 8, 2005, p. A1.
A profile of one of New Orleans' aristocrats brings the city's social inequalities to light in dispassionate fashion.

McQuaid, John, and Mark Schleifstein, "In Harm's Way," "Evolving Danger," "Left Behind," "The Big One," "Exposure's Cost," "Building Better," "Model Solutions," "Tempting Fate," "Shifting Tides," [series] *The Times-Picayune*, June 23-June 26, 2002.
Three years before Katrina, two reporters spell out the city's growing vulnerability to a massive hurricane, virtually telling the Katrina story.

Sontag, Deborah, "Delrey Street," *The New York Times*, Oct. 12, 2005, p. A1; Oct. 24, 2005, p. A1; Nov. 12, 2005, p. A9; Nov. 14, 2005 p. A1; Dec. 2, 2005, p. A20; Jan. 9, 2006, p. A1.
In a series of detailed profiles, a *New York Times* reporter examines how the lives of families from New Orleans' Lower Ninth Ward have been upended by Katrina.

"Tempting Fate," "Shifting Tides," [series] *The Times-Picayune*, June 23-June 26, 2002.
Three years before Katrina, two reporters spell out the city's growing vulnerability to a massive hurricane, virtually telling the Katrina story.

Tizon, Alex Tomas, and Doug Smith, "Evacuees of Hurricane Katrina Resettle Along a Racial Divide," *Los Angeles Times*, Dec. 12, 2005, p. A1.
Two reporters analyzed change-of-address data to draw early conclusions on the racial effects of the disaster.

Reports and studies

"Action Plan for New Orleans: The New American City," Bring New Orleans Back Commission, Urban Planning Committee, Jan. 11, 2006, www.bringnew orleansback.org.
Civic leaders and officials provided the first detailed plan for redevelopment of New Orleans.

"An Unnatural Disaster: The Aftermath of Hurricane Katrina," Scholars for Progressive Reform, Sept. 2005, www.progressivereform.org/Unnatural_Disaster_512. pdf.
A liberal organization analyzes the disaster as a failure of unrestrained energy development and inadequate government regulation.

Katz, Bruce, *et al.*, "Katrina Index: Tracking Variables of Post-Katrina Reconstruction," updated Dec. 6, 2005, The Brookings Institution, www. brookings.edu/metro/pubs/200512_katrinaindex.htm.
To be updated periodically, this report compiles and organizes statistics in order to show economic and social trends as New Orleans recovers.

Seed, R. B., *et al.*, "Preliminary Report on the Performance of the New Orleans Levee Systems in Hurricane Katrina on August 29, 2005," University of California at Berkeley, American Society of Civil Engineers, National Science Foundation, Nov. 2, 2005, www.berkeley.edu/news/media/releases/2005/11/levee report_prelim.pdf.
Engineering experts provide an early look at the failures of the levee system that led to disaster.

For More Information

Bring New Orleans Back Commission, www.bringnew orleansback.org. The commission has been issuing detailed redevelopment plans.

The Brookings Institution, Katrina Issues and the Aftermath Project, Metropolitan Policy Program, 1775 Massachusetts Ave., N.W., Washington, DC 20036; (202) 797-6139; www.brookings.edu/metro/katrina.htm. The think tank provides policy proposals, commentary and statistics.

Center for the Study of Public Health Impacts of Hurricanes, CEBA Building, Suite 3221, Louisiana State University, Baton Rouge, LA 70803; (225) 578-4813; www.publichealth.hurricane.lsu.edu. A research center focusing on disaster prevention and mitigation.

Federal Emergency Management Agency, 500 C St., S.W., Washington, DC 20472; (800) 621-FEMA; www. fema.gov. The lead federal agency on disaster recovery; provides information on relief program requirements and application deadlines.

Greater New Orleans Community Data Center, www.gnocdc.org. A virtual organization that provides links to the city's most recent social, economic and demographic statistics.

Louisiana Recovery Authority, 525 Florida St., 2nd Floor, Baton Rouge, LA 70801; (225) 382-5502; http:// lra.louisiana.gov. The state government's post-disaster reconstruction agency; provides information on the aid flowing to New Orleans.

New Orleans Area Habitat for Humanity, P.O. Box 15052, New Orleans, LA 70175-1732; (504) 861-2077, www.habitat-nola.org. A self-help housing organization building new homes in the city and nearby suburbs.

Savenolamusic, www.savenolamusic.com. An exhaustive listing of performance bookings and other resources (including medical assistance) for New Orleans musicians, including those forced out of the city.

Urban Land Institute, 1025 Thomas Jefferson St., N.W., Suite 500 West, Washington, DC 20007; (202) 624-7000. The nonprofit organization for land-use and development professionals is the New Orleans city government's disaster-recovery consultant.

9

Illegal Immigration

Peter Katel and Patrick Marshall

Mexican immigrants in Homestead, Fla., negotiate with a man seeking four workers on May 7, 2004. Illegal immigrants make up only about 5 percent of the U.S. work force, but critics say they are taking many Americans' jobs by offering to work for low wages and no benefits. Immigration advocates counter that immigrants do the jobs Americans don't want and bolster the economy.

From *CQ Researcher,*
May 6, 2005 (updated May 2006).

T he only future awaiting María and Juan Gomez in their tiny village in Mexico was working the fields from sunup to sundown, living mostly on tortillas and beans. So 11 years ago, when they were both 17, they crossed into the United States illegally, near San Diego. Now ensconced in the large Latino community outside Washington, D.C., they are working hard at building a life for themselves and their young son.

Juan and María (not their real names) follow a simple strategy — staying out of trouble and undercutting competitors. Juan does landscaping, charging about $600 for major yard work — about $400 less than the typical legal contractor. María cleans houses for $70; house-cleaning services normally charge $85 or more.

They aren't complaining, but María and Juan know they offer bargain-basement prices. "You walk down the street, and every house being built, Hispanics are building it," María says in Spanish. "This country is getting more work for less money."

Indeed, some sectors of the economy might have a hard time functioning without illegal workers. Brendan Flanagan, director of legislative affairs for the National Restaurant Association, insists, "Restaurants, hotels, nursing homes, agriculture — a very broad group of industries — are looking for a supply of workers to remain productive," he says, because in many parts of the country, native workers aren't available at any price. Moreover, lobbyists for employers insist that their members can't tell false papers from the real ones that employees present to prove they're here legally.

But Harvard economist George Borjas counters that when an American employer claims he cannot find a legal or native-born worker willing to do a certain job, "He is leaving out a very key part

Most Illegal Immigrants Live in Four States

More than half of the nation's more than 10 million illegal immigrants live in four states — California, Texas, Florida and New York.

Estimated Distribution of Illegal Immigrants
(average of data from 2002-2004)

Legend:
- 300,000-2.4 Million
- 200,000-250,000
- 100,000-150,000
- 55,000-85,000
- 20,000-35,000
- Under 10,000

Source: Jeffrey S. Passel, "Estimates of the Size and Characteristics of the Undocumented Population," Pew Hispanic Center, March 21, 2005, based on data from the March 2004 "Current Population Survey" by the Census Bureau and Department of Labor

of that phrase. He should add 'at the wage I'm going to pay.' " [1]

Many Americans blame illegal immigrants like María and Juan not only for depressing wages but also for a host of problems, including undermining U.S. security.

But the U.S. government refuses to tighten up the border, they say.

"The reason we do not have secure borders is because of an insatiable demand for cheap labor," says Rep. Tom Tancredo, R-Colo., a leading immigration-control advocate in Congress. "We have the ability to secure the border; we choose not to. The Democratic Party sees massive immigration — legal and illegal — as a massive source of voters. The Republican Party looks at the issue and says, 'Wow, that's a lot of cheap labor coming across that border.' "

Some other politicians are following Tancredo's lead. In April 2005, California Gov. Arnold Schwarzenegger ratcheted up his anti-illegal immigration rhetoric. Praising anti-immigration activists monitoring the Mexican border in Arizona, he said, "Our federal government is not doing their job. It's a shame that the private citizen has to go in there and start patrolling our borders."

There are more than 10 million immigrants living illegally in the United States, compared with 3.5 million only 15 years ago, according to the non-profit Pew Hispanic Center. [2] And since 2000 the illegal population has been growing by a half-million illegal immigrants a year — nearly 1,400 people a day, according to the Census Bureau and other sources. [3]

While illegal immigrants make up only about 5 percent of the U.S. work force, they are rapidly making their presence known in non-traditional areas such as the Midwest and South. Willing to work for low wages, undocumented workers are creating a political backlash among some residents in the new states, which have seen a nearly tenfold increase in illegal immigration since 1990.

"Immigration is now a national phenomenon in a way that was less true a decade ago," Mark Krikorian, executive director of the nonpartisan Center for Immigration Studies said. "In places like Georgia and Alabama, which had little experience with immigration before, people are experiencing it firsthand. Immigrants are working in chicken plants, carpet mills and construction. It's right in front of people's faces now." [4]

The debate has taken on populist undertones, says Dan Stein, president of the Federation for American Immigration Reform (FAIR), because some in the public perceive a wide gap between policymakers' positions and popular sentiment in affected regions. "The issue is about elites, major financial interests and global economic forces arrayed against the average American voter," said Stein, whose group favors strict immigration policies. "The depth of anger should not be underestimated." [5]

Grass-roots organizations have formed in seven states to push for laws denying public services for illegal immigrants and Rep. Tancredo hints he may run for president to "build a fire" around the need for immigration reform. [6]

But reform means different things to different people.

To Rep. F. James Sensenbrenner Jr., R-Wis., chairman of the House Judiciary Committee, reform means imposing new restrictions on asylum seekers, blocking states from issuing driver's licenses to illegal immigrants and finishing a border fence near San Diego. "We will never have homeland security if we don't have border

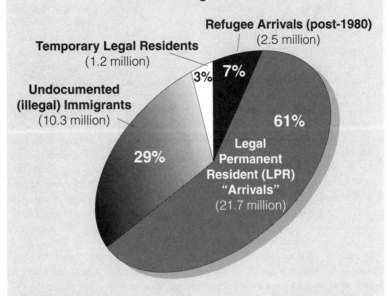

Majority of Immigrants in U.S. Are Legal

More than 21 million legal "permanent" immigrants live in the United States — more than twice the number of illegal immigrants.

Status of Immigrants in U.S.

Refugee Arrivals (post-1980)
(2.5 million)

Temporary Legal Residents
(1.2 million)

Undocumented
(illegal) Immigrants
(10.3 million)

3%   7%

61%

29%   Legal Permanent Resident (LPR) "Arrivals"
(21.7 million)

Sources: Jeffrey S. Passel, "Estimates of the Size and Characteristics of the Undocumented Population," Pew Hispanic Center, March 21, 2005, based on data from the March 2004 "Current Population Survey" by the Census Bureau and Department of Labor

security," Sensenbrenner said in March 2005. [7] Sensenbrenner's tough, new Real ID bill, which requires proof of citizenship or legal status in the United States in order to get a driver's license, was signed into law in May 2005 and will take effect in May 2008.

To Sen. John McCain, R-Ariz., reform means enabling illegal immigrants to stay here legally because, he contends, the nation's economy depends on them. "As long as there are jobs to be had . . . that won't be done by Americans [illegal immigrants] are going to come and fill those jobs," he said in April 2005. [8]

Echoing McCain, President Bush has endorsed the creation of a "guest worker" program that would grant temporary legal status to illegal workers. "If there is a job opening which an American won't do . . . and there's a willing worker and a willing employer, that job ought to be filled on a legal basis, no matter where the person

Immigration Debate Moves Behind the Wheel

The tension was high in suburban Atlanta in October 2005 when protesters confronted hundreds of illegal immigrants who were marching to demand the right to obtain driver's licenses.

The peaceful, sign-waving march soon turned ugly, as angry epithets were hurled back and forth across busy Buford Highway. "This is my country! You are criminals! You cannot have my country!" shouted D.A. King, a former insurance salesman and self-styled anti-immigrant vigilante. Boos and hisses erupted from the mostly Hispanic immigrants across the street. [1]

The heated exchange, caught by a CNN television crew, captured the intensifying debate over driver's licenses for illegal immigrants. Eleven states now issue such licenses, and several others are considering permitting similar laws, but a growing grass-roots movement opposes the licenses, including groups like the American Resistance Foundation, founded by King.

The immigrants' supporters say illegal workers are the backbone of the nation's economic success and that being able to drive legally would allow them to open bank accounts and do other tasks requiring an official identification card. It would also make America's roads safer, the proponents say, by holding immigrants to the same driving and insurance requirements as U.S. citizens. Unlicensed drivers are nearly five times more likely to be in a fatal crash than licensed drivers, and uninsured drivers cause 14 percent of all accidents, according to the AAA Foundation for Traffic Safety. [2]

But King and others say uncontrolled immigration depresses wages, increases crime and causes neighborhood blight, and that granting undocumented workers driver's licenses would only legalize illegal behavior.

Until now the debate over immigrant driver's licenses has been restricted to a few traditional border states, like California, where a new law permitting undocumented workers to get licenses helped defeat Democratic Gov. Gray Davis during the 2003 gubernatorial recall election. Lawmakers repealed the law shortly after Arnold Schwarzenegger was inaugurated as governor, and Schwarzenegger has since vetoed related bills. He wants the licenses of undocumented workers to bear a unique mark.

Now the debate has moved to states throughout the country. In Utah and Tennessee, state laws now give illegal workers so-called "driving privilege cards," which warn in bold, red letters they cannot be used as legal identification. [3] New York State's motor-vehicles commissioner in April 2005 denied license renewals and suspended the licenses of illegal immigrants without a Social Security card or acceptable visa. [4] The state's Supreme Court, which made a preliminary ruling rejecting the commissioner's action, is currently hearing the issue.

Now some in Congress want to jump into the fray — even though issuing driver's licenses has long been the domain of the states. In January 2005, Wisconsin Republican Rep. F. James Sensenbrenner Jr. proposed the Real ID Act, which would establish national driver's license standards, toughen asylum requirements and speedy completion of a fence on the U.S.-Mexico border near San Diego. But the driver's license provision has caused the most debate.

"My bill's goal is straightforward: It seeks to prevent another 9/11-type attack by disrupting terrorist travel," Sensenbrenner said. The bill would require states to verify that driver's-license applicants reside legally in the United States before issuing a license that could be used for federal identification purposes, such as boarding an airplane. [5]

The bill, which Sensenbrenner attached to a "must-pass" emergency military-spending bill, was approved by Congress and signed into law on May 11, 2005, and is scheduled to go into effect in May 2008.

The bill's supporters say providing secure driver's licenses to illegal immigrants will improve national security, because licenses are now the de facto form of identification in the United States. The 9/11 Commission, which investigated the Sept. 11, 2001, terrorist attacks, found that the attackers used driver's licenses rather than passports to avoid creating suspicion. [6]

"At many entry points to vulnerable facilities, including gates for boarding aircraft," the commission's 2004 report noted, "sources of identification are the last opportunity to ensure that people are who they say they are and to check whether they are terrorists." [7]

comes from," Bush said after a meeting at his Texas ranch on March 23, 2005, with Mexican President Vicente Fox and Canadian Prime Minister Paul Martin. [9]

The issue of immigration has, in fact, set the Republican Party against itself, with the more conservative elements of the party arguing for strict enforcement

During House debate, Sensenbrenner said that the Real ID bill might have prevented the Sept. 11 attacks because it requires that any license or ID card issued to visitors expire on the same date the person's visa expires.

"Mohamed Atta, ringleader of the 9/11 murderers, entered the United States on a six-month visa [which] expired on July 9, 2001. He got a [six-month] driver's license from the state of Florida on May 5, 2001," Sensenbrenner said. "Had this bill been in effect at the time, that driver's license would have expired on July 9, and he would not have been able to use that driver's license to get on a plane." [8]

Jack Martin, special projects director for the Federation for American Immigration Reform (FAIR), which seeks to halt illegal immigration, says the difficulty of distinguishing between "illegal aliens merely looking for jobs and potential terrorists looking to carry out attacks" argues against granting licenses to non-citizens. "People who have entered the country illegally — regardless of their motives — should not be able to receive a driver's license," he says.

But critics of the law say denying driver's licenses to illegal immigrants would pose a greater threat to U.S. safety. "Allowing a driver the possibility to apply for a license to drive to work means that person's photograph, address and proof of insurance will be on file at the local DMV," a recent *Los Angeles Times* editorial argued. "And that is something to make us all feel safer." [9]

The Real ID Act "threatens to handcuff state officials with impossible, untested mandates, such as requiring

Immigrants and community leaders in New York City protest on April 13, 2004, against a state policy that denies driver's licenses to hundreds of thousands of immigrants. The protest followed a crackdown on individuals without Social Security numbers.

Getty Images/Stephen Chernin

instant verification of birth certificates, without providing the time or resources needed," says the National Conference of State Legislatures. [10]

Moreover, says Joan Friedland, a policy attorney with the National Immigration Law Center, the law is just "smoke and mirrors" because it is "an inadequate and meaningless substitute for real, comprehensive reform and doesn't resolve the problem of national security."

But Martin says a national law that coordinates driver's-license policies across the nation is vital to security. "Right now, there is virtually a different approach in every state," he says. "People who wish to take advantage of the system can easily target whichever state has the most lax requirements."

— Kate Templin

[1] Quoted from "CNN Presents: Immigrant Nation: Divided Country," Oct. 17, 2004.

[2] www.aaafoundation.org/pdf/UnlicensedToKill2.pdf.

[3] T. R. Reid and Darryl Fears, "Driver's License Curtailed as Identification," *The Washington Post,* April 17, 2003, p. A3.

[4] Nina Bernstein, "Fight Over Immigrants' Driving Licenses Is Back in Court," *The New York Times,* April 7, 2005, p. B6.

[5] www.house.gov/sensenbrenner/newsletterapril2005.pdf.

[6] For background, see Kenneth Jost, "Re-examining 9/11," *CQ Researcher,* June 4, 2004, pp. 493-516.

[7] National Commission on Terrorist Attacks Upon the United States, p. 390.

[8] Frank James, "Immigrant ID Rules Debated," *Chicago Tribune,* March 12, 2005, News Section, p. 1.

[9] "Real ID, Unreal Expectations," *Los Angeles Times,* April 6, 2005.

[10] National Conference of State Legislatures, www.ncsl.org.

of the borders and expulsion of illegal aliens. The Republican-controlled House passed HR4437 in December 2005, a measure that contains procedures for securing the borders, harsher penalties for those assisting illegal entry into the country and provisions for deporting illegal aliens. The legislation does not provide for a

Illegal Migrants Leaving Traditional States

Eighty-eight percent of the nation's illegal immigrants lived in the six traditional settlement states for immigrants in 1990, but the same states had only 61 percent of the total in 2004. In other words, an estimated 3.9 million undocumented migrants lived in other states — nearly a tenfold increase.

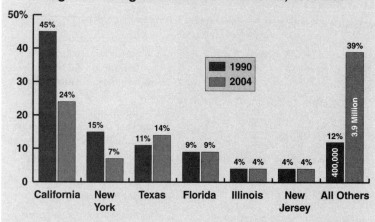

Changes in Immigrant Settlement Patterns, 1990-2004

Source: Jeffrey S. Passel, "Estimates of the Size and Characteristics of the Undocumented Population," Pew Hispanic Center, March 21, 2005, based on data from the March 2004 "Current Population Survey" by the Census Bureau and Department of Labor

guest worker program or any type of amnesty for illegal aliens.

At the same time, the Republican-controlled Senate has proposed more liberal legislation. Bipartisan backing for an immigration bill that would allow illegal immigrants already here to apply for legal residence after six years of temporary legal status nearly resulted in Senate passage in April 2006. S2612, sponsored by Republican senators Chuck Hagel of Nebraska and Mel Martinez of Florida, and cosponsored by Sen. Edward M. Kennedy (D-Mass.), fell victim to a controversial attempt by some Republican senators to insert amendments into the compromise legislation. Senate leaders, however, promised to grapple with the issue again immediately after Congress' spring recess.

Despite vociferous debate within the Republican Party, S2612 attracted the tepid support of President Bush. "Massive deportation of the people here is unrealistic," Bush said in a speech on April 24, 2006. "It's just not going to work." [10]

At the state level, controversy over illegal immigration has helped build and destroy political careers. In California, for example, Schwarzenegger's promise to repeal legislation allowing illegal immigrants to obtain driver's licenses helped him topple Democrat Gray Davis in the 2003 recall election for governor. Tensions are still running high outside the political arena.

Some activists go so far as to call immigration a product of organized crime. "The same people responsible for drug shipments from the south are also dealing in sex slaves and illegal labor and weapons," claims William Gheen, president of Americans for Legal Immigration, in Raleigh, N.C. "Our businesses should not be working with these people or encouraging these people. Some companies want more Third World labor on the territory of 'we the people' of the USA."

But Juan Hernandez, former director of the Center for U.S.-Mexico Studies at the University of Texas at Dallas, says immigration opponents are simply appealing to primitive fears. "There are many jobs that would not be performed if undocumented people were not here. Why can't we come up with ways in which individuals who want to come from Mexico to the United States can get a quick permit, come up, do a job and go back?"

Immigration control has long been a hot-button issue, but the concern in previous years was largely about jobs and wages. In post-9/11 America, many observers view illegal immigration as a national security matter.

"The borders are out of control," says T.J. Bonner, president of the National Border Patrol Council, the union representing some 10,000 border officers. He claims the patrol catches no more than a third of illegal border crossers. "We have a situation where business is controlling our immigration policy rather than sound decisions that take into account all the factors, including homeland security.

While some may dismiss Bonner's concerns as overly alarmist, others point out that stepped-up border-security spending is not stopping the growing illegal immigration.

Over the past 13 years, billions of dollars have been spent on border-control measures, including walls and fences in urban areas, electronic sensors and more personnel. From 1993 to 2004, the federal government quintupled border enforcement spending to $3.8 billion and tripled the Border Patrol to more than 11,000 officers, according to Wayne Cornelius, director of the Center for Comparative Immigration Studies at the University of California, San Diego. [11]

Customs and Border Protection Commissioner Robert Bonner (no relation to T.J. Bonner) told lawmakers in March that a reorganization that combined the Border Patrol, Immigration and Naturalization Service and the Customs Service into one agency under the Department of Homeland Security had improved deterrence. "This consolidation has significantly increased our ability to execute our anti-terrorism and traditional missions at our nation's borders more effectively than ever before," he said." [12]

Then why have illegal border crossings been increasing?

For one thing, the government has nearly stopped enforcing 1986 sanctions on employers who hire illegal immigrants. According to Mary Dougherty, an immigration statistician at the Homeland Security Department, in 2003 the agency levied only $9,300 in fines against employers. Dougherty cautioned that her data might be incomplete, but *Time* reported in 2004 that the number of fines imposed on employers dropped 99 percent during the 1990s from 1,063 in 1992 to 13 in 2002. [13]

Demetrios Papademetriou, director of the Migration Policy Institute, a Washington think tank, says that illegal immigration "maintains a standard of living for everyone in America that is, in a sense, beyond what we can really afford. When you continue to have low-wage workers streaming in, all products and services become cheaper. It has actually become a subsidy to every person in America. We have all become hooked."

For instance, at least 50 percent of the nation's farmworkers are poorly paid illegal immigrants. Americans spend less on food than the citizens of any other industrialized country, the Agriculture Department's Economic Research Service found. [14]

In the final analysis, the lack of enforcement benefits employers and hurts workers, says Ana Avendaño

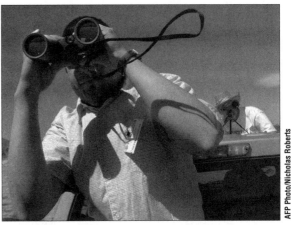

Members of the Minutemen activist group search for illegal immigrants crossing into the United States along a stretch of the Mexican border near Douglas, Ariz., on April 4, 2005. Members of the controversial group said they wanted to aid the understaffed U.S. Border Patrol.

Denier, director of the AFL-CIO Immigrant Worker Program. "Employers have a very vulnerable population to whom they can pay lower wages, and because of business control over public policy, it is OK to have this class of workers that is fully exploitable."

But problems here are unlikely to force illegal immigrants like Juan and María to return home.

"If it were just about us, yes," she says. "But for the sake of our son, no. Here he has a chance to go to college. In Mexico, no matter how hard we work we don't have the possibility of paying for him to go to college. What we want is that he not suffer the humiliations we have had to suffer."

As Congress, the states and citizens' groups debate the effects of illegal immigration, here are some of the key questions being asked:

Does illegal immigration hurt American workers?

Virtually every immigrant comes to the United States for one reason: to work.

About 96 percent of the 4.5 million illegal immigrant men now in the country are working, concludes Jeffrey Passel, a former U.S. Census Bureau demographer who is now senior research associate at the Pew Hispanic Center. All told, some 6 million immigrants — about 5 percent of the labor force — are in the country illegally.

Getty Images/Gary Williams

A group of 130 Mexicans who entered the United States illegally board a charter flight in Tucson, Ariz., to Mexico City on July 12, 2004. The flight is part of a "voluntary repatriation" program run jointly by the U.S. and Mexican governments.

Is the illegal work force large enough to hurt the job security of U.S. citizens?

Quite the contrary, argues John Gay, co-chairman of the Essential Worker Immigration Coalition, a lobbying group of 34 employers — including hotels, restaurants and building firms — that depend on immigrants. "I think back to the 1990s, a decade of economic growth," he says. "We ended with 30-year lows in unemployment and a decade of record-setting immigration, legal and illegal. That tells me immigrants didn't displace millions of Americans; they helped employ Americans."

Gay says low-paid workers help businesses thrive, allowing them to hire the native-born and legal immigrants for higher-paying jobs. In addition, immigrants are consumers themselves, so they boost the national economy.

But what helps business doesn't necessarily help Americans who share the lowest rungs of the socioeconomic ladder with illegal immigrants, according to Jared Bernstein, director of the Economic Policy Institute's Living Standards Program, which has strong ties to organized labor. "There is solid evidence that a large presence of low-wage immigrants lowers wages of domestic workers in low-wage sectors," Bernstein says. "Most economists should bristle at the notion that immigrants are filling jobs that native workers won't take. Maybe they won't take them because of low compensation and poor working conditions. In the absence of immigrants, the quality of some of those jobs probably would improve, and American workers probably would take them."

Bernstein favors controlling the flow of immigrant workers, rather than trying to bar them altogether.

But Michael McGarry, a maintenance worker in Aspen, Colo., and spokesman for the controversial Minuteman Project, says illegals hurt the economy and that they all should be kept out. The group deployed more than 100 volunteers — some of them armed — to spot and report illegal immigrants along a stretch of the Mexican border in April 2005. "People keep forgetting there is something called the law of supply and demand," says McGarry, who represented the group in April 2005 when it recruited citizens to report illegal immigrants along the Mexican border in Arizona. "If you flood the country with workers, that is going to compete down wages and benefits and conditions."

Harvard economist Borjas, whom many consider the leading expert on the economic effects of immigration, calculated that in the late 1990s immigration added a modest $10 billion to the economy — not a lot in a country with a national income in 1998 of about $8 trillion, Borjas wrote. [15]

The key, he argues, is not the overall gain but who won and who lost because of illegal immigration. [16] "Some businesses gain quite a bit and are not willing to give up the privilege — agriculture, the service industry and upper-middle-class Californians who hire nannies and gardeners. People who gain, gain an incredible amount."

Borjas calculated that immigrants' work in 1998 helped those businesses gain roughly $160 billion, including the savings from the lower wages they were paying, plus their overall economic growth. [17] The figures don't distinguish between illegal and legal immigrants, but among low-skilled entrants to the United States, illegal immigrants are in the majority.

Economist Philip Martin, an expert on U.S.-Mexico relations at the University of California, Davis, generally agrees with Borjas on the supply/demand side of the situation. "The economy would not come screeching to a halt," Martin says, without illegal immigrants. At the same time, he acknowledges, they are "important to particular industries."

A detailed 2002 study of illegal Latino immigrants in Chicago — where they made up 5 percent of the work force — supports Martin's analysis. Two-thirds of the workers held low-wage jobs, including cleaning, packaging, child care, restaurant labor, grounds keeping and maintenance. Wages were depressed by an average of 22 percent for men and 36 percent for women. (Wages of undocumented Eastern European men and women were depressed by 20 percent.) "Attaining additional levels of education, having English proficiency and accumulating additional years of U.S. residency *do not neutralize the negative wage effect of working without legal status*," the report said (emphasis in original). [18]

The AFL-CIO's Avendaño acknowledges that undocumented workers push wages down. "Mexican workers are walking into a situation where an employer, with a wink and a nod, will say, 'I'll pay you less than the minimum wage.' It is very important for the AFL-CIO to not be put in a position where we're choosing domestic workers over foreign workers. To us, the answer is a reasonable immigration system."

Stein, of the Federation for American Immigration Reform (FAIR) argues that "earned legalization" proposals that include guest worker provisions, such as the legislation currently being debated in the Senate, amount to schemes to provide employers with a ready supply of low-wage workers. Once immigrants get legal permanent residence, they can't be exploited as readily as illegal immigrants, Stein says, so the six-year legalization process keeps employers supplied with cheap labor.

"These are replacement workers for a very large swath of the American work force," he says. "I say, stop trying to shift the costs for cheap labor onto the backs of hard-working families. They try to sell us all on the idea that low-cost, illegal labor cuts consumer costs, but there are enormous, incalculable costs imposed on society at large [by illegal immigrants] — public education, emergency medical care, housing assistance, housing itself and criminal justice costs."

Are tougher immigration controls needed to protect national security?

"We have some people who are coming in to kill you and your children and your grandchildren," says Rep. Tancredo, who has made immigration control his political mission. "Anyone seeking to come into this country without getting a lot of attention drawn to him would naturally choose the borders and come in under the radar screen along with thousands and thousands and thousands of others."

Tancredo worries about men like Mohamed and Mahmud Abouhalima, who were convicted for their roles in the 1993 bombing of the World Trade Center. The two Middle Eastern terrorists illegally took advantage of one of two immigration-reform programs to acquire "green cards" (which signify legal permanent resident status) under the 1986 Special Agricultural Workers Program for farmworkers.

The brothers obtained the green cards through flaws in the Immigration and Naturalization Service (INS) inspection system, according to the National Commission on Terrorist Attacks Upon the United States (the 9/11 Commission). The agency's "inability to adjudicate applications quickly or with adequate security checks made it easier for terrorists to wrongfully enter and remain in the United States throughout the 1990s." [19]

In a sense, that failure followed logically from Justice Department policy. The report continues, "Attorney General [Janet] Reno and her deputies, along with Congress, made their highest priorities shoring up the Southwest border to prevent the migration of illegal aliens and selectively upgrading technology systems," the 9/11 commission staff concluded. [20] (The INS was then part of the Justice Department.)

Unlike immigrants trekking across the desert, the 19 9/11 terrorist attackers, including 15 Saudis and a citizen of the United Arab Emirates (UAE), flew into the United States on airliners, their passports stamped with legally obtained student or tourist visas. [21]

To be sure, one airport immigration inspector stopped a member of the 9/11 attack team from entering the United States. Mohammed al Kahtani of Saudi Arabia was turned around at Orlando International Airport because he had a one-way ticket, little money, couldn't speak much English and couldn't explain the reason he was visiting. "The inspector relied on intuitive experience . . . more than he relied on any objective fac-

CHRONOLOGY

1800s *After waves of European immigrants are welcomed, anti-immigrant resentment builds.*

1882 Chinese Exclusion Act specifically bars additional Chinese immigrants.

1920s *Public concern about the nation's changing ethnic makeup and hard economic times prompt Congress to limit immigration and set quotas intended to preserve the nation's ethnic makeup.*

1921-1929 Congress establishes a national-origins quota system, effectively excluding Asians and Southern Europeans.

1924 U.S. Border Patrol is created to stem the flow of illegal immigrants, primarily across the Mexican border.

1940s-1950s *Labor shortages and expansion of U.S. economy during World War II attract Mexican laborers. U.S. accepts war survivors, welcomes refugees from communist countries and overhauls immigration laws.*

1942 U.S. creates Bracero guest worker program, allowing immigrant Mexican farmworkers to work temporarily on American farms.

1948 Congress authorizes extra 200,000 visas for concentration camp survivors, later raised to more than 400,000.

1952 Congress passes landmark Immigration and Nationality Act, codifying existing quota system favoring immigrants from northern Europe but exempting Mexican farmworkers in Texas.

1953 U.S. exempts refugees fleeing communist countries from quota system.

1960s-1970s *Amid growing Civil Rights Movement, U.S. scraps the biased quota system and admits more Asians and Latin Americans.*

1965 Major overhaul of immigration law scraps national quotas, giving preference to relatives of immigrants.

1966 Congress orders those fleeing Fidel Castro's Cuba to be admitted automatically if they reach U.S. shores.

1980s *Tide of illegal immigrants rises dramatically, prompting policy makers to act.*

1986 Number of illegal immigrants apprehended on U.S.-Mexican border reaches a peak of 1.7 million. Congress again overhauls immigration law, legalizing undocumented workers and for the first time imposing sanctions on employers of illegal immigrants.

1990s-2000s *Immigration laws fail to deter illegal immigrants, creating backlash that prompts another overhaul of immigration laws; national-security concerns cloud immigration debate after two terrorist attacks on U.S. soil by Middle Eastern visitors.*

1993 World Trade Center is bombed by Middle Eastern terrorists, two of whom had green cards; mastermind had applied for political asylum.

1996 Number of illegal immigrants in U.S. reaches 5 million; Congress passes major immigration-reform law beefing up border security and restricting political asylum.

1997 Most of California's anti-illegal immigrant statute is declared unconstitutional.

Sept. 11, 2001 Terrorists with visas attack World Trade Center and Pentagon; anti-immigrant backlash ensues.

2004 The 9/11 Commission points to "systemic weaknesses" in border-control and immigration systems.

Jan. 20, 2005 President Bush calls for a "temporary worker" program that would not include "amnesty" for illegal immigrants.

May 2005 Sen. F. James Sensenbrenner's Real ID bill, which would block states from issuing driver's licenses to illegal immigrants, is signed into law.

April 9, 2006 Hundreds of thousands of demonstrators march in the streets of cities across the United States, calling for legal status for illegal immigrants.

April 20, 2006 Homeland Security Secretary Michael Chertoff announces a federal crackdown on employers who hire illegal aliens.

May 1, 2006 Hundreds of thousands of immigrants again took to the streets in cities across the country to call for legal status. Many of the participants left work and schools in an effort to demonstrate the economic importance of illegal immigrants.

tor that could be detected by 'scores' or a machine," the commission observed.

As a result, the commission said: "We advocate a system for screening, not categorical profiling. A screening system looks for particular, identifiable suspects or indicators of risk." [22]

Sensenbrenner says the driver's-license prohibition in his Real ID bill will complicate life for terrorists who do manage to slip in. "If you read the 9/11 report, they highlight how al Qaeda studied document fraud and other vulnerabilities in the system," said Jeff Lungren, a spokesman for the House Judiciary Committee. "They undertook the risk and effort to get valid U.S. driver's licenses and state I.D. cards . . . because they allow you to fit in." [23]

Immigrant-rights advocates argue, however, that Sensenbrenner's driver's-license provisions will complicate the lives of citizens and legal residents without damaging terrorists' capabilities.

Timothy Sparapani, legislative counsel for the American Civil Liberties Union (ACLU), says the law "is not going to do anything to deter people coming to this country." Instead, he argues, "the provisions . . . will make it much more complicated and burdensome for every American to get their first driver's licenses or renewals. They will not only have to prove they are citizens of a particular state, they will have to provide certified birth certificates; you'll have to go to a state birth certification agency. Some states don't have them."

Although terrorists have a track record for finding holes in the border-control system, border enforcement isn't actually targeting terrorists, says Jennifer Allen, director of the Border Action Network, a Tucson-based immigrant-defense organization. "A border wall is not going to deter terrorists," she argues. What stepped-up enforcement is achieving, she says, is "ongoing harassment" of people on the U.S. side of the border — particularly those whose Latin features identify them as possible foreigners.

Border Patrol union President Bonner acknowledges that most illegal immigrants are only looking for jobs. But he suggests that concentrating patrol forces on the 2,000-mile Southwest border is leaving the 3,145-mile Canadian border relatively unprotected. Some 9,000 officers are assigned to the Mexican border, he says, compared with only about 1,000 on the Canadian line. "We'll get a call from the Royal Canadian Mounted Police, and they'll say — 'Sixty Koreans landed here, and they're heading your way.' Sometimes we see them and sometimes we don't."

The Mexican and Canadian borders are indeed vulnerable, Papademetriou of the Migration Policy Institute acknowledges. But a 2003 institute report concludes that immigration policy is not an effective anti-terrorism tool. A report he co-authored concluded: "The government's major successes in apprehending terrorists have not come from post-Sept. 11 immigration initiatives but from other efforts, such as international intelligence activities, law enforcement cooperation and information provided by arrests made abroad." [24]

Should illegal immigrants in the United States be allowed to acquire legal status?

Legalization is one of the major dividing lines between illegal-immigration-control forces and employers and other immigrants'-rights advocates.

The guest worker proposal currently being considered in the Senate would allow foreigners to take jobs in the United States for a specified period, perhaps three years. Foreigners already here illegally also would be able to join the program and then apply for permanent residence after six years. Although President Bush generally supports the temporary worker portion of the proposal, he has not said whether he favors legalization.

Backers of the plan reject the term "amnesty," which implies a mass pardon for those covered by the proposal. "For security reasons, for human-rights reasons and for labor reasons, there is a vested interest in legalizing or regularizing the status of individuals," says a member of Sen. John McCain's staff. "Sen. McCain doesn't believe it's possible to round up everyone and send them home. [But] it can't be an amnesty. With high fines, background checks [for criminal violations] and through the temporary-worker program, people will be proving their reliability."

Critics of the Senate legislation argue that guest worker programs amount to amnesty, even if the term itself is not used. "The whole supposed guest worker program is really an amnesty," says McGarry, of the Minuteman Project. "This would be a disaster. An amnesty, by definition, is something the government forgives. Breaking into the country is a crime."

Supporters of legalization say that the main argument in favor of their position is that it is the only effective way to deal with the fact that undocumented immigrants are

Mexico's Call for Reform Still Unheard

To some Americans, undocumented Mexicans are job-stealing, non-English-speaking threats to American culture, economic well-being and national security.

"I'm afraid that America could become a Third World country," Atlanta-area realtor Jimmy Herchek told CNN. "We're importing poverty by millions every year." [1]

To other observers, Mexicans and other illegal workers are crucial to the economy. "There are major benefits to both employers and consumers — in other words, all of us. [T]his supply of labor makes it possible to produce your goods and services more cheaply," said Wayne Cornelius, director of the Center for Comparative Immigration Studies at the University of California at San Diego. "So there are literally hundreds of thousands of employers in this country that have a major stake in continued access to this kind of labor."

And in Mexico, the 6 million illegal *migrantes* in the United States are viewed as heroes, often braving death in desert crossings to take tough construction and service jobs in the United States to support families back home. More than 3,000 Mexicans died trying to cross the border between 1996 and 2004, but those who arrive safely and find work in the United States sent home $16 billion last year — Mexico's third-largest source of revenue. [2]

However, the immigrants' courage and dedication to their families — not to mention the benefit to the U.S. economy from their low-wage labor — haven't earned them the right to work legally in the United States. Far from it, says Mexico's ambassador to the United States, Carlos de Icaza, who supports a program to allow *migrantes* to live and work legally in the United States.

"Migrants are very vulnerable," he says in an interview at his office near the White House. "The difficult situation of these hard-working people makes them subject to abuse."

Many are mistreated once they arrive in the United States — either by anti-immigrant activists, abusive border guards or unscrupulous employers, who know illegal workers are reluctant to report salary and other abuses to author-

ities. Indeed, stories about U.S. mistreatment of migrants are daily fare in Mexico. *El Universal*, one of Mexico City's most influential newspapers, reported in April that 4,400 Mexicans were injured or mistreated by anti-immigrant civilians or Border Patrol agents in 2004. [3]

Icaza says that setting up a legal way for Mexicans to work in the United States would direct them to communities where their labor is needed and wanted, helping to dissipate the tensions that arise now when lots of Mexicans arrive suddenly in communities offering seasonal jobs.

Illegal immigrants have traditionally settled in California, Florida, New York and a few other states, but in recent years enclaves have sprung up in North Carolina, Georgia, Tennessee and other states unaccustomed to the phenomenon. [4]

Often, local residents complain the new immigrants cost taxpayers money for health care, schools and social services and bring gang-related crime. "What I saw happen in California over 30 years is happening here in just a few years," James Burke, 57, a retired ironworker from Cullman, Ala., said as he signed up volunteers to push for immigration control. [5]

Burke is part of a grass-roots movement seeking tougher immigration rules and border patrols. "Our goal is to stop illegal immigration and get rid of the illegal immigrants who are here," he said. [6]

Those goals are clearly at odds with the Mexican government's campaign to forge an immigration accord with the United States that would allow Mexicans to work here legally. Drawing on his apparent friendship with George W. Bush, Mexican President Vicente Fox began his presidency five years ago promising to strike an immigration deal with the United States.

Shortly after taking office, Fox invited his newly elected American counterpart to his ranch. The two presidents assigned top officials to start negotiating a deal. "Geography has made us neighbors," Bush said, standing next to Fox, both men in cowboy boots. "Cooperation and respect will make us partners." [7]

already here. And having illegal immigrants in the work force allows employers to pay them less than they'd be able to earn as legal residents. Such exploitation makes legalization "so crucial," says the AFL-CIO's Avendaño.

She says a December 2004 decision by the Appellate Division of the New York State Supreme Court proves that an unfair, two-tiered labor system is acquiring legal status. The court ruled an illegal immigrant who was

In fact, the pre-9/11 climate was so immigration-friendly that Mexico's foreign minister confidently bragged that Mexico wouldn't settle for anything less than a deal legalizing Mexicans already in the United States. "It's the whole enchilada or nothing," Jorge G. Castañeda said. [8]

So far, it's been *nada*. Nothing. For Fox the politician, the lack of action is especially bad news for his legacy. Mexico's constitution allows only one six-year term, and Fox's term ends in July 2006. Yet, comprehensive immigration reform in the United States seems as distant as ever.

"Fox staked his presidency on getting a bilateral [immigration] agreement with the United States," says Manuel García y Griego, a specialist on U.S-Mexico relations at the University of Texas, Arlington. On the other hand, "Mr. Bush has spent his political capital very selectively, only on things that are close to his heart — making tax cuts permanent, Iraq. I don't see immigration in that category."

But Icaza insists the United States needs an accord as urgently as Mexico. For security reasons alone, he says, the United States must know who is living in the country illegally — and a legalization program would allow illegal residents to step forward with impunity.

Moreover, Icaza says, citing almost word-for-word the Council of Economic Advisers' latest annual report to the president: "The benefits to the U.S. economy are larger than the costs associated with Social Security, health and education." [9]

But the amnesty proposal may not go very far if Bush perceives the issue as alienating his political base in the Southern and Midwestern "red states" that are now attracting many migrantes.

President Bush and Mexican President Vicente Fox discussed immigration at Bush's Texas ranch in March 2004. Bush supports a guest worker program for illegal immigrants in the U.S. but opposes legalization.

Getty Images/Rod Aydelotte

"Folks here could always go out and get a construction job for a decent wage," said Lee Bevang, in Covington, Ga. "But the contractors have totally taken advantage of illegal aliens, paying them wages no American can live on. My husband has been laid off. The concern about this is just huge." [10]

[1] Quoted on "Immigrant Nation: Divided Country," CNN Presents, Oct. 17, 2004.

[2] The desert death figure comes from Wayne Cornelius, "Controlling 'Unwanted' Immigraton: Lessons from the United States, 1993-2004," Center for Comparative Immigration Studies, University of California-San Diego, Working Paper No. 92, December, 2004, p. 14, www.ccis-ucsd.org/PUBLICA-TIONS/wrkg92.pdf. The remittances figure comes from "Las Remesas Familiares en Mexico," Banco de Mexico, noviembre, 2004,http://por-tal.sre.gob.mx/ime/pdf/Remesas_Familiares.pdf. In English, a study by the Inter-American Development Bank has slightly older statistics: "Sending Money Home: Remittance to Latin America and the Caribbean," May 2004, www.iadb.org/mif/v2/files/StudyPE2004 eng.pdf.

[3] Jorge Herrera, "Impulsa Senado protecciÛn a connacionales," p. 17, www.eluniversal.com.mx/pls/impreso/version_himprimir?p_id=12435 3&p_seccion=2.

[4] Jeffrey S. Passel, "Estimates of the Size and Characteristics of the Undocumented Population," Pew Hispanic Center, March 21, 2005, www.pewhispanic.org.

[5] David Kelly, "Illegal Immigration Fears Have Spread; Populist calls for tougher enforcement are being heard beyond the border states," *Los Angeles Times*, April 25, 2005.

[6] *Ibid.*

[7] Mike Allen and Kevin Sullivan, "Meeting in Mexico, Presidents Agree to Form Immigration Panel," *The Washington Post*, Feb. 16, p. A1.

[8] Patrick J. O'Donnell, "Amnesty by Any Name is Hot Topic," *Los Angeles Times*, July 22, 2001, p. A1.

[9] "Economic Report of the President," February 2005, p. 115, http://www.ewic.org/documents/ERP2005-Immigration.pdf.

[10] Quoted in Kelly, *op. cit.*

injured while working on a construction site was entitled to lost wages — but valued only at what he would have earned in his home country. "It is our view that plaintiff, as an admitted undocumented alien, is not entitled to recover lost earnings damages based on the wages he might have earned illegally in the United States. . . . [W]e limited plaintiff's recovery for lost earnings to the wages he would have been able to earn in his home country." [25]

Illegal Immigrants Mostly From Latin America

More than 80 percent of the more than 10 million undocumented immigrants in the United States in March 2004 were from Latin America, including 57 percent from Mexico.

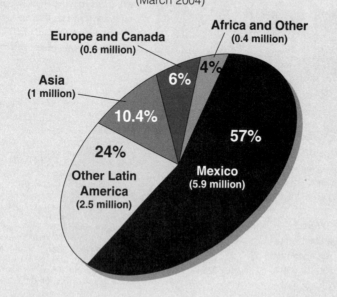

Illegal Immigrants in the U. S.
(March 2004)

Africa and Other
(0.4 million)

Europe and Canada
(0.6 million)

Asia
(1 million)

4%

6%

10.4%

57%

24%

Mexico
(5.9 million)

Other Latin
America
(2.5 million)

Note: Percentages do not add to 100 due to rounding.

Source: Jeffrey S. Passel, "Estimates of the Size and Characteristics of the Undocumented Population," Pew Hispanic Center, March 21, 2005, based on data from the March 2004 "Current Population Survey" by the Census Bureau and Department of Labor

In effect, Avendaño says, the ruling "legitimizes Third World labor conditions" in the United States.

Immigration-control advocates say the solution lies in keeping out the bulk of illegal immigrants trying to enter while cracking down on businesses that employ illegal workers. "If you enforce the law against employers," Rep. Tancredo says, "people who cannot get employment will return" to their home countries. "They will return by the millions."

That way, Tancredo says, a mass roundup would not be required.

Bernstein of the Economic Policy Institute favors a variant of the Tancredo approach that avoids its punitive aspects. Illegal immigrants "ought to have labor protection," he says. "That's not contradictory to the notion that

illegals shouldn't be here. Employers should be held accountable for labor standards for all employees. The beauty part of erasing employer advantage is that it dampens the incentive for illegal flows."

BACKGROUND

Earlier Waves

The United States was created as a nation of immigrants who left Europe for political, religious and economic reasons. After independence, the new nation maintained an open-door immigration policy for 100 years. Two great waves of immigrants — in the mid-1800s and the late 19th and early 20th centuries — drove the nation's westward expansion and built its cities and its industrial base. [26]

But while the Statue of Liberty says America accepts the world's "tired . . . poor . . . huddled masses," Americans themselves vacillate between welcoming immigrants and resenting them — even those who arrive legally. For both legal and illegal immigrants, America's actions have been inconsistent and often racist.

In the 19th century, thousands of Chinese laborers were brought here to build the railroads and then were excluded — via the Chinese Exclusion Act of 1882 — in a wave of anti-Chinese hysteria. Other Asian groups were restricted when legislation in 1917 created "barred zones" for Asian immigrants. [27]

The racist undertones of U.S. immigration policy were by no means reserved for Asians. Describing Italian and Irish immigrants as "wretched beings," *The New York Times* on May 15, 1880, editorialized: "There is a limit to our powers of assimilation, and when it is exceeded the country suffers from something very like indigestion."

Nevertheless, from 1880 to 1920, the country admitted more than 23 million immigrants — first from

Northern and then from Southern and Eastern Europe. In 1890, Census Bureau Director Francis Walker said the country was being overrun by "less desirable" newcomers from Southern and Eastern Europe, whom he called "beaten men from beaten races."

In the 1920s, public concern about the nation's changing ethnic makeup prompted Congress to establish a national-origins quota system. Laws in 1921, 1924 and 1929 capped overall immigration and limited influxes from certain areas based on the share of the U.S. population with similar ancestry, effectively excluding Asians and Southern Europeans.

But the quotas only swelled the ranks of illegal immigrants — particularly Mexicans, who only needed to wade across the Rio Grande. To stem the flow, the United States in 1924 created the U.S. Border Patrol, the enforcement arm of the INS, to guard the 6,000 miles of U.S. land bordering Canada and Mexico.

During the early 1940s the United States relaxed its immigration policies, largely for economic and political reasons. The Chinese exclusion laws were repealed in 1943, after China became a wartime ally against Japan in 1941. And in 1942 — partly to relieve wartime labor shortages and partly to legalize and control the flow of Mexican agricultural workers into the country — the United States began the Bracero (Spanish for "laborer") guest worker program, which allowed temporary workers from Mexico and the Caribbean to harvest crops in Western states.

After the war, Congress decided to codify the scores of immigration laws that had evolved over the years. The landmark Immigration and Nationality Act of 1952, retained a basic quota system that favored immigrants from Northern Europe — especially the skilled workers and relatives of U.S. citizens among them. At the same time, it exempted immigrants from the Western Hemisphere from the quota system — except for the black residents of European colonies in the Caribbean.

Mass Deportation

The 1952 law also attempted to address the newly acknowledged reality of Mexican workers who crossed the border illegally. Border Patrol agents were given more power to search for illegal immigrants and a bigger territory in which to operate.

"Before 1944, the illegal traffic on the Mexican border . . . was never overwhelming," the President's Commission on Migratory Labor noted in 1951, but in

An immigrant works on new homes being built in Homestead, Fla., on May 7, 2004. An estimated 337,000 undocumented immigrants live in Florida, according to the Department of Homeland Security.

the past seven years, "the wetback traffic has reached entirely new levels. . . . [I]t is virtually an invasion." [28]

In a desperate attempt to reverse the tide, the Border Patrol in 1954 launched "Operation Wetback," transferring nearly 500 INS officers from the Canadian perimeter and U.S. cities to join the 250 agents policing the U.S.-Mexican border and factories and farms. More than 1 million undocumented Mexican migrants were deported.

Although the action enjoyed popular support and bolstered the prestige — and budget — of the INS, it exposed an inherent contradiction in U.S. immigration policy. The 1952 law contained a gaping loophole — the Texas Proviso — a blatant concession to Texas agricultural interests that relied on cheap labor from Mexico.

"The Texas Proviso said companies or farms could knowingly hire illegal immigrants, but they couldn't harbor them," said Lawrence Fuchs, former executive director of the U.S. Select Commission on Immigration and Refugee Policy. "It was a duplicitous policy. We never really intended to prevent illegals from coming."

Immigration Reform

The foundation of today's immigration system dates back to 1965, when Congress overhauled the immigration rules. From the 1920s to the 1960s, immigration had been markedly reduced, thanks largely to the effects of the Great Depression, World War II and the quota system established in the 1920s.

From 1930 to 1950, for instance, fewer than 4 million newcomers arrived — more than a 50 percent drop from the high immigration rates of the early 20th century. The heated debates that had accompanied the earlier waves of immigration faded. "Immigration didn't even really exist as a big issue until 1965 because we just weren't letting that many people in," said Peter Brimelow, author of the 1995 bestseller *Alien Nation.*

That all changed in 1965, when Congress scrapped the national-origin quotas in favor of immigration limits for major regions of the world and gave preference to immigrants with close relatives living in the United States. The 1965 amendments to the 1952 Immigration and Nationality Act capped annual immigration at 290,000 — 170,000 from the Eastern Hemisphere and 120,000 from the Western Hemisphere. By giving priority to family reunification as a basis for admission, the amendments repaired "a deep and painful flaw in the fabric of American justice," President Lyndon B. Johnson declared at the time.

However, the law also dramatically changed the immigration landscape. Most newcomers now hailed from the developing world — about half from Latin America. While nearly 70 percent of immigrants had come from Europe or Canada in the 1950s, by the 1980s that figure had dropped to about 14 percent. Meanwhile, the percentage coming from Asia, Central America and the Caribbean jumped from about 30 percent in the 1950s to 75 percent during the '70s.

The government had terminated the Bracero program in December 1964, bowing to pressure from unions and exposés of the appalling conditions under which the braceros were living and working. But after having allowed millions of temporary Mexican laborers into the country legally for years, the government found that it was now impossible to turn off the spigot. Despite beefed-up Border Patrol efforts, the number of illegal migrants apprehended at the border jumped from fewer than 100,000 in 1965 to more than 1.2 million by 1985.

In 1978 the Select Commission on Immigration and Refugee Policy concluded that illegal immigration was the most pressing problem facing immigration authorities, a perception shared by the general public. [29] The number of border apprehensions peaked in 1986 at 1.7 million, driven in part by a deepening economic crisis in Mexico. Some felt the decade-long increase in illegal immigration was particularly unfair to the tens of thousands of legal petitioners waiting for years to obtain entry visas.

"The simple truth is that we've lost control of our own borders," declared President Ronald Reagan, "and no nation can do that and survive." [30]

In the mid-1980s, a movement emerged to fix the illegal immigration problem. Interestingly, the debate on Capitol Hill was marked by bipartisan alliances described by Sen. Alan K. Simpson, R-Wyo., as "the goofiest ideological-bedfellow activity I've ever seen." [31] Conservative anti-immigration think tanks teamed up with liberal labor unions and environmentalists favoring tighter restrictions on immigration. Pro-growth and business groups joined forces with longtime adversaries in the Hispanic and civil rights communities to oppose the legislation.

After several false starts, Congress passed the Immigration Reform and Control Act (IRCA) in October 1986 — the most sweeping revision of U.S. immigration policy in more than two decades. Using a carrot-and-stick approach, IRCA granted a general amnesty to all undocumented aliens who were in the United States before 1982 and imposed monetary sanctions — or even prison — against employers who knowingly hired undocumented workers for the first time. The law also included a commitment to beef up enforcement along the Mexican border.

IRCA allowed 3.1 million undocumented aliens to obtain legal status. Within two years, the number of would-be immigrants detained at the border each year fell from a peak of more than 1.7 million in 1986 to fewer than 900,000 in 1989.

"Once word spreads along the border that there are no jobs for illegals in the U.S., the magnet no longer exists," INS Commissioner Alan Nelson said in 1985. But that assessment was premature.

Political Asylum

Nowadays, illegal migrants come not only from neighboring countries but also from the world's far corners. Homeland Security Department officials have seized ships off the U.S. East and West coasts loaded with would-be illegal Chinese immigrants. Hundreds of others arrive on airplanes with temporary visas and simply stay past their visa-expiration dates.

As it is policing the borders, the department must also determine whether those immigrants seeking political asylum are truly escaping persecution or are merely seeking greener economic pastures. Historically, U.S. immi-

AT ISSUE

Are today's immigrants assimilating into U.S. society?

YES Tamar Jacoby
Senior Fellow, Manhattan Institute; editor,
Reinventing the Melting Pot: The New
Immigrants and What it Means to be
American *(2004)*

From "Think Tank," Public Broadcasting Service, June 24, 2004

It's always been true that Americans have loved the immigrants of a generation or two ago and been frightened by the immigrants of their era. They think the past worked perfectly, and they look around and exaggerate how difficult it is in the present.

Your average American says, "Well, I hear all this Spanish spoken." But in the second generation, if you grow up here you may not learn [Spanish] in school; you may learn it on the street, but you become proficient in English. By the third generation, about two-thirds of Hispanics speak only English. You can be in Mexican-American neighborhoods in California and hear all the adults speaking to each other in Spanish, and the little siblings speak to each other in English.

The bulk of immigrants who are coming now are people who understand cultural fluidity, understand intermarriage [and] find that a natural, easy thing. They understand the mixing of cultures and find the binary nature of our views of race and our views of out and in very alien. And that bodes well for assimilation.

One statistic tells the story. In 1960, half of American men hadn't finished high school. Today, only 10 percent of American men have not finished high school. The people who used to drop out of high school in 1960 did a kind of job that Americans don't want to do anymore. Immigrants don't tend to displace American workers. They have some effect on wages — a small, temporary effect. But it's not a zero-sum game. They help grow the economy.

The key is [for immigrants to] buy into our political values and play by the rules. It's a balance between that sense of shared values and shared political ideals — and then [doing] whatever you want to do at home.

After 9/11, Americans were very frightened. Polls showed huge numbers — two-thirds or higher — thought that the borders should be closed or that we should have much lower [immigration] numbers. Some of those surface fears are ebbing, but I think people [remain] uneasy. [Yet] there's a kind of optimism and a faith in America and in America's power to absorb people that you could tap into. If you said we have control but we are absorbing them, I think you could get people to go for higher [immigration] numbers. And when you look at the big picture — are today's immigrants assimilating? The evidence is: Yes.

NO Victor Davis Hanson
Fellow, Hoover Institution; author, Mexifornia: A
State of Becoming *(2003)*

From *World Magazine*, April 2, 2005

With perhaps as many as 20 million illegal aliens from Mexico, and the immigration laws in shreds, we are reaching a state of crisis. Criminals abound to prey on illegal aliens because they assume their victims are afraid to call the police, carry mostly cash, don't speak English, live as transients among mostly young males and are not legal participants in their communities.

If there were not a perennial supply of cheap labor, wages would rise and would draw back workers to now despised seasonal jobs; something is terribly wrong when central California counties experience 15 percent unemployment and yet insist that without thousands of illegal aliens from Oaxaca crops won't be picked and houses not built. At some point, some genius is going to make the connection that illegal immigration may actually explain high unemployment by ensuring employers cheap labor that will not organize, can be paid in cash and often requires little government deductions and expense.

Attitudes about legality need to revert back to the pre-1960s and 1970s, when immigration was synonymous with integration and assimilation. We need to dispense with the flawed idea of multiculturalism and return to the ideal of multiracialism under the aegis of a unifying Western civilization.

First-generation meritocratic Asians at places like University of California at Berkeley and the University of California at Los Angeles provide an example. What is the Asian community doing that its Mexican counterpart is not? Is it family emphasis on education, a sense of separation from the motherland, a tendency to stress achievement rather than victimization, preference for private enterprise rather than government entitlement? We need to discuss these taboo and politically incorrect paradoxes if we really wish to end something like four of 10 California Hispanic high-school students not graduating. Too many are profiteering and finding careers out of perpetuating the failure of others — others who will be the dominant population of the American Southwest in another decade.

In all public discourse and debate, when the racial chauvinist screams "racist" in lieu of logic, we all need to quit recoiling or apologizing, and instead rejoin with "Shame on you, shame, shame, shame for polluting legitimate discussion with race."

We need to return to what is known to work: measured and legal immigration, strict enforcement of our existing laws, stiff employer sanctions, an end to bilingual documents and interpreters — in other words, an end to the disastrous salad bowl and a return to the successful melting pot.

gration law has been more receptive to political refugees if they come from communist countries.

"It used to be clear," said Doris Meissner, former INS commissioner. "Mexicans were economic, Cubans and Vietnamese were political. That changed when the Haitian boat people started coming in the 1970s. Their reasons for leaving were both political and economic." [32]

Unlike Cuban refugees arriving on boats — who are automatically admitted under the 1966 "Cuban Adjustment Act" — Haitian "boat people" in the 1970s were routinely imprisoned while their applications were being processed. In 1981, the U.S. government began intercepting Haitians' boats on the high seas and towing them back to Haiti. That practice continues. As for Cubans, the Clinton administration established a "wet foot/dry foot" policy — still in effect — that sends fleeing Cubans who don't actually touch U.S. soil back to Cuba; those who make a case for "credible fear of persecution" in Cuba are sent on to third countries.

Complicating the asylum picture, in the 1980s growing numbers of Central Americans began fleeing noncommunist regimes in war-torn countries like El Salvador and Guatemala. But their chances of obtaining political asylum were slim, so many came in illegally.

Human rights advocates argued that the inconsistencies in the treatment of Central American and Haitian refugees amounted to racial and political discrimination. From 1981 through 1986, the federal government deported nearly 18,000 Salvadorans while granting permanent-resident status to 598. [33] During the same period, half of the immigrants from Poland — then under communist rule — were granted asylum.

"Cubans and Poles were accepted without significant questioning," said Ernesto Rodriguez, an immigration expert at the University of Houston, "Central Americans were grilled and usually not accepted, despite the fact that lives were endangered. [Polish President] Lech Walesa would never have survived in Guatemala."

Responding to the unequal treatment, churches and some U.S. communities — Berkeley, Los Angeles, Chicago and others — began offering sanctuary to Central American refugees. By 1985, the sanctuary movement had spread to more than 200 parishes of all denominations. In 1985 several leaders of the movement were tried for being part of an "alien-smuggling conspiracy."

Four years later, the sanctuary movement was vindicated when the U.S. government (in settling a lawsuit filed by a coalition of religious and refugee organizations) agreed to reconsider the cases of tens of thousands of Central Americans previously rejected for political asylum. A 1990 immigration law created a new "temporary protected status" shielding from immediate deportation people whose countries were torn by war or environmental disaster. The provision was written with Central Americans in mind. Eventually, so many cases clogged the system that in 1997 Congress passed the Nicaraguan Adjustment and Central American Relief Act, which allowed thousands of Central Americans to bypass the backlogged asylum system and apply directly for permanent legal residence.

But the 1990 law also made broader changes. It increased the number of foreigners allowed to enter the United States each year from 500,000 to 700,000 (dropping to 675,000 in 1995). More important, it nearly tripled the annual quota for skilled professionals from 55,000 to 144,000. To alter the 1965 law's preference for Latin American and Asian immigrants, it set new quotas for countries seen as having been unfairly treated by the earlier law, with newcomers from Europe and skilled workers receiving a greater share of entry visas.

Changes in 1996

In the 1990s nearly 10 million newcomers arrived on U.S. shores, the largest influx ever — with most still coming from Latin America and Asia.

President Bill Clinton realized early in his presidency that the so-called "amnesty" program enacted in 1986 had not solved the illegal-immigration problem. And in the Border States, concern was growing that undocumented immigrants were costing U.S. taxpayers too much in social, health and educational services. On Nov. 8, 1994, California voters approved Proposition 187, denying illegal immigrants public education or non-essential public-health services. Immigrants'-rights organizations immediately challenged the law, which a court later ruled was mostly unconstitutional. But the proposition's passage had alerted politicians to the intensity of anti-illegal immigrant sentiment. [34]

House Republicans immediately included a proposal to bar welfare benefits for legal immigrants in its "Contract with America," and in 1995, after the GOP had won control of the House, Congress took another stab at reforming the rules for both legal and illegal immigration. But business groups blocked efforts to reduce legal immigration, so the new law primarily focused on curbing illegal immigration.

The final legislation, which cleared Congress on Sept. 30, 1995, nearly doubled the size of the Border Patrol and provided 600 new INS investigators. It appropriated $12 million for new border-control devices, including motion sensors, set tougher standards for applying for political asylum and made it easier to expel foreigners with fake documents or none at all. [35] The law also severely limited — and in many cases completely eliminated — non-citizens' ability to challenge INS decisions in court. [36]

But the new law did not force authorities to crack down on businesses that employed illegal immigrants even though there was wide agreement that such a crackdown was vital. As the Commission on Immigration Reform had said in 1994, the centerpiece of any effort to stop illegal entrants should be to "turn off the jobs magnet that attracts them."

By 1999, however, the INS had stopped raiding work sites to round up illegal immigrant workers and was focusing on foreign criminals, immigrant-smugglers and document fraud. As for cracking down on employers, an agency district director told *The Washington Post*, "We're out of that business." The idea that employers could be persuaded not to hire illegal workers "is a fairy tale." [37]

Terrorism and Immigrants

The debate over immigration heated up dramatically after the 9/11 terrorist attacks. Although none of the terrorists were immigrants, all were foreigners. And some had received help in obtaining housing and driver's licenses from members of Middle Eastern immigrant communities. [38]

There were no indications that Middle Eastern immigrants in general had anything to do with the attacks or with terrorism. But in the days and weeks following the attacks, federal agents rounded up more than 1,200 Middle Easterners on suspicion of breaking immigration laws, being material witnesses to terrorism or supporting the enemy. By August 2002, most had been released or deported. [39]

Nevertheless, a senior Justice Department official said the jailings had "incapacitated and disrupted some ongoing terrorist plans." [40]

Whatever the effects on terrorism, there is no question that 9/11 and the government response to the attacks put a dent in legal immigration. In fiscal 2002-

2003 — the latest period for which statistics are available — the number of people granted legal permanent residence (green cards) fell by 34 percent; 28,000 people were granted political asylum, 59 percent fewer than were granted asylum in fiscal 2000-2001. [41]

But the growth of illegal immigration under way before 9/11 continued afterward, with 57 percent of the illegal immigrants coming from Mexico. [42]

Due to the family-reunification provision in immigration law, Mexico is also the leading country of origin for legal immigrants — with 116,000 of the 705,827 legal immigrants in fiscal 2002-2003 coming from Mexico. [43] No Middle Eastern or predominantly Muslim countries have high numbers of legal immigrants, although Pakistan was 13th among the top 15 countries of origin for legal immigrants in 1998. [44]

CURRENT SITUATION

A Party Divided

Driven by concerns over national security, and with midterm congressional elections approaching, the intensity of the debate over immigration has increased markedly over the past year, both in Congress and in the streets.

In Congress — both houses of which are controlled by Republicans — the immigration issue has divided the Republican Party, with the conservative House favoring more restrictive controls on immigration and the Senate stalled by debate over somewhat more liberal legislation that includes guest worker provisions and a path to legalization for illegal immigrants.

In December 2005, the House passed HR 4437, which would amend the Immigration and Nationality Act to strengthen enforcement of immigration laws and enhance border security, by a vote of 239-182. Significantly, the bill included no provisions for a guest worker program, for amnesty or for a path to legalization for illegal immigrants.

Several immigration bills were introduced in the Senate in 2005 and early 2006 but each failed to attract enough support to proceed. Senate Majority Leader Bill Frist, R-Tenn., for example, sponsored S2454, a bill that would have provided for additional border controls but which did not address illegal immigrants already in the United States. Sen. John McCain, R-Ariz., sponsored S1033. Backed by business groups and by Sen. Edward

M. Kennedy, D-Mass., S1033 would have allowed illegal immigrants to remain in the country and, after six years, apply for legal staus after passing a background check and paying a $1,000 fine.

The one piece of legislation that came close to passage in early 2006 was S2612, sponsored by Republican senators Chuck Hagel of Nebraska and Mel Martinez of Florida, and cosponsored by Sen. Edward M. Kennedy (D-Mass.). The bill would strengthen border security, create a temporary guest worker program and provide a path to U.S. citizenship for most of the illegal immigrants already here. Bipartisan backing for the bill disappeared just prior to Congress' spring recess, however, over the issue of numerous amendments proposed by the Republican leadership.

Upon returning from recess, Republican and Democratic Senate leaders promised, on April 26, to work together to revive the sweeping immigration bill.

Even if Senate Republicans and Democrats are able to work out their differences, however, any resulting legislation is likely to face a tough battle in the House, which has already passed its much more conservative immigration bill.

Reacting to the proposed revival of S2612 by Senate leadership, Rep. John A. Boehner, R-Ohio, the House majority leader, said that any such legislation that would put a vast majority of illegal immigrants on a path to citizenship would face strong opposition. "I don't think that would be supported by the American people," Boehner told reporters. [45]

While the battle over pending legislation heats up in Congress, the prospect of implementing the Real ID law, signed into law in 2005, is generating increasing controversy among the states. The law, which requires states to verify the citizenship of those applying for or renewing driver's licenses, is scheduled to go into effect in May 2008. But many state officials are warning that two years is not enough time and the job is far too expensive for the states to shoulder the burden alone.

Indeed, at the end April 2006, the National Governors Association and the National Conference of State Legislators issued a report saying that the states had been given neither enough time nor enough money to comply with the law and that implementation would take at least eight years.

"It's absolutely absurd," Gov. Mike Huckabee of Arkansas, chairman of the National Governors Association, told reporters. "The time frame is unrealistic; the lack of funding is inexcusable." [46]

Public opinion is also growing more divided as midterm elections approach. In mid-April 2006, demonstrations in cities across the country drew hundreds of thousands of marchers. On May 1, hundreds of thousands more people participated in what some billed as "the Great American Boycott of 2006." The idea was for immigrants, legal and illegal, to demonstrate their economic contribution to the country by staying away from their jobs on May Day.

In terms of numbers alone, the demonstrations of April and May were impressive. But they may also have spurred a backlash among some sectors of the public. "The size and magnitude of the demonstrations had some kind of backfire effect," John McLaughlin, a Republican pollster, told reporters after the first round of marches. "The Republicans that are tough on immigration are doing well right now." [47]

Rep. Steve King, an Iowa Republican, agrees. He told reporters his office had received a number of calls from angry voters. "It is one thing to see an abstract number of 12 million illegal immigrants," King told reporters. "It is another thing to see more than a million marching through the streets demanding benefits as if it were a birthright. I think people resent that." [48]

Perhaps coincidentally, in mid-April the federal government also announced a crackdown against those who hire illegal immigrants. Announcing the arrest of more than 1,100 illegal immigrant employees at a pallet supply company in Houston on April 20, Homeland Security Secretary Michael Chertoff pledged to take stronger action against companies that do such illegal hiring.

"We target those organizations, we use intelligence to define the scope of the organization, and then we use all of the tools we have — whether it's criminal enforcement or the immigration laws — to make sure we come down as hard as possible and break the back of those organizations," Mr. Chertoff said at a news conference. [49]

State Debate

The hard-line approach is no less evident at the state level. In April 2005, for example, the Arkansas State Senate rejected legislation that would have made illegal immigrants eligible for in-state tuition. The state attorney general had ruled that the bill might have violated the 1996 immigration law. Similar bills are pending in North Carolina, Massachusetts, Oregon and Nebraska.

Arizona voters in 2004 approved Proposition 200, which requires proof of citizenship before voting. The new law also requires the state and local governments to check the immigration status of anyone applying for unspecified "public benefits" and to report any illegal immigrants who apply. [50]

Proponents said the law's "benefits" provision was designed to plug a loophole that enabled illegal immigrants to obtain welfare because of holes in the system. "Such benefits are an incentive for illegal aliens to settle in Arizona and hide from federal authorities," state Rep. Russell Pearce, R-Mesa, said. [51]

But the law didn't actually prohibit anything that wasn't already forbidden, opponents said. Ray Ybarra, who was observing the Minuteman Project for the American Civil Liberties Union, told a reporter that it simply restated existing prohibitions on illegal immigrants voting or getting welfare. He called the new law an outgrowth of "fear and misunderstanding." [52]

The law has led immigration-control forces to propose legislation that would bar illegal immigrants from state colleges, adult-education classes and utility and child-care assistance. The proposed legislation, which was under consideration in early May 2005, set off a new round of debate. Arizonans shouldn't have to subsidize services for people in the country illegally, argued state Rep. Tom Boone, R-Glendale, the bill's sponsor. Opponents countered that Hispanic citizens would have to suffer extra scrutiny simply because of their appearance. [53]

A Democratic opponent tried to add sanctions against employers who hire illegal immigrants. Republicans voted that down on the first attempt.

Perhaps because Arizona is on the border and its Proposition 200 passed by referendum, the legislation received more national attention than a similar measure enacted in Virginia this year.

As in Arizona, the Virginia law requires anyone applying for non-emergency public benefits — such as Medicaid and welfare — to be a legal U.S. resident. Democratic Gov. Mark Warner downplayed the measure's effects, even as he signed it into law, saying it restated federal prohibitions against illegal immigrants receiving some public benefits. [54]

Arizona's law is a model for immigration-control forces in other states. In Colorado, organizations that want to cut back illegal immigrants' access to state services are planning to follow the Arizona pattern by bringing the proposal before voters in a referendum, since the state legislature didn't act on the idea. But among voters at large, organizers of the referendum drive predict they'll have no trouble getting more than the 70,000 signatures needed to put the proposal on the 2006 election ballot. [55]

The legislation is "playing to the worst fears and instincts of people," said Democratic state Rep. Terrence Carroll, an opponent. "It has a very good chance of passing." [56]

In North Carolina, meanwhile, five proposals are designed to crack down on illegal immigration by denying driver's licenses to undocumented immigrants and forcing employers who hire them to cover some of their medical expenses. Immigration is a recent phenomenon in the state, and a big one. An estimated 300,000 illegal immigrants have settled in North Carolina — a 43 percent increase from 2000 to 2004 — driven by demand from farmers, the service industry and construction companies. [57]

And most recently, on April 17 of this year, Georgia enacted a tough new immigration law that requires those seeking many state benefits to prove they are in the United States legally. The law also provides sanctions for employers who knowingly hire illegal immigrants.

Assimilation Debate

In small communities experiencing unprecedented waves of new immigrants, many residents feel that the overwhelming numbers of Latinos showing up in their towns are changing American culture. They say that Mexican immigrants — perhaps because they need only walk across the border to return home — stick to themselves and refuse to learn English or to assimilate as readily as previous waves of immigrants.

"They didn't want to socialize with anybody," said D.A. King, describing the Mexicans who moved into a house across the street from his Marietta, Ga., home. "They filled their house full of people. At one time, there were 18 people living in this home." [58]

Harvard historian Samuel Huntington, in his controversial new book *Who Are We: The Challenges to America's National Identity*, worries that the sheer number of Latino immigrants has created a minority with little incentive to assimilate, potentially creating an America with a split identity.

"Continuation of this large immigration [without improved assimilation] could divide the United States into a country of two languages and two cultures," writes Huntington, who heads the Harvard Academy for

International and Area Studies. "Demographically, socially and culturally, the *reconquista* (reconquest) of the Southwestern United States by Mexican immigrants is well under way. Hispanic leaders are actively seeking to transform the United States into a bilingual society." [59]

But many reject Huntington's argument. "The same thing was said about African-Americans . . . about the Irish," a Georgia restaurant owner, who asked not to be identified, told CNN. "It's the same old song and over time it's proved to be a bunch of bologna. I believe these people are just like any other newcomers to this country. They can immigrate in and they're doing a great job here. And why should they be any different?" [60]

Those like Huntington and King say they are not against legal immigrants but oppose unchecked illegal immigration. King, in particular, is so furious with the government's refusal to enforce immigration laws against what he sees as the "invasion and the colonization of my country and my state and my city" that he founded the Marietta, Ga.-based American Resistance Foundation, which pushes for stricter enforcement of immigration laws.

Whenever he calls the INS to report seeing dozens of undocumented workers milling on local street corners waiting for employers seeking day laborers, he says, "I have never gotten through to a person, and I've never gotten a return phone call." [61]

"To whom does an American citizen turn when his government will not protect him from the Third World?" King asks. "What do we do now?"

Asa Hutchinson, former undersecretary of the Department of Homeland Security, which oversees the INS, had a mixed message in addressing King's frustration.

"I would certainly agree with him that we have to enforce our law, and it's an important part of my responsibilities," Hutchinson told CNN last October. "But whenever you look at the family that is being very productive and has a great family life contributing to American society, but in fact they came here illegally, I don't think you could excuse the illegal behavior. But you also recognize they're not terrorists. They're contributing to our society. We understand the humanitarian reasons that brought them here." [62]

Hutchinson said the dilemma for U.S. officials is particularly difficult when those illegal immigrants have had children born here, who are now U.S. citizens. "Do you jerk the parents up and send them back to their home country and leave the two children here that are U.S. citizens?

"Those are the problems that we're dealing with every day. Yes, we certainly want to enforce the law, but we have to recognize we also are a compassionate country that deals with a real human side as well."

Asylum

Political asylum accounts for few immigrants but plays an outsized role in the immigration debate. Most legal immigrants settle in the United States because the government decides to allow them in, and illegal immigrants come because they can. But asylum-seekers are granted refuge because the law requires it — not just federal law but international humanitarian law as well. The Convention Relating to the Status of Refugees of 1951, which was updated in 1967, says that no one fleeing political, racial or religious persecution can be returned involuntarily to a country where he or she is in danger. [63]

However, the United States and all other countries that grant asylum can determine who qualifies for that protection and who doesn't. "Irresponsible judges have made asylum laws vulnerable to fraud and abuse," Rep. Sensenbrenner said in promoting his Real ID bill, which would limit the right to asylum by raising the standard for granting asylum and allowing judges to take an applicant's demeanor into account.

"We will ensure that terrorists like Ramzi Yousef, the mastermind of the first World Trade Center attack in 1993, no longer receive a free pass to move around America's communities when they show up at our gates claiming asylum," Sensenbrenner said. [64]

Civil liberties advocates say terrorists today could not breeze through an immigration inspection by demanding asylum because the 1996 immigration overhaul tightened after Yousef and others abused it. Above all, the 1996 immigration act authorized immigration inspectors to refuse entry to foreigners without passports or with illegally obtained travel documents. [65]

In addition, says Erin Corcoran, a Washington-based lawyer in the asylum-rights program of Human Rights First (formerly, the Lawyers Committee for Human Rights), asylum seekers now get their fingerprints and photos checked at each stage in the process. "Real ID just heightens the burden of proof that a genuine applicant must meet," Corcoran says, arguing that terrorists are more than capable of adjusting to the new security environment. "A terrorist would have everything in order."

The 1996 law tightened up the process in other ways as well. If a foreigner asks for asylum when trying to enter the United States, he must get a so-called "credible fear interview." If an asylum officer concludes that a "significant possibility" exists for the foreigner to win asylum, a judge might rule that the foreigner shouldn't be deported. If the asylum officer decides that foreigners haven't met the "credible fear" standard, they are held and then deported. But those who do meet the standard may be released while they await hearings on their asylum claims. [66]

And even getting to the first step of the asylum process is difficult. In fiscal 1999 through 2003, asylum was requested by 812,324 foreigners, but only 35,566 were granted credible fear interviews. [67] Of the 36,799 asylum applicants whose cases were decided during the same period, 5,891 were granted asylum or allowed to remain in the United States under the international Convention Against Torture; 19,722 applicants were ordered deported, and 1,950 withdrew their applications. Another 2,528 were allowed to become legal permanent residents. [68]

OUTLOOK

Focus on Mexico

Immigration predictions have a way of turning out wrong. The 1986 Immigration Reform and Control Act didn't control illegal immigration. The 1994 North American Free Trade Agreement didn't create enough jobs in Mexico to keep Mexicans from migrating. The 1996 Immigration Enforcement Improvement Act didn't lessen the flow of illegal immigrants. Cracking down on illegal crossings in big cities like San Diego and El Paso only funneled migrants into the deadly desert of northern Mexico. And announced measures to step up border enforcement didn't stop illegals from coming in — both before or after 9/11 — although legal immigration did drop.

Faced with such a track record, many immigration experts say legislation and law enforcement may not be the best ways to change immigration patterns, especially where illegal immigration is concerned.

"The absence of consensus on alternatives locks in the current policy mix, under which unauthorized immigrants bear most of the costs and risks of 'control' while benefits flow impressively to employers and consumers,"

Cornelius of the University of California has concluded. "Promised future experiments with guest worker programs, highly secure ID cards for verifying employment eligibility and new technologies for electronic border control are unlikely to change this basic dynamic. [69]

"The back door to undocumented immigration to the United States is essentially wide open," he said. "And it is likely to remain wide open unless something systematic and serious is done to reduce the demand for the labor." [70]

Steven Camarota, research director of the Washington-based Center for Immigration Studies, which advocates tougher immigration controls, agrees. "There is a fundamental political stalemate," he says. "You have a divide in the country between public opinion and elite opinion. Elite opinion is strong enough to make sure that the law doesn't get enforced but is not strong enough to repeal the law. Public opinion is strong enough to ensure that the law doesn't get repealed but not strong enough to get the law enforced. For most politicians a continuation of the status quo doesn't have a huge political downside."

Nevertheless, Stein of FAIR argues that Beltway insiders are only slowly catching on to what's happening in the country at large. "The issue is building very rapidly in terms of public frustration," he says. "You talk to [congressional] representatives, they'll tell you that you go to a town meeting and talk about the budget or one of the issues that the party wants to talk about, and the discussion will last five minutes. Mention immigration and two hours later you're still on it. It's on fire out there."

Developments in Mexico may be as important to the future of U.S. immigration policy as anything that Washington politicians do, says Martin, at the University of California. If the populist mayor of Mexico City, Manuel López Obrador, wins the presidency of Mexico in 2006, he says, the mutual distrust between the international business community and left-leaning politicians who favor government intervention in the economy could play a key role in immigration to the United States: "That will slow down foreign investment," making it likely that illegal immigration would continue at a high level, he says.

Martin doubts there is much potential for political violence and destabilization in Mexico. Nevertheless, hundreds of thousands of people turned out in Mexico City in April to protest a move to prosecute López Obrador for a minor legal violation, raising the specter of serious political conflict. [71] If that happens, immigration could be seen as a political — as well an economic — safety valve.

"That may be the best rationale for letting illegal immigration be what it is," says Borjas of Harvard, who otherwise opposes that trend. "I could see the point to that."

With little likelihood of substantial change to the immigration picture, virtually all observers agree that there is one potential exception: a major terrorist act committed in the United States by an illegal border-crosser. In that event, Borjas says, "Who knows what the outcome would be?"

NOTES

1. Quoted in "CNN Presents: Immigrant Nation: Divided Country," Oct. 17, 2004.

2. Jeffrey S. Passel, "Estimates of the Size and Characteristics of the Undocumented Population," March 21, 2005, Pew Hispanic Center, www.pewhispanic.org.

3. Census Bureau, Statistical Abstract of the United States, 2004-2005, p. 8; www.census.gov/prod/2004pubs/04statab/pop.pdf; Office of Policy and Planning, U.S. Immigration and Naturalization Service, "Estimates of the Unauthorized Immigration Population Residing in The United States: 1990 to 2000," http://uscis.gov/graphics/shared/statistics/publications/Ill_Report_1211.pdf; Steven A. Camarota, "Economy Slowed, But Immigration Didn't: The Foreign-Born Population 2000-2004," Center for Immigration Studies, November 2004,www.cis.org/articles/2004/back1204.pdf.

4. Quoted in David Kelly, "Illegal Immigration Fears Have Spread; Populist calls for tougher enforcement are being heard beyond the border states," *Los Angeles Times*, April 25, 2005.

5. *Ibid.*

6. *Ibid.*

7. Seth Hettena, "Congressmen call on Senate to pass bill to fortify border fence," The Associated Press, March 29, 2005.

8. PR Newswire, "Senator John McCain Surprises U.S. Constitutional Development Class at Annapolis . . . ," April 21, 2005.

9. "President Meets with President Fox and Prime Minister Martin," White House, March 23, 2005, www.whitehouse.gov/news/releases/2005/03/print/20050323-5.html.

10. Elisabeth Bumiller, "In Immigration Remarks, Bush Hints He Favors Senate Plan," *The New York Times*, April 25, 2006, p. 22.

11. Wayne Cornelius, "Controlling 'Unwanted' Immigration: Lessons from the United States, 1993-2004," Center for Comparative Immigration Studies, University of California, San Diego, December 2004, p. 5, www.ccis-ucsd.org/PUBLICATIONS/wrkg92.pdf.

12. Statement, March 15, 2005; www.cbp.gov/xp/cgov/newsroom/commissioner/speeches_statements/mar17_05.xml.

13. Donald L. Bartlett and James B. Steele, "Who Left the Door Open," *Time*, Sept. 20, 2004, p. 51.

14. Birgit Meade, unpublished analysis, Economic Research Service, U.S. Dept. of Agriculture.

15. George J. Borjas, *Heaven's Door: Immigration Policy and the American Economy* (1999), pp. 87-104.

16. *Ibid*, pp. 103-104.

17. *Ibid*, pp. 90-91.

18. Chirag Mehta *et al.*, "Chicago's Undocumented Immigrants: An Analysis of Wages, Working Conditions, and Economic Contributions," February 2002, www.uic.edu/cuppa/uicued/npublications/recent/undocimmigrants.htm.

19. "Immigration and Border Security Evolve, 1993 to 2001," Chapter 4 in "Staff Monograph on 9/11 and Terrorist Travel," National Commission on Terrorist Attacks Upon the United States, 2004, www.9-11commission.gov/staff_statements/911_TerrTrav_Ch4.pdf.

20. *Ibid.*

21. *Ibid.*

22. *The 9/11 Commission Report* (2004), pp. 248, 387.

23. T. R. Reid and Darryl Fears, "Driver's License Curtailed as Identification," *The Washington Post*, April 17, 2005, p. A3.

24. Muzaffar A. Chishti *et al.*, "America's Challenge: Domestic Security, Civil Liberties, and National

Unity After September 11," Migration Policy Institute, 2003, p. 7.

25. Gorgonio Balbuena, *et al. v. IDR Realty LLC, et al*; 2004 N.Y. App. Div.

26. Unless otherwise noted, material in the background section comes from Rodman D. Griffin, "Illegal Immigration," *CQ Researcher*, April 24, 1992, pp. 361-384; Kenneth Jost, "Cracking Down on Immigration," *CQ Researcher*, Feb. 3, 1995, pp. 97-120; and David Masci, "Debate Over Immigration," *CQ Researcher*, July 14, 2000, pp. 569-592.

27. For background, see Richard L. Worsnop, "Asian Americans," *CQ Researcher*, Dec. 13, 1991, pp. 945-968.

28. Quoted in Ellis Cose, *A Nation of Strangers: Prejudice, Politics and the Populating of America* (1992), p. 191.

29. Cited in Michael Fix, ed., *The Paper Curtain: Employer Sanctions' Implementation, Impact, and Reform* (1991), p. 2.

30. Quoted in Tom Morganthau *et al.*, "Closing the Door," *Newsweek*, June 25, 1984.

31. Quoted in Dick Kirschten, "Come In! Keep Out!," *National Journal*, May 19, 1990, p. 1206.

32. For background, see Peter Katel, "Haiti's Dilemma," *CQ Researcher*, Feb. 18, 2005, pp. 149-172.

33. Cose, *op. cit.*, p. 192.

34. Ann Chih Lin, ed. *Immigration*, CQ Press (2002), pp. 60-61.

35. William Branigin, "Congress Finishes Major Legislation; Immigration; Focus is Borders, Not Benefits," *The Washington Post*, Oct. 1, 1996, p. A1.

36. David Johnston, "Government is Quickly Using Power of New Immigration Law," *The New York Times*, Oct. 22, 1996, p. A20.

37. William Branigin, "INS Shifts 'Interior' Strategy to Target Criminal Aliens," *The Washington Post*, March 15, 1999, p. A3.

38. *The 9/11 Commission*, *op. cit.*, pp. 215-223.

39. Adam Liptak, Neil A. Lewis and Benjamin Weiser, "After Sept. 11, a Legal Battle On the Limits of Civil Liberty," *The New York Times*, Aug. 4, 2002, p. A1. For background, see Patrick Marshall, "Policing the Borders," *CQ Researcher*, Feb. 22, 2002, pp. 145-168.

40. *Ibid.*

41. Deborah Meyers and Jennifer Yau, US Immigration Statistics in 2003, Migration Policy Institute, Nov. 1, 2004, www.migrationinformation.org/USfocus/display.cfm?id=263; and Homeland Security Department, "2003 Yearbook of Immigration Statistics," http://uscis.gov/graphics/shared/statistics/yearbook/index.htm.

42. Passel, *op. cit.*, p. 8.

43. Meyers and Yau, *op. cit.*

44. Lin, *op. cit.*, p. 20.

45. Jim Rutenberg and Rachel L. Swarns, "Senate Leaders Work to Resuscitate Immigration Bill," *The New York Times*, April 26, 2006, p. 16.

46. Pam Belluck, "Mandate for ID Meets Resistance From States," *The New York Times*, May 6, 2006.

47. David D. Kirkpatrick, "Demonstrations on Immigration are Hardening a Divide," *The New York Times*, April 17, 2006, p. 16.

48. *Ibid.*

49. Eric Lipton, "U.S. Crackdwon Set Over Hiring of Immigrants," *The New York Times*, April 21, 2006, p. 1.

50. "Proposition 200," Arizona Secretary of State, http://www.azsos.gov/election/2004/info/PubPamphlet/english/prop200.htm.

51. *Ibid.*

52. Jacques Billeaud, "Congressman: Prop 200's passage was key moment in effort to limit immigration," The Associated Press, April 2, 2005.

53. Jacques Billeaud, "Arizona lawmakers try to add restrictions for illegal immigrants," The Associated Press, March 24, 2005.

54. Chris L. Jenkins, "Warner Signs Limits on Immigrant Benefits," *The Washington Post*, March 30, 2005, p. B5.

55. David Kelly, "Colorado Activists Push Immigration Initiative," *Los Angeles Times*, March 13, 2005, p. A23.

56. *Ibid.*

57. Michael Easterbrook, "Anger rises toward illegal immigrants," *Raleigh* [N.C.] *News & Observer*, April 17, 2005, p. A1.

58. CNN, *op. cit.*

59. Samuel Huntington, "The Hispanic Challenge," *Foreign Policy*, March/April 2004.

60. CNN, *op. cit.*

61. King's quotes are from *ibid.*

62. Hutchinson's quotes are from *ibid.*

63. "The Wall Behind Which Refugees Can Shelter," U.N. High Commissioner for Refugees, 2001; www.unhcr.org.

64. Dan Robinson, "Congress — Immigration," Voice of America, Dec. 8, 2004, www.globalsecurity.org/security/library/news/2004/12/sec-041208-3c7be91f.htm.

65. "Asylum Seekers in Expedited Removal," United States Commission on International Religious Freedom, Executive Summary, pp. 1-2, Feb. 8, 2005, www.uscirf.gov/countries/global/asylum_refugees/2005/february/index.html.

66. *Ibid.*

67. *Ibid*, p. 295.

68. *Ibid.*

69. Cornelius, *op. cit.*, p. 24.

70. CNN, *op. cit.*

71. Ginger Thompson and James C. McKinley Jr., "Opposition Chief at Risk in Mexico," *The New York Times*, April 8, 2005, p. A1.

BIBLIOGRAPHY

Books

Borjas, George J., *Heaven's Door: Immigration Policy and the American Economy*, **Princeton University Press, 2000.**
A Harvard economist who is a leading figure in the debate over immigration and the economy argues for encouraging immigration by the highly skilled while discouraging the entry of low-skilled workers.

Dow, Mark, *American Gulag: Inside U.S. Immigration Prisons*, **University of California Press, 2004.**
A freelance journalist penetrates the secretive world of immigrant detention and finds widespread abuse of prisoners who are granted few, if any, legal rights.

Huntington, Samuel P., *Who Are We?: The Challenges to America's National Identity*, **Simon & Schuster, 2004.**
A Harvard professor argues that mass immigration, especially from Latin America, is flooding the United States with people who are not assimilating into mainstream society.

Jacoby, Tamar, ed., *Reinventing the Melting Pot: The New Immigrants and What It Means To Be An American*, **Basic Books, 2004.**
Authors representing strongly differing views and experiences on immigration contribute essays on how the present wave of immigrants is changing — and being changed by — the United States. Edited by a pro-immigration scholar at the moderately libertarian Manhattan Institute.

Lin, Ann Chih, ed., and Nicole W. Green, *Immigration*, **CQ Press, Vital Issues Series, 2002.**
This useful collection of information on recent immigration policy and law changes also includes steps that other countries have taken to deal with issues similar to those under debate in the United States.

Articles

Cooper, Marc, "Last Exit to Tombstone," *L.A. Weekly*, **March 25, 2005, p. 24.**
A reporter visits the Mexican desert border towns where immigrants prepare to cross illegally into the United States and finds them undaunted by the dangers ahead.

Jordan, Miriam, "As Border Tightens, Growers See Threat to 'Winter Salad Bowl,'" *The Wall Street Journal*, **March 11, 2005, p. A1.**
Lettuce farmers plead with immigration officials not to crack down on illegal immigration at the height of the harvest season in Arizona.

Kammer, Jerry, "Immigration plan's assumption on unskilled workers contested," *San Diego Union-Tribune*, **March 31, 2005, p. A1.**
Even immigrants who once lacked legal status themselves are worried about the continued influx of illegal immigrants, because they drive down wages.

Porter, Eduardo, "Illegal Immigrants are Bolstering Social Security With Billions," *The New York Times,* **April 5, 2005, p. A1.**
Government figures indicate that illegal immigrants are subsidizing Social Security by about $7 billion a year by paying taxes from which they will never benefit.

Seper, Jerry, "Rounding Up All Illegals 'Not Realistic,'" *Washington Times,* **Sept. 10, 2004, p. A1.**
The undersecretary of homeland security acknowledges that law enforcement officials are not hunting for all illegal immigrants, something he said would be neither possible nor desirable.

Reports and Studies

Lee, Joy, Jack Martin and Stan Fogel, "Immigrant Stock's Share of U.S. Population Growth, 1970-2004," Federation for American Immigration Reform, 2005.
The authors conclude that more than half of the country's population growth since 1970 stems from increased immigration, raising the danger of overpopulation and related ills.

Orozco, Manuel, "The Remittance Marketplace: Prices, Policy and Financial Institutions," Pew Hispanic Center, June 2004.
A leading scholar of remittances — money sent back home by immigrants — analyzes the growth of the trend and the regulatory environment in which it operates.

"Refugees, Asylum Seekers and the Department of Homeland Security: One Year Anniversary — No Time for Celebration," *Human Rights First,* **April 2004.**
Some rights of asylum-seekers are being eroded as the number of people granted asylum drops, the advocacy organization concludes, urging changes in procedures.

Stana, Richard M., "Immigration Enforcement: Challenges to Implementing the INS Interior Enforcement Strategy," General Accounting Office (now Government Accountability Office), testimony before House Judiciary Subcommittee on Immigration, June 19, 2002.
A top GAO official finds a multitude of reasons why immigration officials have not been able to deport criminal illegal immigrants, break up people-smuggling rings and crack down on employers of illegal immigrants.

For More Information

Center for Comparative Immigration Studies, University of California-San Diego, La Jolla, CA 92093-0548; (858) 822-4447; www.ccis-ucsd.org. Analyzes U.S. immigration trends and compares them with patterns in Europe and Asia.

Center for Immigration Studies, 1522 K St., N.W., Suite 820, Washington, DC 20005-1202, (202) 466-8185; www.cis.org. A think tank that advocates reduced immigration.

Federation for American Immigration Reform, 1666 Connecticut Ave., N.W., Suite 400, Washington, DC 20009; (202) 328-7004; http://fairus.org. A leading advocate for cracking down on illegal immigration and reducing legal immigration.

Migration Dialogue, University of California, Davis, 1 Shields Ave., Davis, CA 95616; (530) 752-1011; http://migration.ucdavis.edu/index.php. An academic research center that focuses on immigration from rural Mexico and publishes two quarterly Web bulletins.

Migration Policy Institute, 1400 16th St., N.W., Suite 300, Washington, DC 20036; (202) 266-1940; www.migrationpolicy.org. Analyzes global immigration trends and advocates fairer, more humane conditions for immigrants.

National Immigration Law Center, 3435 Wilshire Blvd., Suite 2850, Los Angeles, CA 90010; (213) 639-3900; http://nilc.org. Advocacy organization aimed at defending the legal rights of low-income immigrants.

10

Latinos' Future

David Masci and Alan Greenblatt

A 5-year-old Hispanic girl in Santa Ana, Calif., protests on Aug. 23, 2002, after illegal immigrants working as janitors and baggage handlers were arrested at Southern California airports during a nationwide crackdown on airport security; most were using fake Social Security numbers. Immigrants'-rights groups and union officials are demanding changes in immigration laws to allow more illegal workers to gain necessary working papers.

From *CQ Researcher,*
October 17, 2003 (updated May 15, 2006).

A day after an April 2006 rally drew 180,000 people to Washington, D.C., to protest a U.S. House bill that would cast illegal immigrants as felons, a woman sat on a bench in the city's Metro subway system chatting about the event on her cell phone. She recapped in Spanish, but switched to English to quote its key slogan: "Today we march, tomorrow we vote." Many commentators took the marchers at their word, believing that the congressional debate over immigration had finally roused Hispanics to become more engaged in the political process. Organizers talk of producing 1 million new citizens and voters in time for the November 2006 elections. "I think this campaign can have 10 times the momentum that we had in 1994, post-Proposition 187," said Mike Garcia, president of Service Employees International Union Local 1877 in Los Angeles. [1] But expressing such optimistic hopes is easier than fulfilling them.

Proposition 187 was a California ballot initiative that denied most government services — including access to public education — to illegal immigrants. Most of its provisions were later voided by courts, but it continued to have an important political impact nonetheless. Immigrants who had long been content to maintain citizenship in their homelands suddenly saw the value of naturalization and the ability to vote to protect their own interests. The number of legal residents who became U.S. citizens more than doubled, from 434,000 in 1994 to 1 million in 1996, according to the National Association of Latino Elected and Appointed Officials. The Hispanic share of those being naturalized jumped from 27 percent to 43 percent during the same period.

States Reflect Influx of Latinos

Almost 43 million Latinos live in the United States, with two-thirds clustered in the Southwest. While Hispanics already comprise key political constituencies in many states — including California, Texas, New York and Florida — some experts predict they will soon wield significant influence in national elections.

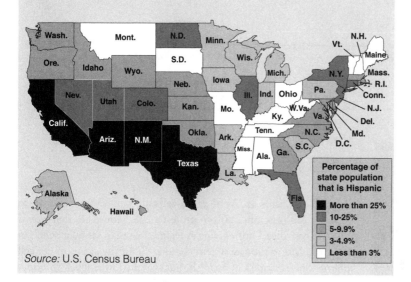

Percentage of state population that is Hispanic

■ More than 25%
▓ 10-25%
▒ 5-9.9%
□ 3-4.9%
□ Less than 3%

Source: U.S. Census Bureau

In Los Angeles County alone, 100,000 residents with Hispanic surnames registered to vote for the first time between 1994 and 1998, according to the Tomas Rivera Policy Institute at the University of Southern California. Nearly 90 percent of them registered as Democrats, largely because Pete Wilson, California's Republican governor at the time, had pushed hard for Proposition 187's passage. After Antonio Villaraigosa was elected mayor of Los Angeles in 2005 — the first Hispanic to win the office in 133 years — he was rewarded with a *Newsweek* cover story entitled, "A Latino Power Surge." [2]

But despite helping to convert California into a solidly "blue" Democratic state, Latinos have been an important swing vote constituency, not strongly favoring one party over the other. Most tend to favor Democrats, but President Bush won an estimated 40 percent of the Latino vote in 2004, increasing his share from his first run. Other demographic trends clearly indicate that Hispanics, long considered the "sleeping giant" of American politics because of their tendency to vote in much lower numbers than African-Americans or whites,

are set to become a potent political force. More than 500,000 Hispanics will turn 18 — and be eligible to vote — every year for the next 20 years, according to Miami-based pollster Sergio Bendixen.

What's more, the Hispanic share of the U.S. population is growing rapidly, and not solely because of immigrants from Mexico and other Latin American countries. Census data indicates that 70 percent of children born in the U.S. in 2005 were Hispanics. Overall, Latinos accounted for 49 percent of the nation's population growth that year. [3] Little wonder that many Republicans have warned for years that their party ignores Hispanic concerns at its own peril. "It's so important to have . . . leaders that stand up and say we will not use our children, the children of immigrants, as a political issue in America," Bush said during a stop in California during his first presidential campaign. [4]

Nonetheless, the loud immigration debate during his second term threatened to tear apart the fabric of the Republican Party coalition. Many party members worried that a bill passed by the House late in 2005, which termed illegal aliens as felons, would come to haunt the party much in the way that Proposition 187 did in California. Passage of the bill kicked off the largest series of demonstrations that the nation had seen for decades, with rallies as large as 500,000 each in Los Angeles and Dallas and dozens more attracting people in the tens of thousands in cities such as New York, Houston and Madison, Wis., throughout the spring and summer of 2006.

On the one hand, GOP supporters in the business community — the party's main source of campaign contributions — favored liberal immigration policies that allowed a steady flow of cheap labor to continue coming into the country, without imposing onerous new regulatory burdens on employers. On the other hand, social conservatives — some of whom seemed to harbor more than a touch of xenophobia — were angry about the constant flood of illegal immigrants into more and more communities.

Both Bush and the U.S. Senate (which, like the House, is controlled by Republicans) favored a lenient approach toward immigration — a stance that left the GOP facing a dilemma. The president's approval ratings had taken a dive early in his second term, due to problems in Iraq and the delayed governmental response to Hurricane Katrina in 2005. But they continued to trend downward, reaching the low 30s during the height of the pro-immigrant demonstration season. Polls indicated that many of Bush's core conservative supporters had turned on him, in part because of his refusal to tighten immigration laws. [5] "Immigration is the only area in which more Republicans disapprove of the president's policy than approve, and they disapprove by a significant margin," wrote Byron York, White House correspondent of the conservative *National Review*. [6]

The political fallout from the immigration debate seeped deep into the political firmament, touching races even at the local level. In Herndon, Va., local officials had favored the creation of a center for day laborers, saying the city needed to offer the facility to replace the impromptu gathering spot that had taken root in a 7-11 parking lot. The debate over the merit of spending taxpayer dollars to provide such services to illegal immigrants drew national attention. So did the defeat in May 2006 of Mayor Michael O'Reilly and two town council members who had supported the center. "Politicians across the country should take note of the results of this election," said Chris Simcox, president of the Minuteman Civil Defense Corps. [7]

What's more, even many immigrants frown upon illegal immigrants. A survey conducted by the Pew Hispanic Center in 2005 found that 23 percent of Hispanics thought that illegal immigrants were hurting the nation's economy and driving down wages. [8] It might have been expected that such attitudes would soften in the wake of the anti-immigrant legislation and pro-immigrant demonstrations, but a poll Bendixen conducted in 2006 showed that 23 percent of legal immigrants favored deportation of undocumented aliens. Claudia Garcia, a naturalized American originally from Mexico, said, "All these people,

Latino Income Lags Behind Others

A higher percentage of Latinos are in the lowest-income bracket than either African-Americans or whites, and fewer Latinos fall into the higher-income brackets.

Annual Household Income of U.S. Latinos
(by race/ethnicity)

Household Income	Latinos	Whites	African-Americans
Less than $30,000	50%	29%	44%
$30,000 - < $50,000	23	27	30
$50,000 +	17	42	22
Don't know	11	3	4

Source: "2002 National Survey of Latinos," Pew Hispanic Center/Kaiser Family Foundation, December 2002

these illegals, are abusing [U.S. freedom]. Americans are giving them everything and they are incapable of saying, 'I broke the law.' Instead they are saying, 'I came to your country illegally and I want to wave my Mexican flag.' " [9]

Even among Hispanics who favor immigrant protections, attempts to translate their anger over anti-immigrant legislation and rhetoric into full participation in the political process proved difficult in the immediate aftermath of the fabulously attended marches. Latinos have never voted at the same rate as whites or African-Americans. Hispanics cast just 6 percent of the ballots in 2004 — even though a year earlier they had surpassed African Americans as the nation's leading minority group. (Blacks cast 11 percent of that year's votes.) "The sleeping giant may have a sleeping sickness," says Larry J. Sabato, director of the University of Virginia's Center for Politics. "Occasionally, he rolls over and yawns, and looks like he's waking, but it's going to be a long time before Hispanic turnout approaches that of other groups."

As experts look to that future, here are the questions they are asking:

Will Latinos' political clout equal their demographic strength in the near future?

A major dynamic of the recent immigration debate is the awareness among politicians in both parties of the increasing importance of the Latino vote. The new attention paid to Latinos is a sign of their rising political importance,

Will Blacks and Latinos Unite Politically?

In just 10 years, African-Americans have slipped from almost half the 150,000 population of Paterson, N.J., to less than a third, while Latinos have vaulted into the majority.

The rapid demographic shift — which mirrors nation-wide demographic changes — has created tension in the city, especially after José "Joey" Torres beat Paterson's first black mayor in his 2003 bid for re-election. The election of the city's first Latino mayor left many African-Americans bitter.

"There's a feeling among some African-Americans that they were cheated out of the office, even though Joey won it fair and square," says the Rev. Stafford Miller, pastor at Paterson's St. Philips United Methodist Church and a leader in the black community. "Some black people are also put off by Spanish; you know, when they go down to city hall or whatever, they feel uncomfortable with all these people speaking another language."

According to Miller, both groups have to work harder to clear up misunderstandings. "There are problems like this in both communities, but I don't see it as the result of malice or anything like that," he says. "It's more like a case of innocent ignorance."

Throughout the nation's history, tensions have been created when large, new immigrant groups have begun competing with more established ethnic communities for political power, resources and social influence. Now it is happening again in some of the nation's largest cities, as African-Americans see Hispanics moving into the majority and threatening the political clout that blacks fought for decades to amass.

In Los Angeles, for instance, the November 2001 mayoral race highlighted a tussle between a white candidate, James Hahn, and Hispanic Antonio Villaraigosa. Although Latinos make up almost half of L.A.'s population, Hahn still won. "African-American leaders unified behind Hahn and helped him win a decisive 80 percent of the black vote — partly because of his longtime family ties to that community and partly because they feared a Latino mayor might tip the local balance of power away from them, according to columnist Ronald Brownstein.[1] In 2005, Villaraigosa successfully reached out to blacks while taking 84 percent of an energized Latino vote to best Hahn in their rematch.

Roland Robuck, a Washington, D.C., political activist who works with both blacks and Hispanics, foresees even greater conflicts between the two groups, as both sides air legitimate grievances. "Latinos are going to make a lot of demands, showing these demographic documents to members of the Afro-American community," he said. "And the Afro-American community is going to say, 'Yeah, but you

have not paid your dues.' So, only through serious and strategic dialogue would you be able to take care of this."[2]

Toni-Michelle Travis, a professor of government and politics at George Mason University, in Fairfax, Va., concurs. "There's going to be a lot of rivalry and jealousy because African-Americans were there first," she says. "People don't want to share power."

But others say both groups should be able to cooperate because they usually have similar agendas. "With the exception of the immigration issue, we are fighting for the same things," says Roderick Harrison, a demographer at the Joint Center for Political and Economic Studies, which focuses on African-American issues. "We both favor more spending on education, housing and health care."

Those convergent agendas eventually will lead to the formation of "real" coalitions, Harrison predicts. "As people in both communities continue lobbying for similar things, they will see that they do better by pooling their resources, energy and strategies," he says.

In fact, noted Lawrence Aaron, a columnist for New Jersey's Bergen County Record, the Congressional Black and Hispanic Caucuses routinely work together on such issues as education and health care.[3]

But Gregory Rodriguez, a senior fellow at the New America Foundation, a Washington think tank, says U.S. demographics do not back up all the talk of either heightened inter-racial tension or greater cooperation. "First of all, the majority of Latinos and blacks don't live in the same regions," he says. Rodriguez notes that while Latinos are moving into non-traditional areas of the United States, two-thirds of Hispanics still live in the Southwest, and more than half of all African-Americans are in the Southeast.

Furthermore, he says, Latinos are not going to form a "minority group" with political and social values in the way that African-Americans have, largely because they don't see themselves as a single racial entity, as blacks do.

"On the last census," he points out, "50 percent of Latinos said they were 'white' and 48 percent said they were 'other,' so it's much too simplistic to call them a group. The idea that you're going to have two big groups either slugging it out or forming grand coalitions is not realistic."

---

[1] Ronald Brownstein, "Latinos Stir Tension in New Brand of Urban Politics," *Los Angeles Times*, Nov. 26, 2001, p. A11.

[2] Quoted in D'Vera Cohn, "Hispanics Declared Largest Minority," *The Washington Post*, June 19, 2003, p. A1.

[3] Lawrence Aaron, "Common Goals Can Unite Blacks and Hispanics" *Bergen County* [New Jersey] *Record*, July 4, 2003, p. L7.

according to Arturo Vargas, executive director of NALEO. "All of a sudden, we have been discovered," he said. "Now, you can't run a national campaign without a Latino strategy. It's a new fixture on the political landscape." [10]

But some observers contend that being the nation's largest minority doesn't automatically guarantee Latinos commensurate political clout. "It was never . . . just about numbers," said Raul Yzaguirre, former president of the Council of La Raza. "It's about trying to capture the attention of decision-makers, about trying to change the way resources are allocated." [11]

Indeed, despite its size, the Latino community has yet to attain significant political clout. For instance, there are only 23 Hispanics in the House of Representatives, compared with 40 African-Americans.

Latinos have less political influence than their numbers would indicate, largely because less than half of them can vote. More than a third of all Latinos are non-citizens, and only citizens can cast ballots. "People who look at the overall size of the Hispanic population and look at the vote think, 'oh my God, what if these people ever get mobilized,' " says Ruy Teixeira, a liberal polling expert at the Century Foundation. "But these people can't vote anyway."

And even among Hispanic citizens, voter registration is about 20 percent lower than among whites or African-Americans. Moreover, Latinos, on average, are younger than other groups. And young Hispanics, just like young Americans of every race, fail to exercise their right to vote in very great numbers. "We know that younger voters tend to vote at lower rates regardless," said Michael McDonald, a visiting fellow at the Brookings Institution.

Finally, Latinos have less income and education than average Americans, says Luis Fraga, a Stanford University political scientist. "Study after study shows that these factors are predictors of voting habits," he notes. "The less income and education you have, the less likely you are to vote."

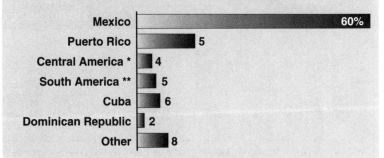

Where Do Latinos Come From?

Nearly two-thirds of adult Latinos in the U.S. have personal or family origins in Mexico. The rest are mainly from Puerto Rico, El Salvador and Colombia.

Origins of U.S. Latino Adults Who Are Registered to Vote
(By percentage of U.S. Latino population)

Mexico	60%
Puerto Rico	5
Central America *	4
South America **	5
Cuba	6
Dominican Republic	2
Other	8

Note: Totals do not add to 100 percent due to rounding.

Source: 2004 National Survey of Latinos, Pew Hispanic Center/Kaiser Family Foundation, July 2004

As a result, Latinos simply don't vote in the same percentages as other Americans: Fewer than 50 percent of voting-age Hispanics (7.6 million) cast ballots during the 2004 election, compared to 56 percent of African-Americans and 60 percent of whites. [12]

Nevertheless, most political analysts agree that Latino clout will increase in the near future. For one thing, the projected growth of the Latino population will produce more eligible voters, and some experts say Latinos are on the verge of making significant political gains that will bring the community's influence more in line with its demographic size.

"The blossoming of Latino power is just an election or two away," says La Raza vice president Celia Muñoz. "We will become the force that we should be."

Muñoz says her assessment is based on the growth of Latino populations in the Midwest and Southeast, where they could soon make the difference between winning and losing a host of states, and hence a national election.

"In the past, you had large concentrations of Latinos in a few states, like California and Texas — states that are generally in one [political] camp or another," she says. "But in the last 10 years you've seen incredible growth of Latinos in new states. In places like Georgia, the Latino population has grown 300 percent in the last 10 years."

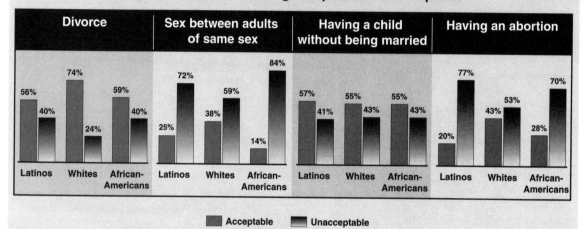

Latinos Are Generally More Conservative Than Whites

Half as many U.S. Latinos as whites approve of abortion, but more Latinos find it acceptable to have a child out of wedlock.

In general, are the following acceptable or unacceptable:

Divorce	Sex between adults of same sex	Having a child without being married	Having an abortion

Divorce:
- Latinos: 56% / 40%
- Whites: 74% / 24%
- African-Americans: 59% / 40%

Sex between adults of same sex:
- Latinos: 25% / 72%
- Whites: 38% / 59%
- African-Americans: 14% / 84%

Having a child without being married:
- Latinos: 57% / 41%
- Whites: 55% / 43%
- African-Americans: 55% / 43%

Having an abortion:
- Latinos: 20% / 77%
- Whites: 43% / 53%
- African-Americans: 28% / 70%

■ Acceptable   ■ Unacceptable

Note: Percentages not included for respondents who did not answer.

Source: "2002 National Survey of Latinos," Pew Hispanic Center/Kaiser Family Foundation, December 2002

Latino population growth in Midwest and the Southern states — including Illinois, Iowa, Colorado, the Carolinas, Georgia and Arkansas — could make Hispanics the key swing vote in most, if not all, of these states, Muñoz claims. "When Latino voters begin to make the difference in these places, then you'll see a change in how we are perceived," she says.

Finally, analysts say, Latinos will benefit from the fact that, unlike African-Americans, they have not been closely tied to one party. "Latinos are not as reliable for the Democratic Party as African-Americans," says Michael Jones-Correa, a government professor at Cornell University, noting that more than a third of Hispanic voters are registered as independents. "This gives them the possibility to influence the policy agendas of both parties, since Republicans and Democrats have to compete for the Latino vote."

But others say predictions of a rising Latino political tide are mostly wishful thinking. "Much of this talk of a new wind blowing is coming from the people who have put their sails up and are waiting for the wind to blow," says Mark Krikorian, executive director of the Center for

Immigration Studies. "A good deal of this is spin to create the impression of clout, which they hope in turn will translate into clout."

Current obstacles to Hispanic political prospects — such as disproportionate numbers of young people and non-citizens — will likely remain in place for the foreseeable future, Krikorian and others say. "You can't change a reality like that over one or two election cycles or even four or five," says the Robert Suro, director of the Pew Hispanic Center. "These trends change very slowly."

Even when today's Latino teenagers reach voting age in the coming years, it won't change the political dynamic much, Suro says. "You have 400,000 Latino youth turning 18 every year, automatically increasing the size of the voting population," he says. "But their political behavior is similar to American teens from other groups — politically apathetic. So it will be hard for Latino politicians to reach this group and mobilize them."

Suro also disputes the notion that burgeoning Latino populations in the South and Midwest will make a big political impact in the coming years. "There's no doubt that the Latino population is growing outside of the traditional Hispanic areas," Suro says, "but they make up less than 5 percent of the electorate in these places, and most of them are foreign-born and so not yet citizens. You can always construct a scenario in one of these states where the Latino vote tips the election, but the numbers aren't big enough to be anything more than one of a host of tipping points."

Even in the handful of states where Hispanics make up a sizable chunk of the electorate, they are not that influential on a national level, Krikorian adds. For example, he says, heavily Democratic California and largely Republican Texas have already been decided in the next presidential election. "Only in Florida, which is a swing state, will Hispanics make a real difference nationally," Krikorian says.

Is the Latino population in the United States growing too fast?

America's Hispanic population has more than doubled since 1980 and is expected to nearly double again — to 61 million — in the next 20 years, according to the Census Bureau. [13] Much of the growth results from high Latino birth rates, which are about 70 percent above the national average. But immigration, including illegal immigration, also plays a role.

Between 2000 and 2005, 7.9 million immigrants entered the United States — the most in any five-year period in the nation's history. About half of these, or 3.7 million, are in the country illegally, according to the Center for Immigration Studies. [14]

The Southwest remains the locus of Hispanic growth, but Latinos are becoming a larger presence in many more states than has traditionally been the case. Since 1990, 25 states have more than doubled their foreign-born populations and nine more have seen their numbers triple. In North Carolina, foreign-born and Hispanic populations grew by 390 percent and 540 percent, respectively,

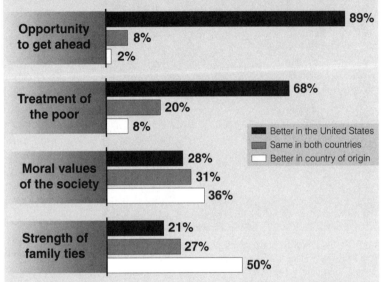

Latinos in U.S. Worry About Family Ties

Latinos overwhelmingly believe the United States offers a better chance to get ahead, but they feel moral and family values are not as strong in the U.S. as in their home countries.

U.S. vs. Country of Origin

Are the following better in the United States, better in the country you or your ancestors came from, or about the same in both?

Opportunity to get ahead: 89% / 8% / 2%

Treatment of the poor: 68% / 20% / 8%

Moral values of the society: 28% / 31% / 36%

Strength of family ties: 21% / 27% / 50%

- Better in the United States
- Same in both countries
- Better in country of origin

Source: "2002 National Survey of Latinos," Pew Hispanic Center/Kaiser Family Foundation, December 2002.

according to William Frey, a demographer with the University of Michigan and the Brookings Institution. [15]

Among the Latino population as a whole, about 40 percent of Latino residents were not born here, and about 40 percent of those are here illegally. Meanwhile, about 65 percent of the nation's Spanish speakers live in the Southwest, mostly in California and Texas. Many cities near the border, including Los Angeles and San Antonio, either have Latino majorities or pluralities.

Some immigration experts worry that the Southwest's large and growing Hispanic influx has arrived too quickly and in too great a number and will fuel separatism.

"We're creating our own Quebec, because we're building a nation within a nation," says Mauro E. Mujica,

Getty Images/David McNew

A U.S. Border Patrol agent examines a Mexican woman suffering from heat-related illness after she was abandoned by her "coyote," or guide, in the desert west of Tucson, Ariz., while entering the U.S. About 600,000 Mexicans illegally cross the border each year, fueling the debate over whether the U.S. Hispanic population is growing too fast.

chairman of U.S. English. "If you take immigration levels from one group and concentrate much of it in one part of the country, as we have done with Hispanics, you are bound to create huge ghettos." [16]

Such "ghettos," with their separate language and different customs, will inevitably want to secede, Mujica worries. "Of course, they will end up identifying with that one area rather than with the whole country," he claims. "It's human nature."

Mujica warns that El Cenizo, Texas, (population 1,399) is an ominous sign of what is coming. In 2000, the community declared Spanish to be its official language. "So what happens when the neighboring town does the same thing, and then it's the whole county, and so on," he says. "After a while, you'll have the whole

Southwest declaring Spanish as its language. Then, you're in trouble."

But immigration lawyer Kathy Culliton dismisses such arguments as "alarmist" and counterproductive. "I don't see what is so scary here," says Culliton, formerly a legislative staff attorney at the Mexican American Legal Defense and Education Fund (MALDEF), in Washington. "Parts of the country have been radically changed by immigrant inflows before. Look at New York with the Irish or California with the inflows of Asian immigrants."

"Look at New Mexico," adds La Raza's Muñoz. "It has been absorbing large numbers of Latinos for 500 years, and it ain't Quebec. If you go there, you'll see that it is a very American place."

Indeed, even in places where Latino immigrants cluster, their children quickly start speaking English, says Jones-Correa. "You go to these places in Texas or Southern California that are 90 percent Latino, and you find that the kids are speaking English and think of themselves as American."

Even in El Cenizo, Spanish is not entirely prevalent. "You go there and sure, most of the adults, who are immigrants, are speaking Spanish," says Gregory Rodriguez, a senior fellow at the New America Foundation, a Washington think tank. "But the kids — they're speaking English and they know who Bart Simpson is."

Culliton and others point out the large influx of Latino immigrants stems, in part, from the demand for their labor. "They are here doing the jobs that Americans don't want to do, in part because the U.S. work force is aging," she says. "If they all disappeared tomorrow, whole sectors of the economy — from agriculture to food service to meatpacking — would literally shut down."

But Krikorian argues that the continuing flood of immigrants is bad for the U.S. economy because it distorts the job market with cheap labor, leaving no incentives to hire native help. "There are no jobs that Americans won't do or that won't get done if the illegal immigrants who are doing them now leave," he says.

If immigrant labor were no longer readily available, Krikorian says, "employers would turn to recruiting in the existing labor force. They would probably have to improve wages and eliminate some of the jobs through automation. They would adapt."

Immigration opponents also contend that hiring Latinos, especially undocumented workers, is essentially exploitative. They say the newcomers take on the most physically demanding jobs — like picking fruit or working construction — often without the same protection and pay enjoyed by American workers.

"People arrive here when they're 18 or 20, strong and hopeful," says Victor Davis Hanson, author of the 2003 book *Mexifornia: A State of Becoming*, which argues for greater controls on illegal Hispanic immigration. "But after 20 or 25 years of backbreaking labor, they become disabled . . . they're essentially unable to do this work anymore. They have no education or other skills, so where do they go?"

"Nowhere," Hanson answers. Such immigrants become dependent on their families and whatever public assistance they can qualify for, he says.

Should greater efforts be made to pass on American values and culture to Latino newcomers?

Perhaps more than any other country, the United States has succeeded in molding newcomers from far-flung nations into Americans — citizens who share the same basic values and cultural traits despite their disparate backgrounds. In the past, this was accomplished through aggressive assimilation policies: Immigrant children were not only taught English but also American history and values in an effort to irrevocably link them to their new country.

Proponents of assimilation contend that today's emphasis on multiculturalism, diversity and ethnic pride is obstructing immigrants' integration into American society. [17] They argue that in addition to learning English, immigrant children also need to embrace American culture and values.

"What are the traditional ingredients for success in America? Is it feeling good about yourself or having ethnic pride?" Hanson asks. "No. It's mastery of the English language, American capitalism and knowledge of the culture around you."

Growing up in central California in the 1960s, Hanson says, he and his classmates — many the children of Mexican immigrants — were given that knowledge. Civic education, far from being crass jingoism, was a crucial means for immigrant children to understand their new country, he says.

"We did not merely review the nuts and bolts of the Constitution, or learn patriotic songs and brief sketches of Washington, Jefferson and Lincoln," he writes. "Our discussions and lectures about American exceptionalism were not the triumphalism of a particular white race or Christian religion, but rather emphasized our own deep appreciation for just how distinctive the culture of the United States had proved to be over some two centuries." [18]

By contrast, Hanson and others say, American schools today are failing Latino students by substituting a curriculum emphasizing maintaining ethnic pride for the teaching of civics. "The results of the decline of civic education are unmistakable," he writes. "It's not just that millions of Americans do not understand fully the mechanics of their own government or the seminal events in their history . . . but they have little idea of what it is to be an American." [19]

As a result, says Ernest W. Lefever, founder of the Ethics and Public Policy Center, a Washington think tank, Latino children are profoundly disadvantaged. "Hispanic kids don't have a chance to become full-fledged Americans because they can't fully participate in our culture and society without understanding it," he says. "They have to know our history — who we are and where we came from and how we got here. It's their history, too, and they're not getting it."

But many Latino-rights advocates argue that forced assimilation would be ineffective and counterproductive. "You can't push people toward assimilation," says John R. Logan, a professor of sociology at the State University of New York, Albany. "Being American is not something that can be taught."

According to Culliton, assimilationists are fighting a non-existent problem. "Surveys show Latinos already identify with the United States more than the countries that they came from," she says. "This just isn't a problem."

In a 2004 survey conducted by the Pew Hispanic Center and the Kaiser Family Foundation, 73 percent of Latinos believed it was "somewhat" or "very" important that Hispanics adapt and blend into the larger American society. In the same survey, however, 93 percent of Latinos said it was important for Hispanics to maintain their distinct cultures. [20]

Cornell's Jones-Correa says it is natural for immigrants to value their native culture, and it poses no societal dangers. "We have this nostalgic view of immigrant groups in the past getting off the boat and Americanizing very quickly, but it took generations for that to happen," he says.

CHRONOLOGY

1800s *Friction between Mexico and the United States leads to war and conquest.*

1848 United States invades Mexico and acquires California and the Southwest after winning the Mexican-American War.

1898 Puerto Rico becomes an American territory after the United States wins the Spanish-American War.

1900-1960 *Greater U.S. involvement in Latin America — coupled with economic growth in the United States — spurs increases in Latino immigration.*

1900 Census Bureau reports half a million people of Mexican descent live in the United States.

1928 U.S. Border Patrol is formed to stem illegal immigration from Mexico.

1942 Labor shortages caused by World War II prompt the government to allow more Mexicans into the U.S. to work.

1959 Fidel Castro seizes power in Cuba, prompting many anti-communist Cubans to flee to the United States.

1960 Civil war breaks out in Guatemala. Unrest in other Central American countries, notably El Salvador and Nicaragua, produces a flood of Latino immigrants to the United States over the next 30 years.

1961 The first U.S. Spanish-language television station begins broadcasting in Texas.

1965 President Lyndon B. Johnson signs the Immigration and Nationality Act, opening the door to more legal immigrants from Latin America.

1970s-1980s *The U.S. Latino community grows dramatically through immigration and high birth rates.*

1975 Congress extends the Voting Rights Act to Latinos.

1980 Census Bureau says U.S. Hispanic population is 12 million.

1984 President Ronald Reagan wins more than 40 percent of the Latino vote, a record for a Republican candidate.

1986 Congress passes the Immigration Control and

Reform Act, which allows millions of illegal immigrants to apply for legal residency.

1990s-2000s *Latinos begin to gain political and economic clout.*

1990 Census Bureau puts Hispanic population at 22.6 million.

1994 Nearly 60 percent of California voters approve Proposition 187, which calls for removing undocumented children from public schools and denying emergency health care to illegal residents. In 1998 a federal judge overturns the law as unconstitutional.

1996 Republican presidential candidate Bob Dole wins about 20 percent of the Latino vote, the lowest amount a Republican has received in recent history.

2000 Gov. George W. Bush, R-Texas, wins 35 percent of the Latino vote in the presidential election, dramatically reversing the recent slide of Hispanic support for GOP presidential candidates. Democrat Bill Richardson, an Hispanic, is elected governor of New Mexico.

2002 Millionaire Texas businessman Tony Sanchez, a Democrat, loses in his bid to become governor of Texas but garners 80 percent of the Latino vote.

June 2003 Census Bureau says Latinos — numbering 38.8 million — are the nation's largest minority, eclipsing African-Americans.

Oct. 2003 California Lt. Gov. Cruz Bustamante comes in second to actor Arnold Schwarzenegger in the gubernatorial recall election. Immediately after taking office, Schwarzenegger overturns a law to allow illegal immigrants to obtain driver's licenses.

2004 Ken Salazar of Colorado and Mel Martinez of Florida are elected to the Senate, giving Hispanics their first presence in that chamber since 1977.

2005 Antonio Villaraigosa is the first Latino elected mayor of Los Angeles since 1872. The House passes a bill classifying illegal immigrants as felons.

2020 U.S. Hispanic population expected to reach 60 million.

2050 Hispanics expected to comprise a quarter of the U.S. population.

"St. Patrick's Day celebrates Irish pride and culture, but no one thinks Irish-Americans are anything but American," Muñoz says.

Moreover, Muñoz and others say, some cultural retention will have a positive impact, and not just for Latinos. "We live in a global economy, and for America to remain strong we need to be able to understand and interact with other languages and cultures," Culliton says. "Latinos help us interact with the Spanish-speaking world, and that gives us an edge."

But assimilationists counter that if Latinos retain a substantial part of their language and culture, they will continue to regard themselves as different. As a result, they say, Latinos will be perceived as different, leading to ethnic tension and segregation.

"A nation is, at its essence, a people with a common historical memory and heritage," Lefever says. "Unless newcomers assimilate this heritage, they ultimately won't feel as if they are part of the nation, and the result inevitably will be fragmentation."

But Stanford political scientist Fraga says today's reality belies Lefever's prediction. "Second-generation Latinos are English-dominant in part because their parents know that to succeed in this new country their kids have to speak the dominant language and be a part of the dominant culture," he says. "This idea of fragmentation or separatism just doesn't have any bearing on reality."

BACKGROUND

Demographic Earthquake

In the 1500s, before the first English settlers landed on the East Coast, the Spanish had established settlements in much of modern-day South and Central America and begun exploring Florida and the American Southeast and Southwest. In 1565, the Spanish established the first permanent European settlement in the United States at present-day St. Augustine, Fla. The Palace of Governors,

built in 1610 by Spanish settlers in Santa Fe, N.M., is the nation's oldest government building.

British settlement of the eastern seaboard in the 17th and 18th centuries eventually pushed the Spanish out of most of the Southeast. But Spanish conquest of the Southwest went unchallenged until the 19th century, when American settlers began moving into Texas, creating friction with Spanish America, now Mexico. The tension came to a head in 1848, when the United States invaded Mexico, grabbing roughly one-third of the country — including what eventually would become California, Texas, New Mexico, Arizona and Colorado.

> ## "If they all disappeared tomorrow, whole sectors of the economy — from agriculture to food service to meatpacking — would literally shut down."
>
> — Kathy Culliton
> Former legislative staff attorney, Mexican American Legal Defense and Education Fund

Victory in the brief Mexican-American War gave the United States control of a large Spanish-speaking territory. Yet for the next 100 years, Hispanics would be little more than an afterthought in the young nation's national psyche, largely because the Southwest was sparsely populated.

Even by 1900, only about 500,000 Mexican-Americans lived in the United States. Although Mexican immigration increased in the first half of the 20th century, along with new arrivals from Cuba and Puerto Rico (conquered during the Spanish-American War of 1898), the number of Hispanics paled in comparison to the huge influxes of immigrants still arriving from Europe. [21]

After World War II, however, waves of immigrants from Puerto Rico, Cuba, the Dominican Republic and Mexico quickly swelled the nation's Latino population. By 1980, the United States had nearly 20 million Hispanics.

---

* The terms Hispanic and Latino are used interchangeably to refer to people who trace their personal or family origins to Central and South America and Spanish-speaking Caribbean nations. Different parts of the country have different preferences, however. In California and New York for example, "Latino" is preferred, while "Hispanic" is more widely used in Texas and Florida. When referring to the national U.S. population, Hispanic/Latino organizations say either term is acceptable.

Midwest Is 'New Frontier' for Latinos

Unlike Texas or Southern California, the Midwest has little, if any, historical or cultural significance to Mexicans and other Latinos. Nor does it offer a similar climate or terrain.

Nevertheless, record numbers of Mexicans and other Latinos have been moving to states like Illinois, Minnesota and Iowa. "There's been incredible growth throughout the region and especially in the last decade," says Marcello Siles, a Latino scholar at Michigan State University.

After Los Angeles, Chicago now has the largest Mexican-American population in the country, surpassing communities in San Antonio, San Diego, Houston and other big cities near the U.S.-Mexican border. Between 1990 and 2000, the number of Mexicans in the Windy City rose 50 percent, to 530,000. Another half-million Latinos, mostly Mexicans, live elsewhere in Illinois. [1]

Meanwhile, the Hispanic populations of Minnesota, Wisconsin, Indiana and Iowa more than doubled between 1990 and 2002. [2] Iowa Governor Tom Vilsack gave three cities $50,000 each in 2000 to assess their workforce needs and develop plans to recruit immigrants. He shelved a more ambitious plan to attract immigrants to his aging state by asking Congress to declare Iowa an "immigration enterprise zone," exempt from federal immigration quotas. That idea had set off a political brawl and even Vilsack's more modest grants drew criticism. [3]

In some communities, like St. James, Minn. (population 4,695), Latinos grew from being a rarity between 1990 and 2000 to one-quarter of the population, and in Postville, Iowa (population 2,273), Latinos climbed from 0 in 1990 to 469 in 2000. [4]

"They have completely changed the demographic makeup of some areas in the span of a very few years," says William Frey, a demographer at the University of Michigan, Ann Arbor.

"Latinos are moving even to the little rural towns," Siles says. "You drive through these places that once were completely white, and now you see a taco shop or a Latino general store."

What are Latinos doing in small towns in one of the coldest and whitest parts of the country — towns that in many cases have been losing young, native-born residents for years?

"It's jobs, plain and simple," Frey says. Latinos have been especially drawn to the region's huge meatpacking industry, where residents have been put off by the smell, the low pay and high risk of injury. "The Iowa work ethic isn't the same anymore," said Doug All, a plant manager in Postville. "Meatpacking isn't glamorous, so they don't want the work." [5]

Indeed, even though the number of meatpacking jobs fell from 168,200 in 1975 to 150,600 in 2001, companies have been recruiting Latinos from Mexico and the Southwest to work in plants in Nebraska and other Northern states. [6] Meatpacking giant Tyson Foods was even charged with bringing in illegal aliens, though it was acquitted in March 2003. [7]

Many meatpacking plants are staffed almost entirely by Latinos. "The meatpacking businesses in southeast Minnesota would have to close up shop without them," said James Kielkopf, president of a St. Paul neighborhood-development group. [8]

Meatpacking and other low-wage, high-risk jobs also have attracted Latinos to the Southeast, another area traditionally

In the next 20 years, the number of Latinos nearly doubled, as leftist insurgencies and rightist government repression — especially in Central America — forced many Hispanics to flee to "el Norte." But most of the newcomers still came from Mexico. Today, nearly two-thirds of all Latinos in the U.S. either arrived from Mexico or are descended from Mexican immigrants.

In June 2003, the Census Bureau announced that African-Americans were no longer the nation's largest minority: The bureau said that the nation's 38.8 million Latinos now made up 13 percent of the U.S population,

compared to 38.3 million blacks, or 12.7 percent of the population. "The black-white divide has been the basic social construct in American history for 300 years," says the Pew Hispanic Center's Suro. "This marks a big change . . . [an] official reminder that we are moving into new territory."

Indeed, census data show that half the nation's population growth is now occurring among Hispanics — due to both immigration and a higher birth rate (3.5 births per each Hispanic woman, compared to 2.7 among African-Americans and 2.1 for the nation's population as a whole). [22] The Latino population had grown to 42.7

devoid of Hispanics (with the exception of Florida). Since 1990, the Hispanic populations of Tennessee, Arkansas, Georgia and North Carolina have grown more than 300 percent.

Besides jobs, Latinos are also moving northward because traditional Latino settlement areas are overcrowded. "California is full," says Jeffrey Passel, an immigration expert at the Urban Institute, a social-policy think tank in Washington, D.C.

"The pioneer immigrant leaves Mexico and goes to California," Passel adds. "After a while, he goes to Iowa and gets a job in a pork-processing plant. He sends word to Mexico that, 'Hey, there are jobs here.'"

A recent census report confirms that fewer immigrants are settling in traditional Hispanic areas — California, Texas, New York, Florida, New Jersey and Illinois. Between 1995 and 2000, only 60 percent of Latino immigrants went to those six states, compared to 73 percent a decade before. [9]

Frey says the migration to the Midwest is likely to continue. "Some of the white population is leaving the region," he says, referring to the fact that 640,000 whites left between 1990 and 2000. [10] "So communities that want to fire up local

Latinos Increasing Fastest in South, Midwest

Since 1990, Hispanic populations have grown fastest in the South and Midwest, but most Latinos still live in Southwestern and border states.

11 States With Largest Percentage Increase in Latinos

	Latino Population		
	1990	2004	% Increase
North Carolina	76,726	517,617	574.63%
Arkansas	19,876	120,820	507.86
Georgia	108,922	598,322	449.31
Tennessee	32,741	167,025	410.14
South Carolina	30,551	130,432	326.93
Alabama	24,629	98,388	299.48
Kentucky	21,984	77,055	250.50
Minnesota	53,884	179,303	232.75
Nebraska	36,969	119,975	224.52
Iowa	32,647	104,119	218.92
Oregon	112,707	343,278	204.57

Source: U.S. Census Bureau

industries will be welcoming more Hispanics to fill these new jobs."

Siles agrees that Hispanics will continue to come, but not just for the jobs. "Latinos like the Midwest," he says. "The people are very open and friendly and receptive to newcomers, and that makes it easier for them to settle here."

[1] "Our Kinda Ciudad," *The Economist*, Jan. 11, 2003.

[2] U.S. Census Bureau, www.census.gov/Press-Release/www/2003/state-est-tb2.xls.

[3] Christopher Conte, "Strangers on the Prairie," *Governing*, Jan. 2002, p. 30.

[4] Noel C. Paul, "A Farm Town Goes Global, and Thrives," *The Christian Science Monitor*, Aug. 20, 2001, p. 16. 2002. Census figures for those cities are not yet available.

[5] Quoted in *Ibid*.

[6] American Meat Institute.

[7] Jeremy Olson, "Migrant Pipeline Fills Meatpackers' Needs," *Omaha* [Nebraska] *World Herald*, Aug. 4, 2003, p. A1.

[8] Quoted in "Our Kinda Ciudad," *op. cit.*

[9] "Migrations by Nativity for the Population 5 Years and Over for the United States and States," Bureau of the Census, www.census.gov/population/www/cen2000/phc-t24.html.

[10] Robert E. Pierre, "In Neb., 'Spanish Now Spoken Here,'" *The Washington Post*, Sept. 2, 2003, p. A3.

million by mid-2005; by 2050, the bureau predicts a quarter of the nation will be Latino.

Moreover, a Pew Center study found that by 2020 nearly half of the growth among Latinos will result from the births of second-generation Hispanics. By then, immigrants' children will outnumber them by 21.7 million to 20.6 million, and nearly 18 million will be third-generation. [23]

This generational shift will have profound implications for the country, the study predicts, since the children of immigrants have different values and priorities than their parents and grandparents. Second-generation Hispanics, for instance, are likely to be more liberal on abortion but less supportive of affirmative action.

While Latinos in America are a diverse group, fully half are in California or Texas. Another 20 percent live in New York, Florida, Illinois, Arizona and New Jersey. By contrast, 39 states each have less than 1 percent of the country's Hispanics, although that is beginning to change.

Meanwhile, experts say, Latinos are already forcing a change in mainstream attitudes toward them. "We're seeing the country [view] Latinos in a new, more positive

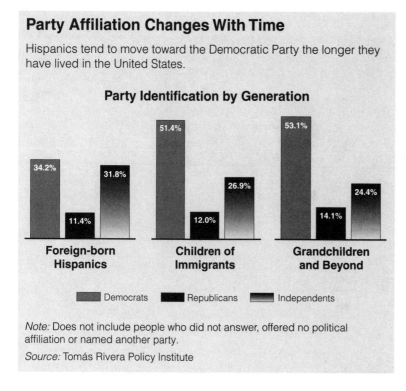

Party Affiliation Changes With Time

Hispanics tend to move toward the Democratic Party the longer they have lived in the United States.

Party Identification by Generation

Foreign-born Hispanics: 34.2% / 11.4% / 31.8%

Children of Immigrants: 51.4% / 12.0% / 26.9%

Grandchildren and Beyond: 53.1% / 14.1% / 24.4%

Democrats ■ Republicans ■ Independents

Note: Does not include people who did not answer, offered no political affiliation or named another party.

Source: Tomás Rivera Policy Institute

way," says economist Carmen Diana Deere, director of the Center for Latin American Studies at the University of Florida.

The "mainstreaming" of Latino culture in recent years reflects the changed attitudes, Deere says. "We now have the Latin Grammy awards," she says, "and white kids are embracing Latino music."

The Same, Yet Different

Latinos come from more than 20 countries in Latin America, including 11 nations in South America, the seven tiny Central American states, Mexico and the Caribbean's Spanish-speaking islands — mainly Cuba, the Dominican Republic and Puerto Rico.

As with people from other sprawling regions, Latin Americans are culturally and even ethnically diverse. Bolivia, with its Indian and Spanish heritage, is different from Brazil, with its large populations of immigrants from Portugal, Africa, Europe and even Asia.

Except for the Portuguese-speaking Brazilians, Latin America's diverse cultures are bound together by the Spanish language and their common religion — Roman Catholicism. When Spain and Portugal conquered Latin

America in the 16th century, they converted the native populations — sometimes forcibly — to Catholicism. Even today, all Latin American countries are predominantly Catholic, although Evangelical Protestant missionaries, mostly from the United States, have made significant inroads in recent decades.

Some experts contend that a common political agenda also ties the community together. "Latinos of all nationalities care about education," says Rodolfo de la Garza, a political scientist at Columbia University. "And because of their working-class status, they care about the economy and jobs."

But unlike African-Americans, Latinos — especially recent immigrants — do not generally think of themselves as a unified ethnic group. "With African-Americans, there is this sense of linked fate, that what happens to any one of us could happen to me," says Cornell's Jones-Correa. "Latinos don't have the same feeling, the same group identity, because they don't have the same group history that blacks do."

Indeed, only 24 percent of Latinos in a recent Pew Hispanic Center/Kaiser Family Foundation survey identified themselves as "Latino" or "Hispanic." A majority of respondents — 54 percent — described themselves by their family's country of origin. Another 21 percent labeled themselves as "American." [24]

Latino identity in America appears to be a paradox, says La Raza's Muñoz, because it defies historical ethnic patterns. "We're not blacks, but we're not Italians either," she says. "We're not a race, but an ethnic group with a diverse ethnicity. So it's very complicated."

The Center for Immigration Studies' Krikorian says a Latino or Hispanic identity does not naturally arise from this complicated mix, but is an artificial construct created by advocacy groups and the government, which needed an easy way to classify people for the census and other programs. "The Latino elite is trying to create a Hispanic identity, and they're making some headway, especially among Hispanics who were born here," Krikorian says.

Critics contend that such efforts are designed to create an identity to perpetuate race and ethnic-based politics. "The so-called Latino leaders want these people to focus on their identity to the exclusion of everything else because it is the basis of their own power," says U.S. English's Mujica. "If people assimilate and stop thinking of themselves as different, groups like La Raza will be out of business."

But Jones-Correa contends the label is legitimate, even if it has been created. "Just because something is artificial doesn't mean that it isn't real," he says. "It has taken on a life of its own." Nevertheless, people still use the "Latino" or "Hispanic" labels sparingly, he says.

"If you ask someone what they are, their first response is unlikely to be 'Latino' or 'Hispanic,' " he says. "But if you ask what they are in certain circumstances, such as concerning Proposition 187 [the 1994 California voter initiative that denied services to illegal immigrants], then it comes into play."

Krikorian hopes the Hispanic or Latino labels don't stick. "It adds a political component to ethnic identity," he says, "and that's bad for democracy."

But Jones-Correa contends that the future fate of words like Latino and Hispanic rests more with society's mainstream than with the group itself.

"These pan-ethnic labels will only be relevant if people feel like they're being singled out as a group," he says. "If rates of intermarriage continue to rise and if Latino upward mobility follows the same path that the Irish or the Italians took, then labels will become increasingly symbolic."

CURRENT SITUATION

Latino Attitudes

Latinos are overwhelmingly optimistic about the future, according to recent polls. A *New York Times*/CBS News poll, for instance, found that 83 percent of foreign-born Hispanics (and 64 percent of the native-born) believed their children would have better lives than they had. By comparison, only 39 percent of non-Hispanics shared their optimism. [25]

The fact that many Latinos are immigrants or only a generation removed from the immigrant experience has much to do with their general hopefulness about the future, experts say.

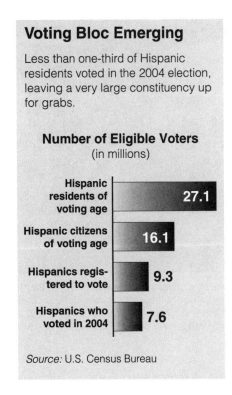

Voting Bloc Emerging

Less than one-third of Hispanic residents voted in the 2004 election, leaving a very large constituency up for grabs.

Number of Eligible Voters
(in millions)

Hispanic residents of voting age	27.1
Hispanic citizens of voting age	16.1
Hispanics registered to vote	9.3
Hispanics who voted in 2004	7.6

Source: U.S. Census Bureau

"You migrate to find a better life," says John A. Garcia, acting director of the Mexican American Studies and Research Center at the University of Arizona. "So if you're an immigrant, it makes sense that you're going to be more optimistic about your future, especially in the first years after you arrive."

Surveys also show that many Latinos are assimilating. According to the *Times*/CBS poll, nearly 70 percent of foreign-born Hispanics said they identify with the United States more than the country they came from. [26] Another survey, from the Latino Coalition, found that a slight majority of Hispanics, 51.2 percent, believed that assimilation is more important than diversity. [27]

Meanwhile, only 31 percent of survey respondents say they themselves or a family member or a friend had experienced discrimination during the last five years, compared to 46 percent for African-Americans and 13 percent for whites. [28]

But some observers say Hispanics may be underreporting incidents of discrimination. "Latinos have a very different view of what discrimination is," says Stanford political scientist Fraga. "If you ask them if they've been treated differently by their white colleagues, they'll say yes.

John Avila, an Albuquerque shop owner, is one of the more than 1.2 million Latino small-business owners in the United States. Hispanic businesses grew by 30 percent between 1992 and 1997, compared to just 7 percent nationwide.

But if you ask them whether that's discrimination, they'll say no. To a Latino immigrant, discrimination means that someone attacks you because of what you are."

The New America Foundation's Rodriguez says the different perceptions about discrimination stem from the fact that so many Latinos are either first- or second-generation Americans who lack a finely honed sense of their rights. "When you feel yourself well ensconced in a society, you're comfortable enough to have grievances," he says. "But if you don't know the system and you're trying to fit in, you don't feel the same sense of grievance. You just want to fit in."

Latino attitudes about political and social issues also produce some surprises. On so-called moral issues, Hispanics tend to be quite conservative, probably because of their Roman Catholicism. For instance, 77 percent find abortion "unacceptable" and 72 percent oppose sexual relations between adults of the same gender. [29] The Catholic Church actively opposes abortion and homosexual relations.

Moreover, many immigrants come from poor, rural areas that tend to be more socially conservative than urban areas. "You have a lot of Mexicans and Central Americans coming from small villages, where they have very traditional values," Garcia says.

However, Latinos tend to be liberal on other issues. Sixty percent, for instance, favor higher taxes to support more government services. [30]

Being conservative on moral issues but not on social policy makes Latinos an anomaly in a country where feelings about both are usually in sync. "Their attitudes don't reflect the American political debate," Rodriguez says. "But given where they're coming from and what they need, it makes perfect sense."

The American Dream

Like many immigrant groups before them, first- and second-generation Latinos are striving to improve their lot. "We believe very strongly in the American dream and are willing to work very hard to fulfill that dream," La Raza's Muñoz says.

And they are succeeding. In recent decades, many Latinos have vaulted into the middle class — a key indicator of economic progress. For instance, since 1972, the percentage of Latinos earning $50,000 or more has doubled — jumping from 15.8 percent to 31 percent in 2001. By comparison, 27.8 percent of African-Americans had comparable earning power in 2001. [31]

Hispanic buying power, currently at $630 billion, is expected to rise 50 percent to $928 billion by 2007. [32]

Hispanics also have made huge progress in another traditional steppingstone toward the American Dream — business ownership. Between 1992 and 1997, the number of Latino-owned businesses grew by 30 percent, compared to just 7 percent overall. Hispanics currently own more than 1.2 million small businesses. [33]

Meanwhile, homeownership among Latinos has risen faster than among either blacks or whites. According to the Joint Center for Housing Studies at Harvard University, Latino homeownership increased by 47 percent, to 4.5 million, between 1994 and 2001, while it increased by only 33 percent among African-Americans and 11 percent among whites. [34]

Almost half of all Latinos now live in the suburbs. Even in expensive housing markets, Latino homeownership rates are increasing. In New York, for instance, 14 percent of all Hispanics owned their own home in 2000, up from 11.6 percent a decade earlier. [35] "The housing numbers are extremely important," Rodriguez says. "They tell us that a lot of Latinos have created enough distance from subsistence poverty and are building something stable and permanent."

Should amnesty be granted to Latinos living illegally in the U.S.?

YES Marisa DeMeo
Regional Counsel, MALDEF (Mexican American Legal Defense & Educational Fund)

Written for *CQ Researcher*, September 2003

A top priority for Latinos is to see Congress legalize the millions of hard-working, taxpaying, undocumented immigrants who can demonstrate they have been living and working in the United States and are not a threat to our national security. The same reasons that existed for legalization before 9/11 still exist today.

Latino immigrants have contributed billions of dollars to our economy. Due to the aging U.S. work force, immigrant workers will become more essential in the years ahead. New immigrants perform jobs U.S. workers do not want, which is why all the major unions, business groups, national faith-based organizations and immigrants' and civil-rights groups support legalization.

Undocumented Latino immigrants do not live in segregated societies among themselves. Forty percent of the Latino community is foreign-born, and many of those who are not are living in families with those who are. Latino undocumented immigrants often work two or three jobs to make ends meet. They are raising their children and going to church in our communities. These individuals are not "aliens" from another planet; they are human beings trying to live out the American dream of a better life for their children.

So long as undocumented Latino immigrants remain without a legal status, they are vulnerable to exploitation. It is easy for unscrupulous employers to pay these workers less than what the law requires and fire them if they complain about unsafe working conditions or sexual harassment. In addition, they often are victims of crime but are too afraid to report the crimes to police because they fear they could be deported. Removing that fear would lead to safer communities for everyone.

Finally, the war against terrorism only further solidifies the reasons for legalizing the undocumented population. Latino immigrants have proven to be extremely patriotic. The first U.S. soldier killed in Iraq was a Guatemalan who first entered the United States illegally. He had been able to change his immigration status and showed his gratitude to his adopted country by joining the military and — in the end — giving his life.

If the U.S. government established a true path to legalization for the undocumented, it would be able to identify and screen these individuals to more easily distinguish the vast majority of immigrants who are contributing to our society from the few immigrants and citizens who mean to do us harm.

NO Mark Krikorian
Executive Director, Center for Immigration Studies

Written for *CQ Researcher*, September 2003

As the number of illegal aliens increases, so do proposals to "solve" the problem through an amnesty. The Bush administration, Sen. John McCain, R-Ariz., and others have floated various proposals, most using a temporary-worker program as a fig leaf to cover the reality of amnesty.

The problem certainly needs to be addressed. Our country is now home to some 9 million illegal aliens — more than a quarter of the total immigrant population — and at least 700,000 new illegals settle each year.

But is legalization likely to solve the problem? Our experience with amnesties leaves little doubt that the answer is "No." In 1986, Congress granted green cards to 2.7 million illegal aliens out of a total of 5 million. But the enforcement measures that were coupled with the amnesty were not implemented in a meaningful way; as a result, by 1994 every amnesty recipient had been replaced by a new illegal.

Amnesty supporters counter that we have to find a way to accommodate this flow of labor from abroad because it is both inevitable and essential to our economy. Neither is true.

Illegal immigration is an artifact of misguided government policies — both sins of commission (like guest-worker programs, amnesties and mass legal immigration) and sins of omission (unwillingness to enforce the law). Though illegal immigration can never be eliminated altogether, it can be radically curtailed, if only we choose to do so.

Nor do we need the labor. In fact, mass, unskilled immigration is actually *harming* the industries where it is concentrated — by slowing the increase in productivity, which is the heart of economic progress. There are enormous labor-saving opportunities — in agriculture, light manufacturing, construction and even services — that remain unrealized because of the continuing flow of low-wage immigrant workers.

The alternative to amnesty is not roundups and mass expulsion. Instead, the solution is the "broken-windows" policing approach pursued by New York Mayor Rudolph Giuliani in the 1990s. A new commitment to enforce order in our lawless immigration system will send the message that the immigration law is back in business and lead many illegals to leave voluntarily; prospective illegals abroad will decide to stay put.

Amnesty is not even an appropriate topic for discussion until after we reassert control over immigration. Only then might it be plausible — as the closing act, tying up the loose ends left over from the irresponsible immigration policies of the past.

Latinos Favor Big Government

A far higher percentage of U.S. Latinos than blacks or whites say they would pay higher taxes if the government could provide more services.

Which of the following statements do you agree with more?

	I'd rather pay higher taxes to support a larger government that provides more services	I'd rather pay lower taxes to support a smaller government that provides fewer services
Latinos	60%	34%
Whites	35%	59%
African-Americans	43%	49%

Note: Totals do not add up to 100 percent because some respondents did not answer.

Source: "2002 National Survey of Latinos," Pew Hispanic Center/Kaiser Family Foundation, December 2002

But the American dream is a mixed picture for Latinos. Educational achievement among Hispanics lags far behind other major groups. According to the Pew Hispanic Center, one-fifth of all Latinos in high school do not graduate, and 33.7 percent of Hispanic immigrant students drop out. [36] By contrast, only 11.7 percent of African-American students and 8.2 percent of whites drop out. [37]

According to the Pew Center's Suro, Latino dropout rates are high primarily for two reasons. "You have a school system that is sliding into crisis, and that hits the poor the hardest because they depend on public education more than others do," Suro says. "And you have a lot of immigrant Latino children who are harder to educate because they live in households where English is not spoken and their parents often don't have much formal education and aren't familiar with the American school system."

Experts worry that the education gap will leave Latinos permanently disadvantaged in the labor market for generations to come. "No community can prosper or move forward without a proper education," says J. R. Gonzales, former chairman of the U.S. Hispanic Chamber of Commerce.

As Latinos become a larger percentage of the labor force in the years ahead, the problem will take on a national dimension, Gonzales and others say. "Baby Boomers are going to be retiring soon, and their replacements are Latinos," Suro says. "They're going to be the largest part of the new labor force, and if they're not properly educated, we're in trouble."

And despite Hispanics' deserved reputation for hard work, their unemployment rate typically runs about 2 percent higher than the national average. According to the Pew Center, much of that employment gap results from Latinos being over-represented in retail and manufacturing, which have been in decline. [38]

But some economists say Latino unemployment is not as bad as the numbers indicate, because many immigrants work in the underground economy, and thus are not counted as employed. Still, Hispanic unemployment could worsen if the housing and real estate bubble bursts, because Latinos do much of the nation's construction work.

Latinos also have a high poverty rate — 21.4 percent in 2001, just under the 22.1 percent for African-Americans and much more than the 7.8 percent for whites. [39]

"They make up a disproportionate number of the working poor," says the University of Florida's Deere. "Earning the minimum wage, which is what a lot of immigrant jobs pay, you simply cannot support a family of four above the poverty line."

Hard Lives for Illegals

Many of the poorest Latinos are living in the United States illegally. Often working for minimum wage without health and other benefits or access to government services, they live very different lives than most Americans.

"It is very, very difficult sometimes," admits 23-year-old "José," an illegal immigrant who recently arrived from Mexico and lives in Arlington, Va., where he works in landscaping. José often works 10 or more hours a day, has no health insurance and lives in a cramped apartment with six other people.

"I am working very hard because I want to help my family," he says. He regularly sends money to his parents and hopes to return home in five or 10 more years to start his own business.

Despite the hardships, José is "grateful" to be in the United States and finds Americans generally "friendly and respectful." But he also is frightened that he may be forced to go back to Mexico before he is ready to return and says he would be apprehensive about going to the police or even to a hospital for fear of being deported. "I would not go to the police if there was a problem," he says. "I don't want to be arrested."

Many immigrant advocates say millions of undocumented Latinos like José, who work hard and pay taxes, should be given a chance — through an amnesty program — to legalize their status. They are doing the work most Americans don't want to do, advocates say, but without the protections legal residents enjoy. An amnesty would be not only fair for immigrants but also right for the country, they say.

But amnesty opponents say such a program would make a mockery of the nation's immigration laws. Moreover, they say, legalizing undocumented foreign workers would unfairly punish would-be immigrants who play by the rules and wait to come to the United States legally, and would also encourage more illegal immigration.

Amnesties have been granted to illegal aliens in the past, most recently in 1986, when Congress legalized 3 million mostly Mexican immigrants as part of a broad immigration-reform package.

In the months leading up to the Sept. 11, 2001, terrorist attacks on New York and the Pentagon, President Bush and Mexican President Vicente Fox talked openly about granting an amnesty for at least some undocumented Latinos. But the attacks led to an abrupt end to the negotiations. [40]

Although Bush and some senators, including John McCain, R-Ariz., favor taking the amnesty approach, the heated politics surrounding the immigration debate make its adoption unlikely. Polls indicate that most Americans favor the tougher approach taken by the U.S. House. In December 2005, the House voted to classify those with illegal status as felons, favored building 698 miles of two-layered fences along the U.S.-Mexico border, and voted to require employers to check the legality of their workers' immigration status.

Senators struggled throughout the spring of 2006 to achieve a compromise that recognized the contributions 11 million illegal immigrants already make to the U.S. economy, while making borders more secure and immigration regulations more stringent. They moved more toward the House's approach — approving a triple-layered border fence, for instance. Bush, too, began to talk

tougher about immigration, proposing to send National Guardsmen to patrol the nation's border with Mexico.

But the House remained far apart from both the Senate and the president, who remained in a more welcoming mood than many members of Congress. "Every generation of immigrants has reaffirmed the wisdom of remaining open to the talents and dreams of the world," Bush said in a televised address devoted to immigration in May 2006. "And every generation of immigrants has reaffirmed our ability to assimilate newcomers — which is one of the defining strengths of our country."

OUTLOOK

Post-Ethnic America?

Futurists Joel Kotkin and Thomas Tseng recently predicted that the United States will enter a "post-ethnic" period in the years ahead. Driven in large part by the influx of Latino immigrants, they contend that longstanding notions of race and ethnicity will melt away, to be replaced by a society where identity is based on personal preferences in things like music, fashion and ideas, rather than skin color or your grandfather's country of origin. [41]

Indeed, they say young Latinos already are beginning to embrace this post-ethnic attitude. "No longer content to hew to a single cultural or racial identity," Kotkin and Tseng wrote, "they are beginning to erase the often unbreachable divide that has marked, and marred, race relations in this country from the earliest European settlements." [42]

In other words, this is not your father's melting pot, but a new one, in which both ethnic and racial barriers disintegrate. "Latinos are not going to create a 'third race,' " Rodriguez of the New America Foundation says, refuting the idea that Hispanics will simply take their place alongside whites and blacks. "They're going to eliminate the notion of race."

But others are more pessimistic. "Race relations are going to get worse as a result of this influx," U.S. English's Mujica says.

Mujica contends that "self-elected" Hispanic leaders are preaching what he calls a "separatist" message, planting the seeds of disunity. "They are encouraging Latinos to think of themselves as different," he claims. "So when, in the future, they make up a huge portion of this country's population and when they have a lot of political power, it's going to be very tense and difficult because we're not going to be able to think of ourselves as one people anymore."

Immigration attorney Culliton shares Mujica's pessimism, but for very different reasons. "Discrimination won't be stopped just because of sheer numbers of Latinos," she says. "We need to match this growth with the right social and legal policies or we will still have ethnic tensions in our country."

Some observers say a post-ethnic America is possible, but only if immigration levels begin dropping. "It's very possible, if we have time to absorb the people we already have," says the University of Arizona's Garcia. "But if we continue to have more and more foreign-born people in this country, Latino or otherwise, it will be hard, because we will have this large group that's going to be different because they come from a different place. A large number of Latino immigrants will also make it easier for the native-born to maintain connections to their old culture, and that will make it harder for them to be part of this post-ethnic America."

Others paint a more mixed picture, predicting that some Latinos will live in the America that Kotkin and Tseng describe, while others will be left behind. "Those Latinos who are whiter, who intermarry and have educational opportunities will live in a world where their identity is largely symbolic," says Cornell's Jones-Correa. "But if you don't look white — say you're a Mexican Indian — then you will continue to be marginalized. Distinction by color is not going to go away."

Suro at the Pew Hispanic Center agrees, although he sees class as more of a dividing line. "If you're poor and you live in the inner city, you're going to still be a minority," he says. "But if you have money and live in the suburbs, you'll end up 'white' regardless of what you look like."

NOTES

1. Teresa Watanabe, "Immigrant Advocates Turn Focus to Ballot Box," *Los Angeles Times*, May 10, 2006, p. B1.

2. Ario Campo-Flores and Howard Fineman, "A Latino Power Surge," *Newsweek*, May 30, 2005, p. 24.

3. D'Vera Cohn and Tara Bahrampour, "Of U.S. Children Under 5, Nearly Half Are Minorities," *The Washington Post*, May 10, 2006, p. A1.

4. Cathleen Decker, "Bush Courts Latinos, Other Californians," *Los Angeles Times*, April 8, 2000, p. A10.

5. Jim VandeHei and Peter Baker, "Bush, GOP Congress Losing Core Supporters," *The Washington Post*, May 11, 2006, p. A1.

6. Byron York, "Inside the President's Terrible Poll Numbers," *National Review Online*, May 9, 2006.

7. Bill Turque and Karin Brulliard, "Vote Fuels Immigration Debate," *The Washington Post*, May 4, 2006, p. B6.

8. Roberto Suro, "Attitudes Toward Immigrants and Immigration Policy: Surveys Among Latinos in the U.S. and in Mexico," Pew Hispanic Center, Aug. 6, 2005, p. 2.

9. S. Mitra Kalita, "Dissonant Voices Inside the Border," *The Washington Post*, May 11, 2006, p. A1.

10. Quoted in Colleen McCain Nelson, "Clout of Hispanics Growing," *The Dallas Morning News*, June 30, 2003, p. A1.

11. Quoted in Scott Shepard, "Democrats, GOP Court Latino Vote," *Austin* [Texas] *American Statesman*, July 13, 2003, p. A1.

12. "Voting and Registration in the Election of 2004," U.S. Census Bureau, March 2006, p. 4.

13. "U.S.-Born Hispanics Increasingly Drive Population Developments," The Pew Hispanic Center, January 2002.

14. Haya El Nasser and Kathy Kiely, "More Immigrants Than Ever Flow Into USA," *USA Today*, Dec. 13, 2005, p. 1A.

15. William Frey, "The Silence Behind America's Immigration Impasse," *Financial Times*, May 3, 2006, p. 13.

16. For background, see Mary H. Cooper, "Quebec Sovereignty," *CQ Researcher*, Oct. 6, 1995, pp. 873-896.

17. For background, see David Masci, "Liberal Arts Education," *CQ Researcher*, April 10, 1998, pp. 313-336, and Kenneth Jost, "Teaching History," *CQ Researcher*, Sept. 29, 1995, p. 858.

18. Victor Davis Hanson, *Mexifornia: A State of Becoming* (2003), p. 93.

19. *Ibid.*

20. "The 2004 National Survey of Latinos: Politics and Civic Participation," Pew Hispanic Center/Kaiser Family Foundation, July 2004.

21. For Background see David Masci, "Hispanic-Americans' New Clout," *CQ Researcher*, Sept. 18, 1998, p. 820.

22. "New Trends in Newborns: Fertility Rates and Patterns in California," Public Policy Institute of California, August 2001.

23. Cohn, *op. cit.*

24. "2002 National Survey of Latinos," Pew Hispanic Center/Kaiser Family Foundation, Dec. 2002, p. 27.

25. Simon Romero and Jenet Elder, "Hispanics in U.S. Report Optimism," *The New York Times*, Aug. 6, 2003, p. A1.

26. *Ibid.*

27. Zev Charles, "Latinos Are Looking Up," *Daily News*, Aug. 27, 2003.

28. 2002 National Survey, *op. cit.*, p. 74.

29. *Ibid.*, p. 47.

30. *Ibid.*, p. 62.

31. Samuel G. Freedman, "Next Step on Affirmative Action? Base It On Income," *USA Today*, June 25, 2003, p. A13.

32. Association of Hispanic Advertising Agencies, www.ahaa.org/Mediaroom/finalfacts0303.htm.

33. Hector V. Barreto, "Latinos Find Opportunity in Free Enterprise," *Bergen County* [New Jersey] *Record*, Aug. 7, 2003, p. L9.

34. Eric Herman, "Latinos Set Pace Among New Homeowners," *Daily News*, March 31, 2003, p. 58.

35. *Ibid.*

36. Pew, "Hispanic Youth Dropping Out," *op. cit.*

37. *Ibid.*

38. "New Lows From New Highs," Pew Hispanic Center, Jan. 24, 2003, p. 3.

39. Bureau of the Census, www.census.gov/hhes/poverty/poverty00/pov00hi.html.

40. For background, see David Masci and Kenneth Jost, "War on Terrorism," *CQ Researcher*, Oct. 12, 2001, pp. 817-840.

41. Joel Kotkin and Thomas Tseng, "Happy to Mix It All Up," *The Washington Post*, June 8, 2003, p. B1.

42. Quoted in *ibid.*

BIBLIOGRAPHY

Books

Hanson, Victor Davis, *Mexifornia: A State of Becoming*, Encounter Books, 2003.
A noted military historian and social commentator argues that illegal immigration — coupled with multiculturalism — is creating a permanent Hispanic underclass in California.

Articles

Barreto, Hector, "Latinos Find Opportunity in Free Enterprise," *Bergen County* [New Jersey] *Record*, Aug. 7, 2003, p. L9.
A new national survey reveals an increase in Latino-owned small businesses in the United States.

Brownstein, Ronald, "Latinos Stir Tension in New Brand of Urban Politics," *Los Angeles Times*, Nov. 26, 2001, p. A11.
Political tensions are brewing between Latinos and African-Americans in Houston, New York, Los Angeles and other cities.

Cohn, D'Vera, "Hispanics Declared Largest Minority; Blacks Overtaken in Census Update," *The Washington Post*, June 19, 2003, p. A1.
Recent Census Bureau data show Hispanics have out-paced African-Americans to become the nation's largest minority — a milestone in U.S. history.

Giroux, Gregory L., "Pursuing the Political Prize of America's Hispanic Vote," *CQ Weekly*, June 29, 2002, p. 1710.
Both major political parties are waking up to the political potential of the Latino community.

Herman, Eric, "Latinos Set Pace Among New Homeowners," *Daily News*, March 31, 2003, p. 58.
A comprehensive look at trends and patterns in Latino homeownership and what they mean for Hispanics and the nation.

Kotkin, Joel, and Thomas Tseng, "Happy to Mix it All Up; For Young America, Old Ethnic Labels No Longer Apply," *The Washington Post*, June 8, 2003, p. B1.

Two futurists argue that the large influx of Latinos will help create a "post-ethnic America," where ethnicity and race are no longer societal dividing lines.

Lefever, Earnest W., "Confronting 'Unmeltable Ethnics'; Check Immigration, End Bilingual Ed and Make English the Official Language," *Los Angeles Times*, May 20, 2003, p. B15.
A senior fellow at the conservative Ethics and Public Policy Center suggests overhauling U.S. policy toward Latino immigrants.

Nather, David, "Issues on Watch List for Growing Voter Bloc," *CQ Weekly*, June 29, 2002, p. 1718.
Congress is not addressing the issues near and dear to Hispanics' hearts, according to Latino leaders.

Nather, David, "Latinos Wait for the Action," *CQ Weekly*, June 29, 2002, p. 1716.
As the two major political parties court them, Hispanics are still waiting for congressional action to match the rhetoric.

Ochoa, Alberto M., "Succeeding in America; Latino Immigrants Are Finding a New World and More Challenges in Assimilating than Immigrants of a Century Ago," *The San Diego Union Tribune*, July 20, 2003, p. G1.
A professor of policy studies at San Diego State University argues that Latinos face challenges that did not exist for past immigrant groups from Europe.

"Our Kinda Ciudad," *The Economist*, Jan. 11, 2003.
Hispanics have been migrating recently to the Midwest, an area not traditionally associated with large Latino populations.

Shepard, Scott, "Democrats, GOP Court Latino Vote; Hispanics Set to Flex Political Clout in Next Election," *Austin-American Statesman*, July 13, 2003, p. A1.
Latinos are poised to become a potent force in next year's elections, both in choosing the Democratic presidential nominee and possibly the president.

Simon, Stephanie, "Latinos Take Root in Midwest," *Los Angeles Times*, Oct. 24, 2004, p. A1.
An examination of some the challenges faced by Latino immigrants in the Midwest.

Reports

"New Lows From New Highs: Latino Economic Losses in the Current Recession," The Pew Hispanic Center, Jan. 24, 2002.
The center has compiled an economic snapshot of the nation's Hispanics during the height of the recession more than a year ago.

"2002 National Survey of Latinos," Pew Hispanic Center and The Henry J. Kaiser Family Foundation, December 2002.
The survey measured Hispanic attitudes on issues ranging from discrimination and religion to living in the United States.

For More Information

Center for Immigration Studies, 1522 K St., N.W., Suite 820, Washington, DC 20005; (202) 466-8185; www.cis.org. Supports a reduction in legal immigration.

League of United Latin American Citizens, 2000 L St., N.W., Suite 610, Washington, DC 20036; (202) 833-6130; www.lulac.org. Advocates political, economic and educational rights for Hispanics.

Mexican American Legal Defense and Educational Fund, 1717 K St., N.W., Suite 311, Washington, DC 20036; (202) 293-2828; www.maldef.org. Maldef aids Latinos in areas ranging from voting rights to immigration.

National Council of La Raza, 1126 16th St., N.W., Washington, DC 20036; (202) 785-1670; www.nclr.org. Studies issues of importance to Latinos.

Pew Hispanic Center, 1615 L St., N.W., Suite 700, Washington, DC 20036; (202) 419-3600; www.pewhispanic.org. Studies Latino social and economic issues.

U.S. English, 1747 Pennsylvania Ave., N.W., Suite 1050, Washington, DC 20006; (202) 833-0100; www.us-english.org. Supports "English-only" policies.

11

Gang Crisis

William Triplett

A wall mural in East Los Angeles marks the 18th Street gang's turf. At least 21,500 gangs are active nationwide, in small communities as well as cities. Recent immigration has energized violent Latino and Asian gangs like Mara Salvatrucha and the Oriental Playboys.

In June 2001, Fredy Reyes-Castillo met four fellow Latino immigrants at a gas station in Reston, an affluent Northern Virginia suburb. With its upscale malls and subdivisions, it's what drug dealers call a "green area" — full of kids with money.

The four were members of Mara Salvatrucha, or MS-13, a nationwide Latino street gang infamous for its drug dealing and violence. Reyes-Castillo, 22, was not a member, but that day he pretended to be. When the real gangsters realized he didn't understand MS-13 slang or sport gang tattoos, they beat him to death so brutally it took weeks to identify his body. [1]

Three months later, in nearby Alexandria, MS-13 members walked into a McDonald's and spotted an acquaintance, Joaquim Diaz, 19. Diaz was not an MS-13 member and didn't pretend to be.

However, one of the gang members, Denis Rivera, suspected Diaz had joined a rival gang. Rivera and another gang member convinced Diaz to accompany them to Washington to buy marijuana. But Diaz soon found himself in a remote area where he was slashed, stabbed, run over and then mutilated.

Rivera's girlfriend, Brenda Paz, later told police Rivera had bragged that he had tried to behead Diaz, comparing it to "preparing a chicken." But his knife had been too dull, so he had cut out Diaz's larynx instead. Paz entered the federal Witness Protection Program but left before Rivera went on trial. Weeks later her pregnant body was found on the banks of the Shenandoah River, stabbed to death. Police believe MS-13 was responsible. [2]

Newspapers across the country report scores of similar crimes in places like Reston that, until now, have not known gang violence. Even Utah, which historically has enjoyed a relatively low crime

From *CQ Researcher*, May 14, 2004.

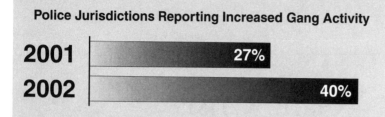

Gang Activity Jumped 50 Percent in 2002

Forty percent of police agencies reported an increase in local gang activity in 2002, a 50 percent rise over 2001, according to a research agency funded by the Department of Justice. Nationwide, there were some 21,500 gangs and 731,000 gang members in 2002.

Police Jurisdictions Reporting Increased Gang Activity

2001	27%
2002	40%

Source: National Youth Gang Center

rate, has at least 250 gangs with 3,000 members operating in the Salt Lake City region alone. [3]

Gang experts say the U.S. gang problem, which had diminished in the 1990s, has worsened dramatically in recent years. In 2001, for instance, 27 percent of police agencies polled by the National Youth Gang Center (NYGC), a research agency funded by the Department of Justice (DOJ), said gang activity was increasing in their jurisdictions. In 2002, however, the figure had jumped to more than 40 percent, with at least 21,500 gangs — and more than 731,000 members — active nationwide. [4] In addition to MS-13, the major groups include the Bloods, Crips, Black Gangster Disciples Nation, Almighty Latin Kings Nation and various so-called Jamaican posses, as well as outlaw motorcycle gangs and prison gangs.

Perhaps most alarmingly, the National Alliance of Gang Investigators Associations (NAGIA) says gangs have morphed from an urban scourge into a nationwide threat. "Gang membership has crossed all socioeconomic, ethnic and racial boundaries and now permeates American society," said an NAGIA report. "The gang problem today is much more pervasive and menacing than at any [other] time in history." [5]

Wesley McBride, president of the California Gang Investigators Association, told a Senate Judiciary Committee hearing on gang violence in September 2003 that while gang activity may wane periodically, it usually roars back at record levels. "While there have been occasional declines in gang activity over the years," McBride said, "the declines never seem to establish a record low [and]

the climactic rise at the end of the decline almost always sets a record." [7]

Moreover, authorities say, today's gangs are surprisingly well organized. The organizational chart of Chicago's 7,000-member Gangster Disciples — recovered during execution of a search warrant — was described by a federal prosecutor as "more sophisticated than many corporations." More than half the size of the Chicago Police Department, the gang had formed a political action committee, bought legitimate businesses and even sponsored community events, the prosecutor said. [9]

In the wake of the Sept. 11, 2001, terrorist attacks on the United States, gangs have even drawn the attention of the State Department and the Department of Homeland Security. Having already diversified from drug dealing into auto theft, extortion, property crimes and home invasion, some East Coast gangs have begun trafficking in fraudulent identification papers that could be used by terrorists trying to enter the country illegally.

While experts agree gangs are a serious problem, few agree on the causes or remedies. Even the definition of a gang is controversial. Some law enforcement officials say a youth gang is three or more 14-to-24-year-olds associating mainly, if not exclusively, to commit crimes. Others, like David Rathbun, a juvenile probation official in Fairfax County, Va., have simpler criteria for identifying gangs: "If it walks like a duck and quacks like a duck, it's probably a duck."

Because different authorities define gangs differently, national figures on gang activity and membership are often only "informed estimates," says NYGC Executive Director John Moore. But according to his organization's "fairly reliable" estimates, he says, 49 percent of U.S. gang members are Latino, 34 percent are black, 10 percent are white and 6 percent are Asian. While Latino and Asian gangs tend to be the most violent, white gangs have expanded into the most new territory over the last decade. [10]

Gangs also commit a disproportionate amount of urban violence. In Rochester, N.Y., for example, gang members who participated in a survey represented only 30 percent of the violent offenders in the region but committed 68 percent of the violent offenses. In Denver, gang members were only 14 percent of those surveyed but admitted to 79 percent of all violent, adolescent offenses committed in the city. [11] In fact, Moore says, 35 percent of Denver's homicides are gang-related.

Many gang victims are potential witnesses, police say. When not killing witnesses, gangs routinely intimidate them, usually through assault or rape. The U.S. attorney in New Orleans recently told Congress that witness intimidation had increased 50 percent in the previous year. [12] "Gangs have even been known to kill police officers who serve as witnesses against them," McBride said. [13]

Yet, the statistics can be tricky. For instance, the data show that overall gang membership and activity in smaller communities have decreased somewhat, but remain as high as ever — if not higher — in large cities and surrounding suburbs, Moore says. "They have decreased in smaller areas, but that's not where their strength ever was," he says.

Most Gang Members Are Latino, Black

Nearly half of all U.S. gang members are Latino, and more than a third are black, according to a research agency funded by the Department of Justice. White gangs reportedly have expanded into the most new territory over the last decade, while Asian gangs have moved into the Northeast, and Latino, black and Asian gangs have migrated into the South.

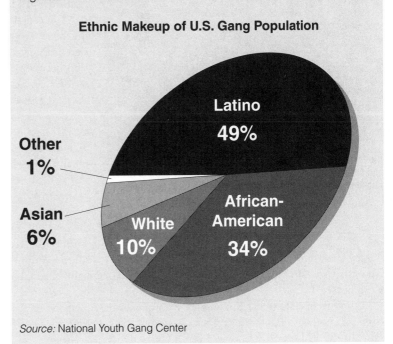

Ethnic Makeup of U.S. Gang Population

Latino 49%, African-American 34%, White 10%, Asian 6%, Other 1%

Source: National Youth Gang Center

As law enforcement officials and policymakers try to assess America's gang problem, here are some of the questions under debate:

Is government doing enough to combat the problem?

Traditionally, state and local authorities have dealt with gangs, since they were not considered a federal problem. In addition to law enforcement, policymakers have tried a variety of prevention programs, such as midnight basketball, designed to give adolescents socially acceptable alternative activities. Other programs, such as vocational training, have offered at-risk youth the promise of legitimate jobs, since unemployment is a major reason kids join gangs.

As gangs migrated — or "franchised" themselves, as some officials describe it — from Los Angeles and other major cities, many police departments set up special gang units. Authorities felt they were keeping pace with the

problem until gangs began increasing in the late 1980s and early '90s, when insufficient resources prevented police from keeping up. Since then, state and local authorities say they haven't been able to keep up with the increase. If the federal government would provide more resources, local law enforcement authorities say they could do more.

Several federal agencies assist in the fight against gangs. Since gang crime often involves guns, the Bureau of Alcohol, Tobacco, Firearms and Explosives (BATFE) investigates gangs. Similarly, gangs' frequent involvement with illegal drugs draws attention from the Drug Enforcement Administration (DEA).

Perhaps foremost among federal anti-gang agencies are the 75 FBI Safe Streets Gang Task Forces (SSGTFs) operating around the country. The SSGTFs emphasize "identification of the major violent street gangs [and] drug enterprises [that] pose significant threats," Grant D.

California Gang Investigators Association

Bloods gang members from Los Angeles display their gang signs and colors. Gang members generally don't wear their colors in public nowadays to avoid trouble from police or rival gangs.

Gang Resistance Education and Training (GREAT) program, which tries to develop positive relationships among local law enforcement, families and at-risk youths.

But McBride says federal law enforcement efforts have been ineffective because they have not been properly coordinated with state and local efforts. For instance, he says Los Angeles law enforcement agencies "hardly ever hear from" the FBI task force on gangs based in Los Angeles.

"You can almost compare [the situation] to the 9/11 hearings," says McBride, referring to the recent commission hearings that revealed a crucial lack of communication between various intelligence agencies before the terrorist attacks. "That's much like what's happening in the gang world."

Riley responds that the SSGTF in Los Angeles is located near the heart of the Watts section and focuses on inner-city gang activity, rather than on the more suburban activity McBride has been battling.

Fairfax County's Rathbun says the FBI task force in Northern Virginia, as well as U.S. immigration officials, works well with local officials, but he acknowledges that the level of cooperation varies from region to region.

But McBride, who recently retired from the Los Angeles County Sheriff's Department after 28 years of fighting gangs, contends that federal prosecution has not been effective. "You'd think they're prosecuting gang members right and left," says McBride, referring to the testimony at last September's Senate Judiciary Committee hearing. "I can tell you that U.S. attorneys don't want to see a gang case. They're very hard to prosecute, very labor-intensive and in their [U.S. attorneys'] defense, they simply can't handle all the cases — we probably arrest 40,000 gang members a year just in L.A. But don't say the feds are doing a great job of prosecuting gang members."

Many state and local authorities say they are best equipped to prosecute gangs, if the federal government would provide the necessary funding. Robert McCulloch, prosecuting attorney of St. Louis County, Mo., and president of the National District Attorneys Association, says 180 gangs with about 4,000 members are fighting a violent turf war in St. Louis. But he says most cases will never be prosecuted because he can't offer witness protection.

"Prosecutors across the county believe witness intimidation is the single, biggest hurdle facing successful gang prosecution," he said. In Denver, a defendant allegedly ordered a sexual assault on a female witness scheduled to testify in a gang homicide. In Savannah, a gang murder

Ashley, assistant director of the FBI's Criminal Investigative Division, told the Senate Judiciary Committee. [14]

"SSGTFs operate under the premise of cooperation between local, state and federal agencies," says Jeff Riley, chief of the FBI's Safe Streets and Gang Unit. "Once established, the SSGTFs are charged with bringing the resources of all the participating agencies to bear on the area's gang problem. This includes using sensitive investigative techniques, with an emphasis on long-term, proactive investigations into the violent criminal activities of the gang's leadership and hierarchy."

Moreover, when appropriate, U.S. attorneys "actively and creatively" prosecute gang crimes in federal courts, according to three U.S. attorneys who testified last September before the Judiciary Committee. In addition to using traditional narcotics and firearms statutes, federal prosecutors are using the Racketeer Influenced and Corrupt Organizations (RICO) law — successfully used to weaken the Mafia — against gangs. The U.S. attorney in Southern California recently convicted 75 members of the 18th Street and Mexican Mafia gangs under the RICO law. [15]

The DOJ also administers the Office of Juvenile Justice and Delinquency Prevention (OJJDP) and the

occurred in front of 300 people, but no one would identify the assailant. [16]

Most state and local jurisdictions cannot afford witness-protection programs or the training and overtime needed for gang investigations. The state budget crisis and tax cuts have sapped local funds, and the war on terrorism has forced the redeployment of anti-gang units. [17]

"There are already plenty of laws to prosecute gangs," says Beryl Howell, a former legislative director for Sen. Patrick J. Leahy, D-Vt., who worked on anti-juvenile-crime legislation in the mid-1990s. The obstacles to pursuing gangs effectively, she says, are "resource issues, not legal issues."

Sens. Orrin G. Hatch, R-Utah, and Dianne Feinstein, D-Calif., hope to remedy that with the Gang Prevention and Effective Deterrence Act of 2003. The bill would authorize approximately $100 million in federal funds annually for five years to underwrite area law enforcement efforts in jurisdictions with "high-intensity interstate gang activity." Another $40 million a year would fund prevention programs.

The Hatch-Feinstein bill would do more than provide desperately needed funds, says Bill Johnson, executive director of the National Association of Police Organizations and a former Florida prosecutor. It would also make participation in a "criminal street gang" and recruiting people to commit "gang crimes" federal offenses, punishable by 10 to 30 years in prison.

"It won't be the only solution, by any stretch of the imagination," he continues. "But if used properly, it'll help crush some of these gangs that really do overrun neighborhoods and communities."

But others are concerned that the bill would expand the federal role in fighting gangs, and in the process hamper local prosecutions. For instance, by redefining some state offenses as federal crimes, the bill could curtail state prosecutors' discretion in bringing charges and

Is There a Gang in Your 'Hood?

The following quiz can help neighborhoods measure potential gang activity. A score of 50 points or more indicates the need for a gang-prevention and intervention program:

In your community:

- Is there graffiti? (5 points)
- Is the graffiti crossed out? (10)
- Do the young people wear colors, jewelry, clothing, flash hand signs or display other behaviors that may be gang related? (10)
- Are drugs available? (10)
- Has there been a significant increase in the number of physical confrontations? (5)
- Is there an increasing presence of weapons? (5)
- Are beepers, pagers or cell phones used by the young people? (10)
- Has there been a "drive-by" shooting? (15)
- Have you had a "show-by" display of weapons? (10)
- Are truancies and/or daytime burglaries increasing? (5)
- Have racial incidents increased? (5)
- Is there a history of local gangs? (10)
- Is there an increasing presence of "informal social groups" with unusual names containing words like: kings, disciples, queens, posse, crew? (15)

Scoring Key

0-20 points = No Problem	50-65 points = You Have Problems
25-45 points = Emerging Problems	70+ points = You Have Serious Problems

Source: Tennessee Gang Investigators Association

negotiating plea agreements, because defendants would be facing federal as well as state prosecution for gang crimes.

"We should be wary of making a federal crime out of everything," said Sen. Leahy. [18]

But Feinstein argues: "It used to be that gangs were local problems, demanding local, law-enforcement-based solutions. But over the last 12 years, I have seen the problem go from small to large and from neighborhood-based to national in scope. What were once loosely organized groups . . . are now complex criminal organizations whose activities include weapons trafficking, gambling, smuggling, robbery, and, of course, homicide. This is why we need a strong federal response."

The Violence of Mara Salvatrucha

David Rathbun has seen a lot of youngsters come through the juvenile justice system in Fairfax County, Va., near Washington, D.C. But he can't shake the memory of the 11-year-old charged with murder.

The boy and his 16-year-old brother belonged to Mara Salvatrucha, a Latino gang known for its violence. The two boys were out early one morning, "looking for trouble," says Rathbun, a juvenile-probation official. When they thought a youth across the street flashed a rival gang's sign at them — a gesture of disrespect — they crossed the street and stabbed him to death.

Violence is a gang's normal stock-in-trade, but gang experts say Mara Salvatrucha — or MS-13 — has made shootings, stabbings, hackings, beatings and rapes its brazen specialties. The gang originated in Los Angeles among refugees of El Salvador's civil war of the 1980s and rapidly spread around the country. The gang was formed in Los Angeles to protect Salvadoran immigrants from other, hostile Latino immigrants, according to veteran gang investigator Wesley McBride. The theory was: strike back twice as violently as you were attacked, and they'll leave you alone. Many MS-13s had been guerrilla fighters in El Salvador's bloody civil war.

MS-13 began as a merger between immigrants who'd been involved with La Mara — a street gang in El Salvador — and former members of the FMNL, a paramilitary group of Salvadoran guerrilla fighters called "Salvatruchas."

MS-13's victims have included innocent people caught in the middle as well as other gang members. In 2002, MS-13's Los Angeles cell reportedly dispatched several members to Fairfax County with instructions to kill a county police officer "at random." They didn't succeed. [1]

The Justice Department says MS-13 now has about 8,000 members in 27 states and the District of Columbia, and 20,000 more members in Central and South America, particularly El Salvador. The gang is involved in smuggling and selling illegal drugs, but different cells (or cliques, as they're sometimes called) may be involved in other activities, including providing "protection" to houses of prostitution, Rathbun says.

The independent National Gang Crime Research Center (NGCRC) ranks gangs by their violence level, with 1 being least dangerous and 3 the most dangerous. MS-13 is ranked a 3. Center Director George W. Knox describes MS-13's level of violence as "extraordinary." [2]

An investigator with the Orange County, Calif., district attorney's office says the gang participates in a broad range of criminal activities across the country. "MS members have been involved in burglaries, auto thefts, narcotic sales, home-invasion robberies, weapons smuggling, car jacking, extortion, murder, rape, witness intimidation, illegal firearm sales, car theft and aggravated assaults. . . . [C]ommon drugs sold by MS members include cocaine, marijuana, heroin, and methamphetamine. Mara Salvatrucha

Others are concerned about the historic conflicts between federal and state/local investigations and prosecutions. While SSGTFs are designed to work cooperatively with local authorities, differences remain in their investigative priorities. For instance, federal investigators' concentration on building cases over time will usually net more convictions, but local authorities often need to respond more quickly to community complaints, usually with street sweeps that can interfere with federal investigations.

Should gun laws be tightened to combat gang violence?

More than 350,000 incidents of gun violence, including 9,369 homicides, were committed in 2002, according to Michael Rand, chief of victimization statistics at the Justice

Department's Bureau of Justice Statistics. But no one knows what percentage of those murders were committed by gang members, partly because of disagreement over what constitutes gang-related crime. To some officials, if two gang members commit an armed robbery, the crime can only be considered gang-related if they share the proceeds with the rest of the gang. To others, any armed robbery committed by gang members qualifies as gang-related.

According to the BATFE, 41 percent of the 88,570 guns used in crimes in 46 large cities in 2000 were traced to people age 24 or younger. [19] Of course, no one knows how many of them were gang members.

But as a recent Justice Department survey concluded: "Although both gang members and at-risk youths admitted

gang members have even placed a 'tax' on prostitutes and non-gang member drug dealers who are working in MS 'turf.' Failure to pay up will most likely result in violence." [3]

One of the gang's signatures is a military-style booby trap used to protect a stash of illegal drugs. The trap usually consists of a tripwire rigged to an anti-personnel grenade.

Joining the gang requires potential members to be "jumped in." Several gangs observe this ritual, which involves a group-administered beating. Typically, gang members surround the candidate and then attack him; other gang members evaluate how well he defends himself and his ability to endure punches. MS-13's jumping-in lasts for 13 seconds.

Most MS-13 members are between ages 11 and 40, but leaving the gang is often difficult. The father of the two

AFP Photo

Police arrested this Mara Salvatrucha leader last year in San Salvador, El Salvador. Thousands of the gang's most violent U.S. members have been deported.

boys who stabbed the suspected rival gang member to death is also an MS-13 member; the mother wholeheartedly supports her husband's and sons' memberships, Rathbun says.

The 16-year-old was tried as an adult and sentenced to a maximum-security prison, but Rathbun has hope for the 11-year-old, who took school classes when he was in the county's juvenile system. "He had a probation officer that worked very closely with him, and his sense of self-worth increased as he did better academically. He stayed in touch with the gang, but he wasn't participating any more. I don't think his father will ever be out of MS-13, but, knock wood, I think we may have changed the son's course."

---

[1] "Focus on Gangs: Salvadoran MS-13 Rated Among Most Violent," *Emergency Net News*, Aug. 24, 2002; http://www.emergency.com/polcpage.htm.

[2] *Ibid.*

[3] Al Valdez, "A South American Import," National Alliance of Gang Investigators Associations, 2000; http://www.nagia.org/mara_salvatrucha.htm.

significant involvement with guns, gang members were far likelier to own guns, and the guns they owned were larger caliber." More than 80 percent of gang members surveyed said either they or their fellow members had carried concealed guns into school, while only one-third of at-risk youths said they or their friends had done the same. [20] The most popular weapons were 9mm semiautomatic pistols. [21]

"Gangs, like any criminals, can never be as effective without firearms," says Joe Vince, a retired BATFE analyst. "Absolutely, guns are a tool of the trade for gangs — you've never heard of a drive-by with a knife."

Vince regularly investigated gangs' gun-show purchases, where unlicensed firearms dealers are exempt from the Brady Handgun Violence Prevention Act, which requires licensed sellers to perform a criminal background check before selling a weapon. Since it is illegal for anyone to sell a firearm to a buyer with a criminal record, gangs often send buyers who don't have criminal records to gun shows. [22]

Such "straw purchases" are also illegal, but unscrupulous unlicensed dealers pretend not to recognize a suspicious purchase, even when an 18-year-old is trying to buy a dozen guns at once, Vince says. "We found a lot of gangs sending someone who didn't have a record to gun shows, and he'd be on a cell phone talking to the gang leaders and saying, 'Hey, this guy's offering this, and that guy's offering that,' " Vince says.

"Some dealers even advertise that they're not licensed, so you can buy from them no-questions-asked," says Garen Wintemute, director of the Violence Prevention Research Program at the University of California, Davis.

In Chicago — which now may have the nation's largest and most active gang population — gangs are blamed for 45 percent of last year's 598 homicides. [23] Authorities also believe Chicago has more illegal firearms than any other city: In 2003, Chicago police seized more than 10,000 illegal guns; Los Angeles police recovered just under 7,000 and New York City under 4,000. [24]

Gun control advocates maintain that tougher gun laws and more stringent enforcement of them could cut gang violence. "Wherever you can reduce the availability and accessibility of firearms to criminals, you reduce violent crime," Vince says. "People just cannot be as violent without a gun."

However, Erich Pratt, communications director for Gun Owners of America (GOA), says, "We've yet to discover any gun control legislation that successfully keeps guns out of the wrong hands. Washington, D.C., is certainly the epitome of that — you have a draconian gun ban there that doesn't let anybody own any guns, and yet the bad guys continue to get firearms."

Data compiled by the Bureau of Justice Statistics show that handgun homicides started decreasing in 1993 — a year before Congress enacted the Brady law — and continued to fall through 2000.

But a study in the *Journal of the American Medical Association* suggests no link between the decrease and the Brady law. "We find no differences in homicide or firearms homicide rates in the 32 . . . states directly subject to the Brady Act provisions compared with the remaining [18] states," the researchers wrote. [25]

Wintemute says the results could be interpreted in two equally valid ways: "One is that the Brady law never went far enough from the beginning," he says, "or that the Brady law is a failure and we should get rid of it."

Supporters of the law say that at the least it has prevented the crime rate from worsening. But Andrew Arulanandam, public affairs director for the National Rifle Association (NRA), says the law's stringent record-keeping provisions make that unlikely.

"You mean to tell me that some guy who's going to commit a heinous crime is going to leave a paper trail?" Arulanandam asks. Gang members are "not going to be deterred by a firearm law. More often than not, they'll obtain the firearm by illegal means."

But record-keeping is diminishing. Because of a provision in the Omnibus Appropriations bill, passed last January, federal authorities who run criminal background checks on gun buyers are no longer required to keep a record of the check for 90 days. In fact, they must now destroy the record within 24 hours.

Moreover, Eric Howard, spokesman for the Brady Campaign to Prevent Gun Violence, says the Department of Justice recently found that Brady background checks blocked more than a million potential purchasers from buying guns. "This flies in the face of what [the NRA] says all the time: That these guys aren't going to get background checks, they'll get guns elsewhere," Howard says. "Well, these guys aren't the sharpest knives in the drawer." The Brady law could very well have kept the nation's crime rate lower than it might otherwise have been in the past decade, Howard argues. [26]

Nonetheless, some states enforce the Brady law less stringently, so gangs go to those states. For instance, gangs in Chicago have established a gun-running pipeline into Mississippi, where Brady enforcement and local gun laws are generally more relaxed. [27]

Opponents of gun control say this proves their point: Regardless of how many prohibited purchases are blocked, criminals will always find a way to get firearms. The best deterrent, they say, is not to limit the number of guns on the street but to increase them — by allowing law-abiding citizens to carry concealed weapons. "States that have adopted concealed-carry legislation are seeing the greatest and most dramatic decreases in the murder rate," Pratt says.

The gun problem is like the drug problem, says the NRA's Arulanandam. "Drugs are outlawed, but people get their hands on them."

The BATFE's Vince agrees with the comparison, but he and other gun control advocates want to close the gun-show loophole, which the gun lobby says would penalize law-abiding, unlicensed dealers.

"If you focus law enforcement only on gun users but not on dealers," he says, "that's like saying we're going to go after everyone that shoots heroin but not the cartel."

Should more minors be tried as adults for gang crimes?

An undercover Chicago police officer working a drug deal in the depressed Humboldt Park neighborhood in April noticed two young men run into an alley. Seconds later, he heard gunshots and saw the men running out. A third man lay dying in the alley.

As the cop chased the suspects, they turned and fired at him. He continued chasing them and eventually caught them. One was 18, the other 15. Both were members of the Maniac Latin Disciples. "I wanted to shoot a Cobra" — a rival gang — "to prove how tough I was," the 15-year-old reportedly said. He was charged as an adult with first-degree murder. [28]

In colonial days, children sometimes faced adult charges and just as often were incarcerated with adults; sometimes they were executed. [29] In the late 19th century, however, social reformers argued that juveniles were developmentally different from adults and could be rehabilitated. The nation established a juvenile justice system — with separate statutes and penalties — at the beginning of the 20th century.

But in cases involving violent crimes, prosecutors sometimes try minors as adults, triggering debate over the tactic's effectiveness and justification. A surge in juvenile crime beginning in the late 1980s — largely triggered by a crack epidemic — led many minors to be charged as adults. A 1989 Supreme Court ruling allowing states to execute juvenile offenders 16 and older has kept the debate alive.

Currently, state prosecutors decide whether minors charged with violent felonies should be charged as adults. But the proposed Hatch-Feinstein bill would allow federal prosecutors to try any gang member 16 or older as an adult.

The legislation has triggered debates over whether more minors should be tried as adults, and whether the federal government should be trying minors at all. "We're always uncomfortable when furthering policies that take things that should be state matters and throw them into federal courts," the GOA's Pratt says. "We agree that if you do an adult crime, you do the adult time, but we think the states [should] handle it."

"The feds don't have any infrastructure set up to deal with juveniles, so they usually defer to the states, and wisely so," says Rathbun of Fairfax County. "We've had a couple of murder cases where the feds got involved, and it was useful because [the accused] got harsher sentences. But that's just a handful of our cases."

However, former legislative director Howell believes that federal authorities can more effectively prosecute gangs than state or local authorities. "The gang problem warrants federal attention because it quickly overtakes local and state boundaries," she says. "It can overtake national boundaries, too."

For example, as a federal prosecutor Howell once went after members of the Flying Dragons, which ran gambling and Mah Jong parlors in New York's Chinatown. But the gang also smuggled heroin from Hong Kong. The investigation had to contend with the respective requirements and laws affecting New York and Hong Kong authorities, not to mention language and cultural complications between both cities.

But prosecuting juveniles as adults won't solve the gang problem, she says. "Where does that get you?" she asks. "The younger you send kids to prison, the better-educated they become at being criminals. Adult prisons have lost much pretense, if they ever had any, of being rehabilitative. With the juvenile system, there's at least a pretense of rehabilitation."

Federal prosecution of minors as adults would be "a good law to have on the books and threaten with, but it's not going to help much," adds McBride, of the California Gang Investigators Association. States have tougher provisions on minors and gangs than federal agencies, he notes, and states aren't making any demonstrable headway against gangs by prosecuting minors as adults.

Trying minors as adults "is an effective tool the same way a sledge hammer is an effective tool," says the National Association of Police Organizations' Johnson. "It ought to be used sparingly, but in those cases where it's necessary, then it ought to be used."

More than 60 child-advocacy organizations oppose the Senate bill's provision to prosecute juveniles as adults for gang crimes. "I understand the desire to respond to gang violence," said Marc Schindler, a staff attorney for the Youth Law Center. "But this is the wrong way to do it. It's basically going to throw kids away to the adult system." [30]

Even law-and-order hard-liners acknowledge that the threat of severe punishment alone will not deter gangs. "A lot of gang members are in gangs because their parents didn't give a rat's behind about them," says McBride, echoing experts on all sides of the issue. "How do you make a momma care for her kid? You can't legislate that."

The best deterrent to gangs, many experts say, is to have parents involved with their children's lives, but in today's economy, that's often nearly impossible. Some observers attribute the rise in immigrant gangs to the fact that both parents often work multiple jobs and have little time to spend with their kids.

CHRONOLOGY

1950s *Southern blacks migrate to Northern inner cities; classic era of teen street gangs; wave of Puerto Rican immigrants arrives in New York City.*

Sept. 26, 1957 Leonard Bernstein's hit musical "West Side Story" opens on Broadway. It looks unflinchingly at the growing menace of gang warfare.

1960s *Gangs take on traits from civil rights, Black Muslim and radical youth movements; government channels some gangs into anti-poverty work.*

1961 President John F. Kennedy signs Juvenile Delinquency and Youth Offenses and Control Act, creating a federal committee to address youth crime.

1967 President's Task Force on Juvenile Delinquency calls for community efforts to curb youth crime. . . . Senate probes fraud in federal grant program for Chicago's Blackstone Rangers gang.

1970s *Police officials and academics shift their strategies on gangs from social work to suppression and control.*

Aug. 21, 1974 Congress creates Office of Juvenile Justice and Delinquency Prevention.

1975 Justice Department launches first national gang survey.

1980s *Latino and Asian immigrants make Los Angeles the nation's gang capital; crack cocaine arrives in inner cities; Reagan administration declares war on drugs.*

1982 FBI designates motorcycle gangs as national investigative priority within its organized-crime program.

1985 California creates State Task Force on Youth Gang Violence; L.A. Police Chief Daryl F. Gates vows to eliminate gangs in five years.

Late 1980s Highly profitable crack cocaine becomes the product of choice for drug-dealing gangs, sparking fights over the most profitable turf and a spike in violent crime.

1988 President Ronald Reagan signs Anti-Drug Abuse Act. . . . California convenes State Task Force on Gangs and Drugs; Los Angeles police crack down on gang neighborhoods.

May 15, 1989 Administration of first President George Bush bans imports of semiautomatic assault weapons used by street gangs.

1990s *Gangs expand out from inner cities; government, police and academics coordinate comprehensive approach to the gang problem.*

1995 Gang homicides in Los Angeles hit a record 809 deaths . . . more than half of all violent crime in Buffalo, N.Y., is gang related.

1997 FBI estimates that 50,000 gang members are active in Chicago. . . . Congress attempts to overhaul the U.S. juvenile justice system, but the bill deadlocks over juvenile sentencing and gun control.

1999 Congress again addresses juvenile justice, but House and Senate negotiators again stall over gun control.

2000s *Police say gang violence begins to rise; Asian and Latino gangs account for most juvenile violence; Congress again attempts to pass anti-gang legislation.*

Sept. 11, 2001 Terrorist strikes against the U.S. cause many police departments to reassign special gang units to counter-terrorist duties.

Jan. 2004 Congress passes Omnibus Appropriations bill, which contains a provision voiding the Brady law's requirement that the National Instant Criminal Background Check system maintain records of criminal checks for 90 days; gun control advocates claim this will make it harder for authorities to trace crime guns to gang members and other criminals.

April 2004 Senate Judiciary Committee begins consideration of the Gang Prevention and Effective Deterrence Act, sponsored by Sens. Dianne Feinstein, D-Calif., and Orrin Hatch, R-Utah. Committee approval is expected in May.

Whatever the causes, the rise in gang crime has made some authorities open to anything that might help. Los Angeles County's sheriff recently estimated that the 96,000 gang members in his jurisdiction commit half the violent offenses each year. "We believe there are teenagers close to 18 who are committing heinous adult acts, and they should be treated as an adult," said Steve Whitmore, a spokesman for the L.A. sheriff's office. [31]

BACKGROUND

Early Gangs

The youth gang phenomenon dates back at least to the days of St. Augustine (A.D. 354-430), who wrote in his *Confessions* of the pleasures of stealing pears with adolescent accomplices: "My pleasure was not in those pears, it was in the offense itself, which the company of fellow sinners occasioned." [32]

In 17th-century London, youth gangs with such names as the Mims, the Bugles and the Dead Boys terrorized the citizenry by breaking windows, destroying taverns and fighting, each group wearing different-colored ribbons. And Charles Dickens often wrote about gangs in the 19th century, perhaps most famously the gang of boy orphans run by the money-grubbing Fagin in the classic *Oliver Twist*.

In the United States, the first recorded youth gang was the Forty Thieves, founded in about 1825 in Lower Manhattan. Others appeared in Philadelphia in the 1840s, such as the Bouncers, the Rats and the Skinners. Mostly they defaced walls with graffiti and carried pistols and knives.

Immigrants usually formed gangs for self-protection. Often not speaking the language of their new country and unfamiliar with its customs, they found assimilation extremely difficult. Discrimination added a sense of victimization to their existing feelings of alienation, and they saw gangs as a refuge from a hostile environment.

Waves of Irish immigrants in New York in the 19th century soon begat such gangs as the Bowery Boys and the Dead Rabbits, who waged three-day rumbles that

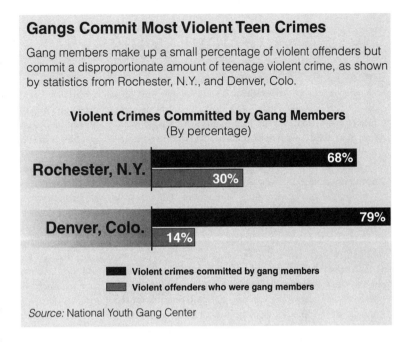

Gangs Commit Most Violent Teen Crimes

Gang members make up a small percentage of violent offenders but commit a disproportionate amount of teenage violent crime, as shown by statistics from Rochester, N.Y., and Denver, Colo.

Violent Crimes Committed by Gang Members
(By percentage)

Rochester, N.Y. — 68% / 30%

Denver, Colo. — 79% / 14%

▇ Violent crimes committed by gang members
▇ Violent offenders who were gang members

Source: National Youth Gang Center

forced helpless police to call in the Army. Their nonchalance toward violence was remarkable: A member of the Plug Uglies is said to have attacked a stranger and cracked his spine in three places just to win a $2 bet. [33] Female gang members also were known in the mid-19th century, among them the celebrated street fighters Hellcat Annie and Battle Annie. [34]

Early New York gangs, as brutally portrayed in the 2002 movie "Gangs of New York," often sold their services to labor unions and company operators maneuvering in the rough and tumble world of politics. "By 1855," a city historian wrote, "it was estimated that the Metropolis contained at least 30,000 men who owed allegiance to gang leaders and through them to the leaders of Tammany Hall and the Know Nothing, or Native American Party." [35] During the Civil War, Irish gang members were blamed for the anti-conscription riots in which many blacks were lynched.

The German and Italian immigrants who arrived in the late 19th century produced equally violent gangs. Some would commit crimes for hire: A slash on the cheek with a knife cost $10; throwing a bomb, $50; murder, $100. "It might be inferred that the New York tough is a very fierce individual [but] it is only when he hunts with the pack that he is dangerous," noted social reformer and photographer Jacob Riis. [36]

When Girls Join Gangs

In Augusta, Ga., six members of an all-girl gang corner a 22-year-old woman on the street and savagely beat her. [1] In San Antonio, Texas, two girls slash a rival gang girl's face with a broken bottle. [2] In Buffalo, N.Y., female members of a mixed gang transport narcotics and sometimes sell drugs on the streets. [3]

Gang members are usually seen as young men wearing distinctive clothes or colors, using a common slang and hand signals and fighting with gangs from other neighborhoods. If females are in the picture at all, they're usually viewed as supporting players — girlfriends, perhaps, or maybe sisters, but never gang members in their own right. Yet, female gangs have existed in America at least since the 19th century.

Relatively little is known about female gangs, however, and most of the knowledge has been acquired only in the last 20 years. Sexist stereotyping has largely been responsible for the lack of awareness, according to the Justice Department's Office of Juvenile Justice and Delinquency Prevention (OJJDP). Researchers historically perceived gangs in terms of vandalism, theft and assault — generally considered male provinces.

"It was often assumed that females did not take part in such behavior, so early researchers were not interested in the delinquency of female gang members," wrote sociologist Joan Moore and criminologist John Hagedorn in an issue of the Juvenile Justice Bulletin devoted to female gangs. [4]

When gang activity escalated in the 1980s and '90s, researchers began noticing that female gangs were either autonomous entities or affiliates of male gangs. With names like Latin Queens, the female counterpart to Latin Kings, and Sisters of the Struggle, they usually had their own identities and structures.

No one knows how many female gangs exist. Law enforcement surveys tend to show that between 4 and 11 percent of gang members are female, but social-service surveys show higher numbers.

Although little is known about female gang activity, some research and anecdotal reports show that most girl gangs are involved in delinquency or non-violent crimes, with drug offenses ranking near the top of the list. Female gang members commit fewer violent crimes than male gang members and in general are more prone to property crime. [5]

"The biggest difference between female gangs and male gangs is violence," says Hagedorn, a professor of criminal justice at the University of Illinois. "Girls are very seldom involved in homicide. The difference between males and females on this issue is massive."

Still, he acknowledges, female gang members can sometimes be just as violent as males. In the mid-1990s, an 11-city survey of eighth-graders revealed that more than 90 percent of male and female gang members admitted to having commit-

The most notorious of the early immigrant gangs in New York was, of course, the Mafia, or La Cosa Nostra ("Our Thing"), which originated as a criminal organization in Sicily. The Mafia rose to power by extorting neighborhood shopkeepers for "protection" money against arson. It consolidated its power during Prohibition, when it controlled the illegal distribution of liquor in many U.S. cities.

By the turn of the century, Jewish gangs and Chinese gangs had been added to the ethnic stew in New York's Bowery, Chinatown and in such rough neighborhoods as Hell's Kitchen on the West Side. During Prohibition, many youth gangs became involved with adult bootleggers. In Southern California, waves of Mexican immigrants arrived to form the first so-called barrio gangs.

But the worst gang problems plagued Chicago. In 1927 criminologist Frederick M. Thrasher published the

first major book on the problem, *The Gang: A Study of 1,313 Gangs in Chicago*, in which he analyzed gangs of every ethnic and racial stripe: Polish, Irish, Anglo-American, Jewish, Slavic, Bohemian, German, Swedish, Lithuanian, black, Chinese and Mexican. "The gang is a conflict group," Thrasher wrote. "It develops through strife and warfare."

The ethnic character of American gangs continued to manifest itself. In the 1930s, the rising numbers of blacks migrating from the South to New York, as well as new immigrants from the British West Indies, set up the first rivalries among black gangs. In the early 1940s, gangs of Latino youths in Southern California frequently clashed with U.S. servicemen stationed in the area, eventually provoking the so-called Zoot Suit Riots, named for a flashy clothing style then popular among Latinos.

ted one or more violent acts in the previous 12 months. Moreover, 78 percent of female gang members reported having been in a gang fight, 65 percent acknowledged carrying a weapon and 39 percent said they had attacked someone with a weapon. [6]

Within mixed gangs, males commonly boast that the females are their sex objects, a claim that has perpetuated the "sex slave" stereotype of female gang members. But OJJDP research done in conjunction with the National Youth Gang Center shows that females deny this, insisting that females of any position or authority in the gang are respected precisely because they do not allow the males to exploit them sexually. Sexual exploitation does occur, they say, but almost always involving girls or young women who are not members of the gang.

Currently, most female gangs are Latina and African-American, though the numbers of Asian and white female gangs have been increasing.

Regardless of ethnicity or race, many girls join gangs for the same reasons as males — seeking friendship and self-affirma-

California Gang Investigators Association

Female gang members commit fewer violent crimes than male gang members, primarily property and drug offenses.

tion. Sometimes the lack of job opportunities pushes girls and young women to join gangs, as it does boys and young men. But many female gang members share a common pain of childhood, which they have tried to escape by seeking refuge in a gang. "Research consistently shows that high proportions of female gang members have experienced sexual abuse at home," Hagedorn and Moore write.

There's another important difference between female and male gang members: Females tend to leave a gang sooner because they get pregnant, usually by age 18.

[1] See "Woman Reports Gang Assault," *The Augusta Chronicle*, Feb. 22, 2004, p. B3.

[2] See Elda Silva, "'Homegirls' Gets Personal, Introspective," *The San Antonio Express-News*, Jan. 29, 2004, p. 1F.

[3] See Lou Michel, "The Bloods, Settling Debts with Death," *Buffalo News*, Dec. 16, 2003, p. A1.

[4] See Joan Moore and John Hagedorn, "Female Gangs: A Focus on Research," *Juvenile Justice Bulletin*, March 2001, p. 1.

[5] *Ibid*, p. 5.

[6] *Ibid*, p. 6.

Seeking Respectability

The classic youth-gang era began after World War II, when Americans migrated from the farms to the cities. The first "teenage" subculture emerged in the postwar period, and gangs severed their earlier ties to adult organized crime.

In Los Angeles, two black gangs appeared — the Businessmen and the Home Street Gang. In the 1950s, CBS News correspondent Edward R. Murrow drew nationwide attention to the conditions that produce gangs with the documentary "Who Killed Michael Farmer?" about the death of a handicapped young man at the hands of a Bronx street gang.

Society responded to gangs by trying to build long-term relationships with gang members and by sponsoring dances or athletic contests, such as a New York City

Youth Board program that sought to reduce gang tensions. "Participation in a street gang or club," a 1950 Youth Board document read, "like participation in any natural group, is part of the growing-up process. . . . Within the structure of the group the individual can develop such characteristics as loyalty, leadership and community responsibility. . . . Some gangs . . . have developed patterns of anti-social behavior . . . [but] members can be reached and will respond to sympathy, acceptance, affection and understanding when approached by adults who possess those characteristics and reach out to them on their own level." [37]

In the 1960s, the Hell's Angels motorcycle gang gained national exposure and greatly influenced the younger, more ethnic urban gangs. "By 1965," wrote counterculture journalist Hunter S. Thompson, later of

The Rev. Greg Boyle, a Jesuit priest, runs a jobs program in East Los Angeles for gang members who want to stop being criminals.

Rolling Stone fame, "[gangs] were firmly established as All-American bogeymen." Meanwhile, the decade's civil rights movement, urban riots and radical politics spilled over into the world of gangs, particularly among blacks, many of whom would become attracted to revolutionary groups like the Black Panthers.

With President Lyndon B. Johnson's War on Poverty pouring millions of federal grant dollars into inner cities, some criminal youth gangs decided to join the Establishment, heralding either an optimistic or opportunistic approach to addressing social problems, depending on one's viewpoint.

In New York City in 1967, for example, leaders of the Puerto Rican gang Spartican Army decided they wanted a role in bettering the social and economic conditions of their Lower East Side neighborhoods. Borrowing from Johnson's Great Society rhetoric, they took the name the Real Great Society and applied for a grant from the federal Office of Economic Opportunity (OEO). They were turned down, but their well-publicized efforts (profiled in *Life* magazine) attracted private foundation money. They opened a Real Great Society nightclub, a child-care service and a leather-goods store, all of which blossomed briefly but failed within a year. [38] They then organized summer classes for inner-city youths and finally won an OEO grant.

In Chicago, meanwhile, another experiment in gang respectability was under way. In 1967, the Blackstone Rangers, led by a fervent black nationalist, Jeff Fort, began toying with the notion of doing anti-poverty work

with a radical white clergyman, John Fry, who was affiliated with a community-organizing group named for Chicago's Woodlawn neighborhood. Because the group opposed Chicago's powerful mayor, Richard J. Daley, its anti-poverty programs had never received federal grant money, over which Daley had de facto control.

But the possible turnaround of the Blackstone Rangers was too tempting to Washington. In June, the OEO awarded the Woodlawn Organization and the Blackstone Rangers $927,000 to operate anti-poverty programs for a year.

Daley was furious at fellow Democrats in the Johnson administration, but he did not have to fume for long. The Woodlawn program quickly became known as a monumental boondoggle: Only 76 of 800 participants in its jobs program got jobs; bookkeeping was lax; gang members encouraged each other to quit school and be paid from the federal grant; by autumn, Fort had been arrested on murder charges. [39]

In Washington, Sen. John L. McClellan, D-Ark., chairman of the Government Operations Committee, held widely publicized hearings into the Woodlawn grant. Many blamed the OEO for poor judgment. While under indictment, Fort appeared as a witness but refused to speak. (The murder charges against him were later dismissed.)

In May 1968, OEO shut down the Woodlawn project, just weeks after the Blackstone Rangers were given credit for keeping Chicago relatively calm during the urban riots that followed the assassination of the Rev. Dr. Martin Luther King, Jr. The idealistic notion of giving government money to reformed gang members had suffered a crippling blow.

The impact of Chicago's gang experiment during the days of the War on Poverty would be felt for decades. Chicago gang members continued to receive foundation money for nearly 20 years. Fort was sentenced to prison in the early 1970s for fraud committed with the OEO grant. In prison, he converted to Islam and changed the Rangers' name to El Rukns (Arabic for "the foundation").

When he and some fellow gang members emerged from prison in the late 1970s, they threw themselves into the violent drug trade. Dozens of El Rukns members were sent to prison in the early 1980s. In 1987, Fort was sentenced to 75 years in prison for soliciting money from Libya to fund terrorist operations in the U.S. [40]

In the 1980s, crack cocaine became the product of choice for drug-dealing gangs: Highly addictive and inexpensive, crack provided a profit margin greater than powdered cocaine. Gangs soon were fighting over the most profitable turf — markets — giving rise to drive-by shootings and a spike in violent crime.

War Refugees

In El Salvador, civil war in the early 1980s prompted many refugees — and former guerrillas — to flee to the United States. The Mara Salvatrucha, or MS-13, gang emerged from a rapidly swelling population of Salvadoran immigrants in Los Angeles. Other gangs with roots in the Central American immigrant communities of Southern California also formed, and violence frequently erupted between them and the area's long-established Mexican gangs.

Asian gangs began appearing around the same time, mostly as a result of massive Asian immigration, including the "boat people," refugees from war-ravaged Southeast Asia. The gangs of Vietnamese, Cambodian and Laotian refugees had roots in the region's refugee camps following the Vietnam War and the post-war atrocities committed by the Khmer Rouge in Cambodia. [41] By the late 1980s and early '90s, Asian gangs had footholds from West Valley City, Utah, to Manhattan. "When I was a prosecutor in New York," Howell recalls, "the Vietnamese gangs were as violent as anybody."

Throughout the late 1980s and early '90s, many Latino gang members in L.A. headed north to Chicago, already teeming with black, white and mixed-race gangs. In 1991, the city's homicide rate hit a record 609 deaths. In response, Mayor Richard M. Daley recalled the gang-grant scandal from the era when his famous father had run city hall. The younger Daley lashed out at the liberal "social workers" of the 1960s and '70s who had "coddled" the teenage gang members who were now, as adults, Chicago's drug kingpins.

In an effort to reduce the nation's crime rate, Congress in 1996 enacted a law that allows deportation of non-citizens sentenced to a year or more in prison for anything ranging from petty theft to murder. Since then, in what constitutes the largest dragnet in the country's history, more than 500,000 "criminal aliens" have been deported to more than 130 countries, including many gang members who originally immigrated to the United States with their parents to escape poverty or civil war. [42]

While the tactic has effectively reduced the number of criminals in the United States, it has overwhelmed the receiving countries, particularly in Latin America and the Caribbean, which have seen crime rates skyrocket since 1996.

Many of the deported have joined local gangs — often home-country versions of the gangs they belonged to in the United States. El Salvador and Honduras have suffered particularly sharp rises in violent gang crime, with beheadings, shootings, rapes and hackings now commonplace, police say. Moreover, vigilante groups often hunt down gang members and murder them on sight — a practice both U.S. and Latin American officials say only causes retaliation and escalation. [43]

By 1997, the chief of the FBI's violent-crime section estimated that Chicago had 50,000 active gang members — more than the combined area membership of the Moose, the Elks, the Knights of Columbus and the Shriners. [44] Meanwhile, in the previous 16 years approximately 7,300 people had died in gang violence in Los Angeles.

But Chicago and L.A. were not alone. In 1995, police blamed gangs for 41 percent of Omaha's homicides, and more than half of all violent crime in Buffalo. In Phoenix, gang-related homicides jumped 800 percent between 1990 and '94. [45] While the overall violent-crime rate across the country was dropping, violent juvenile crime remained high.

In response, lawmakers drafted the Violent and Repeat Juvenile Justice Act of 1997. The House passed its version of the bill, but the Senate's version — opposed by countless advocacy groups — never made it to a floor vote. Liberals felt it was too harsh, citing its intention to prosecute juveniles as adults and house them with adults in prison. Conservatives felt it penalized law-abiding gun merchants and owners.

Congress tried again in early 1999 with Democrats and Republicans apparently determined to compromise on the issue. But the bipartisan spirit was shattered in April, when two teenagers in Littleton, Colo., went on a shooting rampage at Columbine High School, killing 13 people before turning the guns on themselves. [46] Both the House and Senate passed juvenile crime bills, but liberals and conservatives deadlocked over gun control, effectively killing the bills in conference.

Starting in 1995, juvenile violent crime began falling, and continued falling through 2001, but in 2002 authorities began seeing an upsurge in gang violence. [47] Latino and Asian gangs were committing the most violent offenses, particularly along the Northeast Corridor. Of the two, the Latinos have drawn the most attention because their numbers are currently the largest. And among the Latinos, MS-13 is widely considered the most dangerous.

CURRENT SITUATION

Invisible Crisis

If many Americans are unaware of the country's gang crisis, it may be because some police departments don't want them to know about it. The National Alliance of Gang Investigators Associations says many law enforcement agencies have refused to cooperate with its nationwide survey of gang activities.

"We're getting so many of those forms back from [police] departments refusing to fill them out," McBride says. "The local authorities say, 'We don't want to ruin our economy, because companies won't move here if they know we have gangs!' " McBride says. "I even had one executive tell me that people don't have a right to know, and no sense scaring them. I was flabbergasted. People absolutely have a right to know and need to know how many gangs are out there."

But sometimes the agencies don't respond because of poor record keeping, he says. In Denver, for example, police records show that the city's 17,000 gang members committed only 89 of the 59,581 crimes in 2002. "I heard that figure, and I just wanted to laugh," said a member of the metropolitan police department's gang crimes unit. [48] Moore, of the National Youth Gang Center, says officers often do not know immediately that a crime is gang related; when they find out, they rarely revise the initial police report.

Another problem is the cyclical nature of gangs and gang prevention. Police departments often set up gang units and then dissolve them once they believe the situation is under control, only to see the problem worsen again. "There's just no continuity of incident reporting," Moore says, so police records on gangs are "notoriously slack."

Four years ago, when acknowledging a gang problem carried less stigma than it does today, the NAGIA assembled a national picture of gangs and gang activities that many say is still essentially accurate. Starting in the late 1990s, gangs began penetrating into suburban areas in the Northeast and Mid-Atlantic regions, particularly in upstate New York, eastern Pennsylvania and Northern Virginia. Increasing numbers of Asian gangs were migrating into the Northeast, while two Latino gangs — the

Latin Kings and the Netas — had become involved in political and social causes to establish some legitimacy. [49]

Along with the increase in gangs has come an increase in crime. Last September, for instance, Christopher Christie, U.S. attorney for Newark, N.J., reported that for the third straight year, the city's murder rate had risen, as well as the number of handguns recovered by police. "The rise in violence and unlawful gun possession corresponds directly to a substantial increase in documented gang activity beginning in 1999," he said. [50]

The South also has seen increased activity among established Asian and Latino gangs, and several Latino and black gangs from Chicago have expanded into the region, particularly in drug dealing. [51] In Charlotte, N.C., authorities have been fighting white motorcycle gangs along with the black Kings, but as in Northern Virginia, the most violent and visible gang is MS-13. [52]

In the Chicago area, gangs have been growing more sophisticated and organized. Asian and Latino gangs account for the greatest growth throughout the region, with the latter expanding in direct relation to a widening of the methamphetamine market. Chicago-based gangs have also extended their reach into various regions of the West, where the epicenter of gang activity continues to be Los Angeles.

National Gang Policy?

Investigating gangs that appear to be operating in several regions is complicated, because different gang factions often have different interests. "Gangs are, more often than not, locally based, geographically oriented criminal associations," Sen. Leahy recently said. "Even gangs that purportedly have the same name on the East and West coast are not necessarily affiliated with one another." [53]

What is needed, McBride says, is a national gang policy that spells out an accepted definition of a gang and gang-related activity and a national gang intelligence center, similar to the Department of Justice's National Drug Intelligence Center.

"We need massive federal aid to local government in a multifaceted approach — it can't be just cops," he continues, adding that the approach should coordinate probation, corrections and community-based programs, as well as prevention and intervention programs. Coordination and communication among all relevant authorities, which currently is lacking, also must be beefed up, he says. "And it all has to be long term. The

Would the Gang Prevention and Effective Deterrence Act proposed by Sens. Orrin Hatch and Dianne Feinstein help in the fight against gangs?

YES
Sen. Orrin G. Hatch, R-Utah

From a statement before the U.S. Senate, Oct. 15, 2003

Mr. President, I rise today to introduce a comprehensive, bipartisan bill to increase gang prosecution and prevention efforts.

The Gang Prevention and Effective Deterrence Act of 2003 also increases funding for the federal prosecutors and FBI agents needed to conduct coordinated enforcement efforts against violent gangs.

Additionally, this bill will create new, criminal, gang-prosecution offenses, enhance existing gang and violent-crime penalties to deter and punish illegal street gangs, propose violent-crime reforms needed to prosecute effectively gang members and propose a limited reform of the juvenile-justice system to facilitate federal prosecution of 16- and 17-year-old gang members who commit serious acts of violence.

Once thought to be only a problem in our nation's largest cities, gangs have invaded smaller communities. Gangs now resemble organized-crime syndicates who readily engage in gun violence, illegal gun trafficking, illegal drug trafficking and other serious crimes.

Recent studies confirm that gang violence is an increasing problem in all of our communities. The most current reports indicate that in 2002 alone, after five years of decline, gang membership has spiked nationwide.

While we all are committed to fighting the global war on terrorism, we must redouble our efforts to ensure that we devote sufficient resources to combating this important national problem — the rise in gangs and gang violence in America.

We must take a proactive approach and meet this problem head on if we wish to defeat it. If we really want to reduce gang violence, we must ensure that law enforcement has adequate resources and legal tools, and that our communities have the ability to implement proven intervention and prevention strategies, so that gang members who are removed from the community are not simply replaced by the next generation of new gang members.

Federal involvement is crucial to control gang violence and to prevent new gang members from replacing old gang members. I strongly urge my colleagues to join with me in promptly passing this important legislation.

NO
Jeralyn Merritt
Criminal Defense Attorney, Denver, Colo.

From talkleft.com: the politics of crime, Dec. 21, 2003

Sens. Diane Feinstein, D-Calif., and Orrin Hatch, R-Utah, have teamed up to sponsor a terrible bill — one that panders to irrational fear but resonates politically.

It is rife with new categories of crimes, added punishments for having a gun or being a gang member and myriad "think twice" measures hoping gang members will reconsider before committing a crime.

Anyone who knows gangs knows that lawmakers cannot conceive of a law that would lead a hard-core gang member to "think twice." We already have enough gang- and gun-related sentencing "enhancements" to send a 17-year-old who has never been in trouble with the law to prison for 35 years to life. And that's without his ever touching a gun or ever being an actual member of a gang. We need to overhaul these enhancements, not add to them.

Gangs are not all that mysterious. Reformers know what works with them and what doesn't. Gang experts, intervention practitioners, social scientists, researchers and enlightened law enforcement officials all agree. What works is prevention, intervention and enforcement.

You prevent kids from joining gangs by offering after-school programs, sports, mentoring and positive engagement with adults. You intervene with gang members by offering alternatives and employment to help redirect their lives. You deal with areas of high gang-crime activity with real community policing.

There are ways that money could make a difference in curbing gangs — but the Feinstein-Hatch bill doesn't acknowledge them.

Law enforcement doesn't need more tools; it needs more officers. Real community policing requires different deployment, which can happen only with increased personnel. Although the Feinstein-Hatch bill would also allocate $200 million for prevention and intervention, more than three-quarters of that money would be administered by law enforcement. That is as misguided as having Homeboy Industries — a gang rehab center — enforce a gang injunction.

What's really going on here is politics. Feinstein and Hatch's ill-advised bill will neither prevent nor deter gang-related crime. It's time to stop funding wasteful law enforcement initiatives and listen to those who know what works — and it's not the politicians. This turkey of a bill needs to die a fast death.

problem with going to federal funding agencies is you get little grants for 18 months at most. That's not enough."

Newark's Christie has called for a special, multi-level unit that would target an entire gang operation — much like the Mafia was targeted — not simply the most visible members on the streets. "It is not uncommon for a single gang to be involved in drug dealing, firearms trafficking, murder, robbery, money laundering and, more recently, mortgage fraud," he said. To deal with such broad-based activities, he suggests, the U.S. attorney's office should lead a team consisting of the FBI, DEA, BATFE and the Marshals Service, along with local authorities. [54]

Without such broad-based coordination and information sharing, many investigations and prosecutions languish, authorities say. Investigations are also hindered by the lack of funds to adequately protect witnesses. "For many prosecutors, a witness-protection program simply consists of a bus ticket or a motel room," said McCulloch, of the National District Attorneys Association, who has pleaded for federal funds for such programs. In Denver, he points out, the number of prosecutions has dropped sharply because of the lack of protection while the number of gang crimes "has increased tremendously." [55]

Lately, Congress appears to be listening: In addition to making some gang activities federal offenses, the proposed Gang Prevention and Effective Deterrence Act would provide approximately $100 million of federal assistance for state and local law enforcement and $40 million for prevention programs over five years. In the Senate the bill was scheduled for markup in mid-May and expected to pass largely intact. A House companion bill has yet to be submitted.

Johnson of the National Association of Police Organizations predicts the measure will eventually become law. "Maybe not in this Congress before the [November presidential] election," he says, "but I do think it will pass. It won't be a cure-all but another tool in the box that will marginally and incrementally help bring down gangs and make communities safer."

However, Denver criminal-defense attorney Jeralyn Merritt calls it "a terrible bill" that "panders to irrational fear but resonates politically." In a scathing criticism of the proposal on the Web site *talkleft.com*, she argues: "We already have enough gang- and gun-related sentencing 'enhancements' to send a 17-year-old who has never been in trouble with the law to prison for 35 years to life. And that's without his ever being an actual member of a gang. We need to overhaul these enhancements, not add to them."

"Gangs are not all that mysterious. Reformers know what works with them . . . What works is prevention, intervention and enforcement. You prevent kids from joining gangs by offering after-school programs, sports, mentoring and positive engagement with adults. You intervene with gang members by offering alternatives and employment to help redirect their lives. You deal with areas of high gang-crime activity with real community policing."

OUTLOOK

More Violence?

In Northern Virginia, probation official Rathbun thinks authorities at every level of government have begun to realize the size and scope of the gang threat. As he puts it, "It's kind of the problem *du jour* now."

But whether effective policies will soon emerge is an open question, he says. "There's still lots of crazy things," he says. "We've got a directive from our agency now that says we can't question anybody about their immigration status, which seems stupid."

Moore, of the National Youth Gang Center, expects gang violence to continue its cyclical patterns, with upswings followed by downturns. "Some cities experience a big flare-up in gang violence every year," he says. "They've either never recognized the problem and it bubbles up to the surface, or they think they've dealt with the problem, but it comes back up again."

To U.S. Attorney Christie in Newark, nothing short of a full-scale, coordinated assault by law enforcement agencies at all levels is going to make a difference. Gang crime is, he said, "the new organized crime in the United States, an organized crime that destroys families, corrupts our children and lays waste to neighborhoods in our most vulnerable communities. We must mount a fight comparable to the fight against La Cosa Nostra in past decades if we expect to have the same success." [56]

But the FBI's Riley believes the resources are coming "at a slow pace." Given the FBI's priority on combating terrorism, Riley envisions "probably a 10-year progression to get [anti-gang resources] to the point I'd like to see." Meantime, he expects increasing gang activity as a result of continued immigration and "the phenomenon of the media making the 'gangsta' lifestyle appealing."

But he's also somewhat optimistic. "I see more cooperation between federal agencies — the FBI, the [BATFE] and the DEA and even the Marshals Service."

Although federal legislation may help bring the problem under control, changing demographics and the inherent dangerousness of gang activity may help staunch the growth of gangs over the long-term, says Johnson of the National Association of Police Organizations. "The Baby Boomlet will get older, and as they do, they'll mature and calm down," he says. "As this generation ages, there will be a decrease in the general crime rate. Plus, the really bad ones either get caught or killed. Gang [activity] is a very high-risk business."

McBride of the California Gang Investigators Association doubts that either the proposed legislation or more federal funds will eliminate the problem. "After you get some federal grants, the statistics decrease, and then the politicians walk away saying the problem's solved," he says. "Then, surprise, surprise — the problem's right back."

But if done right, he says, the legislation could help. "If the funding goes for local prosecution and for local gang units, that's going to be a tremendous help. But if it stays federally based, it's not going to have the impact they want it to have."

Rathbun, who deals with juvenile gangs daily, is pessimistic. Some gangs that had seemed to disband in Northern Virginia, such as TRG, are revitalizing, and becoming shrewder.

"The kids are less apt to get the tattoos now, and less apt to dress like gang-bangers," he says, so authorities are less apt to immediately recognize them. Their actions, however, won't be any different than before. Rathbun says the rival 18th Street Gang and the Latin Kings, as well as the new South Side Locos, are beginning to move into MS-13 territory.

"We're expecting turf battles," he says. "Machetes, knives and guns. I think it's going to be a bad summer."

It has already begun with machetes. A 16-year-old boy thought to be a South Side Locals member was walking along a suburban street on May 10 when reputed MS-13 members jumped him and nearly hacked his hands off. His screams woke residents, who called police. Doctors saved both hands, but four fingers were permanently lost, and it is too soon to tell if he will recover use of his hands. [57]

"They were trying to send a message," said Robert Walker, a former Drug Enforcement Administration special agent who runs a gang-identification training program for law enforcement officers. "Gangs deal in what we call the three R's. The first is reputation, and they want to do all they can to build that. The second is respect . . . and the third is retaliation or revenge."

NOTES

1. See Maria Glod, "Man Gets 30 Years in Gang Slaying; Va. Judge Cites Brutal Beating in Sentencing 1 of 4 Charged," *The Washington Post*, Sept. 28, 2002, p. B6. See also Maria Glod, "Gangs Get Public's Attention: Dozen Actively Contributing to Area Crime," *The Washington Post*, Sept. 18, 2003, p. T1.

2. See Maria Glod, "Prosecutors Describe Gang-Style Execution as MS-13 Trial Opens," *The Washington Post*, Nov. 6, 2003, p. B6. See also Maria Glod, "Guardian of Slain Woman Replaces Her as Witness; Authorities Believe Teen was Silenced by Gang," *The Washington Post*, Nov. 7, 2003, p. B4.

3. Sen. Orrin G. Hatch, opening statement before Senate Judiciary Committee hearing on "Combating Gang Violence in America: Examining Effective Federal, State and Local Law Enforcement Strategies," Sept. 17, 2003.

4. Office of Juvenile Justice and Delinquency Prevention, U.S. Department of Justice, "Highlights of the 2001 National Youth Gang Survey," April 2003. See also Neely Tucker, "Gangs Growing in Numbers, Bravado Across Area," *The Washington Post*, Sept. 18, 2003, p. A1.

5. National Alliance of Gang Investigators Associations, "Threat Assessment, 2000."

6. Office of Juvenile Justice and Delinquency Prevention, *op. cit.*

7. Wesley McBride, testimony before Senate Judiciary Committee hearing, Sept. 17, 2003.

8. *Ibid.*

9. Patrick Fitzgerald, testimony before Senate Judiciary Committee hearing, Sept. 17, 2003.

10. National Youth Gang Center, www.iir.com/nygc/faq.htm#q6.

11. *Ibid.*

12. Eddie Jordan, testimony before Senate Judiciary Committee hearing, Sept. 17, 2003.

13. McBride, *op. cit.*

14. Grant D. Ashley, testimony before Senate Judiciary Committee hearing, Sept. 17, 2003.

15. Debra Yang, testimony before Senate Judiciary Committee hearing, Sept. 17, 2003.

16. Robert McCulloch, testimony before Senate Judiciary Committee hearing, Sept. 17, 2003.

17. For background, see William Triplett, "State Budget Crisis," *CQ Researcher*, Oct. 3, 2003, pp. 821-844.

18. See Keith Perine, "Senators Pushing for Increased Federal Role in Fighting Crime Linked to Gangs," *CQ Today*, April 9, 2004.

19. Bureau of Alcohol, Tobacco and Firearms and Explosives (BATFE), "Crime Gun Trace Reports: National Report," June 2002, pp. ix, x.

20. C. Ronald Huff, "Criminal Behavior of Gang Members and At-Risk Youths," presentation to the National Institute of Justice.

21. BATFE, *op. cit.*

22. For background, see Richard L. Worsnop, "Gun Control," *CQ Researcher*, June 10, 1994, pp. 505-528, and Kenneth Jost, "Gun Control Standoff," *CQ Researcher*, Dec. 19, 1997, pp. 1105-1128.

23. Fitzgerald, *op. cit.*

24. See David Heinzmann, "Gangs Run Gun Pipeline from Delta to Chicago; Lenient Laws Make Buying Weapons Easier in South," *Chicago Tribune*, Feb. 5, 2004, p. C1.

25. Jens Ludwig and Phil Cook, "Homicide and Suicide Rates Associated with Implementation of the BHVPA," *Journal of the American Medical Association*, Aug. 2, 2000, Vol. 284, p. 585.

26. Jost, *op. cit.*

27. Heinzmann, *op. cit.*

28. See Carlos Sandovi, "Teen Charged in Humboldt Park Gang Rival's Killing; Police say Suspect also Took Shots at Undercover Cop," *Chicago Tribune*, April 21, 2004, p. C2.

29. For background see Brian Hansen, "Kids in Prison," *CQ Researcher*, April 27, 2001, pp. 345-376.

30. See Lisa Friedman, "Anti-Gang Bill Draws Critics; Juvenile Advocacy Groups Oppose Adult Sentencing," *Los Angeles Daily News*, Nov. 24, 2003, p. N4.

31. *Ibid.*

32. Quoted in Armando Morales and Bradford W. Sheafor, *Social Work: A Profession of Many Faces* (1989), p. 415.

33. For background see Charles S. Clark, "Youth Gangs," *CQ Researcher*, Oct. 11, 1991, pp. 753-776.

34. Anne Campbell, *The Girls in the Gang* (1984), p. 9.

35. Quoted in Irving A. Spergel, *Crime and Justice: A Review of Research*, "Youth Gangs: Continuity and Change," Michael Tonry and Norval Morris, eds., Vol. 12 (1990), p. 172.

36. Quoted in James Haskins, *Street Gangs: Yesterday and Today* (1974), p. 48.

37. *Ibid*, p. 99.

38. *Ibid*, p. 112.

39. See Nicholas Lemann, *The Promised Land* (1991), p. 245.

40. See Michael Abramowitz, "Street Gang Convictions Challenged in Chicago," *The Washington Post*, Dec. 22, 1992, p. A3.

41. See Matt Canham and Tim Sullivan, "Asian Gangs a Scourge: Violent Rivals in the Vietnamese, Lao and Cambodia Communities are Settling Scores at Malls, Amusement Parks; Asian Gangs Target Their Own People," *The Salt Lake Tribune*, April 14, 2003, p. D1.

42. The Associated Press, "U.S. Deportees Cart Crime to Native Lands," *Los Angeles Times*, Jan. 4, 2004, p. A5.

43. Kevin Sullivan, "Spreading Gang Violence Alarms Central Americans," *The Washington Post*, Dec. 1, 2003, p. A1.

44. Steven Wiley, testimony before Senate Judiciary Committee hearing on gang violence, April 23, 1997.

45. Sen. Dianne Feinstein, statement before Senate Judiciary Committee hearing on gang violence, April 23, 1997.

46. For background, see Sarah Glazer, "Boys' Emotional Needs," *CQ Researcher*, June 18, 1999, pp. 521-544 and Kathy Koch, "School Violence," *CQ Researcher*, Oct. 9, 1998, pp. 881-904.

47. National Center for Juvenile Justice, "Juvenile Arrest Rates by Offense, Sex, and Race," May 31, 2003.

48. See Chuck Plunkett, "Gangs' Hidden Fingerprint," *The Denver Post*, Nov. 9, 2003, p. A1.

49. National Alliance of Gang Investigators Associations, *op. cit.*

50. Christopher Christie, testimony before Senate Judiciary Committee hearing, Sept. 17, 2003.

51. National Alliance of Gang Investigators Associations, *op. cit.*

52. See Arian Campo-Flores, "Gangland's New Face," *Newsweek*, Dec. 8, 2003, p. 41.

53. Sen. Patrick Leahy, opening statement before Senate Judiciary Committee hearing, Sept. 17, 2003.

54. Christie, *op. cit.*

55. McCulloch, *op. cit.*

56. Christie, *op. cit.*

57. Maria Glod and Tom Jackman, "Teen's Hands Severed In Northern Va. Machete Attack," *The Washington Post*, May 11, 2004, p. B1.

BIBLIOGRAPHY

Books

Hernandez, Arturo, *Peace in the Streets: Breaking the Cycle of Gang Violence*, **Child Welfare League of America, 1998.**
Hernandez tells the riveting story of his experience as a young teacher in South Central Los Angeles and the positive effect he had on the gang members who were his students.

Kinnear, Karen L., *Gangs: A Reference Handbook*, **ABC-CLIO, 1996.**
This compendium on juvenile gangs by a journalist focuses on their activities, membership, motivations and their relation to society and the law.

Lloyd, J.D., ed., *Gangs*, **Greenhaven Press, 2002.**
A collection of informational essays by a journalist examines why gangs exist, their history, their day-to-day actions and what can be done to lessen the damage they do.

The Truth about Street Gangs, **Gang Prevention Inc., 2001.**
This publication is designed to help communities identify and understand gangs, focusing on how they operate and how they conceal their activities.

Articles

Campo-Flores, Arian, "Gangland's New Face," *Newsweek*, Dec. 8, 2003, p. 41.
The surge of Latino gangs is reflected in their relatively new and overwhelming presence in Charlotte, N.C.

Canham, Matt, and Tim Sullivan, "Asian Gangs a Scourge; Gunplay: Violent rivals in the Vietnamese, Lao and Cambodian communities are settling scores at malls, amusement parks; Asian Gangs Target Their Own People," *Salt Lake Tribune*, April 14, 2003, p. D1.
Asian gangs wreak havoc in the greater Salt Lake area, mostly within the immigrant community but sometimes outside of it.

Heinzmann, David, "Gangs run pipeline from Delta to Chicago; Lenient laws make buying weapons easier in the South," *Chicago Tribune*, Feb. 5, 2004, p. 1.
To skirt tough gun control laws, Chicago gangs use the proceeds of illegal drug sales to buy weapons in Mississippi.

Jackson, Chriscia, "Asian gangs have reputation for living 'giang ho,' or crazy life," Associated Press, May 25, 2000.
A look at the violence and destructiveness of Asian gangs as seen in the story of two juvenile members of Vietnamese gangs in Port Arthur, Texas.

Plunkett, Chuck, "Gangs' Hidden Fingerprint," *The Denver Post*, Nov. 9, 2003, p. A1.
Plunkett details the extensive gang activity throughout the Denver area and the police department's lack of accurate records on gangs.

Tucker, Neely, "Gangs Growing in Numbers, Bravado Across Area," *The Washington Post*, Sept. 18, 2003, p. A1.
Latino gangs are growing rapidly in Washington, D.C., and other areas of the country not previously known for intense gang activity.

"U.S. Deportees Cart Crime to Native Lands; More than 500,000 have been banished under 1996 law," The Associated Press, *Los Angeles Times*, Jan. 4, 2004, p A5.
The federal government's tactic of deporting non-U.S. citizens convicted of crimes has sent many gang members back to their homeland, where they resume gang activity.

Reports and Studies

"Highlights of the 2001 National Youth Gang Survey," Office of Juvenile Justice and Delinquency Prevention, Department of Justice, April 2003.
This annual survey documents national trends, activities and developments among youth gangs.

Huff, C. Ronald, "Comparing the Criminal Behavior of Youth Gangs and At-Risk Youths," National Institute of Justice, Department of Justice, October 1998.
A survey shows that criminal activity of youth-gang members is significantly higher than that of at-risk youths.

Moore, Joan, and John Hagedorn, "Female Gangs: A Focus on Research," *Juvenile Justice Bulletin*, Office of Juvenile Justice and Delinquency Prevention, U.S. Department of Justice, March 2001.
This summary of research attempts to address the imbalance between research on male and female gangs.

"National Youth Gang Center Bibliography of Gang Literature," Office of Juvenile Justice and Delinquency Prevention, U.S. Department of Justice, 1997.
An exhaustive bibliography of gang literature — dating as far back as the 1940s — reviewed and compiled by the National Youth Gang Center for the Office of Juvenile Justice and Delinquency Prevention.

Reed, Winifred L., and Scott H. Decker, "Responding to Gangs: Evaluation and Research," National Institute of Justice, U.S. Department of Justice, July 2002.
A comprehensive review of recent research about gang behavior as well as anti-gang strategies.

For More Information

Bajito Onda, P.O. Box 270246, Dallas, TX 75227; (214) 275-6632; www.bajitoonda.org/. Foundation dedicated to giving Latino youths positive alternatives to gangs, drugs and violence through education.

Juvenile Justice Clearinghouse, P.O. Box 6000, Rockville, MD 20849-6000; (800) 851-3420; http://ojjdp.ncjrs.org/programs/ProgSummary.asp?pi=2. A component of the National Criminal Justice Reference Service that maintains information and resources on juvenile-justice topics.

National Alliance of Gang Investigators Associations; www.nagia.org. An online coalition of criminal-justice professionals dedicated to promoting a coordinated anti-gang strategy.

National Criminal Justice Reference Service, P.O. Box 6000, Rockville, MD, 20849-6000; (800) 851-3420; http://virlib.ncjrs.org/juv.asp?category=47&subcategory=66. A federally funded service that provides information on jus-

tice and substance abuse to support research, policy and program development worldwide.

National Major Gang Task Force, 338 S. Arlington Ave., Suite 112, Indianapolis, IN 46219; (317) 322-0537; www.nmgtf.org. An independent organization specializing in intervention, management strategies, networking, training and information-sharing regarding gangs.

National Youth Gang Center, P.O. Box 12729, Tallahassee, FL 32317; (850) 385-0600; www.iir.com/nygc. A Department of Justice-funded group that collects and analyzes information on gangs.

Office of Juvenile Justice and Delinquency Prevention, 810 7th St., N.W., Washington, D.C. 20531; (202) 307-5911; http://ojjdp.ncjrs.org. A Justice Department office providing leadership, coordination and resources on preventing juvenile delinquency and victimization.

12

American Indians

Peter Katel

Getty Images/Mario Tama

Jerolyn Fink lives in grand style in the housing center built by Connecticut's Mohegan Tribe using profits from its successful Mohegan Sun casino. Thanks in part to booming casinos, many tribes are making progress, but American Indians still face daunting health and economic problems, and tribal leaders say federal aid remains inadequate.

From *CQ Researcher*, April 28, 2006.

I t's not a fancy gambling palace, like some Indian casinos, but the modest operation run by the Winnebago Tribe of Nebraska may just help the 2,300-member tribe hit the economic jackpot.

Using seed money from the casino, it has launched 12 businesses, including a construction company and an Internet news service. Projected 2006 revenues: $150 million.

"It would be absolutely dumb for us to think that gaming is the future," says tribe member Lance Morgan, the 37-year-old Harvard Law School graduate who runs the holding company for the dozen businesses. "Gaming is just a means to an end — and it's done wonders for our tribal economy."

Indian casinos have revived a myth dating back to the early-20th-century Oklahoma oil boom — that Indians are rolling in dough. [1] While some of the 55 tribes that operate big casinos indeed are raking in big profits, the 331 federally recognized tribes in the lower 48 states, on the whole, endure soul-quenching poverty and despair.

Arizona's 1.8-million-acre San Carlos Apache Reservation is among the poorest. The rural, isolated community of about 13,000 people not only faces devastating unemployment but also a deadly methemphetamine epidemic, tribal Chairwoman Kathleen W. Kitcheyan, told the Senate Indian Affairs Committee in April.

"We suffer from a poverty level of 69 percent, which must be unimaginable to many people in this country, who would equate a situation such as this to one found only in Third World countries," she said. Then, speaking of the drug-related death of one of her own grandsons, she had to choke back sobs.

"Our statistics are horrific," says Lionel R. Bordeaux, president

Conditions on Reservations Improved

Socioeconomic conditions improved more on reservations with gambling than on those without gaming during the 1990s, although non-gaming reservations also improved substantially, especially compared to the U.S. population. Some experts attribute the progress among non-gaming tribes to an increase in self-governance on many reservations.

Socioeconomic Changes on Reservations, 1990-2000*
(shown as a percentage or percentage points)

	Non-Gaming	Gaming	U.S.
Real per-capita income	+21.0%	+36.0%	+11.0%
Median household income	+14.0%	+35.0%	+4.0%
Family poverty	-6.9	-11.8	-0.8
Child poverty	-8.1	-11.6	-1.7
Deep poverty	-1.4	-3.4	-0.4
Public assistance	+0.7	-1.6	+0.3
Unemployment	-1.8	-4.8	-0.5
Labor force participation	-1.6	+1.6	-1.3
Overcrowded homes	-1.3	-0.1	+1.1
Homes lacking complete plumbing	-4.6	-3.3	-0.1
Homes lacking complete kitchen	+1.3	-0.6	+0.2
College graduates	+1.7	+2.6	+4.2
High school or equivalency only	-0.3	+1.8	-1.4
Less than 9th-grade education	-5.5	-6.3	-2.8

* The reservation population of the Navajo Nation, which did not have gambling in the 1990s, was not included because it is so large (175,000 in 2000) that it tends to pull down Indian averages when it is included.

Source: Jonathan B. Taylor and Joseph P. Kalt, "Cabazon, The Indian Gaming Regulatory Act, and the Socioeconomic Consequences of American Indian Governmental Gaming: A Ten-Year Review, American Indians on Reservations: A Databook of Socioeconomic Change Between the 1990 and 2000 Censuses," Harvard Project on American Indian Economic Development, January 2005

- Nearly one in five Indians age 25 or older in tribes without gambling operations had less than a ninth-grade education. But even members of tribes with gambling had a college graduation rate of only 16 percent, about half the national percentage. [5]
- Death rates from alcoholism and tuberculosis among Native Americans are at least 650 percent higher than overall U.S. rates. [6]
- Indian youths commit suicide at nearly triple the rate of young people in general. [7]
- Indians on reservations, especially in the resource-poor Upper Plains and West, are the nation's third-largest group of methemphetamine users. [8]

The immediate prognosis for the nation's 4.4 million Native Americans is bleak, according to the Harvard Project on American Indian Economic Development. "If U.S. and on-reservation Indian per-capita income were to continue to grow at their 1990s' rates," it said, "it would take half a century for the tribes to catch up." [9]

Nonetheless, there has been forward movement in Indian Country, though it is measured in modest steps. Among the marks of recent progress:

of Sinte Gleska University, on the Rosebud Sioux Reservation in South Dakota. "We're at the bottom rung of the ladder in all areas, whether it's education levels, economic achievement or political status." [2]

National statistics aren't much better:

- Indian unemployment on reservations nationwide is 49 percent — 10 times the national rate. [3]
- The on-reservation family poverty rate in 2000 was 37 percent — four times the national figure of 9 percent. [4]

- Per-capita income rose 20 percent on reservations, to $7,942, (and 36 percent in tribes with casinos, to $9,771), in contrast to an 11 percent overall U.S. growth rate. [10]
- Unemployment has dropped by up to 5 percent on reservations and in other predominantly Indian areas. [11]
- Child poverty in non-gaming tribes dropped from 55 percent of the child population to 44 percent (but the Indian rate is still more than double the 17 percent average nationwide). [12]

More than two centuries of court decisions, treaties and laws have created a complicated system of coexistence between tribes and the rest of the country. On one level, tribes are sovereign entities that enjoy a government-to-government relationship with Washington. But the sovereignty is qualified. In the words of an 1831 Supreme Court decision that is a bedrock of Indian law, tribes are "domestic dependent nations." [13]

The blend of autonomy and dependence grows out of the Indians' reliance on Washington for sheer survival, says Robert A. Williams Jr., a law professor at the University of Arizona and a member of North Carolina's Lumbee Tribe. "Indians insisted in their treaties that the Great White Father protect us from these racial maniacs in the states — where racial discrimination was most developed — and guarantee us a right to education, a right to water, a territorial base, a homeland," he says. "Tribes sold an awful lot of land in return for a trust relationship to keep the tribes going."

Today, the practical meaning of the relationship with Washington is that American Indians on reservations, and to some extent those elsewhere, depend entirely or partly on federal funding for health, education and other needs. Tribes with casinos and other businesses lessen their reliance on federal dollars.

Unlike other local governments, tribes don't have a tax base whose revenues they share with state governments. Federal spending on Indian programs of all kinds nationwide currently amounts to about $11 billion, James Cason, associate deputy secretary of the Interior, told the Senate Indian Affairs Committee in February.

But the abysmal conditions under which many American Indians live make it all too clear that isn't enough, Indians say. "This is always a discussion at our tribal leaders' meetings," says Cecilia Fire Thunder, president of the Oglala Sioux Tribe in Pine Ridge, S.D. "The biggest job that tribal leaders have is to see that the government lives up to its responsibilities to our people. It's a battle that never ends."

Indeed, a decades-old class-action suit alleges systematic mismanagement of billions of dollars in Indian-owned assets by the Interior Department — a case that has prompted withering criticism of the department by the judge (*see p. 281*).

Government officials insist that, despite orders to cut spending, they've been able to keep providing essential services. Charles Grim, director of the Indian Health

Revenues From Casinos Almost Doubled

Revenue from Indian gaming operations nearly doubled to $19.4 billion from 2000-2004. The number of Indian casinos increased from 311 to 367 during the period.

Indian Gaming Revenues
(2000-2004)

Revenue (in $ billions)

$10.9 $12.8 $14.7 $16.8 $19.4
2000 2001 2002 2003 2004

Source: Indian Gaming Commission

Service, told the Indian Affairs Committee, "In a deficit-reduction year, it's a very strong budget and one that does keep pace with inflationary and population-growth increases."

In any event, from the tribes' point of view, they lack the political muscle to force major increases. "The big problem is the Indians are about 1 percent of the national population," says Joseph Kalt, co-director of the Harvard Project. "The voice is so tiny."

Faced with that grim political reality, Indians are trying to make better use of scarce federal dollars through a federally sponsored "self-governance" movement. Leaders of the movement say tribes can deliver higher-quality services more efficiently when they control their own budgets. Traditionally, federal agencies operate programs on reservations, such as law enforcement or medical services.

But since the 1990s, dozens of tribes have stepped up control of their own affairs both by building their own

AP Photo/William Lauer

Controversial Whiteclay, Neb., sells millions of cans of beer annually to residents of the nearby Pine Ridge Reservation in South Dakota. Alcohol abuse and unemployment continue to plague the American Indian community.

businesses and by signing self-governance "compacts" with the federal government. Compacts provide tribes with large chunks of money, or block grants, rather than individual grants for each service. Then, with minimal federal oversight, the tribes develop their own budgets and run all or most services.

The self-governance trend gathered steam during the same time that Indian-owned casinos began booming. For many tribes, the gambling business provided a revenue stream that didn't flow from Washington.

According to economist Alan Meister, 228 tribes in 30 states operated 367 high-stakes bingo halls or casinos in 2004, earning an estimated $19.6 billion. [14]

The gambling houses operate under the 1988 Indian Gaming Regulatory Act (IGRA), which was made possible by a U.S. Supreme Court ruling upholding tribes' rights to govern their own activities. [15] A handful of tribes are doing so well that $80 million from six tribes in 2000-2003 helped fuel the scandal surrounding one-time Washington super-lobbyist Jack Abramoff, whose clients were among the most successful casino tribes. [16]

If the Abramoff scandal contributed to the notion of widespread Indian wealth, one reason may be the mis-impression that tribes don't pay taxes on their gambling earnings. In fact, under the IGRA, federal, state and local governments took in $6.3 billion in gambling-generated

tax revenues in 2004, with 67 percent going to the federal government. In addition, tribes paid out some $889 million in 2004 to state and local governments in order to get gambling operations approved. [17]

The spread of casinos has prompted some cities and counties, along with citizens' groups and even some casino-operating tribes, to resist casino-expansion plans.

The opposition to expansion is another reason tribal entrepreneur Morgan doesn't think gaming is a good long-range bet for Indians' future. His vision involves full tribal control of the Indians' main asset — their land. He argues for ending the "trust status" under which tribes can't buy or sell reservation property — a relic of 19th-century protection against rapacious state governments.

Indian Country needs a better business climate, Morgan says, and the availability of land as collateral for investments would be a big step in that direction. "America has a wonderful economic system, probably the best in the world, but the reservation tends to be an economic black hole."

As Indians seek to improve their lives, here are some of the issues being debated:

Is the federal government neglecting Native Americans?

There is wide agreement that the federal government bears overwhelming responsibility for Indians' welfare, but U.S. and tribal officials disagree over the adequacy of the aid Indians receive. Sen. John McCain, R-Ariz., chairman of the Senate Indian Affairs Committee, and Vice Chairman Byron L. Dorgan, D-N.D., have been leading the fight for more aid to Indians. "We have a full-blown crisis . . . particularly dealing with children and elderly, with respect to housing, education and health care," Dorgan told the committee on Feb. 14. He characterized administration proposals as nothing more than "nibbling around the edges on these issues . . . making a few adjustments here or there.' "

Administration officials respond that given the severe federal deficit, they are focusing on protecting vital programs. "As we went through and prioritized our budget, we basically looked at all of the programs that were secondary and tertiary programs, and they were the first ones on the block to give tradeoffs for our core programs in maintaining the integrity of those," Interior's Cason told the committee.

For Indians on isolated reservations, says Bordeaux of the Rosebud Sioux, there's little alternative to federal money. He compares tribes' present circumstances to those after the buffalo had been killed off, and an Army general told the Indians to eat beef, which made them sick. "The general told them, 'Either that, or you eat the grass on which you stand.' "

But David B. Vickers, president of Upstate Citizens for Equality, in Union Springs, N.Y., which opposes Indian land claims and casino applications, argues that accusations of federal neglect are inaccurate and skirt the real problem. The central issue is that the constitutional system is based on individual rights, not tribal rights, he says. "Indians are major recipients of welfare now. They're eligible. They don't need a tribe or leader; all they have to do is apply like anybody else."

Pat Ragsdale, director of the Bureau of Indian Affairs (BIA), acknowledges that Dorgan's and McCain's criticisms echo a 2003 U.S. Commission on Civil Rights report, which also called underfunding of Indian aid a crisis. "The government is failing to live up to its trust responsibility to Native peoples," the commission concluded. "Efforts to bring Native Americans up to the standards of other Americans have failed in part because of a lack of sustained funding. The failure manifests itself in massive and escalating unmet needs." [18]

"Nobody in this government disputes the report, in general," says Ragsdale, a Cherokee. "Some of our tribal communities are in real critical shape, and others are prospering."

The commission found, for example, that in 2003 the Indian Health Service appropriation amounted to $2,533 per capita — below even the $3,803 per capita appropriated for federal prisoners.

Concern over funding for Indian programs in 2007 centers largely on health and education. Although 90 percent of Indian students attend state-operated public schools, their schools get federal aid because tribes don't pay property taxes, which typically fund public schools. The remaining 10 percent of Indian students attend schools operated by the BIA or by tribes themselves under BIA contracts.

"There is not a congressman or senator who would send his own children or grandchildren to our schools," said Ryan Wilson, president of the National Indian Education Association, citing "crumbling buildings and outdated structures with lead in the pipes and mold on the walls." [19]

Cason told the Indian Affairs Committee the administration is proposing a $49 million cut, from $157.4 million to $108.1 million, in school construction and repair in 2007. He also said that only 10 of 37 dilapidated schools funded for replacement by 2006 have been completed, with another 19 scheduled to finish in 2007. Likewise, he said the department is also behind on 45 school improvement projects.

McCain questioned whether BIA schools and public schools with large Indian enrollments would be able to meet the requirements set by the national No Child Left Behind Law. [20] Yes, replied Darla Marburger, deputy assistant secretary of Education for policy. "For the first time, we'll be providing money to . . . take a look at how students are achieving in ways that they can tailor their programs to better meet the needs of students." Overall, the Department of Education would spend about $1 billion on Indian education under the administration's proposed budget for 2007, or $6 million less than in 2006.

McCain and Dorgan are also among those concerned about administration plans to eliminate the Indian Health Service's $32.7 million urban program, which this year made medical and counseling services available to some 430,000 off-reservation Indians at 41 medical facilities in cities around the nation. (*See Sidebar, p. 278.*) The administration argues that the services were available through other programs, but McCain and Dorgan noted that "no evaluation or evidence has been provided to support this contention." [21]

Indian Health Service spokesman Thomas Sweeney, a member of the Citizen Potawatomi Nation of Oklahoma, says only 72,703 Indians used urban health centers in 2004 and that expansion of another federal program would pick up the slack. [22]

In Seattle, elimination of the urban program would cut $4 million from the city's Indian Health Board budget, says Executive Director Ralph Forquera. "Why pick on a $33 million appropriation?" he asks. In his skeptical view, the proposal reflects another "unspoken" termination program. You take a sub-population — urban Indians — and eliminate funding, then [you target] tribes under 1,000 members, and there are a lot of them. Little by little, you pick apart the system."

The IHS's Grim told the Senate committee on Feb. 14 the cuts were designed to protect funding that "can be used most effectively to improve the health status of American Indian and Alaskan Native people."

Have casinos benefited Indians?

Over the past two decades, Indian casinos have become powerful economic engines for many tribal economies. But the enthusiasm for casinos is not unanimous.

"If you're looking at casinos in terms of how they've actually raised the status of Indian people, they've been an abysmal failure," says Ted Jojola, a professor of planning at the University of New Mexico and a member of Isleta Pueblo, near Albuquerque. "But in terms of augmenting the original federal trust-responsibility areas — education, health, tribal government — they've been a spectacular success. Successful gaming tribes have ploughed the money either into diversifying their economies or they've augmented funds that would have come to them anyway."

Tribes with casinos near big population centers are flourishing. The Coushatta Tribe's casino near Lake Charles, La., generates $300 million a year, enough to provide about $40,000 to every member. [23] And the fabled Foxwoods Resort Casino south of Norwich, Conn., operated by the Mashantucket Pequot Tribe, together with Connecticut's other big casino, the Mohegan Tribe's Mohegan Sun, grossed $2.2 billion just from gambling in 2004. [24]

There are only about 830 Coushattas, so their benefits also include free health care, education and favorable terms on home purchases. [25] The once poverty-stricken Mashantuckets have created Connecticut's most extensive welfare-to-work program, open to both tribe members and non-members. In 1997-2000, the program helped 150 welfare recipients find jobs. [26]

Most tribes don't enjoy success on that scale. Among the nation's 367 Indian gambling operations, only 15 grossed $250 million or more in 2004 (another 40 earned $100 million to $250 million); 94 earned less than $3 million and 57 earned $3 million to $10 million. [27]

"We have a small casino that provides close to $3 million to the tribal nation as a whole," says Bordeaux, on the Rosebud Sioux Reservation. The revenue has been channeled into the tribe's Head Start program, an emergency home-repair fund and other projects. W. Ron Allen, chairman of the Jamestown S'Klallam Tribe in Sequim, Wash., says his tribe's small casino has raised living standards so much that some two-dozen students a year go to college, instead of one or two.

Efforts to open additional casinos are creating conflicts between tribes that operate competing casinos, as well as with some of their non-Indian neighbors. Convicted lobbyist Abramoff, for example, was paid millions of dollars by tribes seeking to block other tribal casinos. [28]

Some non-Indian communities also oppose casino expansion. "We firmly believe a large, generally unregulated casino will fundamentally change the character of our community forever," said Liz Thomas, a member of Tax Payers of Michigan Against Casinos, which opposes a casino planned by the Pokagon Band of Potawotami Indians Tribe in the Lake Michigan town of New Buffalo, where Taylor and her husband operate a small resort.

"People are OK with Donald Trump making millions of dollars individually," says Joseph Podlasek, executive director of the American Indian Center of Chicago, "but if a race of people is trying to become self-sufficient, now that's not respectable."

Nevertheless, some American Indians have mixed feelings about the casino route to economic development. "I don't think anyone would have picked casinos" for that purpose, says the University of Arizona's Williams. "Am I ambivalent about it? Absolutely. But I'm not ambivalent about a new fire station, or Kevlar vests for tribal police fighting meth gangs."

"There's no question that some of the money has been used for worthwhile purposes," concedes Guy Clark, a Corrales, N.M., dentist who chairs the National Coalition Against Legalized Gambling. But, he adds, "If you do a cost-benefit analysis, the cost is much greater than the benefit." Restaurants and other businesses, for example, lose customers who often gamble away their extra money.

Even some Indian leaders whose tribes profit from casinos raise caution flags, especially about per-capita payments. For Nebraska's Winnebagos, payments amount to just a few hundred dollars, says CEO Morgan. What bothers him are dividends "that are just big enough that you don't have to work or get educated — say, $20,000 to $40,000."

But there's no denying the impact casinos can have. At a January public hearing on the Oneida Indian Nation's attempt to put 17,000 acres of upstate New York land into tax-free "trust" status, hundreds of the 4,500 employees of the tribe's Turning Stone Resort and Casino, near Utica, showed up in support. "When I was a kid, people worked for General Motors, General Electric, Carrier and Oneida Ltd.," said casino Human Resources Director Mark Mancini. "Today, people work for the Oneida Indian Nation and their enterprises." [29]

For tribes that can't build independent economies any other way, casinos are appealing. The 225,000-member Navajo Nation, the biggest U.S. tribe, twice rejected gaming before finally approving it in 2004. [30] "We need that infusion of jobs and revenue, and people realize that," said Duane Yazzie, president of the Navajos' Shiprock, N.M., chapter. [31]

But the Navajos face stiff competition from dozens of casinos already in operation near the vast Navajo reservation, which spreads across parts of Arizona, New Mexico and Utah and is larger than the state of West Virginia.

Would money alone solve American Indians' problems?

No one in Indian Country (or on Capitol Hill) denies the importance of federal funding to American Indians' future, but some Indians say it isn't the only answer.

"We are largely on our own because of limited financial assistance from the federal government," said Joseph A. Garcia, president of the National Congress of American Indians, in his recent "State of Indian Nations" speech. [32]

Fifty-two tribal officials and Indian program directors expressed similar sentiments in March before the House Appropriations Subcommittee on the Interior. Pleading their case before lawmakers who routinely consider billion-dollar weapons systems and other big projects, the tribal leaders sounded like small-town county commissioners as they urged lawmakers to increase or restore small but vital grants for basic health, education and welfare services.

"In our ICWA [Indian Child Welfare Act] program, currently we have a budget of $79,000 a year," said Harold Frazier, chairman of the Cheyenne River Sioux, in South Dakota. "We receive over 1,300 requests for assistance annually from 11 states and eight counties in South Dakota. We cannot give the type of attention to these requests that they deserve. Therefore, we are requesting $558,000."

To university President Bordeaux, federal funding is vital because his desolate reservation has few other options for economic survival. "What's missing is money," he says.

A National Indian Gaming Association advertisement touts the benefits of tribal gaming operations to American Indian communities. Some 228 tribes in 30 states operated 367 high-stakes bingo halls or casinos in 2004.

Money is crucial to improving Indians' health, says Dr. Joycelyn Dorscher, director of the Center of American Indian and Minority Health at the University of Minnesota-Duluth. Especially costly are programs to combat diabetes and other chronic diseases, says Dorscher, a Chippewa. While health programs have to be carefully designed to fit Indian cultural patterns, she says, "Everything comes down to time or money in the grand scheme of things."

But with funding from Washington never certain from year to year, says the Harvard Project's Kalt, "The key to economic development has not been federal funding" but rather "tribes' ability to run their own affairs."

For tribes without self-government compacts, growing demands for services and shrinking funding from Washington make keeping the dollars flowing the highest priority. "We're always afraid of more cutbacks," says Oglala Sioux President Fire Thunder.

But an Indian education leader with decades of federal budgetary negotiations acknowledges that problems go beyond funding shortfalls. "If you ask students why they dropped out, they say, 'I don't see a future for myself,' " says David Beaulieu, director of Arizona State University's Center for Indian Education. "Educators need to tie the purposes of schooling to the broad-based purposes of society. We're more successful when we tie education to the meaning of life."

The University of Arizona's Williams says a tribe's success and failure may be tied more to the way its government is organized than to how much funding it gets.

Williams says the first priority of tribes still using old-style constitutions should be reorganization, because they feature a weak executive elected by a tribal council. "That's what the BIA was used to," he explains. "It could play off factions and families, and the economic system would be based on patronage and taking care of your own family." Under such a system, he adds, "there's not going to be any long-term strategic planning going on." [33]

Yet other needs exist as well, says the American Indian Center's Podlasek. "It's so difficult for us to find a place to do a traditional ceremony," he says. "We had a traditional healer in town last month, and he wanted to build a sweat lodge. We actually had to go to Indiana. Doing it in the city wasn't even an option."

BACKGROUND

Conquered Homelands

Relations between Indian and non-Indian civilizations in the Americas began with the Spanish Conquistadors' explorations of the 1500s, followed by the French and British. By turns the three powers alternated policies of enslavement, peaceful coexistence and all-out warfare against the Indians. [34]

By 1830, with the Europeans largely gone, white settlers moved westward into Georgia, Mississippi and Alabama. Unwilling to share the rich frontier land, they pushed the Indians out. President Andrew Jackson backed the strategy, and Congress enacted it into the Indian Removal Act of 1830, which called for moving the region's five big tribes into the Oklahoma Territory.

If the law didn't make clear where Indians stood with the government, the treatment of Mississippi's Choctaws provided chilling evidence. Under a separate treaty, Choctaws who refused to head for Oklahoma could remain at home, become citizens and receive land. In practice, none of that was allowed, and Indians who stayed in Mississippi lived marginal existences.

Georgia simplified the claiming of Cherokee lands by effectively ending Cherokee self-rule. The so-called "Georgia Guard" reinforced the point by beating and jailing Indians. Jackson encouraged Georgia's actions, and when Indians protested, he said he couldn't interfere. The lawsuit filed by the Cherokees eventually reached the Supreme Court.

Chief Justice John Marshall's 1831 majority opinion, *Cherokee Nation v. Georgia*, would cast a long shadow over Indians' rights, along with two other decisions, issued in 1823 and 1832. "Almost all Indian policy is the progeny of the conflicting views of Jackson and Marshall," wrote W. Dale Mason, a political scientist at the University of New Mexico. [35]

In concluding that the court couldn't stop Georgia's actions, Marshall defined the relationship between Indians and the U.S. government. While Marshall wrote that Indians didn't constitute a foreign state, he noted that they owned the land they occupied until they made a "voluntary cession." Marshall concluded the various tribes were "domestic dependent nations." In practical terms, "Their relations to the United States resembles that of a ward to his guardian." [36]

Having rejected the Cherokees' argument, the University of Arizona's Williams writes, the court "provided no effective judicial remedy for Indian tribes to protect their basic human rights to property, self-government, and cultural survival under U.S. law." [37]

Along with the *Cherokee* case, the other two opinions that make up the so-called Marshall Trilogy are *Johnson v. M'Intosh* (also known as *Johnson v. McIntosh*), and *Worcester v. State of Georgia.* [38]

In *Johnson*, Marshall wrote that the European empires that "discovered" America became its owners and had "an exclusive right to extinguish the Indian title of occupancy, either by purchase or by conquest. The tribes of Indians inhabiting this country were fierce savages. . . . To leave them in possession of their country was to leave the country a wilderness." [39]

However, Marshall used the 1832 *Worcester* opinion to define the limits of state authority over Indian tribes, holding that the newcomers couldn't simply eject Indians.

"The Cherokee nation . . . is a distinct community occupying its own territory . . . in which the laws of Georgia can have no force," Marshall wrote. Georgia's conviction and sentencing of a missionary for not swearing allegiance to the state "interferes forcibly with the relations established between the United States and the Cherokee nation." [40] That is, the federal government — not states — held the reins of power over tribes.

According to legend, Jackson remarked: "John Marshall has made his decision — now let him enforce it." Between Jackson's disregard of the Supreme Court and white settlers' later manipulation of the legal system to vacate Indian lands, the end result was the dispossession of Indian lands.

Forced Assimilation

The expulsions of the Native Americans continued in the Western territories — especially after the Civil War. "I instructed Captain Barry, if possible to exterminate the whole village," Lt. Col. George Green wrote of his participation in an 1869 campaign against the White Mountain Apaches in Arizona and New Mexico. "There seems to be no settled policy, but a general policy to kill them wherever found." [41]

Some military men and civilians didn't go along. But whether by brute force or by persuasion, Indians were pushed off lands that non-Indians wanted. One strategy was to settle the Indians on reservations guarded by military posts. The strategy grew into a general policy for segregating Indians on these remote tracts.

Even after the Indians were herded onto lands that no one else wanted, the government didn't respect reservation boundaries. They were reconfigured as soon as non-Indians saw something valuable, such as mineral wealth.

The strategy of elastic reservation boundaries led to the belief — or rationalization — that reservations served no useful purposes for Indians themselves. That doctrine led to a policy enshrined in an 1887 law to convert reservations to individual landholdings. Well-meaning advocates of the plan saw it as a way to inculcate notions of private property and Euro-American culture in general.

All tribal land was to be divided into 160-acre allotments, one for each Indian household. The parcels wouldn't become individual property, though, for 25 years.

Indian consent wasn't required. In some cases, government agents tried persuading Indians to join in; in others, the divvying-up proceeded even with many Indians opposed. In Arizona, however, the government backed off from breaking up the lands of the long-settled Hopis, who resisted attempts to break up their territory. The vast Navajo Nation in Arizona, Utah and New Mexico was also left intact.

While widely reviled, the "forced assimilation" policy left a benign legacy for the affected Indians: the grant of citizenship. Beyond that, the era's Indians were restricted to unproductive lands, and with little means of support many fell prey to alcoholism and disease.

The bleak period ended with President Franklin D. Roosevelt. In his first term he appointed a defender of Indian culture, John Collier, as commissioner of Indian affairs. Collier pushed for the Indian Reorganization Act of 1934, which ended the allotment program, financed purchases of new Indian lands and authorized the organization of tribal governments that enjoyed control over revenues.

Termination

After World War II, a new, anti-Indian mood swept Washington, partly in response to pressure from states where non-Indians eyed Indian land.

Collier resigned in 1945 after years of conflict over what critics called his antagonism to missionaries proselytizing among the Indians and his sympathies toward the tribes. The 1950 appointment of Dillon S. Myer — fresh from supervising the wartime internment of Japanese-Americans — clearly reflected the new attitude. Myer showed little interest in what Indians themselves thought of the new policy of shrinking tribal land holdings. "I realize that it will not be possible always to obtain Indian cooperation. . . . We must proceed, even though [this] may be lacking." [42]

Congress hadn't authorized a sweeping repeal of earlier policy. But the introduction of dozens of bills in the late 1940s to sell Indian land or liquidate some reservation holdings entirely showed which way the winds were blowing. And in 1953, a House Concurrent Resolution declared Congress' policy to be ending Indians' "status as wards of the United States, and to grant them all of the rights and privileges pertaining to American citizenship." A separate law granted state jurisdiction over Indian reservations in five Midwestern and Western states and extended the same authority to other states that wanted to claim it. [43]

CHRONOLOGY

1800s *United States expands westward, pushing Indians off most of their original lands, sometimes creating new reservations for them.*

1830 President Andrew Jackson signs the Indian Removal Act, forcing the Cherokees to move from Georgia to Oklahoma.

1832 Supreme Court issues the last of three decisions defining Indians' legal status as wards of the government.

1871 Congress makes its treaties with tribes easier to alter, enabling non-Indians to take Indian lands when natural resources are discovered.

Dec. 29, 1890 U.S. soldiers massacre at least 150 Plains Indians, mostly women and children, at Wounded Knee, S.D.

1900-1950s *Congress and the executive branch undertake major shifts in Indian policy, first strengthening tribal governments then trying to force cultural assimilation.*

1924 Indians are granted U.S. citizenship.

1934 Indian Reorganization Act authorizes expansion of reservations and strengthening of tribal governments.

1953 Congress endorses full assimilation of Indians into American society, including "relocation" from reservations to cities.

1960s-1980s *In the radical spirit of the era, Native Americans demand respect for their traditions and an end to discrimination; federal government concedes more power to tribal governments, allows gambling on tribal lands.*

1969 American Indian Movement (AIM) seizes Alcatraz Island in San Francisco Bay to dramatize claims of injustice.

July 7, 1970 President Richard M. Nixon vows support for Indian self-government.

Feb. 27, 1973 AIM members occupy the town of Wounded Knee on the Pine Ridge, S.D., Sioux Reservation, for two months; two Indians die and an FBI agent is wounded.

1988 Indian Gaming Regulatory Act allows tribes to operate casinos under agreements with states.

1990s *Indian-owned casinos boom; tribal governments push to expand self-rule and reduce Bureau of Indian Affairs (BIA) supervision.*

1994 President Bill Clinton signs law making experimental self-governance compacts permanent.

March 27, 1996 U.S. Supreme Court rules states can't be forced to negotiate casino compacts, thus encouraging tribes to make revenue-sharing deals with states as the price of approval.

June 10, 1996 Elouise Cobell, a member of the Blackfeet Tribe in Montana, charges Interior Department mismanagement of Indian trust funds cheated Indians out of billions of dollars. The case is still pending.

Nov. 3, 1998 California voters uphold tribes' rights to run casinos; state Supreme Court later invalidates the provision, but it is revived by a 1999 compact between the tribes and the state.

2000s *Indian advocates decry low funding levels, and sovereignty battles continue; lobbying scandal spotlights Indian gambling profits.*

2000 Tribal Self-Governance Demonstration Project becomes permanent.

2003 U.S. Commission on Civil Rights calls underfunding for Indians a crisis, saying federal government spends less for Indian health care than for any other group, including prison inmates.

Feb. 22, 2004 *Washington Post* reports on Washington lobbyist Jack Abramoff's deals with casino tribes.

March 29, 2005 U.S. Supreme Court blocks tax exemptions for Oneida Nation of New York on newly purchased land simply because it once owned the property.

April 5, 2006 Tribal and BIA officials testify in Congress that methamphetamine addiction is ravaging reservations.

The following year, Congress "terminated" formal recognition and territorial sovereignty of six tribes. Four years later, after public opposition began building (spurred in part by religious organizations), Congress abandoned termination. In the meantime, however, Indians had lost 1.6 million acres.

At the same time, though, the federal government maintained an associated policy — relocation. The BIA persuaded Indians to move to cities — Chicago, Denver and Los Angeles were the main destinations — and opened job-placement and housing-aid programs. The BIA placed Indians far from their reservations to keep them from returning. By 1970, the BIA estimated that 40 percent of all Indians lived in cities, of which one-third had been relocated by the bureau; the rest moved on their own. [44]

Activism

Starting in the late 1960s, the winds of change blowing through American society were felt as deeply in Indian Country as anywhere. Two books played a crucial role. In 1969, Vine Deloria Jr., member of a renowned family of Indian intellectuals from Oklahoma, published his landmark history, *Custer Died For Your Sins*, which portrayed American history from the Indians' viewpoint. The following year, Dee Brown's *Bury My Heart at Wounded Knee* described the settling of the West also from an Indian point of view. The books astonished many non-Indians. Among young Indians, the volumes reflected and spurred on a growing political activism.

It was in this climate that the newly formed American Indian Movement (AIM) took over Alcatraz Island, the former federal prison site in San Francisco Bay (where rebellious Indians had been held during the Indian Wars), to publicize demands to honor treaties and

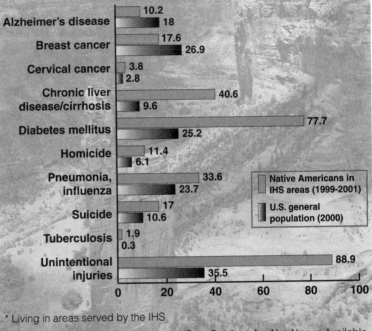

Disease Toll Higher Among Indians

American Indians served by the Indian Health Service (IHS) — mainly low-income or uninsured — die at substantially higher rates than the general population from liver disease, diabetes, tuberculosis, pneumonia and influenza as well as from homicide, suicide and injuries. However, Indians' death rates from Alzheimer's disease or breast cancer are lower.

Health Status of American Indians *
Compared to General Population
(deaths per 100,000 population)

	Native Americans in IHS areas (1999-2001)	U.S. general population (2000)
Alzheimer's disease	10.2	18
Breast cancer	17.6	26.9
Cervical cancer	3.8	2.8
Chronic liver disease/cirrhosis	40.6	9.6
Diabetes mellitus	77.7	25.2
Homicide	11.4	6.1
Pneumonia, influenza	33.6	23.7
Suicide	17	10.6
Tuberculosis	1.9	0.3
Unintentional injuries	88.9	35.5

* Living in areas served by the IHS

Source: "Indian Health Service: Health Care Services Are Not Always Available to Native Americans," Government Accountability Office, August 2005

Background image: Canyon de Chelly, Navajo Nation, Arizona (Navajo Tourism)

respect Native Americans' dignity. The takeover lasted from Nov. 20, 1969, to June 11, 1971, when U.S. marshals removed the occupiers. [45]

A second AIM-government confrontation took the form of a one-week takeover of BIA headquarters in Washington in November 1972 by some 500 AIM members protesting what they called broken treaty obligations. Protesters charged that government services to Indians were inadequate in general, with urban Indians neglected virtually completely.

Budget Cuts Target Health Clinics

When Lita Pepion, a health consultant and a member of the Blackfeet Nation, learned that her 22-year-old-niece had been struggling with heroin abuse, she urged her to seek treatment at the local Urban Indian Clinic in Billings, Mont.

But the young woman had so much trouble getting an appointment that she gave up. Only recently, says Pepion, did she overcome her addiction on her own.

The clinic is one of 34 federally funded, Indian-controlled clinics that contract with the Indian Health Service (IHS) to serve urban Indians. But President Bush's 2007 budget would kill the $33-million program, eliminating most of the clinics' funding.

Indians in cities will still be able to get health care through several providers, including the federal Health Centers program, says Office of Management and Budget spokesman Richard Walker. The proposed budget would increase funding for the centers by nearly $2 billion, IHS Director Charles W. Grim told the Senate Indian Affairs Committee on Feb. 14, 2006. [1]

But Joycelyn Dorscher, president of the Association of American Indian Physicians, says the IHS clinics do a great job and that, "It's very important that people from diverse backgrounds have physicians like themselves."

Others, however, including Pepion, say the clinics are poorly managed and lack direction. Ralph Forquera, director of the Seattle-based Urban Indian Health Institute, says

that while the clinics "have made great strides medically, a lack of resources has resulted in services from unqualified professionals." In addition, he says, "we have not been as successful in dealing with lifestyle changes and mental health problems."

Many Indian health experts oppose the cuts because Indians in both urban areas and on reservations have more health problems than the general population, including 126 percent more chronic liver disease and cirrhosis, 54 percent more diabetes and 178 percent more alcohol-related deaths. [2]

Indian health specialists blame the Indians' higher disease rates on history, lifestyle and genetics — not just on poverty. "You don't see exactly the same things happening to other poor minority groups," says Dorscher, a North Dakota Chippewa, so "there's something different" going on among Indians.

In the view of Donna Keeler, executive director of the South Dakota Urban Indian Health program and an Eastern Shoshone, historical trauma affects the physical wellness of patients in her state's three urban Indian clinics.

Susette Schwartz, CEO of the Hunter Urban Indian Clinic in Wichita, Kan., agrees. She attributes Indians' high rates of mental health and alcohol/substance abuse to their long history of government maltreatment. Many Indian children in the 19th and early 20th centuries, she points out, were taken from their parents and sent to government boarding schools where speaking native languages was pro-

Another protest occurred on Feb. 27, 1973, when 200 AIM members occupied the village of Wounded Knee on the Oglala Sioux's Pine Ridge Reservation in South Dakota. U.S. soldiers had massacred at least 150 Indians at Wounded Knee in 1890. AIM was protesting what it called the corrupt tribal government. And a weak, involuntary manslaughter charge against a non-Indian who had allegedly killed an Indian near the reservation had renewed Indian anger at discriminatory treatment by police and judges.

The occupation soon turned into a full-blown siege, with the reservation surrounded by troops and federal law-enforcement officers. During several firefights two AIM members were killed, and an FBI agent was wounded. The occupation ended on May 8, 1973.

Self-Determination

Amid the surging Indian activism, the federal government was trying to make up for the past by encouraging tribal self-determination. [46]

In 1975, Congress passed the Indian Self-Determination and Education Assistance Act, which channeled federal contracts and grants directly to tribes, reducing the BIA role and effectively putting Indian communities in direct charge of schools, health, housing and other programs.

And to assure Indians that the era of sudden reversals in federal policy had ended, the House in 1988 passed a resolution reaffirming the "constitutionally recognized government-to-government relationship with Indian tribes." Separate legislation set up a "self-governance

hibited. "Taking away the culture and language years ago," says Schwartz, as well as the government's role in "taking their children and sterilizing their women" in the 1970s, all contributed to Indians' behavioral health issues.

Keeler also believes Indians' low incomes cause their unhealthy lifestyles. Many eat high-fat, high-starch foods because they are cheaper, Pepion says. Growing up on a reservation, she recalls, "We didn't eat a lot of vegetables because we couldn't afford them."

Opponents of the funding cuts for urban Indian health centers also cite a recent letter to President Bush from Daniel R. Hawkins Jr., vice president for federal, state and local government for the National Association of Community Health Centers. He said the urban Indian clinics and community health centers are complementary, not duplicative.

While Pepion does not believe funding should be cut entirely, she concedes that alternative health-care services are often "better equipped than the urban Indian clinics." And if American Indians want to assimilate into the larger society, they can't have everything culturally separate, she adds. "The only way that I was able to assimilate into an urban society was to make myself do those things that were

Native Americans in downtown Salt Lake City, Utah, demonstrate on April 21, 2006, against the elimination of funding for Urban Indian Health Clinics.

uncomfortable for me," she says.

But Schwartz believes a great benefit of the urban clinics are their Indian employees, "who are culturally competent and sensitive and incorporate Native American-specific cultural ideas." Because of their history of cultural abuse, it takes a long time for Native Americans to trust non-Indian health providers, says Schwartz. "They're not just going to go to a health center down the road."

Dorscher and Schwartz also say the budget cuts could lead to more urban Indians ending up in costly emergency rooms because of their reluctance to trust the community health centers. "Ultimately, it would become more expensive to cut the prevention and primary care programs than it would be to maintain them," Dorscher says.

— *Melissa J. Hipolit*

---

[1] Prepared testimony of Director of Indian Health Service Dr. Charles W. Grim before the Senate Committee on Indian Affairs, Feb. 14, 2006.

[2] Urban Indian Health Institute, "The Health Status of Urban American Indians and Alaska Natives," March 16, 2004, p. v.

---

demonstration project" in which eligible tribes would sign "compacts" to run their own governments with block grants from the federal government. [47]

By 1993, 28 tribes had negotiated compacts with the Interior Department. And in 1994, President Bill Clinton signed legislation that made self-governance a permanent option.

For the general public, the meaning of newly strengthened Indian sovereignty could be summed up with one word: casinos. In 1988, Congress enacted legislation regulating tribal gaming operations. That move followed a Supreme Court ruling (*California v. Cabazon*) that authorized tribes to run gambling operations. But tribes could not offer a form of gambling specifically barred by the state.

The law set up three categories of gambling operations: Class I, traditional Indian games, controlled exclusively by tribes; Class II, including bingo, lotto, pull tabs and some card games, which are allowed on tribal lands in states that allow the games elsewhere; and Class III, which takes in casino games such as slot machines, roulette and blackjack, which can be offered only under agreements with state governments that set out the size and types of the proposed casinos.

Limits that the Indian Gaming Regulatory Act put on Indian sovereignty were tightened further by a 1996 Supreme Court decision that the Seminole Tribe couldn't sue Florida to force negotiation of a casino compact. The decision essentially forced tribes nation-

Native American children and adults in the Chicago area keep in touch with their cultural roots at the American Indian Center. About two-thirds of the nation's Indians live in urban areas.

American Indian Center/Warren Perlstein

wide to make revenue-sharing deals with states in return for approval of casinos. [48]

Meanwhile, particularily on reservations from Minnesota to the Pacific Northwest, a plague of methamphetamine addiction and manufacturing is leaving a trail of death and shattered lives. By 2002, Darrell Hillaire, chairman of the Lummi Nation, near Bellingham, Wash., said that members convicted of dealing meth would be expelled from the tribe. [49]

But the Lummis couldn't stop the spread of the scourge on other reservations. National Congress of American Indians President Garcia said early in 2006: "Methamphetamine is a poison taking Indian lives, destroying Indian families, and razing entire communities." [50]

CURRENT SITUATION

Self-Government

Some Indian leaders are advocating more power for tribal governments as the best way to improve the quality of life on reservations.

Under the Tribal Self-Governance Demonstration Project, made permanent in 1994, tribes can replace program-by-program grants by entering into "compacts" with the federal government, under which they receive a single grant for a variety of services. Some 231 tribes and

Alaskan Native villages have compacts to administer a total of about $341 million in programs. Of the Indian communities now living under compacts, 72 are in the lower 48 states. [51]

Under a set of separate compacts, the Indian Health Service has turned over clinics, hospitals and health programs to some 300 tribes and Alaskan villages, 70 of them non-Alaskan tribes.

The self-governance model has proved especially appropriate in Alaska, where the majority of the native population of 120,000 is concentrated in 229 villages, many of them remote, and compact in size, hence well-suited to managing their own affairs, experts say.

Another advantage of Alaska villages is the experience they acquired through the 1971 Alaska Native Claims Settlement Act, which granted a total of $962 million to Alaska natives born on or before Dec. 18, 1971, in exchange for giving up their claims to millions of acres of land. Villages formed regional corporations to manage the assets. In addition, all Alaska residents receive an annual dividend ($946 in 2005) from natural-resource royalty income. [52]

"The emergence of tribal authority is unprecedented in Indian Country's history," says Allen, of the Jamestown S'Klallam Tribe, one of the originators of the self-governance model. "Why not take the resources you have available and use them as efficiently as you can — more efficiently than currently being administered?" [53]

But the poorer and more populous tribes of the Great Plains and the Southwest have turned down the self-governance model. "They can't afford to do it," says Michael LaPointe, chief of staff to President Rodney Bordeaux of the Rosebud Sioux Tribe. "When you have a lot of poverty and not a lot of economic activity to generate tribal resources to supplement the unfunded mandates, it becomes impossible."

In contrast with the Jameston S'Klallam's tiny membership of 585 people, there are some 24,000 people on the Rosebud Siouxs' million-acre reservation. The tribe does operate law enforcement, ambulances and other services under contracts with the government. But it can't afford to do any more, LaPointe says.

A combined effect of the gambling boom and the growing adoption of the self-governance model is that much of the tension has gone out of the traditionally strained relationship between the BIA and tribes. "BIA people are getting pushed out as decision-makers," Kalt says. Some strains remain, to be sure. Allen says he senses a growing reluctance by the BIA to let go of tribes. "They use the argument that that the BIA doesn't have the money [for block grants]," he says.

BIA Director Ragsdale acknowledges that tougher financial-accounting requirements sparked by a lawsuit over Interior Department handling of Indian trust funds are slowing the compact-approval process. (*See "Trust Settlement" below.*) But, he adds, "We're not trying to hinder self-governance."

Limits on Gambling

Several legislative efforts to limit Indian gaming are pending. Separate bills by Sen. McCain and House Resources Committee Chairman Richard Pombo, R-Calif., would restrict tribes' ability to acquire new land for casinos in more favorable locations.

More proposals are in the pipeline. Jemez Pueblo of New Mexico wants to build a casino near the town of Anthony, though the pueblo is 300 miles away. [54]

In eastern Oregon, the Warm Springs Tribe is proposing an off-reservation casino at the Columbia River Gorge. And in Washington state, the Cowlitz and Mohegan tribes are planning an off-reservation casino near Portland. [55] The process has been dubbed "reservation shopping."

Under the Indian Gaming Regulatory Act of 1988, a tribe can acquire off-reservation land for casinos when it is:

- granted as part of a land claim settlement;
- granted to a newly recognized tribe as its reservation;
- restored to a tribe whose tribal recognition is also restored; or
- granted to a recognized tribe that had no reservation when the act took effect.

The most hotly debated exemption allows the secretary of the Interior to grant an off-reservation acquisition that benefits the tribe without harming the community near the proposed casino location. Both Pombo and McCain would repeal the loophole created by this so-called "two-part test." Under Pombo's bill, tribes acquiring land under the other exemptions would have to have solid historic and recent ties to the property. Communities, state governors and state legislatures would have to approve the establishment of new casinos, and tribes would reimburse communities for the effects of casinos on transportation, law enforcement and other public services.

McCain's bill would impose fewer restrictions than Pombo's. But McCain would give the National Indian Gaming Commission final say over all contracts with outside suppliers of goods and services.

The bill would also ensure the commission's control over big-time gambling — a concern that arose from a 2005 decision by the U.S. Court of Appeals for the District of Columbia that limited the agency's jurisdiction over a Colorado tribe. The commission has been worrying that applying that decision nationwide would eliminate federal supervision of casinos.

McCain told a March 8 Senate Indian Affairs Committee hearing that the two-part test "is fostering opposition to all Indian gaming." [56]

If the senator had been aiming to soften tribal opposition to his bill, he didn't make much headway. "We believe that it grows out of anecdotal, anti-Indian press reports on Indian gaming, the overblown issue of off-reservation gaming, and a 'pin-the-blame-on-the-victim' reaction to the Abramoff scandal," Ron His Horse Is Thunder, chairman of the Standing Rock Sioux Tribe of North Dakota and South Dakota, told the committee. He argued that the bill would amount to unconstitutional meddling with Indian sovereignty.

But the idea of restricting "reservation-shopping" appeals to tribes facing competition from other tribes. Cheryle A. Kennedy, chairwoman of the Confederated Tribes of the Grand Ronde Community of Oregon, said her tribe's Spirit Mountain Casino could be hurt by the Warm Springs Tribes' proposed project or by the Cowlitz and Mohegan project. [57]

Pombo's bill would require the approval of new casinos by tribes that already have gambling houses up and running within 75 miles of a proposed new one.

The House Resources Committee heard another view from Indian Country at an April 5 hearing. Jacquie Davis-Van Huss, tribal secretary of the North Fork Rancheria of the Mono Indians of California, said Pombo's approval clause would doom her tribe's plans. "This provision is anti-competitive," she testified. "It effectively provides the power to veto another tribe's gaming project simply to protect market share."

Trust Settlement

McCain's committee is also grappling with efforts to settle a decade-old lawsuit that has exposed longstanding federal mismanagement of trust funds. In 1999, U.S.

Urban Indians: Invisible and Unheard

Two-thirds of the nation's 4.4 million American Indians live in towns and cities, but they're hard to find. [1] "Indians who move into metropolitan areas are scattered; they're not in a centralized geographical area," says New Mexico Secretary of Labor Conroy Chino. "You don't have that cohesive community where there's a sense of culture and language, as in Chinatown or Koreatown in Los Angeles."

Chino's interest is professional as well as personal. In his former career as a television journalist in Albuquerque, Chino, a member of the Acoma Pueblo, wrote an independent documentary about urban Indians. His subjects range from a city-loving San Franciscan who vacations in Hawaii to city-dwellers who return to their reservations every vacation they get. Their lives diverge sharply from what University of Arizona anthropologist Susan Lobo calls a "presumption that everything Indian is rural and long, long ago." [2]

Indian society began urbanizing in 1951, when the Bureau of Indian Affairs (BIA) started urging reservation dwellers to move to cities where — it was hoped — they would blend into the American "melting pot" and find more economic opportunity and a better standard of living. [3]

But many found the urban environment oppressive and the government assistance less generous than promised. About 100,000 Indians were relocated between 1951 and 1973, when the program wound down; unable to fit in, many fell into alcoholism and despair. [4]

Still, a small, urban Indian middle class has developed over time, partly because the BIA began systematically hiring Indians in its offices. Indians keep such a low profile, however, that the Census Bureau has a hard time finding them. Lobo, who consulted for the bureau in 1990, recalls that the agency's policy at the time was to register any household where no one answered the door as being in the same ethnic group as the neighbors. That strategy worked with urban ethnic groups who tended to cluster together, Lobo says, but not with Native Americans because theirs was a "dispersed population."

By the 2000 census that problem was resolved, but another one cropped up. "American Indians are ingenious at keeping expenses down — by couch-surfing, for instance," Lobo says. "There's a floating population that doesn't get counted because they weren't living in a standard residence."

But other urban Indians live conventional, middle-class lives, sometimes even while technically living on Indian land. "I am highly educated, a professor in the university, and my gainful employment is in the city of Albuquerque," says Ted Jojola, a professor of planning at the University of New Mexico (and a member of the Census Bureau's advi-

sory committee on Indian population). "My community [Isleta Pueblo] is seven minutes south of Albuquerque. The reservation has become an urban amenity to me."

Some might see a home on Indian land near the city as a refuge from discrimination. "There have been years where you couldn't reveal you were native if you wanted to get a job," says Joseph Podlasek, executive director of the American Indian Center of Chicago.

Joycelyn Dorscher, president of the Association of American Indian Physicians, recalls a painful experience several years ago when she rushed her 6-year-old daughter to a hospital emergency room in Minneapolis-St. Paul, suspecting appendicitis. The young intern assigned to the case saw an Indian single mother with a sick child and apparently assumed that the daughter was suffering from neglect. "She told me if I didn't sit down and shut up, my daughter would go into the [child-protective] system," recalls Dorscher, who at the time was a third-year medical student.

Even Chino, whose mainstream credentials include an M.A. from Princeton, feels alienated at times from non-Indian city dwellers. He notes that Albuquerque officials ignored Indians' objections to a statue honoring Juan de Oñate, the 16th-century conqueror who established Spanish rule in what is now New Mexico. "Though native people protested and tried to show why this is not a good idea," Chino says, "the city went ahead and funded it." [5]

In the long run, Chino hopes a growing presence of Indian professionals — "we're not all silversmiths, or weavers" — will create more acceptance of urban Indians and more aid to combat high Indian dropout rates and other problems. "While people like having Indians in New Mexico and like visitors to get a feel for the last bastion of native culture," he says, "they're not doing that much for the urban Indian community, though we're paying taxes, too."

---

[1] Urban Indians were 64 percent of the population in 2000, according to the U.S. Census Bureau. For background, see, "We the People: American Indians and Alaska Natives in the United States," U.S. Census Bureau, 2000, p. 14, www.census.gov/prod/2006pubs/censr-28.pdf.

[2] "Looking Toward Home," *Native American Public Telecommunications,* 2003, www.visionmaker.org.

[3] Donald L. Fixico, *The Urban Indian Experience in America* (2000), pp. 9-11.

[4] *Ibid.,* pp. 22-25.

[5] Oñate is especially disliked at Acoma, Chino's birthplace, where the conqueror had the feet of some two-dozen Acoma men cut off in 1599 after Spanish soldiers were killed there. For background, see Wren Propp, "A Giant of Ambivalence," *Albuquerque Journal,* Jan. 25, 2004, p. A1; Brenda Norrell, "Pueblos Decry War Criminal," *Indian Country Today,* June 25, 2004.

Should tribes open casinos on newly acquired land?

YES — Ernest L. Stevens, Jr.
Chairman, National Indian Gaming Association

From statement before U.S. House Committee on Resources, Nov. 9, 2005

Indian gaming is the Native American success story. Where there were no jobs, now there are 553,000 jobs. Where our people had only an eighth-grade education on average, tribal governments are building schools and funding college scholarships. Where the United States and boarding schools sought to suppress our languages, tribal schools are now teaching their native language. Where our people suffer epidemic diabetes, heart disease and premature death, our tribes are building hospitals, health clinics and wellness centers.

Historically, the United States signed treaties guaranteeing Indian lands as permanent homes, and then a few years later, went to war to take our lands. This left our people to live in poverty, often on desolate lands, while others mined for gold or pumped oil from the lands that were taken from us.

Indian gaming is an exercise of our inherent right to self-government. Today, for over 60 percent of Indian tribes in the lower 48 states, Indian gaming offers new hope and a chance for a better life for our children.

Too many lands were taken from Indian tribes, leaving some tribes landless or with no useful lands. To take account of historical mistreatment, the Indian Gaming Regulatory Act (IGRA), provided several exceptions to the rule that Indian tribes should conduct Indian gaming on lands held on Oct. 17, 1988.

Accordingly, land is restored to an Indian tribe in trust status when the tribe is restored to federal recognition. For federally recognized tribes that did not have reservation land on the date IGRA was enacted, land is put into trust. Or, a tribe may apply to the secretary of the Interior. The secretary consults with state and local officials and nearby Indian tribes to determine whether an acquisition of land in trust for gaming would be in the tribe's "best interest" and "not detrimental to the surrounding community."

Now, legislation would require "newly recognized, restored, or landless tribes" to apply to have land taken in trust through a five-part process. Subjecting tribes to this new and cumbersome process discounts the fact that the United States mistreated these tribes by ignoring and neglecting them, taking all of their lands or allowing their lands to be stolen by others.

We believe that Congress should restore these tribes to a portion of their historical lands and that these lands should be held on the same basis as other Indian lands.

NO — State Rep. Fulton Sheen, R-Plainwell
Michigan House of Representatives

From statement to U.S. House Committee on Resources, April 5, 2006

The rampant proliferation of tribal gaming is running roughshod over states' rights and local control and is jeopardizing everything from my own neighborhood to — as the Jack Abramoff scandal has demonstrated — the very integrity of our federal political system.

In 1988, Congress passed the Indian Gaming Regulatory Act (IGRA) in an effort to control the development of Native American casinos and, in particular, to make sure that the states had a meaningful role in the development of any casinos within their borders. At that time, Native American gambling accounted for less than 1 percent of the nation's gambling industry, grossing approximately $100 million in revenue.

Since that time, the Native American casino business has exploded into an $18.5 billion industry that controls 25 percent of gaming industry revenue. Despite this unbridled growth, IGRA and the land-in-trust process remain basically unchanged.

When Congress originally enacted IGRA, the general rule was that casino gambling would not take place on newly acquired trust land. I believe Congress passed this general rule to prevent precisely what we see happening: a mad and largely unregulated land rush pushed by casino developers eager to cash in on a profitable revenue stream that is not burdened by the same tax rates or regulations that other businesses have to incur. "Reservation shopping" is an activity that must be stopped. And that is just one component of the full legislative overhaul that is needed.

IGRA and its associated land-in-trust process is broken, open to manipulation by special interests and in desperate need of immediate reform. It has unfairly and inappropriately fostered an industry that creates enormous wealth for a few select individuals and Las Vegas interests at the expense of taxpaying families, small businesses, manufacturing jobs and local governments.

Our research shows that while local and state governments receive some revenue-sharing percentages from tribal gaming, the dollars pale in comparison to the overall new costs to government and social-service agencies from increased infrastructure demands, traffic, bankruptcies, crime, divorce and general gambling-related ills.

I do not think this is what Congress had in mind. Somewhere along the way, the good intentions of Congress have been hijacked, and it is time for this body to reassert control over this process. It is imperative that Congress take swift and decisive steps today to get its arms around this issue before more jobs are lost and more families are put at risk.

District Judge Royce Lamberth said evidence showed "fiscal and governmental irresponsibility in its purest form." [58]

The alternative to settlement, McCain and Dorgan told the Budget Committee, is for the case to drag on through the courts. Congressional resolution of the conflict could also spare the Interior Department further grief from Lamberth. In a February ruling, he said Interior's refusal to make payments owed to Indians was "an obscenity that harkens back to the darkest days of United States-Indian relations." [59]

Five months later, Lamberth suggested that Congress, not the courts, may be the proper setting for the conflict. "Interior's unremitting neglect and mismanagement of the Indian trust has left it in such a shambles that recovery may prove impossible." [60]

The court case has its roots in the 1887 policy of allotting land to Indians in an effort to break up reservations. Since then, the Interior Department has been responsible for managing payments made to landholders, which later included tribes, for mining and other natural-resource extraction on Indian-owned land.

But for decades, Indians weren't receiving what they were owed. On June 10, 1996, Elouise Cobell, an organizer of the Blackfeet National Bank, the first Indian-owned national bank on a reservation, sued the Interior Department charging that she and all other trust fee recipients had been cheated for decades out of money that Interior was responsible for managing. "Lands and resources — in many cases the only source of income for some of our nation's poorest and most vulnerable citizens — have been grossly mismanaged," Cobell told the Indian Affairs Committee on March 1.

The mismanagement is beyond dispute, said John Bickerman, who was appointed to broker a settlement. Essentially, Bickerman told the Senate Indian Affairs Committee on March 28, "Money was not collected; money was not properly deposited; and money was not properly disbursed."

As of 2005, Interior is responsible for trust payments involving 126,079 tracts of land owned by 223,245 individuals — or, 2.3 million "ownership interests" on some 12 million acres, Cason and Ross Swimmer, a special trustee, told the committee.

Bickerman said a settlement amount of $27.5 billion proposed by the Indian plaintiffs was "without foundation." But the Interior Department proposed a settlement of $500 million based on "arbitrary and false assumptions," he added. Both sides agree that some $13 billion should have been paid to individual Indians over the life of the trust, but they disagree over how much was actually paid.

Supreme Court Ruling

Powerful repercussions are expected from the Supreme Court's latest decision in a centuries-long string of rulings involving competing claims to land by Indians and non-Indians.

In 2005, the high court said the Oneida Indian Nation of New York could not quit paying taxes on 10 parcels of land it owns north of Utica. [61]

After buying the parcels in 1997 and 1998, the tribe refused to pay property taxes, arguing that the land was former tribal property now restored to tribal ownership, and thereby tax-exempt. [62]

The court, in an opinion written by Ruth Bader Ginsburg, concluded that though the tribe used to own the land, the property right was too old to revive. "Rekindling the embers of sovereignty that long ago grew cold" is out of the question, Ginsburg wrote. She invoked the legal doctrine of "laches," in which a party who waits too long to assert his rights loses them. [63]

Lawyers on both sides of Indian law cases expect the case to affect lower-court rulings throughout the country. "The court has opened the cookie jar," Williams of the University of Arizona argues. "Does laches only apply to claims of sovereignty over reacquired land? If a decision favoring Indians is going to inconvenience too many white people, then laches applies — I swear that's what it says." Tribes litigating fishing rights, water rights and other assets are likely to suffer in court as a result, he argues.

In fact, only three months after the high court decision, the 2nd U.S. Circuit Court of Appeals in New York invoked laches in rejecting a claim by the Cayuga Tribe. Vickers of Upstate Citizens for Equality says that if the 2nd Circuit "thinks that laches forbids the Cayugas from making a claim because the Supreme Court said so, you're going to find other courts saying so."

In Washington, Alexandra Page, an attorney with the Indian Law Resource Center, agrees. "There are tribes in the West who have boundary disputes on their reservations; there are water-law cases where you've got people looking back at what happened years ago, so the

Supreme Court decision could have significant practical impact. The danger is that those with an interest in limiting Indian rights will do everything they can to expand the decision and use it in other circumstances."

OUTLOOK

Who Is an Indian?

If advocates of Indian self-governance are correct, the number of tribes running their own affairs with minimal federal supervision will keep on growing. "The requests for workshops are coming in steadily," says Cyndi Holmes, self-governance coordinator of the Jamestown S'Klallam Tribe.

Others say that growth, now at a rate of about three tribes a year, may be nearing its upper limit. "When you look at the options for tribes to do self-governance, economics really drives whether they can," says LaPointe of the Rosebud Sioux, whose tribal government doesn't expect to adopt the model in the foreseeable future.

But the longstanding problems of rural and isolated reservations are not the only dimension of Indian life. People stereotypically viewed as tied to the land have become increasingly urban over the past several decades, and the view from Indian Country is that the trend will continue.

That doesn't mean reservations will empty out or lose their cultural importance. "Urban Indian is not a lifelong label," says Susan Lobo, an anthropologist at the University of Arizona. "Indian people, like everyone else, can move around. They're still American Indians."

For Indians, as for all other peoples, moving around leads to intermarriage. Matthew Snipp, a Stanford University sociologist who is half Cherokee and half Oklahoma Choctaw, notes that Indians have long married within and outside Indian society. But the consequences of intermarriage are different for Indians than for, say, Jews or Italians.

The Indian place in American society grows out of the government-to-government relationship between Washington and tribes. And most tribes define their members by what's known as the "blood quantum" — their degree of tribal ancestry.

"I look at it as you're kind of USDA-approved," says Podlasek of the American Indian Center. "Why is no other race measured that way?"

Harvard Law School graduate Lance Morgan, a member of Nebraska's Winnebago Tribe, used seed money from his tribe's small casino to create several thriving businesses. He urges other tribes to use their casino profits to diversify. "Gaming is just a means to an end," he says.

Podlasek is especially sensitive to the issue. His father was Polish-American, and his mother was Ojibway. His own wife is Indian, but from another tribe. "My kids can be on the tribal rolls, but their kids won't be able to enroll, unless they went back to my tribe or to their mother's tribe to marry — depending on what their partners' blood quantum is. In generations, you could say that, by government standards, there are no more native people."

Snipp traces the blood-quantum policy to a 1932 decision by the Indian Affairs Commission, which voted to make one-quarter descent the minimum standard. The commissioners were concerned, Snipp says, reading from the commission's report, that thousands of people "more white than Indian" were receiving "shares in tribal estates and other benefits." Tribes are no longer bound by that decision, but the requirement — originally inserted at BIA insistence — remains in many tribal constitutions.

On the Indian side, concern over collective survival is historically well-founded. Historian Elizabeth Shoemaker of the University of Connecticut at Storrs calculated that the Indian population of what is now the continental United States plummeted from a top estimate of 5.5 million in 1492 to a mere 237,000 in 1900. Indian life expectancy didn't begin to rise significantly until after 1940. [64]

Now, Indians are worrying about the survival of Indian civilization at a time when Indians' physical survival has never been more assured.

Even as these existential worries trouble some Indian leaders, the living conditions that most Indians endure also pose long-term concerns.

Conroy Chino, New Mexico's Labor secretary and a member of Acoma Pueblo, says continuation of the educational disaster in Indian Country is dooming young people to live on the margins. "I'm out there attracting companies to come to New Mexico, and these kids aren't going to qualify for those good jobs."

Nevertheless, below most non-Indians' radar screen, the Indian professional class is growing. "When I got my Ph.D. in 1973, I think I was the 15th in the country," says Beaulieu of Arizona State University's Center for Indian Education. "Now we have all kinds of Ph.D.s, teachers with certification, lawyers." And Beaulieu says he has seen the difference that Indian professionals make in his home state of Minnesota. "You're beginning to see an educated middle class in the reservation community, and realizing that they're volunteering to perform lots of services."

In Albuquerque, the University of New Mexico's Jojola commutes to campus from Isleta Pueblo. Chairman of an advisory committee on Indians to the U.S. Census Bureau, Jojola shares concerns about use of "blood quantum" as the sole determinant of Indian identity. "A lot of people are saying that language, culture and residence should also be considered," he says.

That standard would implicitly recognize what many Indians call the single biggest reason that American Indians have outlasted the efforts of those who wanted to exterminate or to assimilate them. "In our spirituality we remain strong," says Bordeaux of the Rosebud Sioux. "That's our godsend and our lifeline."

NOTES

1. For background, see "The Administration of Indian Affairs," *Editorial Research Reports 1929* (Vol. II), at *CQ Researcher Plus Archive*, CQ Electronic Library, http://library.cqpress.com.

2. For background see Phil Two Eagle, "Rosebud Sioux Tribe, Demographics," March 25, 2003, www.rosebudsiouxtribe-nsn.gov/demographics.

3. "American Indian Population and Labor Force Report 2003," p. ii, Bureau of Indian Affairs, cited in John McCain, chairman, Senate Indian Affairs Committee, Byron L. Dorgan, vice chairman, letter to Senate Budget Committee, March 2, 2006, http://indian.senate.gov/public/_files/Budget5.pdf.

4. Jonathan B. Taylor and Joseph P. Kalt, "American Indians on Reservations: A Databook of Socioeconomic Change Between the 1990 and 2000 Censuses," Harvard Project on American Indian Economic Development, January 2005, pp. 8-13; www.ksg.harvard.edu/hpaied/pubs/pub_151.htm. These data exclude the Navajo Tribe, whose on-reservation population of about 175,000 is 12 times that of the next-largest tribe, thus distorting comparisons, Taylor and Kalt write.

5. *Ibid.*, p. 41.

6. McCain and Dorgan, *op. cit.*

7. "Injury Mortality Among American Indian and Alaska Native Youth, United States, 1989-1998," Morbidity and Mortality Weekly Report, Centers for Disease Control and Prevention, Aug. 1, 2003, www.cdc.gov/mmwr/preview/mmwrhtml/mm5230a2.htm#top.

8. Robert McSwain, deputy director, Indian Health Service, testimony before Senate Indian Affairs Committee, April 5, 2006.

9. *Ibid.*, p. xii.

10. Taylor and Kalt, *op. cit.*

11. *Ibid.*, pp. 28-30.

12. *Ibid.*, pp. 22-24.

13. The decision is *Cherokee Nation v. Georgia*, 30 U.S. 1 (1831), http://supreme.justia.com/us/30/1/case.html.

14. Alan Meister, "Indian Gaming industry Report," Analysis Group, 2006, p. 2. Publicly available data can be obtained at, "Indian Gaming Facts," www.indiangaming.org/library/indian-gaming-facts; "Gaming Revenues, 2000-2004," National Indian Gaming Commission, www.nigc.gov/TribalData/GamingRevenues2004 2000/tabid/549/Default.aspx.

15. The ruling is *California v. Cabazon Band of Mission Indians*, 480 U.S. 202 (1987), http://supreme.justia.com/us/480/202/case.html.

16. For background, see Susan Schmidt and James V. Grimaldi, "The Rise and Steep Fall of Jack Abramoff," *The Washington Post*, Dec. 29, 2005, p. A1. On March 29, Abramoff was sentenced in Miami to 70 months in prison after pleading to fraud, tax evasion and conspiracy to bribe public officials in charges growing out of a Florida business deal. He is cooperating with the Justice Department in its Washington-based political-corruption investigation. For background see Peter Katel, "Lobbying Boom," *CQ Researcher*, July 22, 2005, pp. 613-636.

17. Meister, op. cit., pp. 27-28. For additional background, see John Cochran, "A Piece of the Action," *CQ Weekly*, May 9, 2005, p. 1208.

18. For background, see, "A Quiet Crisis: Federal Funding and Unmet Needs in Indian Country," U.S. Commission on Civil Rights, July, 2003, pp. 32, 113. www.usccr.gov/pubs/na0703/na0731.pdf.

19. Ryan Wilson, "State of Indian Education Address," Feb. 13, 2006, www.niea.org/history/SOIEAddress06.pdf.

20. For background see, Barbara Mantel, "No Child Left Behind," *CQ Researcher*, May 27, 2005, pp. 469-492.

21. McCain and Dorgan, *op. cit.*, pp. 14-15.

22. According to the Health and Human Services Department's budget proposal, recommended funding of $2 billion for the health centers would allow them to serve 150,000 Indian patients, among a total of 8.8 million patients. For background, see "Budget in Brief, Fiscal Year 2007," Department of Health and Human Services, p. 26, www.hhs.gov/budget/07budget/2007BudgetInBrief.pdf.

23. Peter Whoriskey, "A Tribe Takes a Grim Satisfaction in Abramoff's Fall," *The Washington Post*, Jan. 7, 2006, p. A1.

24. Meister, *op. cit.*, p. 15.

25. Whoriskey, *op. cit.*

26. For background see Fred Carstensen, *et al.*, "The Economic Impact of the Mashantucket Pequot Tribal National Operations on Connecticut," Connecticut Center for Economic Analysis, University of Connecticut, Nov. 28, 2000, pp. 1-3.

27. "Gambling Revenues 2004-2000," National Indian Gaming Commission, www.nigc.gov/TribalData/GamingRevenues20042000/tabid/549/Default.aspx.

28. Schmidt and Grimaldi, *op. cit.*

29. Alaina Potrikus, "2nd Land Hearing Packed," *The Post-Standard* (Syracuse, N.Y.), Jan. 12, 2006, p. B1.

30. For background see "Profile of the Navajo Nation," Navajo Nation Council, www.navajonationcouncil.org/profile.

31. Leslie Linthicum, "Navajos Cautious About Opening Casinos," *Albuquerque Journal*, Dec. 12, 2004, p. B1.

32. For background, see "Fourth Annual State of Indian Nations," Feb. 2, 2006, www.ncai.org/News_Archive.18.0.

33. For background see Theodore H. Haas, *The Indian and the Law* (1949), p. 2; thorpe.ou.edu/cohen/tribalgovtpam2pt1&2.htm#Tribal%20Power%20Today.

34. Except where otherwise noted, material in this section is drawn from Angie Debo, *A History of the Indians of the United States* (1970); see also, Mary H. Cooper, "Native Americans' Future," *CQ Researcher*, July 12, 1996, pp. 603-621.

35. W. Dale Mason, "Indian Gaming: Tribal Sovereignty and American Politics," 2000, p. 13.

36. *Cherokee Nation v. Georgia*, op. cit., 30 U.S.1, http://supct.law.cornell.edu/supct/html/historics/USSC_CR_0030_0001_ZO.html.

37. Robert A. Williams Jr., *Like a Loaded Weapon: the Rehnquist Court, Indians Rights, and the Legal History of Racism in America* (2005), p. 63.

38. *Johnson v. M'Intosh*, 21 U.S. 543 (1823), www.Justia.us/us21543/case.html; *Worcester v. State of Ga.*, 31 U.S. 515 (1832), www.justia.us/us/31/515/case.html.

39. *Johnson v. M'Intosh, op. cit.*

40. *Worcester v. State of Ga., op. cit.*

41. Quoted in Debo, *op. cit.*, pp. 219-220.

42. Quoted in *ibid.*, p. 303.

43. The specified states were Wisconsin, Minnesota (except Red Lake), Nebraska, California and Oregon (except the land of several tribes at Warm Springs). For background, see Debo, *op. cit.*, pp. 304-311.

44. Cited in Debo, *op. cit.*, p. 344.

45. For background see Troy R. Johnson, *The Occupation of Alcatraz Island: Indian Self-Determination and the Rise of Indian Activism* (1996).

46. For background, see Mary H. Cooper, "Native Americans' Future," *CQ Researcher*, July 12, 1996, pp. 603-621.

47. For background see "History of the Tribal Self-Governance Initiative," Self-Governance Tribal Consortium, www.tribalselfgov.org/Red%20Book/SG_New_Partnership.asp.

48. Cochran, *op. cit.*

49. For background see Paul Shukovsky, "Lummi Leader's Had It With Drugs, Sick of Substance Abuse Ravaging the Tribe," *Seattle Post-Intelligencer*, March 16, 2002, p. A1.

50. "Fourth Annual State of Indian Nations," *op. cit.*

51. Many Alaskan villages have joined collective compacts, so the total number of these agreements is 91.

52. For background see Alexandra J. McClanahan, "Alaska Native Claims Settlement Act (ANCSA)," Cook Inlet Region Inc., http://litsite.alaska.edu/aktraditions/ancsa.html; "The Permanent Fund Dividend," Alaska Permanent Fund Corporation, 2005, www.apfc.org/alaska/dividendprgrm. cfm?s=4.

53. For background see Eric Henson and Jonathan B. Taylor, "Native America at the New Millennium," Harvard Project on American Indian Development, Native Nations Institute, First Nations Development Institute, 2002, pp. 14-16, www.ksg.harvard.edu/hpaied/pubs/pub_004.htm.

54. Michael Coleman, "Jemez Casino Proposal At Risk," *Albuquerque Journal*, March 10, 2006, p. A1; Jeff Jones, "AG Warns Against Off-Reservation Casino," *Albuquerque Journal*, June 18, 2005, p. A1.

55. For background see testimony, "Off-Reservation Indian Gaming," House Resources Committee, Nov. 9, 2005, http://resourcescommittee.house.gov/archives/109/full/110905.htm.

56. Jerry Reynolds, "Gaming regulatory act to lose its 'two-part test,' " *Indian Country Today*, March 8, 2006.

57. Testimony before House Resources Committee, Nov. 9, 2005.

58. Matt Kelley, "Government asks for secrecy on its lawyers' role in concealing document shredding," The Associated Press, Nov. 2, 2000.

59. "Memorandum and Order," Civil Action No. 96-1285 (RCL), Feb. 7, 2005, www.indiantrust.com/index.cfm?FuseAction=PDFTypes.Home&PDFType_id=1&IsRecent=1.

60. "Memorandum Opinion," Civil Action 96-1285 (RCL), July 12, 2005, www.indiantrust.com/index.cfm?FuseAction=PDFTypes.Home&PDFType_id=1&IsRecent=1.

61. Glenn Coin, "Supreme Court: Oneidas Too Late; Sherrill Declares Victory, Wants Taxes," *The Post-Standard* (Syracuse), March 30, 2005, p. A1.

62. *Ibid.*

63. *City of Sherrill, New York, v. Oneida Indian Nation of New York*, Supreme Court of the United States, 544 U.S._(2005), pp. 1-2, 6, 14, 21.

64. Elizabeth Shoemaker, *American Indian Population Recovery in the Twentieth Century* (1999), pp. 1-13.

BIBLIOGRAPHY

Books

Alexie, Sherman, *The Toughest Indian in the World*, Grove Press, 2000.
In a short-story collection, an author and screenwriter draws on his own background as a Spokane/Coeur d'Alene Indian to describe reservation and urban Indian life in loving but unsentimental detail.

Debo, Angie, *A History of the Indians of the United States*, University of Oklahoma Press, 1970.
A pioneering historian and champion of Indian rights provides one of the leading narrative histories of the first five centuries of Indian and non-Indian coexistence and conflict.